Donald C. Bryant, Ph.D., Cornell University, is Professor of Speech at The University of Iowa. He was formerly Professor of English and Speech and Chairman of the Department of English at Washington University.

Carroll C. Arnold, Ph.D., University of Iowa, is Professor of Speech at The Pennsylvania State University. He was formerly Professor of Speech and Chairman of the Department of Speech and Drama at Cornell University.

Frederick W. Haberman, Ph.D., Cornell University, is Professor of Speech and Chairman of the Department of Speech at the University of Wisconsin.

Richard Murphy, Ph.D., University of Pittsburgh, is Professor of Speech at the University of Illinois.

Karl R. Wallace, Ph.D., Cornell University, is Professor of Speech and Chairman of the Department of Speech at the University of Illinois.

An Historical Anthology of
Select British Speeches

Edited by

DONALD C. BRYANT
THE UNIVERSITY OF IOWA

CARROLL C. ARNOLD
THE PENNSYLVANIA STATE UNIVERSITY

FREDERICK W. HABERMAN
UNIVERSITY OF WISCONSIN

RICHARD MURPHY
UNIVERSITY OF ILLINOIS

KARL R. WALLACE
UNIVERSITY OF ILLINOIS

THE RONALD PRESS COMPANY · NEW YORK

Library of Congress Catalog Card Number: 67–21676
PRINTED IN THE UNITED STATES OF AMERICA

Preface

This volume is intended as a textbook for undergraduate and graduate students in courses on British Public Address. It provides, with few exceptions, complete texts representing notable recorded public speaking in the British Isles from the earliest times to the present.

In choosing speakers and speeches we have preferred those which in our opinion are both excellent and characteristic. Where feasible we have tried to include selections which are seldom conveniently available to the student or general reader. The inclusion of sermons, especially early homilies, is one of the distinguishing features of our selection. Some new translations of Latin, Old French, and Middle English sermons and speeches have been made for this volume. For all the speeches we have done our best to use authoritative texts, though the reader must realize that until very recent times verbatim reports of public speeches have been rare. The source of each speech is identified, and usually some estimate is given of the reliability of the text.

The speeches are grouped into five historical periods, each of which is introduced by an essay on the events and cultural factors in British society which gave rise to the problems which the speakers faced and the kinds of speeches men made and heard.

Our intention in this anthology is to present the largest practicable selection of complete speeches in the space available, annotated as usefully as possible. Hence in the introductions and headnotes we minimize historical narrative and focus upon those issues, institutions, social factors, and distinguishing features of the speaking to which the student should give special attention. These headnotes and the footnotes and bibliographical notes supply also recommendations of up-to-date, authoritative readings in pertinent history, biography, and criticism, and include suggestions of additional speeches by the speakers represented and by their contemporaries.

The book is truly a joint venture of all the editors, but we have divided primary responsibility for the several sections. Richard Murphy prepared Part I, Ethelbert to Mary Tudor; Karl R. Wallace, Part II, The Reigns of Elizabeth and the Stuarts; Donald C. Bryant, Part III, The Eighteenth Century; and Carroll C. Arnold and Frederick W. Haberman, Parts IV and V, The Nineteenth and Twentieth Centuries.

We wish to acknowledge gratefully the patient assistance and sound advice which we have received from our colleagues and graduate students. Especially do we thank Theresa Kahn Murphy for preparing new translations of six of the early speeches.

Donald C. Bryant
Carroll C. Arnold
Frederick W. Haberman
Richard Murphy
Karl R. Wallace

October, 1967

General Introductory
and Bibliographical Note

Speeches are springs of public action and concomitants of popular decision. Speakers and audiences have always struggled with ideas, motives, and events, striving to animate ideas, to harmonize motives, to resolve doubts, to take action. In speeches the leaders of all societies publicly formulate their choices, as they come to decisions amidst and before and conjointly with their fellows. They bring into the forum of public conflict the internal motives that compel and constrain and confuse men and the external possibilities with which somehow they must harmonize their aspirations. Speeches, therefore, are windows through which the observer may glimpse the dynamics of society and may view the public life of the human spirit. Speeches, also, are historical records of politics, society, and language. Obviously, too, they are biographical sources of great value. First and foremost, however, they are verbal artifacts, and often in them "moral truth and human passion are touched with a largeness, sanity, and attractiveness of form." Then they become what Lord Morley called literature.[1]

If speeches, then, are to be studied as speeches, they must be studied as whole works of fine and useful art rather than as mere documents or purple passages; and more essentially even than plays, poems, and other works of literary art, they must be studied in the context of their times as well as of all time. In this volume we have put prime emphasis upon full texts, and we have not attempted to furnish extensive historical backgrounds and contexts. These we expect the reader to derive from other sources. For general history of England we suggest the textbooks which are currently recommended in departments of history in colleges and universities. Besides these the "Penguin" *History of England* and the authoritative *Oxford History of England,* each in several volumes, will be found useful. In each introduction we recommend special histories of the period.

For basic introductory biographies of all except the most recent living speakers, the *Dictionary of National Biography* is a standard convenient source. Other biographical dictionaries and encyclopedias, such as the *Encyclopaedia Britannica,* are sometimes more easily available. The 11th edition of the *Britannica* (1910–1911) is especially good on the lives of orators and on the facts of English history.

The most comprehensive source for texts of parliamentary speeches from the earliest times to 1803 is *The Parliamentary History of England . . . to the Year 1803* [compiled and edited by William Cobbett; 36 volumes (London: T. C. Hansard, 1806–1820)], often referred to simply as "Cobbett." Parliamentary reporting was neither official, systematic, nor impartial until comparatively re-

---

[1] "Address at the Mansion House," *Pall Mall Gazette,* February 28, 1887, p. 11.

cently, and the early reports are found in many forms—in pamphlets, in newspapers (beginning in the eighteenth century), in magazines, in published and unpublished diaries, letters, and memoirs. From all such sources Cobbett collected the most satisfactory texts he could find, sometimes including alternative versions in footnotes. For some limited periods there are now more complete and accurate texts than Cobbett's, but his is still the accepted standard collection of parliamentary debates. Succeeding the *Parliamentary History* is Hansard's *Parliamentary Debates,* beginning where Cobbett stopped and continuing to the present time. Parliamentary reporting improved greatly in the late eighteenth and the nineteenth centuries, and "Hansard" came to be the quasi-official and then the official record of the proceedings of Parliament. In 1878 the Treasury first subsidized *Hansard;* and in 1892 appeared the first authorized edition, with the speeches summarized. Since 1909 *Hansard* has published full verbatim texts. It is the British equivalent of the U. S. *Congressional Record.*

Another important collection of British political speeches is *Select British Eloquence,* by Chauncey A. Goodrich, the mid-nineteenth-century American clergyman and Professor of Oratory at Yale. First published in 1852 and reprinted at various times through the rest of the century, this invaluable volume had long been out of print until reissued in 1963 (Indianapolis: Bobbs-Merrill & Company) with a Preface by Bower Aly. Containing nearly a thousand pages of double-columned small print, *Select British Eloquence* offers the most extensive selection of British speeches now in print in a single volume. Though Goodrich included speeches from the Reign of Elizabeth I onward, he gave all but twenty pages to the years 1700–1831. Goodrich's lengthy introductions to the several speakers make up as comprehensive a critical examination of British speakers as was ever undertaken, by one of the best-informed, most penetrating, and at the same time most affectionate students of the subject. Used with the realization that they were composed over a hundred years ago, before the great histories of the period were written, and without the benefit of the documentary and critical researches of the past century, Goodrich's critical essays are the students' most valuable single resource. These introductions, edited by Professor A. Craig Baird, were reprinted in a convenient, readable volume in 1963 by the Southern Illinois University Press. Additional selections from many British speakers may be found, of course, in various multivolume collections of oratory, usually available in libraries. Among such collections, two are perhaps more useful than the rest: David J. Brewer's *The World's Best Orations* (10 vols., 1899) and Thomas B. Reed's *Modern Eloquence* (15 vols., 1900–1903). Brewer is the best critic after Goodrich; and the lists and chronologies of the world's speakers, in the last volume, are very useful. Reed's is the best source for occasional speeches, such as after-dinner speeches, not given in most anthologies. Houston Peterson's *A Treasury of the World's Great Speeches* (1954; enlarged ed., 1965) has introductions and connecting passages which give a sense of themes and continuity to a single-volume assembly chiefly of excerpts from great speeches and speakers.

The sophisticated student of speeches should be something of a social and political historian; something of a philosopher, political scientist, and psychologist; a person well read in literature and well versed in literary criticism. In addition he should be master of the special equipment of the rhetorical critic. That equipment begins, of course, with extensive familiarity with speeches and speaking. It should be built upon wide acquaintance with the theory of public address—

that is, rhetoric—from Plato and Aristotle, Cicero and Quintilian, Thomas Wilson of Tudor England, Fénelon of Louis XIV's France, and Hugh Blair, George Campbell, and Richard Whately of eighteenth- and nineteenth-century England, to I. A. Richards, Kenneth Burke, and the logicians, linguists, literary critics, and social scientists of the present time who are re-examining the phenomena of verbal communication. These, of course, become the studies of the specialist. The inexperienced reader seeking the equipment for his study might begin with the brief treatment of the study of speeches in Chapter 27 of *Fundamentals of Public Speaking* by Donald C. Bryant and Karl R. Wallace (3rd ed.; New York: Appleton-Century-Crofts, 1960); and the Introduction on "The Study of Speeches" in *American Speeches,* edited by W. M. Parrish and Marie Hochmuth [Nichols] (New York: Longmans, Green, 1954). Of about the same scope is A. Craig Baird's "Introduction" to *American Public Addresses, 1740–1952* (New York: McGraw-Hill, 1956). Hochmuth's critical analysis of Lincoln's First Inaugural, in *American Speeches,* is a good example of the extended treatment of a single speech. Besides Goodrich's, which we have mentioned, and Lord Brougham's (see below, page 323), there is no extensive collection of critical essays or studies of British speakers. In *A History and Criticism of American Public Address,* edited by W. Norwood Brigance and Marie Hochmuth (New York: McGraw-Hill, Vols. I and II, 1943, reprinted by Russell & Russell, 1960; and Longmans, Green, Vol. III, 1955, reprinted by Russell & Russell, 1965), however, the student may observe various approaches to the criticism of speakers and speaking. Hochmuth's "The Criticism of Rhetoric," the opening chapter of Volume III, provides a more advanced treatment of principles and methods than those by Parrish and Baird.

The twentieth-century development of speech criticism probably began with Herbert A. Wichelns' distinction between literary and rhetorical criticism in "The Literary Criticism of Oratory," in *Studies in Rhetoric and Public Speaking in Honor of James Albert Winans* (New York: The Century Company, 1925; reprinted, New York: Russell & Russell, 1962). That essay, still a standard introduction to the subject, was reprinted in *The Rhetorical Idiom* (edited by Donald C. Bryant; Ithaca, N. Y.: The Cornell University Press, 1958; reprinted, New York: Russell & Russell, 1965). Of the many useful contributions to the theory and principles of speech criticism since Wichelns' essay, the best would certainly include *Speech Criticism* by Lester Thonssen and A. Craig Baird (New York: The Ronald Press Company, 1948), *Rhetorical Criticism: a Study in Method* by Edwin Black (New York: Macmillan, 1965), and *Rhetoric and Criticism* by Marie Hochmuth Nichols (Baton Rouge: Louisiana State University Press, 1963). Interesting special ways of viewing speeches and speakers are presented in Richard Murphy's "The Speech as Literary Genre," *Quarterly Journal of Speech,* XLIV (1958), 117–27; Albert J. Croft's "The Functions of Rhetorical Criticism," *ibid.,* XLII (1956), 283–91; and Leland M. Griffin's "The Rhetoric of Historical Movements," *ibid.,* XXXVIII (1952), 184–88.

The first necessity, however, is familiarity with speeches, speakers, and circumstances. In this book students should find the essentials for beginning the quest.

Acknowledgments

Eyre and Spottiswood, Ltd., for permission to quote Wulfstan, "The Sermon of the Wolf to the English . . . ," from Dorothy Whitelock (ed.), *English Historical Documents.*

Ginn and Company, for permission to quote Aelfric, "A Sermon on the Sacrifice on Easter Day," from *Select Translations from Old English Prose.*

Her Majesty's Stationery Office, for permission to quote Stanley Baldwin, "The Debate in the House of Commons (on the abdication of Edward VIII)," and Winston Spencer Churchill, "On the Munich Agreement," and "A Solemn Hour."

Oxford University Press, for permission to quote "A Sermon for the Third Sunday after Trinity," from Woodburn O. Ross (ed.), *Middle English Sermons 1940* (Early English Text Society Original Series 209).

Oxford University Press, Inc., for permission to quote Wulfstan, "The Sermon of the Wolf to the English . . . ," from Dorothy Whitelock (ed.), *English Historical Documents.*

G. P. Putnam's Sons & Coward-McCann, Inc., for permission to quote materials regarding Edward VIII, "Farewell Message," from *A King's Story: The Memoirs of the Duke of Windsor,* 1951.

Grace Roe, Executrix of Dame Christabel Pankhurst, for permission to quote Emmeline G. Pankhurst, "The Importance of the Vote," and "Speech at the Bow Street Police Court."

Robert W. Smith, for permission to quote Edward VIII, "Farewell Message," from *Speech Monographs,* November 1963.

S. P. C. K. (Society for Promoting Christian Knowledge), for permission to quote the Venerable Bede, "On the Nativity of the Apostles Peter and Paul," from G. F. Browne, *Venerable Bede: His Life and Writing,* 1919.

St. Martin's Press and the author for permission to quote Queen Elizabeth I, "Speech at the Dissolution of Parliament," from J. E. Neale, *Elizabeth I and Her Parliament, 1559–1581* (Vol. I).

The Society of Authors, Miss D. E. Collins through the courtesy of A. P. Watt & Son, and the Hilaire Belloc Estate, for permission to quote G. B. Shaw and G. K. Chesterton, "Do We Agree?" 1927.

The Times, for permission to quote David Lloyd George, "Speech at Limehouse," July 31, 1909.

William E. White, for permission to quote Daniel O'Connell, "The Speech at Tara" from "Daniel O'Connell: Ireland's Orator for Repeal," unpublished doctoral dissertation.

Contents

General Introductory and Bibliographical Note v

I. Ethelbert to Mary Tudor

Introduction 1
ETHELBERT: *On Augustine's Mission to England* (597) 3
EDWIN OF DEIRA'S ALDERMAN: *On the Flight of a Sparrow and the Life of Man* (627) 5
THE VENERABLE BEDE: *On the Nativity of the Apostles Peter and Paul* (710) 7
AELFRIC: *A Sermon on the Sacrifice on Easter-Day* (994) 14
WULFSTAN: *The Sermon of the Wolf to the English* . . . (1014) 21
WILLIAM THE CONQUEROR: *Speech to His Troops Before the Battle of Hastings* (1066) 27
UNKNOWN MEDIEVAL PREACHER: *A Sermon for the Third Sunday After Trinity* (1378–1417) 31
JOHN WYCLIF: *Sermon for the Sunday Within the Week of the Twelfth Day After Christmas* . . . (c. 1381) 38
JOHN BALL: *"Let Us Go to the King!"* (1381?); *Speech at the Peasants' Rising* (1381) 42
HUGH LATIMER: *Sermon on the Ploughers* (1548) 45
THOMAS CRANMER: *Speech at the Stake* (1556) 60

II. The Reigns of Elizabeth and the Stuarts

Introduction 65
QUEEN ELIZABETH I: *Speech on Marriage and Succession* . . . (1566); *Speech at the Dissolution of Parliament* (1567); *Speech at the Proroguing of Parliament* (1585) 69
PETER WENTWORTH: *On the Liberty of the House of Commons* (1576) 79
FRANCIS BACON: *Upon the Motion of Subsidy* (1598); *Against Dueling* (1613) 90
SIR WALTER RALEIGH: *Speech on the Scaffold* (1618) 104
JOHN DONNE: *Sermon Preached at St. Paul's* (1625) 109
SIR JOHN ELIOT: *For the Petition of Right* (1628) 123
THOMAS WENTWORTH, EARL OF STRAFFORD: *Speech of the Earl of Strafford at His Trial for Treason* (1641) 131
OLIVER CROMWELL: *Speech to the First Protectorate Parliament* (1654) ... 144
JOHN TILLOTSON: *Sermon Against Evil Speaking* (1694) 156

xi

III. The Eighteenth Century

Introduction   173
SIR ROBERT WALPOLE (from Johnson's Debates): *Debate on the Seamen's Bill* (1741)   176
JOHN WESLEY: *The Use of Money* (1744)   190
WILLIAM PITT, THE ELDER, EARL OF CHATHAM: *On Restoring Peace With America* (1777)   201
EDMUND BURKE: *Burke to His Constituents* (1780); *Declining the Poll* (1780)   211
HENRY GRATTAN: *A Free People* (1782)   244
CHARLES JAMES FOX: *On Electoral Reform* (1797)   254
WILLIAM PITT, THE YOUNGER: *The Deliverance of Europe* (1799)   281
LORD THOMAS ERSKINE: *In Behalf of Hadfield* (1800)   294

IV. The Nineteenth Century

Introduction   317
HENRY LORD BROUGHAM: *Speech on Parliamentary Reform* (1831)   322
DANIEL O'CONNELL: *The Speech at Tara* (1843)   358
BENJAMIN DISRAELI, LORD BEACONSFIELD: *Third Reading of the Corn Importation Bill* (1846)   371
CHARLES KINGSLEY: *The Massacre of the Innocents* (1859)   392
JOHN BRIGHT: *On Punishment of Death* (1864)   398
WILLIAM EWART GLADSTONE: *Campaign Speech* (1879)   413
WILLIAM MORRIS: *Art, Wealth, and Riches* (1883)   422

V. The Twentieth Century

Introduction   439
EMMELINE G. PANKHURST: *The Importance of the Vote* (1908); *Speech at the Bow Street Police Court* (1908)   442
DAVID LLOYD GEORGE: *Speech at Limehouse* (1909)   461
G. B. SHAW, G. K. CHESTERTON, and HILAIRE BELLOC: *Do We Agree?* (1927)   474
STANLEY BALDWIN: *The Debate in the House of Commons (on the Abdication of Edward VIII)* (1936)   491
EDWARD VIII: *Farewell Message* (1936)   515
WINSTON SPENCER CHURCHILL: *On the Munich Agreement* (1938); *A Solemn Hour* (1940)   521

Index of Speakers   539

An Historical Anthology of
Select British Speeches

I

Ethelbert to Mary Tudor

Introduction

The speeches in this first Part cover the vast span of ten centuries. The period begins dramatically with Ethelbert's kindly reception of Christianity. It ends even more dramatically with the Protestant Reformation and the Catholic Reformation, when Bishop John Fisher and Sir Thomas More were beheaded for refusing to acknowledge Henry VIII as supreme head of the church, and Hugh Latimer and Thomas Cranmer were burned for refusing to acknowledge the supremacy of the papacy. Under Ethelbert, St. Augustine became the first Archbishop of Canterbury. Under Mary Tudor, "Bloody Mary" as she was called by the Protestants, the sixty-ninth Archbishop, Cranmer, was martyred. Politically the scene opens with the king-states of the early period and closes with the consolidation of the English kingdom under the Tudors.

Most of the speeches are translations from Latin or French, or renderings from Anglo-Saxon or Middle English. The originals are more satisfactory, but translation is necessary to make these early specimens of British public address more accessible.

Some characteristics of the period should be noted. During most of the time, "books" were collections of script on parchment—printing did not come to England until 1476—and were a substitute for the spoken word rather than a medium in themselves. Letters were run together, and the conveniences of paragraphing, capital letters, punctuation, and standardized spelling were unknown. Individual copies of books were laboriously made by scribes, and readers intoned as they read—the image was acoustic rather than visual. The reader's carrel in our libraries today is a memorial to attempts to cut down the mumblings of the monks as they voiced their way along the parchment, perhaps reading a book or two a year.[1]

It was an oral society. Devices for spoken and visual communication were lavishly used. The speaker stored his memory with *exempla*, stories, illustrations, and anecdotes, to illustrate points and to help recall. Devices of repetition were

---

[1] See H. J. Chaytor, *From Script to Print* (Cambridge, 1945).

used, for there was little chance of reading the speech on the morrow. There was much alliteration, imagery, and rhyme. Here is a passage from a rhymed sermon on Pater Noster, the Lord's Prayer:

> Ne beo þu nawiht monslaht;
> *Be thou not manslayer;*
>
> Ne in hordom dei ne naht.
> *Nor be in whoredom, day or night.*
>
> Ne þu naȝest for to stele,
> *Nor oughtest thou to steal,*
>
> Ne nan þefþe for to heole.
> *Nor any theft to conceal.*[2]

The medieval preacher was not to be outdone by the minstrel or troubadour. Chaucer's Pardoner displayed a pillow case of "oure lady," and a piece of sail St. Peter used on his boat, but his best feat was singing the offertory for his collection. Devices for interest were drawn on increasingly. At the appropriate moment, one preacher drew from his cloak a skull, to illustrate dramatically the horrors of death. Latimer drew from the sleeve of his gown a pack of cards and preached from them a "Sermon on the Card," at St. Mary's, Cambridge, in 1529. A few days later, a rival, Buckenham, preached his "Sermon on the Dice," illustrating his points by rolling the cubes.

Forms of speaking during the period were various. There were speeches in the witenagemot—the precursor of parliament—as witness the remarks of Edwin of Deira's alderman; speeches before battle, such as William the Conqueror's; speeches at trials, such as Sir Thomas More's; and speeches at church trials and disputations. The predominant form, however, was the sermon. There were sermons in the streets, at cemeteries, at outdoor crosses, at fairs, weddings, and funerals, in processions for the health of the king, or to ward off plagues and bad harvests. At the end of the period came the sermon before the burning of heretics. In an attempt to "save" Friar Forest from immediate flames at the stake and eternal hell-fire, Latimer preached for three hours to a crowd of ten thousand, but Forest refused to recant even as Latimer did when his faggots were lighted seventeen years later, after Dr. Richard Smith had preached from the text, "Though I give my body to be burned, and have not charity . . . ."

The earliest form of sermon was the homily, a simple religious address, with practical exposition of a passage of scripture, designed to give the communicant better understanding of a precept or a service such as communion. Examples are seen in Bede and Aelfric. The homily probably developed from expositions of scripture in the Jewish synagogue. It was used in the morality plays, as in the fifteenth-century *Everyman*, in which God, Death, and other characters preach from the stage.[3]

During the thirteenth, fourteenth, and fifteenth centuries, the friars used homiletical forms to attack social injustice.[4] John Ball's homily is an example.

---

[2] *Old English Homilies and Homiletic Treatises . . . of the Twelfth and Thirteenth Centuries,* ed. Richard Morris (London, 1868), pp. 56–57.

[3] See G. R. Owst, *Literature and Pulpit in Medieval England* (2nd rev. ed.; Oxford, 1961), p. 527.

[4] See Homer G. Pfander, *The Popular Sermon of the Medieval Friar in England* (New York, 1937).

As Owst says, "It is to the glory of the mendicant preachers of all the orders that, as champions of the poor, they attacked the tyranny and oppression of lords, the weaknesses of knights, the ravages of retainers, the cunning and extortion of merchants, the corruption of the law, in short, every conceivable form of injustice in the land. . . . Nothing escapes their notice."[5] But they, too, became corrupt, and Chaucer's Pardoner is depicted as a mercenary fraud, although he put on a good show.

From the homily evolved the sermon, a religious oration designed to induce or bolster faith, frequently with applications to social and political matters beyond the literal text. This form, usually ascribed to St. Augustine, Bishop of Hippo, who adapted pagan rhetoric to Christian uses, can be seen in Wulfstan, Wyclif, and Latimer. It became an art form of precision, as can be observed in the sample Middle English sermon in the collection. There were collections of sermons and many manuals on how to design them.[6]

By the end of the period,[7] rhetoric and public address had developed in many ways. In the next period, the age of Elizabeth, they were to enjoy one of their greatest flowerings in the history of the kingdom.

Ethelbert

(*Fl.* 560–616)

Ethelbert (Aethelberht), King of Kent, came to the throne about 560. He was reputed to be the great-great-grandson of Hengist, who, with his brother chieftain Horsa, led the first Saxon bands which settled in England in the fifth century. In a period of regional rulers, before there was a nation–state of England, he reigned over the East and South Saxons, the East Angles, the Lindiswaras, and the Mercians, from Kent north to the Humber. He was the most powerful king on the Island, and the first English king to receive baptism. *The Anglo-Saxon Chronicle* says he died in 616, after reigning fifty-six years. One of his main claims to fame is a short speech made on the occasion of Augustine's mission to convert the English.

Many details of that mission are recorded in Bede's *Ecclesiastical History*.[1] The story begins with Gregory the Great, before he became pope. One day he

---

[5] G. R. Owst, *Preaching in Medieval England; an Introduction to Sermon Manuscripts of the Period* (Cambridge, 1926), p. 80.

[6] *Ibid.*, chaps. vi–viii: "The Sermon Literature and Its Types," "Manuals and Treatises," "Sermon-Making or the Theory and Practice of Sacred Eloquence."

[7] For treatment of sermons in the last part of the period, including technical discussions of *dispositio* and *elocutio,* and particularly for Catholic preachers who usually are neglected, see *Preaching in England in the Late Fifteenth and Sixteenth Centuries* by J. W. Blench (Oxford, 1964).

[1] See J. A. Giles, *Bede's Ecclesiastical History of England* (London, 1903), Bk. I, chaps. xxiii–xxvi; Bk. II, chap. i.

saw in the marketplace at Rome, among the slaves for sale, some boys of fair countenance and flaxen hair. When he asked what they were called, he was told, "Angles." He replied that this was appropriate, since they looked like angels. Asking what province they were from, and being told "Deira" (Durham and Yorkshire), he commented, "Truly are they *De ira,* withdrawn from wrath." Gregory then asked who was king of the province. Told it was Aella, he replied, "Hallelujah, the praise of God the Creator must be sung in those parts."

In 596, Gregory, then pope, dispatched Augustine and forty monks to England. It took them ten months to journey through Europe. In the spring of 597, with some Frankish priests for interpreters, Augustine and his company left France, probably from Boulogne, and landed on the Isle of Thanet, on the southeast coast of England. The Isle was then separated from the main island by the River Stour, which was fordable in several places. Augustine did not know what his reception would be, and Thanet was a good point for reconnoitering.

Ethelbert had some knowledge of Christianity. His wife Bertha, daughter of Charibert, King of Paris, was a Christian, and had as her chaplain a French bishop, Luidhard. Ethelbert was suspicious of Augustine, however, and refused to see him at the seat in Canterbury. The king was afraid to meet indoors lest a spell be cast upon him; so with his soldiers he journeyed to Thanet to see Augustine. There they met. Augustine, a huge man towering a head above the others, moved with his company to meet the king. They carried a large silver cross and a gilded picture of Jesus, and chanted a litany as they walked. The sight must have been one to strike terror into the heart of the heathen. The two groups sat on the ground facing each other, and a dialogue was carried on. Augustine spoke in Latin and Ethelbert in the Kentish dialect of Saxon. Ethelbert, convinced by the dialogue that he should give asylum to Augustine, then spoke his famous speech.

The qualities of the speech have been well described by Arthur Penryhn Stanley, former canon at Canterbury and Dean of Westminster:

> Such an answer, simple as it was, really seems to contain the seeds of all that is excellent in the English character—exactly what a king should have said on such an occasion—exactly what, under the influence of Christianity, has grown up into all our best institutions. There is the natural dislike to change, which Englishmen still retain; there is the willingness at the same time to listen favourably to anything which comes recommended by the energy and self-devotion of those who urge it; there is, lastly, the spirit of moderation and toleration, and the desire to see fair play, which is one of our best gifts, and which, I hope, we shall never lose. We may, indeed, well be thankful, not only that we had an Augustine to convert us, but that we had an Ethelbert for our king.[2]

The two companies then went to Canterbury. Ethelbert granted to Augustine an old Roman church, and was himself converted to Christianity about 600. On this site later was built the Premier Cathedral Church of Canterbury.

∽

[2] Arthur P. Stanley, *Historical Memorials of Canterbury* (new ed.; London, 1875), p. 34.

ON AUGUSTINE'S MISSION TO ENGLAND *

Isle of Thanet
Spring, 597

In truth, the words and promises you bring to us are fair; but inasmuch as they are new and unproved, I cannot bring myself to accept them, and to put away from me those beliefs which I, together with all the people of the English nation, have observed for so long a time. But since you have come to us as strangers from a distant place, and since I seem to perceive that you believe the concepts you wish to impart to us to be true and ennobling, we desire that no harm befall you; rather we wish to receive you with warm hospitality and to bestow upon you whatever is necessary to your well-being; moreover, we shall do nothing to prevent you from preaching and from converting all those whom you can to the faith of your religion.

∾

BIBLIOGRAPHICAL NOTE

For documents on Augustine's mission, including Pope Gregory's letters to Ethelbert and Bertha and to courts where Augustine stayed on his way, see Arthur James Mason's *The Mission of St Augustine to England According to the Original Documents, Being a Handbook for the Thirteenth Centenary* (1897).

Edwin of Deira's Alderman

(*Fl. 627*)

Edwin of Deira (585–633), son of Aella, ruled over Northumbria from 617 to 633. At the height of his power his domain extended from the Humber north to Edinburgh (Edwin's burgh). He was superior over all English regions except Kent.

* This is a new translation of the original Latin text as given in Carolus Plummer's *Venerabilis Baedae* (Oxford, 1896), I, 46. Since Bede wrote his history in 731, the speech was recorded 134 years after it was delivered. Of Bede's account in general, the Right Reverend Abbot Snow, O.S.B., says in *The Coming of St. Augustine by Venerable Bede* (London, 1897), p. 3: "Few historical documents have so clearly upon them the stamp of accuracy and truth. Whatever may be thought of some details— e.g., the words put into the mouth of King Ethelbert, the incident of rising or sitting at the conference with the Britons, and other immaterial particulars, the outline and substance of the narrative stand out as incontestable as any record of the past."

Edwin was married to Ethelberga, daughter of Ethelbert, in 625. Her brother, Eabold, who succeeded his father as King of Kent, insisted that her Christian beliefs be respected, and arranged for Bishop Paulinus to accompany her as chaplain. Edwin was a pagan, but was troubled about it. He had seen a vision. He had also made a pledge, after he had been stabbed by a supposedly peaceful emissary from the West Saxon area, that if he should recover and could avenge himself on the enemies who plotted his destruction, he would give some thought to the Christian religion. He lived, and in successful raids destroyed those who had plotted against him. No doubt his wife and Paulinus in their own ways had tried to influence him. In addition he had received a letter from Pope Boniface V, urging him to embrace Christianity. Edwin spent hours brooding on what to do. He decided to call a gemot (meeting) of his witan (wise men and councilors). This was a century before the witenagemot became an institution and the fore-runner of the British parliament. The meeting was held at Edwin's castle, Alby, eight miles from York.

In opening the council, the king asked each member what he thought of the new doctrine. Coifi, chief of the pagan priests, replied that something was lack-ing in the old religion; it did not seem to be working in the interests of prosperity, either for himself or in general. "None of your people has applied himself more diligently to the worship of the gods than I," said Coifi, "and yet there are many who receive greater favors from you, and are more preferred than I, and are more prosperous in all their undertakings." He could, he said, see no virtue in the present religion, either for himself or the realm, nor could be believe that "the gods were good for anything."

After Coifi's crass appeal for material gain through religion, an "ealdor-mann" (the chief officer of a shire) spoke on the theme of man's relation to God. Using the single and simple figure of the sparrow, he made his appeal. Bede, who records the details in his *Ecclesiastical History,* says that "the other elders and king's counsellors, by Divine inspiration, spoke to the same effect."

Edwin then publicly gave Paulinus license to preach, and declared himself converted to Christianity. He asked Coifi what to do about the heathen temple and its images. The high priest said that he would himself destroy them. Riding swiftly to Goodmanham, he and his companions set fire to the temple. Edwin was baptized April 12, 627, in a church at York which he built while he was being catechised and instructed to receive baptism. These events would make the date of the assembly about January, 627, at a time of storms of rain and snow.

The beauty of the alderman's simple speech has been described by Emile Legouis, the French historian of English literature:

> Nowhere else is there anything at once so exact and so ample. The image is as great as it is intimate, precise although mysterious. Shakespeare never pro-duced one which was more striking or which better conveyed the feeling of life's strangeness. Nothing equal to it is to be found in the whole of Anglo-Saxon poetry.[1]

Bede's introductory sentence for the speech is given below in three versions: Anglo-Saxon, Bede's Latin, and modern English:

Þæs wordum ōþer cyninges wita ǫnd ealdormann geþafunge sealde, ǫnd tō þære sprǣece fēng ǫnd þus cwæð;

[1] Emile Legouis and Louis Cazamian, *A History of English Literature* (new ed.; New York, 1929), p. 12.

Cuius suasioni uerbisque prudentibus alius optimatum regis tribuens assensum, continuo subdidit;

Another of the king's counselors, one of his chief men, assented to his words, and taking up the discussion, thus spoke.

∽

On the Flight of a Sparrow and the Life of Man *

Edwin's Castle, Alby, Northumbria
January, 627

The present life of man on this earth, oh king, in comparison to that existence which is not revealed to us, appears to me like the very swift flight of a sparrow, which for a moment flies through the room in which you, your leaders, and ministers on a wintry day are seated at supper around a warm fire, while out of doors rage the whirling storms of wintry rains and snows; the bird entering through one door quickly passes out through the other. For the brief moment it is within the room, it is safe from the wintry blast, but after a moment of calm from the storm, it quickly returns from winter to winter, and slips away from sight. So, for such a little time, seems this present life of man. But what has gone before, and what comes after, we know not. Therefore if this new doctrine can dispel the mystery, there seems to be merit in following it.

The Venerable Bede

(673–735)

Bede has been called the "father of English literature," and the "father of English history." He might also be called the "father of English oratory," and the "father of English rhetoric." His two books of homilies, although recorded in Latin, are the oldest collection of speeches by an Englishman, and his *On Figures and Tropes,* also in Latin, is the oldest work on rhetoric by an Englishman.

Bede was born in Northumbria, at or near Yarrow. At the age of seven he was placed in the monastic school near there, St. Peter's, founded in 674 at Wearmouth. The monasteries were a development following Edwin of Deira's conversion. When the monastery at Yarrow, St. Paul's, was founded about eight years after Wearmouth, Bede was transferred there. Benedict was abbot of the two monasteries, and Bede was placed in his care. At nineteen Bede was made

---

* This is a new translation from Bede's *Ecclesiastical History,* following the Latin text in Carolus Plummer's *Venerabilis Baedae* (Oxford, 1896), I, 112. Incidental remarks and setting are from J. A. Giles, *Bede's Ecclesiastical History of England* (London, 1903), Bk. II, chaps. v, ix–xiv.

a deacon, and at thirty was ordained a priest. Except for short travels, he lived at Yarrow the rest of his life, declining the office of abbot lest it interfere with his pursuit of learning.

Bede wrote hagiography, biblical commentaries, history, letters, poems, hymns, and scientific works in addition to his homilies and the work on rhetoric. He has not been much studied by students of speech and rhetoric because of the scarcity of translations. His work on rhetoric was not published in translation until 1962, 1,260 years after it had been written, and his books of homilies have never been translated.

The homilies were delivered to the brethren at the monastery. They were composed from time to time and recorded, probably by a boy-scribe. The translator of the homily given here estimates that about eighteen minutes was an average length for the homilies, with the longest running to twenty-eight minutes. The form of the homilies is consistent. There is an occasion, such as a holy day; then the text, taken from one of the four Gospels, is explained section by section along moral and patristic lines, with development by figure; finally, there is a peroration. Notice that in the homily given here the gates of hell are a symbol for all temptation, rather than a literal gateway. As the translator of this homily notes, "It is to be feared that many of Bede's sermons would be stigmatized in these days as 'doctrinal,' or, by those who say more distinctly what they mean, as 'dull.'" In justice to Bede, it should be recognized that the homilies recorded were to be read and pondered by monastics in the early days of orthodox English learning. Through the centuries there was to develop first the English division from Rome—an idea that would have pained Bede severely—and then the evangelical movement, with Congregationalists, Friends, Baptists, Unitarians, and other sects breaking away from the Anglican tradition. Bede's homilies are a landmark in British preaching.

Some homilies attributed to Bede, as given in several speech anthologies, are spurious. One of them, however, "A Sermon for Sundays," is so delightfully terrorizing that a part is given below:

> There Paul beheld many souls of sinners plunged, some to the knees, some to the loins, some to the mouth, some to the eyebrows; and every day and eternally they are tormented. And Paul wept, and asked who they were that were therein plunged to the knees. And the Angel said, These are detractors and evil speakers; and those up to the loins are fornicators and adulterers, who returned not to repentance; and those to the mouth are they who went to Church, but they heard not the word of God; and those to the eyebrows are they who rejoiced in the wickedness of their neighbour. . . . And after this, he saw between heaven and earth the soul of a sinner, howling betwixt seven devils, that had on that day departed from the body. And the Angels cried out against it and said, Woe to thee, wretched soul! What hast thou done upon earth? Thou hast despised the commandments of God, and hast done no good works; and therefore thou shalt be cast into outer darkness, where shall be weeping and gnashing of teeth. And after this, in one moment, angels carried a soul from its body to heaven; and Paul heard the voice of a thousand angels rejoicing over it, and saying, O most happy and blessed soul! rejoice to-day, because thou hast done the will of God. And they set it in the Presence of God. . . . And the angel said, Whoso keepeth the Sunday shall have his part with the angels of God. And Paul demanded of the angel, how many kinds of punishment there were in hell. And the angel said, There are a hundred and forty-four thousand; and if there were a hundred

eloquent men, each having four iron tongues, that spoke from the beginning of the world, they could not reckon up the torments of hell. But let us, beloved brethren, hearing of these so great torments, be converted to our Lord, that we may be able to reign with the angels.

All this is by some unknown contemporary of Bede, six centuries before Dante, and evidently addressed to a very sinful audience. Bede's homilies were for the monks of Yarrow, who, whatever their omissions, must have kept the Sunday.

Carolus Plummer [1] has noted some of Bede's characteristics. His "command of Latin is excellent, and his style is clear and limpid, and it is very seldom that we have to pause to think of the meaning of a sentence. There is no affectation of a false classicality, and no touch of . . . puerile pomposity." He relied chiefly on Augustine, Jerome, Ambrose, and Gregory the Great for his patristic comments. He knew Virgil and Horace, but thought pagan literature should be used with caution. His use of figure and allegory shows the "influence of the Alexandrian schools upon the early church."

ᖇ

On the Nativity of the Apostles Peter and Paul [*]

Yarrow Monastery
circa 710

(Matthew 16; Mark 8; Luke 9.) *When Jesus came into the coasts of Caesarea Philippi, he asked his disciples, saying, Whom do men say that I, the Son of man, am? etc.*

The holy Gospel which has been read to you, my brethren, is worthy of your utmost attention, and should be kept in constant remembrance. For it commends to us perfect faith, and shows the strength of such perfect faith against all temptations. If you would know how one ought to believe in Christ, what can be more clear than this which Peter says to Him, "Thou art the Christ, the Son of the living God"? If you would hear of what avail is this belief, what can be more plain than this which the Lord says of the Church to be builded upon Him, "The gates of hell shall not prevail against it"? These points will be more fully considered hereafter, each in its own place. I will now proceed to the explanation of the whole passage, taking the sentences in their natural order.

And first, of the place in which the Lord's words were spoken. *"Jesus came*

[1] *Venerabilis Baedae* (Oxford, 1896), I, l–lvi.
[*] This English rendering was made by the Rev. G. F. Browne in his *The Venerable Bede—His Life and Writing* (London, 1919), pp. 256–66. Browne translated from the text in *The Complete Works of Venerable Bede, in the Original Latin* by the Rev. J. A. Giles (London, 1843), V, 193–200. Giles took his text from a manuscript in the public library of Boulogne—a large quarto of the eighth or ninth century, and formerly belonging to the monastery of St. Bertin at St. Omer; it is written in double columns on parchment, divided into two books, and contains fifty homilies (pp. xi–xii). Browne studied all the homilies and selected this as representative. The sermon text is translated from Giles, Homilia XXVII.

into the coasts of Caesarea Philippi." Philip, as Luke informs us, was tetrarch of Iturea and of the region of Trachonitis. He built a city in the district where the Jordan rises, at the foot of Mount Lebanon, a district which bounds Judea towards the north, and he named it Caesarea Philippi, after his own name, and at the same time in honour of Tiberius Caesar, under whom he governed the country.

"Jesus asked His disciples, saying, Whom do men say that I, the Son of Man, am?" He does not ask as though He knew not what His disciples and others thought of Him. He questions the disciples as to their opinion, in order that He may worthily reward their confession of a true faith. For as, when all were questioned, Peter alone answered for all, so what the Lord answered to Peter, in Peter He answered to all. And He asks what others think of Him, in order that the erroneous opinions of others might be exposed, and so it would be shown that the disciples received the truth of their confession not from the common belief, but from the very secrets of revelation from the Lord. "Whom do men say that I, the Son of Man, am?" He asks. Right well does He call them "men" who spoke of Him only as Son of Man, because they knew not the secrets of His Divinity. For they who can receive the mysteries of His Divinity are deservedly said to be more than men. The Apostle [meaning of course St. Paul, known in the mediaeval times as "The Apostle"] himself beareth witness, "Eye hath not seen nor ear heard, nor have entered into the heart of man, the things which God hath prepared for them that love Him." And having premised this of men, that is, of those whose knowledge is from the human heart, the human ear, the human eye, the Apostle presently adds, of himself and of those like him who surpassed the ordinary knowledge of the human race, "but God hath revealed them unto us by His Spirit." In the same way here, when the Lord had questioned the disciples as to whom men held Him to be, and they had stated the different views of different persons, He says to them:

"But whom do ye say that I am?" as though setting them apart from ordinary men, and implying that they were made gods and sons of God by adoption, according to that saying of the Psalmist, "I have said, Ye are gods, and ye are all the children of the Most Highest."

"Simon Peter answered and said, Thou art the Christ, the Son of the living God." He calls Him the "living" God by way of distinction from the false gods which heathendom in its various delusions made to itself to worship, either of dead men, or—greater folly still—of insensate matter. Of which false gods it is sung in the Psalm, "their idols are silver and gold, the work of men's hands." And mark well, my beloved, for it is worthy of all admiration, how, when the true view of both the natures of the same Lord our Saviour is to be expressed, it is the Lord who sets forth the humility of the manhood He had taken upon Him, the disciple who shows the excellency of the divine eternity. The Lord says of Himself that which is the less, the disciple says of the Lord that which is the greater. So, too, in the Gospel, the Lord was accustomed to speak of Himself much more often as Son of Man than as Son of God, that He might admonish us of the dispensation which He undertook for us. And we ought the more humbly to reverence the high things of His divinity, the more we remember that for our exaltation He descended to the low estate of manhood. For if among the mysteries of the Incarnation, by which we have been redeemed, we cherish always in pious memory the power of the divinity by which we have been

created, we too with Peter are rewarded with blessing from on high. For when Peter confesses Him to be the Christ, the Son of the living God, see what follows: *"Jesus answered and said, Blessed art thou, Simon Bar-Jona."* It is certain, then, that after true confession of Christ there remain the true rewards of blessedness.

Let us now consider attentively what and how great is that name with which He glorifies the perfect confessor of His name, that by a true confession we may deserve to be partakers of this also. "Blessed art thou, Simon Bar-Jona." Bar-Jona in Syriac signifies "son of a dove." And rightly is the Apostle Peter called son of a dove, for the dove is without guile, and Peter followed his Lord in prudent and pious guilelessness, mindful of that precept of guilelessness and truth which he and his fellow-disciples received from the same Master—"Be ye wise as serpents, and harmless as doves." And surely, since the Holy Spirit descended upon the Lord in the form of a dove, he is rightly called "Son of a Dove" who is shown to have been filled with the grace of the Spirit. And justly does the Lord reward him who loved Him and confessed Him, by declaring that he, who asserted Him to be Son of the living God, is son of the Holy Spirit. Of course no faithful man doubts that these two sonships are very different. For the Lord Christ is Son of God by nature: Peter, as also the other elect, son of the Holy Spirit by grace. Christ is Son of the living God, because He is born of Him: Peter is son of the Holy Spirit, because he is born again of Him. Christ is Son of God before all time, for He is that virtue of God and wisdom of God which saith, "The Lord possessed Me in the beginning of His way, before His works of old." Peter is son of the Holy Spirit from the time when, illumined by Him, he received the grace of divine knowledge. And because the will of the Holy Trinity is one, and the operation one, when the Lord had said, "Blessed art thou, Simon Bar-Jona," that is, son of the grace of the Spirit, He rightly proceeded to say:

"For flesh and blood hath not revealed it unto thee; but my Father which is in Heaven." It was indeed the Father who revealed it: for the grace of the Father and of the Holy Spirit is one, as also that of the Son, which may be proved very easily from sacred Scripture. For the Apostle says of the Father, "God hath sent forth the Spirit of His Son into your hearts." The Son Himself says of the Holy Spirit, "But when the Comforter is come, whom I will send unto you from the Father." The Apostle says of the Holy Spirit, "But all these worketh that one and the selfsame Spirit, dividing to every man severally as He will." The Father therefore sends the Spirit, the Son sends the Spirit: the Spirit Himself breatheth where He listeth, because, as we have said, the will and the operations of the Father, the Son, and the Holy Spirit, is one. And hence it is fittingly said, that the Father which is in heaven revealed to the son of the dove that mystery of faith which flesh and blood could not reveal. Now flesh and blood we rightly understand to mean men puffed up with the wisdom of the flesh, ignorant of the guilelessness of the dove, and thus as far as possible removed from the wisdom of the Spirit. Of whom it has been said above, that in their ignorance of Christ some said that He was John the Baptist; some Elias; and others Jeremias, or one of the prophets. Of such men the Apostle saith: "But the natural man receiveth not the things of the Spirit of God."

To proceed. *"And I say unto thee, That thou art Peter, and upon this rock I will build my Church."* Peter, who was before named Simon, received from the Lord the name of Peter on account of the strength of his faith and the constancy of his confession; for his mind clung firmly to That of which it is written, "that rock was Christ." "And upon this rock," that is, upon the Lord and Saviour who gave to him that knew Him, loved Him, confessed Him, a share in His own name, so that from the Rock he should be called Peter; on which Rock the Church is builded, because only by believing and loving Christ, by receiving the Sacraments of Christ, by observing the commandments of Christ, can man arrive at the lot of the elect, at eternal life. To this the Apostle [again of course St. Paul] beareth witness when he saith, "For other foundation can no man lay than that is laid, which is Jesus Christ."

"*And the gates of Hell shall not prevail against it.*" The gates of Hell are wicked doctrines, which seduce men and bring them to Hell. The gates of Hell, further, are the tortures and the blandishments of persecutors, who by terrifying and enticing unstable souls, open unto them an entrance into eternal death. Further, the gates of Hell are the evil deeds and the unseemly words of believers, inasmuch as they show the way of perdition to those who allow them or follow their example. For even faith, if it have not works, is dead in itself, and evil communications corrupt good manners. Many, then, are the gates of Hell; but not one of them prevails against the Church which is builded on the Rock: for one who has received the faith of Christ with the inmost love of his heart, easily puts down every temptation from without. But a believer who has depraved and betrayed his belief, either by wrongdoing or by denial, is to be taken as having built the house of his confession, not on a rock with the Lord as his helper, but on sand with no foundation: that is, he must be held to have made pretence of being a Christian, with no simple and true determination to follow Christ, but with some frail earthly purpose.

"*And I will give unto thee the keys of the kingdom of Heaven.*" He who confessed the King of Heaven with a devotion beyond that of others, had worthily conferred upon him beyond others the keys of the kingdom of Heaven; that all might know, how that without such confession and faith none may enter into the kingdom of Heaven. And He describes, as "the keys of the kingdom of Heaven," that knowledge and power of discerning by which the worthy would be received into the kingdom, the unworthy rejected. It is evidently on this account that He added:

"*And whatsoever thou shalt bind on earth shall be bound in Heaven: and whatsoever thou shalt loose on earth shall be loosed in Heaven.*" This power of binding and of loosing seems to be given by the Lord to Peter alone; but without the slightest doubt it is given to the other Apostles also. Christ Himself bears witness to this, for after the triumph of His Passion and Resurrection He appeared to them, and breathing on them said, "Receive ye the Holy Ghost: whosoever sins ye remit, they are remitted unto them; and whosoever sins ye retain, they are retained." Nay, the same function is committed now, in the person of the bishops and priests, to the whole Church, so that after knowledge of the case of sinners it may take pity on those whom it sees to be humble and truly penitent, and absolve them from the fear of eternal death; while it marks as bound under everlasting punishments those whom it finds to be persistent in their sins. Whence in another place the Lord says of one who is once and again taken in a fault and yet repenteth not—"But if he neglect to hear the Church, let him be unto thee as an heathen man and a publican." And lest any should deem it a light thing to be condemned by the judgment of the Church, He adds presently these terrible words, "Verily I say unto you, whatsoever ye shall bind on earth shall be bound

in Heaven; and whatsoever ye shall loose on earth shall be loosed in Heaven."
To the whole Church, then, of the elect is there given authority to bind and
loose according to the measure of sins and of repentance. But the blessed Peter,
who confessed Christ with a true faith, and followed Him with a true love,
received in a special manner the keys of the kingdom of Heaven and the first
place of the power of judgment; in order that all believers throughout the world
may understand that no man who in any way separates himself from the unity
of faith and fellowship can be absolved from the chains of sin or enter the gate
of the kingdom of Heaven. So that, my dearest brethren, we must of necessity
learn with the utmost care the sacraments of the faith which he taught, and show
forth works meet for faith. We must with all vigilance beware of the manifold
and subtle snares of the gates of Hell, that so we may be worthy to enter into the
gates of the daughter of Sion, that is, into the joys of the city which is on high.
And let us not suppose that it suffices for salvation that we be like unto the
crowds of careless and ignorant persons in faith or in deeds, for there is in the
sacred writings one only rule laid down for faith and life. But as often as the
examples of those who err are brought before us, let us turn away the eyes of our
mind lest they behold vanity, and carefully investigate what truth itself teaches.
Let us follow the example of the blessed Peter, who rejected the errors of others,
and made with the mouth an unwavering profession of the hidden things of the
true faith which he had learned, and kept them in his heart with invincible
care. For in this place we learn of the faithfulness of confession; while of the
virtue of single love for Christ He beareth witness Himself in another place,
when some of His disciples went back, and He said unto the twelve, "Will ye
also go away?" Peter answered Him, "Lord, to whom shall we go? Thou hast
the words of eternal life. And we believe and are sure that Thou art that Christ,
the son of the living God." If we set ourselves to follow his example, my brethren,
according to our ability, we too shall be able with him to be called blessed and to
be blessed; to us, too, the name of Simon will be meet, that is, of one that obeys
Christ; we too, on account of the guilelessness of our faith that is not feigned,
and the grace we receive from the Lord, shall be called sons of the virtue of the
dove; and He Himself, rejoicing with us in the spiritual progress of our soul,
shall say, "Behold, thou art fair, my love; behold, thou art fair; thou hast dove's
eyes." And so it cometh to pass that if we build on the rock of faith, gold, silver,
precious stones, that is, the perfect works of virtues, the fires of tribulation shall
bring no harm, the storms of temptation shall not prevail. Nay, rather, proved
by adversity, we shall receive the crown of life, promised before the ages by Him
who liveth and reigneth God, with the Father, in the unity of the Holy Spirit,
for ever and ever. Amen.

∽

BIBLIOGRAPHICAL NOTE

Bede's work on rhetoric, *De Schematibus Et Tropis*, was translated by Gussie Hecht
Tanenhaus and published in *The Quarterly Journal of Speech*, XLVIII (October 1962),
237–53.

The four spurious homilies anthologized are: "Sermon on All Saints"; "The Meeting of Mercy and Justice"; "A Sermon for Any Day"; "A Sermon for Sundays." These

were translated by J. M. Neale in *Mediaeval Preachers and Mediaeval Preaching* (1856), pp. 2–18. Neale noted that the homilies were rejected by Giles, and explained that "these discourses, if not Bede's, are of the age of Bede." William Jennings Bryan, in anthologizing "Sermon on All Saints" in his *The World's Famous Orations* (1906), III, 3–7, used the Neale translation, but printed it as genuine. David J. Brewer, in his *The World's Best Orations* (1899), I, 340–45, printed "The Meeting of Mercy and Justice," "A Sermon for Any Day," and "A Sermon for Sundays," in the Neale text, without noting his qualifications. To touch up the horrors, Brewer changed the title of "A Sermon for Sundays" to "The Torments of Hell," which was the top-page line in Neale.

For a checklist of what is spurious, what genuine in Bede, see M. L. W. Laistner and H. H. King, *A Hand-List of Bede Manuscripts* (1943).

Aelfric

(955–1020-25)

Aelfric was the greatest prose writer of his age. In an attempt to bring worthy works to the people, he wrote English compositions on grammar, astronomy, and pedagogy, in addition to lives of the saints, pastoral letters, and sermons, and he made translations from the Bible.

Not much is known of his life. He was a Wessex boy, and went to school at the Old Monastery of Winchester, operated by the Benedictines. By 987 he was a priest at the newly founded abbey at Cernel in Dorsetshire. About 1005 he became abbot of the new abbey at Eynsham, on the Thames above Oxford. He is not to be confused with other Aelfrics, such as the Bishop of Crediton, the Archbishop of York, or the Archbishop of Canterbury.

Aelfric's active life began in a period of great discouragement in England. In 793 the Danes began their raids on the Island, and destroyed many abbeys, including Bede's Yarrow and Wearmouth. The result was a great decline in monastic learning. In the pattern of King Alfred before him, Aelfric sought to preserve the best that had been recorded, and to make it available to the people. Like others of his time, he believed the world would end in the year 1000: "Men have need of good instruction, especially at this time, which is the ending of the world," he wrote in the preface to his first volume of sermons.

So that people in the churches might have intelligent instruction given in English, Aelfric composed two volumes of sermons to be read to congregations by the priests. Originally there were forty sermons in each volume, to be delivered on Sundays and general feastdays; not all ordinary Sundays were provided for. "I thought that it were less tedious to hear, if the one book were read in the course of one year, and the other in the year following," he wrote in the preface to the second volume. Although he wrote for a popular audience, he tried to keep alive the best traditions of scholarship, and his adjuration in the same preface might well be noted by contemporary writers of dissertations and scholarly articles:

I now pray and implore, in the name of God, if any one will transcribe this
book, that he carefully rectify it by the copy, lest, through negligent writers, we
be blamed. He does great evil who writes false, unless he rectify it, as though
he brought the true doctrine to false heresy; therefore should every one correct that
which he had perverted to wrong, if he will be guiltless at God's doom.

Since the sermons were composed to be read aloud, they have rhythm and
informality. Of his writing, Emile Legouis says: "Aelfric's prose, unlike that of
Alfred, is written not to be read but to be spoken to the people, in the conventional tone of a priest delivering a sermon. It has therefore a rhythm which brings
it near to verse: its sentences are divided into sections, more or less equivalent to
the metrical line, and it is frequently alliterative." [1]

The sermons were not intended to be original, but were rather adaptations
from the Latin fathers. In his Latin preface to the first volume, Aelfric gives as
his sources Augustine, Jerome, Bede, Gregory, Smaragdus, and Haymo.

This Easter homily has become a document in English church history. As the
translators say, "The date (1567) of the publication, in Elizabeth's reign, of the
Easter Homily, may conveniently be reckoned as that which marks the beginning
of the study of English, as we now understand that term." English Protestants
used this sermon in various reprintings to show that the old English church did
not believe in transubstantiation. Whatever the merits of this issue, on its own
merits this sermon is a delightful example of tightly reasoned and patristically
supported high imagery in exposition of the true significance of Easter Communion.

&

A Sermon on the Sacrifice on Easter-Day [*]

994

Dearly beloved, you have frequently been told about the resurrection of our
Saviour—how, on this day, after His passion, He mightily arose from death. We
will now, through the grace of God, enlighten you concerning the holy eucharist
to which you are about to go, and guide your understanding with regard to that
mystery, according to the teaching of both the Old Testament and the New, lest
any doubt as to that banquet of life do you harm.

[1] Emile Legouis and Louis Cazamian, *A History of English Literature* (new ed.; New
York, 1929), p. 54.

[*] Aelfric wrote his first volume of sermons in 990–991, and the second volume in
994. About 1020 he made a revised edition. The first volume of forty sermons was
collected and edited by Benjamin Thorpe (London: Aelfric Society, 1844) as *The
Sermones Catholici, or Homilies of Aelfric.* The second volume of forty-five sermons
was issued in 1846. The Thorpe edition was transcribed from an old English manuscript of the first edition in the Cambridge University Library, a copy coeval with
Aelfric but probably not an autograph. The sermon here given is Number 15 in the
second volume (pp. 263–83). The text is a translation by Albert S. Cook and Chauncey B. Tinker, in their edition of *Select Translations from Old English Prose* (Boston,
1908), pp. 164–73, except the last paragraph, which is from Thorpe. The Cook–
Tinker translation has been preferred to Thorpe's because the style is freer flowing and
the compression of about a third makes the sermon more compact and artistic.

God Almighty directed Moses, the leader in Egypt, to command[1] the people of Israel that, on the night in which they were to depart thence to the promised land, they should take a yearling lamb for every hearth, offer that lamb to God, and then kill it, making with its blood the sign of the cross over their door-posts and lintels, and afterwards eat of the lamb's flesh roasted, together with unleavened bread and wild lettuce.

.   .   .

[A paragraph of twenty-one lines is here omitted; it is an aside about cooking and eating the lamb, burning the remains, and crossing the Red Sea.]

To-day Christian men may not keep the old law literally, but at least they are bound to know its spiritual significance. The innocent lamb which the ancient Israel used to slay was a symbol, spiritually interpreted, of the passion of Christ, who, though innocent, shed His holy blood for our sins. Wherefore at every mass God's servants sing, *Agnus Dei, qui tollis peccata mundi, miserere nobis,* which, being interpreted, is, "O Lamb of God, who takest away the sins of the world, have mercy upon us." The people of Israel were delivered from sudden death, and from bondage to Pharaoh, through the offering of the lamb, which signified Christ's passion, by which we are redeemed from eternal death and from the power of the raging devil, if we rightly believe on the true Redeemer of the whole world, Jesus Christ. The lamb was offered at evening, and our Saviour suffered in the sixth age of the world, which is considered the evening of this transitory world. Over their door-posts and lintels was marked with the blood of the lamb *Tau,* that is, the sign of the cross, and thus were they protected from the angel that slew the first-born children of the Egyptians. And we must mark our foreheads and our hearts with the sign of Christ's cross, in order that, being thus marked with the blood of our Lord's passion, we may be saved from destruction.

The people of Israel ate the flesh of the lamb at their Eastertide, when they were delivered, and we now partake spiritually of Christ's body and drink His blood, when with true faith we receive the holy eucharist. The time when they had been saved from Pharaoh, and had departed from the country, they were accustomed to keep for seven days with great honor, as their Eastertide. And in like manner, we Christian men keep Christ's resurrection for seven days as our Eastertide, because through His passion and resurrection we are redeemed, and we shall be purified by partaking of the holy sacrament, even as Christ Himself said in His gospel:[2] "Verily, verily I say unto you, except ye eat my flesh and drink my blood, ye have no life in you. He that eateth my flesh and drinketh my blood dwelleth in me and I in him, and he hath eternal life, and I will raise him up at the last day. I am the living bread which came down from heaven. Not as your fathers did eat heavenly food in the wilderness, and are dead: he that eateth of this bread shall live for ever." He blessed bread before His passion, and gave it to His disciples, saying, "Eat this bread, it is my body; this do in remembrance of me." Afterwards He blessed wine in a cup, saying, "Drink ye all of it, this is my blood which is shed for many for the remission of sins." The

[1] Exod. 12:3 ff.
[2] Cf. John 6:53 ff.; Matt. 26:26–28.

apostles did as Christ had commanded them, in that they were afterwards wont to bless bread and wine in remembrance of Him.[3] So also, according to Christ's behest, their successors and all priests consecrate bread and wine for communion in His name, and with the apostolic blessing.

Some men have often wondered, and frequently wonder still, how bread prepared from grain, and baked by the heat of the fire, can be changed to Christ's body; or how wine, pressed from many grapes, can by any blessing be changed to the Lord's blood. Now we say to such men that some things are related of Christ figuratively, and some literally. It is certain that Christ was born of a virgin, and by His own will suffered death and was buried, and on this day arose from death. He is called in a figurative sense Bread, and Lamb, and Lion, and so on. He is called Bread, since He is our life, and that of the angels; He is called Lamb on account of His innocence, and Lion because of the strength with which He overcame the powerful devil. Yet according to His true nature Christ is neither bread, nor a lamb, nor a lion. Why then is the holy eucharist called Christ's body, if it is not truly that which it is called? The bread and the wine which are consecrated through the mass of priests appear one thing to our human understanding, as viewed from without, and quite another to believing souls, as viewed from within. From without, both in appearance and taste, they seem bread and wine, but after the consecration they are truly, through a spiritual mystery, the body and blood of Christ. When a heathen child is baptized, its outward appearance is not altered, though its inner nature is changed. Through Adam's transgression it is sinful when brought to the font, but it is cleansed of all inward sins, although its outward appearance is not transformed. In like manner the holy baptismal water, which is called the well of life, in appearance resembles other water, and is subject to corruption; but when, through the priestly benediction, the power of the Holy Ghost is brought nigh this corruptible water, by its spiritual efficacy it cleanses body and soul from all sins. In this one element we find two characteristics: in its true nature the water is a corruptible fluid, but according to a spiritual mystery it has healing power. So also if we consider the holy eucharist in a physical sense, we see that it is a corruptible and changeable substance, but if we discern its spiritual efficacy, then we perceive that there is life in it, and that upon those who receive it in true faith it confers immortality. Great is the difference between the corruptible virtue of the holy sacrament and its visible aspect. By nature it is corruptible bread and wine, but through the power of the divine word it is indeed the body and the blood of Christ, not however in a literal sense, but spiritually. Very different is the body in which Christ suffered from the body which is consecrated to the eucharist. The body in which Christ suffered was born of Mary's flesh, with blood and bones, skin and sinews and human limbs, quickened by a rational soul; whereas His spiritual body, which we call the eucharist, is gathered from many grains, is without blood and bone and limbs, and hath no soul; wherefore it is to be interpreted in no wise literally, but wholly in a spiritual sense. Whatever the sacrament contains of life-giving power comes from its spiritual virtue and invisible efficacy. Hence the holy eucharist is called a mystery, because whereas one thing is seen, another is to be understood, that which is seen having a material aspect, and that which it symbolizes possessing spiritual efficacy. Verily Christ's body, which suffered death

[3] Cf. I Cor. 11:24, 25.

and rose from death, shall henceforth never die, but is eternal and impassible. The sacrament is temporal, not eternal, corruptible, distributed in fragments, chewed between the teeth and sent into the stomach, but nevertheless, by reason of spiritual power, its parts are all one. Many partake of the holy body, and yet, through a spiritual mystery, the whole of it is in each several part. Although a smaller part fall to one man, yet there is no more efficacy in the greater part than in the less, because, through its invisible virtue, it is complete in each man.

This mystery is a pledge and a symbol; Christ's body is truth. This pledge we hold mystically until we come to the truth, and then will it be fulfilled. Verily it is, as we said before, the body and the blood of Christ, not literally, but spiritually. Nor must ye wonder how this is brought about, but have faith that it is thus effected.

. . .

[A paragraph of eighteen lines is here omitted. It is a narrative of how at Mass "God's angel" dismembered a child's body and poured its blood into a cup. Later the flesh was turned to bread and the blood to wine.]

Paul the apostle, in an epistle to believers, wrote thus [4] of the ancient people Israel: "All our forefathers were baptized in the cloud and in the sea, and they did all eat the same spiritual meat, and did all drink the same spiritual drink. They drank from that Rock that followed them, and that Rock was Christ." The rock from which the water flowed was not Christ literally, but it symbolized Christ, who declared unto all believers: "If any man thirst, let him come unto me and drink, and out of his belly shall flow living water." [5] This He said of the Holy Ghost, whom those received who believed on Him. The apostle Paul said that the people of Israel ate the same spiritual meat, and drank the same spiritual drink, because the heavenly food which fed them for forty years, and the water which flowed from the rock, symbolized Christ's body and His blood, which are now offered daily in God's Church. They were the same which we now offer, not literally, but spiritually.

We told you a little while ago that before His passion Christ blessed bread and wine for communion, saying, "This is my body and my blood." He had not yet suffered, but nevertheless through invisible power He turned the bread into His own body, and the wine into His blood, even as He had formerly done in the wilderness before He was born as man, when He changed the heavenly meat into His flesh, and the water that flowed from the rock into His blood. Many did eat of the heavenly meat in the wilderness, and drink the spiritual drink, and then died, even as Christ said. Christ did not mean that death which no man can escape, but He meant the eternal death which, because of unbelief, some of the people had merited. Moses and Aaron, and many others of the people who pleased God, ate the heavenly bread, and did not suffer eternal death, although they died the common death. They perceived that the heavenly meat was visible and corruptible, but they understood the visible thing in a spiritual sense, and partook of it spiritually. Jesus said, "Whoso eateth my flesh, and drinketh my blood, hath eternal life." He did not command men to eat the body with which

[4] Cf. I Cor. 10:1–4.
[5] Cf. John 7:37–39.

He was invested, nor to drink the blood which He shed for us, but by these words He meant the holy eucharist, which is spiritually His body and His blood, and he who tastes of that with believing heart hath eternal life.

Under the old law believers offered to God divers gifts that prefigured Christ's body, which He Himself afterwards offered to His heavenly Father as a sacrifice for our sins. Verily this sacrament which is now consecrated at God's altar is a memorial of Christ's body, which He offered for us, and of His blood, which He shed for us, even as He Himself commanded, "This do in remembrance of me."

Christ suffered once through Himself,[6] but nevertheless His passion is daily renewed through the mystery of the holy eucharist at holy mass. Wherefore, as has often been manifested, the holy mass greatly benefits both the living and the dead. We must also consider that, according to a spiritual mystery, the holy sacrament is both the body of Christ and that of all believers, as the wise Augustine said of it: "If you will understand concerning the body of Christ, hear the apostle Paul, who says, 'You are truly the body and the members of Christ.' Now your mystery is laid on God's table, and you receive your mystery, to which you yourselves have been transformed. Be what you see on the altar, and receive what you yourselves are."[7] Again the apostle Paul said on this point, "We, being many, are one bread and one body in Christ."[8] Understand now and rejoice: it is many who constitute one bread and one body in Christ. He is our Head, and we are His members. The bread is not made of one grain, but of many, nor the wine of one grape, but of many.[9] In like manner we must have unity in our Lord, as it is written concerning the multitude of them that believed that they were in as great unity as if they had had one heart and one soul.[10]

Christ blessed on His table the mystery[11] of our peace and our unity. He who receives the mystery of unity, and holds not the bond of true peace,[12] receives not the mystery for himself, but as a witness against himself.[13] Much do Christian men gain by going frequently to communion, if in their hearts they bear innocence to the altar, and if they are not beset with sins. To the wicked man it brings no good, but rather destruction, if he taste of the sacrament unworthily.[14] Holy books command that water be mixed with the wine used for communion, because water is typical of the people, even as wine is of the blood of Christ, and therefore neither should be offered without the other at holy mass, that Christ may be with us, and we with Christ, the Head with the members, and the members with the Head.

.   .   .

[6] Cf. I Pet. 3:18.

[7] Augustine, Sermo CCXXIX (Migne, *Patrologiae Latinae*, XXXVIII, 1103): *Quia passus est pro nobis, commendavit nobis in isto sacramento corpus et sanguinem suum; quod etiam fecit et nos ipsos. . . .*

[8] I Cor. 10:17.

[9] Augustine, Sermo CCXXVII (Migne, 1099): *Unus panis, unum corpus, multi sumus. . . .*

[10] Acts 4:32.

[11] Perhaps in the sense of "sacrament."

[12] Eph. 4:3.

[13] See note 7, above.

[14] Cf. I Cor. 11:29.

[Four paragraphs of eighty-three lines are here omitted. Various symbolisms are explained, such as the significance of bitter field lettuce and unleavened bread.]

This tide [15] is in the Hebrew tongue called Pascha, that is in Latin, *Transitus*, and in English, *Passover*; because on this day God's folk passed from the land of Egypt over the Red sea, from thraldom to the promised country. Our Lord also passed at this time, as the evangelist John said, from this world to His Heavenly Father.[16] We should follow our Head, and pass from the devil to Christ, from this unsteady world to His steadfast kingdom; but we should first, in our present life, pass from sins to holy virtues, from vices to good morals, if we desire, after this transitory life, to pass to the life everlasting, and, after our resurrection, to Jesus Christ. May He lead us to His Living Father, who gave Him to death for our sins. Be to Him glory and praise for that beneficence to all eternity. Amen.

◇

BIBLIOGRAPHICAL NOTE

For the life of Aelfric, descriptions of his works, and detailed bibliography, see *Aelfric—A New Study of His Life and Writings* by Caroline Louisa White, "Yale Studies in English" (1898).

As an example of studies of Aelfric's artistry, see *Studies in the Word-Order of Aelfric's Catholic Homilies and Lives of the Saints* by Charles Robin Barrett (1953).

The source of Aelfric's ideas in the sermon is attributed to Bertram by John Lingard in his *The History and Antiquities of the Anglo-Saxon Church* (2nd ed.; 1858; II, 414): "There is scarcely a sentence in the homily which may not be traced to the work of Bertram." (By Bertram, Lingard means Ratramnus, a ninth-century monk of the Benedictine abbey of Corbie, near Amiens; his treatise on the Eucharist, *De Corpore et Sanguine Domini* [On the Body and Blood of Christ] is in Migne, *Patrologiae Latinae*, CXXI, 126–70, especially col. 147.)

In 1567, as noted above, Aelfric's homily was published as a document in the history of the English church. The edition was made by Archbishop Matthew Parker and his chaplain, John Joscelyn, as *A Testimonie of Antiquitie, shewing the auncient Fayth in the Church of England touching the Sacrament of the Body and Bloude of the Lord*. The work was reprinted in 1623, 1638, and 1687. The edition of 1638 was titled *A Sermon of the Paschall Lambe, and of the Sacramental Body and Bloud of Christ Our Saviour. Written In The Old Saxon Tongue, before the Conquest, and appointed in the reigne of the saxons to bee spoken unto the people at Easter, before they should receive the Communion.* In the margin opposite the fifth paragraph (of this text) and the lines, "By nature it is corruptible bread and wine, but through the power of the divine word it is indeed the body and the blood of Christ, not however in a literal sense, but spiritually," is printed *no transubstantiation*, with a list of four arguments following.

[15] Time.
[16] John 22:17.

Wulfstan

(?–1023)

Wulfstan, statesman, reformer, legislator, canonist, and homilist, was Bishop of London, 996–1002, Bishop of Worcester, 1002–1016, and Bishop of York from 1002 until his death. He was adviser to King Ethelred from 1008 to 1012, and upon Cnut's becoming King of all England in 1016, served as counselor and lawgiver. Nothing is known of his early life. One of his main claims to fame is the sermon given below, titled in Latin, *Sermo Lupi Ad Anglos Quando Dani Maxime Persecuti Sunt Eos, Quod Fuit Anno Millesimo XIII Ab Incarnatione Domini Nostri Iesu Cristi*, but recorded in Anglo-Saxon.

The sermon was given in a period of great tribulation for the English. For over three centuries the Danes had raided and invaded England. In 1011 Canterbury was beset; Archbishop Aelfheah, an abbess, monks, and nuns were carried off as hostages. In 1012, on Palm Sunday, Aelfheah was dragged out of prison at Greenwich, and pelted to death with bones of oxen slaughtered for a feast. That year Ethelred paid 48,000 pounds of silver in an attempt to placate the Danes. In the year Wulfstan's sermon was preached, Cnut the Dane put ashore at Sandwich English hostages from Wessex and the Midlands with their noses, ears, and hands cut off. It was under these conditions that Wulfstan preached his sermon. Curiously, he does not blame the Danes for their atrocities, but puts responsibility for punishment of their sins on the English. It should be noted that Cnut later delegated much of his administration to the English, and became, as monarchs go, benevolent.

In comparing Wulfstan's sermon with Aelfric's, one notes a more powerful, argumentative appeal, with little attention to figurative language or to biblical support. As Dorothy Bethurum (pp. 91, 89) says, "All the figures of sound taught by the manuals of rhetoric appear in abundance," but "severely absent are most of the *figurae sententiarum*, particularly metaphor and simile, or any of the analogical interpretations of scripture . . . ; whatever the tone, the sermons show the most careful adjustment to his audience, whether they are addressed *ad clerum* or *ad populum*, and above all, they are designed for public delivery." John S. Westlake (p. 144) has contrasted Aelfric's relatively mild exposition and exhortation with Wulfstan's vigorous pleading:

> Wulfstan's style is much more vehement than that of Aelfric. He is preacher rather than teacher, appealing more to the emotions than to the reason of his hearers, fertile in concrete illustrations, and avoiding the subtle symbolism in which Aelfric delighted. His sentences, though not deficient in lucidity, are very long; synonym is heaped on synonym and clause upon clause; yet the chanting sense of rhythm is always present; epithets are balanced, and the effect is often heightened by the use of antithesis. But, as might be expected from one whose life was so much absorbed by the administration of public affairs, his style is that of the rhetorician rather than of the philosopher.

∾

The Sermon of the Wolf to the English When the Danes Persecuted Them Most, Which Was in the Year 1014 From the Incarnation of Our Lord Jesus Christ *

1014

Beloved men, realize what is true: this world is in haste and the end approaches; and therefore in the world things go from bad to worse, and so it must of necessity deteriorate greatly on account of the people's sins before the coming of Antichrist, and indeed it will then be dreadful and terrible far and wide throughout the world.[1]

Understand well also that now for many years the devil has led astray this people too greatly and there has been little loyalty among men, though they spoke fair enough; and too many wrongs prevailed in the land, and there were never many men who sought after a remedy as zealously as one should; but daily evil was piled on evil and wrongs and many lawless acts committed far too widely throughout all this people; also we have on that account suffered many losses and insults, and, if we are to experience any improvement, we must then deserve better of God than we have previously done. For with great deserts have we merited the miseries which oppress us, and with very great deserts must we obtain relief from God if henceforward things are to start to improve. For lo! we know full well that a great breach will require much repair, and a great fire no little water, if the fire is to be quenched at all; and great is the necessity for every man that he keep henceforward God's laws eagerly and pay God's dues rightly.

Among heathen peoples one dare not withhold little or much of what is appointed to the worship of false gods; and we everywhere withhold God's dues all too often. And one dare not among heathen peoples curtail within the sanctuary or outside any of the things which are brought to the false gods and delivered for sacrifices, and we have entirely despoiled God's houses inside and out. And the servants of God[2] are everywhere deprived of respect and protection; while among heathen peoples one dare not in any way ill-use the servants of false gods as one now does the servants of God too widely, where Christians ought to keep God's law and protect God's servants.

But it is true what I say, there is need of that relief, for God's dues have dwindled too long in every district within this nation, and the laws of the people

---

* This translation is by Dorothy Whitelock as given in *English Historical Documents*, Vol. I, ed. Dorothy Whitelock (London: Eyre & Spottiswoode, 1955), pp. 854–59, and is printed here with permission of the publishers. The notes are also Miss Whitelock's. For the text she used an eleventh-century MS, Cotton Nero A; fol. 110 ff. in the British Museum, and collated it with other MSS, as indicated in the notes.

[1] MS. C (C.C.C.C., 201) incorporates what was probably a marginal note: "This was composed in the days of King Ethelred, four years before he died. Let him who will, pay heed how it then was and what happened afterwards." As this gives an impossible date for the text as it has come down, it seems possible that the scribe of C wrote "four years" for "few years."

[2] Wulfstan defines this expression elsewhere as covering "bishops and abbots, monks and nuns, priests and women under religious vows."

have deteriorated all too much,[3] and sanctuaries are violated far and wide, and the houses of God are entirely despoiled of ancient privileges and stripped inside of all that is seemly.[4] And widows are wrongfully forced into marriage, and too many are reduced to poverty and greatly humiliated. And poor men are sorely deceived and cruelly defrauded [5] and sold far and wide out of this country into the power of foreigners, although quite innocent; and children in the cradle are enslaved for petty theft [6] by cruel injustice widely throughout this people. And the rights of freemen are withdrawn and the rights of slaves are restricted and charitable obligations are curtailed; [7] and, in short, God's laws are hated and his precepts despised. And therefore we all through God's anger are frequently disgraced, let him perceive it who can; and this injury will become common to all this people, though one may not think so, unless God protect us.

For it is clear and manifest in us all that we have previously transgressed more than we have amended, and therefore much is assailing this people. Things have not gone well now for a long time at home or abroad, but there has been devastation and famine, burning and bloodshed in every district again and again; and stealing and killing, sedition and pestilence, murrain and disease, malice and hate and spoliation by robbers have harmed us very grievously, and monstrous taxes have afflicted us greatly, and bad seasons have very often caused us failure of crops. For now for many years, as it may seem, there have been in this country many injustices and wavering loyalties among men everywhere.

Now too often a kinsman does not protect a kinsman any more than a stranger, neither a father his son, nor sometimes a son his own father, nor one brother another; nor has any one of us ordered his life as he should, neither ecclesiastics according to rule nor laymen according to law. But we have made desire a law unto us all too often, and have kept neither the precepts nor laws of God or man as we should. Nor has anyone had loyal intentions towards another as justly as he should, but almost everyone has deceived and injured another by word or deed; and in particular almost everyone wrongly stabs another in the back with shameful attack [8]—let him do more, if he can.

For here in the country there are great disloyalties both in matters of Church and State, and also here in the country there are many who are traitors in various ways. And it is the greatest of all treachery in the world that a man betray his

[3] MS. E (Bodleian MS. Hatton 113) adds: "since Edgar died." Wulfstan's writings often refer to the happier conditions of this king's reign.

[4] Three MSS., C, B (C.C.C.C. 419), and H Bodleian MS. 343), add: "and ecclesiastical orders have now for a long time been greatly despised."

[5] MSS. B and H add: "both of reputation (?) and of sustenance and of money and all too often of life."

[6] The laws of Ine state that if a man steal with the knowledge of his household, all are liable to penal slavery. Cnut's laws, drawn up by Wulfstan, legislate against the application of this to young children.

[7] MS. C has an important addition here: "Free men are not allowed to keep their independence, nor go where they wish, nor to deal with their own property as they wish; and slaves are not allowed to keep what they have gained by toil in their own free time, or what good men have granted them in God's favour, and given them in charity for the love of God. But every charitable obligation which ought by rights to be paid eagerly in God's favour every man decreases or withholds, for injustice is too widely common to men and lawlessness dear to them."

[8] MS E adds: "and with accusations."

lord's soul; [9] and a full great treachery it is also in the world that a man should betray his lord to death, or drive him in his lifetime from the land; and both have happened in this country: Edward was betrayed and then killed, and afterwards burnt, [10] [and Ethelred was driven out of his country]. [11] And too many sponsors and godchildren have killed one another far and wide throughout this people. [12] And far too many holy foundations far and wide have come to grief because some men have previously been placed in them, who should not have been, if one wished to show respect to God's sanctuary. And too many Christian people have been sold out of this country now all the time; and all this is hateful to God, let him believe it who will. And it is shameful to speak of what has happened too widely, and it is terrible to know what too many do often, who commit that miserable deed that they contribute together and buy a woman between them as a joint purchase, and practise foul sin with that one woman, one after another, just like dogs, who do not care about filth; and then sell for a price out of the land into the power of strangers God's creature and his own purchase, that he dearly bought. Also we know well where that miserable deed has occurred that a father has sold his son for a price, and a son his mother, and one brother has sold another, into the power of strangers. And all these are grave and terrible deeds, let him understand who will. And yet, what is injuring this people is still greater and even more manifold: many are forsworn and greatly perjured, and pledges are broken again and again; and it is obvious in this people that God's anger violently oppresses us, let him perceive it who can.

And lo! how can greater shame befall men through God's anger than often does us for our own deserts? Though any slave runs away from his master and, deserting Christianity, becomes a viking, and after that it comes about that a conflict takes place between thegn and slave, if the slave slays the thegn, no wergild is paid to any of his kindred; but if the thegn slays the slave whom he owned before, he shall pay the price of a thegn. [13] Very base laws and shameful tributes are common among us, through God's anger, let him understand it who can; and many misfortunes befall this people again and again. Things have not gone well now for a long time at home or abroad, but there has been devastation and persecution in every district again and again, and the English have been for a long time now completely defeated and too greatly disheartened through God's anger; and the pirates so strong with God's consent that often in battle one puts

[9] I.e., by persuading him to do evil, or by failing to carry out religious benefactions for his soul after his death.

[10] Edward the Martyr, murdered in 978. No other authority mentions the burning of the body, but strictly contemporary records are reticent about the whole business, and this categorical statement by a man who must have been at least a youth at the time, and who later had opportunity of learning the facts, deserves attention.

[11] Three MSS., including Nero A I, omit the reference to Ethelred, possibly from motives of policy, for the reason for Ethelred's flight to Normandy late in 1013 was that Swegn, King Cnut's father, had been accepted as king by the English. It is clear, however, that the clause is necessary to complete the sentence, and I have added it from MSS. B and H.

[12] MS. E adds: "in addition to far too many other innocent people who have been destroyed all too widely"; and this is added in the margin of the Nero text.

[13] The Danish freeman was equated for purposes of the wergild with the English thegn, and presumably the Danes claimed this for any member of their forces, even English run-aways.

to flight ten,[14] and sometimes less, sometimes more, all because of our sins. And often ten or a dozen, one after another, insult disgracefully the thegn's wife, and sometimes his daughter or near kinswoman, whilst he looks on, who considered himself brave and mighty and stout enough before that happened. And often a slave binds very fast the thegn who previously was his master and makes him into a slave through God's anger. Alas for the misery, and alas for the public shame which the English now have, all through God's anger. Often two seamen, or maybe three, drive the droves of Christian men from sea to sea, out through this people, huddled together, as a public shame to us all, if we could seriously and rightly feel any shame. But all the insult which we often suffer we repay with honouring those who insult us; we pay them continually and they humiliate us daily; they ravage and they burn,[15] plunder and rob and carry on board; and lo, what else is there in all these events except God's anger clear and visible over this people?

It is no wonder that things go wrong with us, for we know full well that now for many years men have too often not cared what they did by word or deed; but this people, as it may seem, has become very corrupt through manifold sins and many misdeeds: through murders and crimes, through avarice and through greed, through theft and robbery, through the selling of men and through heathen vices, through betrayals and frauds, through breaches of law and through deceit, through attacks on kinsmen and through slayings, through injury of men in holy orders and through adultery, through incest and through various fornications. And also, far and wide, as we said before, more than should be are lost and per-jured through the breaking of oaths and of pledges and through various false-hoods; and failure to observe fasts and festivals widely occurs again and again. And also there are here in the country degenerate apostates[16] and fierce perse-cutors of the Church and cruel tyrants all too many, and widespread scorners of divine laws and Christian virtues, and foolish deriders everywhere among the people, most often of those things which God's messengers command, and espe-cially of those things which always belong to God's law by rights. And there-fore things have now come far and wide to that full evil pass that men are more ashamed now of good deeds than of misdeeds, for too often good deeds are re-viled with derision and godfearing people are blamed all too greatly, and espe-cially are those reproached and all too often treated with contempt who love right and possess the fear of God in any extent. And because people behave thus, blaming all that they should praise, and loathing too much what they should love, they bring all too many to evil intentions and wicked acts, so that they are not ashamed, although they sin greatly and commit wrongs even against God himself, but because of idle calumny they are ashamed to atone for their mis-deeds as the books teach,[17] like those fools who because of their pride will not protect themselves from injury until they cannot, although they much wish it.

Here, in the country as it may seem, too many are sorely blemished with the stains of sin. Here there are manslayers and slayers of their kinsmen, and slayers

[14] MS. C adds: "and two often twenty."

[15] MS. C has instead of "burn": "cut down, bind and insult."

[16] MS. C explains this foreign term by adding "God's adversaries," and MSS. B and H replace apostates by this gloss.

[17] I.e., the penitentials used in the Anglo-Saxon Church, some of which have sur-vived.

of priests and persecutors of monasteries,[18] and here there are perjurers and murderers,[19] and here there are harlots and infanticides and many foul adulterous fornicators, and here there are wizards and sorceresses,[20] and here there are plunderers and robbers and spoliators,[21] and, in short, a countless number of all crimes and misdeeds. And we are not ashamed of it, but we are greatly ashamed to begin the atonement as the books teach, and that is evident in this wretched corrupt people. Alas, many can easily call to mind much besides this which a single man could not quickly investigate, showing how wretchedly things have gone all the time now widely throughout this people. And, indeed, let each examine himself eagerly and not put it off all too long. But lo! in God's name, let us do as is needful for us, save ourselves as we best can, lest we all perish together.

There was a historian in the times of the Britons, called Gildas,[22] who wrote about their misdeeds, how with their sins they angered God so excessively that finally he allowed the army of the English to conquer their land and to destroy the host of the Britons entirely. And that came about, according to what he said,[23] through robbery by the powerful, and through the coveting of ill-gotten gains, through the lawlessness of the people and through unjust judgments, through the sloth [24] of the bishops and the wicked cowardice of God's messengers, who mumbled with their jaws where they should have cried aloud; also through the foul wantonness of the people and through gluttony and manifold sins they destroyed their country and themselves they perished. But let us do as is necessary for us, take warning from such; and it is true what I say, we know worse deeds among the English than we have heard of anywhere among the Britons; and therefore it is very necessary for us to take thought for ourselves and to intercede eagerly with God himself. And let us do as is necessary for us, turn to the right and in some measure leave wrong-doing, and atone very zealously for what we have done amiss; [25] and let us love God and follow God's laws and perform very eagerly what we promised when we received baptism, or those who were our advocates at our baptism; and let us order our words and deeds rightly, and eagerly cleanse our thoughts, and keep carefully oath and pledge, and have some loyalty between us without deceit. And let us often consider the great Judgment to which we all must come, and save ourselves from the surging fire of hell torment, and earn

[18] MS. E adds: "and traitors and open apostates."

[19] MS. E adds: "and here there are injurers of men in orders and adulterers and people greatly corrupt through incest and various fornications."

[20] Wulfstan used the word "valkyries," but it is clear from the context that it does not here refer to a goddess or supernatural being. It originally meant "choosers of the slain." It is used in Old English to gloss classical names, e.g., the Furies, a Gorgon, Bellona, and even Venus.

[21] MS. E adds: "and thieves and injurers of the people and breakers of pledges and treaties."

[22] Gildas wrote *Liber Querulus de Excidio Brittaniae* near the middle of the sixth century. Much of this paragraph is translated literally from a passage in one of Alcuin's letters written after the sack of Lindisfarne by the Danes in 793 (Dümmler, No. 17).

[23] MS. E adds: "through breach of rule by the clergy and breach of law by the laity."

[24] MS. E adds: "and folly."

[25] MS. C adds: "Let us kneel to Christ and with a trembling heart invoke him frequently and gain his mercy."

for ourselves the glories and the joys which God has prepared for those who do his will in the world. God help us. Amen.

⌣

BIBLIOGRAPHICAL NOTE

The student of Wulfstan should consult two scholarly works, *Sermo Lupi Ad Anglos* by Dorothy Whitelock (1939), and *The Homilies of Wulfstan* by Dorothy Bethurum (1957). Miss Whitelock gives the Anglo-Saxon text with detailed notes. Miss Bethurum also gives the text with independent notes. See especially her chapter on "Style," where Wulfstan's sources of rhetoric are detailed; "Wulfstan's practice seems to have been modelled on the teachings of Cicero, particularly as they were interpreted by Augustine" (pp. 88–89). For another translation of the sermon, see Elizabeth W. Manwaring's in Albert S. Cook and Chauncey B. Tinker, *Select Translations from Old English Prose* (1908), pp. 194–99.

See also "From Alfred to the Conquest," by John S. Westlake, *Cambridge History of English Literature,* I, chap. vii, and John W. Lamb, *Saint Wulfstan Prelate and Patriot—A Study of his Life and Times* (1933).

For those reading Wulfstan's sermon in Anglo-Saxon, *A Glossary of Wulfstan's Homilies* by Loring Holmes Dodd (1908) will be helpful.

"The Wolf" was the literary alias used by Wulfstan.

William the Conqueror

(1027?–1087)

William, surnamed the Conqueror, was the son of Robert the Devil, Duke of Normandy. At the death of his father, when the lad was eight years old, he acceded to the dukedom. In 1051 he visited England, and supposedly received from Edward the Confessor a promise of the English succession. One of William's claims was consanguinity—a remote connection through Edward's mother, Emma, second wife of Aethelred II, king of England, who was the daughter of Richard I, Duke of Normandy, William's great grandfather. William fortified his claim by marrying Matilda, a daughter of Baldwin V of Flanders, who traced her descent from Alfred the Great. William also laid claim to the throne by declaring that Harold, on a forced visit to Normandy when he was shipwrecked in 1064, had pledged his support to William when Edward died. Instead, Harold claimed the throne himself. The reference in the speech, "Harold, perjured as he was in your presence," is to this sequence.

William decided to use invasion as a final measure for his claim to the English throne. With his army he landed at Pevensey, on the southeast coast, September 28, 1066. Harold refused various proposals by William, and marched south with his army. The two forces met beyond Hastings. The battle raged from nine in the morning until nightfall. Harold was pierced in the eye by an arrow and was slain. William had conquered, and on Christmas Day he was crowned at Westminster.

Reports of William's speech, and of the circumstances, vary. William of Malmesbury says William began the Song of Roland, called on God for assistance, and then commenced the battle. Robert Wace says William spoke to his men from a mound before he put on his hauberk (coat of mail) and mounted his horse. He spoke so long, Wace says, that William Fitz-Osbert, the duke's steward, warned him of the delay: "'Sire,' dist il, 'trop demoron, / Armez uos tost, alon, alon!'" Henry of Huntingdon reports the speech as given at the beginning of battle, a circumstance which would explain why William spoke from his horse. Huntingdon agrees with Wace that William overdid it: "Duke William had not concluded his harangue, when all the squadrons, inflamed with rage, rushed on the enemy with indescribable impetuosity, and left the duke speaking to himself." [1]

Estimates of the size of William's army, and hence his audience, vary, but it seems likely it was about 10,000 men, whereas Harold had between 12,000 and 15,000. That William should address his troops was not unusual. It was customary for leaders to sing battle songs and encourage their followers. Harold rode among his men before the battle, spoke words of encouragement, answered questions of strategy, and then dismounted for the fray.

〜

Speech to His Troops Before the Battle of Hastings [*]

October 14, 1066

What I have to say to you, ye Normans, the bravest of nations, does not spring from any doubt of your valour or uncertainty of victory, which never by any chance or obstacle escaped your efforts. If, indeed, once only you had failed of conquering, it might be necessary to inflame your courage by exhortation. But how little does the inherent spirit of your race require to be roused!

Most valiant of men, what availed the power of the Frank king, with all his people, from Lorraine to Spain, against Hastings,[1] my predecessor? What he wanted of the territory of France he appropriated to himself; what he chose, only, was left to the king; what he had, he held during his pleasure; when he was satisfied, he relinquished it, and looked for something better.

Did not Rollo,[2] my ancestor, the founder of our nation, with your progenitors, conquer at Paris the king of the Franks in the heart of his dominions; nor could he obtain any respite until he humbly offered possession of the country which from you is called Normandy, with the hand of his daughter? Did not your

---

[1] See F. Baring, "The Battle Field of Hastings," *English Historical Review*, XX (1905), 65–70.

[*] This is as recorded in *The Chronicle of Henry of Huntingdon*, edited and translated from the Latin by Thomas Forester (London, 1853), pp. 210–11. The part of *The Chronicle* drawn upon was published about 1135.

[1] Hastings—Hasting or Haesten, Viking leader, who terrorized the western Franks for thirty years in the latter part of the ninth century.

[2] Rollo, first ruler in the Ducal House of Normandy, who reigned from 911 until his death in 927.

fathers take prisoner the king of the French,[3] and detain him at Rouen till he restored Normany to your Duke Richard,[4] then a boy; with this stipulation, that in every conference between the King of France and the Duke of Normandy, the duke should have his sword by his side, while the king should not be allowed so much as a dagger? This concession your fathers compelled the great king to submit to, as binding for ever. Did not the same duke lead your fathers to Mirmande, at the foot of the Alps, and enforce submission from the lord of the town, his son-in-law, to his own wife, the duke's daughter? Nor was it enough to conquer mortals; for he overcame the devil himself, with whom he wrestled, and cast down and bound him, leaving him a shameful spectacle to angels.

But why do I go back to former times? When you, in our own time, engaged the French at Mortemer,[5] did not the French prefer flight to battle, and use their spurs instead of their swords; while—Ralph, the French commander, being slain—you reaped the fruits of victory, the honour and the spoil, as natural results of your wonted success?

Ah! let any one of the English whom our predecessors, both Danes and Norwegians, have defeated in a hundred battles, come forth and show that the race of Rollo ever suffered a defeat from his time until now, and I will submit and retreat. Is it not shameful, then, that a people accustomed to be conquered, a people ignorant of the art of war, a people not even in possession of arrows,[6] should make a show of being arrayed in order of battle against you, most valiant? Is it not a shame that this King Harold, perjured as he was in your presence, should dare to show his face to you? It is a wonder to me that you have been allowed to see those who by a horrible crime beheaded your relations and Alfred[7] my kinsman, and that their own accursed heads are still on their shoulders.

Raise, then, your standards, my brave men, and set no bounds to your merited rage. Let the lightning of your glory flash, and the thunders of your onset be heard from east to west, and be the avengers of the noble blood which has been spilled.

∽

Bibliographical Note

There are other versions of William's speech. Robert Wace records William as thanking his men and promising them rewards: " 'Se io conquier, uos conquerreiz, / Se io prenc terre, uos l'aureiz.' " This was written about 1160. See *Roman De Rou Et Des Ducs De Normandie,* edited by Hugo Andresen (Heilbronn, 1879), vss. 7415–7515.

William of Poitiers gives a version in which William puts his men on their mettle;

---

[3] King Louis IV of France was captured at Rouen.

[4] Richard I of Normandy, third in line from Rollo.

[5] William Busas, Count of Eu and Montreuil, claimed Normandy, and was supported by Henry I of France. The French forces were defeated at Mortemer in 1054.

[6] Harold had a few bowmen.

[7] Alfred, a son of Emma of Normandy (King Aethelred's widow and later wife of King Cnut), who was brought up by his uncle, Richard II of Normandy. In 1036, with 600 soldiers, he landed in England to lay claim to the throne during the confusion following the death of Cnut. Harold Harefoot put out Alfred's eyes, incarcerated him, and slew his forces or sold them into slavery.

the unknown foe is before them and the sea and Harold's warships are behind them: "Hic arma et inimica ignotaque regio obsistant, illinc pontus et arma." See Guillaume De Poitiers, *Histoire De Guillaume Le Conquérant* (Paris, 1952), edited and translated (from Latin into French) by Raymonde Foreville (pp. 182–85). William of Poitiers was a contemporary of William the Conqueror, and wrote his version of the speech about 1073. Foreville cites a sixteenth-century MS, *Oratio Willelmi ducis Normannorum ad exercitum ante pugnandum cum Haralde rege Anglorum*, in the Bibliothèque Nationale de Paris, ms. lat. 6238, anciennement ms. Colbert 5336 et ancien n° 6244 de la "Bibl. du roi" as another version of "cette harangue" (p. 183, n. 4).

William of Malmesbury's *Gesta Regum* (secs. 241–42), written about 1120, does not give a text of the speech. He notes the English spent the night before the battle "without sleep, in drinking and singing," whereas the Normans "passed the whole night in confessing their sins, and received the communion of the Lord's Body in the morning."

Thomas Arnold in his edition of Henry of Huntingdon (1879), says: "This speech of William before the battle is a rhetorical flight of Henry's own invention; no contemporary author mentions any thing of the kind" (p. 200, n. a). This is too cynical, and not quite accurate. There is abundant evidence that William said something on that fateful day. The version of the speech here given has some semblance of reality. What William actually said, we may never know exactly.

For the life of William, see *William The Conqueror* by Frank Merry Stenton (1908). For background and detail, see *The History of the Norman Conquest of England, Its Causes and Its Results* by Edward A. Freeman (rev. ed.; 1873), Vol. III. Hope Muntz in *The Golden Warrior* (1949), a historical novel, gives colloquies between Harold and his men, and William and his followers, before and during the battle.

A contemporary Norman tapestry, now in the old bishopric at Bayeux, France, depicts William addressing his soldiers from his horse (see Freeman, p. 304, n. 2). This tapestry, stitched on linen in eight colors of thread, is about 230 feet long and 20 inches wide, and is a primary source for details of the invasion. Reproductions can be found in various books. See these three, all titled *The Bayeux Tapestry*: by F. R. Fowke (1875); by Sir Eric Maclagan (1943); by Sir F. Stenton and others (1957).

A handy collection of documents about William and the invasion can be found in *English Historical Documents—1042–1189*, ed. David C. Douglas and George W. Greenaway (1953). Reproductions of the Bayeux tapestry showing William harranguing his soldiers appear on pages 268–71.

In 1966 the 900th anniversary of Hastings was commemorated in various ways. University students reenacted the battle, and a number of books and articles were published. See Alan Lloyd's *The Making of the King—1066* for a short version of William's speech (p. 209) adapted from Wace; and Rupert Furneaux's *Invasion 1066* for another short version (p. 127) taken from William of Poitiers.

William's physical appearance is described by David C. Douglas in his *William The Conqueror* (1964) with details taken from many sources, including a reported examination of the bones in William's coffin, made in 1522. He was about five feet ten inches in height, "a burly warrior," with exceptional strength and excellent health, although he became corpulent in his middle years. He spoke in "a harsh, guttural voice."

Unknown Medieval Preacher (Middle English)

(1378–1417)

By the fourteenth century, the sermon had developed into an artistic form. Although the rather formless homily—the "ancient" style (see pages 2, 7–9)—was still used, the "modern" or "university" style was in vogue for sophisticated audiences on formal occasions. The new design added aesthetic pleasure to the usual emotive response of the homily. By this time, pulpits, raised above the congregation, were in general use, and the preacher spoke less as a homiletic conversationalist than as a pronouncer or orator. Before this period the congregation in the church stood, or leaned against the walls, or sat on stone ledges, or sat or squatted on rushes spread over the stone floor. By now pews had been installed, and the audience was in a position to enjoy an aesthetic experience rather than suffer through elementary instruction and vehement castigation. The audience was not, however, ideal for the sermonizer's purpose. Some members came in late. Included among the latecomers were women—and women were the majority of the congregation—who had spent too much time preening. Other members left before the sermon ended. Others slept and snored, and still others heckled, demanding scriptural proof of assertions. Less attentive members talked with one another, so the sermonizer had to penetrate the buzz of conversation. Even so, the English church audience seems to have been better behaved than some on the Continent, where members sometimes engaged in trade and even diced as the preacher strove to save souls.

Formal sermons were given on many occasions, but the two most frequent times were during the morning Mass, between the Creed and the Offertory, and during the afternoon service following the main Sunday dinner. The sermon at Mass was short, five to ten minutes; the long sermon, such as the one here given, was generally used at the early afternoon service. The time of day explains much of the sleeping and snoring.

This particular sermon may have been delivered, or it may have been written as a model. It exhibits many adaptations to the occasion, such as the repeated theme for those who came late or left early, and the quick proof of point to ward off doubters and hecklers. The use of proverb, reference to familiar custom, composition in the vernacular rather than in Latin, the general tone of simple exposition and pleading, indicate that this was a sermon for a lay audience.

The Middle English language of the sermon is about the same as Chaucer's, although in a different dialect. The printed version can be read, with the help of a glossary, by a person who reads modern English. The transcription from the manuscript, however, could have been made only by an expert in the period, such as Professor Ross. To show how the original looks in print, here is a sentence, the first of the protheme:

Frendes, ȝe shall vndirstonde þat experiens of resonable doying techiþ vs þis day þat ȝiff a man had trespassed aȝeyns þe kynge of þis londe, and ȝiff he myght not askape is lordeshippe but nedis must be dede or els haske hym forȝenes and put hym in ys grace, þan iij þinges þer ben þat shuld comforte hym well.

The "modern" sermon had six parts:

1. The statement of text, a statement from the Bible appropriate for the particular Sunday or saint's day, interrelated with the theme. The theme was comprehensive enough to be divided into three main topics.
2. Short exordium, usually for introduction of a prayer. The theme in the exordium was called the protheme or antetheme. The principal theme was then repeated for the latecomers and those who had been nodding.
3. Introduction to the theme.
4. Division of the theme—statement of subtopics.
5. Further subdivision was sometimes used.
6. Discussion—amplification. The means of amplification were: (a) derivation of a word; (b) argument, such as syllogism, enthymeme, induction; (c) biblical authorities; (d) natural qualities in life—analogies with animals, plants, and so on; (e) exposition of passages literally and morally, heavenly comparisons, figurative meanings; (f) cause and effect relationships.

In the medieval period, this structure of the sermon was put in pictorial form as *Arbor de Arte Predicandi,* the Tree of the Art of Sermonizing. In the visual scheme, the trunk of the tree is the theme. Two side branches near the ground, one on each side, show the protheme and the prayer. The trunk divides into three main branches, the three parts of the theme, which produce three branches each, the subdivisions. These branches grow leaves, amplifications of the theme. This picturing of the sermon design does not provide for any review or summary. Evidently once the leaves were put in place, the sermon amplified, that was the culmination and summit.

Although this scheme of organization for a formal sermon was precise, it was not always followed absolutely. The following sermon lacks a prayer after the protheme, and the first member of the division is not confirmed by authority. The use of verse is unusual in the sermon of this period, although prominent in homilies.

∽

A Sermon for the Third Sunday After Trinity *

1378–1417

[Text]
"Hic recipit peccatores," Luke xv.[1]

---

* This is a translation from the Middle English text of Sermon 32 in *Middle English Sermons,* ed. Woodburn O. Ross, published for the Early English Text Society by Oxford University Press (1940). The sermons were taken from British Museum MS. Royal 18 B. xxiii. The manuscript is paper with some vellum. The photostat is in the Modern Language Association of America collection, Library of Congress (No. 158). As Ross explains, the signature of Thomas Looke is the name of the scribe. The sermons in Ross's collection were gathered at Oxford about 1450. Insofar as possible, the word order, vocabulary, and style of the original sermon have been followed. Inconsistencies in the use of archaic pronoun and verb forms have been retained as in the text. The Latin, with some deviations from standard usage, is as Ross reconstructed it from the original manuscript.

[1] Luke 15:2.

[Theme]

Friends, these words be written in the gospel of St. Luke and may be said in English for your understanding: "He receiveth sinful men"; or else, "Here are received sinners."

[Protheme]

Friends, ye shall understand that experience of reasonable doing teacheth us this day that if a man had trespassed against the king of this land, and if he might not escape his lordship but needs must be dead or else ask him forgiveness and so put him in his grace, then three things there be that should comfort him well. One is, if he knows in what place that the king would grant a man readily his asking; another is this, if he knows at what time that the king would most readily forgive a man his trespass; and the third is this, if he knew that the king received a wicked doer as readily to his grace as a good doer.

These be three things that would most comfort a man against his trouble in this world. And rightly so and much more they ought to be for every man's spiritual comfort when they have sinned against God almighty. And that this is true, I may show you by the three words that I took for my theme.

First question
Second question
Third question
[Prayer lacking]
Restatement of theme

For if thou, sinful man, ask me where and in what place that God will have mercy upon thee, which is the first thing for you to know, I may answer thee by the first word of my theme, and say to thee, "Hic"; that is, "Here." If thou ask me when is the best time, or in what time that God taketh a sinful man unto his grace, I answer thee by the second word of my theme, when I say by the words of present time, "Recipit"; that is, "He receiveth now." And if thou ask me if God will receive a wicked doer to his grace as readily as a good doer, I answer thee by the third word of my theme, when I say, "Peccatores"; that is to say, "A sinful man." Thus I may well conclude the words that I took at the beginning, that he it is who receiveth sinners to his grace.

[Introduction]

Authority
Division

Friends, to show you a ground for my theme, ye shall understand as witness the great doctor Ambrose, *De Opere Tercij Diei.*[2] He says that all manner of sin that may be done standeth on three things; that is to say, in thought, word, and deed; so that what sin thou doest, either it is in thinking or in speaking or in deed doing. Now that God hath mercifully forgiven these sins, I may show you by three worshipful persons that are now in the bliss of heaven—God bring us all thereto.

First person cited

First to tell you of the sin of ill thinking. Where, I pray you, was ever a sinfuller thinker than was Saint Paul? Was he a sinful thinker? Yea, forsooth, for when that he saw that in his power he had not the power to destroy Christ's law, then he went and asked for letters patent[3] of the keepers of the land, whereby he might take any men that believed in Christ and bind them as thieves and put them in prison. This, I trow, was a wicked thought. But be thou certain that God forsook him not therefore, but graciously received him to his grace. And that seemeth

[2] Ross could not locate this reference in Ambrose; it may have been a commonplace of the day.
[3] Acts 9:1–2.

well, since that he gave him so much wisdom that he was and is the greatest preacher that ever was in holy church. Thus then thou may well see, though thou be never so sinful a thinker, and thou wilt repent thee and ask forgiveness, God will receive thee and take thee to his high mercy and grace. Wherefore I may of him say the words that I took for my theme, that he it is who receiveth sinners.

If thou look furthermore at the sin of speaking, where was there
Second   ever a sinfuller speaker than was Saint Peter, the apostle? For how
person   might any man worse speak than he that with his tongue forsook
cited   God almighty? Saint Peter said before the passion of Christ that he
would die with Christ and that he would never forsake him,[4] and yet long ere midnight he forsook him thrice [5] and swore that he never knew him. Thinketh thou that Christ forsook him therefore? Nay, forsooth; but as soon as he wept and asked mercy,[6] Christ forgave him his trespass and loved him better after than ever he had done before. And thereto he made him prince and master of all his apostles. So that by this example thou may well see that though thou have spoken never so ill with thy tongue, yet he will not forsake thee but take thee
to his grace in case that thou ask forgiveness. For thus sayeth our
Authority   Savior, Luke v: "Non ueni uocare iustos, sed peccatores—I come
not," says Christ, "to call righteous men, but I come to call sinful men to penance." [7]

If we look then furthermore to the sin of deed doing, I pray thee
Third   who was or where was a more sinful doer than was Mary Magda-
person   lene? For as I read in the gospel, Luke xl, she was filled with seven
cited   deadly devils of sin,[8] that is to say, with all the seven deadly sins.
And yet the gospel sayeth, "Dismissa sunt ei peccata multa, quoniam
Authority   dilexit multum." That is to say, "Many sins were forgiven her, for
she loved much." [9] What loved she? Truly, to ask forgiveness and mercy of God for her evil doing.

So that thou may well see that if a man have been never so ill a doer nor never so ill a thinker nor never so ill a speaker, he shall not be forsaken by God, if he
will ask forgiveness. Thus beareth witness Christ himself, where
Authority   he says this by the prophet, "Nolo mortem peccatoris, sed ut magis
conuertatur et viuat—I wish not," sayeth God, "the death and the destruction of sinners, but that they be converted from their sin and live." [10] Since, friends, that it is so, that for any sin that man may do God will not have him lost, but when he asketh mercy, then he is ready to take him to his grace, I may then skillfully verify and say of him the words that I took for my theme, that he it is that receiveth sinners.

[Division]

In which words I see two things. First I see of a person repenting, that he will save what he has so dearly bought, when I say ibi, "Hic recipit."

[4] Matt. 26:35.
[5] Matt. 26:69–75.
[6] This request for forgiveness lacks biblical support.
[7] Luke 5:32.
[8] Luke 8:2.
[9] Luke 7:47.
[10] Ezek. 33:11.

[Authority lacking] Also as to wrongdoing—that bringeth a man from something to nothing—id est, peccatum.

Authority

Friends, ye shall understand what the great clerk Saint Augustine [11] says on the gospel of Saint John, "In principia erat," et cetera, he says that deadly sin is rightly nothing. And this is the reason, for it changeth a man from something to nothing. In evidence hereof thou seest well with thine own eyes that if a man leave his son his lands and his rents in order to live by it after his days a worshipful life, and his son gives himself to riot, sin, and folly, and spend it up, and sell away all that was his father's; then if he afterward fall into misfortune that he is fain to beg his bread what will men say of him? Forsooth, men will say that his cursed living and his sin hath brought him to nothing.

Truly, right so spiritually I may say of every sinner, for a truer beggar is there none bodily than is a sinful man spiritually. This I may well prove by the conditions that belongeth to a beggar. For a beggar lacketh his home and also his clothing and also he lacketh his food. Spiritually, thus it fareth with a sinful man.

Division

First want cited

First I say he lacketh his food. For what thinketh thou should be a man's spiritual food? Forsooth, the preaching and the teaching of God's word. For Christ sayeth himself, "Non in solo pane viuit homo, sed in omni verbo quod procedit de ore Dei." That is to say, "Man liveth not only on bread but on the word that cometh out of the mouth of God." [12] But what savour hath a sinful man in preaching? Forsooth, little or none; no, but as little as an ass hath in piping. Bartholomew, De Proprietatibus Rerum,[13] tells about an ass that had right good liking for his food, and he heard a pipe or a trumpet, anon he will lift his head out of the manger and be full glad in his way as long as that he heareth it. But as soon as that he heareth the pipe or trumpet hath ceased, then at once he putteth down his head again to his food and thinketh no more thereof. Forsooth just so it fareth with a sinful man. Though he listen never so well to God's word and holy preaching for the time that a man preacheth, think thou that it feeds his soul spiritually? Nay, forsooth, for it cometh in at one ear and goeth out by the other. So I say he hath no savour in spiritual food, and yet his soul is hungry thereafter. But the false flesh will not let him be fed therewith. In this manner is his soul an actual beggar for spiritual food. Against such speaketh Christ in the gospel of Saint John, John vi, "Qui est ex Deo, verba Dei audit. Propteria vos non auditis quia ex Deo non estis." Christ sayeth, "He that is on God's side he heareth God's words. And for thou, sinful man, thou art not one with God's law, therefore thou heareth not that thing that is agreeable unto God and profitable to thy soul." [14] So by this process, thou seest well that whose soul is not fed with spiritual food, he is but a beggar for food.

Authority

Second want cited

Also I said that he lacks housing. For the house that man should rest in is the high bliss of heaven, concerning which Christ speaketh and sayeth thus, "Si quis diligit me," et cetera, "et pater meus diliget eum et ad eum veniemus et mansionem apud eum faciemus," John.[15]

[11] Joannis Evangelium, I:1.
[12] Matt. 4:4.
[13] Ross could not locate this reference.
[14] John 8:47.
[15] John 14:23.

Christ sayeth, "He that loveth me, my Father in heaven shall love him, and unto him he shall come, and with him, we shall make our dwelling." But Christ and a sinful man may not dwell together, as the apostle says. And thus I say a sinful man is a beggar for housing.

Third want cited   The third point that belongeth to a beggar is that he lacks clothing. Hath a sinful man this misery? Yes, forsooth; for if we look at what should be the clothing of every Christian, I say it should be mundicia, that is chastity. And what supposeth thou forsooth both in body and soul is a token thereof when thou comest into the world? For inasmuch as thou art filled with original sin, therefore thou art not clean in the sight of God. Therefore thy friends bring thee to holy church in a clean white cloth that is a chrisom, with the which thou shalt appear before God at the Day of Doom. And inasmuch as thou cannot speak there, therefore there cometh with thee a man and a woman, thy godfather and thy godmother, for they are and shall be thy witnesses before God at the Day of Doom that thou there forsook the devil and his foul works and made a covenant there to live chastely. And in token thereof thy chrisom is white. And there the priest says to thee, "Accipe vestem candidam," et cetera. "Take here a white cloth so holy and clean," et cetera. But thinkest thou that this cloth of chastity stays with thee when thou doeth a deadly sin? For I say nay, for as soon as thou commiteth a deadly sin, then thou breaketh thy vow that thou madest at the font and putteth away the cloth of chastity and of light, and putteth upon thee a cloth of darkness. And so thou maketh thy soul a beggar for clothing.

Authority   And therefore to such men speaketh the holy apostle Saint Paul, Corinthians, iii, where he speaks thus, "Abiciamus opera tenebrarum et induamur arma lucis—Cast away the works of darkness and put upon thee the armor of light." [16] For if thou wilt be shriven of thy trespass and ask God's forgiveness, then know well that God is full of mercy and is ever ready to take thee to his grace.

[Discussion]

In likeness and figure hereof I read in the gospel of Saint Luke, Luke xv,[17] that there was upon a time a man who had two sons. And that younger son was weary of dwelling with his father and spoke thus, "Pater, da mihi porcionem substancie que mihi contingit," et cetera—"Give me," he said, "part of my inheritance and let me go from thee." The father was wise and wished no discord with his son, and divided all his goods and gave him part, and let him go. What did this young man, but travel and take himself to a great city where there was much mirth and riot? And there in the sin of lechery he wasted all his goods. And when he had spent it all up and had exactly nothing, there happened to be a great famine in that land, and for the hunger that he had he was fain to take care of swine; and for the great hunger and misery that he felt, he would fain have eaten the husks of the peas that the swine ate, and no man would give him them. I trow that he had great suffering. So one day he thought and said to himself, "In my father's house," he said, "there is great abundance, and every servant hath food and drink enough and I," he said, "perish here for want of food. I will rise," he said, "and go to my father and acknowledge all my trespasses and

16 Rom. 13:12.
17 Luke 15:11–32.

put myself wholly in his grace, beseeching him to have mercy on me." And he rose up and went thither. And when he had come to the place where his father was he fell down low, sighing and weeping, saying these words, "Pater, peccavi in celum et coram te. Iam non sum dignus vocari filius tuus,"[18] et cetera—

> For my sin that I have wrought
> I am not worthy to be thy own,
> For I have sinned in wish and thought;
> Therefore I make full dreary moan.
> To thee acknowledge each misdeed
> My lowliness of heart thou see.
> Therefore, father, thy grace I plead
> And all my sins forgive thou me.

"If it be thy will, father, have mercy and pity on me, and let me not perish." He had not completely said these words but his father had pity on him and ran to him and took him up and kissed him and welcomed him with joy, and did make a great feast and asked his neighbors all to come and to make his son merry.

And when they were all at their greatest mirth, the elder brother who had been in the field came home from his work to his food. And when he came near the house he heard a great din and noise of minstrelsy; and anon he called a servant to him and asked him what that mirth was. The servant answered and said that it was because his brother had come home. Then this man was so wroth that he would not come into his father's house, but fast he went away. The father heard tell of this and rose up and went out of his own gate, and earnestly with a great will cried after his son and asked why and wherefore he was so wroth. His son answered and said, "Forsooth, father," he said, "I have great cause to be wroth. For I," he said, "have been a good child to thee and many years have served and much labor have I undergone, and I never failed to do thy bidding, and yet did thou never make such a celebration for me. But my brother, that never did thee good but hath wasted all his goods and lived in lechery, to him thou hast given great comfort and not to me. Forsooth, father," he said, "thou art unkind to me." "How so, son?" said the father. "Son, well thou knowest that what I have, all is thine at thine own wish. And forsooth it is a very great joy to me that thou didst nothing amiss. But forsooth, son," he said, "it is a thousand times more joy to me that he that hath done so much amiss, hath now repenteth him and will be a good man and forsake his sin."

Now to my purpose in a spiritual sense. By this father that hath

Application   two sons, I represent the Father of heaven. By the two sons, I represent righteous and sinful men. The righteous is always ready for God and therefore he is saved and may take the bliss of heaven for his good living when he will. But, forsooth, know thou well that it is more joy to the Father of heaven for one sinful man that is nearly lost through sin—when he will cry mercy and amend himself, there is more to God's liking in such a one than in many

Authority   righteous men that never did sin, as Christ witnesses in the gospel where he says thus, "Maius gadium erit in celo super vno peccatore penitenciam agente quam super nonagint[a] nouem iustis,"[19] et cetera —"there is more joy in heaven over one sinful man that does penance than over ninety and nine righteous men that need no penance."

[18] Luke 15:21.
[19] Luke 15:7.

And therefore, thou sinful men, be thou never so sinful, know thou well that the mercy of God is much more than is thy sin, and therefore say to God as the young man said who had trespassed, to his father, "For my trespass," ut supra. Then if thou be in this state of lowliness, know well that our Lord God shall take thee to his grace and forgive thee all thy sins and thy trespasses. And so shall be fulfilled what he himself sayeth, Luke xvi, "Recipient vos in eterna tabernacula." [20] Ad que perducat nos Ihesus Cristus.[21] Amen.

Quoth Thomas Looke

∿

BIBLIOGRAPHICAL NOTE

The form of the sermon here described is given by Woodburn O. Ross in his Introduction. For further descriptions see these articles by Harry Caplan: "A Late Medieval Tractate on Preaching," *Studies in Rhetoric and Public Speaking in Honor of James Albert Winans* (1925), pp. 61–90; "Classical Rhetoric and the Mediaeval Theory of Preaching," *Classical Philology*, XXVIII (April 1933), 73–96; " 'Henry of Hesse' on the Art of Preaching," *PMLA*, XLVIII (June 1933), 340–61.

A drawing of the "Tree of the Art of Sermonizing" is given in "Artes Praedicandi Contribution à l'Histoire de la Rhétorique au Moyen Age," by Th.-M. Charland, O.P., *Publications de l'Institut d'Études Médiévales d'Ottawa*, VII (1936), 1–2. For a detailed treatment, see *"Arbor Picta: The Medieval Tree of Preaching"* by Otto A. Dieter, *Quarterly Journal of Speech*, LI (April 1965), 123–44; three plates of the tree are reproduced.

For a description of the medieval English church audience, see G. R. Owst, "The Preaching Scene," *Preaching in Medieval England* (1926), pp. 144–94.

Trinity Sunday was established by Thomas Becket when he became Archbishop of Canterbury, 1162. It is the Sunday following Whitsunday (Pentecost). The story of the prodigal son is on the Roman Catholic calendar for the third Sunday after Pentecost.

John Wyclif

(1328?–1384)

John Wyclif, called "The Morning Star of the Reformation," "The First Protestant," "The First Puritan," was born on his father's estate, Wyclif, in the Richmond district of Yorkshire. He entered Oxford about 1345. By 1360 he was Master of Balliol College. He received the Regent Master of Arts degree in 1361, the B.D. degree in 1369, and in 1372, after several years of lecturing on theology and passing his public disputations, the full Doctorate in Theology.

During his years at Oxford he held several livings and prebends in other places. In 1374 he was granted by the crown the rectory of Lutterworth, in

[20] Luke 16:9. "That they may receive you into everlasting habitation."
[21] "To which may Jesus Christ lead us."

Leicestershire, fifty miles north of Oxford. When in 1380 he was declared a
heretic by the Oxford doctors, he retired to Lutterworth and served as the parish
priest. He had a stroke while hearing Mass in his church and died three days
later. By order of the Council of Constance in 1415, Wyclif's books were to be
burned and his bones cast from consecrated ground. In 1428 his bones were ex-
humed and burned, and the ashes cast into the river Swift.

Wyclif's ideas have been the subject of much controversy. In theological matters he opposed transubstantiation, but accepted consubstantiation; he objected to
the use of images in the church, and to gaudy buildings, rich holdings of the
church, and elaborate singing in the service. He advocated more preaching, less
ceremony, and the supremacy of the Bible over church doctrine, and he deprecated
the importance of some of the sacraments. In matters of politics and society, he
opposed the power of church over state, objected to wars and crusades, and opposed serfdom. Although not involved in the Peasants' Rising, he wrote and spoke
in defense of their cause (see Workman, II, 243). Wyclif lived in a time of great
theological and social controversy. It was the period of removal of the papal see
from Rome to Avignon, and the "Great Schism." Wyclif was a part of many of
the controversies of his day.

Although revolutionary in many of his theories, on the style of preaching he
was a "fundamentalist." He opposed the friars' pandering to popularity with their
allegories and fables, jingles and songs; he opposed the "new" style of preaching
(see the "Sermon for the Third Sunday after Trinity" earlier in the book) as artificial. Although simple in form, Wyclif's English sermons are more than homilies;
they go beyond textual illumination into the realms of political, social, and religious reform.

While at Oxford, Wyclif preached mainly in Latin, but at Lutterworth he
spoke in English. He wrote many tracts and pamphlets in which he made more
use of scorn and invective than in his sermons. He has been called by J. R.
Green (A Short History of the English People, chap. v, sec. 3) "the father of
our later English prose" as "Chaucer is the father of our later English poetry."
Wyclif sponsored the first complete English translation of the Bible, the "Early
Version," published about 1382.

His English sermons were not only preached for his congregation at Lutterworth, but were written down for his "Poor Preachers," who roamed the country.
In some sermons (see the first four in Arnold) the conclusion includes hints on
how to amplify and apply. Wyclif's followers, called Lollards (babblers, mum-
blers), dressed in long russet gowns, staff in hand, preached over the country, in
streets, graveyards, any place available.

The sermon here given shows Wyclif's plain speaking, his desire for fundamental truth, his devotion to the Bible, his desire for the use of English in the
service, and his general awareness of the necessity of getting "true" meaning
through words. The ideas expressed may seem rather commonplace today, but
the time and scene should be kept in mind. Actually Wyclif gave a diatribe
against practices which he felt interfered with honest communication: the con-
volutions of the "modern" sermon; the minutiæ of divisions and distinctions; the
logic chopping of the scholastics and their sophistical "dialectical" prolusions on
simple matters, and the arbitrary use of "authority."

Sermon for the Sunday Within the Week of the Twelfth Day After Christmas, January 6—on Meaning *

c. 1381

Vidit Johannes Jesum venientum ad se.[1]

This gospel tells about a witness, how [John the] Baptist testified to Christ, concerning both his godhood and his manhood. The story relates *that John saw Jesus coming unto him and said* thus of our Lord, *Lo, the lamb of God; lo, him that taketh away the sins of this world,* for he is both God and man. Christ is called God's lamb for many reasons according to the law. In the old law they were accustomed to offer a lamb without blemish which should be one year old, for the sins of the people. Thus Christ, who was without blemish, and one year an elder[2] was offered on the cross for the sins of all this world, and just as some lambs that were offered sometimes fell to the priests, this lamb that died for others fell to God's hand. And other lambs in a way wiped out the sins of a region, but this lamb of himself wiped out the sins of all this world. And thus he was the shape and form of lambs of the old law, and thus Baptist showed by his double speaking[3] the manhood of Christ and his godhood; for only God might thus wipe out sin, for all other lambs had blemishes and might not themselves wipe out sin. And so, although priests have the power as Christ's vicars to wipe out sin, they have this power to the degree that they are in accord with Christ; so that if their power and Christ's will are in disagreement, they falsely attempt to grant absolution, and then they neither release nor bind; so that in each act of this kind the godhead of Christ must first work.

And therefore Baptist said of Christ: *This is he that I spoke of. After me is to come a man, for whom I made the way, for he was* straightway *my prior.* For as Christ was truly a man the first time that he was conceived, so God then made him head of all his religion; and he was abbot, as Paul[4] said, of the highest rank. *And first I knew him not;* I knew in my soul that he was born, but I could not with my bodily eye know him from any other man. And this usually happened; but, *to make him manifest in Israel, therefore I baptized thus in water. And John bore witness and said that he saw a spirit come down as a dove from heaven and left all others and dwelt with him. But God, who sent me to baptize with water, taught me and spoke thus: Upon whom thou shalt see the spirit descend and remain upon him, that is he that baptizeth men in the Holy Ghost. And I say and bear witness that this is God's begotten son.*

We know that this dove was a bird like other birds; and so it was not the third person in the Trinity taking its substance for this person as God's son took his

---

* This is a rendering from Middle English of Sermon XXX in *Select English Works of John Wyclif,* ed. Thomas Arnold (Oxford, 1869), I, 77–79. It was taken from Bodleian MS. 788, a fourteenth-century parchment.

[1] John 1:29.

[2] The meaning of this phrase may not be clear; it reads "of o ȝeer in mannis elde."

[3] Double meaning.

[4] Eph. 1:22; Col. 1:18.

manhood; but because of the meekness of the dove and more good properties that she had, she signifies the third person; and the third person is ascribed to her, for John said, The spirit came down and dwelt long with Christ; and this spirit was this dove. And so it seems that this dove was God; and so, although it may be argued that two persons are creatures, nevertheless the trinity may not be construed in this way. But it seems that we may grant that this dove was the Holy Ghost, as we grant that this person came down in this dove. And thus, as God says in his law that seven oxen are seven years, and that the sacred bread is truly God's body, so it seems that he says, that this dove is the Holy Ghost. But scholars know that there are two kinds of sayings; there is the literal and the figurative. This dove by its substance may not be God, but by some association it signifies God, and thus by the authority of God it is God. And you might say that by this reasoning each thing should be God, since each of God's creatures signifies its maker, just as smoke signifies kinship with fire; indeed Paul [5] seemed to speak in this way when he said that Christ would be all things in all things to men who understood him. [To carry the argument further] after the day of doom, all this world shall be a book and in each part thereof God shall be written, since God by his nature shall be in every part of the world. Thus since God is shown to be first and foremost in every thing, why may we not argue that God is each thing? In answer to this, men must understand that there is a diversity in words, and must understand the intent of the words. And thus by authority of the law of God, men should speak their words as God's law speaks, and not in strange speech that is not understood by the people; they should always take care that the people fully understand, and so should use the speech that is native to the people; and if they speak in Christ's person the words of his law, see to it that they speak as Christ, for fear of privy errors.

And we scorn the arguments that fools make here, but we should speak with the same kind of skill that God thus spoke in the words of his law. Such likeness to apes surpasses the folly of beasts for they would show by this that each man was God. And so let us give God leave to speak as pleases him, and let us not speak except by the same authority; these words that God speaks, let us always affirm, and proclaim him to true understanding. And let us not deal in arguments that sophists make, when we contest, affirming what we deny, for we intend the meaning and not merely the words, for the words pass away as soon as we have spoken them. And as Aristotle [6] said, contradiction exists not only in words but both in words and the meaning of words. And by this we see that Christ's speech is not contrary to his nature, nor one part of his law contradictory to another. And thus if we grant that Christ is all things, it does not follow therefore that Christ is an ass, nor that Christ is each thing, or whatever we want to name. For God said the one, and he did not say the other. But we grant that Christ is both a lamb and a sheep, for God's law ascribes both of these to him; and so Christ is a lion and a worm; and thus of many things that holy writ tells us. And it is enough to say of contradiction, that God has a special meaning for one and not for the other. And thus we should always appeal to the common understanding, but only if God's word has taught us his true meaning. And such

[5] Col. 3:11.

[6] *Analytica Priora* ii. 15.64a–64b. Aristotle here discusses figures of the syllogism, and the relations of words in terms.

strife in words is of no value, nor does it prove that God's word is in any way false. In this matter we have striven enough in Latin [7] with adversaries of God's law who maintain that it is the falsest law that God ever permitted in this world.

～

BIBLIOGRAPHICAL NOTE

For a checklist of writings, see *A Catalogue of the Original Works of John Wyclif*, ed. Walter Waddington Shirley (1865); rev. ed. by Johann Loserth (1924). Wyclif's *Sermones*, in Latin, were edited by J. Loserth, 4 vols. (1887–1890). In 1882, the Wyclif Society was founded at Oxford, and has published many of his works. *The English Works of Wyclif Hitherto Unprinted*, ed. F. D. Matthew (1880), contains a number of tracts, some of doubtful authorship and so indicated by the editor. For a sampling of compositions, see *Wyclif—Select English Writings*, ed. Herbert E. Winn (1929). For biography, see *John Wyclif* by Herbert B. Workman, 2 vols. (1926), and *John Wiclif and His English Precursors* by Gotthard Lechler, 2 vols., trans. Peter Lorimer (1878).

John Ball

(?–1381)

By the latter part of the fourteenth century, the feudal system, which had flourished under William the Conqueror and his successors, was breaking up. Many villeins had been able to purchase their freedom, and many feudal services such as ploughing and threshing were being remitted for cash payments. The Black Death of 1349 reduced the population by a third to a half, and services later became much in demand. Deserting the lands to which they were bound, many villeins became fugitive laborers in other areas. Resentment toward the manorial system spread among the lower classes as desire for conditions of free contract increased.

A spokesman for discontent was John Ball, called by Froissart "the mad priest of Kent." He had been a priest in the North, but became an itinerant friar preaching for social justice, and he finally lived as an agitator in the regions around London. The first speech given below is a kind of political homily which could be given over and over. Froissart says: "This priest used often times on Sundays after Mass, when the people were going out of the minster, to go into the cloister and preach, and made the people to assemble about him." As to the effect of the speeches, Froissart reports: "Many of the common people loved him, and such as intended to no goodness said how he spoke truth; and so they would murmur one with another in the fields and in the ways as they went together, affirming how John Ball said truth." Such was Ball's generic incitement to rebellion.

---

[7] Wyclif evidently refers here to his own treatise, *De Veritate Scripturae*, written in 1378 or 1379. Arnold (p. xv) cites this reference as evidence of the authenticity of the sermon. It is also evidence that the sermon was not composed before these dates.

Discontent prevailed, and was increased by the head tax in 1377 to pay for the unsuccessful wars in France. The Peasants' Rising of 1381 started in Essex and spread to other counties. The most dramatic events, however, were associated with the Kentish risers. "For four days," says Trevelyan (p. 223), "a drama was played out, second to none in the history of England for appalling situations, horrible possibilities, and memorable actions." Rebellion in Kent began June 2, with the assault on the monastery of Lesness. On June 5 the protesters entered Dartford. The next day they took the castle at Rochester, and at Maidstone released John Ball who had been locked in prison there since April on orders of the Archbishop of Canterbury. On June 7 Wat Tyler was selected as leader. Canterbury was taken June 10. In a two-day march to London, the company encamped at Blackheath, an open common in the south end of London, June 12. The following morning Ball preached his sermon with Adam and Eve as the text. The company was by now about 10,000. Gathered on the rising shores of the Thames above Greenwich, with two great banners of St. George's cross and forty pennons, they heard Ball's specific incitement to rebellion.

The march on London began. That evening the forces gutted the Archbishop of Canterbury's residence, Lambeth Palace, but could not seize him for he was in the Tower. They sought out John of Gaunt; he was in Scotland, but his house, Savoy, was destroyed. Robert Hales, Treasurer of England, held responsible for taxes, was sought, but he, too, was ensconced in the Tower; so his house was destroyed. The Temple and Inns of Court were leveled, and records burned. Persons along the way who incurred displeasure were put to death. The insurgents tried hard, however, to follow their ethical precepts against stealing and looting, and confined themselves mainly to violence, destruction, and assassination.

The following day, June 14, Richard II, then only a boy of fourteen, conferred with the rioters at Mile End, on the northeast edge of London, where the Essex men were mainly encamped. The crowd, swollen by Londoners, was about 100,000. The king agreed to all demands. Serfdom and all servile dues were to be abolished. A pardon for all those involved in the rebellion was to be granted. Thirty clerks were set to work writing out pardons and charters of liberty. (None of the promises was kept.) Some of the insurrectionists left for home, but the majority stayed on. They broke into the Tower, murdered John of Gaunt *in absentia* in the form of his adviser and physician, William Appleton, cut off the head of Simon Sudbury, Archbishop of Canterbury, and did the same to Hales. The heads were paraded and placed on London Bridge.

On June 15, the king agreed to another conference at Smithfield, a market square to the north of London. Wat Tyler on a pony confronted the king on his charger. There was a long harangue, interrupted when a heckler in the king's company was heard to say Tyler was a highwayman. In the ensuing altercation, Tyler was wounded by Walworth, Lord Mayor of London, whom he had attacked with a knife. Tyler was finished off promptly by another in the king's company. When Tyler fell, the king shouted, "I will be your chief and your captain," and led the throng north to St. John's Fields at Clerkenwell. There he parleyed until the Lord Mayor, who had set off for London, returned with a force of 7,000 armed men, and rescued the king. The rebels were dispersed. John Ball fled westward, but was captured at Coventry, tried at St. Albans on July 13, hanged, drawn, and quartered on July 15 in the presence of the king.

"Let Us Go to the King!" *

1381?

Good people, matters go not well in England, nor shall they until all things be held in common and there shall be neither vassals nor lords, but we shall all be united together, and the lords shall be no more masters than ourselves.

Why have they mistreated us? Why should they hold us in bondage? Are we not all descended from one father and one mother, Adam and Eve? How can they maintain or show that they are more masters than we, except that they force us to gain and labor for what they spend?

They are clothed in velvet and rich cloth ornamented with ermine and other furs, while we are clothed in wretched rags. They have wine, spices, and fine bread, while we have rye, the shrunken grains from the chaff, and drink water. They have fine dwellings and manors while we have the pain and suffering, the rain and wind in the fields, and it is with our strength and labor that they support their estates. We are called their bondsmen and are beaten if we do not readily perform their services, and we have no sovereign to whom we can complain, nor any to hear us or right our wrongs.

Let us go to the king; he is young; let us remonstrate with him concerning our bondage, and tell him we shall have it otherwise, or we shall provide for ourselves our own remedy. And certainly, if we go there together, all manner of people who are called slave and held in bondage will follow us, to be made free. And when the king shall see us, some remedy will be provided us, either peacefully or otherwise.

〜

Speech at the Peasants' Rising *

Blackheath
June 13, 1381

Whan Adam dalf, and Eve span,
Wo was thanne a gentilman?

In the beginning, all men were by nature created equal; slavery was introduced—contrary to the will of God—by unjust oppression by evil men. For if it had been pleasing to God to create men to be slaves, He would, in the beginning of the world, most certainly have determined those who were to be slaves and those who were to be masters.

* This is a new translation from the French in Jean Froissart's *Chroniques* as edited by Gaston Raynaud (Paris, 1897), X, 96. Froissart lived from 1338–1410? and was a French poet, raconteur, and chronicler. He traveled in England before and after the Peasants' Rising, but was not there at the time.

* This is a new translation from the Latin of *Historia Anglicana* by Thomas Walsingham, as edited by Henry Thomas Riley in the "Rolls Series" (London, 1864), II, 32–33. Walsingham, a monk at St. Albans, was a contemporary; he died about 1422.

So mark ye now, that the time appointed by God has come. Ye can, if ye will, cast off the yoke of your long slavery and seize upon that long coveted liberty. Be ye like the good husbandman who tills his field and roots out and cuts off the noxious weeds that are wont to choke the fruit. So now, ye must hasten to cleanse your land.

First, kill the great lords of the realm; then destroy the judges, court officials, and those who establish taxes throughout the land. Destroy those who might sometime be a threat to the people. So finally, may ye secure unto yourselves peace and security. If the powerful are destroyed, then there shall dwell among you liberty for all, and all shall have the same degree of nobility, dignity, and power.

〜

Bibliographical Note

For events of the rising, see George Macaulay Trevelyan, *England in the Age of Wycliffe* (new ed.; 1909), Chap. vi, "The Peasants' Rising of 1381." A map of the events from June 12 to June 15 is given. Note (p. 203) that "the union of the lower classes" was called the "Great Society." See also *The Great Revolt of 1381* by Charles Oman (Oxford, 1906).

For a biography of John Ball, see *Lives of English Popular Leaders in the Middle Ages—Tyler, Ball, and Oldcastle* (1875) by C. Edmund Maurice.

Several literary works are associated with the Peasants' Rising. *Piers Plowman*, written several years before, describes sympathetically events which led to the revolt. Of the priests who taught communism, the author wrote (Passus XX, ll. 270–74):

> Envy heard this and had the friars to schooling,
> To learn logic and law and contemplation also,
> To preach from Plato and to prove by Seneca
> That all things under heaven ought to be in common.

(Although Ball asks that "all things be held in common," he advocated some sort of Christian democracy rather than a communal state.) John Gower's *Vox Clamantis,* in Latin elegiac verse, is built around the rising. He was a contemporary Kentishman, and the insurrection started not far from his land. William Morris, in *A Dream of John Ball* (1888), fictionizes the yearnings of man from Ball's sermon and the Adam and Eve theme.

Hugh Latimer

(1492?–1555)

Hugh Latimer was born at Thurcaston, Leicestershire, the son of a yeoman who rented a farm. When he was fourteen he entered Cambridge University, where he received the B.A. degree in 1510 and the M.A. degree in 1514. He was ordained a priest in 1515. He received a B.D. degree in 1524, the subject of his oration and disputations being an attack on Melanchthon's *Rhetoric*.

It was the time of the "new learning" at Cambridge, and debates and disputations were rampant. Erasmus taught at the university, but Latimer did not study with him. The Reformation was in full bloom, and Wyclif's works, especially his translations of the New Testament, were widely circulated, although often surreptitiously.

Latimer's powers as a preacher became known generally after his two sermons "On the Card," delivered at St. Mary's, Cambridge, in 1529. He preached before Henry VIII and advised him on his divorce. In 1531, through royal patronage, he was given the living at West Kington, in Wiltshire. In 1532 he was brought before the Convocation in London and then interrogated for three months, three times refused to confess error, and was remanded to custody in the episcopal palace at Lambeth. He appealed to the King as head of the church—the first such appeal in English history—confessed his errors on advice of the King, was released, and returned to West Kington. About 1534 he was appointed one of the King's chaplains, and became Bishop of Worcester in 1535, but resigned in 1539 shortly after the Statute of the Six Articles. These articles, anti-reformatory in nature, imposed the death penalty for denial of transubstantiation, and prohibited marriage of the clergy.

From 1540 to 1546 Latimer was inactive as a preacher because his theories were dangerously heretical. In 1546 he was called before the Council in Greenwich and sent to the Tower. He was released under the general pardon issued by Edward VI, February 20, 1547, and preached in London and in the country. Two months after the accession of Mary in 1553, when attempts were made to restore Roman Catholicism, Latimer was called before the Privy Council, September 4, 1553, and sent to the Tower. He was removed to Oxford in March of the following year. After trial and public disputations which went on and on, he was executed by burning at the stake in front of Balliol College, the morning of October 16, 1555. Cranmer, who was to suffer the same fate six months later, watched from the roof of Bocardo jail. It was at the stake that Latimer supposedly said in encouraging Nicholas Ridley, who was beginning to mutter as the faggots were lighted: "Be of good comfort, Mr. Ridley, and play the man! We shall this day light such a candle, by God's grace, in England, as I trust never shall be put out." [1]

The sermon here given was the last of four sermons "On the Plow." The other three have not been preserved. There is so much of particular setting in this sermon that some of the historic details should be mentioned. When Henry VIII died on January 28, 1547, he was succeeded by his nine-year-old son by his third wife, Jane Seymour. Although Henry had broken with Rome, he retained many of his Catholic beliefs. Some of the hopes of the Protestants that the new King, Edward VI, and his advisors would be less orthodox were fulfilled. The Six Articles were repealed December 2, 1547. Edward's Injunctions to the Visitors, issued in May 1547, put restrictions on the use of images, and required that a chapter of the English Bible be read at matins and evensong. When released from the Tower, Latimer began to preach actively. Chester (p. 163) reckons

[1] This famous adjuration was first recorded by John Foxe in the third edition of his *Acts and Monuments of These Later and Perilous Days* . . . (London, 1576). In the Bramley-Moore edition it appears on page 470. An abridged printing of the fifth (1596–97) edition was issued in 1966 (Boston), edited by G. A. Williamson. See page 311.

that he preached eight sermons at St. Paul's Cross in January 1548: four on Sundays, and the series "On the Plow" on Wednesdays. There is disagreement as to where the sermon was preached. It was scheduled for the Cross, but because of bad weather it was given in "The Shrouds." Some think this was the roofed shed by the side of the church, used mainly for protection of horses. Others think "Shrouds" means the crypt or undercroft, a vault under the main part of the church, used for burial and as a chapel or oratory. In Latimer's day, parishioners were permitted to use the crypt for services. The sermon has no internal evidence as to place of delivery. The very day the sermon was given, the Lord Protector and Council forbade carrying of candles, taking of ashes, bearing of palms, creeping to the cross. The Reformation went on apace.

The sermon below is a fine specimen of evangelical preaching, in contrast to the labored, impersonal textual illuminations of the early English homilies. Notable are the personal tone, the reference to the preacher's days at Cambridge and what he had heard of London then; references to the audience, and how he must treat them differently from a country congregation; the sustained metaphor of ploughing and sowing; the abundant concreteness; the teasing of the audience —"who is the most diligentest bishop and prelate in all England?"—until the auditors seem to cry out for the answer. One gets the impression that "Old Latimer" would be able to hold his own in Hyde Park today.

∽

SERMON ON THE PLOUGHERS *

Preached in The Shrouds of St. Paul's, London
January 18, 1548

Quaecumque scripta sunt ad nostram doctrinam scripta sunt.[1]

"All things which are written, are written for our erudition and knowledge. All things that are written in God's book, in the Bible book, in the book of the holy scripture, are written to be our doctrine."

I told you in my first sermon, honourable audience, that I purposed to declare unto you two things. The one, what seed should be sown in God's field, in God's plough land; and the other, who should be the sowers: that is to say, what doc-

* This sermon was first printed by John Daye in London, 1548. It is not known who supplied the copy. It was titled "A Notable Sermon of ye reverende father Maister Hughe Latimer, whiche he preached in ye Shrouds at paules churche in London, on the xviii daye of Januarye—The yere of oure Loorde MD XLviii." The title of "The Ploughers" is used here because Latimer so announced his theme early in the sermon. It was included in the first collection of Latimer's sermons, "27 Sermons Preached by the ryght Reverende father in God and Constant Matir of Jesus Christe, Maister Hugh Latimer . . ." (London: John Day, 1562).

The text here printed is a modernization in spelling and punctuation of a 1548 printing, by George Elwes Corrie who edited *Sermons by Hugh Latimer* in volume 27 of "Publications for the Parker Society" (Cambridge, 1844), 59–78.

A facsimile of the first edition was issued in 1868 and 1869, ed. Edward Arber (London).

[1] Rom. 15:4.

trine is to be taught in Christ's church and congregation, and what men should be the teachers and preachers of it. The first part I have told you in the three sermons past, in which I have assayed to set forth my plough, to prove what I could do. And now I shall tell you who be the ploughers: for God's word is a seed to be sown in God's field, that is, the faithful congregation, and the preacher is the sower. And it is in the gospel: *Exivit qui seminat seminare semen suum;* "He that soweth, the husbandman, the ploughman, went forth to sow his seed." [2] So that a preacher is resembled to a ploughman, as it is in another place: *Nemo admota aratro manu, et a tergo respiciens, aptus est regno Dei.* "No man that putteth his hand to the plough, and looketh back, is apt for the kingdom of God." [3] That is to say, let no preacher be negligent in doing his office. Albeit this is one of the places that hath been racked,[4] as I told you of racking scriptures. And I have been one of them myself that hath racked it, I cry God mercy for it; and have been one of them that have believed and expounded it against religious persons that would forsake their order which they had professed, and would go out of their cloister: whereas indeed it toucheth not monkery, nor maketh any thing at all for any such matter; but it is directly spoken of diligent preaching of the word of God.

For preaching of the gospel is one of God's ploughworks, and the preacher is one of God's ploughmen. Ye may not be offended with my similitude, in that I compare preaching to the labour and work of ploughing, and the preacher to a ploughman: ye may not be offended with this my similitude; for I have been slandered of some persons for such things. It hath been said of me, "Oh, Latimer! nay, as for him, I will never believe him while I live, nor never trust him; for he likened our blessed lady to a saffron-bag": where indeed I never used that similitude. But it was, as I have said unto you before now, according to that which Peter saw before in the spirit of prophecy, and said, that there should come after men *per quos via veritatis maledictis afficeretur;* there should come fellows "by whom the way of truth should be evil spoken of, and slandered." [5] But in case I had used this similitude, it had not been to be reproved, but might have been without reproach. For I might have said thus: as the saffron-bag that hath been full of saffron, or hath had saffron in it, doth ever after savour and smell of the sweet saffron that it contained; so our blessed lady, which conceived and bare Christ in her womb, did ever after resemble the manners and virtues of that precious babe that she bare. And what had our blessed lady been the worse for this? or what dishonour was this to our blessed lady? But as preachers must be wary and circumspect, that they give not any just occasion to be slandered and ill spoken of by the hearers, so must not the auditors be offended without cause. For heaven is in the gospel likened to a mustard-seed: it is compared also to a piece of leaven; and as Christ saith, that at the last day he will come like a thief: and what dishonour is this to God? or what derogation is this to heaven? Ye may not then, I say, be offended with my similitude, for because I liken preaching to a ploughman's labour, and a prelate to a ploughman. But now you will ask me, whom I call a prelate? A prelate is that man, whatsoever he be, that hath a flock

[2] Luke 8:5.
[3] Luke 9:62.
[4] Tortured, twisted, as on the rack.
[5] II Pet. 2:2.

to be taught of him; whosoever hath any spiritual charge in the faithful congregation, and whosoever he be that hath cure of souls.

And well may the preacher and the ploughman be likened together: first, for their labour of all seasons of the year; for there is no time of the year in which the ploughman hath not some special work to do: as in my country in Leicestershire, the ploughman hath a time to set forth, and to assay his plough, and other times for other necessary works to be done. And then they also may be likened together for the diversity of works and variety of offices that they have to do. For as the ploughman first setteth forth his plough, and then tilleth his land, and breaketh it in furrows, and sometime ridgeth it up again; and at another time harroweth it and clotteth it, and sometime dungeth it and hedgeth it, diggeth it and weedeth it, purgeth and maketh it clean: so the prelate, the preacher, hath many diverse offices to do. He hath first a busy work to bring his parishioners to a right faith, as Paul calleth it, and not a swerving faith; but to a faith that embraceth Christ, and trusteth to his merits; a lively faith, a justifying faith; a faith that maketh a man righteous, without respect of works: as ye have it very well declared and set forth in the Homily.[6] He hath then a busy work, I say, to bring his flock to a right faith, and then to confirm them in the same faith: now casting them down with the law, and with threatenings of God for sin; now ridging them up again with the gospel, and with the promises of God's favour: now weeding them, by telling them their faults, and making them forsake sin; now clotting them, by breaking their stony hearts, and by making them supplehearted, and making them to have hearts of flesh; that is, soft hearts, and apt for doctrine to enter in: now teaching to know God rightly, and to know their duty to God and their neighbours: now exhorting them, when they know their duty, that they do it, and be diligent in it; so that they have a continual work to do. Great is their business, and therefore great should be their hire. They have great labours, and therefore they ought to have good livings, that they may commodiously feed their flock; for the preaching of the word of God unto the people is called meat: scripture calleth it meat; not strawberries, that come but once a year, and tarry not long, but are soon gone: but it is meat, it is no dainties. The people must have meat that must be familiar and continual, and daily given unto them to feed upon. Many make a strawberry of it, ministering it but once a year; but such do not the office of good prelates. For Christ saith, *Quis putas est servus prudens et fidelis? Qui dat cibum in tempore.* "Who think you is a wise and a faithful servant? He that giveth meat in due time."[7] So that he must at all times convenient preach diligently: therefore saith he, "Who trow ye is a faithful servant?" He speaketh it as though it were a rare thing to find such a one, and as though he should say, there be but a few of them to find in the world. And how few of them there be throughout this realm that give meat to their flock as they should do, the Visitors can best tell. Too few, too few; the more is the pity, and never so few as now.

By this, then, it appeareth that a prelate, or any that hath cure of soul, must

[6] Corrie cites this as reference to "Of a True and Lively Faith." This is one of the twelve homilies in *Homilies—Certayne Sermons, or Homelies, appoynted by the kynges Maiestie, to be declared and redde, by all persones, Vicars, or Curates, every Sondaye in their churches, where they have cure* (London, July 31, 1547). Cranmer sponsored the publication and wrote three of the homilies, including the one cited.

[7] Matt. 24:45.

diligently and substantially work and labour. Therefore saith Paul to Timothy, *Qui episcopatum desiderat, hic bonum opus desiderat:* "He that desireth to have the office of a bishop, or a prelate, that man desireth a good work." [8] Then if it be a good work, it is work; ye can make but a work of it. It is God's work, God's plough, and that plough God would have still going. Such then as loiter and live idly, are not good prelates, or ministers. And of such as do not preach and teach, nor do their duties, God saith by his prophet Jeremy, *Maledictus qui facit opus Dei fradulenter;* "Cursed be the man that doth the work of God fraudulently, guilefully or deceitfully:" [9] some books have it *negligenter,* "negligently or slackly." How many such prelates, how many such bishops, Lord, for thy mercy, are there now in England! And what shall we in this case do? shall we company with them? O Lord, for thy mercy! shall we not company with them? O Lord, whither shall we flee from them? But "cursed be he that doth the work of God negligently or guilefully." A sore word for them that are negligent in discharging their office, or have done it fraudulently; for that is the thing that maketh the people ill.

But true it must be that Christ saith, *Multi sunt vocati, pauci vero electi:* "Many are called, but few are chosen." [10] Here have I an occasion by the way somewhat to say unto you; yea, for the place I alleged unto you before out of Jeremy, the forty-eighth chapter. And it was spoken of a spiritual work of God, a work that was commanded to be done; and it was of shedding blood, and of destroying the cities of Moab. For, saith he, "Cursed be he that keepeth back his sword from shedding of blood." [11] As Saul, when he kept back the sword from shedding of blood at what time he was sent against Amaleck, was refused of God for being disobedient to God's commandment, in that he spared Agag the king. So that that place of the prophet was spoken of them that went to the destruction of the cities of Moab, among the which there was one called Nebo, which was much reproved for idolatry, superstition, pride, avarice, cruelty, tyranny, and for hardness of heart; and for these sins was plagued of God and destroyed.

Now what shall we say of these rich citizens of London? What shall I say of them? Shall I call them proud men of London, malicious men of London, merciless men of London? No, no, I may not say so; they will be offended with me then. Yet must I speak. For is there not reigning in London as much pride, as much covetousness, as much cruelty, as much oppression, and as much superstition, as was in Nebo?[12] Yes, I think, and much more too. Therefore I say, repent, O London; repent, repent. Thou hearest thy faults told thee, amend them, amend them. I think, if Nebo had had the preaching that thou hast, they would have converted. And, you rulers and officers, be wise and circumspect, look to your charge, and see you do your duties; and rather be glad to amend your ill living than to be angry when you are warned or told of your fault. What ado was there made in London at a certain man, because he said, (and indeed at that time on a just cause,) "Burgesses!" quoth he, "nay, Butterflies." Lord, what ado there was for that word! And yet would God they were no worse than butterflies! Butterflies do but their nature: the butterfly is not covetous, is not greedy, of other men's goods; is not full of envy and hatred, is not malicious, is not cruel, is not

[8] I Tim. 3:1.
[9] Jer. 48:10.
[10] Matt. 22:14.
[11] Jer. 48:10.
[12] Pisgah.

merciless. The butterfly glorieth not in her own deeds, nor preferreth the traditions of men before God's word; it committeth not idolatry, nor worshippeth false
gods.

But London cannot abide to be rebuked; such is the nature of man. If they be
pricked, they will kick; if they be rubbed on the gall, they will wince; but yet
they will not amend their faults, they will not be ill spoken of. But how shall
I speak well of them? If you could be content to receive and follow the word of
God, and favour good preachers, if you could bear to be told of your faults, if you
could amend when you hear of them, if you would be glad to reform that is amiss;
if I might see any such inclination in you, that you would leave to be merciless,
and begin to be charitable, I would then hope well of you, I would then speak
well of you. But London was never so ill as it is now. In times past men were
full of pity and compassion, but now there is no pity; for in London their brother
shall die in the streets for cold, he shall lie sick at the door between stock and
stock, I cannot tell what to call it, and perish there for hunger: was there ever
more unmercifulness in Nebo? I think not.

In times past, when any rich man died in London, they were wont to help the
poor scholars of the Universities with exhibition. When any man died, they
would bequeath great sums of money toward the relief of the poor. When I was
a scholar in Cambridge myself, I heard very good report of London, and knew
many that had relief of the rich men of London: but now I can hear no such
good report, and yet I inquire of it, and hearken for it; but now charity is waxen
cold, none helpeth the scholar, nor yet the poor. And in those days, what did
they when they helped the scholars? Marry, they maintained and gave them
livings that were very papists, and professed the pope's doctrine: and now that
the knowledge of God's word is brought to light, and many earnestly study and
labour to set it forth, now almost no man helpeth to maintain them.

Oh London, London! repent, repent; for I think God is more displeased with
London than ever he was with the city of Nebo. Repent therefore, repent, London,
and remember that the same God liveth now that punished Nebo, even the
same God, and none other; and he will punish sin as well now as he did then:
and he will punish the iniquity of London, as well as he did then of Nebo.
Amend therefore. And ye that be prelates, look well to your office; for right
prelating is busy labouring, and not lording. Therefore preach and teach, and
let your plough be doing. Ye lords, I say, that live like loiterers, look well to
your office; the plough is your office and charge. If you live idle and loiter, you
do not your duty, you follow not your vocation: let your plough therefore be
going, and not cease, that the ground may bring forth fruit.

But now methinketh I hear one say unto me: Wot ye what you say? Is it a
work? Is it a labour? How then hath it happened that we have had so many
hundred years so many unpreaching prelates, lording loiterers, and idle ministers?
Ye would have me here to make answer, and to shew the cause thereof. Nay,
this land is not for me to plough; it is too stony, too thorny, too hard for me to
plough. They have so many things that make for them, so many things to lay
for themselves, that it is not for my weak team to plough them. They have to lay
for themselves long customs, ceremonies and authority, placing in parliament,
and many things more. And I fear me this land is not yet ripe to be ploughed:
for, as the saying is, it lacketh weathering: this gear lacketh weathering; at least
way it is not for me to plough. For what shall I look for among thorns, but

pricking and scratching? What among stones, but stumbling? What (I had almost said) among serpents, but stinging?

But this much I dare say, that since lording and loitering hath come up, preaching hath come down, contrary to the apostles' times: for they preached and lorded not, and now they lord and preach not. For they that be lords will ill go to plough: it is no meet office for them; it is not seeming for their estate. Thus came up lording loiterers: thus crept in unpreaching prelates; and so have they long continued. For how many unlearned prelates have we now at this day! And no marvel: for if the ploughmen that now be were made lords, they would clean give over ploughing; they would leave off their labour, and fall to lording outright, and let the plough stand: and then both ploughs not walking, nothing should be in the commonweal but hunger. For ever since the prelates were made lords and nobles, the plough standeth; there is no work done, the people starve. They hawk, they hunt, they card, they dice; they pastime in their prelacies with gallant gentlemen, with their dancing minions, and with their fresh companions, so that ploughing is set aside: and by their lording and loitering, preaching and ploughing is clean gone. And thus if the ploughmen of the country were as negligent in their office as prelates be, we should not long live, for lack of sustenance. And as it is necessary for to have this ploughing for the sustentation of the body, so must we have also the other for the satisfaction of the soul, or else we cannot live long ghostly. For as the body wasteth and consumeth away for lack of bodily meat, so doth the soul pine away for default of ghostly meat. But there be two kinds of inclosing, to let or hinder both these kinds of ploughing; the one is an inclosing to let or hinder the bodily ploughing, and the other to let or hinder the holiday-ploughing, the church-ploughing.

The bodily ploughing is taken in and inclosed through singular commodity. For what man will let go, or diminish his private commodity for a commonwealth? And who will sustain any damage for the respect of a public commodity? The other plough also no man is diligent to set forward, nor no man will hearken to it. But to hinder and let it all men's ears are open; yea, and a great many of this kind of ploughmen, which are very busy, and would seem to be very good workmen. I fear me some be rather mock-gospellers, than faithful ploughmen. I know many myself that profess the gospel, and live nothing thereafter. I know them, and have been conversant with some of them. I know them, and (I speak it with a heavy heart) there is as little charity and good living in them as in any other; according to that which Christ said in the gospel to the great number of people that followed him, as though they had had any earnest zeal to his doctrine, whereas indeed they had it not; *Non quia vidistis signa, sed quia comedistis de panibus.* "Ye follow me," saith he, "not because ye have seen the signs and miracles that I have done; but because ye have eaten the bread, and refreshed your bodies, therefore you follow me." [13] So that I think many one now-a-days professeth the gospel for the living's sake, not for the love they bear to God's word. But they that will be true ploughmen must work faithfully for God's sake, for the edifying of their brethren. And as diligently as the husbandman plougheth for the sustentation of the body, so diligently must the prelates and ministers labour for the feeding of the soul: both the ploughs must still be going, as most necessary for man.

[13] John 6:26.

And wherefore are magistrates ordained, but that the tranquillity of the commonweal may be confirmed, limiting both ploughs?

But now for the fault of unpreaching prelates, methink I could guess what might be said for excusing of them. They are so troubled with lordly living, they be so placed in palaces, couched in courts, ruffling in their rents, dancing in their dominions, burdened with ambassages, pampering of their paunches, like a monk that maketh his jubilee; munching in their mangers, and moiling in their gay manors and mansions, and so troubled with loitering in their lordships, that they cannot attend it. They are otherwise occupied, some in the king's matters, some are ambassadors, some of the privy council, some to furnish the court, some are lords of the parliament, some are presidents, and comptrollers of mints.

Well, well, is this their duty? Is this their office? Is this their calling? Should we have ministers of the church to be comptrollers of the mints? Is this a meet office for a priest that hath cure of souls? Is this his charge? I would here ask one question: I would fain know who controlleth the devil at home in his parish, while he controlleth the mint? If the apostles might not leave the office of preaching to the deacons, shall one leave it for minting? I cannot tell you; but the saying is, that since priests have been minters, money hath been worse than it was before. And they say that the evilness of money hath made all things dearer. And in this behalf I must speak to England. "Hear, my country, England," as Paul said in his first epistle to the Corinthians, the sixth chapter; for Paul was no sitting bishop, but a walking and a preaching bishop. But when he went from them, he left there behind him the plough going still; for he wrote unto them, and rebuked them for going to law, and pleading their causes before heathen judges: "Is there," saith he, "utterly among you no wise man, to be an arbitrator in matters of judgment? What, not one of all that can judge between brother and brother; but one brother goeth to law with another, and that under heathen judges? *Constituite contemptos qui sunt in ecclesia*, etc. Appoint them judges that are most abject and vile in the congregation." [14] Which he speaketh in rebuking them; "For," saith he, *ad erubescentiam vestram dico*—"I speak it to your shame." [15] So, England, I speak it to thy shame: is there never a nobleman to be a lord president, but it must be a prelate? Is there never a wise man in the realm to be a comptroller of the mint? "I speak it to your shame. I speak it to your shame." If there be never a wise man, make a water-bearer, a tinker, a cobbler, a slave, a page, comptroller of the mint: make a mean gentleman, a groom, a yeoman, or a poor beggar, lord president.

Thus I speak, not that I would have it so; but "to your shame," if there be never a gentleman meet nor able to be lord president. For why are not the noblemen and young gentlemen of England so brought up in knowledge of God, and in learning, that they may be able to execute offices in the commonweal? The king hath a great many of wards, [16] and I trow there is a Court of Wards: why is there not a school for the wards, as well as there is a Court for their lands? Why are they not set in schools where they may learn? Or why are they not sent to the universities, that they may be able to serve the king when they come to

---

[14] I Cor. 6:4.
[15] I Cor. 6:5.
[16] Minors of rank were regarded as wards of the crown.

age? If the wards and young gentlemen were well brought up in learning, and in the knowledge of God, they would not when they come to age so much give themselves to other vanities. And if the nobility be well trained in godly learning, the people would follow the same train. For truly, such as the noblemen be, such will the people be. And now, the only cause why noblemen be not made lord presidents, is because they have not been brought up in learning.

Therefore for the love of God appoint teachers and schoolmasters, you that have charge of youth; and give the teachers stipends worthy their pains, that they may bring them up in grammar, in logic, in rhetoric, in philosophy, in the civil law, and in that which I cannot leave unspoken of, the word of God. Thanks be unto God, the nobility otherwise is very well brought up in learning and godliness, to the great joy and comfort of England; so that there is now good hope in the youth, that we shall another day have a flourishing commonweal, considering their godly education. Yea, and there be already noblemen enough, though not so many as I would wish, able to be lord presidents, and wise men enough for the mint. And as unmeet a thing it is for bishops to be lord presidents, or priests to be minters, as it was for the Corinthians to plead matters of variance before heathen judges. It is also a slander to the noblemen, as though they lacked wisdom and learning to be able for such offices, or else were no men of conscience, or else were not meet to be trusted, and able for such offices. And a prelate hath a charge and cure otherwise; and therefore he cannot discharge his duty and be a lord president too. For a presidentship requireth a whole man; and a bishop cannot be two men. A bishop hath his office, a flock to teach, to look unto; and therefore he cannot meddle with another office, which alone requireth a whole man: he should therefore give it over to whom it is meet, and labour in his own business; as Paul writeth to the Thessalonians, "Let every man do his own business, and follow his calling." [17] Let the priest preach, and the noblemen handle the temporal matters. Moses was a marvellous man, a good man: Moses was a wonderful fellow, and did his duty, being a married man: we lack such as Moses was. Well, I would all men would look to their duty, as God hath called them, and then we should have a flourishing christian commonweal.

And now I would ask a strange question: who is the most diligentest bishop and prelate in all England, that passeth all the rest in doing his office? I can tell, for I know him who it is; I know him well. But now I think I see you listening and hearkening that I should name him. There is one that passeth all the other, and is the most diligent prelate and preacher in all England. And will ye know who it is? I will tell you: it is the devil. He is the most diligent preacher of all other; he is never out of his diocess; he is never from his cure; ye shall never find him unoccupied; he is ever in his parish; he keepeth residence at all times; ye shall never find him out of the way, call for him when you will, he is ever at home; the diligentest preacher in all the realm; he is ever at his plough: no lording nor loitering can hinder him; he is ever applying his business, ye shall never find him idle, I warrant you. And his office is to hinder religion, to maintain superstition, to set up idolatry, to teach all kind of popery. He is ready as he can be wished for to set forth his plough; to devise as many ways as can be to deface and obscure God's glory. Where the devil is resident, and hath his plough going, there away with books, and up with candles; away with bibles, and up with beads; away with

17 I Thess. 4:11.

the light of the gospel, and up with the light of candles, yea, at noon-days. Where the devil is resident, that he may prevail, up with all superstition and idolatry; censing, painting of images, candles, palms, ashes, holy water, and new service of men's inventing; as though man could invent a better way to honour God with than God himself hath appointed. Down with Christ's cross, up with purgatory pickpurse, up with him, the popish purgatory, I mean. Away with clothing the naked, the poor and impotent; up with decking of images, and gay garnishing of stocks and stones: up with man's traditions and his laws, down with God's traditions and his most holy word. Down with the old honour due to God, and up with the new god's honour. Let all things be done in Latin: there must be nothing but Latin, not so much as *Memento, homo, quod cinis es, et in cinerem reverteris:* "Remember, man, that thou art ashes, and into ashes thou shalt return": which be the words that the minister speaketh unto the ignorant people, when he giveth them ashes upon Ash-Wednesday; but it must be spoken in Latin: God's word may in no wise be translated into English.

Oh that our prelates would be as diligent to sow the corn of good doctrine, as Satan is to sow cockle and darnel! And this is the devilish ploughing, the which worketh to have things in Latin, and letteth the fruitful edification. But here some man will say to me, What, sir, are ye so privy of the devil's counsel, that ye know all this to be true? Truly I know him too well, and have obeyed him a little too much in condescending to some follies; and I know him as other men do, yea, that he is ever occupied, and ever busy in following his plough. I know by St. Peter, which saith of him, *Sicut leo rugiens circuit quærens quem devoret:* "He goeth about like a roaring lion, seeking whom he may devour." [18] I would have this text well viewed and examined, every word of it: *"Circuit,"* he goeth about in every corner of his diocess; he goeth on visitation daily, he leaveth no place of his cure unvisited: he walketh round about from place to place, and ceaseth not. *"Sicut leo,"* as a lion, that is, strongly, boldly, and proudly; stately and fiercely with haughty looks, with his proud countenances, with his stately braggings. *"Rugiens,"* roaring; for he letteth not slip any occasion to speak or to roar out when he seeth his time. *Quærens,* he goeth about seeking, and not sleeping, as our bishops do; but he seeketh diligently, he searcheth diligently all corners, where as he may have his prey. He roveth abroad in every place of his diocess; he standeth not still, he is never at rest, but ever in hand with his plough, that it may go forward. But there was never such a preacher in England as he is. Who is able to tell his diligent preaching, which every day, and every hour, laboureth to sow cockle and darnel, that he may bring out of form, and out of estimation and room, [19] the institution of the Lord's supper and Christ's cross? For there he lost his right; for Christ said, *Nunc judicium est mundi, princeps seculi hujus ejicietur foras.* [20] *Et sicut exaltavit Moses serpentem in deserto, ita exaltari oportet Filium hominis.* [21] *Et cum exaltatus fuero a terra, omnia traham ad meipsum.* [22] "Now is the judgment of this world, and the prince of this world shall be cast out. And as Moses did lift up the serpent in the wilderness, so must the Son of man be lift up. And when I shall be lift up from the

---

[18] I Pet. 5:8.
[19] Place or office.
[20] John 12:31.
[21] John 3:14.
[22] John 12:32.

earth, I will draw all things unto myself." For the devil was disappointed of his purpose: for he thought all to be his own; and when he had once brought Christ to the cross, he thought all cocksure. But there lost he all reigning: for Christ said, *Omnia traham ad meipsum:* "I will draw all things to myself." He meaneth, drawing of man's soul to salvation. And that he said he would do *per semetipsum,* by his own self; not by any other body's sacrifice. He meant by his own sacrifice on the cross, where he offered himself for the redemption of mankind; and not the sacrifice of the mass to be offered by another. For who can offer him but himself? He was both the offerer and the offering. And this is the prick, this is the mark at the which the devil shooteth, to evacuate the cross of Christ, and to mingle the institution of the Lord's supper; the which although he cannot bring to pass, yet he goeth about by his sleights and subtil means to frustrate the same; and these fifteen hundred years he hath been a doer, only purposing to evacuate Christ's death, and to make it of small efficacy and virtue. For whereas Christ, according as the serpent was lifted up in the wilderness, so would he himself be exalted, that thereby as many as trusted in him should have salvation; but the devil would none of that: they would have us saved by a daily oblation propitiatory, by a sacrifice expiatory, or remissory.

Now if I should preach in the country, among the unlearned, I would tell what propitiatory, expiatory, and remissory is; but here is a learned auditory: yet for them that be unlearned I will expound it. Propitiatory, expiatory, remissory, or satisfactory, for they signify all one thing in effect, and is nothing else but a thing whereby to obtain remission of sins, and to have salvation. And this way the devil used to evacuate the death of Christ, that we might have affiance in other things, as in the sacrifice [23] of the priest; whereas Christ would have us to trust in his only sacrifice. So he was, *Agnus occisus ab origine mundi;* "The Lamb that hath been slain from the beginning of the world," [24] and therefore he is called *juge sacrificium,* "a continual sacrifice;" [25] and not for the continuance of the mass, as the blanchers have blanched it, and wrested it; and as I myself did once betake [26] it. But Paul saith, *per semetipsum purgatio facta:* [27] "By himself," and by none other, Christ "made purgation" and satisfaction for the whole world.

Would Christ this word, "by himself," had been better weighed and looked upon, and *in sanctificationem,* to make them holy; for he is *juge sacrificium,* "a continual sacrifice," in effect, fruit and operation; that like as they, which seeing the serpent hang up in the desert, were put in remembrance of Christ's death, in whom as many as believed were saved; so all men that trusted in the death of Christ shall be saved, as well they that were before, as they that came after. For he was a continual sacrifice, as I said, in effect, fruit, operation, and virtue; as though he had from the beginning of the world, and continually should to the world's end, hang still on the cross; and he is as fresh hanging on the cross now, to them that believe and trust in him, as he was fifteen hundred years ago, when he was crucified.

[23] Editions of 1562 and 1571 give "daily sacrifice."
[24] Rev. 13:8.
[25] Dan. 8:11–12.
[26] Editions of 1562 and 1571 give "mistake it."
[27] Heb. 1:3.

Then let us trust upon his only death, and look for none other sacrifice propitiatory, than the same bloody sacrifice, the lively sacrifice; and not the dry sacrifice, but a bloody sacrifice. For Christ himself said, *consummatum est:* "It is perfectly finished: I have taken at my Father's hand the dispensation of redeeming mankind, I have wrought man's redemption, and have despatched the matter." [28] Why then mingle ye him? Why do ye divide him? Why make you of him more sacrifices than one? Paul saith, *Pascha nostrum immolatus est Christus:* "Christ our passover is offered;" [29] so that the thing is done, and Christ hath done it, and he hath done it *semel,* once for all; and it was a bloody sacrifice, not a dry sacrifice. Why then, it is not the mass that availeth or profiteth for the quick and the dead.

Wo worth thee, O devil, wo worth thee, that hast prevailed so far and so long; that hast made England to worship false gods, forsaking Christ their Lord. Wo worth thee, devil, wo worth thee, devil, and all thy angels. If Christ by his death draweth all things to himself, and draweth all men to salvation, and to heavenly bliss, that trust in him; then the priests at the mass, at the popish mass, I say, what can they draw, when Christ draweth all, but lands and goods from the right heirs? The priests draw goods and riches, benefices and promotions to themselves; and such as believed in their sacrifices they draw to the devil. But Christ is he that draweth souls unto him by his bloody sacrifice. What have we to do then but *epulari in Domino,*[30] to eat in the Lord at his supper? What other service have we to do to him, and what other sacrifice have we to offer, but the mortification of our flesh? What other oblation have we to make, but of obedience, of good living, of good works, and of helping our neighbours? But as for our redemption, it is done already, it cannot be better: Christ hath done that thing so well, that it cannot be amended. It cannot be devised how to make that any better than he hath done it. But the devil, by the help of that Italian bishop yonder, his chaplain, hath laboured by all means that he might to frustrate the death of Christ and the merits of his passion. And they have devised for that purpose to make us believe in other vain things by his pardons; as to have remission of sins for praying on hallowed beads; for drinking of the bakehouse bowl; as a canon of Waltham Abbey once told me, that whensoever they put their loaves of bread into the oven, as many as drank of the pardon-bowl should have pardon for drinking of it. A mad thing, to give pardon to a bowl! Then to pope Alexander's holy water, to hallowed bells, palms, candles, ashes, and what not? And of these things, every one hath taken away some part of Christ's sanctification; every one hath robbed some part of Christ's passion and cross, and hath mingled Christ's death, and hath been made to be propitiatory and satisfactory, and to put away sin. Yea, and Alexander's holy water yet at this day remaineth in England, and is used for a remedy against spirits and to chase away devils; yea, and I would this had been the worst. I would this were the worst. But wo worth thee, O devil, that hast prevailed to evacuate Christ's cross, and to mingle the Lord's supper. These be the Italian bishop's devices, and the devil hath pricked at this mark to frustrate the cross of Christ: he shot at this mark long before Christ came, he shot at it four thousand years before Christ hanged on the cross, or suffered his passion.

[28] John 19:30.
[29] I Cor. 5:7.
[30] I Cor. 11:20.

For the brasen serpent was set up in the wilderness, to put men in remembrance of Christ's coming; that like as they which beheld the brasen serpent were healed of their bodily diseases, so they that looked spiritually upon Christ that was to come, in him should be saved spiritually from the devil. The serpent was set up in memory of Christ to come; but the devil found means to steal away the memory of Christ's coming, and brought the people to worship the serpent itself, and to cense him, to honour him, and to offer to him, to worship him, and to make an idol of him. And this was done by the market-men that I told you of. And the clerk of the market did it for the lucre and advantage of his master, that thereby his honour might increase; for by Christ's death he could have but small worldly advantage. And so even now so hath he certain blanchers belonging to the market, to let and stop the light of the gospel, and to hinder the king's proceedings in setting forth the word and glory of God. And when the king's majesty, with the advice of his honourable council, goeth about to promote God's word, and to set an order in matters of religion, there shall not lack blanchers that will say, "As for images, whereas they have used to be censed, and to have candles offered unto them, none be so foolish to do it to the stock or stone, or to the image itself; but it is done to God and his honour before the image." And though they should abuse it, these blanchers will be ready to whisper the king in the ear, and to tell him, that this abuse is but a small matter; and that the same, with all other like abuses in the church, may be reformed easily. "It is but a little abuse," say they, "and it may be easily amended. But it should not be taken in hand at the first, for fear of trouble or further inconveniences. The people will not bear sudden alterations; an insurrection may be made after sudden mutation, which may be to the great harm and loss of the realm. Therefore all things shall be well, but not out of hand, for fear of further business." These be the blanchers, that hitherto have stopped the word of God, and hindered the true setting forth of the same. There be so many put-offs, so many put-byes, so many respects and considerations of worldly wisdom: and I doubt not but there were blanchers in the old time to whisper in the ear of good king Hezekiah, for the maintenance of idolatry done to the brasen serpent, as well as there hath been now of late, and be now, that can blanch the abuse of images, and other like things. But good king Hezekiah would not be so blinded; he was like to Apollos, "fervent in spirit." He would give no ear to the blanchers; he was not moved with the worldly respects, with these prudent considerations, with these policies: he feared not insurrections of the people: he feared not lest his people would not bear the glory of God; but he, without any of these respects, or policies, or considerations, like a good king, for God's sake and for conscience sake, by and by plucked down the brasen serpent, and destroyed it utterly, and beat it to powder. He out of hand did cast out all images, he destroyed all idolatry, and clearly did extirpate all superstition. He would not hear these blanchers and worldly-wise men, but without delay followeth God's cause, and destroyeth all idolatry out of hand. Thus did good king Hezekiah; for he was like Apollos, fervent in spirit, and diligent to promote God's glory.[31]

And good hope there is, that it shall be likewise here in England; for the king's majesty[32] is so brought up in knowledge, virtue, and godliness, that it is not to be

[31] II Kings 18:4.
[32] Edward VI was a boy of ten at this time.

mistrusted but that we shall have all things well, and that the glory of God shall be spread abroad throughout all parts of the realm, if the prelates will diligently apply their plough, and be preachers rather than lords. But our blanchers, which will be lords, and no labourers, when they are commanded to go and be resident upon their cures, and preach in their benefices, they would say, "What? I have set a deputy there; I have a deputy that looketh well to my flock, and the which shall discharge my duty." "A deputy," quoth he! I looked for that word all this while. And what a deputy must he be, trow ye? Even one like himself: he must be a canonist; that is to say, one that is brought up in the study of the pope's laws and decrees; one that will set forth papistry as well as himself will do; and one that will maintain all superstition and idolatry; and one that will nothing at all, or else very weakly, resist the devil's plough: yea, happy it is if he take no part with the devil; and where he should be an enemy to him, it is well if he take not the devil's part against Christ.

But in the mean time the prelates take their pleasures. They are lords, and no labourers: but the devil is diligent at his plough. He is no unpreaching prelate: he is no lordly loiterer from his cure, but a busy ploughman; so that among all the prelates, and among all the pack of them that have cure, the devil shall go for my money, for he still applieth his business. Therefore, ye unpreaching prelates, learn of the devil: to be diligent in doing of your office, learn of the devil: and if you will not learn of God, nor good men, for shame learn of the devil; *ad erubescentiam vestram dico,* "I speak it for your shame:"[33] if you will not learn of God, nor good men to be diligent in your office, learn of the devil. Howbeit there is now very good hope that the king's majesty, being by the help of good governance of his most honourable counsellors trained and brought up in learning, and knowledge of God's word, will shortly provide a remedy, and set an order herein; which thing that it may so be, let us pray for him. Pray for him, good people; pray for him. Ye have great cause and need to pray for him.

∽

BIBLIOGRAPHICAL NOTE

A number of biographies of Latimer have been written. For intimate contemporary details, see *Acts & Monuments* . . . by John Foxe (see note under Cranmer's speech which follows.) *Hugh Latimer—Apostle to the English,* by Allan G. Chester (1954), has a detailed bibliography and gives special attention to the sermons. For a sympathetic interpretation of Latimer see Robert Demaus' *Hugh Latimer* (new ed., 1903). For the setting of Latimer in the stream of preaching, see *A History of Preaching* by Edwin Charles Dargan (new ed., 1954). Dargan calls Latimer "the most powerful and popular preacher of the Reformation in England" (I, 487–88).

---

[33] I Cor. 6:5.

Thomas Cranmer

(1489–1556)

Thomas Cranmer, Archbishop of Canterbury, was born at Aslockton, Nottinghamshire, July 2, 1489. His father was a country gentleman, and saw that his son had a schoolmaster and that he learned horsemanship and archery. In 1503 he went to Cambridge, and after eight years, in 1511, took the B.A. degree. In 1514 he received the M.A. degree and became a fellow. By 1520, having been ordained, he was one of the university preachers, and in 1521 he received a B.D. degree. He became a Doctor of Divinity in 1526.

Cranmer, who supported Henry VIII in his break with Rome, was appointed Archbishop in 1533. He soon declared Henry's marriage to Catherine of Aragon null and void, and five days later declared the marriage of Henry to Anne Boleyn valid. He stood godfather that year to the future Queen Elizabeth. He was with Henry when he died, and officiated at the coronation of Edward VI.

On the death of the boy-king, Cranmer supported Lady Jane Grey for the succession in opposition to Mary Tudor. Two months after Mary's accession, September 14, 1553, Cranmer was sent to the Tower; in November he was condemned for treason, and ordered to be hanged, drawn, and quartered. The execution was stayed, and in March, 1554, Cranmer (with Ridley and Latimer) was transferred from the Tower to Bocardo prison in Oxford. The next month disputations on the Real Presence were held before a papal commission. On March 12 and 13 of the following year, at St. Mary's, Oxford, Cranmer was tried before a papal commission on sixteen charges of blasphemy, perjury, and heresy. The transcript was sent to Rome, and Cranmer had eighty days in which to appear and defend himself, a rather difficult feat since he was kept incarcerated at Oxford. In December he was pronounced contumacious for his absence, excommunicated for his heresy, and ordered to be delivered to the secular powers for punishment. In February of 1556, he was publicly degraded from his office as archbishop, in a ceremony in the church of Christ Church, Oxford. On February 24, Mary signed a warrant for his committal to the flames.

It was damp and rainy on the morning the order was executed, not good weather for a burning; the conditions would have been uncomfortable for the spectators, and so much dampness would have made the faggots soggy. The ceremonies were therefore held in St. Mary's, a convenient place since the fires were being prepared a pace down Broad Street, the same spot where Ridley and Latimer had preferred burning to recanting. Dr. Henry Cole, Provost of Eton, had been sent by the Queen to preach the prefatory sermon. Cranmer was put on a platform, a "stage," erected across from the pulpit. Cole recalled Cranmer's errors and justified his execution even though there had been recantation. It was a time of strong expression of feelings, and according to Strype (p. 386), Cranmer presented a "sorrowful countenance," although with "heavy cheer." Sometimes he lifted his eyes to heaven in hope, and then cast them "down to the earth for shame." He was "an image of sorrow, the dolour of his heart bursting out at his eyes in plenty of tears," but "retaining ever a quiet and grave behaviour." At the conclusion of his sermon, as the spectators were preparing to leave to get places for viewing the burning outside, Cole asked for prayers. "There never was such a number so earnestly praying together" (Strype, p. 386). Cole then asked Cranmer to "now perform what you promised not long ago," evidently thinking he would elaborate on the six recantations he had previously signed and admit full error. Cranmer replied he would speak "with a good will." He then took off his cap, pulled a paper from his bosom, and supposedly read and spoke as recorded below.

The speech is a curious blend of confession, contrition, and fearless defiance. There is a possible explanation. During the days before his death Cranmer had prepared a statement to be made at the stake, and had been guided in it by his inquisitors, who expected full confession of error. During the night before his death, Cranmer prepared another statement (see Ridley, p. 400 f.); the speech as recorded is probably a combination of the two speeches, the first part being his earlier apologetic, the second his expression of growing defiance.

Cranmer is the ecclesiastic most closely associated with the Reformation in England. He steadily forsook Catholicism and sponsored Protestantism. In his office as Archbishop of Canterbury his influence was powerful. The *Homilies* (1547), which he sponsored for reading in service, and his *Book of Common Prayer* (1549), substituting English for Latin, and still used in the Church of England, were instruments of the English Reformation. He was one of the sponsors of the translation known as *The Great Bible* (because of its size), 1539; the second edition, 1540, is known as *Cranmer's Bible* because of his preface. He befriended Latimer and gave him abode at Lambeth Palace. Although a tolerant man for the age—he was one of the few public men to intercede for Sir Thomas More and Bishop John Fisher, who perished for their Catholic beliefs— he presided at hearings which sent heretics to the stake. Cranmer stood for supremacy of the state over church and individual, a doctrine acceptable when the crown was Anglican. When Mary Tudor, a Catholic, acceded, Cranmer was caught in his own dilemma. His motives, beliefs, and ambitions were controverted during his life, and have been argued about ever since. One detail seems to be certain, however; as the flames mounted at the stake, he held his right hand in them, as he had vowed.

∽

SPEECH AT THE STAKE *

St. Mary's, Oxford
March 21, 1556

Good Christian people, my dearly beloved brethren and sisters in Christ, I beseech you most heartily to pray for me to Almighty God, that he will forgive me all my sins and offences, which be many without number, and great above

* This is the earliest recorded version of the speech as given in the first English edition of *Acts and Monuments of These Later and Perilous Days* . . . by John Foxe (London: John Day, 1563), pp. 1500–1. Interpolations and descriptions are from this source unless otherwise noted. This work went through many later editions as *The*

measure. But yet one thing grieveth my conscience more than all the rest, whereof, God willing, I intend to speak more hereafter. But how great and how many soever my sins be, I beseech you to pray God of his mercy to pardon and forgive them all.[1]

[Kneeling down, he said the following prayer:]

O Father of heaven, O Son of God, Redeemer of the world, O Holy Ghost, three persons and one God, have mercy upon me, most wretched caitiff and miserable sinner. I have offended both heaven and earth more than my tongue can express. Whither, then, may I go, or whither should I fly? To heaven I may be ashamed to lift up mine eyes, and in earth I find no place of refuge or succour. To thee, therefore, O Lord, do I run; to thee do I humble myself, saying, O Lord my God, my sins be great, but yet have mercy upon me for thy great mercy. The great mystery that God became man was not wrought for little or few offences. Thou didst not give thy Son, O heavenly Father, unto death for small sins only, but for all the greatest sins of the world, so that the sinner return to thee with his whole heart, as I do here at this present. Wherefore have mercy on me, O God, whose property is always to have mercy; wherefore have mercy upon me, O Lord, for thy great mercy. I crave nothing, O Lord, for mine own merits, but for thy name's sake, that it may be hallowed thereby, and for thy dear Son Jesus Christ's sake. And now, therefore, Our Father of heaven, hallowed be thy name. . . .

[After repeating the Lord's Prayer, he rose and continued:]

Every man, good people, desireth at that time of their death to give some good exhortation, that others may remember the same before their death, and be the better thereby; so I beseech God grant me grace that I may speak something at this my departing, whereby God may be glorified, and you edified.

First, it is an heavy case to see that so many folk be so much doted upon the love of this false world, and [be] so careful for it, that of the love of God, or the

---

Book of Martyrs, and became the stereotype of Catholic persecution of Protestants. See, for example, the illustrated edition by William Bramley-Moore (London, 1865, 1872, 1877). The source of Foxe's copy is not known.

A later version appeared in *Memorials of the Most Reverend Father in God, Thomas Cranmer . . .* by John Strype (London: Richard Chiswell, 1694), pp. 386–88. Strype says his text was recorded by one "J. A.," "a certain grave person unknown, but a papist, who was an eye and ear witness." Pollard (p. 379, n. 3) notes that the British Museum has two documents on the speech, one the letter of "J. A.," the other a paper headed "Cranmer's Words before his Death" (Harleian MS. 422, ff. 48–53). Strype, says Pollard, "manipulated these two documents so as to form a continuous narrative." For an edited sequence of Strype, see *Strype's Memorials of Archbishop Cranmer,* 4 vols. (Oxford: Ecclesiastical History Society, 1848–54).

[1] Strype gives this version of the opening: "Good people, I had intended indeed to desire you to pray for me; which because Mr. Doctor hath desired, and you have done already, I thank you most heartily for it. And now I will pray for myself, as I could best devise for mine own comfort, and say the prayer, word for word, as I have here written it."

world to come, they seem to care very little or nothing. Therefore, this shall be my first exhortation:—That you set not your minds over much upon this glosing [2] world, but upon God, and upon the world to come, and to learn to know what this lesson meaneth which St. John teacheth, that the love of this world is hatred against God.[3]

The second exhortation is, that next, under God, you obey your king and queen willingly and gladly, without murmuring or grudging; not for fear of them only, but much more for the fear of God, knowing that they be God's ministers, appointed by God to rule and govern you; and therefore, whosoever resisteth them, resisteth the ordinance of God.

The third exhortation is, that you love altogether like brethren and sisters. For, alas! pity it is to see what contention and hatred one Christian man beareth to another, not taking each other as brother and sister, but rather as strangers and mortal enemies. But I pray you, learn and bear well away this one lesson, to do good unto all men, as much as in you lieth, and to hurt no man, no more than you would hurt your own natural loving brother or sister. For this you may be sure of, that whosoever hateth any person, and goeth about maliciously to hinder or hurt him, surely, and without all doubt, God is not with that man, although he think himself never so much in God's favour.

The fourth exhortation shall be to them that have great substance and riches of this world, that they will well consider and weigh three sayings of the scripture. One is of our Saviour Christ himself, who saith, "It is hard for a rich man to enter into the kingdom of heaven." [4] A sore saying, and yet spoken by him who knoweth the truth. The second is of Saint John, whose saying is this: "He that hath the substance of this world, and seeth his brother in necessity, and shutteth up his mercy from him, how can he say that he loveth God?" [5] The third is of Saint James, who speaketh to the covetous rich man, after this manner: "Weep you and howl for the misery that shall come upon you; your riches do rot, your clothes be moth-eaten, your gold and silver doth canker and rust, and their rust shall bear witness against you, and consume you like fire; you gather a hoard or treasure of God's indignation against the last day." [6] Let them that be rich ponder well these three sentences; for if ever they had occasion to show their charity, they have it now at this present, the poor people being so many, and victuals so dear.

And now, forasmuch as I am come to the last end of my life, whereupon hangeth all my life past and all my life to come, either to live with my Master Christ for ever in joy, or else to be in pain for ever with wicked devils in hell, and [I] see before mine eyes presently either heaven ready to receive me, or else hell ready to swallow me up; I shall therefore declare unto you my very faith, how I believe, without any colour of dissimulation, for now is no time to dissemble, whatsoever I have said or written in times past.

First, I believe in God the Father Almighty, maker of heaven and earth, etc. And I believe every article of the catholic faith, every word and sentence taught

---

[2] I.e., deceitful.
[3] I John 2:15, 16.
[4] Luke 18:24.
[5] I John 3:17.
[6] James 5:1–3.

by our Saviour Jesus Christ, his apostles and prophets, in the New and Old Testament.

And now I come to the great thing that so much troubleth my conscience, more than anything that ever I did or said in my whole life, and that is the setting abroad of a writing contrary to the truth; which now here I renounce and refuse, as things written with my hand contrary to the truth which I thought in my heart, and written for fear of death, and to save my life if it might be; and that is, all such bills and papers which I have written or signed with my hand since my degradation, wherein I have written many things untrue. And forasmuch as my hand offended, writing contrary to my heart, my hand shall first be punished therefore; for may I come to the fire, it shall be first burned.

And as for the pope, I refuse him, as Christ's enemy and antichrist, with all his false doctrine.

And as for the sacrament, I believe as I have taught in my book against the Bishop of Winchester; [7] the which my book teacheth so true a doctrine of the sacrament, that it shall stand at the last day before the judgment of God, where the papistical doctrine contrary thereto shall be ashamed to show her face.

["Here the standers-by were all astonished." Some began to admonish him and to accuse him of falsehood. The Doctors "began to let down their ears, to rage, fret, and fume." Cranmer continued:]

Ah, my masters, do not you take it so. Always since I lived hitherto I have been a hater of falsehood, and a lover of simplicity, and never before this time have I dissembled. . . .

["He began to speak more of the sacrament and of the papacy," whereupon Cole cried out, " 'Stop the heretic's mouth, and take him away!' " "And then Cranmer being pulled down from the stage, was led to the fire. . . ."]

～

BIBLIOGRAPHICAL NOTE

In addition to the lives cited under the text, see *Thomas Cranmer and the English Reformation* by Albert Frederick Pollard (new ed.; 1926) for the traditional Protestant view, and *Cranmer, Archbishop of Canterbury* (1931) by Joseph Hilaire Pierre Belloc, for the view of a Catholic. *Thomas Cranmer* by Jasper Ridley (1962) presents new materials and has a bibliography. Two volumes of the works of Cranmer, including some of his disputations at Oxford, were edited by John Edmund Cox for The Parker Society (Vols. 15, 16; 1844, 1846).

---

[7] Reference is to Cranmer's book, *A Defence of the True and Catholic Doctrine of the Sacrament*, an answer to Stephen Gardiner, Bishop of Winchester, published in 1550.

II

The Reigns of Elizabeth and the Stuarts

Introduction

In the period from Queen Elizabeth I (1558) to William III (1688) may be seen conditions that gave rise to memorable eloquence. The dominant force of the period was religion. The religious feeling that permeated the Reformation reached its first political climax under Henry VIII, when an English church was formally declared, distinct from the Church of Rome. The second political climax came with the execution of King Charles I, the "reign" of the Long Parliament, and the ascendancy of Cromwell and the Commonwealth government. The third climax occurred when nearly all religious forces united to depose James II and make William of Orange King of England.

Elizabeth strengthened the position of Protestant Episcopalianism as embodied in the Church of England, by steering a middle way between extreme Roman Catholics and extreme Protestants. The established church and the Anglican preacher suffered little competition from Protestant dissenters and splinter sects during Elizabeth's years. After Elizabeth's death and after the first years of James, the number and power of dissident groups—collectively and loosely called Puritans—increased until they dominated Parliament, deposed Charles I, and sorely troubled Cromwell. The predominant rhetorical instrument of these struggles was the sermon, and on through the Restoration the sermon remained an important feature of intellectual, emotional, and public life.

The discussion of religion during the period centered on three main topics: religious creeds and their expression in "prayer books," in church services, and in religious objects and vestments as symbols of faith and belief; the kinds of church institution and government; the preparation and competence of the preaching ministry. Such matters are reflected in *The First Admonition to Parliament* (1572) and in the subsequent debate it stimulated. There was little pointed and extensive debate between Catholicism and Protestantism. The Anglican state church would not allow it. Rather, the debate was chiefly among the Protestants,

65

By the 1580's the Presbyterians were disputing with the Anglicans, and by the 1650's, the Independents were at odds with the Presbyterians and with a number of smaller dissenting groups, sufficiently distinct to have acquired labels like Latitudinarians, Arminians, Socinians. On the whole, however, questions of church government, creed, and theology, especially in their technical aspects, did not reach the general public, but were debated in pamphlets and books by learned disputants for the sophisticated reader. One of the great treatises was Richard Hooker's *Laws of Ecclesiastical Policy*. There were doctrinal sermons as well as books and pamphlets, of course, mostly delivered by learned divines who, knowing that their utterances were to be set into type, aimed at audiences of readers as well as hearers. Into this category fall the sermons by Donne and Tillotson included in this volume. Other great preachers, to name but a few, were Launcelot Andrewes, Jeremy Taylor, Richard Baxter, William Bates, Isaac Barrow, and Robert South. Most sermons, however, were addressed to rural parishes of hearers of mixed education whose common denominator was a familiarity with the Scriptures far beyond that possessed by the modern churchgoer. Of such sermons we have found no reliable texts. The homily was another form of religious message still widely used in the rural parishes; an example is included in the previous section (pages 9–13). The content of the homily was officially sanctioned by the church, and its ideas and language were designed to be understood by everyone.

Rivaling religion in public controversy was the political struggle between the Crown and Parliament. At bottom the struggle was for power, with Parliament seeking greater influence over the Crown than it had been able to exert through partial control of the purse, the Crown determined to protect its traditional and "divine" prerogatives, and willing, when necessary, to govern without Parliament. As an extreme resort, the king undertook to live on his hereditary revenues and to invent new ways of securing monies instead of depending entirely an parliamentary grants and subsidies. In many concrete ways, the struggle centered on this question: Whose voice should be effective in advising the Crown, the voice of councillors chosen by the king and responsible only to him, or the voice of Parliament, particularly of the House of Commons?

Parliament became more and more insistent that Tudor and Stuart rulers live according to law and custom. When a monarch found constitutional ways too restrictive, he tried to govern without Parliament, with the aid of a small council and the advice of personal favorites. When personal rule became unbearably arbitrary, when it endangered the realm, the established religion, and the liberty of the subject, Parliament found ways of getting rid of the king's advisors—in extremities, of deposing kings themselves—and of making its voice prevail. The constitutional voice of Parliament became supreme with the agreement between monarch and subject that brought William III to the throne.

Parliament found that giving effective advice required attention to a larger number of subjects and more complex problems than had been necessary in earlier centuries. The safety and peace of the realm were of almost constant concern. The conflict and intrigues of Catholics and Protestants for control of religion through control of the monarch went on without end, both in England and on the continent. At home there were also rivalries and conflicts within Protestant ranks. Some Presbyterians could be as intolerant of Quakers as of Papists. The continent was rarely free of war, and the conflicts among Europe's kings usually represented Catholic–Protestant animosities. Because England and Parliament were dominantly Protestant, whenever they could, the English supported with money and men the "anti-Popish" forces abroad.

Economic problems multiplied in number and complexity. There were competitive trade ventures into the new world, and competition became sharper among old rivals in Europe. In England, national pride became associated with commerce and sea power as well as with Protestantism. The English population grew faster in the towns and cities than in the countryside, and the size and power of the mercantile groups grew rapidly. Their interests, represented in the House of Commons by the burgesses, and the interests of the country gentry, represented in Commons by the knights, sometimes coincided and sometimes did not. Membership in the House of Lords was drawn from the titled families of the realm, the great landowners, and from the governors of the Church, the bishops. In the struggle for power between Crown and Parliament, the upper estates—lords and bishops—usually found their sympathies on the side of the king, and the lower estates—the commoners—often had to carry the burden of discussion, debate, and negotiation without much effective help from the House of Lords.

England's relationships with Ireland and with Scotland introduced complexities both religious and political. Both Crown and Commons used the dominant religious feeling of the Irish and the Scots in ways that they believed best served their interests and the good of the nation. With the crowning of James VI of Scotland as James I of England in 1603, the economic and business interests of the Scots and the English came into conflict and into the focus of public attention.

That Parliament thought of itself in the role of councillor may be seen in D'Ewes's *Journals* of the Parliaments of Elizabeth and James. In these *Journals*, for example, one section is headed: "That the advice and consent of the Common-Council, or Parliament, was often required for the Marrying of the Kings of England." Parliament gave advice by means of debate and discussion that took place on the floor of each House and by means of committees. It communicated its advice to the monarch and his council through petition, "address," and conference. The "messenger" for the House of Commons was its "Speaker," although for special reasons other trusted persons were sometimes selected to report the substance of negotiations. Both Crown and Parliament knew that the amount, kind, and effectiveness of advice depended upon the members' freedom of speech and discussion, freedom from harassment and arrest, and freedom of "access" to each other. The Crown used its powers indirectly, by influencing the machinery for electing knights and burgesses from the shires and towns, and sometimes directly by intimidation and arrest of members while the House was in session. On its part, the House of Commons used its powers of purse and persuasion to protect and extend its "ancient privileges" of free discussion and immunity from arrest. Time after time during this period, Commons would in effect say to the Crown: "We will grant, or we will increase, your subsidy if you will reaffirm our privileges to speak freely on all matters vital to the realm without fear of reprisal and if you will prefer our counsel to that of your particular favorites." Consequently, the struggle to protect the *privilege* of free discussion gradually became, as the period unfolded, a struggle to strengthen and extend the *right* of free discussion. The orators of the House of Commons contended that the

Anglican Church and the cause of Protestantism in general could not be secured unless, at critical junctures, Parliament's advice were final.

So, in general the interest of the English people in religion, and in particular the interest of the Crown and Parliament in their powers, privileges, and rights, found a common focal point in freedom of speech and of person. The English church could not be sustained and freedom of worship could not be extended unless Parliament wielded effective power, and Parliament could not wield effective power unless the Commons could debate what it wished without restraints, threats, and reprisals. These interests, together with related ones, may be seen in four pivotal documents: the Petition of Right (1628), the Grand Remonstrance (1641), the Declaration of Right (1688), and the Bill of Rights (1689). In them are stated concisely the values that permeated and the premises that underlay the critical political controversies of the period.

The conflicts in political and religious life produced not only significant oratory but also widespread and sustained interest in language and the arts of language. The interest in the arts of speech and language is reflected in the education of the period. The schoolboy learned grammar, logic, and rhetoric as these disciplines were applied and illustrated in both Latin and English. He worked with limited materials, selected chiefly from classical writers, which he virtually memorized. He was engaged in rigorous "double" translation. He was exercised in composition, writing letters, constructing speeches and parts thereof, according to models. In the University, if not earlier, he learned dialectic, the art of disputation, which, combined with reading and listening to lectures, provided the method for studying any subject. The bachelor's degree required lectures on grammar, logic, and rhetoric, to which was added "philosophy," a general study that included metaphysics, ethics, politics, and a survey of much other knowledge. Advanced degrees represented specialization in civil law, medicine, and theology. But no matter what the subject or degree of learning, the education of the period emphasized grammar and logic as instruments of thought and intellectual analysis, and treated rhetoric as the instrument of communication in practical discourse and in poetry.

It was a verbal age. Generations of listeners stood for long hours taking in speeches and sermons. Men like Milton were deeply concerned over the control and dissemination of ideas through the "liberty" of the press and the theatre. Practitioner and theorist alike showed new concern for language as a medium of communication. There was a movement away from Latin in favor of English, accompanied by learned disputes over the merits of the two languages. Was English, for example, as capable of precision, subtleties, and niceties of thought as Latin? Francis Bacon believed that English would never meet the standards of exactness desired by learned men; hence he put his scientific and philosophical works into Latin. There were experiments in styles of English, ranging from the imitation of Cicero through the artfulness of Euphuism and the complicated figures and diction of metaphysical poetry to the plain austerity of scientific prose. In the speeches printed here from Elizabeth to Tillotson, the reader can discern some of the rough and awkward effects that resulted when English syntax fought with Latin syntax; he will discover moments of cadenced, poetical language in which the speaker seems to be more interested in the architecture and adornment of his discourse than in communication; and he will find moments of direct unadorned utterance in which English is adapting to the immediate demands of an audience. During these centuries, English became a working language for both poet and speaker, for the communicator was aware of an audience willing to listen and read. By the end of the period John Bunyan was speaking the English of the English, a language, says David Brewer, of "short sentences, compact, earnest, decisive," bearing an idea in every clause.

Bibliographical Note

For general histories of the period one may consult John B. Black, *The Reign of Elizabeth, 1558–1603* (*The Oxford History of England,* Vol. VIII, 1959); and the monumental work of S. R. Gardiner issued under various titles and covering the period from 1603 to 1660. Still standard is G. M. Trevelyan's *England Under the Stuarts* (21st ed.; 1949).

For social and political history, there is M. M. Knappen, *Constitutional and Legal History of England* (1942); and Trevelyan's *English Social History* (1944). The principal religious attitudes, Anglican and Puritan, are well analyzed by Perry Miller, *The New England Mind: The Seventeenth Century* (1939); and Norman Sykes, *Old Priest and New Presbyter* (1956).

For preaching and rhetoric, one should consult W. F. Mitchell, *English Pulpit Oratory from Andrewes to Tillotson: A Study of its Literary Aspects* (1932); Caroline F. Richardson, *English Preachers and Preaching, 1640–1670* (1928); Richard Foster Jones, *The Triumph of the English Language* (1953); and W. S. Howell, *Logic and Rhetoric in England, 1500–1700* (1956). Short, reliable accounts of education in the late sixteenth and early seventeenth centuries are Craig R. Thompson's *Schools in Tudor England* (1958), and *Universities in Tudor England* (1959).

Valuable sources of bibliography are *Bibliography of British History, Tudor Period, 1485–1603,* ed. Conyers Read (2nd ed., 1959); and *Bibliography of British History, Stuart Period, 1603–1714,* ed. Godfrey Davies (1928). For the Stuart period see Robert Walcott, "The Later Stuarts (1600–1714): Significant Work of the Last Twenty Years (1939–1959)," *American Historical Review,* LXVII (January 1962), 352–70.

Queen Elizabeth I

(1533–1603)

Elizabeth I succeeded "Bloody" Mary Tudor in 1558. Her father, Henry VIII, had given political sanction to the Reformation by setting up an English church distinct from the Church of Rome. Her brother, the child king, Edward VI (1547–1553), governed through privy councillors, one of whom, the Earl of Warwick and Duke of Northumberland, took advantage of Protestant zeal to extend his own power. To strengthen and protect the English church, Protestant extremists in Parliament were encouraged to pass new acts of uniformity in religious worship, revise anew the Book of Common Prayer, and specify extreme penalties for failure to conform. One of the severest of penalties stipulated that "any one neglecting to attend service on Sunday and holidays was liable to excommunication, and the penalty for attending any other form [of worship] was six months' imprisonment for the first offense, a year for the second, and life for the third." [1] When Mary succeeded Edward in 1553 she had most of his church legislation repealed, supported laws to restore Catholicism, and burned heretics and flagrant dissenters. By the time Mary died in 1558, England had had its fill of religious extremism. Elizabeth re-established the Anglican Church and modified the forms of worship in ways thought to be offensive to Catholic moderates. She protected her Church from radical reformists—from the Puritans and their attacks, as may be seen in the famous *Admonitions to Parliament,* and from Catholic diehards who lent their support to her enemies, both domestic and foreign. Her foes questioned her legitimacy, as the daughter of Anne Boleyn, and intrigued to dethrone or kill her. They incited Mary Stuart and the Scots to rise against her, and brought Philip of Spain's mighty Armada to her shores. The history of her land and the history of her own life led Elizabeth to seek two chief goals: stability and peace.

The three speeches of hers included here are incidents in the dispute between Elizabeth and Parliament over her marriage and the succession and over attempts to "purify" the church. Parliament and the people knew that the absence of an heir apparent or of an heir designate to the throne invited bold, ambitious claimants of power to hatch plots, uprisings, and invasions. They wanted Elizabeth to marry and have issue, or to name her successor. Despite her love of peace and security, she would do neither. The first two speeches reveal Elizabeth's characteristic responses to Parliament when it pressed her hard enough on the matter of marriage to make her answer. The third speech came at a time when Presbyterians and dissenters had provoked her on religious matters.

Elizabeth was well equipped for speechmaking. Among her tutors had been William Grindal, a professor at Cambridge, and Roger Ascham, whose ideals and methods of education may be seen in his *The Scholemaster* (1570). Under these tutors, and perhaps other unknown to us, Elizabeth received a sound education that included the study of classical authors, grammar, rhetoric, and logic, and the writing and speaking of Latin, French, and Italian, and perhaps some Greek. With Ascham she read some of the orations of Isocrates and much of Cicero. She could make a Latin oration fit for an Oxford audience. She herself admitted that she was well read in the Scriptures, history, and "philosophy." Her feeling for languages, her training in composition, her knowledge of literature, of men, and of practical affairs led Ascham to remark that she liked "a style that grows out of the subject," and was fond of "modest metaphors" and antitheses when "happily opposed." [2]

Doubtless the Queen was listened to in part because she was a queen. Yet there is no doubt that she was both respected and loved by the court, the men of Parliament and government, and the people. She held the utmost good will for her subjects. She demonstrated her prudence by conducting a frugal government, avoiding extraordinary taxes, and securing much peace and prosperity. She could be courageous and afraid, magnificent and scolding, direct and evasive, tactful and insulting, clear and ambiguous, endearing and exasperating. Withal, she

---

[1] Arthur Lyon Cross, *A Shorter History of England and Greater Britain* (New York, 1925), p. 234.

[2] See George P. Rice, Jr., *The Public Speaking of Queen Elizabeth* (New York, 1951), p. 47.

was popular. She believed, as did all Tudor and Stuart monarchs, in the divine right of the ruler, but unlike the Stuarts who came after her, she knew how to accommodate divine right to the wishes of her subjects without yielding much of her power or any of her prerogatives to Parliament. Much of Elizabeth's effectiveness in act and speech was due to good acts and good will.

Little trustworthy information about Elizabeth's voice and speech has yet been uncovered. One observer reported that her speech was high-keyed and rapid. She was taller than most women. "Her head was good—aquiline nose, high forehead, long chin, gray-green eyes, and reddish blonde hair."[3] Gay and witty in spirit and active in body, she never lost the facial signs of youth and energy.

The texts of Elizabeth's speeches represent a variety of sources. Among recent scholars, J. E. Neale has had the best opportunity to uncover and compare texts. Auditors like Stow reported some speeches as accurately as they could. Neale's general opinion is that the speeches, "as we can tell from the style and from the specimens we still possess in Elizabeth's own hand, were always composed and written by herself. She played with their wording in the manner of a precious stylist, improving here, inverting phrases there."[4] Possibly she had help from advisors—William Cecil, for example. She read most of the speeches that opened and closed Parliament, yet at times, if we may judge from her version of a speech compared with versions given by others, she abandoned the manuscript and spoke from memory. Her words as made available to us demonstrate that she knew whereof she spoke. They mix reason with emotion, partly by acknowledging the realities of a situation, evoking familiar facts and events, and revealing in the speaker the indignation and affection that she touched off in others. Ever present is the impression of a strong will and a knowing intelligence employed in a spirit of good will and love. Some contrasts and comparisons there are; yet the style is not richly figurative, and antithetical ideas are not worked out in measured euphuistic patterns. Her utterances do not smell of lamp and learning, as do those of her successor, James I.

◌

Speech on Marriage and Succession, to a Delegation from the Lords and Commons *

Westminster Palace
November 5, 1566

[When the Parliament of 1563 settled down to business it addressed itself to the question of the succession. Events were sufficiently critical to cause talk of

---

[3] *Ibid.*, p. 29.

[4] J. E. Neale, *Elizabeth I and her Parliaments, 1559–1581* (New York, 1958), p. 50.

* The text closely follows that in Neale, *Elizabeth and Her Parliaments 1559–1581*, pp. 146–50, but incorporates minor readings from the version printed by Rice, pp. 77–81. (See Bibliographical Note, below.) Neale's text is basically that of the Cambridge University Library MS., Gg. III, 34, fols. 208 seq., with some readings from the version in the British Museum Stowe MS. 354, fols. 18–19, and used by Neale in the *English Historical Review*, XXXVI, 514–17.

civil war if Elizabeth were to die without naming a successor. Smallpox had broken out and the Queen was one of its victims. She nearly died. There were two legitimate lines of succession. One focused on Lady Catherine Grey, whom Elizabeth would not abide. The other line pointed to Mary Queen of Scots, but the country feared her French associations and her Catholic religion. By marrying Darnley she had alienated the Scots and had sought help from Catholic France. Early in 1566, Elizabeth herself had been conducting a series of marriage negotiations with Archduke Charles of Austria. The bargaining had alternately blown hot and cold. Court, councillors, and Parliament had become exasperated with "that woman ruler."

[The House of Commons, numbering 400, contained a small but strong minority of Puritan-minded enthusiasts. These stirred the House to action, and the arguments and appeals for marriage and for settling the succession were reviewed and strengthened. Certain Lords informally persuaded the Queen to say that she would marry, but she added, "at my convenience." Parliament was not satisfied, and a formal petition was being readied by both Commons and Lords when Elizabeth sent word that she would receive a delegation. Thirty persons from each House assembled in the afternoon at Westminster Palace. The Queen addressed them as follows.]

If that order had been observed in the beginning of the matter, and such consideration had in prosecuting of the same, as the gravity of the cause had required, the success thereof might have been otherwise than now it is. But those unbridled persons whose mouth was never snaffled by the rider, did rashly ride into it in the Common House, a public place; where Mr. [Robert] Bell with his complices [accomplices] alleged that they were natural Englishmen and were bound to their country, which they saw must needs perish and come to confusion unless some orders were taken for limitation of the succession of the crown. And further to help the matter, [they] must needs prefer their speeches to the Upper House, to have you, my Lords, consent with them; whereby you were seduced, and of simplicity did assent unto it, which you would not have done if you had foreseen before considerately the importance of the matter. So that there was no malice in you, and so I do ascribe it. For we think and know you have just cause to love us, considering our mercifulness showed to all our subjects since our reign. But there, two bishops, with their long orations, sought to persuade you also with solemn matters, as though you, my Lords, had not known that when my breath did fail me I had been dead unto you, and that then, dying without issue, what a danger it were to the whole State: which you had not known, before they told it you![1]

[1] There is another version of the opening paragraph, which Neale believes is a first draft:

"If the order of our cause had matched the weight of your matter, the one might well have craved reward, and the other much the sooner be satisfied. But when I call to mind how far from dutiful care, yea rather how nigh a traitorous trick this tumbling cast did spring, I muse how men of wit can so hardly use that gift they hold. I marvel not much that bridleless colts do not know their rider's hand whom bit of kingly rein did never snaffle yet. Whether it was fit that so great a cause as this should have had this beginning in such a public place as that, let it be well weighed. Must all evil bodings that might be recited be found little enough to hap to my share? Was it well

And so it was easily to be seen *quo oratio tendit*.[2] For those that should be stops and stays[3] of this great good, and [responsible for] avoiding of so many dangers and perils, how evil might they seem to be! And so to aggravate the cause against me! Was I not born in the realm? Were my parents born in any foreign country? Is there any cause I should alienate myself from being careful over this country? Is not my kingdom here? Whom have I oppressed? Whom have I enriched to other's harm? What turmoil have I made in this Commonwealth that I should be suspected to have no regard to the same? How have I governed since my reign? I will be tried [tormented] by envy itself. I need not to use many words, for my deeds do try [test] me.

Well, the matter whereof they would have made their petition (as I am informed) consisteth in two points—in my marriage and in the limitation of the succession of the Crown, wherein my marriage was first placed, as for manner's sake. I did send them answer by my Council I would marry (although of mine own disposition I was not inclined thereunto). But that was not accepted nor credited, although spoken by their Prince. And yet I used so many words that I could say no more: and were it not now I had spoken those words, I would never speak them again. I will never break the word of a prince, spoken in a public place, for my honour's sake. And therefore I say again, I will marry as soon as I can conveniently, if God take not him away with whom I mind to marry, or myself, or else some other great let happen. I can say no more, except the party were present. And I hope to have children, otherwise I would never marry.

A strange order of petitioners, that will make a request and [that] cannot be otherwise ascertained [proved] but by their Prince's word, and yet will not believe it when it is spoken! But they (I think) that moveth the same will be as ready to mislike him with whom I shall marry, as they are now to move it. And then it will appear they nothing meant it. I thought they would have been rather ready to have given me thanks than to have made any new request for the same. There hath been some that have ere this said unto me they never required more than that they might once hear me say I would marry. Well, there was never so great a treason but might be covered under as fair a pretence.

The second point was the limitation of the succession of the crown: wherein was nothing said for my safety but only for themselves. A strange thing that the foot should direct the head in so weighty a cause; which cause hath been so diligently weighed by us, for that it toucheth us more than them. I am sure there was not one of them that ever was a second person, as I have been, and have tasted of the practices against my sister—who, I would to God were alive again.[4] I had great occasions to hearken to their motions, of whom some of them are of the Common House. But when friends fall out, truth doth appear, ac-

---

meant, think you, that those that knew not how fit this matter was to be granted by the prince, would prejudice their prince in aggravating the matter? so [that] all their arguments tended to my careless care of this my dear realm."

Both Neale and Froude derive this passage from *Calendar of State Papers, Domestic, Elizabeth*, XLI.

[2] . . . *quo oratio tendit*—the way the wind was blowing.

[3] Props and supports.

[4] Elizabeth's sister was Queen Mary, her predecessor, to whom she was second in line to the throne.

cording to the old proverb; and were it not for my honour, their knavery should be known. There were occasions in me at that time. I stood in danger of my life, my sister was so incensed against me: I did differ from her in religion, and I was sought for divers ways. And so shall never be my successor.

I have conferred before this time with those that are well learned, and have asked their opinions touching the limitation of succession; who have been silent— not that by their silence, after lawlike manner, they have seemed to assent to it, but that indeed they could not tell what to say, considering the great peril to the realm, and most danger to myself. But now the matter must needs go trimly and pleasantly when the bowl runneth all on the one side. And, alas, not one amongst them all would answer for us, but all their speeches were for the surety of their country. They would have twelve or fourteen limited in succession, and the more the better.[5] And those shall be of such uprightness and so divine as in them shall be divinity itself. Kings were wont to honour philosophers; but if I had such I would honour them as angels, that should have such piety in them that they would not seek where they are the second, to be the first, and where the[y are] third to be the second, and so forth.

It is said, I am no divine. Indeed, I studied nothing else but divinity till I came to the crown; and then I gave myself to the study of that which was meet for government, and am not ignorant of stories wherein appeareth what hath fallen out for ambition of kingdoms—as in Spain, Naples, Portugal, and at home; and what cocking hath been between the father and the son for the same. You would have a limitation of succession. Truly, if reason did not subdue will in me, I would cause you to deal in it, so pleasant a thing it should be unto me. But I stay it for your benefit. For if you should have liberty to treat of it, there be so many competitors—some kinfolks, some servants, and some tenants; some would speak for their master, and some for their mistress, and every man for his friend— that it would be an occasion of a greater charge [burden] than a subsidy. And if my will did not yield to reason, it should be that thing I would gladliest desire to see you deal in.

Well, there hath been error: I say not errors, for there were too many in the proceeding in this matter. But we will not judge that these attempts were done of any hatred to our person, but even for lack of good foresight. I do marvel, though *Domini Doctores* with you, my Lords, did so use themselves therein, since after my brother's death they openly preached and set forth that my sister and I were bastards.[6] Well, I wish not the death of any man, but only this I desire: that they which have been the practisers herein may before their deaths repent the same, and show some open confession of their fault, whereby the scabbed sheep may be known from the whole.[7]

[5] The exasperated allusion is to Parliament's consideration of all possible lines of succession. Perhaps some persons were looking for lines to themselves or their families. Only angels could be trusted not to covet the throne.

[6] Upon the death of Elizabeth's brother, Edward VI, the Duke of Northumberland tried to put Lady Jane Grey on the throne and questioned the legitimacy of Mary and Elizabeth.

[7] Froude has another version of this passage addressed to the doctors, i.e., bishops, to whom Elizabeth alluded early in the speech. He says that she turned round to where Grindal and Pilkington were standing, and said:

"And you *doctors,* you I understand make long prayers about this business. One

As for my own part, I care not for death; for all men are mortal. And though I be a woman, yet I have as good a courage, answerable to my place, as ever my father had. I am your anointed Queen. I will never be by violence constrained to do anything. I thank God I am endued with such qualities that if I were turned out of the realm in my petticoat, I were able to live in any place in Christendom.

Your petition is to deal in the limitation of the succession. At this present it is not convenient; nor never shall be without some peril unto you and certain danger unto me. But were it not for your peril, at this time I would give place, notwithstanding my danger. Your perils are sundry ways; for some may be touched, who resteth now in such terms with us as is not meet to be disclosed, either in the Common House or in the Upper House. But as soon as there may be a convenient time, and that it may be done with least peril unto you—although never without great danger unto me—I will deal therein for your safety, and offer it unto you as your Prince and head, without request; for it is monstrous that the feet should direct the head.

And therefore this is my mind and answer, which I would have to be showed in the two Houses. And for the doing thereof, you, my Lord Chief Justice, are meetest to do it in the Upper House, and you, Cecil, in the Nether House.

⌒

SPEECH AT THE DISSOLUTION OF PARLIAMENT *

January 2, 1567

[Following the speech of November 5, the delegates returned to their Houses and reported their impression informally. The formal digest of the speech was made to the Commons by Cecil, as the Queen had instructed. It was the duty

---

of you dared to say in times past that I and my sister were bastards; and you must needs be interfering in what does not concern you. Go home and amend your own lives and set an honest example in your families. The Lords in Parliament should have taught you to know your places; but if they have forgotten their duty I will not forget mine. Did I so choose I might make the impertinence of the whole set of you an excuse to withdraw my promise to marry; and I will take a husband that will not be to the taste of some of you. I have not married hitherto out of consideration for you, but it shall be done now, and you who have been so urgent with me will find the effects of it to your cost. Think you the prince who will be my consort will feel himself safe with such as you, who thus dare to thwart and cross your natural queen?"

History of England . . . to . . . Elizabeth, VIII, 324.

* The text is from the *Journals of All the Parliaments during the Reign of Queen Elizabeth . . . by Sir Simonds D'Ewes,* pp. 116–17 (see Bibliographical Note, below). We have adjusted spelling and some punctuation to suit the modern eye. Neale has seen a manuscript of the speech in Elizabeth's handwriting and reproduces it in *Elizabeth I and Her Parliaments 1559–1581,* pp. 173–76. D'Ewes's version is somewhat shorter than the manuscript text. It contains all the chief ideas and almost all of their elaboration, and is more direct and oral in style and tone. For these reasons, among others, we believe that the Queen on this occasion spoke from memory rather than from manuscript.

of the Speaker to make such reports, but in this case the Speaker, Richard Onslow, had not been a member of the delegation.

[The Queen had intended to quiet talk of marriage and succession and to put Parliament on the track of its "proper" business. But Parliament was obviously in a slow down. It liked neither the monarch's attempts to stifle discussion of marriage and religion nor the new "commission of inquisitors" set up by the Queen better to enforce the penal laws against those who failed to observe the prescribed ceremonies of worship. So Elizabeth resolved to end the session, and sent her legislators home after delivering a speech to them.

[The setting was that which customarily marked the opening and closing of a Parliament. Lords and Commons met in the Lord's quarters, a large oblong room having bleacher-like benches ranged along either side. These faced into the room. Between them was open space in which the only objects were large, sausage-shaped wool sacks that provided additional seating. At one end of the room stood the barons and members of the Commons; at the other on a raised platform was a throne chair from which the monarch spoke. Standing on either side of the monarch were Crown officers and privy councillors. On the benches and wool sacks sat marquesses, earls, bishops, and judges. About 500 persons were present on this occasion. (An engraving of the Queen in Parliament forms the frontispiece of Neale's *The Elizabethan House of Commons*.)

[The proceedings began with the Speaker's oration. Worked into it amidst the conventional praises of the Queen and of monarchy were plain advice to marry without further delay and to put away "all hurtful or unprofitable ceremonies in any wise contrary to God's word" in church worship, and warning that "princely prerogatives and royalties" cannot be exercised by the Prince "at his own pleasure." The Lord Keeper responded with a speech of praise and reproof, followed by the Clerk's announcement of those laws the Queen had approved and those she had vetoed. This done, Elizabeth spoke as follows.]

My Lords, and others, the Commons of this assembly, although the Lord Keeper hath, according to order, very well answered in my name, yet as a periphrasis I have a few words further to speak unto you, notwithstanding I have not been used, nor love to do it, in such open assemblies; yet now (not to the end to amend this talk) but remembering that commonly Prince's own words be better printed in the hearers' memory than those spoken by her command, I mean to say thus much unto you.

I have in this assembly found so much dissimulation, where I always professed plainness, that I marvel thereat, yea two faces under one hood, and the body rotten, being covered with two vizors, Succession and Liberty, which they determined must be either presently granted, denied or deferred. In granting whereof, they had had their desires, and denying or deferring thereof (those things being so plaudable, as indeed to all men they are) they thought to work me that mischief, which never foreign enemy could bring to pass, which is the hatred of my Commons. But alas they began to pierce the Vessel before the Wine was fined, and began a thing not foreseeing the end, how by this means I have seen my well-willers from mine Enemies, and can, as me seemeth, very well divide the House into four.

First the broachers and workers thereof, who are in the greatest fault. Secondly, the speakers, who by eloquent tales persuaded others, are in the next degree. Thirdly, the agreers, who being so light of credit, that the eloquence of the tales so overcame them that they gave more credit thereunto than unto their own wits. And lastly, those that sat still mute, and meddled not therewith, but rather wondered, disallowing the matter; who in my opinion, are most to be excused.

But do you think, that either I am unmindful of your surety by succession, wherein is all my care, considering I know myself to be mortal? No, I warrant you. Or that I went about to break your liberties? No, it was never in my meaning, but to stay you before you fell into the ditch. For all things have their time. And although perhaps you may have after me one better learned, or wiser, yet I assure you, none more careful over you. And therefore henceforth, whether I live to see the like assembly or no, or whoever it be, yet beware however you prove your Prince's patience, as you have now done mine.

And now to conclude, all this notwithstanding (not meaning to make a Lent of Christmas) the most part of you may assure yourselves that you depart in your Prince's grace.

~

Speech at the Proroguing of Parliament *

March 29, 1585

[The Court of High Commission had been established to curb mounting violations of the Act of Uniformity. In practice the Court was dominated by the Archbishop of Canterbury, at this time John Whitgift. He interpreted and enforced the famous Thirty-Nine Articles, designed to keep the clergy strictly within the prescribed Anglican forms of worship and church practices. Teams of inquisitors were at work searching out violators, who were deprived of their pulpits, or fined or jailed. The harassment fell chiefly upon Puritans. Among these the largest group were the Presbyterians.

[Prior to 1572, the Presbyterians and all non-conformists had sought to liberalize the Act of Uniformity by agitation and debate within the official channels and convocations of the church. But they were ineffective within the ranks of the clergy; so they sought to secure their ends through Parliament. Thomas Cartwright's *An Admonition to the Parliament* in 1572 warned Parliament of the growing rebellion against the abuses and restrictions of the state church. Furthermore, it frightened Elizabeth, because Cartwright asserted the absolute supremacy of Presbyterianism over the State as well as over all other religious institutions. The *Admonition* found some adherents already in the House of Commons. From 1572 onward, the number steadily increased until in 1585 they constituted a substantial and powerful minority. There were Presbyterian sympathizers among the Lords and bishops, and even in the Queen's privy council. In the fall of 1584 and the early months of 1585, Parliament had petitioned Whitgift for fair treatment and relief of Dissenters, but had received no answer. Elizabeth forbade any more talk about religion. The Commons especially was

* The text is taken from D'Ewes, *Journal of All of the Parliaments* . . . , pp. 328–29.

in a sensitive mood. It protested over some minor bills requested by the Queen, and it set a precedent by refusing to give even a first reading to one bill that had originated with the Lords. The Queen and her councillors saw that the time had come to give Parliament a rest.

[In the closing ritual speech, the Lord Chancellor, Sir Thomas Bromley, chastised the Commons. Some members would have to be "punished," for they had meddled with Church and religion against the commandment of Her Majesty, and they had "contemptuously and disdainfully rejected such matters as came from their betters, the Lords of the Higher House, whose proceedings they ought with all reverent and dutiful manner to have received." Bromley scarcely improved the mood of the burgesses, knights, and citizens. When the Queen spoke, she had to maintain and explain her own inflexible position on religion and at the same time she had to conciliate. She would need this same Parliament before many months, for the machinations of Spain were apparent, and the advent of Philip's Armada was already to be foreseen.]

My Lords and ye of the Lower House, my silence must not injure the owner so much as to suppose a substitute sufficient to render you the thanks that my heart yieldeth you, not so much for the safe keeping of my life, for which your care appears so manifest, as for the neglecting your private future peril, not regarding other way than my present state.

No Prince herein, I confess, can be surer tied or faster bound than I am with the link of your good will, and can for that but yield a heart and a head to seek for ever all your best. Yet one matter toucheth me so near, as I may not overskip, religion, the ground on which all other matters ought to take root, and being corrupted, may mar all the tree. And that there be some fault-finders with the order of the clergy, which so may make a slander to my self and the Church, whose over-ruler God hath made me, whose negligence cannot be excused if any schisms or errours heretical were suffered. Thus much I must say that some faults and negligences may grow and be, as in all other great charges it happeneth, and what vocation without? All which if you my Lords of the clergy do not amend, I mean to depose you. Look ye therefore well to your charges. This may be amended without heedless or open exclamations.

I am supposed to have many studies, but most philosophical. I must yield this to be true, that I suppose few (that be no professors) have read more. And I need not tell you that I am so simple, that I understand not, nor so forgetful, that I remember not; and yet amidst my many volumes I hope God's Book hath not been my seldomest lectures, in which we find that which by reason (for my part) we ought to believe—that seeing so great wickedness and griefs in the world in which we live but as way-faring pilgrims, we must suppose that God would never have made us but for a better place, and of more comfort than we find here. I know no creature that breatheth, whose life standeth hourly in more peril for it [i.e., religion] than mine own, who entered not into my state without sight of manifold dangers of life and Crown, as one that had the mightiest and greatest to wrestle with. Then it followeth that I regarded it so much, as I left my life behind my care.

And so you see that you wrong me too much (if any such there be) as doubt my coldness in that behalf; for if I were not persuaded that mine were the true way of God's will, God forbid that I should live to prescribe it to you. Take you heed lest *Ecclesiastes* say not too true, *They that fear the hoary frost, the snow shall fall upon them.* I see many over-bold with God Almighty, making too many subtle scannings of his blessed will, as lawyers do with humane testaments. The presumption is so great, as I may not suffer it (yet mind I not hereby to animate Romanists, which what adversaries they be to mine estate, is sufficiently known), nor tolerate new fangleness. I mean to guide them both by God's holy true rule. In both parts be perils, and of the latter I must pronounce them dangerous to a Kingly rule, to have every man according to his own censure to make a doom of the validity and privity of his Prince's government with a common veil and cover of God's Word, whose followers must not be judged but by private men's exposition. God defend you from such a ruler that so evil will guide you.

Now I conclude that your love and care neither is nor shall be bestowed upon a careless Prince, but such as but for your good will passeth as little for this World as who careth least. With thanks for your free subsidy, a manifest shew of the abundance of your good wills, the which I assure you but to be employed to your weal, I could be better pleased to return than receive.

〜

Bibliographical Note

The most available, and perhaps the most authoritative, source of Elizabeth's speeches is J. E. Neale's two volumes, *Elizabeth I and her Parliaments 1559–1581,* and *Elizabeth I and her Parliaments 1584–1601* (1958). The same volumes detail much of the political history of the reign. Knowledge of the composition and procedures in the lower House is found in the same author's *The Elizabethan House of Commons* (1949). *Journals of All the Parliaments during the Reign of Queen Elizabeth, both of the House of Lords and the House of Commons, collected by Sir Simonds D'Ewes,* revised and published by Paul Bowes (1682), contains "texts" and summaries of speeches of persons prominent in debate and in the machinery of government. J. A. Froude's *History of England from the Fall of Wolsey to the Death of Elizabeth* (12 Vols., 1870) allots Volumes VI–XII to the reign of the Queen and often affords epitomes and extracts of important speeches of the period. A recent social history is A. L. Rowse's *The England of Elizabeth* (1961). The background and the specific documents that illuminate the controversy over church and worship may be found in *Puritan Manifestoes, A Study of the Origin of the Puritan Revolt, with a Reprint of the Admonition to the Parliament and Kindred Documents,* ed. W. H. Frere and E. C. Douglas (1954). For the speaker herself, there is Neale's *Queen Elizabeth* (1934), and for a general estimate of her speechmaking, together with a number of texts, there is George P. Rice, Jr., *The Public Speaking of Queen Elizabeth* (1951).

Peter Wentworth

(1524–1596)

Peter Wentworth entered Parliament in 1571 at the age of about forty-six. He sat in six parliaments and was a member of the House of Commons for twenty-two years. Perhaps his interest in politics was aroused by his brother Paul, who had preceded him in Parliament. More probably he saw membership in the Commons as a way of securing non-Anglican, non-Catholic modes of religion. His first wife was a cousin of Henry VIII's queen, Katherine Parr; his second wife was the sister of Sir Francis Walsingham, Queen Elizabeth's secretary. Both families were Protestant and Puritan. His highest education was at the Inns of Court, and his association with the law may have led him to ponder a monarch's prerogatives and divine right and a parliament's rights and privileges. In any event, Wentworth held convictions and believed he had the right to express them. His views were rebuked not only by his Queen but also at times by his fellow Commoners. He was repeatedly arrested and imprisoned. He died in the Tower rather than submit to authority.

Wentworth's speech printed here reveals the circumstances that gave it birth. The Parliament of 1572 met in two sessions. The session in 1572 was prorogued in May and nearly four years went by before the second session opened on the day of Wentworth's speech. In the first session Wentworth had been active in the attempts to persuade the Queen to protect herself and the realm by dealing promptly and summarily with Mary Queen of Scots, who was at the center of plots that would pit France against England and restore Catholicism. Elizabeth had vacillated then, and had done nothing in the meantime. In the earlier session a speech by a Member of the House had not only been reported to the higher powers—such leaks were not unusual—but had been distorted. Wentworth rose to declare that the freedom of the House was being taken away by tale-bearers. Somewhat earlier, as one of a delegation pressing the bishops to modify the Articles of Religion (known also as the Thirty-nine Articles), he had crossed wits directly with Archbishop Parker. In the speech of February 8 he narrated his version of this encounter.

From the Crown's point of view, there was to be no yielding in matters of religion. Elizabeth rejected all efforts of Parliament to amend the Articles. Furthermore, when she detected subtle attempts by Commons *to initiate* bills—a practice widely regarded as a right of the monarch—she insisted that legislation on all "matters of state" (i.e., matters of Church, the succession, and finance) be proposed by her or her councillors and bishops. She directed, also, that Parliament's grievances be handled in the historic way—by petition, not by "bill." Thomas Cartwright and the forces behind the *Admonition* had raised grave fears that the Presbyterians intended to substitute one religious dynasty for another. Indeed, toleration was a century or more away. During the interval between sessions Peter Wentworth had been thinking deeply. His speech, he said, had been in writing for two or three years.

The speech tells us nearly as much about the speaker as about its circumstances. Wentworth's credo is clearly implied, though nowhere is it stated with the crispness he used when called to account for his utterance. Even if her Majesty sent "messages" specifically banning the discussion of certain subjects, "I will never hold my tongue," he said, on any matter "wherein God is dishonored, the Prince perilled, or the Liberties of the Parliament impeached." The thrust of this statement is consistent with an observation of one of Wentworth's contemporaries, that he was a man "of a whet and vehement spirit." There is nothing of the sycophant in him; he stands as one of the great examples of intellectual integrity and moral courage. He may have been more deeply motivated by religious interests than by the principle of free debate, but he knew that freedom of religion could not be served without freedom of discussion among the people's representatives. In both the Commons and the Lords, he had Puritan friends. The Parliament of 1571 had contained a sizable minority of Puritan-minded members, and this Parliament certainly contained a larger number of them, for the Presbyterians, once they had determined to advance their cause through Parliament rather than through the channels of the Church, began to use, as the Crown always had, the arts of pressure politics to elect their men. Wentworth, moreover, was in the company of many members of both Houses who were old hands at parliamentary debate and discussion, and they loved to talk. Neale tells us that of the 438 members in Wentworth's first Parliament (1571) about 115 had been in the sessions of 1563 and 1566. In this Parliament there sat over 200 former members. Without doubt the *habit* of discussion was growing in amount and respect, despite Elizabeth's caustic remark that the Commons were too fond of long tales. Such tendencies, nevertheless, do not impugn Wentworth's courage. The principle of free discussion was so little valued by the Commons that they stopped him before he finished his speech. They then set up an examining commission, found that he had trod on ground specifically forbidden by Elizabeth, and sent him to the Tower "until such time as this House shall have further consideration of him." Ironically, his fellows did not get around to restoring him to their midst before Elizabeth herself did so on March 12.

We do not know the precise place in the text at which Wentworth was forced to cease speaking. He was criticizing Her Majesty in unambiguous terms; and the Privy Councillors in the House, the Speaker, and many other listeners became alarmed. They determined to act when he reminded the House that Parliament had been called in 1572 to deal with the treason of Mary Queen of Scots—called "of purpose to prevent traitorous perils" to Her Majesty's person. Did they not, he said, assent to her two bills, and did she not "in the end refuse all our travails?" As a result, "hath not Her Majesty left us all open" to the revenge of our enemies? Within minutes of these utterances the House had stopped him. The examining commission made him produce the complete manuscript of his speech, and thus the entire speech was seen, perhaps heard, by a little group of the audience that had heard most of it earlier.

~

On the Liberty of the House of Commons *

House of Commons
February 8, 1576

Mr. Speaker, I find in a little volume these words, in effect: Sweet is the name of Liberty, but the thing itself a value beyond all inestimable treasure. So much the more it behoveth us lest we, contenting ourselves with the sweetness

---

* The text of this speech follows closely that printed by Sir Simonds D'Ewes, *Journals of All of the Parliaments during the Reign of Queen Elizabeth* . . . (1682), pp. 236–41, emended rarely by a reading from Neale. Neale offers a running account of the speech and includes long extracts from his preferred source, the Petyt MS. 538/17, fols. 1–6. Spelling and punctuation have been modernized.

of the name, lose and foregoe the thing, being of the greatest value that can come unto this noble realm. The inestimable treasure is the use of it in this House. And, therefore, I do think it needful to put you in remembrance that this honourable assembly are come together here in this place for three special causes of most weighty and great importance. The first and principal is to make and abrogate such laws as may be most for the preservation of our noble sovereign; the second . . .[1] the third is to make or abrogate such laws as may be to the chiefest surety, safe-keeping, and enrichment of this noble realm of England. So that I do think that the part of a faithful-hearted subject is to do his endeavour to remove all stumbling-blocks out of the way that may impair or any manner of way hinder these good and godly causes of this our coming together.

I was never of Parliament but the last, and the last session, at both of which times I saw the liberty of free speech, the which is the only salve to heal all the sores of this Commonwealth, so much and so many ways infringed, and so many abuses offered to this honourable council, as hath much grieved me, even of very conscience and love to my Prince and State. Wherefore, to avoid the like, I do deem it expedient to open the commodities [advantages] that grow to the Prince and the whole State by free speech used in this place; at least, so much as my simple wit can gather it, the which is very little in respect of that, that wise heads can say therein, and so it is of more force.

First, all matters that concern God's honour, through free speech, shall be propagated here and set forward, and all things that do hinder it removed, repulsed, and taken away. Next, there is nothing commodious, profitable, or any way beneficial for the Prince or State but faithful and loving subjects will offer it in this place. Thirdly, all things discommodious, perilous, or hurtful to the Prince or State shall be prevented, even so much as seemeth good to our merciful God to put into our minds, the which no doubt shall be sufficient if we do earnestly call upon Him and fear Him (for Solomon saith, "The fear of God is the beginning of wisdom.[2] Wisdom breatheth life into her children, receiveth them that seek her, and will go beside them in the way of righteousness"), so that our minds shall be directed to all good, needful, and necessary things, if we call upon God with faithful hearts. Fourthly, if the envious do offer anything hurtful or perilous, what incommodity doth grow thereby? Verily, I think none; nay, will you have me to say my simple opinion therein—much good cometh thereof. How, forsooth? Why, by the darkness of the night the brightness of the sun showeth more excellent and clear; and how can truth appear and conquer until falsehood and all subtleties that should shadow and darken it are found out? For it is offered in this place as a piece of fine needlework to them that are most skilful therein, for there cannot be a false stitch (God aiding us) but will be found out. Fifthly, this good cometh thereof—a wicked purpose may the easier be prevented when it is known. Sixthly, an evil man can do the less harm when it is known. Seventhly, sometime it happeneth that a good man will in this place (for argument sake) prefer an evil cause, both for that he would have a doubtful truth to be opened and manifested, and also the evil prevented. So that to this point I conclude, that in this House, which is termed a place of free speech, there is nothing so necessary for the preservation of the Prince and State as free

---

[1] Every text we have seen contains this lacuna.
[2] Prov. 9:10.

speech; and without [this] it is a scorn and mockery to call it a Parliament House, for in truth it is none but a very school of flattery and dissimulation, and so a fit place to serve the devil and his angels in, and not to glorify God and benefit the Commonwealth.

Now to the impediments thereof, which, by God's grace and my little experience, I will utter plainly and faithfully. I will use the words of Elcha—"Behold, I am as the new wine which has no vent, and bursteth the new vessels in sunder";[3] therefore, I will speak that I may have a vent. I will open my lips and make answer. I will regard no manner of person, no man will I spare; for if I go about to please men, I know not how soon my Maker will take me away. My text is vehement, which, by God's sufferance, I mean to observe, hoping therewith to offend none; for that of very justice none ought to be offended for seeking to do good and saying of the truth.

Amongst other [things], Mr. Speaker, two things do great hurt in this place, of which I do mean to speak. The one is a rumour which runneth about the House, and this it is—Take heed what you do; the Queen liketh not such a matter; whosoever preferreth it, she will be offended with him. Or the contrary—Her Majesty liketh of such matter; whosoever speaketh against it, she will be much offended with him. The other: sometimes a message is brought into the House, either of commanding or inhibiting, very injurious to the freedom of speech and consultation. I would to God, Mr. Speaker, that these two were burned in hell— I mean rumours and messages, for wicked they undoubtedly are. The reason is, the devil was the first author of them, from whom proceedeth nothing but wickedness. Now I will set down reasons to prove them wicked. For if we be in hand with anything for the advancement of God's glory, were it not wicked to say the Queen liketh not of it, or commandeth that we shall not deal in it? Greatly were these speeches to Her Majesty's dishonour; and an hard opinion were it, Mr. Speaker, that these things should enter into Her Majesty's thought. Much more wicked were it that Her Majesty should like or command anything against God or hurtful to herself and the State. The Lord grant that this thing may be far from Her Majesty's heart! Here this may be objected, that, if the Queen's Majesty have intelligence of anything perilous or beneficial to Her Majesty's person or the State, would you not have Her Majesty give knowledge thereof to the House, whereby her peril may be prevented and her benefit provided for? God forbid! Then were Her Majesty in worse case than any of her subjects. And, in the beginning of our speech, I showed it to be a special cause of our assembling; but my intent is, that nothing should be done to God's dishonour, to Her Majesty's peril, or the peril of the State. And, therefore, I will show the inconveniences that grow of these two. First, if we follow not the Prince's mind, Solomon saith, "The king's displeasure is a messenger of death."[4] This is a terrible thing to a weak nature; for who is able to abide the fierce countenance of his Prince? But if we will discharge our consciences, and be true to God and Prince and State, we must have due consideration of the place and the occasion of our coming together, and especially have regard unto the matter wherein we both shall serve God and our Prince and State faithfully, and not dissembling as eye-pleasers, and so justly avoid all displeasures both to God and our Prince; for Solomon saith,

[3] The words of Elihu, Job 32:19.
[4] Prov. 16:14.

"In the way of the righteous there is life." [5] As for any other way, it is the path to death. So that, to avoid everlasting death and condemnation with the high and mighty God, we ought to proceed in every cause according to the matter, and not according to the Prince's mind.

And now I will show you a reason to prove it perilous always to follow the Prince's mind. Many a time it falleth out that a Prince may favour a cause perilous to himself and the whole State. What are we then if we follow the Prince's mind? Are we not unfaithful unto God, our Prince, and State? Yes, truly; we are chosen of the whole realm, of a special trust and confidence by them reposed in us, to foresee all such inconveniences. Then I will set down my opinion herein; that is to say, he that dissembleth to Her Majesty's peril to be accounted as a hateful enemy, for that he giveth unto Her Majesty a detestable Judas's kiss; and he that contrarieth her mind to her preservation, yea, though Her Majesty would be much offended with him, is to be judged an approved lover. For "faithful are the wounds of a lover," saith Solomon; "but the kisses of an enemy are deceitful." [6] "And 'tis better," saith Antisthenes, "to fall amongst ravens than amongst flatterers; for ravens do but devour the dead corpse, and flatterers the living." And it is both traitorous and hellish, through flattery, to seek to devour our natural Prince; and that do flatterers. Therefore, let them leave it with shame enough.

Now to another great matter that riseth of this grievous rumour. What is it, forsooth? Whatsoever thou art that pronounceth it, thou doth pronounce thy own discredit. Why so? For that thou doth what lieth in thee to pronounce the Prince to be perjured, the which we neither will nor may believe. For we ought not, without too manifest proof, to credit any dishonour to our anointed. No; we ought not without it to think any evil of Her Majesty, but rather to hold him a liar, what credit soever he be of; for the Queen's Majesty is the head of the law, and must of necessity maintain the law, for by the law Her Majesty is made justly our queen, and by it she is most chiefly maintained. Hereunto agreeth the most excellent words of Bracton [7] who saith, "The King hath no peer nor equal in his kingdom." He hath no equal, for otherwise he might lose his authority of commanding, since that an equal hath no power of commandment over an equal. The King ought not to be under man, but under God, and under the law, because the law maketh him a King. Let the King, therefore, attribute that the law attributeth unto him, that is, dominion and power; for he is not a King in whom Will, and not the law, doth rule; and therefore he ought to be under the law. I pray you mark the reason why my authority saith the King ought to be under the law; for, saith he, "He is God's vicegerent upon earth;" that is, His lieutenant, to execute and do His will, the which is law or justice, and thereunto was Her Majesty sworn at her coronation, as I have heard learned men in this place sundry times affirm. Unto which I doubt not Her Majesty will, for her honour and conscience' sake, have special regard. For free speech and conscience in this place are granted by a special law, as that without which the Prince and State cannot be preserved or maintained. So that I would wish that every man that feareth God, regardeth the Prince's honour, or esteemeth his own

[5] *Ibid.* 11:19.

[6] *Ibid.* 27:6.

[7] Henry de Bracton (d. 1268), author of *De legibus et consuetudinibus Angliae*, a broad philosophical treatise on the laws and customs of England. Sir Edward Coke and other Puritan-minded lawyers often based legal arguments on Bracton.

credit, to fear at all times hereafter to pronounce any such horrible speeches, so much to the Prince's dishonour; for in so doing he showeth himself an open enemy to Her Majesty, and so worthy to be contemned of all faithful hearts.

Yet there is another inconvenience that riseth of this wicked rumour. The utterers thereof seem to put into our heads that the Queen's Majesty hath conceived an evil opinion, diffidence, and mistrust in us, her faithful and loving subjects; for, if she hath not, Her Majesty would wish that all things dangerous to herself should be laid open before us, assuring herself that loving subjects as we are would, without schooling and direction, with careful mind to our powers, prevent and withstand all perils that might happen unto Her Majesty. And this opinion I doubt not but Her Majesty hath conceived of us; for undoubtedly there was never prince that had faithfuller hearts than Her Majesty hath here, and surely there were never subjects had more cause heartily to love their Prince for her quiet government than we have. So that he that raiseth this rumour still increaseth but discredit, in seeking to sow sedition as much as lieth in him between our merciful Queen and us, her loving and faithful subjects, the which, by God's grace, shall never lie in his power; let him spit out all his venom, and therewithal show out his malicious heart. Yet I have collected sundry reasons to prove this a hateful and detestable rumour, and the utterer thereof to be a very Judas to our noble Queen. Therefore, let any hereafter take heed how he publish it, for as a very Judas unto Her Majesty, and an enemy to the whole State, we ought to accept [perceive] him.

Now the other was a message, Mr. Speaker, brought the last session into the House that we should not deal in any matters of religion, but first to receive from the bishops.[8] Surely this was a doleful message; for it was as much as to say, "Sirs, ye shall not deal in God's causes; no! ye shall no wise seek to advance His glory!" And in recompense of your unkindness, God in His wrath will look upon your doings that the chief cause that ye were called together for, the which is the preservation of their Prince, shall have no success. If some one of this House had presently made this interpretation of this said message, had he not seemed to have the spirit of prophecy? Yet, truly, I assure you, Mr. Speaker, there were divers of this House that said with grievous hearts, immediately upon the message, that God of His justice could not prosper the session. And let it be holden for a principle, Mr. Speaker, that council that cometh not together in God's name cannot prosper. For God saith, "Where two or three are gathered together in my name, there am I in the midst amongst them."[9] Well, God, even the great and mighty God, whose name is the Lord of Hosts, great in council and infinite in thought, and who is the only good director of all hearts, was the last session shut out of doors! But what fell out of it, forsooth? His great indignation was therefore poured upon this House; for He did put into the Queen's Majesty's heart to refuse good and wholesome laws for her own preservation, the which caused many faithful hearts for grief to burst out with sorrowful tears and moved

[8] In May 1571, under the influence of Presbyterian pressure from Thomas Cartwright's followers, the Commons was hotly debating two versions of a bill that would purge certain rites and ceremonies from the Book of Common Prayer. The Queen demanded that the two versions be shown to her. She ordered, also, that henceforth the Commons must not deal with bills on religion unless the bishops had first considered and approved them.

[9] Matt. 18:20.

all Papists, traitors to God and Her Majesty, who envy good Christian government, in their sleeves to laugh all the whole Parliament House to scorn. And shall I pass over this weighty matter so lightly? Nay! I will discharge my conscience and duties to God, my Prince, and country. So certain it is, Mr. Speaker, that none is without fault, no, not our noble Queen, sith [seeth] then Her Majesty hath committed great fault, yea, dangerous faults to herself.

Love, even perfect love, void of dissimulation, will not suffer me to hide them to Her Majesty's peril, but to utter them to Her Majesty's safety. And these they are: It is a dangerous thing in a Prince unkindly to abuse his or her nobility and people; and it is a dangerous thing in a Prince to oppose or bend herself against her nobility and people, yea, against most loving and faithful nobility and people. And how could any Prince more unkindly entreat, abuse, and oppose herself against her nobility and people than Her Majesty did the last Parliament? Did she call it of purpose to prevent traitorous perils to her person, and for no other cause? Did not Her Majesty send unto us two bills, willing us to make choice of that we liked best for her safety, and thereof to make a law, promising Her Majesty's assent thereunto? And did we not first choose the one, and Her Majesty refused it, yielding no reason; nay, yielding great reasons why she ought to have yielded to it? Yet did we nevertheless receive the other, and, agreeing to make a law thereof, did not Her Majesty in the end refuse all our travails? [10] And did not we, Her Majesty's faithful nobility and subjects, plainly and openly decipher ourselves unto Her Majesty and our hateful enemies, and hath not Her Majesty left us all open to their revenge? Is this a just recompense in our Christian Queen for our just dealings? The heathen do requite good for good; then how much more is it to be expected in a Christian Prince? And will not this Her Majesty's handling, think you, Mr. Speaker, make cold dealing in any of Her Majesty's subjects toward her again? I fear it will. And hath it not caused many already, think you, Mr. Speaker, to seek a salve for the head that they have broken? I fear it hath; and many more will do the like, if it be not prevented in time. And hath it not marvellously rejoiced and encouraged the hollow hearts of Her Majesty's hateful enemies and traitorous subjects? No doubt but it hath. And I beseech God that Her Majesty may do all things that may grieve the hearts of her enemies, and may joy the hearts that unfeignedly love Her Majesty; and I beseech the same God to endue Her Majesty with His wisdom, whereby she may discern faithful advice from traitorous, sugared speeches, and to send Her Majesty a melting, yielding heart unto sound counsel, that Will may not stand for [want of] a Reason. And then Her Majesty will stand where her enemies have fallen; for no estate will stand where the Prince will not be governed by advice. And I doubt not but that some of Her Majesty's council have dealt plainly and faithfully with Her Majesty herein. If any have, let it be a sure sign to Her Majesty to know them for approved subjects; and whatsoever they be that did persuade

[10] In the Parliament of 1572, two bills had been directed against Mary Queen of Scots, who had fled Scotland and was being held prisoner in England. One bill called for her execution, the other denied her any rights of succession to the English throne. The occasion of both was the Ridolfi plot, a scheme to declare Mary Queen and to depose or kill Elizabeth. Parliament had worked hard on both bills only to see them fail, one after the other, through Elizabeth's indecisiveness. The House was thoroughly frustrated—and so was Wentworth who had eagerly supported both bills by speech and vote.

Her Majesty so unkindly to entreat, abuse, and to oppose herself against her nobility and people, or commend Her Majesty for so doing, let it be a sure token to Her Majesty to know them for sure traitors and underminers of Her Majesty's life, and remove them out of Her Majesty's presence and favour; for, the more cunning they are the more dangerous are they unto Her Majesty. But was this all? No, for God would not vouchsafe that His Holy Spirit should all that session descend upon our bishops; so that in that session nothing was done to the advancement of His glory. I have heard of old Parliament men that the banishment of the Pope and Popery and the restoring of true religion had their beginning from this House, and not from the bishops; and I have heard that few laws for religion had their foundation from them. And I do surely think, before God I speak it, that the bishops were the cause of that doleful message.

And I will show you what moveth me so to think. I was, amongst others, the last Parliament sent unto the Bishop of Canterbury for the Articles of Religion that then passed this House. He asked us why we did put out of the book the homilies, consecrating of bishops, and such like. "Surely, sir," said I, "because we were so occupied with other things that we had no time to examine them how they agreed with the Word of God." "What!" said he, "surely you mistook the matter; you will refer yourself wholly to us therein?" "No! by the faith I bear to God," said I, "we will pass nothing until we understand what it is; for that were but to make you popes. Make you popes who list," said I, "for we will make you none." And sure, Mr. Speaker, the speech seemed to me a pope-like speech; and I fear lest our bishops do attribute this of the Pope's canons unto themselves, "papa non potest errare";[11] for surely, if they did not, they would reform things amiss, and not to spurn against God's people for writing therein as they do. But I can tell them news: they do but kick against the prick; for undoubtedly they both have [erred] and do err; for God will reveal His truth maugre [in spite of] the hearts of them and all His enemies; for great is the truth, and it will prevail. And, to say the truth, it is an error to think that God's spirit is tied only in them; for the Heavenly Spirit saith, "First seek the kingdom of God and the righteousness thereof, and all these things (meaning temporal) shall be given you."[12] These words were not spoken to the bishops only, but to all. And the writ, Mr. Speaker, that we are called up by, is chiefly to deal in God's cause, so that our commission, both from God and our Prince, is to deal in God's causes. Therefore, the accepting of such messages, and taking them in good part, do highly offend God, and is the acceptation of the breach of the liberties of this honourable council. For is it not all one thing to say, sirs, "you shall deal in such matters only," as to say "you shall not deal in such matters"? and is it as good to have fools and flatterers in the House as men of wisdom, grave judgment, faithful hearts, and sincere consciences; for they, being taught what they shall do, can give their consents as well as others? Well, "He that hath an office," saith Saint Paul, "let him wait on his office," or give diligent attendance on his office. It is a great and special part of our office, Mr. Speaker, to maintain the freedom and consultation of speech; for by this, good laws that do set forth God's glory and for the preservation of the Prince and State, are made. Saint Paul, in the same place, saith: "Hate that which is evil, cleave unto that which is good."[13] Then with Saint

---

[11] The Pope cannot err.
[12] Matt. 6:33.
[13] Rom. 12:9.

Paul I do advise you all here present, yea, and heartily and earnestly desire you, from the bottom of your hearts, to hate all messengers, tale-carriers, or any other thing, whatsoever it be, that any way infringes the liberties of this honourable council; yea, hate it or them as poisonous unto our Commonwealth, for they are venomous beasts that do use it. Therefore, I say unto you again and again, "Hate that which is evil, and cling unto that which is good." And thus, being loving and faithful-hearted, I do wish to be conceived in fear of God and of love of our Prince and State; for we are incorporated into this place to serve God and all England, and not to be time-servers, as humour-feeders, as cancers that would pierce the bone, or as flatterers that would fain beguile all the world, and so worthy to be condemned both of God and man; but let us show ourselves a people endued with faith, I mean a lively faith that bringeth forth good works,[14] and not as dead. And these good works I wish to break forth in this sort, not only in hating the enemies before spoken against, but also in openly reproving them as enemies to God, our Prince, and State, that do use them, for they are so. Therefore, I would have none spared or forborne that shall from henceforth offend herein, of what calling soever he be; for the higher place he hath the more harm he may do. Therefore, if he will not eschew offences, the higher I wish him hanged.

I speak this in charity, Mr. Speaker; for it is better that one should be hanged than that this noble State should be subverted. Well, I pray God with all my heart to turn the hearts of all the enemies of our Prince and State, and to forgive them that wherein they have offended; yea, and to give them grace to offend therein no more. Even so, I do heartily beseech God to forgive us for holding our peace when we have heard any injury offered to this honourable council; for surely it is no small offence, Mr. Speaker, for we offend therein against God, our Prince, and State, and abuse the confidence by them reposed in us. Wherefore God, for His great mercies' sake, grant that we may from henceforth show ourselves neither bastards nor dastards therein, but that as rightly-begotten children we may sharply and boldly reprove God's enemies, our Princes, and State; and so shall every one of us discharge our duties in this our high office, wherein He hath placed us, and show ourselves haters of evil and cleavers to that that is good to the setting forth of God's glory and honour, and to the preservation of our noble Queen and Commonwealth, for these are the marks that we ought only in this place to shoot at.

I am thus earnest, I take God to witness, for conscience' sake, love unto my Prince and Commonwealth, and for the advancement of Justice; "for Justice," saith an ancient father, "is the prince of all virtues," yea, the safe and faithful guard of man's life, for by it empires, kingdoms, people, and cities, be governed, the which, if it be taken away, the society of man cannot long endure. And a king, saith Solomon, "that sitteth in the throne of judgment, and looketh well about him, chaseth away all evil";[15] in the which State and throne God, for His great mercies' sake, grant that our noble Queen may be heartily vigilant and watchful; for surely there was a great fault committed both in the last Parliament and since also that was, as faithful hearts as any were unto the Prince and State

---

[14] James 2:14. Possibly there is an allusion to the Presbyterian position that for purposes of salvation, faith is primary, good deeds secondary.
[15] Prov. 20:8.

received most displeasure, the which is but a hard point in policy to encourage the enemy, to discourage the faithful-hearted, who of fervent love cannot dissemble, but follow the rule of Saint Paul, who saith, "Let love be without dissimulation." [16]

Now to another great fault I found the last Parliament, committed by some of this House also, the which I would desire of them all might be left. I have seen right good men in other causes, although I did dislike them in that doing, sit in an evil matter against which they had most earnestly spoken. I mused at it, and asked what it meant, for I do think it a shameful thing to serve God, their Prince, or country, with the tongue only and not with the heart and body. I was answered that it was a common policy in this House to mark the best sort of the same, and either to sit or arise with them.[17] That same common policy I would gladly have banished this House, and have grafted in the stead thereof either to rise or sit as the matter giveth cause; "for the eyes of the Lord behold all the earth, to strengthen all the hearts of them that are whole with him." [18] These be God's own words; mark them well, I heartily beseech you all; for God will not receive half-part; He will have the whole. And again, He misliketh these two-faced gentlemen, and here be many eyes that will to their great shame behold their double-dealing that use it.

Thus I have holden you long with my rude speech, the which since it tendeth wholly with pure conscience to seek the advancement of God's glory, our honourable Sovereign's safety, and to the sure defence of this noble isle of England, and all by maintaining of the liberties of this honourable council, the fountain from whence all these do spring—my humble and hearty suit unto you all is to accept my good-will, and that this that I have here spoken out of conscience and great zeal unto my Prince and State may not be buried in the pit of oblivion, and so no good come thereof.

∽

Bibliographical Note

For an account of Parliamentary activity and the principal actors, one must consult J. E. Neale's three volumes that deal with Parliament and the Commons. Neale draws upon Parliamentary diarists and manuscript materials that are not widely available. See also his "Peter Wentworth," *English Historical Review*, XXXIX (1924), 36–54, 175–205; and his "The Commons' Privilege of Free Speech in Parliament," *Tudor Studies*, ed. R. W. Seton-Watson (1925), pp. 257–86. In addition to D'Ewes's *Journal*, already cited, is Heywood Townshend's *An Exact Account of the Proceedings of the Four Last Parliaments of Queen Elizabeth of Famous Memory* (1680).

[16] Rom. 12:9.
[17] Thus the House voted.
[18] Compare I Pet. 3:12.

Francis Bacon

(1561–1626)

A remarkable example of the versatile Renaissance man, Francis Bacon was lawyer and judge, legislator and privy councillor, popular essayist and philosopher of science and the advancement of learning. Although his reputation today rests on his essays, he was regarded in his time as an outstanding political speaker. Ben Jonson praised him highly, and Dudley Carleton, looking back on parliamentary speakers he had heard over three decades, considered him the best of all. The two speeches in this volume present him in two roles, first as a deft political speaker at his best even on the dull but unavoidable subject of taxes; and second as a lawyer and statesman arguing against dueling.

Bacon's education and career indicate the strength and authority he brought to speechmaking. His father, Sir Nicholas Bacon, councillor and adviser to both Queen Mary and Queen Elizabeth, and his mother, a woman who could translate Greek and Latin and argue theology, were responsible for his early tutorial learning and his enrollment at Cambridge. He knew much of Cicero, Plato, and Aristotle, and from them acquired sufficient knowledge of logic and rhetoric to formulate principles of reasoning for science and to make suggestions for the practice of writing and speaking. While at Cambridge he began the habit of keeping commonplace books of materials and ideas that might be useful in speechmaking and public life. In 1576 he entered legal circles at Gray's Inn, establishing living quarters there that he maintained, in addition to his estates, throughout his life. Beginning with his election to Parliament in 1584, Bacon lived among lawyers, legislators, and courtiers for 36 years. He counseled both Elizabeth and James, and was judge in the Court of Chancery. In James's reign he progressed through the offices of Solicitor General, Attorney General, Lord Keeper, and Lord Chancellor. The "dignities" he enjoyed were those of Knight, Baron of Verulam, and Viscount St. Alban. In 1621 he was punished for taking bribes as a judge and retired to Gray's Inn where he concentrated wholly upon revising and extending his program for the advancement of science and learning. With Roger Bacon he is counted among the first of the English philosophers; yet he chose a public life, informing and tempering it with broad knowledge and speculative thought.

Bacon's hearers recognized his learning; there was no need to display his erudition and employ the flattering compliment, beyond what any Jacobean audience would expect. Sometimes an idea is reinforced in Latin, but to persons of the period, whose education always included the reading, writing, and speaking of that language, a little latinity bore the pleasure of the familiar and the sign of deftness. Bacon's rhetorical strength lay in *decorum*. He was at home with any of his audiences. He readily found and phrased the general principle relative to the matter at issue and fitted it to circumstances and to his audience with appropriate examples and specific references. He could handle the language of the court masque and the essay with facility; he could manage also the language of direct address with consummate ease and deftness. Quite characteristic are his sense of point and order, always made evident in any setting. Often the thrust of structure is emphasized and relieved by the balance of phrase and contrast in idea. His clarity is sharp, a quality reflecting Bacon's passion for accuracy. His habits of clearness and accuracy won him a high reputation as a reporter of both Court and parliamentary business and utterance. Ben Jonson, applying some of Seneca's phraseology to Bacon, declared that "no man ever spake more neatly, more pressly, more weightily, or suffered less emptiness, less idleness, in what he uttered. . . . He commanded where he spoke."

The speech on the Subsidy Bill was designed to secure prompt consideration and passage by Parliament of what we would call a general appropriations bill. Partly because of rising prices and extraordinary expenses incurred in defending the realm against Spain, Parliament in 1593 had voted a sum twice as large as ever before, and had of course increased taxes proportionately. Despite fears to the contrary, the country had borne the increase without much murmur. Now Parliament was being asked that this same amount be paid by taxes collected over a three-year period instead of the usual four. The House of Commons was in a calm mood; hence the aim of the sponsors of the bill was to stir up sufficient enthusiasm for wide support and swift passage. The initial motion was made by the Chancellor of the Exchequer, who emphasized what the Queen had done in defense of the kingdom. It was seconded by Sir Robert Cecil, who warned at large of the dangerous designs of the King of Spain. Sir Edward Hoby moved to have the proposal sent to committee, and Bacon spoke in support. He felt he should treat the matter from the point of view of "persons of generality," i.e., persons at large, because prior speakers had represented "persons of authority." With little or no obstruction, the proposal went through committee and both Houses within a month.

The speech against dueling was presented to the Court of Star Chamber. Although dueling to the death did not disappear in the western world until about 1900, civilized states have always made periodic attempts to stamp it out. In the reign of James I dueling was growing and had become so obnoxious that the government felt it must take action. England had laws against the evil, but enforcement was feeble for the reasons indicated by Bacon to his audience. John Chamberlain had written of "the many private quarrels among great men . . . which may breed dangerous diseases, if they be not purged and prevented." He had cited a number of instances, the latest being that of the Earl of Essex challenging Henry Howard for "certain disgraceful speeches." A general advertisement issued by the King in the autumn of 1613, calling attention to the laws and warning of vigorous enforcement, was so unclear and feeble as to seem ineffective. So Bacon in his new role as Attorney General saw a way of acting. There was pending the case of William Priest and Richard Wright, confessed challengers to a duel that had been refused. He asked the Star Chamber to let him make the case the occasion for discussing the seriousness of the evil, for clarifying the laws, and for announcing a policy of prompt enforcement. He hoped, also, that his opening speech—his charge to the Court—would be considered as an appropriate proclamation for wide distribution. Upon concluding the case, the judges, ten Lords and three Knights, specified where and how the speech was to be publicized along with the decree of the Court.

We know that the speech was prepared with great care. Bacon was among those councillors who had discussed with the King the growing number of duels and the means of checking them. He had drawn up an early memorandum on the steps to be taken. These facts, and the fact that the speech was Bacon's first major effort as Attorney General, suggest full provision of idea and meticulous planning of detail.

∽

UPON THE MOTION OF SUBSIDY *

House of Commons
November 15, 1598

And please you, Mr. Speaker, I must consider the time which is spent, but yet so as I must consider also the matter which is great. This great cause was at the first so materially and weightily propounded, and after in such sort persuaded and enforced, and by him that last spake [1] so much time taken and yet to good purpose; as I shall speak at a great disadvantage. But because it hath been always used, and the mixture of this House doth so require it, that in causes of this nature there be some speech and opinion as well from persons of generality as by persons of authority, I will say somewhat and not much: wherein it shall not be fit for me to enter into or to insist upon secrets either of her Majesty's coffers or of her counsel; but my speech must be of a more vulgar nature.[2]

I will not enter, Mr. Speaker, into a laudative speech of the high and singular benefits which by her Majesty's most politic and happy government we receive, thereby to incite you to a retribution; partly because no breath of man can set them forth worthily; and partly because I know her Majesty in her magnanimity doth bestow her benefits like her freest patents *absque aliquo inde reddendo,* not looking for anything again (if it were in respect only of her particular) but love and loyalty.

Neither will I now at this time put the case of this realm of England too precisely how it standeth with the subject in point of payments to the Crown, though I could make it appear by demonstration (what opinion soever be conceived) that never subjects were partakers of greater freedom and ease; and that whether you look abroad into other countries at this present time, or look back to former times

---

* There is a manuscript of this speech in the hand of one of Bacon's servants and carefully corrected in his own. It is the only full record of a speech by Bacon in the House of Commons during Elizabeth's reign, and this fact, as Spedding suggests, indicates the value and importance Bacon placed upon it. Although in later life he apparently preferred to speak from notes, he may have written this speech out in full beforehand. We have accepted Spedding's version of the text, *Life and Letters,* II (1862), 85–89 (see Bibliographical Note, below).

[1] Sir Edward Hoby, scholar and monarchist, friend of learned men; accomplished parliamentary speaker.

[2] The words "must be of a more vulgar nature" represent a revision of Bacon's, perhaps with a view to publication. The original words were: "must be like those propositions which when they are once demonstrated every man thinks he knows them before, though perchance knowing them he did not so observe them, or observing them he did not apply them so fully." Bacon thus states a criterion of comprehension for the popular audience.

in this our own country, we shall find an exceeding difference in matter of taxes; which now I reserve to mention; not so much in doubt to acquaint your ears with foreign strains, or to dig up the sepulchres of buried and forgotten impositions, which in this case (as by way of comparison) it is necessary you understand; but because speech in the House is fit to persuade the general point, and particularity is more proper and seasonable for the committee.

Neither will I make any observations upon her Majesty's manner of expending and issuing treasure, being not upon excessive and exorbitant donatives, nor upon sumptuous and unnecessary triumphs, buildings, or like magnificence; but upon the preservation, protection, and honour of the realm: for I dare not scan upon her Majesty's actions, which it becometh me rather to admire in silence, than to gloss or discourse upon them. Sure I am that the treasure that cometh from you to her Majesty is but as a vapour which riseth from the earth and gathereth into a cloud, and stayeth not there long, but upon the same earth it falleth again: and what if some drops of this do fall upon France or Flanders? It is like a sweet odour of honour and reputation to our nation throughout the world. But I will only insist upon the natural and inviolate law of preservation.

It is a truth, Mr. Speaker, and a familiar truth, that safety and preservation is to be preferred before benefit or increase, insomuch as those counsels which tend to preservation seem to be attended with necessity, whereas those deliberations which tend to benefit seem only accompanied with persuasion. And it is ever gains and no loss, when at the foot of the account there remains the purchase of safety. The prints of this are everywhere to be found. The patient will ever part with some of his blood to save and clear the rest. The seafaring man will in a storm cast over some of his goods to save and assure the rest. The husbandman will afford some foot of ground for his hedge and ditch to fortify and defend the rest. Why, Mr. Speaker, the disputer will if he be wise and cunning grant somewhat that seemeth to make against him, because he will keep himself within the strength of his opinion, and the better maintain the rest. But this place advertiseth me not to handle the matter in a commonplace.[3] I will now deliver unto you that which upon a *probatum est*[4] hath wrought upon myself, knowing your affections to be like mine own.

There hath fallen out since the last parliament four accidents or occurrents of state, things published and known to you all, by every one whereof it seemeth to me in my vulgar understanding that the danger of this realm is increased; which I speak not by way of apprehending fear, for I know I speak to English courages, but by way of pressing provision. For I do find, Mr. Speaker, that when kingdoms and states are entered into terms and resolutions of hostility one against the other, yet they are many times refrained from their attempts by four impediments.

The first is by this same *aliud agere*;[5] when they have their hands full of other matter which they have embraced, and serveth for a diversion of their hostile purposes.

---

[3] Bacon means that his subject matter and the occasion do not yield ideas and arguments drawn from traditional rhetorical *topoi* and commonplaces.

[4] *Probatum est* as used here cannot be literally translated. It refers to the analysis of the subject and to the facts and arguments which convinced Bacon himself: "that which served to prove the matter to me."

[5] Doing of something else.

The next is when they want the commodity or opportunity of some places of near approach.

The third, when they have conceived an apprehension of the difficulty and churlishness of the enterprise, and that it is not prepared to their hand.

And the fourth is when a state through the age of the monarch groweth heavy and indisposed to actions of great peril and motion, and this dull humour is not sharpened nor inflamed by any provocations or scorns.

Now if it please you to examine whether by removing the impediments in these four kinds the danger be not grown so many degrees nearer us, by accidents, as I said, fresh and all dated since the last parliament.

Soon after the last parliament you may be pleased to remember how the French king revolted from his religion,[6] whereby every man of common understanding may infer that the quarrel between France and Spain is more reconciliable, and a greater inclination of affairs to a peace than before: which supposed, it followeth Spain shall be more free to intend his malice against this realm.

Since the last parliament, it is also notorious in every man's knowledge and remembrance that the Spaniards have possessed themselves of that avenue and place of approach for England, which was never in the hands of any king of Spain before, and that is Calais;[7] which in true reason and consideration of estate of what value or service it is I know not, but in common understanding it is a knocking at our doors.

Since the last parliament also that ulcer of Ireland, which indeed brake forth before, hath run on and raged more, which cannot but be a great attractive to the ambition of the counsel of Spain, who by former experience knows of how tough a complexion this realm of England is to be assailed; and therefore (as rheums and fluxes of humours) is like to resort to that part which is weak and distempered.[8]

And lastly, it is famous now, and so will be many ages hence, how by these two sea-journeys we have braved him and objected him to scorn, so that no blood can be so frozen or mortified but must needs take flames of revenge upon so mighty disgraces.

So as this concurrence of occurrents, all since our last assembly, some to deliver and free our enemy, some to advance and bring him on his way, some to tempt and allure him, some to spur on and provoke him, cannot but threaten an increase of our peril in great proportion.

Lastly, Mr. Speaker, I will but reduce to the memory of this House one other argument for ample and large providing and supplying treasure, and this it is:

I see men do with great alacrity and spirit proceed when they have obtained a course they long wished for and were refrained from. Myself can remember, both in this honourable assembly and in all other places of this realm, how forward and affectionate men were to have an invasive war. Then we would say, a defensive war was like eating and consuming interest, and needs would we be

[6] Henry IV declared himself a Catholic in 1593.

[7] This French city, directly across the English Channel from Dover, had often been held by England and had been regarded as an English bastion. In 1592 the forces of Philip II of Spain had taken it.

[8] In this paragraph Bacon may be alluding to the severe Irish uprisings in 1579, encouraged and supported by the Pope and Philip II. More likely he is alluding to the constant unrest which Philip sought to capitalize on by sending fleets against England and Ireland in 1596 and 1597. Neither reached its destination.

adventurers and assailants. *Habes quod tota mente petisti:*[9] shall we not now make it good? especially when we have tasted so prosperous fruit of our desires.

The first of these expeditions invasive was achieved with great felicity,[10] ravished a strong and famous port in the lap and bosom of their high countries, brought them to such despair as they fired themselves and their Indian fleet in sacrifice, as a good odour and incense unto God for the great and barbarous cruelties which they have committed upon the poor Indians, whither that fleet was sailing, disordered their reckonings, so as the next news we heard of was of nothing but protesting of bills and breaking credit.

The second journey was with notable resolution borne up against weather and all difficulties,[11] and besides the success in amusing him and putting him to infinite charge, sure I am it was like a Tartar's or Parthian's bow, which shooteth backward, and had a most strong and violent effect and operation both in France and Flanders, so that our neighbours and confederates have reaped the harvest of it, and while the life-blood of Spain went inward to the heart, the outward limbs and members trembled and could not resist. And lastly, we have a perfect account of all the noble and good blood that was carried forth, and of all our sea-walls and good shipping, without mortality of persons, wreck of vessels, or any manner of diminution. And these have been the happy effects of our so long and so much desired invasive war.

To conclude, Mr. Speaker, therefore I doubt not but every man will consent that our gift must bear these two marks and badges, the one of the danger of the realm by so great a proportion since the last parliament increased, the other of the satisfaction we receive in having obtained our so earnest and ardent desire of an invasive war.

〜

[9] You now have what you wanted so badly.

[10] Bacon is referring to the first of the two sea journeys he mentioned above. It was to Cádiz, where the English fleet burned some thirteen Spanish ships and the town itself. Some two years before the events of Cádiz, England had had news of Sir Francis Drake's successes against shipping along the Spanish coast and the outposts of Spain in the New World.

[11] The reference is to the Earl of Essex's expedition to the Azores to harass Spanish commerce. The venture at least had the effect, as Bacon says, of keeping Spain's attention at home. Note that Spain's fortunes under Philip II are compressed into a single analogy.

Against Dueling *

Court of Star Chamber
November 18, 1613

My Lords:

I thought it fit for my place, and for these times, to bring to hearing before your Lordships some cause touching private *Duels,* to see if this Court can do any good to tame and reclaim that evil which seems unbridled. And I could have wished that I had met with some greater persons, as a subject for your censure, both because it had been more worthy of this presence, and also the better to have shewed the resolution myself hath to proceed without respect of persons in this business. But finding this cause on foot in my predecessor's time,[1] and published and ready for hearing, I thought to lose no time, in a mischief that groweth every day; and besides it passeth not amiss sometimes in government, that the greater sort be admonished by an example made in the meaner, and the dog to be beaten before the lion. Nay I should think (my Lords) that men of birth and quality will leave the practice, when it begins to be vilified, and come so low as to barbers, surgeons, and butchers, and such base mechanical persons.

And for the greatness of this presence, in which I take much comfort, both as I consider it in itself, and much more in respect it is by his Majesty's direction, I will supply [make up] the meanness of the particular cause by handling of the general point, to the end that by occasion of this present cause, both my purpose of prosecution against *Duels* and the opinion of the Court (without which I am nothing) for the censure of them may appear, and thereby offenders in that kind may read their own case, and know what they are to expect; which may serve for a warning until example may be made in some greater person, which I doubt the times will but too soon afford.

Therefore before I come to the particular whereof your Lordships are now to judge, I think it time best spent to speak somewhat,

First, of the nature and greatness of this mischief.

Secondly, of the causes and remedies.

Thirdly, of the justice of the law of England, which some stick not to think defective in this matter.

Fourthly, of the capacity of this Court, where certainly the remedy of this mischief is best to be found.

And fifthly, touching mine own purpose and resolution, wherein I shall humbly crave your Lordships' aid and assistance.

---

* The version here is printed by Spedding, *Letters and Life,* IV (1868), 399–409. He took it from the original edition (1614) as published with the following title: *The charge of Sir Francis Bacon, knight, his Majesties Attourney generall, touching Duells, upon an information in the Star-chamber against Priest and Wright. With the Decree of the Star-chamber in the same cause.* The language of the text may have received some editing before printing; nevertheless, the speech as it stands is replete with the marks of direct address. This fact is strikingly evident when the speech is compared with the Court's very full summary of it.

[1] Sir Henry Hobart had recently been raised to the King's Bench. Bacon was then made Attorney General.

For the mischief itself, it may please your Lordships to take into your consideration that when revenge is once extorted out of the magistrate's hand contrary to
God's ordinance, *Mihi vindicta, ego retribuam,*[2] and every man shall bear the
sword not to defend but to assail, and private men begin once to presume to give
law to themselves, and to right their own wrongs, no man can foresee the dangers
and inconveniencies that may arise and multiply thereupon. It may cause sudden
storms in Court, to the disturbance of his Majesty, and unsafety of his person. It
may grow from quarrels to banding, and from banding to trooping, and so to
tumult and commotion, from particular persons to dissension of families and
alliances, yea to national quarrels, according to the infinite variety of accidents,
which fall not under foresight: so that the state by this means shall be like to
a distempered and unperfect body, continually subject to inflammations and
convulsions.[3]

Besides, certainly, both in divinity and in policy, *offences of presumption are
the greatest.* Other offences yield and consent to the law *that it is good,* not daring to make defence, or to justify themselves; but this offence expressly gives the
law an affront, as if there were two laws, one a kind of *gown-law,* and the other
a law of *reputation,* as they term it; so that Paul's and Westminster, the pulpit and
the courts of justice, must give place to the law (as the King speaketh in his
proclamation[4]) of *Ordinary* tables, and such reverend assemblies; the year-books
and statute-books must give place to some French and Italian pamphlets, which
handle the doctrine of *Duels,* which if they be in the right, *transeamus ad illa,*
let's receive them, and not keep the people in conflict and distraction between
two laws.

Again (my Lords) it is a miserable effect, when young men full of towardness
and hope, such as the poets call *auroræ filii,* sons of the morning, in whom the
expectation and comfort of their friends consisteth, shall be cast away and destroyed
in such a vain manner; but much more it is to be deplored when so much noble
and gentle blood shall be spilt upon such follies, as, if it were adventure in the
field in service of the King and realm, were able to make the fortune of a day,
and to change the fortune of a kingdom. So as your Lordships see what a
desperate evil this is; it troubleth peace, it disfurnisheth war, it bringeth calamity
upon private men, peril upon the State, and contempt upon the law.

Touching the causes of it: the first motive no doubt is a false and erroneous
imagination of honour and credit; and therefore the King, in his last proclamation, doth most amply and excellently call them *bewitching Duels.* For, if one
judge of it truly, it is no better than a sorcery, that enchanteth the spirits of young
men, that bear great minds, with a false shew, *species falsa;* and a kind of satanical
illusion and apparition of honour; against religion, against law, against moral virtue,
and against the precedents and examples of the best times and valiantest nations,
as I shall tell you by and by, when I shall shew you that the law of England is not
alone in this point.

But then the seed of this mischief being such, it is nourished by vain discourses,

[2] Heb. 10:30. "Vengeance is mine, I will repay."

[3] John Chamberlain supplies a considerable list of duelists or near-duelists. See
Spedding, *Letters and Life of Francis Bacon,* IV (1868), 396.

[4] King James had issued his proclamation against duels in October. Bacon and others
felt that it had had little effect, chiefly becaues the Crown's position had not been
clearly expressed.

and green and unripe conceits, which nevertheless have so prevailed, as though a man were staid and sober-minded, and a right believer touching the vanity and unlawfulness of these *Duels*, yet the stream of vulgar opinion is such, as it imposeth a necessity upon men of value to conform themselves; or else there is no living or looking upon men's faces. So that we have not to do, in this case, so much with particular persons, as with unsound and depraved opinions, like the dominations and spirits of the air which the Scripture speaketh of.

Hereunto may be added, that men have almost lost the true notion and understanding of *Fortitude* and *Valour*. For *Fortitude* distinguisheth of the grounds of quarrels, whether they be just; and not only so, but whether they be worthy; and setteth a better price upon men's lives than to bestow them idly. Nay it is weakness and dis-esteem of a man's self, to put a man's life upon such ledgier [5] performances. A man's life is not to be trifled away; it is to be offered up and sacrificed to honourable services, public merits, good causes, and noble adventures. It is in expense of blood as it is in expense of money. It is no liberality to make a profusion of money upon every vain occasion, nor no more it is fortitude to make effusion of blood, except the cause be of worth. And thus much for the causes of this evil.

For the remedies, I hope some great and noble person will put his hand to this plough, and I wish that my labours of this day may be but forerunners to the work of a higher and better hand. But yet to deliver my opinion, as may be proper for this time and place, there be four things that I have thought on, as the most effectual for the repressing of this depraved custom of particular combats.

The first is, that there do appear and be declared a constant and settled resolution in the State to abolish it. For this is a thing (my Lords) must go down at once, or not at all. For then every particular man will think himself acquitted in his reputation, when he sees that the State takes it to heart, as an insult against the King's power and authority, and thereupon hath absolutely resolved to master it; like unto that which was set down in express words in the edict of Charles the ninth of France touching *Duels, That the King himself took upon him the honour of all that took themselves grieved or interested* [injured] *for not having performed the combat.* So must the State do in this business; and in my conscience there is none that is but of a reasonable sober disposition, be he never so valiant, (except it be some furious person that is like a firework) but will be glad of it, when he shall see the law and rule of State disinterest him of a vain and unnecessary hazard.

Secondly, care must be taken that this evil be no more cockered [coddled], nor the humour of it fed; wherein I humbly pray your Lordships that I may speak my mind freely, and yet be understood aright. The proceedings of the great and noble Commissioners Marshall I honour and reverence much, and of them I speak not in any sort. But I say the compounding of quarrels, which is otherwise in use, by private noblemen and gentlemen, is so punctual, and hath such reference and respect unto the received conceits, what's before-hand, and what's behind-hand, and I cannot tell what, as without all question it doth in a fashion

---

[5] Comparative form of *ledgy*. Dueling is like standing on the edge of a precipice since the outcome may be quite as sudden and final.

countenance and authorize this practice of *Duels,* as if it had in it somewhat of right.[6]

Thirdly, I must acknowledge that I learned out of the King's last proclamation the most prudent and best applied remedy for this offence (if it shall please his Majesty to use it) that the wit of man can devise. This offence (my Lords) is grounded upon a false conceit of honour, and therefore it would be punished in the same kind. *In eo quis rectissime plectitur, in quo peccat.*[7] The fountain of honour is the King, and his aspect and the access to his person continueth honour in life, and to be banished from his presence is one of the greatest eclipses of honour that can be; if his Majesty shall be pleased that when this Court shall censure any of these offences in persons of eminent quality, to add this out of his own power and discipline, that these persons shall be banished and excluded from his Court for certain years, and the Courts of his Queen and Prince, I think there is no man that hath any good blood in him will commit an act that shall cast him into that darkness, that he may not behold his Sovereign's face.

Lastly, and that which more properly concerneth this Court, we see (my Lords) the root of this offence is stubborn; for it depiseth death, which is the utmost of punishments, and it were a just but a miserable severity, to execute the law without all remission or mercy, where the case proveth capital. And yet the late severity in France was more, where by a kind of martial law established by ordinance of the King and Parliament, the party that had slain another was presently had to the gibbet; insomuch as gentlemen of great quality were hanged, their wounds bleeding, lest a natural death should prevent the example of justice. But (my Lords) the course which we shall take is of far greater lenity, and yet of no less efficacy; which is to punish, in this Court, all the middle acts and proceedings which tend to the *Duel* (which I will enumerate to you anon), and so to hew and vex the root in the branches; which, no doubt, in the end will kill the root, and yet prevent the extremity of law.

Now for the law of England, I see it excepted to, though ignorantly, in two points:

The one, that it should make no difference between an insidious and foul murder, and the killing of a man upon fair terms, as they now call it.

The other, that the law hath not provided sufficient punishment and reparations for contumely of words, as the Lie, and the like.

But these are no better than childish novelties, against the divine law, and against all laws in effect, and against the examples of all the bravest and most virtuous nations of the world.

For first for the law of God, there is never to be found any difference made in homicide, but between homicide voluntary and involuntary, which we term misadventure. And for the case of misadventure itself, there were cities of refuge; so that the offender was put to his flight, and that flight was subject to

---

[6] Bacon refers obliquely to some minor government officials and lawyers who obligingly ignored duels or even aided the disputants in various ways. Some would help a man decide whether he had grounds for a duel, the "what's before-hand," and what would be the probable consequences, the "what's behind-hand." Later in the speech Bacon issues a half-veiled threat to such lawyers.

[7] Men are most correctly punished in that in which they have sinned.

accident, whether the revenger of blood should overtake him before he had gotten sanctuary or no. It is true that our law hath made a more subtle distinction between the will inflamed and the will advised, between manslaughter in heat and murder upon prepensed [planned] malice, or cold blood, as the soldiers call it; and indulgence not unfit for a choleric and warlike nation; for it is true, *ira furor brevis;* [8] a man in fury is not himself. This privilege of passion the ancient Roman law restrained, but to a case: that was, if the husband took the adulterer in the manner; to that rage and provocation only it gave way, that it was an homicide was justifiable. But for a difference to be made in case of killing and destroying man, upon a fore-thought purpose, between foul and fair, and as it were between single murder and vied [9] murder, it is but a monstrous child of this later age, and there is no shadow of it in any law divine or human. Only it is true, I find in the Scripture that Cain inticed his brother into the field and slew him treacherously, but Lamed vaunted of his manhood *that he would kill a young man and if it were in his hurt:* So as I see no difference between an insidious murder and a braving or presumptuous murder, but the difference between Cain and Lamed. [10]

As for examples in civil states, all memory doth consent that Greece and Rome were the most valiant and generous nations of the world; and, that which is more to be noted, they were free estates, and not under a monarchy, whereby a man would think it a great deal the more reason that particular persons should have righted themselves; and yet they had not this practice of *Duels,* nor anything that bare show thereof. And sure they would have had it, if there had been any virtue in it. Nay as he saith, *Fas est et ab hoste doceri,* [11] it is memorable, that is reported by a counsellor and ambassador of the Emperor's, touching the censure of the Turks of these *Duels.* There was a combat of this kind performed by two persons of quality of the Turks, wherein one of them was slain, the other party was convented before the council of *Bassaes;* the manner of the reprehension was in these words: *How durst you undertake to fight one with the other? Are there not Christians enough to kill? Did you not know that whether of you should be slain, the loss would be the Great Seigneours?* So as we may see that the most warlike nations, whether generous or barbarous, have ever despised this wherein now men glory.

It is true (my Lords) that I find combats of two natures authorized, how justly I will not dispute as to the later of them.

The one, when upon the approaches of armies in the face one of the other, particular persons have made challenges for trial of valours in the field, upon the public quarrel.

This the Romans called *pugna per provocationem.* [12] And this was never . . . [permitted except] between the generals themselves, who were absolute, or between particulars by licence of the generals; never upon private authority. So you see David asked leave when he fought with Goliah, and Joab, when the armies were met, gave leave, and said, *Let the young men play before us;* and of this

---

[8] Horace, *Epistles* i. 2. 62. "Rage is a short madness."

[9] *Vied* carries the ideas of contest, rivalry, chance or gamble; hence Bacon's meaning is that of persons in conflict, as in a duel.

[10] Lamech, a descendant of Cain.

[11] "One may be taught even by the enemy."

[12] "Combat by challenge."

kind was that famous example in the wars of Naples, between twelve Spaniards and twelve Italians, where the Italians bare away the victory—besides other infinite like examples worthy and laudable, sometimes by singles, sometimes by numbers.

The second combat is a judicial trial of right, where the right is obscure, introduced by the Goths and the Northern nation, but more anciently entertained in Spain; and this yet remains in some cases as a divine lot of battle, though controverted by divines touching the lawfulness of it. So that a wise writer saith, *Taliter pugnantes videntur tentare Deum, quia hoc volunt ut Deus ostendat et faciat miraculum, ut justam causam habens victor efficiatur, quod sæpe contra accidit.*[13] But howsoever it be, this kind of fight taketh his warrant from law. Nay, the French themselves, whence this folly seemeth chiefly to have flown, never had it but only in practice and toleration, but never as authorized by law. And yet now of late they have been fain to purge their folly with extreme rigour, in so much as many gentlemen left between death and life in the *Duels* (as I spake before) were hastened to hanging with their wounds bleeding. For the State found it had been neglected so long, as nothing could be thought cruelty which tended to the putting of it down.

As for the second defect pretended in our law, that it hath provided no remedy for *lies* and *fillips*, it may receive like answer. It would have been thought a madness amongst the ancient lawgivers, to have set a punishment upon the *lie given*, which in effect is but a word of denial, a negative of another's saying. Any lawgiver, if he had been asked the question, would have made Solon's answer: *that he had not ordained any punishment for it, because he never imagined the world would have been so fantastical as to take it so highly.* The civilians, they dispute whether an action of *injury* lie for it,[14] and rather resolve the contrary. And Francis the first of France, who first set on and stamped this disgrace so deep, is taxed by the judgment of all wise writers for beginning the vanity of it; for it was he, that when he had himself given the lie and defy to the Emperor, to make it current in the world, said in a solemn assembly, *That he was no honest man that would bear the lie;* which was the fountain of this new learning.

As for words of *reproach* and *contumely* (whereof the lie was esteemed none) it is not credible (but that the orations themselves are extant) what extreme and exquisite reproaches were tossed up and down in the senate of Rome and the places of assembly, and the like in Greece, and yet no man took himself fouled by them, but took them but for breath and the style of an enemy, and either despised them or returned them, but no blood was spilt about them.

So of every touch or light blow of the person, they are not in themselves considerable, save that they have got upon them the stamp of a disgrace, which maketh these light things pass for great matter. The law of England, and all laws, hold these degrees of injury to the person, *slander, battery, maim,* and *death;* and if there be extraordinary circumstances of despite and contumely, as in case of libels and bastinadoes, and the like, this Court taketh them in hand, and punisheth them exemplarly. But for this apprehension of a disgrace, that a fillip to the person should be a mortal wound to the reputation, it were good that men

---

[13] In this manner [i.e., battle involving divine lot] combatants appear to tempt God, because they want God to show himself and perform a miracle so that the party having just cause might win—the contrary of which often happens.

[14] *Lie* appears here in the sense of "be admissible."

did hearken unto the saying of Consalvo, the great and famous commander, that was wont to say, *a gentleman's honour should be de tela crassiore*, of a good strong warp or web, that every little thing should not catch in it, when as now it seems they are but of cobweb-lawn or such light stuff, which certainly is weakness, and not true greatness of mind, but like a sick man's body, that is so tender that it feels every thing. And so much in maintenance and demonstration of the wisdom and justice of the law of the land.

For the capacity of this Court, I take this to be a ground infallible: *that wheresoever an offence is capital, or matter of felony, if it be acted, there the combination or practice tending to that offence is punishable in this Court as a high misdemeanor.* So practice to impoison, though it took no effect; waylaying to murder, though it took no effect, and the like, have been adjudged heinous misdemeanors punishable in this Court. Nay, inceptions and preparations in inferior crimes (that are not capital), as suborning and preparing of witnesses that were never deposed, or deposed nothing material, have likewise been censured in this Court, as appeareth by the decree in Garnon's case.

Why then, the major proposition being such, the minor cannot be denied: for every appointment of the field is but combination and plotting of murder; let them gild it how they list, they shall never have fairer terms of me in place of justice. Then the conclusion followeth, that it is a case fit for the censure of this Court. And of this there be precedents in the very point of challenge.

It was the case of Wharton, plaintiff, against Ellekar and Acklam defendants, where Acklam being a follower of Ellekar's, was censured for carrying a challenge from Ellekar to Wharton, though the challenge was not put in writing, but delivered only by word of message; and there are words in the decree, that such challenges are to the subversion of government.

These things are well known, and therefore I needed not so much to have insisted upon them, but that in this case I would be thought not to innovate anything of mine own head, but to follow the former precedents of the Court, though I mean to do it more thoroughly, because the time requires it more.

Therefore now to come to that which concerneth my part: I say that by the favour of the King and the Court, I will prosecute in this Court in the cases following.

If any man shall appoint the field, though the fight be not acted or performed.

If any man shall send any challenge in writing, or any message of challenge.

If any man carry or deliver any writing or message of challenge.

If any man shall accept or return a challenge.

If any man shall accept to be a second in a challenge of either side.

If any man shall depart the realm, with intention and agreement to perform the fight beyond the seas.

If any man shall revive a quarrel by any scandalous bruits or writings, contrary to a former proclamation published by his Majesty in that behalf.

Nay I hear there be some Counsel learned of *Duels*, that tell young men when they are before-hand, and when they are otherwise,[15] and thereby incense and incite them to the *Duel*, and make an art of it. I hope I shall meet with some of them too. And I am sure (my Lords) this course of preventing *Duels* in nipping them in the bud, is fuller of clemency and providence than the suffering

[15] I.e., when they have cause or grounds of dishonor and when they do not.

them to go on, and hanging men with their wounds bleeding, as they did in France.

To conclude, I have some petitions to make, first to your Lordship, my Lord Chancellor,[16] that in case I be advertised of a purpose in any to go beyond the sea to fight, I may have granted his Majesty's writ of *Ne exeat regnum* [17] to stop him, for this giant bestrideth the sea, and I would take and snare him by the foot on this side; for the combination and plotting is on this side, though it should be acted beyond sea. And your Lordship said notably the last time I made a motion in this business, that a man may be as well *fur de se*, as *felo de se*,[18] if he steal out of the realm for a bad purpose; and for the satisfying of the words of the writ, no man will doubt but he doth *machinari contra coronam* [19] (as the words of the writ be) that seeketh to murder a subject; for that is ever *contra coronam et dignitatem*.[20] I have also a suit to your Lordships all in general, that for justice sake, and for true honour's sake, honour of religion, law, and the King our master, against this fond and false disguise or puppetry of honour, I may in my prosecution, which it is like enough it may sometimes stir coals (which I esteem not for my particular, but as it may hinder the good service) I may (I say) be countenanced and assisted from your Lordships. Lastly, I have a petition to the noblesse and gentlemen of England, that they would learn to esteem themselves at a just price. *Non hos quæsitum munus in usus*,[21] their blood is not to be spilt like water or a vile thing; therefore that they would rest persuaded there cannot be a form of honour, except it be upon a worthy matter. But for this, *ipsi viderint*,[22] I am resolved. And thus much for the general, now to the present case.

∽

Bibliographical Note

For knowledge of Bacon's life, his times, the circumstances and texts of his speeches, the best single source is *The Letters and the Life of Francis Bacon, Including All his Occasional Works* . . . , ed. James Spedding, 7 vols. (1861–1874). The best interpretation of Bacon's thought and philosophy is by Fulton H. Anderson, in *The Philosophy of Francis Bacon* (1948), and in *Francis Bacon: His Career and Thought* (1962). Suggestive at times is Robert Hannah, "Francis Bacon, the Political Orator," in *Studies in Rhetoric and Public Speaking in Honor of James A. Winans*, ed. A. M. Drummond (1925). For a treatment of Bacon's principles of rhetoric and of discussion, see Karl R. Wallace, *Francis Bacon on Communication and Rhetoric* (1943), and "Discussion in Parliament and Francis Bacon," *The Quarterly Journal of Speech*, XLIII (February, 1957), 11–21.

[16] Thomas, Lord Ellesmere. Other members of the Court are listed by Spedding, IV, 409.

[17] "Let him not leave the realm."

[18] *Fur de se*, stealing himself from himself; *felo de se*, suicide. He who flees his country is like a man who commits suicide: he himself steals himself.

[19] "Plot some evil against the Crown."

[20] "Against the Crown and its dignity."

[21] "Service does not demand these uses."

[22] "They themselves will see."

Sir Walter Raleigh

(1552?–1618)

Sir Walter Raleigh was a Renaissance man, versatile in interests, abilities, and action. He was soldier and sailor, adventurer and explorer, businessman and ship-designer, parliamentarian and debater, courtier to Elizabeth, Captain of the Queen's Guard, and writer of poetry and history. Leaving Oxford to fight for the Huguenots, he charged on through life, subduing the Irish, pillaging treasure ships, warring on Spain and helping to repulse the Armada, exploring the Americas and colonizing Virginia. His courage and arrogance, his ambition and ruthlessness, his remarkable intellect, his skill at intrigue and the manipulation of men brought him a number of powerful, bitter enemies and few friends. His rivalry with Essex for the Queen's favor and his ambiguous behavior at the scaffold when Essex was beheaded were widely known and often misinterpreted. In 1603, Raleigh's enemies succeeded in implicating him in a plot against James. The sentence of death was suspended in favor of imprisonment in the Tower, from which Sir Walter was not released until 1616.

The circumstances of his release are Raleighesque, and help to explain the scaffold speech. Raleigh took advantage of his popularity among the people and of James's greed to propose a voyage up the Orinoco River, whose great valley was called Guiana, to secure gold from a mine that he and his supporters believed to exist. The King drove a hard bargain. He coveted a marriage alliance with Spain; so the royal commission stipulated not only that the venture be privately financed, but that any loss of Spanish life and property on sea or land should be recompensed by Raleigh's death. It was a bad bargain for Sir Walter. Some Spanish ships were pirated and a Spanish-held village was burned by men Raleigh could not control. His son was killed. He returned to England as he had promised, apparently hoping that his persuasions would prevail on the King and Council. On October 28, James signed the death warrant and decreed that the execution should take place the next morning.

The scaffold had been erected in the Old Palace Yard at Westminster. A large crowd had collected. Most persons were standing; some were on horseback. Nearby were some houses, among which was Sir Randall Carew's. Standing before the windows or on the balcony was Lord Arundel, who had given money to the Guiana expedition, and other lords. In the crowd, also, stood Sir John Eliot (see below, pages 123–25).

Raleigh went to the scaffold ushered by two sheriffs and the Rev. Robert Tounson, Dean of Westminster. Oldys reports that "he had on a wrought night-cap under his hat; a ruff band; a black wrought velvet nightgown over a hair-coloured satin doublet, and a black wrought waistcoat; a pair of black cut taffeta breeches, and ash-coloured silk stockings." Persons remarked on his proud carriage and cheerful countenance. The speech had been well prepared beforehand, a summary of it having been signed by Raleigh himself. At one point in delivery he cast his eye upon "his note of remembrance."

An attendant, John Porry, recorded his impression: "Every man that saw Sir

Walter Raleigh die said it was impossible for any man to show more decorum, courage, or piety; and that his death will do more hurt to the faction that sought it, than ever his life could have done."

∽

Speech on the Scaffold *

October 29, 1618

I thank God, that he has sent me to die in the light, and not in darkness.[1] I likewise thank God, that he has suffered me to die before such an assembly of honourable witnesses, and not obscurely in the Tower; where, for the space of thirteen years together, I have been oppressed with many miseries. And I return him thanks, that my fever hath not taken me at this time, as I prayed to him it might not, that I might clear myself of some accusations unjustly laid to my charge, and leave behind me the testimony of a true heart both to my king and country.

There are two main points of suspicion that his majesty hath conceived against me, and which, I conceive, have specially hastened my coming hither; therefore I desire to clear them to your lordships, and resolve you in the truth thereof. The first is, that his majesty hath been informed, I have had some plot or confederacy with France, for which he had some reasons, though grounded upon a weak foundation. One was, that when I returned to Plymouth, I endeavoured to go to Rochelle, which was because I would fain have made my peace before I came to England. Another reason was, that again I would have bent my course to

* Except for one change in a place name in the interest of accuracy, this version of Raleigh's speech is that of Oldys, who explains that he took it "partly from an old MS copy in the Harleian library, and another MS also before me, but principally from three of the most ancient copies we have of it in print, at the end of Overbury's Narrative of his Arraignment, and in his Remains; each supplying something the others are wanting in, yet none varying considerably from the rest, either in form of expression or matter of fact." (*Works,* VIII, 557–63.) The text in Edwards is smoother than the one that we print. He derived it from Archbishop Sancroft's transcript of a contemporary account, which is in the Tanner MSS collection, Oxford. Perhaps it is the version referred to by Tounson, Dean of Westminster, in a letter to Sir John Isham: ". . . one Craford, who was sometimes Mr. Rodeknight's pupil, hath penned it prettily, and meaneth to put it to the press, and came to me about it, but I hear not that it is come forth." (*Ibid.,* VIII, 781.)

[1] Raleigh had trouble getting started, for he was uncertain whether his voice was carrying to the Lords standing in the windows off Carew's balcony. "I have had fits of ague," he said, "for these two days. If, therefore, you perceive any weakness in me, ascribe it to my sickness, rather than to myself." From the balcony, Lord Arundel called out, "We will come down to you." The Lords made their way to the scaffold, shook hands with Raleigh, and stood to one side. Raleigh then began again. The description of the opening moments is reported by Edwards, Oldys, and Wallace. The letter writers present add some color. For their accounts see William S. Powell, "John Pory on the Death of Sir Walter Raleigh," *William and Mary Quarterly,* IX (1952), 532–38; and R. F. Williams, *The Court and Times of James the First,* 2 vols. (London, 1849), II, 95–103.

France, upon my last intended escape from London, being the place where I might have the best means of making such peace, and the best safeguard during that terror from above. These, joined with the coming of the French agent to my house here in London, only to confer about my said voyage, together with the report of my having a commission from the king of France, might occasion my being so suspected in this particular, and his majesty to be so displeased with me.[2] But this I say; for a man to call God to witness at any time to a falsehood, is a grievous sin. To call him as witness to a falsehood at the point of death, when there is no time for repentance, is a crime far more impious and desperate; therefore, for me to call that Majesty to witness an untruth, before whose tribunal I am instantly to appear, were beyond measure sinful, and without hope of pardon. I do yet call that great God to witness, that, as I hope to see him, to be saved by him, and live in the world to come, I never had any plot or intelligence with the French king; never had any commission from him, nor saw his hand or seal; that I never had any practice or combination with the French agent, nor ever knew or saw such a person, till I met him in my gallery unlooked-for. If I speak not true, O Lord, let me never enter into thy kingdom.

The second suspicion or imputation was, that his majesty had been informed I had spoken disloyally of him. The only witness of this was a base Frenchman, a runagate [renegade], a chemical fellow,[3] whom I soon knew to be perfidious; for being drawn by him into the action of freeing myself at Salisbury, in which I confess my hand was touched, he, being sworn to secrecy overnight, revealed it the next morning. It is strange, that so mean a fellow could so far encroach himself into the favour of the lords; and, gaping after some great reward, could so falsely accuse me of seditious speeches against his majesty, and be so credited. But this I here speak, it is no time for me to flatter or to fear princes, I, who am subject only unto death; and for me, who have now to do with God alone, to tell a lie to get the favour of the king were in vain; and yet, if ever I spake disloyally or dishonestly of the king, either to this Frenchman or any other, ever intimated the least thought hurtful or prejudicial of him, the Lord blot me out of the book of life.

I confess, I did attempt to escape, and it was only to save my life. I likewise confess, that I feigned myself to be indisposed at Salisbury, but I hope it was no sin; for the prophet David did make himself a fool, and suffered spittle to fall upon his beard to escape from the hands of his enemies, and it was not imputed unto him as a sin. What I did was only to prolong time, till his majesty came, in hopes of some commiseration from him.

But I forgive that Frenchman, and likewise Sir Lewis Stukely, the wrongs he

---

[2] The passage refers to these circumstances: When Raleigh was raising money for the Guiana adventure, he had conversed with the French ambassador, des Marets. A French commission was offered him—and apparently refused—by Admiral de Montmorency. Raleigh was known to have had a long-time French friend, Captain Faige, of the anti-Spanish party in France. So Sir Walter's critics argued that he had intended to find protection in France if the expedition failed.

[3] A French physician, one Dr. Manourie. Raleigh obtained some pills from him to produce the "feigned" sickness referred to in the next paragraph. After landing at Plymouth, he lingered at Salisbury. He needed time to prepare his *Apology*, later published, so he used various stratagems of delay.

hath done me, with all my heart;[4] for I have received the sacrament this morning of Mr. Dean, and I have forgiven all men; but, in charity to others, am bound to caution them against him, and such as he is. For Sir Lewis Stukely, my keeper and kinsman, hath affirmed, that I should tell him, my lord Carew and my lord of Doncaster here, did advise me to escape; but I protest before God I never told him any such thing; neither did these lords advise me to any such matter. It is not likely that I should acquaint two privy-counsellors of my escape; nor that I should tell him, my keeper, it was their advice; neither was there any reason to tell it him, or he to report it; for it is well known he left me six, eight, or ten days together alone, to go whither I listed, while he rode about the country. He further accused me, that I should shew him a letter, whereby I did signify that I would give him ten thousand pounds to escape. But God cast my soul into everlasting fire if ever I made such proffer of ten thousand pounds, or one thousand pounds; but indeed I shewed him a letter, that if he would go with me, there should be order taken for the discharge of his debts when he was gone; neither had I one thousand pounds, for, if I had, I could have made my peace better with it otherwise than by giving it Stukely. Further, he gave out, when I came to Sir Edward Parham's house, who had been a follower of mine, and gave me good entertainment, I had there received some dram of poison. When I answered, [I said] that I feared no such thing, for I was well assured of those in the house; and therefore wished him to have no such thought. Now I will not only say, that God is the God of revenge, but also of mercy; and I desire God to forgive him, as I hope to be forgiven.

It was told the king, that I was brought perforce into England; and that I did not intend to return again: whereas captain Charles Parker, Mr. Tresham, Mr. Leak, and divers others, that knew how I was dealt withal by the common soldiers, will witness to the contrary. They were an hundred and fifty of them who mutinied against me, and sent for me to come to them; for unto me they would not come. They kept me close prisoner in my cabin, and forced me to take an oath, that I would not go into England without their consent, otherwise they would have cast me into the sea. After I had taken this oath, I did, by wine, gifts, and fair words, so work upon the master-gunner, and ten or twelve of the faction, that I won them to desist from their purposes, and intended, when I returned home, to procure their pardon; in the meanwhile [I] proposed, that I would dispose of some of them in Ireland; to which they agreed, and would have gone into the north parts, from which I dissuaded them, and told them, they were red-shanks[5] who inhabited there, so drew them to the south; and the better to clear myself of them, was forced to get them a hundred and fifty pounds at Kinsale,[6] otherwise I had never got from them.

There was a report also, that I meant not to go to Guiana at all; and that I knew not of any mine, nor intended any such matter, but only to get my liberty, which I had not the wit to keep. But it was my full intent to go for gold, for the benefit of his majesty, myself, and those who went with me, with the rest of my

[4] Stukely, a cousin, had plotted with the authorities to encourage Raleigh to escape and catch him in the act. The staged affair involved a boat chase on the Thames, with Stukely personally in charge of Raleigh's boat and thus assuring capture.

[5] A derisive allusion to poor Irish whose bare legs appeared red.

[6] A town in Ireland.

countrymen: though he that knew the head of the mine would not discover it when he saw my son was slain, but made himself away. [He turned to the Earl of Arundel.] My lord, you being in the gallery of my ship at my departure, I remember you took me by the hand, and said, you would request one thing of me; which was, whether I made a good voyage or a bad, that I would return again into England; which I then promised, and gave you my faith I would. "So you did," said his lordship; "it is true, and they were the last words I said to you."

Another slander was raised of me, that I should have gone away from them, and have left them at Guiana. But there were a great many worthy men, who accompanied me always, as my sergeant-major, and divers others, [whom he named] that knew it was none of my intention. Also it hath been said, that I stinted them of fresh water; to which I answer, every one was, as they must be in a ship, furnished by measure, and not according to their appetites. This course all seamen know must be used among them, and to this strait were we driven.

Another opinion was held, that I carried with me sixteen thousand pieces of gold; and that all the voyage I intended, was but to gain my liberty, and this money into my hands. But, as I shall answer it before God, I had no more in all the world, directly or indirectly, than one hundred pounds; whereof I gave about forty-five pounds to my wife. But the ground of this false report was, that twenty thousand pounds being adventured, and but four thousand appearing in the surveyor's books, the rest had my hand to the bills for divers adventures; but, as I hope to be saved, I had not a penny more than one hundred pounds.[7] These are the material points I thought good to speak of; I am at this instant to render my account to God, and I protest, as I shall appear before him, this that I have spoken is true.

I will borrow but a little time more of Mr. Sheriff, that I may not detain him too long; and herein I shall speak of the imputation laid upon me through the jealousy of the people, that I had been a persecutor of my lord of Essex; that I rejoiced in his death, and stood in a window over-against him when he suffered, and puffed out tobacco in defiance of him; when as, God is my witness, that I shed tears for him when he died; and, as I hope to look God in the face hereafter, my lord of Essex did not see my face at the time of his death; for I was far off, in the armoury, where I saw him, but he saw not me. It is true, I was of a contrary faction; but I take the same God to witness, that I had no hand in his death, nor bare him any ill affection, but always believed it would be better for me that his life had been preserved; for after his fall, I got the hatred of those who wished me well before: and those who set me against him, set themselves afterwards against me, and were my greatest enemies. And my soul hath many times been grieved, that I was not nearer to him when he died; because, as I understood afterwards, he asked for me at his death, and desired to have been reconciled to me.

And now I entreat, that you all will join with me in prayer to that great God of heaven whom I have grievously offended, being a man full of all vanity, who has lived a sinful life in such callings as have been most inducing to it; for I have been a soldier, a sailor, and a courtier, which are courses of wickedness and vice; that his almighty goodness will forgive me; that he will cast away my sins from

---

[7] The expedition cost thirty thousand pounds of joint stock money and the remainder of Raleigh's personal fortune. Sir Walter is distinguishing between money ventured on the enterprise and money he had for his own use.

me; and that he will receive me into everlasting life. So I take my leave of you all, making my peace with God.

～

BIBLIOGRAPHICAL NOTE

The most recent biography is Willard M. Wallace's *Sir Walter Raleigh* (1959). Good also are Edward Edwards, *The Life of Sir Walter Raleigh, together with his Letters*, 2 Vols. (1868); and William Oldys and Theodore Birch, *The Works of Sir Walter Raleigh, Kt.*, 8 Vols. (1829). A description and judicious interpretation of events prior to the scaffold scene are afforded by James Spedding, *The Letters and Life of Francis Bacon*, 7 Vols. (1861–1874), VI (1872), 342–74.

John Donne

(1573–1631)

Donne had been Dean of St. Paul's some three years when he preached the Easter sermon in 1625. He had thoroughly settled into preaching at last. In his early sermons he often addressed courtiers, lawyers, and other special groups. He *built* sermons, played with metaphysical conceits, polished and balanced antitheses, demonstrated his sharp and subtle wit. He was the self-conscious artist. Now the Cathedral congregation brought together everybody: courtier and commoner, the nimble-brained and the slow-witted, the well-to-do and the poor, the master and the apprentice. Donne made this auditory *his*—his to possess, to instruct and move. The sermon here printed illustrates his greatest strength: clear, imaginative explanation of the Scriptures according to the Anglican Church. Donne intends to be unmistakably clear, and he goes about his task with directness and ease. Evident are the careful partition of the scriptural text and the methodical development of it—much after the formula of medieval preaching—avoiding woodenness through sharpness of idea and relaxed statement. Illuminating the idea are the sensuous, direct images of experience and the human body, shorn of all intricate, fanciful, or grotesque imagery. Of course there are the sounds and rhythms of speech, to which Donne was supersensitive, particularly in moments of strong emotion; and there are antitheses of idea, neatly proportioned and balanced. But they are so businesslike as almost to escape notice. Donne is here in his middle style, perhaps illustrating, as he said, how rhetoric "will make absent and remote things present to your understanding . . . . Poetry is a counterfeit creation, and makes things that are not, as though they were." Donne knew that his effectiveness lay in his ability, not to stir his auditors to live in a world of the poet's making, but to set out rational images of Christian principles in ways that moved men to live in a world of their own making. In the sermon Donne is terribly concerned, not with the resurrection of Christ, or of any remote man, but with the resurrection of present hearers' souls from sin and present hearers' bodies from death. There were hundreds jammed together before him—a sermon by Dean Donne was a great event in London—standing eagerly for an hour in the ancient transepts and the nave stretching over 350 feet westward from his pulpit. He commanded men's understanding that he might bring God's meaning to command men's hearts.

Many persons in Donne's congregation knew well the chief facts of their preacher's life. Was he not King James's favorite divine? Had not the King encouraged him to take orders and commanded Cambridge University to make him a Doctor of Divinity? Had he not in his young days been a libertine, an adventurer with the Earl of Essex to the Azores, an intimate with English diplomats in France, Spain, and Italy? They knew that the man before them had suffered as the devoted son of Roman Catholics, had been sorely punished for a secret marriage, had achieved fame as the author of brilliant poetry, of pungent satires, of a brittle attack on the Jesuits, and had finally renounced his years of agnosticism to become a preacher. Now he could speak to them as both Christian and humanist, Catholic and Protestant.

Alford prints an impression of Donne in the pulpit, written by a Mr. Mayne of Cambridge. It testifies to the vividness, energy, and expressiveness of Donne's delivery:

> Thou with thy words coulds't charm thine audience,
> That at thy sermons, ear was all our sense;
> Yet have I seen thee in the pulpit stand,
> Where we might take notes, from thy look, and hand;
> And from thy speaking action bear away
> More sermon, than some teachers use to say.
> Such was thy carriage, and thy gesture such,
> As could divide the heart, and conscience touch.
> Thy motion did confute, and we might see
> An error vanquished by delivery.

∽

SERMON PREACHED AT ST. PAUL'S *

Easter Day, 1625

Marvel not at this; for the hour is coming, in the which, all that are in the graves, shall hear his voice; and shall come forth; they that have done good, unto

---

* The precise relationship of written word to delivered word in Donne's case is still a problem. There exists no known "reported" text. Donne speaks of his "sermon-notes." Some of his hearers say he referred to notes when speaking, others that he spoke from memory. He wrote out sermons, some of them soon after delivery. But precisely when Donne did what we cannot say with assurance. The language of this sermon adheres to that appearing in Potter and Simpson, Volume VI. These scholars based their work on the folio volumes presided over by Donne's son: LXXX Sermons (1640), Fifty Sermons (1661), and XXVI Sermons (1661). These represent whatever Donne did when he readied a sermon for publication. His habits of writing are discussed by Mrs. Simpson in the Introduction of the Potter and Simpson edition, and with reference to a particular sermon in the Preface to her Donne's Sermon of Valediction at his Going into Germany, Preached at Lincoln's Inn, April 8, 1619 (London, 1932). We are following the spelling and punctuation of the sermon as printed in Alford, Works, I.

the resurrection of life; and they that have done evil, unto the resurrection of damnation.—John 5:28–29.

As the sun works diversely, according to the diverse disposition of the subject, (for the sun melts wax, and it hardens clay) so do the good actions of good men: upon good men they work a virtuous emulation, a noble and a holy desire to imitate, upon bad men they work a vicious, and impotent envy, a desire to disgrace, and calumniate. And the more the good is that is done, and the more it works upon good men, the more it disaffects the bad: for so the Pharisees express their rancor and malignity against Christ, in this Gospel, *If we let him thus alone, all men will believe in him;* [1] and that they foresaw would destroy them in their reputation. And therefore they enlarged their malice, beyond Christ himself, to him, upon whom Christ had wrought a miracle, to *Lazarus, They consulted to put him to death, because by reason of him, many believed in Jesus.* [2] Our text leads us to another example of this impotency in envious men; Christ, in this chapter had, by his only word, cured a man that had been eight and thirty years infirm; and he had done this work upon the Sabbath. They envied the work in the substance, but they quarrel the circumstance; and they envy Christ, but they turn upon the man, who was more obnoxious to them; and they tell him, *That it was not lawful for him to carry his bed that day.* [3] He discharges himself upon Christ; I dispute not with you concerning the Law; this satisfies me, *He that made me whole, bade me take up my bed and walk.* [4] Thereupon they put him to find out Jesus; and when he could not find Jesus, Jesus found him, and in his behalf offers himself to the Pharisees. Then they direct themselves upon him, and (as the Gospel says) *They sought to slay him, because he had done this upon the Sabbath:* [5] and, as the patient had discharged himself upon Christ, Christ discharges himself upon his Father; doth it displease you that I work upon the Sabbath? Be angry with God, be angry with the Father, for the Father works when I work. And then this they take worse than his working of miracles, or his working upon the Sabbath, *That he would say, that God was his Father;* and therefore in the averring of that, that so important point, *That God was his Father,* Christ grows into a holy vehemence, and earnestness, and he repeats his usual oath, *Verily, verily,* three several times: First, verse 19: *That whatsoever the Father doth, He, the Son, doth also,* and then verse 24: *He that believeth on me, and him that sent me, hath life everlasting.* And then again, verse 25: *The hour is coming, and now is, when the dead shall hear the voice of the Son of God, and they that hear it shall live.* At this, that the dead should live, they marvelled; but because he knew that they were men more affected with things concerning the body, than spiritual things, as in another story, when they wondered that he would pretend to forgive sins, because he knew, that they thought it a greater matter to bid that man that had the palsy, take up his bed and walk, than to forgive him his sins, therefore he took that way which was hardest in their opinion, he did bid him take up his bed and walk; so here, when they wondered at his speaking of a spiritual resurrection, to hear him say, that at his preaching,

[1] John 9:48.
[2] John 12:10.
[3] John 5:10.
[4] John 5:11.
[5] John 5:16.

the dead (that is, men spiritually dead in their sins) should rise again, to them who more respected the body, and did less believe a real resurrection of the body, than a figurative resurrection of the soul, he proceeds to that which was, in their apprehension, the more difficult, *Marvel not at this,* says he, here in our text; not at that spiritual resurrection by preaching, *for the hour is coming, in the which, all that are in the graves, [shall hear his voice and come forth].* And so he establishes the resurrection of the body.

That then which Christ affirms and avows, is, that he is the Son of God; and that is the first thing that ever was done in heaven, the eternal generation of the Son: that by which he proves this to these men, is, that by him, there shall be a resurrection of the body; and that is the last thing that shall be done in heaven, for, after that there is nothing, but an even continuance in equal glory. Before that, says he, that is, before the resurrection of the body, there shall be another resurrection, a spiritual resurrection of the soul from sin; but that shall be by ordinary means, by preaching, and sacraments, and it shall be accomplished every day; but fix not upon that, determine not your thoughts upon that, marvel not at that, make that no cause of extraordinary wonder, but make it ordinary to you, feel it, and find the effect thereof in your souls, as often as you hear, as often as you receive, and thereby provide for another resurrection, *For, the hour is coming, in which, all that are in their graves, [shall hear his voice and come forth].*

Where we must necessarily make thus many steps, though but short ones. First, the dignity of the resurrection, marvel at nothing so much, as at this, nothing is so marvelous, so wonderful as this; and secondly, the approach of the resurrection, *The hour is coming;* and thirdly, the generality, *All that are in the graves;* and then the instrument of the resurrection, *The voice of Christ; that shall be heard;* and lastly, the diverse end of the resurrection, *They shall come forth, they that have done good, [unto the resurrection of life].* God hath a care of the body of man, that is first; and he defers it not, that is next; and he extends it to all, that is a third; and a fourth is, that he does that last act, by him, by whom he did the first, the creation, and all between, the redemption, that is, by his Son, by Christ; and then the last is, that this is an everlasting separation and divorce of the good and the bad. The bad shall never be able to receive good from the good, nor to do harm to the good, after that.

First then, Christ says, *Ne miremini, Marvel not at this,* not at your spiritual resurrection, not that a sermon should work upon man, not that a sacrament should comfort a man, make it not a miracle, nor an extraordinary thing, by hearing to come to repentance, and so to such a resurrection. For though St. Augustine say, that to convert a man from sin, is as great a miracle as creation, yet St. Augustine speaks that of a man's first conversion, in which the man himself does nothing, but God all—then he is made of nothing. But after God hath renewed him, and proposed ordinary means in the Church still to work upon him, he must not look for miraculous working, but make God's ordinary means, ordinary to him. This is *Panis quotidianus,* the daily bread which God gives you as often as you meet here, according to his ordinances. *Ne miremini, Stand not to wonder,* as though you were not sure, but come to enjoy God's goodness, in his ordinary way here.

But it is, *Ne miremini hoc, Wonder not at this.* But yet, there are things which we may wonder at. *Nil admirari,* is but the philosopher's wisdom; he thinks it a weakness to wonder at anything, that any thing should be strange to him. But Christian philosophy that is rooted in humility tells us, in the mouth of Clement of Alexandria,[6] *Principium veritatis est res admirari,* The first step to faith is to wonder, to stand, and consider with a holy admiration, the ways and proceedings of God with man; for admiration, wonder, stands as in the midst, between knowledge and faith, and hath an eye towards both. If I know a thing, or believe a thing, I do no longer wonder; but when I find that I have reason to stop upon the consideration of a thing, so as that I see enough to induce admiration, to make me wonder, I come by that step, and God leads me by that hand, to a knowledge, if it be of a natural or civil thing, or to a faith, if it be of a supernatural and spiritual thing.

And therefore be content to wonder at this, that God would have such a care to dignify, and to crown, and to associate to his own everlasting presence, the body of man. God himself is a Spirit, and heaven is his place; my soul is a spirit, and so proportioned to that place. That God, or angels, or our souls, which are all Spirits, should be in heaven, *Ne miremini, Never wonder at that.* But since we wonder, and justly, that some late philosophers have removed the whole earth from the centre,[7] and carried it up, and placed it in one of the spheres of heaven, that this clod of earth, this body of ours should be carried up to the highest heaven, placed in the eye of God, set down at the right hand of God, *Miremini hoc, Wonder at this,* that God, all Spirit, served with Spirits, associated to Spirits,[8] should have such an affection, such a love to this body, this earthly body, this deserves wonder. The Father was pleased to breathe into this body, at first, in the creation; the Son was pleased to assume this body himself, after, in the redemption; the Holy Ghost is pleased to consecrate this body, and make it his temple, by his sanctification. In that *Faciamus hominem, Let us,* all us, *make man,* that consultation of the whole Trinity in making man is exercised even upon this lower part of man, the dignifying of his body. So far, as that amongst the ancient Fathers, very many of them, are very various, and irresolved, which way to pronounce, and very many of them clear in the negative, in that point, that the soul of man comes not to the presence of God, but remains in some out-places till the resurrection of the body. That observation, that consideration of the love of God to the body of man, withdrew them into that error, that the soul itself should lack the glory of heaven, till the body were become capable of that glory too.

They therefore oppose God in his purpose of dignifying the body of man, first, who violate and mangle this body, which is the organ in which God breathes; and they also, which pollute and defile this body in which Christ Jesus is apparelled; and they likewise, who profane this body which the Holy Ghost, as the high Priest, inhabits and consecrates.

[6] Titus Flavius Clemens, flourished about 200 A.D. He was a Greek theologian and head of the Catechetical School of Alexandria.

[7] Galileo and his followers, who put the sun at the center of the universe.

[8] Donne is alluding swiftly here to two conceptions of spirit widely held by his educated contemporaries. There was a substantial, material spirit, atom-like, and analyzable into three kinds: natural, animal, and vital. The vital spirit in particular had a special affection, or love, for the body. All three kinds were the proper subject of study by science and natural philosophy. There was another conception of spirit, not the object of scientific study, that was reserved for the theologians to speculate about. It was sometimes called the divine spirit, and quite possibly was "pure" form. Donne clearly has both conceptions of spirit in mind. He holds that the divine spirit (or soul) and the body, permeated with its material spirits, never separate. On this point Donne bases his criticism of some of the Fathers and his denunciation of torture.

Transgressors in the first kind, that put God's organ out of tune, that discompose and tear the body of man with violence, are those inhuman persecutors, who with racks, and tortures, and prisons, and fires, and exquisite inquisitions, throw down the bodies of the true God's true servants, to the idolatrous worship of their imaginary gods; that torture men into hell, and carry them through the inquisition into damnation. St. Augustine moves a question, and institutes a disputation, and carries it somewhat problematically, whether torture be to be admitted at all, or no. That presents a fair probability, which he says against it. We presume, says he, that an innocent man should be able to hold his tongue in torture. That is no part of our purpose in torture, says he, that he that is innocent should accuse himself by confession in torture. And if an innocent man be able to do so, why should we not think that a guilty man who shall save his life by holding his tongue in torture, should be able to do so? And then, where is the use of torture? *Res fragilis, et periculosa quaestio,*[9] says that lawyer, who is esteemed the law, alone, Ulpian: It is a slippery trial, and uncertain, to convince by torture. For, many times, says St. Augustine again, *Innocens luit pro incerto scelere certissimas poenas:* He that is yet but questioned, whether he be guilty or no, before that be known, is, without all question, miserably tortured. And whereas, many times, the passion of the judge, and the covetousness of the judge, and the ambition of the judge, are calamities heavy enough upon a man that is accused, in this case of torture, *Ignorantia judicis est calamitas plerumque innocentis,* says that Father, For the most part, even the ignorance of the judge, is the greatest calamity of him that is accused. If the judge knew that he were innocent, he should suffer nothing; if he knew he were guilty, he should not suffer torture; but because the judge is ignorant, and knows nothing, therefore the prisoner must be racked, and tortured, and mangled, says that Father.

There is a whole epistle in St. Hierome,[10] full of heavenly meditation, and of curious expressions; it is his forty-ninth epistle, *Ad Innocentium,* where a young man tortured for suspicion of adultery with a certain woman, *Ut compendio cruciatus vitaret,* says he, for his ease, and to abridge his torment, and that he might thereby procure and compass a present death, confessed the adultery, though false. His confession was made evidence against the woman: and she makes that protestation, *Tu testis Domini Jesu,* Thou Lord Jesus be my witness, *non ideo me negare velle, ne peream, sed ideo mentiri nolle, ne peccem:* I do not deny the fact for fear of death, but I dare not belie myself, nor betray mine innocence, for fear of sinning, and offending the God of truth. And as it follows in that story, though no torture could draw any confession, any accusation from her, she was condemned; and one executioner had three blows at her with a sword, and another four, and yet she could not be killed.

And therefore, because story [history] abounds with examples of this kind, how uncertain a way of trial and conviction, torture is, though St. Augustine would not say that torture was unlawful, yet he says, It behooves every judge to make that prayer, *Erue me Domine a necessitatibus meis,* If there be some cases in which the judge must necessarily proceed to torture, O Lord, deliver me from having any such brought before me.

[9] Donne's rendering of this saying by the Roman jurist, Ulpian, is delayed but a moment: a slippery trial and uncertain. Observe that similar delaying tactics are often employed.

[10] St. Jerome.

But what use soever there may be for torture for confession, in the Inquisition they torture for a denial, for the denial of God, and for the renouncing of the truth of his Gospel: as men of great place, think it concerns their honour, to do above that which they suffer, to make their revenges, not only equal, but greater than their injuries; so the Roman Church thinks it necessary to her greatness, to inflict more tortures now, than were inflicted upon her in the Primitive Church; as though it were a just revenge, for the tortures she received then for being christian, to torture better christians than herself, for being so. In which tortures, the Inquisition hath found one way, to escape the general clamour of the world against them, which is to torture to that height that few survive, or come abroad after, to publish how they have been tortured. And these, first, oppose God's purpose, in the making, and preserving, and dignifying the body of man.

Transgressors herein, in the second kind, are they that defile the garment of Christ Jesus, the body in which he hath vouchsafed to invest and enwrap himself, and so apparel a harlot in Christ's clothes, and make that body, which is his, hers. That Christ should take my body, though defiled with fornication, and make it his, is strange; but that I, in fornication, should take Christ's body, and make it hers, is more. *Know ye not,* says the Apostle, *that your bodies are the members of Christ?* And again, *Know you not, that he that is joined to a harlot, is one body?* [11] Some of the Roman Emperors made it treason to carry a ring that had their picture engraved in it to any place in the house of low office. What name can we give to that sin, to make the body of Christ, the body of a harlot? And yet, the Apostle there, as taking knowledge that we loved ourselves better than Christ, changes the edge of his argument and argues thus: *He that committeth fornication, sinneth against his own body;* if ye will be bold with Christ's body, yet favour your own. No man ever hated his own body; and yet, no outward enemy is able so to macerate our body, as our own licentiousness. Christ who took all our bodily infirmities upon him, hunger, and thirst, and sweat, and cold, took no bodily deformities upon him; he took not a lame, a blind, a crooked body; and we, by our intemperance and licentiousness, deform that body which is his, all these ways. The licentious man, most of any, studies bodily handsomeness, to be comely, and gracious, and acceptable, and yet, soonest of any, deforms, and destroys it, and makes that loathsome to all, which all his care was to make amiable. And so they oppose God's purpose of dignifying the body.

Transgressors in a third kind are they that sacrilegiously profane the temple of the Holy Ghost, by neglecting the respect and duties belonging to the dead bodies of God's saints, in a decent and comely accompanying them to convenient [appropriate] funerals. Heirs and executors are oftentimes defective in these offices, and pretend better employments of that, which would be (say they) vainly spent so. But remember you, of whom (in much such a case) that is said in St. John, *This he said, not because he cared for the poor, but because he was a thief, and had the bag, and bore that which was put therein.* [12] This executors say, not because they intend pious uses, but because they bear, and bear away the bags. Generally thy opinion must be no rule for other men's actions; neither in these cases of funerals must thou call all too much, which is more than enough.

[11] I Cor. 6:15, 16.
[12] John 12:6.

That woman's ointment poured upon Christ's feet, that hundred pound weight of perfumes to embalm his one body, was more than enough, necessarily enough; yet it was not too much for the dignity of that person, nor for the testimony of their zeal, who did it, in so abundant manner.

Now, as in all these three ways, men may oppose the purpose of God in dignifying the body; so in concurring with God's purpose, for the dignifying thereof, a man may exceed and go beyond God's purpose, in all three. God would not have the body torn and mangled with tortures in those cases; but then, he would not have it pampered with wanton delicacies, nor varnished with foreign complexion. It is ill, when it is not our own heart, that appears in our words; it is ill too when it is not our own blood, that appears in our cheeks; it may do some ill offices of blood; it may tempt; but it gives over when it should do a good office of blood: it cannot blush. If when they are filling the wrinkles and graves of their face, they would remember that there is another grave, that calls for a filling with the whole body; so, even their pride would flow into a mortification. God would not have us put on a sad countenance, nor disfigure our face, not in our fastings, and other disciplines; God would not have us mar his work; nor God would not have us go about to do his last work, which he hath reserved to himself in heaven, here upon earth, that is, to glorify our bodies, with such additions here, as though we would need no glorification there.

So also in the second way of giving due respect to the body of man, a man may exceed God's purpose. God would not have the body corrupted and attenuated, shrunk and deformed with incontinency and licentiousness. But God would not have that sparing of the body, to dishonour, or undervalue, or forbear marriage, nor to frustrate that which was one of God's purposes in the institution of marriage, procreation of children. Marriage without possibility of children lacks one half of God's purpose in the institution of marriage; for, the third reason of marriage, after the other two (which two were, for a helper, and for children) which is, that marriage should be for a remedy, that third came in after; for at the time of the institution of marriage, man was not fallen into any inordinate concupiscences, and so, at that time, needed no remedy. Marriage without possibility of children, lacks one of God's two reasons for children; but marriage with a contract against children, or a practice against children, is not (says St. Augustine) a marriage, but a solemn, an avowed, a daily adultery. To choose to be ill in the sight of God, rather then to look ill in the sight of men, is a perverse and a poisonous physic. The sin of *Er* and *Onan* in married men; the sin of procured abortions in married women, do in many cases equal, in some, exceed, the sin of adultery. To rob a husband, or a wife, of a future child, may be in the wife, or husband, as great a sin, as to bring a supposititious, or a spurious child, into the father's inheritance. God would not have the comeliness, the handsomeness of the body defaced by incontinency and intemperance, but he would not have the care of that comeliness and handsomeness frustrate his purpose of children in marriage.

And as in those two (God would not have the body tortured, nor mangled, God would not have the body deformed by licentiousness) so, in his third respect to man's body, God would not have the bodies of his dead saints neglected, God's purpose may be exceeded too. God's purpose therein is that all men should be decently, and honourable persons, honourably, buried. But his purpose herein is exceeded, when any rag of their skin, or chip of their bones, or lock of their hair, is kept for a relic, and made an universal balm, and amulet, and antidote, against all temporal, and all spiritual diseases, and calamities, not only against the rage of a fever, but of hell itself. What their counterfeit relics may do against their counterfeit hell, against their purgatory, I know not: that powerful, and precious, and only relic, which is given to us against hell itself, is only the communion of the body, and blood of Christ Jesus, left to us by him, and preserved for us, in his church, though his body be removed out of our sight.

To end this, *Miramini hoc*, marvel at this, at the wonderful love of God to the body of man, and thou wilt favour it so, as not to macerate thine own body, with uncommanded and inhuman flagellations, and whippings, nor afflict their bodies, who are in thy charge, with inordinate labour. Thou wilt not dishonour this body, as it is Christ's body, nor deform it, as it is thine own, with intemperance, but thou wilt behave thyself towards it so, as towards one whom it hath pleased the king to honour with a resurrection (which was our first [step]) and not to defer that resurrection long, which is our next step, *Venit hora, The hour is coming.*

Non talem Deum tuum putes, qualis nec tu debes esse, is excellently said by St. Augustine: Never presume upon any other disposition in God, than such as thou findest in thine own heart, that thou art bound to have in thyself; for we find in our hearts, a band of conformity and assimilation to God, that is to be as like God as we can. Therefore whatsoever thou findest thyself bound to do to another, thou mayest expect at God's hand. Thou art bound to help up another that is fallen; therefore thou mayest assure thyself that God will give thee a resurrection. So, thou findest in thy heart that the soul of an alms, the soul of a benefit, that that gives it life, is the speedy, the present doing of it; therefore thou mayest be sure that God will make speed to save thee, that he will not long defer this thy resurrection, *hora venit.* St. Augustine, comparing the former resurrection,[13] which is the spiritual resurrection of the soul, with this in the text, which is the resurrection of the body, observes that there Christ says, *Hora venit, et nunc est, the hour is coming, and now is;* because in every private inspiration of the Holy Ghost, in every sermon, in every meeting of the congregation, the dead may hear and live; *nunc est,* they may do it now. But that in this resurrection in the text, the resurrection of the body, it is not said, *nunc est,* that the hour is now; for, the son of man who says it (as he is the son of man) knows not when it shall be; but he says *Hora venit, It is coming,* and coming apace, and coming quickly, shortly.

As soon as God had made man, he gave him his patent, *Dominamini,* Dominion over the creature. As soon as man was fallen, God gave him the promise of a Messiah. And of his second coming, himself, says, *Ecce, venio cito, Behold, I come speedily: Venit,* he comes, he is upon the way; and *Ecce, venit, Behold, he comes,* he is within sight, you may see him in his forerunning tokens; and *Ecce cito,* as little way as he hath to go, he makes haste; and there is a Jesuit that makes the haste so great, as that he says, Howsoever St. Augustine make use of that note, that it is not said in the text, *nunc est,* that the hour of the resurrection is now; yet he does believe that Christ did say so, though the evangelist left it out. We need not say so; we do not; so much less liberty do we take in departing from the Fathers, than the Roman authors do. But yet, so as St. John speaks, *Hora novis-*

---

13 John 5:25.

sima, This is the last time. (*Now there are many antichrists, whereby we know that this is the last time.*) [14] And so, as St. Peter speaks, *Be not ignorant of this one thing, that one day is with the Lord as a thousand years, and a thousand years as one day.*[15] So as this *Nunc* may signify *ultimum statum,* the last course of times, the time not of nature, nor of law, but of grace; so we admit that addition in this resurrection, too, *Hora venit, et nunc est, The hour is coming, and now is,* because there are no other means to be hereafter instituted for the attaining of a happy resurrection, than those that now are established in the Church, especially at a man's death, may we very properly say, *Nunc est,* now is the resurrection come to him—not only because the last judgment is involved in the first (for that judgment which passeth upon every man at his death stands for ever without repeal, or appeal, or error)—but because after the death of the body, there is no more to be done with the body, till the resurrection. For as we say of an arrow, that it is overshot, it is gone, it is beyond the mark, though it be not come to the mark yet, because there is no more to be done to it till it be; so we may say, that he that is come to death is come to his resurrection, because he hath not another step to make, another foot to go, another minute to count, till he be at the resurrection.

The resurrection, then, being the coronation of man, his death and lying down in the grave is his enthroning, his sitting down in that chair, where he is to receive that crown. As then the Martyrs, under the altar, though in heaven, yet do cry out for the resurrection; so let us, in this miserable life, submit ourselves cheerfully to the hand of God, in death, since till that death we cannot have this resurrection, and the first thing that we shall do after this death, is to rise again. To the child that is now born, we may say, *Hora venit,* The day of his resurrection is coming; to him that is old, we may say, The hour is come; but to him that is dead, the minute is come, because to him there are no more minutes till it do come.

Miramini hoc, marvel at this, at the descent of God's love: he loves the body of man; and *Miramini hoc,* marvel at his speed; he makes haste to express this love: *Hora venit.* And then *Miramini hoc,* marvel at the generality, it reaches to all, all that are in the grave: *All that are in the graves shall hear his voice,* [*and shall come forth*]. God hath made the body as a house for the soul, till he call her out, and he hath made the grave as a house for the body, till he call it up. The misery and poor estate that Christ submitted himself unto for man was not determined in that, *That foxes had holes, but he nowhere to lay his head,*[16] while he lived; but he had no grave that he could claim, when he was dead. It is some discontinuance of the communion of saints, if I may not be buried with the saints of God. Every man that hath not divested humanity hath a desire to have his bones lie at rest, and we cannot provide for that so well, any way, as to bury them in consecrated places, which are, in common intendment [disposition], safest from profane violences. Even that respect, that his bones might lie at rest, seems to have moved one prophet, to enjoin his sons, to bury him in the Sepulchre, where the other prophet was buried. He knew that Josiah would burn the bones of all the other graves, upon the altar of Bethel, as was prophesied; and he presumed that he would spare the bones of that prophet, and so his bones should be

[14] John 2:18.
[15] II Pet. 3:8.
[16] I Kings 13:31.

safe, if they were mingled with the other. God expressed his love to Moses, in that particular, *That he buried him;* [17] and, to deliver, and remove him, from the violence of any that loved him not, and so might dishonor his memory, and from the superstition of any that over-loved him, and so might over-honour his memory, God buried him in secret. In more than one place doth David complain, *That there was none to bury God's saints;* and the dignity that is promised here in the text, is appropriated to them, *who are in the graves,* who are buried.

But then, was that general? Is it simply, plainly, literally of them, and them only, who are in graves, who are buried? Shall none enjoy a resurrection, that have not enjoyed a grave? Still I say, it is a comfort to a dying man, it is an honour to his memory, it is a discharge of a duty in his friends, it is a piece of the communion of saints, to have a consecrated grave. But the word here is, *In monumentis,* all that are in monuments, that is, in receptacles of bodies, of what kind soever they be: wheresoever the hand of God lays up a dead body, that place is the receptacle, so the monument, so the grave of that body. *God keeps all the bones of the righteous, so that none of them are broken:* [18] though they be trod to dust in our sight, they are entire in his, because he can bid them be whole again in an instant. Some nations burnt their dead; there the fire is the grave; some drowned their dead; there the sea is the grave; some hung them up upon trees; and there the air is their grave; some nations eat their dead themselves, and some maintained dogs to eat the dead; and as they called those dogs, *Canes Sepulchrales,* Sepulchral dogs, so those men were sepulchral men, those men and those dogs were graves. *Death and hell shall deliver up their dead,* says St. John.[19] That is, the whole state, and mansion of the dead, shall be emptied: the state of the dead is their grave, and upon all that are in this state, shall the testimony of God's love to the body of man, fall. And that is the generality, *All that are in the grave, [shall come forth].*

Our next step is, The instrument, the means by which this first so speedy, and then so general love of God to man, to man in his lowest part, his body, is accomplished unto him. These, all these that are in graves, in all these kind of graves, *shall hear his voice,* and that is the means. First, whose voice? That is expressed immediately before, *The Son of man.* In the other resurrection, in that of the dead soul, in verse 25, there it is said, *The dead shall hear the voice of the Son of God.* In this, which is the resurrection to judgment, it is *The Son of man.* The former resurrection (that of a sinner to repentance by preaching) is wrought by a plain and ordinary means here in the church, where you do but hear a man in a pew read prayers, and pronounce absolution, and a man in a pulpit preach a sermon, and a man at a table consecrate, and administer a sacrament. And because all this, though it be the power of life, and the means of your spiritual resurrection, is wrought by the ministry of man, who might be contemptible in your eye, therefore the whole work is referred to God, and not the Son of man, but *the Son of God,* is said to do it.

In this resurrection of the text, which is a resurrection to judgment, and to an account with God, that God whom we have displeased, exasperated, violated, wounded in the whole course of our life, lest we should be terrified, and dejected

[17] Deut. 34:6.
[18] Ps. 34:20.
[19] Rev. 20:13.

at the presence of that God, the whole work is referred to *the Son of Man,* which hath himself formerly felt all our infirmities, and hath had as sad a soul at the approach of death, as bitter a cup in the form of death, as heavy a fear of God's forsaking him in the agony of death, as we can have. And for sin itself, I would not, I do not extenuate my sin, but let me have fallen, not seven times a day, but seventy-seven times a minute, yet what are my sins, to all those sins that were upon Christ? The sins of all men, and all women, and all children, the sins of all nations, all the East and West, and all the North and South, the sins of all times and ages, of nature, of law, of grace, the sins of all natures, sins of the body, and sins of the mind, the sins of all growth, and all extentions, thoughts, and words, and acts, and habits, and delight, and glory, and contempt, and the very sin of boasting, nay of our belying ourselves in sin—all these sins, past, present and future, were at once upon Christ, and in that depth of sin, mine are but a drop to his ocean; in that treasure of sin, mine are but single money to his talent. And therefore, that I might come with a holy reverence to his ordinance in this place, though it be but in the ministry of man, that first resurrection is attributed to the Son of God, to give a dignity to that ministry of man, which otherwise might have been under-valued, that thereby we might have a consolation, and a cheerfulness towards it. It is he, that is, the Son of God, and the Son of man, Christ, which remembers [reminds] us also, that all that belongs to the expressing of the law of God to man must be received by us, who profess ourselves Christians, in, and by, and for, and through Christ.

We use to ascribe the creation to the Father, but the Father created by the word, and his word is his Son, Christ; *When he prepared the heavens, I was there* (says Christ, of himself in the person of Wisdom) *and when he appointed the foundations of the earth, then was I by him, as one brought up with him.* It is not as one brought in to him, or brought in by him, but with him; one as old, that is, as eternal, as much God as he. We use to ascribe sanctification to the Holy Ghost; but the Holy Ghost sanctifies in the church, and the church was purchased by the blood of Christ, and Christ remains Head of the church, *usque in consummationem,* till the end of the world. I look upon every blessing that God affords me, and I consider whether it be temporal, or spiritual; and that distinguishes the metal. The temporal is my silver, and the spiritual is my gold; but then I look again upon the inscription, *Cujus Imago,* whose image, whose inscription it bears, and whose name; and except I have it, in, and for, and by Christ Jesus, temporal, and spiritual things too, are but imaginary, but illusory shadows; for God conveys himself to us no other way but in Christ.

The benefit then in our text, the resurrection, is by him; but it is limited thus: it is by hearing him; *They that are in their graves shall hear* [*his voice*]. So it is in the other resurrection too, the spiritual resurrection, verse 25. There, they must *hear* him, that will *live.* In both resurrections, that in the church, now, by grace, and that in the grave hereafter, by power, it is said, *They shall hear him.* They shall, which seems to imply a necessity, though not a coaction.[20] But that necessity [is] not of equal force, not equally irresistible in both: in the grave, *They shall;* though they be dead, and senseless as the dust (for they are dust itself) though they bring no concurrence, no cooperation, *They shall hear,* that is,

[20] One meaning of *coact* is to work together or, close to the Latin *coacto,* compel; accordingly the meaning of the phrase is that man may not *choose* to hear; he *shall,* as Donne says.

they shall not choose but hear. In the other resurrection, which is, in the church, by grace, in God's ordinance, *They shall hear too,* that is, there shall be a voice uttered so, as that they may hear, if they will, but not whether they will or no, as in the other case, in the grave. Therefore when God expresses his gathering of his church, in this world, it is *Sibilabo et congregabo, I will hiss, or chirp for them, and so gather them:* [21] He whispers in the voice of the spirit, and he speaks a little louder, in the voice of a man. Let the man be a *Boanerges,* a son of thunder, never so powerful a speaker, yet no thunder is heard over all the world.[22] But for the voice that shall be heard at the resurrection, *He shall send his angels, with a great sound of a trumpet;* [23] a great sound, such as may be made by a trumpet, such as an Angel, all his Angels can make in a trumpet, and more than all that, *The Lord himself shall descend from heaven,*[24] and that, *with a shout, and with the voice of an archangel.* That is, says St. Ambrose, of Christ himself, *and in the trumpet of God,* that is also, Christ himself.

So then, you have the person, Christ; the means, a voice, and the powerfulness of that voice, in the name of an Archangel, which is named but once more in all the Scriptures. And therefore, let no man, that hath an holy anhelation [25] and panting after the resurrection, suspect that he shall sleep in the dust, forever; for this is a voice that will be heard, he must rise. Let no man, who because he hath made his course of life like a beast would therefore be content his state in death might be like a beast too, hope that he shall sleep in the dust, forever, for this is a voice that must be heard; *And all that hear shall come forth, they that have done good, [unto the resurrection of life].*

He shall come forth; even he that hath done ill, and would not, shall come forth. You may have seen moral men, you may have seen impious men go in confidently enough; not afrighted with death, not terrified with a grave; but when you shall see them come forth again, you shall see them in another complexion. That man that died so, with that confidence, thought death his end. It ends his seventy years, but it begins his seventy millions of generations of torments, even to his body, and he never thought of that: indeed, *Judicii, nisi que vitae aeternae praedestinatus est, non potest reminisci,* says St. Ambrose, No man can, no man dares think upon the last judgment, but he that can think upon it with comfort, he that is predestinated to eternal life. Even the best are sometimes shaked with the consideration of the resurrection, because it is impossible to separate the consideration of the resurrection from the consideration of the judgment; and the terrors of that may abate the joy of the other. *Sive comedo, sive bibo,* says St. Hierome, whether I eat, or drink, still methinks I hear this sound: *Surgite mortui, et venite ad judicium;* Arise you dead, and come to judgment. When it calls me up from death, I am glad, [but] when it calls me to judgment, that impairs my joy. Can I think that God will not take a strict account; or, can I be without fear, if I think he will? *Non expavescere requisiturum est dicere, non requiret,* is excellently said by St. Bernard, if I can put off all fear of that judgment, I have put off all imagination that any such judgment shall be. But, when

---

[21] Zech. 10:8.

[22] A mythical figure, possibly Aramaic, meaning "sons of the thunder," and hence a declamatory and vociferous orator.

[23] Matt. 24:31.

[24] I Thes. 4:16.

[25] Short and rapid breathing.

I begin this fear in this life, here, I end this fear in my death, and pass away cheerfully. But the wicked begin this fear, when the trumpet sounds to the resurrection, and then shall never end it; but, as a man condemned to be half hanged, and then quartered, hath a fearful addition in his quartering after, and yet had no ease in his hanging before, so they that have done ill, when they have had their hanging, when they have suffered in soul, the torments of hell, from the day of their death, to the day of judgment, shall come to that day with fear, as to an addition to that, which yet, was infinite before. And therefore the vulgat edition [26] hath rendered this well, *Procedent, They shall proceed,* they shall go farther and farther in torment.

But this is not the object of our speculation, the subject of our meditation, now. We proposed this text for the contemplation of God's love to man, and therefore we rather comfort ourselves with that branch, and refresh ourselves with the shadow of that, *That they who have done good, shall come forth unto the resurrection of life.* Alas, the others shall live as long as they; Lucifer is as immortal as Michael, and Judas as immortal as St. Peter. But *Vita damnatorum, mors est,* that which we call immortality in the damned is but a continual dying; howsoever it must be called life, it hath all the qualities of death, saving the ease, and the end, which death hath, and damnation hath not. They must come forth; they that have done evil must do so too. Neither can stay in their house, their grave; for, their house (though that house should be the sea) shall be burnt down, all the world dissolved with fire. But then, they who have done evil shall pass from that fire into a farther heat, without light; they who have done good, into a farther light, without heat.

But fix upon the conditions, and perform them: they must *have done good.* To have known good, to have believed it, to have intended it, nay to have preached it to others, will not serve; they must have done good. They must be rooted in faith, and then bring forth fruit, and fruit in season; and then is the season of doing good, when another needs that good at thy hands. God gives the evening rain, but he gave the morning rain before; a good man gives at his death, but he gives in his lifetime too. To them belongs this resurrection of the body to life upon which, since our text inclines us to marvel rather than to discourse, I will not venture to say with David, *Narrabo omnia mirabilia tua, I will show all thy wondrous works* [27] (an angel's tongue could not show them), but I will say with him, *Mementote mirabilium, Remember the marvellous works he hath done.* [28] And by that, God will open your eyes, that you may behold the wondrous things that he will do. Remember with thankfulness the several resurrections that he hath given you; from superstition and ignorance, in which, you, in your fathers lay dead; from sin, and a love of sin, in which, you, in the days of your youth, lay dead; from sadness, and dejection of spirit, in which, you, in your worldly crosses, or spiritual temptations, lay dead. And assure yourself, that that God that loves to perfect his own works, when you shall lie dead in your graves, will give you that resurrection to life, which he hath promised to all them that do good, and will

---

[26] The reference is to the Latin vulgate translation of the Scriptures prepared originally by St. Jerome in the fourth century and accepted by the Council of Trent in 1546 as the official basis of Roman Catholic worship.

[27] Ps. 9:2.

[28] Ps. 105:5; 119:18.

extend to all them, who having done evil, do yet truly repent the evil they have done.

◇

BIBLIOGRAPHICAL NOTE

The best edition of Donne's sermons is that by George R. Potter and Evelyn M. Simpson (10 vols., 1953–1962). Another good edition is *The Works of John Donne . . .* by Henry Alford (6 vols., 1839). Conveniently available in paperback is *The Sermons of John Donne*, selected and introduced by Theodore Gill, "Living Age Books" (1958). For the student of speechmaking perhaps the most satisfactory life is Isaac Walton's *The Lives of Dr. John Donne, Sir Henry Wotton . . .* (1675); Walton heard Donne many times.

Sir John Eliot

(1590–1632)

Eliot's speech played an essential role, perhaps the critical role, in persuading Charles I to sign the Petition of Right, which would secure Englishmen from the billeting of troops upon them, the exercise of martial law, arbitrary taxation, and arbitrary imprisonment. On June 2, 1628, the King appeared before the assembled Lords and Commons, directed that the Petition be read aloud, and declared that his subjects had no cause to complain of violations of their rights and privileges. When the Commons returned to their own quarters, there was thick silence, disbelief, and bitter disappointment. Charles had not given them a direct answer. The House adjourned until the next day. When it met on the morrow, writes Harold Hulme, Sir John Eliot, "inspired by hatred and love, hatred of a fellow man and his policies and love of his country, launched into an oratorical denunciation of the English Government such as never before had been heard in the House of Commons" (*Life of Sir John Eliot*, p. 243). Better at criticism than at constructive legislation, Eliot reached his greatest powers in this discourse. He had prepared the speech with benefit of some counsel from like-minded parliamentarians, and the right moment had come. He reviewed the causes of discontent, only alluding to some, pointing directly to others, and contriving to lay the blame on Parliament's nemesis, the King's favorite, the Duke of Buckingham. Eliot thus sustained the emotional pitch of the crisis until the King replied on June 7: "It will be as you wish." His fellows promptly undertook to impeach Buckingham, only to be checked when the King sent Parliament home.

The intensity and pitch of feeling aroused at the crisis of the Petition can be compared to the excitement that surrounds a declaration of war. It was emotion inspired by principle, fed by distrust and insult. The state of mind is incredible to the modern student unless he appreciates, to a degree at least, the forces at work during the rule of James I. His son, Charles, had only added fuel to an already huge, long-smoldering fire.

The English deeply resented the attempt of the first two Stuarts to continue in the tradition of the former Tudor absolutism. Although Elizabeth had made the realm safe, united, and prosperous, she had remained inflexible against innovations in religion and increase of Parliament's power; yet her subjects were loyal and loving—albeit somewhat resentful—to the end. The middle classes had grown in numbers and wealth, and desiring to protect their position against arbitrary levies and taxes, they tended to join ranks with the Presbyterians and Puritans. So except for the bishops—the Lords spiritual—who were devoted to Episcopacy, the chief political groups were in the mood for innovation. They expected much of the new monarch. But James soon made clear that he would rule by the Divine Right of Kings, and consequently he conceded virtually nothing to the Presbyterians. He tried to foist Episcopacy upon the Scots. He refused to redress economic grievances in any significant way, and Parliament in reprisal would barely open its purse. So James ruled alone as long as he could, supporting his establishment by special levies, indirect taxes, and grants of monopoly. He hesitated to provide military support for the Protestant cause in the Thirty Years' War on the Continent; and his marriage negotiations with the Spanish king aroused fears of partiality on his part toward Catholics both at home and abroad. The political climax came when James had to summon Parliament in 1621. The Commons framed petitions and debated a long backlog of grievances. The House approved a "protestation": their liberties and privileges were an inherited birthright; the State, the defense of the realm, all laws and grievances were proper matters of debate; members had liberty of speech, and freedom from all imprisonment during sessions. James stopped the session. He sent for the Commons' *Journal* and tore out the offending pages with his own hand. Surprisingly, the Parliament following in 1624 was a "happy" one. James removed most of the restrictions on free discussion. Sir John Eliot, elected to the House of Commons for the second time, was deeply gratified. The King gave up his attempts to marry Prince Charles into Spain's royal family and agreed to the persuasions of everybody, including Buckingham and the young Prince, to fight Spain instead. All good Commoners felt that the liberty of Parliament had been won.

But Charles the King was unlike Charles the popular prince. He called three Parliaments in rapid succession; he quarrelled with them all, and they refused to vote taxes. So he resorted to treasure ships and forced loans, advised and encouraged by his favorite, the detested Duke of Buckingham. An expedition to Cádiz to capture Spanish galleons was a failure, and Eliot, then vice-admiral of Devon, witnessed the tragic return of the soldiers and sailors. He rose in the Parliament of 1626, demanded an inquiry into the disaster, and laid the blame on Buckingham. The Commons started impeachment proceedings against the Duke, and Charles, to save him, ordered dissolution. Eliot, with eighty others, refused to pay the forced assessments and was imprisoned. Five knights among those who were imprisoned sued for a writ of *habeas corpus,* but the judges sent them back to prison. These are some of the circumstances and facts on which Eliot capitalized in his speech.

The tenacity and heat of the conflict were intensified by religious alignments, which sometimes paralleled political feelings and sometimes crossed them. The dominant religious group in Parliament was Puritan, consisting mainly of Presbyterians who fought for their own supremacy against Catholics, Episcopalians, and Puritan extremists. Among the Lords, the largest group supported the Es-

tablished Church; it feared Presbyterian rule, and gave solid support to political
and religious monarchy, if not to some of Charles's acts. Most of the bishops
were royalists in their church and state commitments. In Eliot's Parliament, then,
the large groupings were finding identity and cohesion. The conflicts among
them were for effective power; they grew increasingly intolerant of each other.

Eliot's formal education seems to have ceased after a year or two at Oxford;
yet from his college days and his early reading he probably derived a lasting
interest in history and government. When in the Tower, he wrote an account
of Charles's first Parliament. From his education, too, he apparently developed
an interest in oratory, and sought opportunities to develop himself as a speaker.
In the Parliament of 1624 he found that the House preferred specific arguments
to large generalities. He appeared on a number of committees, and we find him
speaking on affairs that show his hatred of Spain and his loyalty to Anglicanism
and to the Crown as an institution; evident also are his impulsive, enthusiastic
nature, and his devotion to a cause. To follow Eliot's parliamentary record is to
see the novice of 1624 growing into the effective, respected Member of Parliament
of 1628. He had found political principles and confidence in himself. By June 3
he was ready to make the great speech of his career. Though he said nothing
that was new to his colleagues, he spoke with force and clarity, summoning a
host of ready examples, touching the chords of indignation, striking the notes of
freedom, and utterly overwhelming the Duke whom he never named.

∽

For the Petition of Right *

House of Commons
June 3, 1628

Mr. Speaker: We sit here as the great Council of the King; and, in that capacity,
it is our duty to take into consideration the state and affairs of the kingdom; and
when there is occasion, to give a true representation of them by way of counsel
and advice, with what we conceive necessary or expedient to be done.

In this consideration, I confess, many a sad thought hath affrighted me; and
that not only in respect of our dangers from abroad (which yet I know are great,
as they have been often pressed and dilated to us), but in respect of our disorders
here at home, which do enforce those dangers, and by which they are occasioned:
for, I believe, I shall make it clear to you, that both at first the causes of these
dangers were our disorders, and our disorders now are yet our greatest dangers;
that not so much the potency of our enemies, as the weakness of ourselves, do
threaten us; so that the saying of one of the Fathers may be assumed by us, *Non*

---

* Our version of the text is very close to that appearing in Cobbett's *Parliamentary
History*, II, 380–85. It is the result of close comparison with texts in the old *Parliamentary History*, John Rushworth's *Collections*, *Ephemeris Parliamentaria*, and the
Everyman Library edition (#714) of *British Orations*. P. H.'s text, the recorder says,
is "taken from Sir John Napier's MS." Contemporaneous versions, of which there are
many, may be derived from Napier. There is some discussion of textual sources in
Harold Hulme, p. 243.

tam potentia sua quam negligentia nostra—"Not so much by their power as by our neglect."

Our want of true devotion to Heaven, our insincerity and doubling in religion, our want of councils, our precipitate actions, the insufficiency or unfaithfulness of our generals abroad, the ignorance and corruption of our ministers at home, the impoverishing of the sovereign, the oppression and depression of the subject, the exhausting of our treasures, the waste of our provisions, consumption of our ships, destruction of our men—these make the advantage of our enemies, not the reputation of their arms. And if in these there be not reformation, we need no foes abroad; time itself will ruin us.

To show this more fully, I believe you will all hold it necessary that what I say should not seem an aspersion on the state or imputation on the government, as I have known such motions misinterpreted. But far is this from me to propose, who have none but clear thoughts of the excellency of the King; nor can I have other ends but the advancement of His Majesty's glory. I shall desire a little of your patience extraordinary as I lay open the particulars, which I shall do with what brevity I may, answerable to the importance of the cause and the necessity now upon us; yet with such respect and observation to the time, as I hope it shall not be thought troublesome.

For the first, then, our insincerity and doubling in religion is the greatest and most dangerous disorder of all others. This hath never been unpunished, and of this we have many strong examples of all states and in all times to awe us. What testimony doth it want? Will you have authority of books? Look on the collections of the Committee for Religion; *there* is too clear an evidence. See then the commission procured for composition with the papists of the North:[1] mark the proceedings thereupon, and you will find them to little less amounting than a toleration in effect: the slight payments, and the easiness of them will likewise show the favour that is intended. Will you have proofs of *men*? Witness the hopes, witness the presumptions, witness the reports of all the papists generally: observe the dispositions of commanders, the trust of officers, the confidence in secretaries to employments in this kingdom, in Ireland, and elsewhere. These will all show that it hath too great a certainty. And to this add but the incontrovertible evidence of that all-powerful Hand, which we have felt so sorely, that gave it full assurance, for as the heavens oppose themselves to us for our impiety, so it is we that first opposed the heavens.

For the second, our want of councils,[2] that great disorder in a state under

---

[1] By "composition" is meant compromise or accommodation. "North" seems to be shorthand for Council of the North. This consisted of a group of men appointed by the King, and directly responsible to him, to govern the northern counties of England. In this paragraph, Eliot is referring to the general relaxation by the King's order of the penal laws and fines against Catholics. Upon marrying the Catholic Henrietta Maria of France, Charles promised the French king that he would make life easier for the adherents of his wife's religion. The promise infuriated the Commons, as did the marriage.

[2] Here and below Eliot and his audience had the Duke of Buckingham in mind. The Duke dominated both the King and the Privy Council, and his advice—bad advice—King Charles followed without question. He saved the Duke from the final step in impeachment proceedings in 1626 by dissolving Parliament. He imprisoned Eliot and Digges for their part in the proceedings.

which there can not be stability. If effects may show their causes (as they are often a perfect demonstration of them), our misfortunes, our disasters serve to prove our deficiencies in council, and the consequences they draw with them. If reason be allowed in this dark age, the judgment of dependencies and foresight of contingencies in affairs do confirm my position. For if we view ourselves at home, are we in strength; are we in reputation, equal to our ancestors? If we view ourselves abroad, are our friends as many? Are our enemies no more? Do our friends retain their safety and possessions? Do not our enemies enlarge themselves, and gain from them and us? To what council owe we the loss of the Palatinate,[3] where we sacrificed both our honour and our men sent thither, stopping those greater powers appointed for the service, by which it might have been defended? What council gave direction to the late action whose wounds are yet bleeding, I mean the expedition to Rhé, of which there is yet so sad a memory in all men? What design for us, or advantage to our state, could that impart?

You know the wisdom of your ancestors, and the practice of their times, how they preserved their safeties. We all know, and have as much cause to doubt [i.e. distrust or guard against] as they had, the greatness and ambition of that kingdom, *which the Old World could not satisfy*.[4] Against this greatness and ambition, we likewise know the proceedings of that princess, that excellent Queen Elizabeth, whose name, without admiration, falls not into mention even with her enemies. You know how she advanced herself, and how she advanced this nation in glory and in state; how she depressed her enemies and how she upheld her friends; how she enjoyed a full security, and made those our scorn who now are made our terror!

Some of the principles she built on were these—and if I mistake, let reason and our statesmen contradict me.

First, to maintain, in what she might, a unity in France, that that kingdom, being at peace within itself, might be a bulwark to keep back the power of Spain by land.

Next, to preserve an amity and league between that state and us, that so we might come in aid of the Low Countries [Netherlands], and by that means receive their ships, and help them by sea.

This treble cord, so working between France, the States [Netherlands], and England, might enable us, as occasion should require, to give assistance unto others; and by this means, as the experience of that time doth tell us, we were not only free from those fears that now possess and trouble us, but then our names were fearful to our enemies. See now what correspondency our actions had with this. Try our conduct by these rules. It did induce, as a necessary consequence, a division in France between the protestants [5] and their king, of which there is too woeful and lamentable experience. It hath made an absolute breach between that state and us, and so entertains us against France, and France in preparation against

---

[3] The Palatinate was a German state lying along the Rhine. Charles's sister was the wife of Frederick V, the country's Protestant ruler, who had been attacked on religious grounds by a combination of Catholic German and Austrian states. Defeated, he was in exile, and his cause was a popular one in Protestant England. Buckingham hurriedly sent 12,000 men into Holland under the command of Count Mansfeld, but the venture was so badly planned that some 9,000 men perished on the way.

[4] Spain is the villain, hated by Eliot and all good Protestants.

[5] Specifically, the Huguenots.

us, that we have nothing to promise to our neighbours, nay, hardly to ourselves. Next, observe the *time* in which it was attempted, and you shall find it not only varying from those principles, but directly contrary and opposite, *ex diametro*, to those ends; and such, as from the issue and success, rather might be thought a conception of Spain than begotten here with us.[6]

Mr. Speaker, I am sorry for this interruption, but much more sorry if there hath been occasion on my part. And, as I shall submit myself wholly to your judgment, to receive what censure you may give me, if I have offended, so, in the integrity of my intentions and the clearness of my thoughts, I must still retain this confidence: *that no greatness shall deter me from the duties I owe to the service of my king and country; but that, with a true English heart, I shall discharge myself as faithfully and as really to the extent of my poor power, as any man whose honours or whose offices most strictly oblige him.*

You know the dangers Denmark is in, and how much they concern us; what in respect of our alliance and the country; what in the importance of the Sound [Baltic Sea]; what an advantage to our enemies the gain thereof would be! What loss, what prejudice to us by this disunion,[7] we breaking in upon France, France enraged by us, and the Netherlands at amazement between both. Neither could we intend to aid that luckless king, whose loss is our disaster.

Can those that express their trouble at the hearing of these things, and have so often told us in this place of their knowledge in the conjunctures and disjunctures of affairs—can they say they advised in this? Was this an act of council, Mr. Speaker? I have more charity than to think it; and unless they make confession of it themselves, I can not believe it.

For the next, the insufficiency and unfaithfulness of our generals (that great disorder abroad), what shall I say? I wish there were not cause to mention it; and, but for the apprehension of the danger that is to come, if the like chance hereafter be not prevented, I could willingly be silent. But my duty to my sovereign, my service to this House, and the safety and honour of my country, are above all respects; and what so nearly trenches to the prejudice of these must not, shall not, be forborn.

At Cádiz,[8] then, in that first expedition we made, when we arrived and found a conquest ready—the Spanish ships, I mean—fit for the satisfaction of a voyage, and of which some of the chiefest then there, themselves have since assured me

[6] Eliot was interrupted here by Sir Humphrey May, a member of the Privy Council, who expressed "dislike." After the speech was over, Eliot, when questioned, imputed to Spain the origin of the advice which led Buckingham and Charles to break with France.

[7] Denmark, a Protestant ally of the Palatinate, had suffered military reverses and was in danger. The English merchants would be hurt if the Baltic were closed to them. Denmark was promised substantial aid in money which Charles tried to raise without a Parliament. In addition to forced loans and other "projects," the King and Buckingham pawned the Crown jewels and plate—circumstances referred to later in the speech.

[8] To raise money, Buckingham set out with eighty ships, some of them Dutch, to plunder Spanish treasure ships as they neared their port of Cádiz. The voyage could easily have met with success ("satisfaction"), but the Spanish galleons were allowed to slip by. Buckingham took the small fort of Puntal; the soldiers, drinking and rioting, became unmanageable, and their commanders had to leave them to die by the knives of the enraged inhabitants.

that the satisfaction would have been sufficient, either in point of honour or in point of profit—*why was it neglected?* Why was it not achieved, it being granted on all hands how feasible it was?

Afterward, when with the destruction of some of our men, and the exposure of others, who (though their fortune since has not been such) by chance came off safe—when, I say, with the loss of our serviceable men, that unserviceable fort was gained, and the whole army landed, *why was there nothing done?* Why was there nothing *attempted?* If nothing was intended, wherefore did they land? If there *was* a service,[9] wherefore were they shipped again? Mr. Speaker, it satisfies me too much [i.e. I am over-satisfied] in this—when I think of their dry and hungry march into that drunken quarter (for so the soldiers termed it), which was the period [termination] of their journey—that divers of our men being left as a sacrifice to the enemy, *that labor was at an end.*

For the next undertaking, at Rhé,[10] I will not trouble you much; only this, in short. Was not that whole action carried against the judgment and opinion of those officers that were of the council? Was not the first, was not the last, was not all in the landing—in the intrenching—in the continuance there—in the assault—in the retreat—without their assent? Did any advice take place of such as were of the council? If there should be made a particular inquisition thereof, these things will be manifest and more. I will not instance the manifesto that was made, giving the reason of these arms; nor by whom, nor in what manner, nor on what grounds it was published, nor what effects it hath wrought, drawing, as it were, almost the whole world into league against us. Nor will I mention the leaving of the wines, the leaving of the salt, which were in our possession, and of a value, as it is said, to answer much of our expense. Nor will I dwell on that great wonder (which no Alexander or Cæsar ever did), the enriching of the enemy by courtesies when our soldiers wanted help; nor the private intercourse and parleys with the fort, which were continually held. What they intended may be read in the success; and upon due examination thereof, they would not want their proofs.

For the last voyage to Rochelle,[11] there need be no observations, it is so fresh in memory; or will I make an inference or corollary on all. Your own knowledge shall judge what truth or what sufficiency they express.

For the next, the ignorance and corruption of our ministers, where can you miss of instances? If you survey the court, if you survey the country; if the church, if the city be examined; if you observe the bar, if the bench, if the ports, if the shipping, if the land, if the seas—all these will render you variety of proofs; and that in such measure and proportion as shows the greatness of our disease to be

[9] Some old meanings of *service* are at issue. "Our serviceable men," meant soldiers, or our willing men. An "unserviceable fort" was a useless fort. "If there *was* a service" therefore meant, "If there was a fealty or loyalty."

[10] In June 1627, Buckingham sailed with a large fleet and 7,000 soldiers to Rochelle in aid of the Huguenots, who, not expecting him, advised him to take the Island of Rhé, just offshore. This he did; in the ensuing uprising of the Huguenots, Buckingham managed his forces badly and lost heavily. He received reinforcements in October and lost most of them. Eliot alludes later to that "manifesto" which the Duke published, inciting the Huguenots to all-out rebellion.

[11] The voyage carrying reinforcements.

such that, if there be not some speedy application for remedy, our case is almost desperate.

Mr. Speaker, I fear I have been too long in these particulars that are past, and am unwilling to offend you; therefore in the rest I shall be shorter, and as to that which concerns the impoverishing of the King, no other arguments will I use than such as all men grant.

The exchequer, you know, is empty, and the reputation thereof gone; the ancient lands are sold; the jewels pawned; the plate engaged; the debts still great; almost all charges, both ordinary and extraordinary, borne up by projects! What poverty can be greater? What necessity so great? What perfect English heart is not almost dissolved into sorrow for this truth?

For the oppression of the subject, which, as I remember, is the next particular I proposed, it needs no demonstration. The whole kingdom is a proof; and for the exhausting of our treasures, that very oppression speaks it. What waste of our provisions, what consumption of our ships, what destruction of our men there hath been. Witness that expedition to Algiers [12]—witness that with Mansfeld— witness that to Cádiz—witness the next—witness that to Rhé—witness the last (I pray God we may never have more such witnesses)—witness, likewise, the Palati- nate—witness Denmark—witness the Turks—witness the Dunkirkers—witness all! What losses we have sustained! How we are impaired in munitions, in ships, in men!

It is beyond contradiction that we were never so much weakened, nor ever had less hope how to be restored.

These, Mr. Speaker, are our dangers; these are they who do threaten us, and these are like the Trojan horse brought in cunningly to surprise us. In these do lurk the strongest of our enemies, ready to issue on us; and if we do not speedily expel them, these are the signs, these are the invitations to others! These will so prepare their entrance that we shall have no means left of refuge or defence. If we have these enemies at home, how can we strive with those that are abroad? If we be free from these, no other can impeach us. Our ancient English virtue (like the old Spartan valour) cleared from these disorders—our being in sincerity of religion and once made friends with Heaven; having maturity of councils, suf- ficiency of generals, incorruption of officers, opulency in the King, liberty in the people, repletion in treasure, plenty of provisions, reparation of ships, preservation of men—our ancient English virtue, I say, thus rectified, will secure us; and unless there be a speedy reformation in these, I know now not what hopes or expecta- tions we can have.

These are the things, sir, I shall desire to have taken into consideration; that as we are the great Council of the Kingdom, and have the apprehension of these dangers, we may truly represent them unto the King, which I conceive we are bound to do by a triple obligation—of duty to God, of duty to His Majesty, and of duty to our country.

And therefore I wish it may so stand with the wisdom and judgment of the House, that these things may be drawn into the body of a remonstrance, and in all humility expressed, with a prayer to His Majesty, that for the safety of him- self, for the safety of the kingdom, and for the safety of religion, he will be pleased to give us time to make perfect inquisition thereof, or to take them into his own

[12] Some years earlier Buckingham had lost thirty ships in a futile attack on Algiers.

wisdom, and there give them such timely reformation as the necessity and justice of the case doth import.

And thus, sir, with a large affection and loyalty to His Majesty, and with a firm duty and service to my country, I have suddenly (and it may be with some disorder) expressed the weak apprehensions I have, wherein, if I have erred, I humbly crave your pardon, and so submit myself to the censure of the House.

~

BIBLIOGRAPHICAL NOTE

The most recent biography of Eliot is most reliable: *Harold Hulme, The Life of Sir John Eliot, 1592–1632, Struggle for Parliamentary Freedom* (1957). See also S. R. Gardiner's article in the *Dictionary of National Biography*, and John Forster, *Sir John Eliot* (2 vols., 1865). For an account of the political ideas in conflict, consult Perez Zagorin, "The English Revolution," *Journal of World History*, II (Pts. 3–4, 1955), 668–81, and "The Social Interpretation of the English Revolution," *Journal of Economic History*, XIX (September 1959), 376–401. Hulme is especially good for the events preceding and succeeding the speech.

Thomas Wentworth, Earl of Strafford

(1593–1641)

The Earl of Strafford was the dominant figure and possibly the most powerful orator in one of the great trials in English history. Great it was, because upon its outcome rested, to a large extent, the future of English parliamentary ideals, and because in its conduct were arrayed some of the keenest political minds and foremost legal talents of the middle seventeenth century. Against Strafford were ranged seven of the Commons' best lawyers: George Lord Digby, John Glyn, John Maynard, Geoffrey Palmer, John Pym, Oliver St. John, and Bulstrode Whitelocke. Opposite them at the bar, alone, imperious in thought and manner, and in speech, quick, sharp, impetuous, and appealing, stood the Earl in defense of himself. The drama was a direct result of political and religious forces.

These forces were assuming identity and shape, as we have seen, in Sir John Eliot's Parliament of 1626. Strafford found them converging upon him. The Commons believed that Wentworth, Buckingham's successor as the King's closest and most trusted adviser, had to be gotten rid of, no matter how. He was an avowed monarchist, and had been haughtily proud of his own powers in the years he had been President of the Council of the North and Lord Lieutenant of Ireland. Many believed him to be a turncoat, for they remembered that in 1626 he had been on the Parliamentary side and had gone to jail rather than pay the forced loan. Most of them believed that he counseled Charles to live without Parliament and to decree whatever revenue measures were necessary. He was thought to have encouraged Archbishop Laud in his "thorough" rule of the Church—a personal rule in which speech and press were systematically muzzled and the Court of High Commission was used to enforce rigid uniformity. Under the influence of his wife, a Catholic who maintained her forms of worship, the King had not been above bargaining with Catholic forces in France and at home. Extremists thought of him as a Catholic and they suspected Strafford, too, of being a Catholic in secret. Much of the Commons' diffuse resentment came to a focus on him; impeachment was voted, and the accused was arraigned before the House of Lords, which functioned as a court of justice.

Despite the Commons' hue and cry, the contest was not entirely one-sided. Many in the Upper House had loyalist leanings, and the Lords endeavored to function as good justices. Wentworth himself was a bold, direct, and ready speaker; he possessed intimate knowledge of the evidence and facts, sometimes to the confusion of the prosecution; and as a veteran administrator in northern England and in Ireland he had had much experience in the role, though not in the office, of judge. His was an excellent mind, methodically trained at Cambridge. He had entered the Inner Temple at the age of fourteen, had been knighted at nineteen, and at twenty-one had been elected to the Addled Parliament (1614). His friend and the custodian of his papers and letters, George Radcliffe, remarked on Wentworth's habits of reading good authors in French, English, and Latin, of hearing the best sermons and public addresses, and of exercising meticulous care in letter writing. Much practice, he believed, made for quickness of wit and clearness of judgment.

The trial took place in Westminster Hall. It was fitted with a throne chair, as well as seats for the Lords, for a number of judges (advisers to the House), and for members of the Commons, who attended in large numbers. Near the throne chair was an enclosure for the King and Queen. Charles was present daily; and some of the arguments and appeals on both sides were obviously directed at him. The presiding officer was the Earl of Arundel, the Lord High Steward. The defendant was dressed in black, his tall, spare frame slightly stooped, his thick hair cut short, his countenance and gesture those of the dignified, haughty lord. For some five hours each day for nearly three weeks he responded one by one to the articles in which were couched the specific accusations. He weighed the testimony, examined witnesses and their evidence, conducted counter-argument and refutation. In all, it was an impressive performance. Not the least remarkable feature was the demonstration of his powerful memory. The participants, of course, took notes and used them, as one onlooker reported; but Gardiner may be right in suggesting that, since Wentworth had far less time to prepare his defense than his prosecutors had to make ready their case, the contrast between John Pym using notes liberally and Strafford speaking "as the thoughts rose within him" must have been striking and telling.

His closing speech, printed below, exhibits the argument and manner of the polished debater, heightened by nobility of appeal, by loyalty to personal principle, to monarch, and to class, and by the pity and fear that attend tragedy. The speech is dramatic rhetoric in which fact, intellect, and imagination work as one for the defense of personal life against public expediency. The impact of idea and the unity of impression are made possible through simplicity of diction and statement together with careful management of verbal structure.

The response to the speech was probably quite in keeping with the response to Strafford's whole case and conduct. At some point in the proceedings shortly before delivery of the speech, it was evident to the major contestants that the charge of treason could not be sustained. So the Commons framed a Bill of Attainder, the effect of which, when signed by Charles some weeks after the formal part of the trial was over, was to declare Strafford, legislatively rather than judicially, guilty. Policy, not law, called for the block. Wentworth's impact on the judicious observer may have been that made upon Whitelocke; one of the Commons' prosecutors: "Never any man acted such a part, on such a theatre with more wisdome, constancy and eloquence, with greater reason, judgment and temper, and with better grace in all his words and actions than did this great and excellent person; and he moved the hearts of all his auditors—some few excepted—to remorse and pity." (*Parliamentary History*, II, 748–49.)

〜

SPEECH OF THE EARL OF STRAFFORD AT HIS TRIAL FOR TREASON *

House of Lords
April 12, 1641

May it please your Lordships, it falls to my turn, by your Lordships' leave and favour, to presume to put you in mind, and to represent to you the proofs, as they have been offered, which I shall do to the best of my memory, with a great deal of clearness. I shall desire to represent them neither better nor worse than they are in themselves, and I wish the like rule may be observed on the other side; for in the proceeding of this cause I heard them allege that, as they conceived, divers articles were fully proved: whence I conceive, there was nothing fully proved.

My Lords, my memory is weak, my health hath been impaired, and I have not had such quiet thoughts as I desired to have had, in a business of so great and weighty importance to me.[1] And therefore I shall most humbly beseech your Lordships, that by your wisdom, your justice and goodness, I may be so much bound to you, as to have my infirmities supplied by your better abilities, better judgments, and better memories.

My Lords, the charge I am to answer is a charge of high treason; and that which makes it the most grievous of all, it is an impeachment of treason from the honourable House of Commons. Were not that in the case, my Lords, it

---

* This version of the speech is that by John Rushworth (see Bibliographical Note, below), one of the Commons' clerks, who was placed close to the speakers where he could hear. He reported the language faithfully, so he said, in "characters." Extracts in Cobbett's *Parliamentary History* correspond closely to Rushworth in style. The version in *Select British Eloquence* presents serious difficulties as to source and style. Rushworth's language seems closer to the high conflict of the trial. About half of Rushworth's text is reproduced, the elisions being indicated by the conventional sign of omission. The full structure of the speech is preserved; so are those points of Strafford's rule and counsel that were of greatest concern to the Commons. There have been minor adjustments in punctuation and capitalization.

[1] Strafford had been imprisoned in the Tower. Since the day the trial opened, March 12, he had had the chief burden of his defense. Until three days before the trial opened, he was given to understand that he was to use no witnesses. Most of his witnesses were in Ireland, but he had pleaded in vain for postponement.

would not press so heavy and sore upon me, as now it doth, having the authority and power of their names upon it. Otherwise, my Lords, the innocency, and the clearness of my own heart from so foul a crime is such that I must with modesty say, if I had no other sin to answer for, it would be easily borne.

My Lords, as I went along article by article, these gentlemen were pleased to say, they [the actions charged] were no treasons in themselves, but conducing to the proof of treason; and, most of the articles being gone over, they come to the point at last. And hence, my Lords, I have all along watched to see if that I could find that poisoned arrow that should invenom all the rest, that deadly cup of wine that should intoxicate a few alleged inconveniences and misdemeanors, to run them up to high treason.

My Lords, I confess it seems very strange to me, that, there being a special difference between misdemeanors, and between felonies and treasons: How is it possible that ever misdemeanors should make felonies, or a hundred felonies make a treason? Or that misdemeanors should be made accessories to treason, where there is not a principal in the case? No treason, I hope, shall be found in me, nor in any thing I hear to be charged, under favour, and not waived.

They say well that if a man be taken threatening of a man to kill him, conspiring his death, and with a bloody knife in his hand, these be great arguments to convince a man of murder. But then, under favour, the man must be killed; for if the man be not killed the murder is nothing. So, all these things that they would make conduce to treason, unless something be treasonable, under favour,[2] they cannot be applied to treason.

My Lords, I have learnt that in this case, which I did not know before, that there be treasons of two kinds: there be statute treasons, there be treasons at common law, or treasons constructive and arbitrary.[3]

My Lords, these constructive treasons have been strangers in this commonwealth a great while, and I trust, shall be still, by your Lordships' wisdom and justice. But as for treasons in the statute, I do with all gladness and humility acknowledge your Lordships to be my judges, and none but you, under favour can be my judges. His Majesty is above it, the King condemns no man; the great operation of his scepter is mercy; his justice is dispensed by his ministry; so he is no judge in the case (with reverence be it spoken) and likewise no Commoner can be judge in the case of life and death, under favour, in regard he is of another body. So that, my Lords, I do acknowledge entirely you are my judges, and do with all cheerfulness in the world submit myself unto you, thinking that I have great cause to give God thanks, that I have you for my judges. And God be praised it is so, and celebrated be the wisdom of our ancestors that have so ordained it.

---

[2] "Under favour" seems to have carried two meanings. First, it was roughly equivalent to the modern "May it please your Honour." Second, Strafford uses it to acknowledge the privilege, the favor, that the Lords had shown in permitting him in their presence to speak in his own behalf.

[3] "Statute" treason was to be determined by the statute of 25 Edward III, the crucial point of which is that any man who "shall intend the death of the king, his queen, their children; kill the chancellor or judge upon the bench, imbase the king's coin, or counterfeit the king's seal . . . shall be convict, and punished as a traytor." The general sense, import, and tenor of the first seven articles were alleged by the prosecution to add up to "constructive" treason.

My Lords, I shall observe these rules: first, I shall (as I hope) clear myself of statute treason, and then shall come to constructive treason, or treason at the common law.

The first point they charge me withal of treason is upon the Fifteenth Article. Wherein nevertheless, before I come to answer the particulars, I must humbly inform your Lordships that, in that Article, two of the most material charges are waived. . . . The matter that stays with me in this Article is the alleged warrant to Mr. Savill, Sergeant-at-Arms, and the execution of it; for that I shall humbly beseech your Lordships, I may mind you with all humility that that warrant is not showed; and I do think that my Lords the judges do, in the trials before them,[4] observe that deeds are to prove themselves in ordinary trials betwixt men and men. Now, how much more in a trial of life, and which is more than that (though my misfortune will have me to own it) in the trial of a Peer?

The witnesses, my Lords, say they have seen such a warrant. But no witness says he knows it and will swear it to be my hand and seal; or that I set my hand or seal to it, for it may be counterfeited for any thing they know.

For Mr. Savill, upon oath, I thought (under favour) he ought not to be admitted against me, for he swears directly to justify himself. For if there be no such warrant, he is answerable for the fact, not I. But, my Lords, admit there were such a warrant, I humbly conceive I gave your Lordships a very clear and full answer to it. I showed you (and proved it, as I conceive) that the [as]sessing[5] of soldiers hath been a coercive means used in Ireland always to enforce obedience to the King's authority. I proved it to have been used to fetch in the King's rents of all kinds, contributions, compositions, exchequer rents. I proved it to have been used to bring in offenders and rebels. . . .

And, my Lords, I beseech your Lordships, how should it be not treason to assess soldiers for the King's debts, and yet the assessing of soldiers on the contempt of the King's authority should be treason? For certainly the King's authority is of far more dignity, and more respect is to be had to it than the getting of a few poor debts. And why it should be treason in one case and not in another, methinks it is very strange. . . .

The next statute treason is an intendment, or design, or what you will have it, for bringing over the Irish army into this Kingdom to reduce it, or to do I know not what, nor I think no body else, for there is no such thing.

But, my Lords, for proof in this case, you have two offered there, and no more, under favour, at all. The first proof is the fears and doubts of my Lord Ranalaugh that tells you he fears such a thing and doubts such a thing. My Lords, if fears and doubts may be sufficient to condemn me for treason, by my faith, I fear, and doubt very much, these fears and doubts might accuse me and condemn me of treason more than once a year. But, my Lords, his fears and doubts he may keep to himself. I hope they shall not be brought any way to the prejudice of me. I am, I thank God, both confident and knowing there is no such thing.

The next is the testimony of Mr. Treasurer Vane;[6] and, the words Mr. Treas-

---

[4] Present were professional judges from the courts of King's Bench and Common Pleas.

[5] It was common practice to press men into service for both domestic and foreign duty.

[6] Sir Harry Vane, anti-Charles, Presbyterian, and ardent defender of the Commons' rights and privileges.

urer doth witness against me in that particular are, as I conceive, these: that I should say to His Majesty, in an argument concerning an offensive or defensive war with Scotland, Your Majesty hath tried all ways and are refused and, in this extreme necessity, for the safety of the Kingdom and your people, you may employ the Irish army to reduce this Kingdom.

My Lords, to this I say that (under favour) Mr. Treasurer was in this (methoughts) a little dubious. He was something doubtful, for at the first he told your Lordships he would deal plainly and clearly with you, that he knew before whom he spoke. And then, my Lords, it was but to the best of his remembrance that these and these words were spoken. At the last, my Lords, being put to it more, he was pleased to say that these were positively the words, or something to that effect. So my Lords, here is but a dubious and uncertain witness, under favour, and these professions of his speaking clearly and plainly, and of his consideration before whom he was (which are something unusual clauses to men that come to swear upon oath) make me conceive him something dubious in this point.

Secondly, my Lords, he is a single witness, and not only so, but under favour, disavowed by all the rest that were present at the Council. My Lord of Northumberland remembered no such thing. My Lord Marquess of Hamilton remembered no such thing. My Lord Treasurer remembered no such thing. My Lord Cottington is very well assured he said no such thing, for if he had he should have taken offence at it himself, which he never did.

My Lords, in the third place, he is pleased to mention that it was in a debate, whether an offensive or defensive war? and, that then I should say, the King had an army in Ireland [which could be used to reduce this kingdom]. My Lords, it falls out in time, to be as I conceive, to be about the fifth of May last, not many days sooner or later, [and] the army of Ireland was not raised till June following. So it seems I should tell the King a great untruth: that he had an army in Ireland which he might employ for his service before that army was raised; for it is a notorious thing, and any of that country knows, that the army was not raised till the fifteenth of June, as I remember.

Lastly, in farther taking away of this testimony, I have proved it by a great many witnesses, beyond all exception that there was never any such intendment of the bringing this army into England. Nay, that the design was quite otherwise, and this hath been apparently cleared before your Lordships by the testimony of my Lord of Northumberland, Marquess of Hamilton, Sir Thomas Lucas, and Mr. Slingsby, and might have been further justified by the testimony of my Lord of Ormond, President of Munster, and Sir John Burlace, Master of the Ordnance in Ireland, if they had been here to have been produced. So that all these laid together, the strong and clear proof on my part, the producing of a single witness which, by the proviso of I Edward 6 cannot rise in judgment against any man for high treason. I trust, all these laid together, I shall appear to your Lordships clear and free from these two points, whereupon they enforce me to be within the compass of treason by the statute alleged. . . .

Then comes in the second condition of treason in the charge, and that is constructive treason. And, it is laid down in the First Article of the general charge.

For, my Lords, I must tell you, the First Articles exhibited are grounds and foundations whereupon the rest are gathered, and to which they resort and apply themselves severally.

I do conceive myself, in a manner, by themselves, clear of seven of these, for they have, in a manner, relinquished five of them, so that the First Article is the main article whereupon I must be touched, and that is laid in the charge thus: That I have traitorously endeavoured to subvert the fundamental laws and government of the realms of England and Ireland; and have, by traiterous words, counsels, and actions, declared the same; and have advised His Majesty to compel his subjects to submit thereunto by force.

My Lords, I must confess I have many times with myself considered with wonder at the wisdom of our ancestors that set the pillars of this monarchy with that singular judgment and providence, that I have ever observed, that so oft as either the prerogative of the Crown, or liberty of the subject, ecclesiastical or temporal powers exceed those modest bounds set and appointed for them, by the sobriety and moderation of former times, the exercise of it over-turned to [turned to] the prejudice and to the detriment of the public weal. All the strings of this government and monarchy have been so perfectly tuned through the skill and attention of our forefathers, that if you wind any of them any thing higher, or let them lower, you shall infallibly interrupt the sweet accord that ought to be entertained of King and people.

With this opinion I had the honour to sit many years in the Commons House; and this opinion I have carried along with me exactly and entirely for fourteen years in the King's service, ever resolving in my heart *stare super vias antiquas,*[7] to prove with equal care the prerogative of the Crown and the liberty of the subject, to introduce the laws of England into Ireland, ever setting before myself a joint and individual well-being of King and people (for either they must be both or neither)—which made my misfortune the greater to be now in my gray hairs charged as an under-worker against that government, a subverter of that law I most affected, and a contriver against that religion, to the whereof I would witness by the sealing of it with my blood.

My Lords, this subversion must be by words, by counsels, and by actions in Ireland and in England.

My Lords, I shall first give you an accompt [account] of the words wherewithall I am charged forth of Ireland: and, the first words are in the Third Article, where I am charged to have said that Ireland is a conquered nation and that the King may do with them as he pleaseth, and to the city of Dublin that their charters are nothing worth and bind the King no farther than he pleaseth. These are the words charged.

My Lords, methinks it is very strange, under favour, that this can be made an inducement to prove this charge, because I said that Ireland is a conquered nation, therefore I endeavour to subvert the fundamental laws when I speak the truth; for certainly it is very true, it was so.

For Lords, under favour, I remember very well there was as much said here at this bar since we began; and yet I dare well swear, and acquit him that spake it, from intending to subvert the laws. For, my Lords, you were told, and told truly, that Ireland was a conquered nation, and that it was subordinate to England (and God forbid that it should be otherwise) and that they have received laws from the conqueror. . . .

For my words concerning their charters, your Lordships remember very well,

---

[7] "To stand fast upon the old paths."

I doubt not, wherefore I said they were void, for their misuse of them; and that I told them so, not with the intent to overthrow their patents, or charters, but to make them more conformable to those things that the state thought fit for increase of religion and trade, and encouraging and bringing English into that town; and, that it was meant so, and no otherwise. Whatsoever was said, it appears by this their charters were never touched nor infringed, nor med[d]led withal by me, during the time I was in that Kingdom, so that [as for] words so spoken, and to such a purpose that they should go to prove such a conclusion, I conceive there is great difference betwixt those premises and that conclusion.

My Lords, these being the words that passed from me in Ireland, there are other words that are charged upon me, to have been spoken in England [in the King's council]. . . .

The next Article . . . chargeth me with words . . . that His Majesty should first try the Parliament here, and if that did not supply him according to his occasions, he might then use his prerogative as he pleased to levy what he needed, and that he should be acquitted both of God and man if he took some other courses to supply himself, though it were against the will of his subjects.

My Lords, as unto this, I conceive the charge is not proved by any witness that hath here produced against me; and in truth my Lords, I must needs say this, under favour (if it be an error in my judgement, I must humbly crave your Lordships' pardon) through the whole cause I have not seen a weaker proof; and if I had had time to have gotten my witnesses out of Ireland, I hope that should be proved, and so clearly, as nothing could be proved more. But I must stand or fall to what I have proved, and so I do my Lords. The proof they offer for this (as I conceive) is the testimony of my Lord Primate,[8] and his testimony is that in some discourse betwixt us two, touching levying upon the subject in case of imminent necessity, he found me of opinion that the King might use his prerogative as he pleased. My Lords, this is (under favour) a single testimony. It is of a discourse between him and me, and there is not any other that witnesses anything concerning it; so that (under favour my Lords) I conceive this will not be sufficient to bring me any ways in danger of treason, being but a single testimony. And my Lords, it is to be thought and to be believed (and it were a great offence for any man to think otherwise) that in this case anything can please the King (he is so gracious and good) but what shall be just and lawful. And then there is no doubt but so far as with justice and lawfulness he may use his prerogative in case of imminent danger, when ordinary means will not be admitted.

At most, he saith it was but an opinion, and opinions may make an heretic, but they shall not, I trust, make a traitor. . . .

My Lords, the next testimony offered for proving this charge is . . . that at the Council-Board, or in the gallery, I did say that seeing the Parliament had not supplied the King, His Majesty might take other courses for the defence of the Kingdom. Truly my Lords (under favour) who doubts but he might. For my part, I see not where the offence is. For another man to have said thus—for if another man will not help me, may not I therefore help myself? (under favour) —I conceive there is no great weight nor crime in these words. But in these likewise he stands a single testimony. There is no man that joins with him in it.

[8] The Archbishop of Canterbury, Charles Laud.

And there is this in the whole cause, concerning the words, that I think there is not any one thing wherein two concur.

The next testimony is that of the Earl of Holland, and he says that at the Council-Board I said the Parliament having denied the King, he had advantage to supply himself other ways. Truly, my Lords, I say still other ways being lawful ways, and just ways, and such ways as the goodness of the King can only walk in; and in no other can he walk. And therefore I conceive they be far from bringing it to so high a guilt as treason. And this likewise his Lordship expresses as the rest do, singly on his own word, as he conceives them, and not on the particular word of any other person, which is I say the case of every one that speaks in the business. And therefore there being so great a difference in the report and conceiving of things, it is very hard my words should be taken to my destruction, when no man agrees what they were.

. . . I have heard some discourse of great weight, and of great authority. And that is certain, the arguments that were used in the case of ship-money,[9] by those that argued against the King in that case, say as much; and [I] will undertake, if any man read those arguments, he shall find as much said there as I said at Council-Board. For there you shall hear that there be certain times and seasons when propriety ceases, as in the case of burning, where a man pulls down the next house to preserve the whole street from being set on fire. In the case of building forts on any man's land, where it is for the public defence of the Kingdom, in both these cases propriety doth cease: nay, he says that in war, *inter arma silent leges.*[10] Now my Lords, these are as highly said as anything you have heard by me, and yet certainly is no subverting of the fundamental laws for all that. And therefore, if a man must be judged, he must not be judged by pieces, but by all together.

My Lords, whatsoever I said at Council-Board was led in by this case, what a King should do in case of a foreign invasion of an enemy when the ordinary ways and means of levying money would not come in seasonably to prevent mischief, for what a King may do in case of absolute necessity. Certainly in these cases, the ordinary rules do not take place. As this was the case that let in [initiated] the discourse, so I most humbly beseech your Lordships (for it is fully proved) to remember what was the conclusion of that discourse, which was that after the present occasion [was] provided for, the King was obliged in honor and justice to vindicate and free the liberty of the subject from all prejudice and harm it might sustain in that extraordinary occasion; and that this was to be done by a Parliament, and no other way but a Parliament; and the King and his people could never be happy, till the prerogative of the Crown [and] the liberty of the subject were so bounded and known that they might go hand in hand together, mutually to the assistance of one another. . . .

My Lords, these are as near as I can gather, all that are charged as unto words, spoken either in England or Ireland Councils. Other than these I am not

[9] Everyone was familiar with ship money and the levy of it. In a time of danger, Charles instead of taking ships had levied a tax. The expedient worked; so he extended the tax to the realm in general. Hampden was jailed for refusal to pay. Strafford here uses one of the Crown's chief arguments: that the King is justified in levying taxes to meet dangers.

[10] "Silent are the laws in the midst of arms." (War suspends the laws.) (Cicero *Pro Milone* iv, 11.)

charged withall, and so there remains nothing but my actions; and, if I can free them as well, as I have freed the words, I conceive then, under favour, I have fully answered all that hath been objected against me.

My Lords, the first of these is the Fifth Article in the case of sentence of the council of war, against my Lord Mountnorris.[11] . . .

They say, he was a Peer, and it is very true; but, as he was a Peer, so he was a captain of the army; and, in this case, we consider men as members of the army, not as Peers; and, if a Peer will not submit himself to an officer of the army, he must submit himself to the order of the army. . . . But, at the worst, this is but an over-exercising of a jurisdiction. . . . That it should be high treason to enlarge jurisdiction is a perilous point. And if it be so, it befits your Lordships, and all judges, to be well certained what you may do, least by going too far, you fall into great inconveniences.

But, my Lords, I say (under favour) that all these, if they had been done without any manner of authority had not been a subversion, but rather a diversion of the law. . . . If **you** will bring in the Thames about Lambeth, to come in again below the bridge, the river is the same, though the course be diverted to another place; I say, the fundamental law is the same, only it is carried in another pipe. And shall this be said to be a subverting? Under favour, as the river is the same, so the law is the same; it is not a subversion, but a diversion. Nor doth it skill [discern] where justice be done (I mean so far as it concerns the subject's interest), for so long as he hath justice speedily, and with least charge, his end is complied with; and it concerns not himself, whether he hath it in the King's Bench, or Common-Pleas, so [long as] he hath it speedily, and with the least charge. And therefore, as long as the laws are the same, though executed by several persons, and in several places, I cannot conceive it to be a subversion.

And I shall humbly beseech your Lordships, to take care that while these strains are put upon me, to make this personal charge against me, ye do not through my sides, wound the Crown of England by taking that power from the deputy which must of necessity be lodged in him, if you will have that Kingdom depend upon the Crown of England, which I hold, in all wisdom and judgment, ought to be cared for. Therefore, I beseech you, prejudice not the deputy, to the disabling him from serving the Crown hereafter, by beating down me, who am this day to answer before you; for if you take away the power of the deputy, you shall not have that Kingdom long depend upon this Crown; for it rests under God and His Majesty, and must principally rest upon the care of him that is entrusted with that charge. And, therefore, give me leave, on the behalf of the Crown of England, to beseech you to be wary of lessening the deputies' power too much; for, if you do, I fear you will find it a great disservice to the Crown. . . .

The next is the business of the tobacco, which is not applicable to treason in any kind. But because I would be clear in every man's judgment that hears me, I beseech your Lordships to call to mind, it was the petition of the Commons-House of Ireland, that the grant of import on the tobacco should be taken in, and converted to the King's use; so that whatsoever was done was persuing their intention and desire.

That there was no way but this, to make benefit and profit of it, is most

---

[11] As Lord Lieutenant of Ireland, Strafford had construed some insolent words of Lord Mountnorris as mutinous and had arraigned him before a council of war.

manifestly showed, that there was a proclamation in England of the like nature, and a command of the King to proceed in it accordingly; and an act of Parliament transmitted here, for passing it to the Crown, according to the intention of the Commons-House. And for the greatness of the bargain, no proof hath been offered to your Lordships, but only the estimate of a merchant; and how far your Lordships will be guided by the estimate of a merchant I know not, but I have had trial of some of them, and their estimates never hold. For they have always told me I shall gain much, and when I came to the point, I gained nothing. And if Sir George Ratcliffe should be sworn to the point, he should say confidently that we are fourscore and six thousand out of purse, and when he came out of Ireland, but fourscore thousand pounds received. And this is the profit estimated by the great merchants, at a hundred and forty thousand pounds a year. But, at the worst it is but a monopoly, and a monopoly of the best condition, because it was begun by a parliament. I have seen many monopolies questioned in Parliament, and many overthrown in Parliament, but I never heard a monopoly charged for a treason.

The Eighteenth [Article] is . . . waived, but it is that which sticks very heavy upon me, and wherein I find myself as much afflicted as in any one part of the charge. For, my Lords, here I am charged up and down to endeavor to draw upon myself a dependance of the papists, in both Kingdoms of Ireland and England; and that I have, during the time of my government, restored diverse Mass-houses in Dublin and elsewhere, that have been by precedent deputies taken away. I am likewise charged to have drawn to myself a dependance of the Irish army, eight thousand, all papists; and likewise to have miscarried myself in a commission entrusted with me, before my going into Ireland, concerning composition for recusants.

This is a very heavy and grievous charge, and hath raised a great deal of ill opinion against me in the world, to be a favourer and contriver with papists, and I know not whom, against the religion I profess. A greater and fouler crime there cannot be against God and man, and yet this goes in print all over the world. And when it comes to the point, here is no proof, nor any part of the charge made good. And, therefore, since it is not made good by the charge, I humbly desire I may be vindicated in your Lordships' noble opinions, and the opinions of all that hear me, that I am, in my religion, what I ought to be, and that which I will die in and maintain against all the world. And I am so far from contriving anything to the hindrance of it, that, if God give me life, I will serve it, and prevent any inconvenience to it; and, my religion and duty to God is so dear, and precious to me, that there is nothing in this world, but I shall lay down, as straw and stubble, under my feet, and trample upon it, rather than in any kind forfeit that. But in the mean time, I suffer, and must be content. . . .

In the Twenty-fourth Article comes in that of the Parliament more fully; and there I am charged falsely, and treacherously, and maliciously, to have declared before His Majesty's Privy-Council, that the Parliament of England had forsaken the King, and given him the advantage to supply himself otherways; and having so maliciously slandered the said House of Commons, that I did, with the advice of the Archbishop of Canterbury, and the Lord Finch, publish a false and traitorous book, called *His Majesties Declaration of the Causes of Dissolving the last Parliament*, etc. This goes very heavy upon me in the world, that I should be a breaker of parliaments, a counsellor against parliaments. My Lords, there is nothing proved of it; and, I hope I shall be cleared by your Lordships, and these noble gentlemen, and all the world, that I had no such thing in my heart.

For the point of the declaration, I was at that time sick in my bed and could do nothing in it, and therefore I trust I shall be acquitted as to that. As to the breaking of the Parliament, or any ill-will to parliaments, I have ever honoured them. And far be it from me to wish that they may not be frequent, for the good of the King and kingdom. But as oft as you shall have it urged and pressed against me, that I should be an endeavourer to subvert the fundamental laws of the land in this kind, I beseech your Lordships, call to mind what hath been proved, that at all public debates, at Council, and privately apart, I have humbly represented to His Majesty, from time to time, that parliaments are the only way to settle himself in quietness in the Kingdom, and to acquire prosperity and happiness to himself and his people. And when you shall hear them press upon me that I have endeavoured to subvert the fundamental laws of the land, I beseech your Lordships to call to mind how frequently and fervently I have advised the King to call for parliaments, which, under God, is the great protection and defence of the fundamental laws of the Kingdom. . . .

And so, my Lords, I am come to the end of these twenty-eight articles that were for my further impeachment. I have gone over them all. And out of these now there remains that other second treason, that I should be guilty of endeavouring to subvert the fundamental laws of the land, in the first of those seven articles.

My Lords, that those should now be treason together that are not treason in any one part, and accumulatively to come upon me in that kind, and where one will not do it of itself, yet woven up with others it shall do it—under favour, my Lords, I do not conceive that there is either statute law, or common law, that hath declared this, endeavouring to subvert the fundamental laws, to be high treason.

I say, neither statute law, nor common law written, that I could hear of; and I have been as diligent to enquire of it as I could be. And your Lordships will believe I had reason so to do. And, sure it is a very hard thing, I should here be questioned for my life and honour, upon a law that is not extant, that cannot be shewed. There is a rule that I have read out of my Lord Coke, *Non apparentibus et non existentibus eadem est Ratio.*[12]

Jesu! My Lords, where hath this fire lain all this while, so many hundred years together, that no smoke should appear till it burst out now, to consume me and my children? Hard it is, and extreme hard, in my opinion, that a punishment should precede the promulgation of a law, that I should be punished by a law subsequent to the act done.[13] I most humbly beseech your Lordships, take that into consideration; for certainly it were better a great deal to live under no law but the will of man, and conform ourselves in human wisdom as well as we could, and to comply with that will, than to live under the protection of a law,

---

[12] "The rule is: non evident, non existent"; i.e., if it is not in the books, it is not law.

[13] In arguing the injustice of retroactive legislation, Strafford here and below has two facts in mind. The House of Commons was already talking of a Bill of Attainder designed to *declare* him guilty of treason. The prosecution, moreover, had been endeavoring to make much out of a *proviso* in the famous statute of 25 Edward III, namely, "That what Parliament should declare to be treasonable in time to come, should be punished as a treason." Later one of Strafford's lawyers pointed out that the provision had kept a sword hanging over men's heads and that it had been repealed in Henry IV's reign.

as we think, and then a law should be made to punish us for a crime precedent to the law. Then I conceive no man living could be safe, if that should be admitted.

My Lords, it is hard in another respect, that there should be no tokens set upon this offence, by which we may know it, no manner of token given, no admonition by which we might be aware of it. If I pass down the Thames in a boat and run and split myself upon an anchor if there be not a buoy to give me warning, the party shall give me damages; but if it be marked out, then it is at my own peril. Now, my Lords, where is the mark set upon this crime? Where is the token by which I should discover? If it be not marked, if it lie under water, and not above, there is no human providence can prevent the destruction of a man presently and instantly. Let us then lay aside all that is human wisdom, let us rely only upon divine revelation; for certainly nothing else can preserve us if you will condemn us before you tell us where the fault is, that we may avoid it.

My Lords, may your Lordships be pleased to have that regard to the peerage of England, as never to suffer yourselves to be put upon those moot points, upon such constructions, and interpretations, and strictness of law, as these are, when the law is not clear nor known. If there must be a trial of wits, I do most humbly beseech your Lordships to consider that the subject may be of something else than of your lives and your honours.

My Lords, we find, that in the primitive time, on the sound and plain doctrine of the blessed apostles, they brought in their books of curious art, and burnt them. My Lords, it will be likewise (under favour, as I humbly conceive) wisdom and providence in your Lordships, for yourselves and posterities, for the whole kingdom, to cast from you into the fire those bloody and mysterious volumes of constructive and arbitrary treasons, and to betake yourselves to the plain letter of the statute, that tells you where the crime is, that so you may avoid it. And let us not, my Lords, be ambitious to be more learned in those killing arts than our forefathers were before us.

My Lords, it is now full two hundred and forty years since any man ever was touched to this height upon this crime before myself; we have lived, my Lords, happily to ourselves at home, we have lived gloriously abroad to the world; let us be content with that which our fathers left us, and let us not awake those sleepy lions to our own destruction by rattling up of a company of records that have lain for so many ages by the wall, forgotten, or neglected.

My Lords, there is this that troubles me extremely, least it should be my misfortune to all the rest (for my other sins, not for my treasons) that my precedent should be of that disadvantage (as this will be, I fear, in the consequence of it) upon the whole *Kingdom*.

My Lords, I beseech you, therefore, that you will be pleased seriously to consider it, and let my particular case be so looked upon as that you do not through me wound the interest of the Commonwealth. For howesoever those gentlemen at the bar say, They speak for the Commonwealth, and they believe so; yet, under favour, in this particular I believe I speak for the Commonwealth too; and, that the inconveniencies and miseries that will follow upon this, will be such, as it will come within a few years to that which is expressed in the statute of Henry the Fourth, it will be of such a condition, that no man shall know what to do, or what to say.

Do not, my Lords, put greater difficulty upon the ministers of state, than that with cheerfulness they may serve the king and the state; for if you will examine them by every grain or every little weight, it will be so heavy that the public affairs of the kingdom will be left waste, and no man will meddle with them, that hath wisdom, and honour, and fortune to lose.

My Lords, I have now troubled your Lordships a great deal longer, than I should have done. Were it not for the interest of those *Pledges* that a saint in heaven left me, I would be loth, my Lords[14]. . . . What I forfeit for myself it is nothing; but, I confess, that my indiscretion should forfeit for them it wounds me very deeply. You will be pleased to pardon my infirmity. Something I should have said. But I see I shall not be able and therefore I will leave it.

And now, my Lords, for myself, I thank God I have been, by His good blessing towards me, taught that the afflictions of this present life are not to be compared with that eternal weight of glory that shall be revealed for us hereafter. And so, my Lords, even so, with all humility, and with all tranquility of mind, I do submit myself clearly and freely to your judgments. And whether that righteous judgment shall be to life, or to death,

Te Deum Laudamus, Te Dominum Confitemur.[15]

◟

BIBLIOGRAPHICAL NOTE

The entire proceedings of the trial are best seen in John Rushworth, *The Tryal of Thomas Earl of Strafford . . . upon an Impeachment of High Treason by the Commons then Assembled in Parliament . . . begun in Westminster Hall March 22, 1640* [1641] *and continued until . . . the 10th of May 1641* (1680), republished, with some modifications in spelling, as Volume VIII of Rushworth's *Historical Collections* (1721). The Earl of Birkenhead, *Famous Trials of History* (1926), offers a useful, brief account of the trial. Helpful biographies are those by Robert Browning, *Prose Life of Strafford* (1892), John Forster, *Thomas Wentworth, A Life,* "Lives of Eminent English Statesmen," II (1836), H. D. Traill, *Lord Strafford* (1899), and C. V. Wedgwood, *Strafford: 1593–1641* (1935).

Oliver Cromwell

(1599–1658)

Cromwell was of a family that had been given clerical lands by Henry VIII, and may be counted among the small landed gentry. His first education in the Free School at Huntingdon, his birthplace, was under Thomas Beard, a Puritan whose *Theatre of God's Judgments* depicted a God who reached into every detail

---

[14] At this juncture Strafford is referring to his children ("pledges") and to his dead wife. The *Parliamentary History* records that here "he stopped a while, letting fall some tears" to her memory.

[15] "We give praise to God, and we confess to the Lord and Master."

of life. The pupil probably knew this book, as well as the Scriptures, by heart. Cromwell's advanced education was at Sidney-Sussex College, Cambridge, a forge of Puritanism. The youth was cast early into a religious mold that was never perceptibly cracked by any amount of legendary foreign travel, professional soldiering, or philandering. Entering Parliament in 1628, he began a political experience which led him into a civil war in which Cavalier and Roundhead were rallying symbols. He became commander of the Model Army, whose discipline and religious fervor gave Parliament the courage to win the war and behead the King, and he rose finally to the position of Lord Protector and virtual political dictator of England until his death in 1658.

Despite his impulsiveness, violence of temper, and unimpressive appearance, Cromwell could lead men. Possessing unquestionable ability and deep sincerity, he saw himself as God's instrument, and wished above all else to see his ideals of religion and government made real and effective. One of his biographers has said that "with parliamentary experience he came to be an influential speaker—not so much because he was eloquent as because he was in earnest." (Tanner, p. 283.) Abbott's estimate emphasizes his uniqueness in English history:

> That in an age of divine right monarchy an obscure Huntingdonshire gentleman should rise not only to the first place in England, but to almost, if not quite, the first place in the European world, seemed then, and still seems, to argue all but superhuman qualities; and so long as human greatness is measured in terms of power over one's fellowmen, Cromwell must be reckoned as perhaps the greatest of Englishmen. (*Writings*, I, 1.)

The Long Parliament had won the wars against Charles's absolute rule; its Rump members found the King treacherous, scheming, dangerous and sent him to the block. They abolished the House of Lords and the kingship, and put down uprisings in Ireland and Scotland. When subsequent Parliaments were unsuccessful, Cromwell and the army set up the Instrument of Government with himself as Lord Protector. The government of the Instrument successfully fought the Dutch, made an alliance with France, and began to break Spain's hold on ocean commerce to the New World. Now Lord Protector Cromwell was facing the first Parliament elected under the Instrument. He knew he must inspire the devout to carry on with "healing and settling" without bickering over religion and questioning the "fundamentals" of government. He knew, too, that his hearers distrusted power backed by an army, doubted the legality of the Instrument, and deplored his sympathy for the Independents. He was unsuccessful in his task.

The opinions represented in Cromwell's Protectorate Parliament were both political and religious. Royalist and Cavalier convictions lived on despite military defeats, and royalist sentiment was strong enough in the Parliament to be bothersome. It stood for a strong constitutional monarchy and a strong Anglican Church. Roundhead and parliamentary convictions were dominant. They called for rule by Parliament and by Presbyterians. The economic estates of the realm were also in evidence. In his speech opening the Parliament of 1654, Cromwell refers to them by name: noblemen, gentlemen, and yeomen. The merchants were present, too; and Cromwell appeals to their interests in assailing Levellers and Fifth Monarchy men—those men who would abolish civil government, establish a Kingdom of God on earth, and make all men equal in rights and goods. But in this Parliament, the militant spirit of religion and of parliamentary supremacy dominated. Members fell to quarrelling over the position and strength of the principle of sovereignty in the Instrument of Government, and Cromwell had to purge the Royalists from Parliament a few days after the speech. In Charles's parliaments, Royalist and Parliamentarian had been able to unite against absolute rule, but in Cromwell's parliaments they could not. The presence of irreconcilable religious positions was most disheartening. The Presbyterians were determined to dominate everything, both government and Church; and the Independents (a loose designation for sects who wanted to govern and worship as each desired) were equally insistent on their own views. Cromwell, more tolerant than most, knew that he was censured for "all the Sects and Heresies of the Nation. I have borne my reproach," he said, "but I have through God's mercy, not been unhappy in hindering any one Religion to impose upon another."

The speech below shows us Cromwell's chief characteristics: profound sincerity, earnestness, and integrity of belief. Supremely confident that God is for him, he calls on his authorities: the Deity, truth, and his conscience that weighs as a thousand witnesses. One hears of his favorite "twin liberties," civil and spiritual, on which part of the speech is built. Characteristic, too, are the appeals to the history of his own making, to both its ills and its goods, appeals that stir apprehension and indignation (his own and that of others). One hears, too, the pride of achievement and the love of property and security. There is the typical Cromwellian style: the Oliverian sentence—so Carlyle called it—whose progress is interrupted by qualifiers, disclaimers, and disavowals, suggesting the speaker's keen sensitivity to himself and others; and the earthy, bloody imagery darting out of diction and impregnating arguments of fear and destruction. Over all there is always the man who speaks for God, a man of much iron and of little clay.

The Cromwell who confronted his Parliament in the Painted Chamber could not have differed in appearance from the Cromwell installed as Lord Protector at the age of fifty-four. S. R. Church offers the description (*Oliver Cromwell*, p. 396):

> His frame was cast in a large mould, and lacked but two inches of six feet in height. His head was massive,—"You might see it," said John Maidstone, "a storehouse and shop—of a vast treasury of natural parts." There was the historic wart above the right eyebrow; nose large and wide at nostril; full lips; deep gray eyes, full of all tenderness, or, if need be, of all fierceness. Rich, dark brown locks, now showing a silver hair, fell flowing below his collar-band. A slight mustache only partially covered his upper lip, while just under his nether lip was a little tuft of beard scarce half-an-inch long. A hero, he was, whose face and figure had been bathed in the storms of battle, and on which the eternal dignities of a great life had set an indelible and distinguished mark.

∽

Speech to the First Protectorate Parliament *

September 4, 1654

Gentlemen: You are met here on the greatest occasion that, I believe, England ever saw, having upon your shoulders the interest of three great nations,[1] with the territories belonging to them. And truly, I believe I may say without any hyperbole, you have upon your shoulders the interest of all the Christian people in the world; and the expectation is that I should let you know, as far as I have cognizance of it, the occasion of your assembling together at this time.

It hath been very well hinted to you this day,[2] that you come hither to settle the interests before mentioned; for it will be made of so large extention in the issue and consequence of it. In the way and manner of my speaking to you I shall study plainness, and to speak to you what is truth, and what is upon my heart, and what will in some measure reach to these concernments.

After so many changes and turnings which this nation hath laboured under, to have such a day of hope as this is, and such a door of hope opened by God to us, truly, I believe some months since, would have been above all our thoughts. I confess it would have been worthy of such a meeting as this is, to have remembered that which was the rise, and gave the first beginning to all those turnings and tossings that have been upon these nations; and to have given you a series of the transactions not of men, but of the providence of God, all along unto our late changes; as also the ground of our first undertaking to oppose that usurpation and tyranny that was upon us, both in civils and spirituals; and the several grounds particularly applicable to the several changes that have been.

But I have two or three reasons which divert me from such a way of proceeding at this time. If I should have gone in that way, that which is upon my heart to have said (which is written there, that if I would blot it out I could not) [I] would have spent this day—the providences and dispensations of God have been so stupendous. As David said in the like case, 'Many, O Lord my God, are thy wonderful works which thou hast done; and thy thoughts which are to us ward, they cannot be reckoned up in order unto thee: if I would declare and speak of them, they are more than can be numbered.'[3]

Truly, another reason, new to me, you had today in the sermon. Much recapitulation of providence; much allusion to a state and dispensation, in respect of discipline and correction; of mercies and deliverances; the only parallel of

---

* The text printed here follows very closely that appearing in Cobbett's *Parliamentary History*, III, 1434–44. In turn it was taken from an original version "printed for G. Sawbridge, at the Bible on Ludgate Hill, 1654 . . ." as taken down "by one who stood very near and published to prevent mistakes." There is no evidence, external or internal, of revision by Cromwell, though presumably the pamphlet had his approval. The paragraphing is ours; and punctuation adheres to that of the source except where minor changes improve reading.

[1] England, Scotland, and Ireland. The free election under the Instrument of Government sent to this Parliament 400 English, 30 Scots, and 30 Irish.

[2] Allusion is to the sermon by Thomas Goodwin preached to Parliament in Westminster Abbey prior to the assembling of the Lords and Commons in the Painted Chamber.

[3] Ps. 40:5.

God's dealing with us that I know in the world, which was largely and wisely held forth to you this day, Israel's bringing out of Egypt through a wilderness, by many signs and wonders, towards a place of rest—I say towards it. And that having been so well remonstrated to you this day, is another argument why I shall not trouble you with a recapitulation of those things; though they are things that I hope will never be forgotten, because written in better books than those of paper —I am persuaded written in the heart of every good man.

The third reason was this, that which I judge to be the end of your meeting, the great end, which was likewise remembered to you this day, to wit, healing and settling. And the remembering transactions too particularly, perhaps instead of healing (at least in the hearts of many of you) may set the wound fresh a-bleeding. I must profess this to you, whatever thoughts pass upon me, that if this day (that is, this meeting) prove not healing, what shall we do? But, as I said before, seeing, I trust, it is in the minds of you all, and much more in the mind of God, which must cause healing. It must be first in his mind, and he being pleased to put it into yours, it will be a day indeed; and such a day as generations to come will bless you for. I say for this, and the other reasons, I have forborne to make a particular remembrance and enumeration of things, and of the manner of the Lord's bringing us through so many changes and turnings as have passed upon us. Howbeit, I think it will be more than necessary to let you know, at least so well as I may, in what condition this, nay these nations were, when this government was undertaken. For order's sake, it is very natural for us to consider what our condition was in civils; [what] in spirituals.

What was our condition? Every man's hand almost was against his brother— at least, his heart, little regarding any thing that should cement and might have a tendency in it to cause us to grow into one. All the dispensations of God, his terrible ones (he having met us in the way of his judgment in a ten-years Civil War, a very sharp one); his merciful dispensations, they did not, they did not work upon us; but we had our humours and interests, and indeed I fear our humours were more than our interests; and certainly, as it fell out in such cases, our passions were more than our judgments. Was not everything almost grown arbitrary? Who knew where, or how, to have right without some obstruction or other intervening? Indeed we were almost grown arbitrary in everything. What was the face that was upon our affairs as to the interest of the nation; to the authority of the nation; to the magistracy; to the ranks and orders of men, whereby England hath been known for hundreds of years? A nobleman, a gentleman, a yeoman, that is a good interest of the nation, and a great one. The magistracy of the nation, was it not almost trampled under foot, under despite and contempt, by men of levelling principles? I beseech you, for the orders of men and ranks of men, did not that levelling principle tend to the reducing all to an equality? [4] Did it think to do so? Or did it practise towards it for property and interest? What was the design, but to make the tenant as liberal a fortune as the landlord? which, I think, if obtained, would not have lasted long. The men of that principle, after they had served their own turns, would have cried up interest and property then fast enough. This instance is instead of many; and that it may appear this thing did extend far, is manifest, because it was a pleasing voice to all poor men, and

---

[4] Politically the Levellers wanted universal suffrage; economically they advocated equal shares of land, "by the law of Righteousness." John Lilburne, their chief spokesman, had caused Parliament—and Cromwell—much grief.

truly not unwelcome to all bad men. To my thinking it is a consideration that, in your endeavours after settlement, you will be so well minded of, that I might well have spared this. But let that pass.

Indeed in spiritual things, the case was more sad and deplorable; and that was told to you this day eminently. The prodigious blasphemies, contempt of God and Christ, denying of him, contempt of him and his ordinances, and of the Scriptures; a spirit visibly acting those things foretold by Peter and Jude; yea, those things spoken of by Paul to Timothy; who, when he would remember some things to be worse than the Antichristian state, of which he had spoken in the first [letter] to Timothy iv. 1, 2, tells them what should be the lot and portion of the last times; and says, [in the] second to Timothy iii. 2, 3, 4, 'In the last days perilous times should come, for men should be lovers of their ownselves, covetous, boasters, proud, blasphemers, disobedient to parents, unthankful, unholy . . . lovers of pleasures more than lovers of God.' And when he remembers that of the Antichristian state, he tells them, [in the] first to Timothy iv. 1, 2, 'That, in the latter days' that State shall come in, 'wherein there shall be a departing from the faith, and a giving heed to seducing spirits, and doctrines of devils, speaking lies in hypocrisy, having their conscience seared with a hot iron.' By which description he makes the state of the last times worse than that under Antichrist. And surely it may well be feared these are our times; for when men forget all rules of law and nature, and break all the bonds that fallen man hath upon him, the remainder of the image of God in his nature, which he cannot blot out, and yet shall endeavour to blot out, 'having a Form of Godliness, without the power'; these are sad tokens of the last times.

And indeed the character wherewith this spirit and principle is described in that place [of Scripture] is so legible and visible that he that runs may read it to be amongst us; for by such the 'Grace of God is turned into wantonness,' and Christ and the spirit of God made the cloak of all villainy and spurious apprehensions. And although these things will not be owned publicly, as to practice, (they being so abominable and odious) yet how this principle extends itself, and whence it had its rise, makes me to think of a second sort of men; who, it is true, as I said, will not practise nor own these things, yet can tell the magistrate that he hath nothing to do with men thus holding; for these are matters of conscience and opinion: they are matters of religion. What hath the magistrate to do with these things? He is to look to the outward man, but not to meddle with the inward. And truly it so happens, that though these things do break out visibly to all, yet the principle wherewith these things are carried on, so forbids the magistrate to meddle with them, as it hath hitherto kept the offenders from punishment. Such considerations and pretensions of liberty, liberty of conscience, and liberty of subjects, two as glorious things to be contended for, as any God hath given us; yet both these also abused for the patronizing of villanies, in so much as that it hath been an ordinary thing to say, and in dispute to affirm, That it was not in the magistrate's power; he had nothing to do with it; not so much as the printing a Bible in the nation for the use of the people, lest it be imposed upon the consciences of men; for they must receive the same traditionally and implicitly from the power of the magistrate, if thus received. The aforementioned abominations did thus swell to this height amongst us. The axe was laid to the root of the ministry. It was Antichristian; it was Babylonish: it suffered under a judgment, that the truth of it is, as the extremity was great on that, I wish it prove not so on this hand. The extremity was that no man having a good testimony, having received gifts from Christ, might preach, if not ordained. So now, many on the other hand affirm that he who is ordained hath a nullity, or Antichristianism, stamped upon his calling, so that he ought not to preach, or not be heard. I wish it may not too justly be said that there was severity and sharpness; yea, too much of an imposing spirit in matters of conscience; a spirit unchristian enough in any times, most unfit for these; denying liberty to those who have earned it with their blood; who have gained civil liberty and religious also for those who would thus impose upon them.[5]

We may reckon among these our spiritual evils, an evil that hath more refinedness in it, and more colour for it, and hath deceived more people of integrity than the rest have done; for few have been catched with the former mistakes, but such as have apostatized from their holy profession—such as being corrupt in their consciences, have been forsaken by God, and left to such noisome opinions. But, I say there are others more refined; many honest people, whose hearts are sincere, many of them belonging to God [who have fallen into an error], and that is the mistaken notion of the Fifth Monarchy. A thing pretending more spirituality than any thing else: a notion, I hope, we all honour, wait, and hope for, that Jesus Christ will have a time to set up his reign in our hearts, by subduing those corruptions, and lusts, and evils that are there, which reign now more in the world than I hope, in due time, they shall do; and when more fulness of the spirit is poured forth to subdue iniquity, and bring in everlasting righteousness, then will the approach of that glory be. The carnal divisions and contentions amongst Christians, so common, are not the symptoms of that kingdom. But for men to entitle themselves, upon this principle, that they are the only men to rule kingdoms, govern nations, and give laws to people; to determine of property, and liberty, and every thing else, upon such a pretence as this is; truly, they had need give clear manifestations of God's presence with them, before wise men will receive or submit to their conclusions.[6] Besides, certainly though many of these men have good meanings, as I hope in my soul they have, yet it will be the wisdom of all knowing and experienced Christians to do as Jude saith: when he had reckoned up those horrible things done upon pretences, and happily by some upon mistakes, 'Of some,' says he, 'have compassion, making a difference; others save with fear, pulling them out of the fire.'[7] I fear they will give opportunity too often for this exercise, and I hope the same will be for their good.

If men do but pretend for justice and righteousness, and be of peaceable spirits, and will manifest this, let them be the subjects of the magistrate's en-

---

[5] Cromwell apparently has been alluding to the consequences of Archbishop Laud's literal, though strict, enforcement of the Act of Uniformity. His position is this: Religious restrictions enforced according to the letter of the law allow outward conformists to believe privately whatever they wish. They may even embrace "popery" or atheism; and all this is bad. Furthermore, the magistrate who is a strict verbalist can, if he wishes, blink at "villanies" that are not spelled out in the law. Moreover, a law specifying ordination as a requirement for preaching works two ways: it prevents a non-ordained person from preaching though he has "good testimony" and "gifts from Christ"; and it does not require the ordained minister to preach if he wishes not to. (Incidentally, the controversy over the qualifications of the preacher had raged in the open since *The First Admonition to Parliament* in 1572.)

[6] Cromwell objected to the Fifth Monarchy because spirituality did not necessarily confer either practical or political wisdom.

[7] Jude 22:23.

couragement. And if the magistrate, by punishing visible miscarriages, save them by that discipline, (God having ordained him for that end) I hope it will evidence love, and no hatred to punish where there is cause. Indeed this is that which doth most declare the danger of that spirit; for if these were but notions, I mean the instances that I have given you both of civil considerations and spiritual; if, I say, they were but notions, they were to be let alone. Notions will hurt none but them that have them: but when they come to such practices, as to tell us, that liberty and property are not the badges of the kingdom of Christ; and tell us, that, instead of regulating laws, laws are to be abrogated, indeed subverted; and perhaps would bring in the Judaical law, instead of our known laws settled amongst us, this is worthy of every magistrate's consideration; especially where every stone is turned to bring confusion.

Whilst these things were in the midst of us, and the nation rent and torn, in spirit and principle from one end to another, after this sort and manner I have now told you; family against family; husband against wife; parents against children; and nothing in the hearts and minds of men but 'Overturn, Overturn, Overturn' (a scripture phrase very much abused, and applied to justify unpeaceable practices by all men of discontented spirits), the common adversary in the mean time sleeps not. And our adversaries, in civil and spiritual respects, did take advantage at these divisions and distractions, and did practice accordingly in the three nations. We know very well that emissaries of the Jesuits never came in those swarms as they have done since these things were set on foot.[8] And I tell you, that divers gentlemen here can bear witness with me, how that they have had a consistory abroad, that rules all the affairs of things in England, from an archbishop down to the other dependents upon him. And they had fixed in England (of which we are able to produce the particular instruments in most of the limits of the cathedrals) an Episcopal power, with archdeacons, and so on; and had persons authorized to exercise and distribute those things, who pervert and deceive the people. And all this, while we were in this sad, and, as I said, deplorable condition. In the mean time, all endeavours possible were used to hinder the work in Ireland, and the progress of the work of God in Scotland, by continual intelligences and correspondences, both at home and abroad; from hence into Ireland, and from hence into Scotland, persons were stirred up and encouraged, from these divisions and discomposure of affairs, to do all they could to encourage and foment the war in both these places. To add yet to our misery: whilst we were in this condition we were deeply engaged in a war with the Portuguese, whereby our trade ceased, and the evil consequences by that war were manifest and very considerable. And not only this, but we had a war with Holland, consuming our treasure, occasioning a vast burden upon the people; a war that cost this nation full as much as the taxes came unto; the navy being 160 ships, which cost this nation above 100,000*l.* a month, besides the contingences, which would make it 120,000*l.* a month. That very one war did engage us to so great a charge. At the same time also we were in a war with France. The advantages that were taken at the discontents and divisions among ourselves, did also foment that war, and at least hinder us of an honourable peace, every man being confident we could not hold out long. And surely they did not calculate amiss, if the Lord had not been exceeding gracious to us. I say, at the same time, we had a war with

---

[8] The Jesuits established a seminary in France in the late sixteenth century, which trained English Catholics and planned a Church hierarchy complete in every detail.

France. And besides the sufferings, in respect of the trade of the nation, 'tis most evident, that the purse of the nation had not possibly been able longer to bear it, by reason of the advantages taken by other states to improve their own and spoil our manufacture of cloth, and hinder the vent [sale] thereof; which is the great staple commodity of this nation.

This was our condition: spoiled in our trade, and we at this vast expense; thus dissettled at home, and having these engagements abroad. These things being thus, what a heap of confusions were upon these poor nations! And either things must have been left to have sunk into the miseries these premises would suppose, or a remedy must be applied.

A remedy hath been applied; that hath been this government, a thing that I shall say little unto.[9] The thing is open and visible to be seen and read by all men; and therefore let it speak for itself. Only let me say this, because I can speak it with comfort and confidence before a greater than you all, that is, before the Lord, that, in the intention of it, as to the approving our hearts to God—let men judge as they please—it is calculated for the interest of the people, for the interest of the people alone, and for their good, without respect had to any other interest. And if that be not true, I shall be bold to say again, let it speak for itself. Truly I may (I hope humbly before God, and [with] modesty before you) say somewhat on the behalf of the government: that is (not to discourse of the particular heads of it), to acquaint you a little with the effects of it; and that not for ostentation's sake, but to the end that I may deal at this time faithfully with you, by acquainting you with the state of things, and what proceedings have been upon this government, that so you may know the state of our affairs. This is the main end of my putting you to this trouble.

It hath had some things in desire, and it hath done some things actually. It hath desired to reform the laws: I say, to reform them; and, for that end, it hath called together persons (without reflection) of as great ability, and as great integrity, as are in these nations, to consider how the laws might be made plain and short, and less chargeable to the people; how to lessen expense for the good of the nation; and those things are in preparation, and bills prepared, which in due time, I make no question, will be tendered to you. There hath been care taken to put the administration of the laws into the hands of just men, men of the most known integrity and ability. The Chancery hath been reformed, and, I hope, to the just satisfaction of all good men; and for the things depending there, which made the burden and work of the honourable persons intrusted in those services beyond their ability, it hath referred many of them to those places where Englishmen love to have their rights tried, the courts of law at Westminster. It hath endeavoured to put a stop to that heady way (touched of likewise this day) of every man making himself a Minister and a Preacher. It hath endeavoured to settle a way for the approbation of men of piety and ability for the discharge of that work: and, I think I may say, it hath committed that work to the trust of persons, both of the Presbyterian and Independent judgments, men of as known ability, piety, and integrity as, I believe, any this nation hath. And I believe also, that in that care they have taken, they have laboured to approve themselves to Christ, the nation, and their own consciences. And indeed I think if

---

[9] By "this government" is meant the Instrument of Government under whose authority Cromwell had called Parliament.

there be anything of quarrel against them, it is, (though I am not here to justify the proceedings of any) I say it is, that they go upon such a character as the Scripture warrants, to put men into that great employment, and to approve men for it, who are men that have received gifts from him that ascended up on high, and gave gifts for the work of the ministry, and for the edifying of the body of Christ. It hath taken care, we hope, for the expulsion of all those who may be judged any way unfit for this work; who are scandalous, and the common scorn and contempt of that administration.

One thing more this government hath done: It hath been instrumental to call a Free Parliament; which, blessed be God, we see here this day—I say, a Free Parliament. And that it may continue so, I hope is in the heart and spirit of every good man in England, save such discontented persons as I have formerly mentioned. It is that which, as I have desired above my life, I shall desire to keep it so above my life. I did before mention to you the plunges we were in, in respect of foreign states, by the war with Portugal, France, the Dutch, the Danes, and the little assurance we had from any of our neighbours round about. I perhaps forgot it, but indeed it was a caution upon my mind, and I desire that it might be so understood, that if any good hath been done, it was the Lord, not we his poor instruments. I did instance in the wars which did exhaust your treasure, and put you into such a condition that you must have sunk therein, if it had continued but a few months longer. This I dare affirm, if strong probability can give me a ground. You have now, though it be not the first in time, peace with Swedeland; an honourable peace, through the endeavours of an honourable person here present [Mr. Whitlocke] as the instrument. I say, you have an honourable peace with a kingdom that, not many years since, was much a friend to France, and lately, perhaps, inclinable enough to the Spaniard. And I believe you expect not very much good from any of your Catholic neighbours; nor yet that they would be very willing you should have a good understanding with your Protestant friends. Yet, thanks be to God, that peace is concluded and, as I said before, it is an honourable peace. You have a peace with the Danes: a state that lay contiguous to that part of this Island which hath given us the most trouble. And certainly, if your enemies abroad be able to annoy you, it is likely they will take their advantage, where it best lies, to give you trouble there. But you have a peace there, and an honourable one; satisfaction for your merchants' ships, not only to their content, but to their rejoicing. I believe you will easily know it is so. You have the Sound [10] open, which was obstructed. That which was, and is, the strength of this nation, the shipping, will now be supplied thence. And whereas you were glad to have any thing of that kind at the second hand, you have all manner of commerce, and at as much freedom as the Dutch themselves, there, and at the same rates and tolls; and, I think I may say, by that peace, they cannot raise the same upon you.

You have a peace with the Dutch: a peace unto which I shall say little, because so well known in the benefit and consequences of it; and I think it was as desirable and as acceptable to the spirit of this nation, as any one thing that lay before us. And, as I believe, nothing so much gratified our enemies as to see us at odds; so, I persuade myself, nothing is of more terror nor trouble to them, than to see us thus reconciled. As a peace with the Protestant states hath much security in it,

[10] The Baltic Sea, which the Danes had closed.

so it hath as much of honour and of assurance to the Protestant interest abroad, without which no assistance can be given thereunto. I wish it may be written upon our hearts to be zealous for that interest; for if ever it were like to come under a condition of suffering, it is now. In all the emperor's patrimonial territories, the endeavour is to drive them out as fast as they can, and they are necessitated to run to Protestant states to seek their bread; and by this conjunction of interests, I hope, you will be in a more fit capacity to help them; and it begets some reviving of their spirits that you will help them as opportunity shall serve.

You have a peace likewise with Portugal; which peace, though it hung long in hand, yet is lately concluded. It is a peace that your merchants make us believe is of good concernment to their trade; their assurance being greater, and so their profit in trade thither, than to other places. And this hath been obtained in that treaty, (which never was since the Inquisition was set up there) that our people which trade thither have liberty of conscience. Indeed, peace is, as you were well told to-day, desireable with all men, as far as it may be had with conscience and honour. We are upon a treaty with France. And we may say this, that if God give us honour in the eyes of the nations about us, we have reason to bless him for it, and so to own it. And I dare say that there is not a nation in Europe, but they are very willing to ask a good understanding with you.

I am sorry I am thus tedious; but I did judge that it was somewhat necessary to acquaint you with these things. And things being thus, I hope you will be willing to hear a little again of the sharp as well as the sweet; and I should not be faithful to you, nor to the interest of these nations which you and I serve, if I should not let you know all. As I said before, when this government was undertaken, we were in the midst of these divisions, and animosities, and scatterings; also thus engaged with these enemies round about us, at such a vast charge, 120,000l. a month for the very fleet, which was the very utmost penny of your assessments; aye, and then all your treasure was exhausted and spent when this government was undertaken; all accidental ways of bringing in treasure, to a very inconsiderable sum, consumed: that is to say, the lands were sold; the treasures spent; rents, fee-farms, king's, queen's, princes', bishops', dean and chapters', delinquents' lands, sold. These were spent when this government was undertaken.[11] I think it is my duty to let you know so much: and that is the reason why the taxes do yet lie so heavy upon the people; of which we have abated 30,000l. a month for the next three months.

Truly I thought it my duty to let you know, that though God hath dealt thus with you, yet these are but entrances and doors of hope; wherein, through the blessing of God, you may enter into rest and peace. But you are not yet entered. You were told to-day of a people brought out of Egypt towards the land of Canaan; but through unbelief, murmuring, repining, and other temptations and sins, wherewith God was provoked, they were fain to come back again, and linger many years in the wilderness before they came to the place of rest. We are thus far through the mercy of God. We have cause to take notice of it, that we are not brought into misery; but, as I said before, a door of hope open. And I may say this to you, if the Lord's blessing and his presence go along with the

---

[11] Cromwell is saying in effect: We are now supporting this government by direct taxes ("assessments"), for long ago we sold off Crown properties and they can be no further source of revenue.

management of affairs at this meeting, you will be enabled to put the top-stone to this work, and make the nation happy. But this must be by knowing the true state of affairs; you are yet, like the people under circumcision, but raw; your peaces are but newly made; and it is a maxim not to be despised, though peace be made, yet it is interest that keeps peace. And I hope you will trust it no further than you see interest upon it: and therefore I wish that you may go forward, and not backward; and that you may have the blessing of God upon your endeavours.

It is one of the great ends of calling this parliament, that this ship of the Commonwealth may be brought into a safe harbour; which, I assure you, it will not well be, without your counsel and advice. You have great works upon your hands. You have Ireland to look unto; there is not much done towards the planting [developing] of it, though some things leading and preparing for it are. It is a great business to settle the government of that nation upon fit terms, such as will bear that work through. You have had likewise laid before you the considerations intimating your peace with some foreign States, but yet you have not made peace with all.

And if they should see we do not manage our affairs with that wisdom which becomes us, truly we may sink under disadvantages for all that is done. And our enemies will have their eyes open and be revived, if they see animosities amongst us; which indeed will be their great advantage. I do therefore persuade you to a sweet, gracious, and holy understanding of one another, and of your business, concerning which you had so good counsel this day; that indeed, as it rejoiced my heart to hear it, so I hope the Lord will imprint it upon your spirits; wherein you shall have my prayers.

Having said this, and perhaps omitted many other material things through the frailty of my memory, I shall exercise plainness and freeness with you, in telling you that I have not spoken these things as one that assumes to himself dominion over you, but as one that doth resolve to be a fellow servant with you, to the interest of these great affairs, and of the people of these nations. I shall therefore trouble you no longer, but desire you to repair to your house, and to exercise your own liberty in the choice of a Speaker, that so you may lose no time in carrying on your work.

Bibliographical Note

Cromwell continues to be a controversial figure and has been much written about. Standard works are Wilbur Cortez Abbott, *The Writings and Speeches of Oliver Cromwell*, 4 vols. (1937); Robert S. Paul, *The Lord Protector: Religion and Politics in the Life of Oliver Cromwell* (1955); and C. V. Wedgwood, *Oliver Cromwell* (1956). Abbott has exercised great care with the texts of the speeches. For an appreciation of social and political ideas and attitudes, see Godfrey Davies, *The Early Stuarts, 1603–1660* (1937), and J. R. Tanner, *English Constitutional Conflicts of the Seventeenth Century* (1928). See also Paul H. Hardacre, "Writings on Oliver Cromwell Since 1929," *Journal of Modern History*, XXXIII (March, 1961), 1–14; and Frederick G. Marcham, "Oliver Cromwell, Orator," in *The Rhetorical Idiom*, ed. D. C. Bryant (1958), pp. 179–200.

John Tillotson

(1630–1694)

Dr. John Tillotson may be said to have made religion reasonable to a whole generation and to have stamped upon the English sermon the mark of plain rationality. Born of a Puritan family and equipped with the traditional grammar school education, Tillotson entered Cambridge at the age of seventeen, and was there attracted by the keenness of Calvinist theologians and deeply impressed by William Chillingworth's *The Religion of Protestants* (1637). He became a close friend of John Wilkins and allied himself with a group who sought to free men "from superstitions, conceits, and fierceness about opinions."

Abandoning Presbyterianism, Tillotson became a good Anglican, chaplain to Charles II, Dean of St. Paul's, and Archbishop of Canterbury. His urban congregations at Lincoln's Inn, St. Lawrence-Jewry, and St. Paul's, composed mostly of professional and middle-class people, admired his good sense, plain preaching, earnestness, and spotless character. He became one of the great preachers of Restoration England.

Tillotson developed a practical theology that emphasized the reasonableness of ethics and morality. In this respect he was not of his age, but of an age to come. His election to the Royal Society in 1672 signified not only that he was acceptable to men of science but that he believed in the rule of universal law. Revealed religion, he held, cannot be contrary to the "natural notions" of man. "The Scripture useth the word faith largely for a real persuasion of anything, whether grounded upon sense or reason, or upon divine revelation." And "if men would be contented to speak justly of things and pretend to no greater assurance than they can bring evidence of, considerate men would be more apt to believe them." He sought to bring all Protestants together in a single creed, a goal most clearly seen, and argued with utmost tact, in the "Sermon at the Yorkshire Feast." We may apply to Tillotson what was said of another divine a century later, that he made Christianity so reasonable that it seemed immoral not to accept it.

The sermon we print is the last one Tillotson preached before a royal audience. It is not so famous as "The Wisdom of Being Religious," an early sermon much too long to include here. But it is an outstanding example of limpid rationality, and it reflects some of the criteria of sermonizing that Tillotson derived from Wilkins' book on preaching, *Ecclesiastes* (1646). Evident is Tillotson's fondness for precise structure, much admired by his Restoration colleagues, and his respect for the chief movements in a sermon: explication, confirmation, and application. The minute, hairsplitting analysis of each word in a scriptural text, so prized by Andrewes and Donne and the scholastics, has given way to a general setting of the text; and the exhortation, in earlier times often vivid, sharp, and emotional, has made way for the quiet, pointed suggestion. The new feature of sermonizing, one that was to be popular in the following fifty years, is an emphasis on straightforward argument, plainly put. As a result, as Bishop Gilbert Burnet said at Tillotson's funeral, few men "ever heard him, but they found some new thought occurred; something that either they had not considered before, or at least not so distinctly, and with so clear a view as he gave them."

Tillotson's style is plain and direct, its transparency perhaps the outcome of a scientific view of diction. In 1668 Wilkins and Tillotson worked on a dictionary, and later published an essay toward "the real character" of a philosophical language. Ever after, the young minister monitored "the truth of language and style" in his own utterance. His general aim, he said in one sermon, was to preach "what men might understand, and what they ought to believe and practice, in a plain and unaffected, and convincing manner." He did not "intend to follow the metaphor too close, and to vex and torture it by pursuing all those little parallels and similitudes, which a lively fancy might make or find." There are no high flights of diction in Tillotson, as there are in Jeremy Taylor, Isaac Barrow, or Robert South. His language is carefully modulated, reminiscent of the essay.

John Beardmore, once Tillotson's sizar at Cambridge, has left a word portrait of his friend. "His countenance was fair and very amiable; his face round, his eyes vivid, and his air and aspect quick and ingenuous; all which were the index of his excellent soul and spirit. His hair was brown and bushy; he was moderately tall; very slender and sparing in his youth; his constitution but tender and frail to outward appearance. He became corpulent and fat, when grown in age, which increased more and more as long as he lived; but yet was neither a burden to himself, nor in the least unseemly to others." If we may accept Burnet, Tillotson always "read his sermons with so due a pronunciation, in so sedate and so solemn a manner, that they were not the feebler, but rather the perfecter, even by that way, which often lessens the grace, as much as it adds to the exactness of such discourses."

∽

Sermon Against Evil Speaking *

Before King William and Queen Mary at Whitehall
February 25, 1694

To speak evil of no man.—Titus 3:2.

General persuasives to repentance and a good life, and invectives against sin and wickedness at large, are certainly of good use to recommend religion and

* The text adheres closely to that in *The Works of Dr. John Tillotson . . . with the Life of the Author by Thomas Birch*, 10 Vols. (1820), III, 249–78. There were a number of separate printings of the sermon, the fifth appearing in 1709. From these it has been possible to remove a few ambiguities in Birch's text. Tillotson presided over the publication of some of his sermons and is not known to have made substantial changes. He would not have needed to create a verbatim text from notes at some time after delivery, for his habit was to read from a complete manuscript. On this point we have testimony other than Burnet's. Birch reports that Dr. Maynard, Tillotson's successor at Lincoln's Inn, was told by the Archbishop himself "that he had always written every word, before he preached it, but used to get it by heart till he found that it heated his head so much a day or two before and after he preached that he was forced to leave it off." (*Life*, p. 416.)

virtue, and to expose the deformity and danger of a vicious course. But it must be acknowledged, on the other hand, that these general discourses do not so immediately tend to reform the lives of men: because they fall among the crowd, but [do] not touch the consciences of particular persons in so sensible and awakening a manner, as when we treat of particular duties and sins, and endeavour to put men upon the practice of the one, and to reclaim them from the other, by proper arguments taken from the word of God, and from the nature of particular virtues and vices.

The general way is, as if a physician, instead of applying particular remedies to the distemper of his patient, should entertain him with a long discourse of diseases in general, and of the pleasure and advantages of health, and earnestly persuade him to be well, without taking his particular disease into consideration, and prescribing remedies for it.

But if we would effectually reform men, we must take to task the great and common disorders of their lives, and represent their faults to them in such a manner, as may convince them of the evil and danger of them, and put them upon the endeavour of a cure.

And to this end I have pitched upon one of the common and reigning vices of the age, calumny and evil speaking, by which men contract so much guilt to themselves, and create so much trouble to others, and from which, it is to be feared, few or none are wholly free.[1] For "Who is he (saith the son of Sirach) that hath not offended with his tongue?"[2] "In many things (saith St. James) we offend all: and if any man offend not in word, the same is a perfect man."[3]

But how few have attained to this perfection: and yet, unless we do endeavour after it, and in some good measure attain it, all our pretence to religion is vain: so the same apostle tells us, "If any man among you seemeth to be religious, and bridleth not his tongue, but deceiveth his own heart, that man's religion is vain."[4]

For the more distinct handling of this argument, I shall reduce my discourse to these five heads:

First, I shall consider the nature of this vice, and wherein it consists.

Secondly, I shall consider the due extent of this prohibition, "To speak evil of no man."

[1] Tillotson is probably alluding to the general situation in Restoration England which he characterized briefly at the time he was preparing Wilkins' sermons for publication. He grouped ten of the sermons together because they tended "to reform the several vices of the tongue," particularly in "atheistical discourses, and blasphemous raillery, and profane swearing . . . when censoriousness, detraction and slander are scarce accounted faults, even with those who would seem to be most strict in other parts and duties of religion." [The Introduction to Wilkins' sermons as reproduced by F. H., *The Life of the Most Reverend Father in God John Tillotson . . . compiled from the Minutes of the Reverend Mr. Young . . .* (1717), pp. 65, 66.] Tillotson himself had come under criticism by the uncharitable and ill-tempered for his fairness in dealing with his enemies, the Socinians. John Jortin, Rector of St. Dunstan's in the East, believed he would never be forgiven because he had "broken an ancient and fundamental rule of theological controversy, *allow not an adversary to have either common sense or common honesty.*" An example of the rule can be taken from Robert South: "The Socinians are impious blasphemers, whose infamous pedigree runs back [*from wretch to wretch*] in a direct line to the devil himself." (Birch, *Life*, p. 427.)

[2] Ecclesiasticus 19:16.

[3] James 3:2.

[4] James 1:26.

Thirdly, I shall shew the evil of this practice, both in the causes and effects of it.

Fourthly, I shall add some farther considerations to dissuade men from it.

Fifthly, I shall give some rules and directions for the prevention and cure of it.

I shall consider what this sin or vice of evil speaking, here forbidden by the apostle, is: μηδένα βλασφημειν, not to defame and slander any man, not to hurt his reputation, as the etymology of the word doth import. So that this vice consists in saying things of others which tend to their disparagement and reproach, to the taking away or lessening of their reputation and good name. And this, whether the things said be true or not. If they be false, and we know it, then it is downright calumny, and if we do not know it, but take it upon the report of others, it is however a slander; and so much the more injurious, because really groundless and undeserved.

If the thing be true, and we know it to be so, yet it is a defamation, and tends to the prejudice of our neighbour's reputation: and it is a fault to say the evil of others which is true, unless there be some good reason for it besides; because it is contrary to that charity and goodness which Christianity requires, to divulge the faults of others, though they be really guilty of them, without necessity, or some other very good reason for it.

Again, it is evil speaking and the vice condemned in the text, whether we be the first authors of an ill report, or relate it from others: because the man that is evil spoken of is equally defamed either way.

Again, whether we speak evil of a man to his face, or behind his back: the former way indeed seems to be the more generous, but yet is a great fault, and that which we call reviling; the latter is more mean and base, and that which we properly call slander or backbiting.

And, lastly, whether it be done directly and in express terms, or more obscurely and by way of oblique insinuation; whether by way of downright reproach, or with some crafty preface of commendation: for so it have the effect to defame, the manner of address does not much alter the case; the one may be more dexterous, but is not one jot less faulty. For many times the deepest wounds are given by these smoother and more artificial ways of slander: as by asking questions, "Have you not heard so and so of such a man? I say no more; I only ask the question." Or by general intimations, that—they are loath to say what they have heard of such an one, are very sorry for, and do not at all believe it—if you will believe them; and this many times without telling the thing, but leaving you in the dark to suspect the worst.

These and such-like arts, though they may seem to be tenderer and gentler ways of using men's reputation, yet in truth they are the most malicious and effectual methods of slander, because they insinuate something that is much worse than is said, and yet are very apt to create in unwary men a strong belief of something that is very bad, though they know not what it is. So that it matters not in what fashion a slander is dressed up; if it tend to defame a man, and to diminish his reputation, it is the sin forbidden in the text.

We will consider the extent of this prohibition, "To speak evil of no man"; and the due bounds and limitations of it. For it is not to be understood absolutely to forbid us to say any thing concerning others that is bad. This in some cases may be necessary and our duty, and in several cases very fit and reasonable. The question is, In what cases, by the general rules of Scripture and right reason, we are warranted to say the evil of others that is true?

In general, we are not to do this without great reason and necessity, as for the prevention of some great evil, or the procuring of some considerable good to ourselves, or others. And this I take to be the meaning of that advice of the son of Sirach: "Whether it be to a friend or a foe, talk not of other men's lives; and if thou canst without offence, reveal them not";[5] that is, if without hurt to anybody thou canst conceal them, divulge them not.

But because this may not be direction sufficient, I shall instance in some of the principal cases wherein men are warranted to speak evil of others, and yet in so doing, do not offend against this prohibition in the text.

First, it is not only lawful, but very commendable, and many times our duty, to do this in order to the probable amendment of the person of whom evil is spoken. In such a case we may tell a man of his faults privately: or, where it may not be so fit for us to use that boldness and freedom, we may reveal his faults to one who is more fit and proper to reprove him, and will probably make no other use of this discovery but in order to his amendment. And this is so far from being a breach of charity, that it is one of the best testimonies of it: for perhaps the party may not be guilty of what hath been reported of him, and then it is a kindness to give him the opportunity of vindicating himself; or, if he be guilty, perhaps being privately and prudently told of it he may reform. In this case the son of Sirach adviseth to reveal men's faults: "Admonish a friend (says he); it may be he hath not done it; and if he have done it, that he do it no more: admonish a friend, it may be he hath not said it; and if he have, that he speak it not again: admonish a friend, for many times it is a slander; and believe not every tale."[6]

But then we must take care that this be done out of kindness, and that nothing of our own passion be mingled with it: and that under pretence of reproving and reforming men, we do not reproach and revile them, and tell them of their faults in such a manner, as if we did not shew our authority rather than our charity. It requires a great deal of address and gentle application so to manage the business of reproof, as not to irritate and exasperate the person whom we reprove instead of curing him.

Secondly, this likewise is not only lawful, but our duty, when we are legally called to bear witness concerning the fault and crime of another. A good man would not be an accuser, unless the public good, or the prevention of some great evil, should require it; and then the plain reason of the thing will sufficiently justify a voluntary accusation. Otherwise it hath always among well-mannered people been esteemed very odious for a man to be officious in this kind, and a forward informer concerning the misdemeanours of others. Magistrates may sometimes think it fit to give encouragement to such persons, and to set one bad man to catch another, because such men are fittest for such dirty work; but they can never inwardly approve them, nor will they ever make them their friends and confidants.

But when a man is called to give testimony in this kind in obedience to the laws and out of reverence to the oath taken in such cases, he is so far from deserving blame for so doing, that it would be an unpardonable fault in him to conceal the truth, or any part of it.

Thirdly, it is lawful to publish the faults of others, in our own necessary de-

---

[5] Ecclesiasticus 19:8.
[6] *Ibid.*, 13–15.

fence and vindication. When a man cannot conceal another's faults without betraying his own innocency, no charity requires a man to suffer himself to be defamed to save the reputation of another man. Charity begins at home; and though a man had never so much goodness, he would first secure his own good name, and then be concerned for other men's. We are to love our neighbour as ourselves; so that the love of ourselves is the rule and measure of our love to our neighbour, and therefore first, otherwise it could not be the rule. And it would be very well for the world if our charity would rise thus high, and no man would hurt another man's reputation, but where his own is in real danger.

Fourthly, this also is lawful for caution and warning to a third person that is in danger to be infected by the company or ill example of another; or may be greatly prejudiced, by reposing too much confidence in him, having no knowledge or suspicion of his bad qualities: but even in this case, we ought to take great care that the ill character we give of any man be spread no further than is necessary to the good end we designed in it.

Besides these more obvious and remarkable cases, this prohibition doth not I think hinder, but that in ordinary conversation men may mention that ill of others which is already made as public as it well can be; or that one friend may not in freedom speak to another of the miscarriage of a third person, where he is secure no ill use will be made of it, and that it will go no further to his prejudice—provided always, that we take no delight in hearing or speaking ill of others. And the less we do it, though without any malice or design of harm, still the better; because this shews that we do not feed upon ill reports and take pleasure in them.

These are all the usual cases in which it may be necessary for us to speak evil of other men. And these are so evidently reasonable, that the prohibition in the text cannot with reason be extended to them. And if no man would allow himself to say anything to the prejudice of another man's good name but in these and the like cases, the tongues of men would be very innocent, and the world would be very quiet.

I proceed, in the third place, to consider the evil of this practice, both in the causes and the consequences of it.

First, we will consider the causes of it. And it commonly springs from one or more of these evil roots.

First, one of the deepest and most common causes of evil speaking is ill-nature and cruelty of disposition; and by a general mistake ill-nature passeth for wit, as cunning doth for wisdom, though in truth they are nothing akin to one another, but as far distant as vice and virtue.

And there is no greater evidence of the bad temper of mankind, than the general proneness of men to this vice. For (as our Saviour says) "out of the abundance of the heart the mouth speaketh."[7] And therefore men do commonly incline to the censorious and uncharitable side, which shews human nature to be strangely distorted from its original rectitude and innocency. The wit of man doth more naturally vent itself in satire and censure, than in praise and panegyric. When men set themselves to commend, it comes hardly from them, and not without great force and straining; and if any thing be fitly said in that kind, it doth hardly relish with most men. But in the way of invective, the invention of men is a plentiful and never-failing spring; and this kind of wit is not more easy than

[7] Luke 6:45.

it is acceptable: it is greedily entertained and greatly applauded, and every man is glad to hear others abused, not considering how soon it may come to his own turn to lie down and make sport for others.

To speak evil of others is almost become the general entertainment of all companies; and the great and serious business of most meetings and visits, after the necessary ceremonies and compliments are over, is to sit down and backbite all the world. It is the sauce of conversation, and all discourse is counted but flat and dull which hath not something of piquancy and sharpness in it against somebody. For men generally love rather to hear evil of others than good, and are secretly pleased with ill reports, and drink them in with greediness and delight, though at the same time they have so much justice as to hate those that propagate them, and so much wit, as to conclude that these very persons will do the same for them in another place and company.

But especially if it concerns one of another party, and that differs from us in matters of religion; in this case, all parties seem to be agreed that they do God great service in blasting the reputation of their adversaries. And though they all pretend to be Christians, and the disciples of him who taught nothing but kindness and meekness and charity, yet it is strange to see with what a savage and murderous disposition they will fly at one another's reputation, and tear it in pieces. And, whatever other scruples they may have, they make none to bespatter one another in the most bitter and slanderous manner.

But if they hear any good of their adversaries, with what nicety and caution do they receive it; how many objections do they raise against it; and with what coldness do they at last admit it. "It is very well (say they) if it be true; I shall be glad to hear it confirmed. I never heard so much good of him before. You are a good man yourself, but have a care you be not deceived."

Nay, it is well if, to balance the matter and set things even, they do not clap some infirmity and fault into the other scale, that so the enemy may not go off with flying colours.

But, on the other side, every man is a good and substantial author of an ill report. I do not apply this to any one sort of men, though all are to blame in this way: *Iliacos intra muros peccatur, et extra.*[8] To speak impartially, the zealots of all parties have got a scurvy trick of lying for the truth.

But of all sorts of people, I have observed the priests and bigots of the church of Rome to be the ablest in this way, and to have the strongest faith for a lusty falsehood and calumny. Others will bandy a false report, and toss it from one hand to another, but I never knew any that would so hug a lie, and be so very fond of it. They seem to be described by St. John in that expression in the Revelation, "whosoever loveth and maketh a lie."[9]

Another shrewd sign that ill-nature lies at the root of this vice is that we easily forget the good that is said of others, and seldom make mention of it; but the contrary sticks with us, and lies uppermost in our memories, and is ready to come out upon all occasions. And which is yet more ill-natured and unjust, many times when we do not believe it ourselves, we tell it to others, with this charitable caution—that we hope it is not true. But in the meantime we give it our pass, and venture it to take its fortune to be believed or not, according to the charity of those into whose hands it comes.

[8] "Error springs within us as well as outside us." Horace, *Epistles*, i.2.6.
[9] Perhaps Revelation 21:27.

Secondly, another cause of the commonness of this vice is, that many are so bad themselves in one kind or other. For to think and speak ill of others is not only a bad thing, but a sign of a bad man. Our blessed Saviour, speaking of the evil of the last days, gives this as the reason of the great decay of charity among men: "Because iniquity shall abound, the love of many shall wax cold." [10] When men are bad themselves, they are glad of any opportunity to censure others, and are always apt to suspect that evil of other men which they know by themselves. They cannot have a good opinion of themselves, and therefore are very unwilling to have so of anybody else; and for this reason they endeavour to bring men to a level, hoping it will be some justification of them if they can but render others as bad as themselves.

Thirdly, another source of this vice is malice and revenge. When men are in heat and passion, they do not consider what is true, but what is spiteful and mischievous; and speak evil of others in revenge of some injury which they have received from them; and when they are blinded by their passions, they lay about them madly and at a venture, not much caring whether the evil they speak be true or not. Nay, many are so devilish, as to invent and raise false reports on purpose to blast men's reputation. This is a diabolical temper, and therefore St. James tells us, that the slanderous tongue is "set on fire of hell"; [11] and the devil hath his very name from calumny and false accusation; and it is his nature too, for he is always ready to stir up and foment this evil spirit among men. Nay, the Scripture tells us that he hath the malice and impudence to accuse good men before God, as he did Job, charging him with hypocrisy to God himself who he knows does know the hearts of all the children of men.

Fourthly, another cause of evil-speaking is envy. Men look with an evil eye upon the good that is in others, and think that their reputation obscures them, and that their commendable qualities do stand in their light; and therefore they do what they can to cast a cloud over them, that the bright shining of their virtues may not scorch them. This makes them greedily to entertain, and industriously to publish anything that may serve to that purpose, thereby to raise themselves upon the ruins of other men's reputation. And therefore, as soon as they have got an ill report of any good man by the end, to work they presently go to send it abroad by the first post; for the string is always ready upon their bow to let fly this arrow with an incredible swiftness, through city and country, for fear the innocent man's justification should overtake it.

Fifthly, another cause of evil-speaking is impertinence and curiosity, an itch of talking and meddling in the affairs of other men, which do no wise concern them. Some persons love to mingle themselves in all business, and are loath to seem ignorant of so important a piece of news as the faults and follies of men, or any bad thing that is talked of in good company. And therefore they do with great care pick up ill stories, as good matter of discourse in the next company that is worthy of them: and this perhaps not out of any great malice, but for want of something better to talk of, and because their parts lie chiefly that way.

Lastly, men do this many times out of wantonness and for diversion. So little do light and vain men consider that a man's reputation is too great and tender a concernment to be jested withal, and that a slanderous tongue bites like a serpent

[10] Matt. 24:12.
[11] James 3:6.

and wounds like a sword. For what can be more barbarous, next to sporting with a man's life, than to play with his honour and reputation, which to some men is dearer to them than their lives?

It is a cruel pleasure which some men take in worrying the reputation of others much better than themselves, and this only to divert themselves and the company. Solomon compares this sort of men to distracted persons: "As a madman (saith he) who casteth fire-brands, arrows and death, so is the man that deceiveth his neighbour": [12] The LXX render it, "so is the man that defameth his neighbour, and saith, Am I not in sport?" [13] Such and so bad are the causes of this vice.

I proceed to consider, in the second place, the ordinary, but very pernicious consequences and effects of it, both to others and to ourselves.

First, to others—the parties I mean that are slandered. To them it is certainly a great injury, and commonly a high provocation, but always matter of no small grief and trouble to them. It is certainly a great injury, and if the evil which we say of them be not true, it is an injury beyond imagination, and beyond all possible reparation. And though we should do our utmost endeavour afterwards towards their vindication, yet that makes but very little amends; because the vindication seldom reacheth so far as the reproach, and because commonly men are neither so forward to spread the vindication, nor is it so easily received, after ill impressions are once made. The solicitous vindication of a man's self is at the best but an after-game; and, for the most part, a man had better sit still, than to run the hazard of making the matter worse by playing it.

I will add one thing more—that it is an injury that descends to a man's children and posterity; because the good or ill name of the father is derived down to them, and many times the best thing he hath to leave them is the reputation of his unblemished virtue and worth. And do we make no conscience to rob his innocent children of the best part of this small patrimony, and of all the kindness that would have been done them for their father's sake, if his reputation had not been so undeservedly stained? Is it no crime by the breath of our mouth at once to blast a man's reputation, and to ruin his children, perhaps to all posterity? Can we make a jest of so serious a matter? Of an injury so very hard to be repented of as it ought, because in such a case no repentance will be acceptable without restitution, if it be in our power. And perhaps it will undo us in this world to make it; and if we do it not, will be our ruin in the other.

I will put the case at the best, that the matter of the slander is true; yet no man's reputation is considerably stained, though never so deservedly, without great harm and damage to him. And it is great odds but the matter by passing through several hands is aggravated beyond truth, every one out of his bounty being apt to add something to it.

But besides the injury, it is commonly a very high provocation. And the consequence of that may be as bad as we can imagine, and may end in dangerous and desperate quarrels. This reason the wise son of Sirach gives why we should defame no man: "Whether it be (says he) to a friend or a foe, talk not of other men's lives. For he hath heard and observed thee"—that is, one way or other it

[12] Prov. 26:18–19.

[13] "LXX" is a reference to the Septuagint, an early version of the Old Testament prepared by seventy (or seventy-two?) Jerusalem scholars working at Alexandria at Ptolemy II's request, about 278–270 B.C.

will probably come to his knowledge—"and when the time cometh, he will shew his hatred" [14]—that is, he will take the first opportunity to revenge it.

At the best, it is always matter of grief to the person that is defamed: and Christianity, which is the best-natured institution in the world, forbids us the doing of those things whereby we may grieve one another. A man's good name is a tender thing, and a wound there sinks deep into the spirit even of a wise and good man. And the more innocent any man is in this kind, the more sensible is he of this hard usage, because he never treats others so, nor is he conscious to himself that he hath deserved it.

Secondly, the consequences of this vice are as bad or worse to ourselves. Whoever is wont to speak evil of others gives a bad character of himself, even to those whom he desires to please, who, if they be wise enough, will conclude that he speaks of them to others, as he does of others to them. And were it not for that fond partiality which men have for themselves, no man could be so blind as not to see this.

And it is very well worthy of our consideration, which our Saviour says in this very case, "That with what measure we mete to others, it shall be measured to us again;" [15] and that many times heaped up and running over. For there is hardly anything wherein mankind do use more strict justice and equality than in rendering evil for evil, and railing for railing.

Nay, revenge often goes further than words. A reproachful and slanderous speech hath cost many a man a duel, and in that the loss of his own life, or the murder of another, perhaps with the loss of his own soul; and I have often wondered that among Christians this matter is no more laid to heart.

And though neither of these great mischiefs should happen to us, yet this may be inconvenient enough many other ways. For no man knows in the chance of things, and the mutability of human affairs, whose kindness and good-will he may come to stand in need of before he dies. So that did a man only consult his own safety and quiet, he ought to refrain from evil-speaking. "What man is he (saith the Psalmist) that desireth life, and loveth many days, that he may see good: keep thy tongue from evil, and thy lips from speaking falsehood." [16]

But there is an infinitely greater danger hanging over us from God. If we allow ourselves in this evil practice, all our religion is good for nothing. So St. James expressly tells us: "If any man among you seemeth to be religious, and bridleth not his tongue, but deceiveth his own heart, that man's religion is vain." [17] St. Paul puts slanderers and revilers amongst those that shall not inherit the kingdom of God. [18] And our blessed Saviour hath told us, that "by our words we shall be justified, and by our words we shall be condemned." [19] To which I will add the counsel given us by the wise man: "Refrain your tongue from backbiting; for there is no word so secret that shall go for nought, and the mouth that slandereth slayeth the soul."

I proceed, in the fourth place, to add some further argument and considerations to take men off from this vice.

[14] Ecclesiasticus 19:8–9.
[15] Matt. 7:2.
[16] Ps. 34:12–13.
[17] James 1:26.
[18] I Cor. 6:10.
[19] Matt. 12:37.

First, that the use of speech is a peculiar prerogative of man above other creatures, and bestowed upon him for some excellent end and purpose: that by this faculty we might communicate our thoughts more easily to one another, and consult together for our mutual comfort and benefit; not to enable us to be hurtful and injurious, but helpful and beneficial, to one another. The Psalmist, as by interpreters is generally thought, calls our tongue our glory: "Therewith we praise God and bless men." Now to bless is to speak well of any, and to wish them well. So that we pervert the use of speech, and turn our glory into shame, when we abuse this faculty to the injury and reproach of any.

Secondly, consider how cheap a kindness it is to speak well, at least not to speak ill of any. A good word is an easy obligation, but not to speak ill requires only our silence, which costs us nothing. Some instances of charity are chargeable, as to relieve the wants and necessities of others; the expense deters many from this kind of charity. But were a man never so covetous, he might afford another man his good word; at least he might refrain from speaking ill of him, especially if it be considered how dear many have paid for a slanderous and reproachful word.

Thirdly, consider that no quality doth ordinarily recommend one more to the favour and good-will of men, than to be free from this vice. Every one desires such a man's friendship, and is apt to repose such a great trust and confidence in him. And when he is dead, men will praise him; and, next to piety towards God, and righteousness to men, nothing is thought a more significant commendation, than that he was never, or very rarely, heard to speak ill of any. It was a singular character of a Roman gentleman, *Nescivit quid esset male dicere,* "He knew not what it was to give any man an ill word."

Fourthly, let every man lay his hand upon his heart, and consider how himself is apt to be affected with this usage. Speak thy conscience man, and say whether, as bad as thou art, thou wouldst not be glad to have every man's, especially every good man's, good word? And to have thy faults concealed, and not to be hardly spoken of, though it may be not altogether without truth, by those whom thou didst never offend by word or deed? But with what face or reason dost thou expect this from others, to whom thy carriage hath been so contrary? Nothing surely is more equal and reasonable than that known rule,—what thou wouldst have no man do to thee, that do thou to no man.

Fifthly, when you are going to speak reproachfully of others, consider whether you do not lie open to just reproach in the same, or some other kind. Therefore give no occasion, no example, of this barbarous usage of one another.

There are very few so innocent and free either from infirmities or greater faults, as not to be obnoxious to reproach upon one account or other, even the wisest, and most virtuous, and most perfect among men, who have some little vanity or affectation which lays them open to the raillery of a mimical and malicious wit; therefore we should often turn our thoughts upon ourselves, and look into that part of the wallet which men commonly fling over their shoulders, and keep behind them, that they may not see their own faults. And when we have searched that well, let us remember our Saviour's rule, "He that is without sin, let him cast the first stone."[20]

Lastly, consider that it is in many cases as great a charity to conceal the evil

[20] John 8:7.

you hear and know of others, as if you relieved them in a great necessity. And we think him a hard-hearted man that will not bestow a small alms upon one in great want. It is an excellent advice which the son of Sirach gives to this purpose: "Talk not of other men's lives; if thou hast heard a word, let it die with thee; and be bold it will not burst thee." [21]

I shall, in the fifth and last place, give some rules and directions for the prevention and cure of this great evil among men.

First, never say any evil of any man but what you certainly know. Whenever you positively accuse and indict any man of any crime, though it be in private and among friends, speak as if you were upon your oath, because God sees and hears you. This not only charity, but justice, and regard to truth, do demand of us. He that easily credits an ill report is almost as faulty as the first inventor of it. For though you do not make, yet you commonly propagate, a lie. Therefore never speak evil of any upon common fame, which for the most part is false, but almost always uncertain, whether it be true or not.

Not but that it is a fault,[22] in most cases, to report the evil of men which is true, and which we certainly know to be so, but if I cannot prevail to make men wholly to abstain from this fault, I would be glad to compound [come together] with some persons, and to gain this point of them however; because it will retrench nine parts in ten of the evil-speaking that is in the world.

Secondly, before you speak evil of any man, consider whether he hath not obliged you by some real kindness, and then it is a bad return to speak ill of him who hath done us good. Consider also, whether you may not come hereafter to be acquainted with him, related to him, or obliged by him whom you have thus injured. And how will you then be ashamed when you reflect upon it, and perhaps have reason also to believe, that he to whom you have done this injury is not ignorant of it?

Consider, likewise, whether, in the chance of human affairs, you may not some time or other come to stand in need of his favour, and how incapable this carriage of yours towards him will render you of it, and whether it may not be in his power to revenge a spiteful and needless word by a shrewd turn; so that, if a man made no conscience of hurting others, yet he should in prudence have some consideration of himself.

Thirdly, let us accustom ourselves to pity the faults of men, and to be truly sorry for them, and then we shall take no pleasure in publishing them. And this common humanity requires of us, considering the great infirmities of human nature, and that we ourselves also are liable to be tempted; considering, likewise, how severe a punishment every fault and miscarriage is to itself, and how terribly it exposeth a man to the wrath of God, both in this world and the other. He is not a good Christian, that is not heartily sorry for the faults even of his greatest enemies; and, if he be so, he will discover [reveal] them no further than is necessary to some good end.

Fourthly, whenever we hear any man evil spoken of, if we know any good of him let us say that. It is always the more humane and the more honourable part to stand up in defence and vindication of others, than to accuse and be-

---

[21] Ecclesiasticus 19:10.

[22] The edition of 1707 reads *nor* for *not*. The sense seems to be, "Nor only is it a fault . . . ."

spatter them. Possibly the good you may have heard of them may not be true, but it is much more probable that the evil which you have heard of them is not true neither. However, it is better to preserve the credit of a bad man, than to stain the reputation of the innocent. And if there were any need that a man should be evil spoken of, it is but fair and equal that his good and bad qualities should be mentioned together; otherwise, he may be strangely misrepresented, and an indifferent man may be made a monster.

They that will observe nothing in a wise man but his oversights and follies, nothing in a good man but his failings and infirmities, may make a shift to render a very wise and good man very despicable. If one should heap together all the passionate speeches, all the froward and imprudent actions of the best man, all that he has said or done amiss in his whole life, and present it all at one view, concealing his wisdom and virtues, the man in this disguise would look like a madman or a fury. And yet if his life were fairly represented, and just in the same manner it was led, and his many and great virtues set over against his failings and infirmities, he would appear to all the world to be an admirable and excellent person. But how many and great soever any man's ill qualities are, it is but just, that with all this heavy load of faults he should have the due praise of the few real virtues that are in him.

Fifthly, that you may not speak ill of any, do not delight to hear ill of them. Give no countenance to busybodies, and those that love to talk of other men's faults; or if you cannot decently reprove them, because of their quality, then divert the discourse some other way; or if you cannot do that, by seeming not to mind it, you may sufficiently signify that you do not like it.

Sixthly, let every man mind himself and his own duty and concernment. Do but endeavour in good earnest to mend thyself, and it will be work enough for one man, and leave thee but little time to talk of others. When Plato withdrew from the court of Dionysius, who would fain have had a famous philosopher for his flatterer, they parted in some unkindness, and Dionysius bade him not to speak ill of him when he was returned into Greece. Plato told him he had no leisure for it—meaning, that he had better things to mind than to take up his thoughts and talk with the faults of so bad a man, so notoriously known to all the world.

Lastly, let us set a watch before the door of our lips, and not to speak but upon consideration. I do not mean to speak finely, but fitly. Especially when thou speakest of others, consider of whom and what thou art going to speak: use great caution and circumspection in this matter; look well about thee, on every side of the thing, and on every person in the company, before thy words slip from thee; which, when they are once out of thy lips are for ever out of thy power.

Not that men should be sullen in company, and say nothing; or so stiff in conversation, as to drop nothing but aphorisms and oracles. Especially among equals and friends, we should not be so reserved as if we would have it taken for a mighty favour that we vouchsafe to say anything. If a man had the understanding of an angel, he must be contented to abase something of this excess of wisdom, for fear of being thought cunning. The true art of conversation, if anybody can hit upon it, seems to be this: an appearing freedom and openness, with a resolute reservedness as little appearing as is possible.

All that I mean by this caution is that we should consider well what we say, especially of others. And to this end we should endeavour to get our minds furnished with matter of discourse concerning things useful in themselves, and not hurtful to others. And if we have but a mind wise enough, and good enough, we may easily find a field large enough, for innocent conversation, such as will harm nobody, and yet be acceptable enough to the better and wiser part of mankind. And why should any one be at the cost of playing the fool to gratify anybody whatsoever?

I have done with the five things I propounded to speak to upon this argument. But because hardly anything can be so clear, but something may be said against it, nor anything so bad, but something may be pleaded in excuse for it, I shall therefore take notice of two or three pleas that may be made for it.

First, some pretend mighty injury and provocation. If in the same kind, it seems thou art sensible of it, and therefore thou of all men oughtest to abstain from it; but in what kind soever it be, the Christian religion forbids revenge. Therefore do not plead one sin in excuse of another, and make revenge an apology for reviling.

Secondly, it is alleged by others, with a little better grace, that if this doctrine were practised, conversation would be spoiled, and there would not be matter enough for pleasant discourse and entertainment.

I answer, the design of this discourse is to redress a great evil in conversation, and that, I hope, which mends it will not spoil it. And, however, if men's tongues lay a little more still, and most of us spake a great deal less than we do, both of ourselves and others, I see no great harm in it. I hope we might for all that live comfortably and in good health, and see many good days. David, I am sure, prescribes it as an excellent receipt, in his opinion, for a quiet and cheerful, and long life, to refrain from evil-speaking: "What man is he that desireth life, and loveth many days, that he may see good? Keep thy tongue from evil, and thy lips from speaking falsehood." [23]

But granting that there is some pleasure in invective, I hope there is a great deal more in innocence; and the more any man considers this, the truer he will find it; and whenever we are serious, we ourselves cannot but acknowledge it. When a man examines himself impartially before the sacrament, or is put in mind upon a death-bed to make reparation for injuries done in this kind, he will then certainly be of this mind, and wish he had not done them. For this certainly is one necessary qualification for the blessed sacrament, that we "be in love and charity with our neighbours," with which temper of mind this quality is utterly inconsistent.

Thirdly, there is yet a more specious plea than either of the former, that men will be encouraged to do ill if they can escape the tongues of men, as they would do, if this doctrine did effectually take place; because by this means one great restraint from doing evil would be taken away, which these good men, who are so bent upon reforming the world, think would be great pity. For many who will venture upon the displeasure of God will yet abstain from doing bad things for fear of reproach from men. Besides that, this seems the most proper punishment of many faults the laws of men can take no notice of.

Admitting all this to be true, yet it does not seem so good and laudable a way to punish one fault by another. But let no man encourage himself in an evil

---

[23] Ps. 34:12–13.

way with this hope, that he shall escape the censure of men: when I have said all I can, there will, I fear, be evil speaking enough in the world to chastise them that do ill; and though we should hold our peace, there will be bad tongues enough to reproach men with their evil doings. I wish we could but be persuaded to make the experiment for a little while, whether men would not be sufficiently lashed for their faults though we sat by and said nothing.

So that there is no need at all that good men should be concerned in this odious work. There will always be offenders and malefactors enough to be the executioners to inflict this punishment upon one another. Therefore let no man presume upon impunity on the one hand; and, on the other, let no man despair but that this business will be sufficiently done one way or other. I am very much mistaken, if we may not safely trust an ill-natured world that there will be no failure of justice in this kind.

And here, if I durst, I would have said a word or two concerning that more public sort of obloquy, by lampoons and libels, so much in fashion in this witty age. But I have no mind to provoke a very terrible sort of men. Yet thus much I hope may be said without offence: that how much soever men are pleased to see others abused in this kind, yet it is always grievous when it comes to their own turn. However, I cannot but hope that every man that impartially considers, must own it to be a fault of a very high nature to revile those whom God hath placed in authority over us; and to slander the footsteps of the Lord's anointed; especially since it is so expressly written, "Thou shalt not speak evil of the rulers of thy people." [24]

Having represented the great evil of this vice, it might not now be improper to say something to those who suffer by it. Are we guilty of the evil said of us? Let us reform and cut off all occasions for the future; and so turn the malice of our enemies to our own advantage, and defeat their ill intentions by making so good a use of it. And then it will be well for us to be evil spoken of.

Are we innocent? We may so much the better bear it patiently, imitating herein the pattern of our blessed Saviour, "who when he was reviled, reviled not again, but committed himself to him that judgeth righteously."

We may consider, likewise, that though it be a misfortune to be evil spoken of, it is their fault that do it, and not ours, and therefore should not put us into passion, because another man's being injurious to me is no good reason why I should be uneasy to myself. We should not revenge the injuries done to us, no not upon them that do them, much less upon ourselves. Let no man's provocation make thee to lose thy patience. Be not such a fool as to part with any one virtue, because some men are so malicious as to endeavour to rob thee of the reputation of all the rest. When men speak ill of thee, do as Plato said he would do in that case, "Live so, as that nobody may believe them."

All that now remains is to reflect upon what hath been said, and to urge you and myself to do accordingly. For all is nothing, if we do not practise what we so plainly see to be our duty. Many are so taken up with the deep points and mysteries of religion that they never think of the common duties and offices of human life. But faith and a good life are so far from clashing with one another, that the Christian religion hath made them inseparable. True faith is necessary in order to [live] a good life, and a good life is the genuine product of a right belief; and therefore the one never ought to be pressed to the prejudice of the other.

[24] Acts 23:5.

I foresee what will be said, because I have heard it so often said in the like case, that there is "not one word of Jesus Christ in all this." [25] No more is there in the text. And yet I hope that Jesus Christ is truly preached, whenever his will and laws, and the duties enjoined by the Christian religion are inculcated upon us.

But some men are pleased to say that this is mere morality. I answer, that this is scripture morality, and Christian morality, and who hath anything to say against that? Nay, I shall go yet farther, that no man ought to pretend to believe the Christian religion, who lives in the neglect of so plain a duty, and in the practice of a sin so clearly condemned by it, as this of evil-speaking is.

But because the word of God is quick and powerful, and sharper than a two-edged sword, yea, sharper than any calumny itself, and pierceth the very hearts and consciences of men, laying us open to ourselves, and convincing us of our more secret as well as of our more visible faults, I shall therefore at one view represent to you what is dispersedly said concerning this sin in the holy word of God.

And I have purposely reserved this to the last, because it is more persuasive and penetrating than any human discourse. And to this end be pleased to consider in what company the Holy Ghost doth usually mention this sin. There is scarce any black catalogue of sins in the Bible but we find this among them, in the company of the very worst actions and most irregular passions of men. "Out of the heart (says our Saviour) proceed evil thoughts, murders, adulteries, fornications, false-witness, evil-speakings." [26] And the apostle [Paul] ranks backbiters with fornicators and murderers and haters of God,[27] and with those of whom it is expressly said, that they shall not inherit the kingdom of God.[28]

And when he enumerates the sins of the last times, "Men (says he) shall be lovers of themselves, covetous, boasters, evil-speakers, without natural affection, perfidious, false accusers. . . ." And which is the strangest of all, they who are said to be guilty of these great vices and enormities are noted by the apostle to be great pretenders to religion; for so it follows in the next words, "Having a form of godliness, but denying the power thereof." [29] So that it is no new thing for men to make a more than ordinary profession of Christianity, and yet at the same time to live in a most palpable contradiction to the precepts of that holy religion, as if any pretence to mystery, and I know not what extraordinary attainments in the knowledge of Christ, could exempt men from obedience to his laws, and set them above the virtues of a good life.

And now, after all this, do we hardly think that to be a sin, which is in Scripture so frequently ranked with murder and adultery, and the blackest crimes, such as are inconsistent with the life and power of religion, and will certainly shut men out of the kingdom of God? Do we believe the Bible to be the word of God? And can we allow ourselves in the common practice of a sin, than which there is hardly any fault of men's lives more frequently mentioned, more severely reproved, and more odiously branded in that holy book?

Consider seriously these texts: "Who shall abide in thy tabernacle, who shall dwell in thy holy hill? He that backbiteth not with his tongue, nor taketh up a

[25] Some "gospel" Puritans believed in only "preaching Christ," and exhorted their followers to "roll upon Christ." There were many such cant phrases.

[26] Matt. 15:19.

[27] Rom. 1:29, 30.

[28] I Cor. 6:10.

[29] II Tim. 3:2–5. The list of epithets is a long one. Most texts at this point have etc.

reproach against his neighbour." [30] Have ye never heard what our Saviour says, that of every idle word we must give an account in the day of judgment; that "by thy words thou shalt be justified, and by thy words thou shalt be condemned?" [31] What can be more severe than that of St. James? "If any man among you seemeth to be religious, and bridleth not his tongue, that man's religion is vain." [32]

To conclude: The sin which I have now warned men against is plainly condemned by the word of God. And the duty which I have now been persuading you to is easy for every man to understand; not hard for any man that can but resolve to keep a good guard upon himself for some time, by the grace of God, to practise; and most reasonable for all men, but especially for all Christians, to observe. It is as easy as a resolute silence upon just occasion; as reasonable as prudence, and justice, and charity, and the preservation of peace and good-will among men, can make it; and of as necessary and indispensable an obligation as the authority of God can render anything.

Upon all which considerations let every one of us be persuaded to take up David's deliberate resolution: "I said, I will take heed to my ways, that I offend not with my tongue." [33] And I do verily believe that would we but heartily endeavour to amend this one fault, we should soon be better men in our whole lives. I mean that the correcting of this vice, together with those that are nearly allied to it, and may at the same time, and almost with the same resolution and care, be corrected, would make us owners of a great many considerable virtues, and carry us on a good way towards perfection, it being hardly to be imagined, that a man that makes conscience of his words should not take an equal or a greater care of his actions. And this I take to be both the true meaning and the true reason of that saying of St. James, and with which I shall conclude: "If any man offend not in word, the same is a perfect man." [34]

Now the God of peace, who brought again from the dead our Lord Jesus Christ, the great Shepherd of the sheep, through the blood of the everlasting covenant, make you perfect in every good word and work, to do his will, working in you always that which is well-pleasing in his sight, through Jesus Christ, to whom be glory for ever. *Amen.*

∽

BIBLIOGRAPHICAL NOTE

The most accessible source to Tillotson's sermons is *The Works of Dr. John Tillotson . . . with the Life of the Author by Thomas Birch*, 10 vols. (1820). A brief sketch of Tillotson's life may be found in the *Dictionary of National Biography*; a book-length treatment is that by Thomas Birch, *Life of Tillotson* (1752). See also Louis Locke, *Tillotson: A Study in Seventeenth-century Literature. Anglistica IV* (Copenhagen, 1954). Useful for understanding points of view in religion are John Hunt, *Religious Thought in England* (1871), and Edward Dowden, *Puritan and Anglican* (3rd ed., 1910).

[30] Ps. 15:1, 3.
[31] Matt. 12:36, 37.
[32] James 1:26.
[33] Ps. 39:1.
[34] James 3:2.

III

The Eighteenth Century

Introduction

The eighteenth century, and especially the reign of George III, saw the full maturity of British eloquence, and probably its golden age. If the seventeenth century had been the age of great preachers, the eighteenth was the age of great parliamentary orators and debaters. The battles for parliamentary supremacy in government had mostly been won. Hence the revolutionary boldness of men such as Eliot, Wentworth, and Pym was no longer needed. Nor were Cromwellian exhortations, and threats to the radicals of the right and of the left appropriate to the contests among the great Whig families for the management of the Hanoverian sovereigns and of the wars and resources of the growing new Empire. Not until the very close of the century did radicalism and revolution again become major issues.

Then as never before, reputations could be made and power and fortune achieved in the House of Commons, and fine public speaking came to be one of the avenues to that sort of success. In educated circles it had become the fashion to exhibit good taste in public speaking as well as in other forms of polite literature. Adam Smith and Hugh Blair were lecturing to the Scottish university students on rhetoric and belles lettres by the 1750's and 1760's. Blair's *Lectures,* when later published, and other books on rhetoric and eloquence such as those of Lord Kames (1762) and George Campbell (1776), were widely sold. Furthermore, the ordinary member of Parliament, though he himself might seldom speak, admired good speaking in others on whichever side of the House; and even when Administration commanded huge majorities at its will, good speaking was thought to matter. Replied Edmund Burke, at Samuel Johnson's Club, to R. B. Sheridan's query as to why he bothered to speak well when he couldn't possibly carry the vote:

> It is very well worth while for a man to take pains to speak well in Parliament. A man, who has vanity, speaks to display his talents; and if a man speaks well, he gradually establishes a certain reputation and consequence in the general opinion, which sooner or later will have its political reward. Besides, though not one vote is gained, a good speech has its effect. Though an act which has been ably

opposed passes into law, yet in its progress it is modelled, it is softened in such a manner, that we see plainly the Minister has been told, that the members attached to him are so sensible of its injustice or absurdity from what they have heard, that it must be altered. (James Boswell, *Life of Samuel Johnson*, April 3, 1778).

Samuel Johnson added, "And, Sir, there is a gratification of pride. Though we cannot out-vote them, we will out-argue them. They shall not do wrong without its being shown both to themselves and to the world."

In the first half of the century, of course, fine parliamentary speaking was to be heard, as for example, Lord Belhaven's plea for the independence of Scotland (1706) and the Earl of Chesterfield's ironic speech on the Spiritous Liquors Bill of 1743. (See Goodrich, *Select British Eloquence*.) Reporting of texts was so infrequent and unreliable, however (see below, pages 176–77), that we know the speakers better from what is said about them than from what is said by them. For the latter part of the century, texts are better and more plentiful, and there is a remarkable concentration of eminent speakers in Parliament, debating questions of increasing scope and consequence: corruption in government and the influence of the Crown on elections and on the voting in Parliament; reforms of the House of Commons and of the franchise; empire and the rivalry of the "natural enemy," France; commercial regulation and the development of trade all over the world; colonial policy and the American Revolution; India and the East India Company; popular unrest at home and in Ireland; the French Revolution abroad; and religious tolerance and Catholic emancipation.

Though records of secular public speaking and debate outside the Houses of Parliament are scarce and even less complete than those of parliamentary speaking, it is clear that such speaking became frequent and important: in political clubs; in debating and literary societies like the one Edmund Burke founded as a student at Trinity College, Dublin, and those he attended in Fleet Street in London, or "The British Inquisition" conducted by Charles Macklin, the actor; in the County Meetings, such as those held in the summer of 1769 during the agitation over the Middlesex Election; in the Guildhalls in London, Bristol, and other cities (Burke's speech at Bristol during the election of 1780 is included here); and in the meetings of the Court of Proprietors (stockholders) of the East India Company. As the century progressed, and especially after 1770, systematic popular political agitation increased rapidly and was reported more and more in the press. Distinguished examples such as remain from the next century, however, have not been preserved.

Political controversy in print was plentiful, and the principal rhetorical activity addressed to the general public was carried on in the press—in letters to the newspapers, in periodical papers, and in broadsides and pamphlets. Notable pamphlets early in the century included Jonathan Swift's *The Conduct of the Allies* (1711) and *Drapier's Letters* (1724). Later came Samuel Johnson's *Taxation No Tyranny* (1775), Burke's *Present Discontents* (1770) and his *Reflections on the Revolution in France* (1790), and Thomas Paine's reply, *The Rights of Man* (1791 and 1792). Some of the most notable periodical papers and letters in the newspapers were Daniel Defoe's *Review* (1704–1713), the anti-Walpole *Craftsman* (1726–1731), John Wilkes's *North Briton* (1762–1763), and the famous *Letters of Junius* (1769–1772). These, perhaps as much as the speeches, represent British public address of the eighteenth century. Since they were not speeches, however, we do not include examples in this volume.

Protestant preaching flourished likewise throughout the century, though not, in the Church of England, with the vigor and grandeur of the previous two centuries. It is said that the poor quality of reading of the service and sermons from the majority of pulpits gave impetus to the popularity of such writers and teachers of elocution and pronunciation as Thomas Sheridan and John Walker. Good preaching there was, of course. Robert South at the beginning of the century, Hugh Blair of Edinburgh later, and Bishop Joseph Butler in between represent the better preaching of the Established Church. That Church and its preaching, like society generally, were devoted to stability and good taste. James Boswell, for example, thought Blair a satisfactory preacher because he was always reassuring, never disturbing. Toward mid-century, however, a new movement in popular preaching arose with the great revival of the Christian spirit, the Methodism of the Wesleys and Whitefield. So far as the masses in city and country were reached by persuasive oratory, it was by the preaching of the Methodists. For that reason, preaching is represented here by a sermon of John Wesley.

Limitations of space require us to exclude examples from the most notable display of forensic oratory of the latter part of the century, the Impeachment of Warren Hastings, Governor General of India, which began before a large and distinguished audience in the House of Lords in 1788. Leading the attack on Hastings as the personification of misgovernment in India was Edmund Burke, in speeches lasting several days each. His principal colleagues, speaking almost as long, were Charles James Fox and Richard Brinsley Sheridan. Fox and Burke, of course, are included in this book, but on other subjects, Burke from an earlier time and Fox from a later. Sheridan, the eminent playwright and theatre manager, owes his remarkable oratorical reputation almost entirely to his great performances on the so-called Begum charges against Hastings. Rather than represent him and the others by excerpts, however, we refer the reader to other sources. One of Sheridan's speeches is available in Goodrich's *Select British Eloquence* and in the Everyman *British Orations*. Burke's are printed in editions of his complete *Works,* and a transcript of most of the speeches in the trial, from a reasonably good shorthand report, was edited by E. A. Bond in four volumes in 1859–1861.

The student of the eighteenth century is well supplied with comprehensive histories. The most extensive is W. E. H. Lecky's *History of England in the Eighteenth Century* in eight volumes (1877), which covers the field in detail to the beginning of the war with France in 1793. Lecky includes substantial essays on the character and achievements of most of the speakers whom we treat and is good on such subjects as religion, colonial affairs, and Ireland. He has a parallel *History of Ireland in the Eighteenth Century* in five volumes (1893). The most recent authoritative general histories are two volumes in the *Oxford History of England*: Basil Williams, *The Whig Supremacy 1714–1760* (1939), and J. Steven Watson, *The Reign of George III 1760–1815* (1960). A brief and excellent survey is J. H. Plumb's *England in the Eighteenth Century* (1950). Chauncey Goodrich's *Select British Eloquence* (1852) is, of course, most helpful to the student of speaking in this period. A useful corrective to Goodrich's mid-nineteenth-century American prejudices and the limitations of his historical perspective may be found in Bonamy Dobrée (ed.), *From Anne to Victoria* (1927), a collection of brief sketches of the most prominent people of the time by various specialists. The greatest resource for the study of the House of Commons in this century is the first completed portion of the comprehensive *History of Parliament*: Sir Lewis Namier and John Brooke, *The House of Commons, 1754–1790*, 3 vols. (New York, 1964). It offers biographical and political accounts of everyone who sat in the House during the period, and analyses of the representation and the politics of all the constituencies.

The period is replete with correspondences, memoirs, and biographies. Especially useful will be Horace Walpole's *Letters* and his *Memoirs* of the reigns of George II and George III, James Boswell's *Life of Samuel Johnson*, and, for the last quarter of the century, Nathaniel Wraxall's *Historical and Posthumous Memoirs*. Other important books are mentioned in the Bibliographical Notes on the various speakers. There are no significant histories of rhetoric or oratory for this period, but a history of its logic and rhetoric by Wilbur Samuel Howell is in preparation.

Sir Robert Walpole (1676–1745); William Pitt, the Elder; * and Others

Sir Robert Walpole sat in the House of Commons, except for a brief misadventure or two, from 1701 to 1742. For the last twenty years of that time he was First Minister and the master of the government. The third son and fifth child of a large family, he succeeded to a comfortable income which he increased to a substantial estate for his sons, the most famous of whom was the memoirist, correspondent, and man of letters, Horace Walpole.

Walpole was a man of business, a brilliant public financier, and a superb political manager. Though viciously opposed and abused by William Pitt and the so-called "Patriots" as an author of corruption on a grand scale who ruled his country by bribery, favoritism, and deceit, Walpole provided stability, prosperity, and peace, and later generations have judged that the "Age of Walpole" was what England needed.

Outshone in reputation for oratory by his contemporary and rival, Lord Bolingbroke, and ultimately eclipsed by his younger opponent, William Pitt, Walpole nonetheless was a skillful and efficient speaker. Like Lord North later, he made his reputation not in opposition but in office; and the Minister's speaking, explanatory and defensive as it is much of the time, never seems so eloquent, so high-minded, so justly vehement as the assault and invective of righteous opposition. But the fact remains that in the English parliamentary system of the eighteenth century, however skilled a man might be at operating behind the scenes, it was most unlikely that he would reach Sir Robert's eminence without the ability to hold his own on the floor of the House. Against a formidable array of talent in the House and of intrigue and propaganda outside, Walpole held his own, and more.

A serious obstacle to the study of the history of oratory is the scarcity of good

* For an introduction to Pitt see below, pp. 201–02.

texts, especially of parliamentary and popular speeches. Throughout this century, much was published in the form of speeches, and much was printed in the newspapers and magazines purporting to be reports of speeches in Parliament. In fact, however, there was very little good reporting of parliamentary speaking, and for almost three-quarters of the century, almost none at all. From Tudor times there had been no legal, much less official, reporting of what was said in either house of Parliament, and from time to time severe punishments were imposed upon printers who violated the prohibition against publishing the debates.

Nevertheless, the appetite of the public for politics grew rapidly with the rise of newspapers and the founding of the great *Gentleman's* and *London* magazines. To satisfy this demand, printers resorted to various not impenetrable disguises for printing parliamentary debates. Edward Cave of *The Gentleman's Magazine,* for example, engaged the young Samuel Johnson to compose debates purporting to be those of the legislature of Gulliver's Lilliput. They concerned matters which Parliament was known to have recently debated, and they presented under transparent Lilliputian names speakers presumed to have taken part. Sometimes the lines of argument followed by the pros and cons were known to the reporter, and occasionally he had available the gist of some of the individual speeches. For the most part, however, like the Greek historian Thucydides, he wrote what he thought might properly have been said; and the debates by Samuel Johnson or his counterpart at *The London Magazine* are often the only reports we have of notable speeches in Parliament by men such as Sir Robert Walpole, the elder William Pitt as a young man, and the Earl of Chesterfield. Because of parliamentary regulations the disguised reports were not printed until long after the actual debates had taken place—often as much as a year or two.

These debates, sometimes fictional, seldom altogether actual, are significant rhetorical records. They are what the literate public knew of the speaking of its leaders. To the extent that parliamentary debates had public importance, these are the influential discourses. Moreover, the debates in *Gentleman's* were composed with the skill of one of England's great literary men.

We think it desirable, therefore, to represent the parliamentary oratory of the early 1740's by a debate written by Samuel Johnson for *The Gentleman's Magazine*. It professes to be the debate in the House of Commons on March 4, 1741, on Walpole's bill to meet the serious shortage of sailors for the Fleet. The particular clause under consideration provided that "no Merchants, or Bodies Corporate or Politic, shall hire Sailors at higher Wages than Thirty-five shillings for the Month, on Pain of forfeiting the treble Value of the Sum so agreed for." There is no important corroborating record of this debate.

The portion which we include may be thought rather to feature Pitt than Walpole, unless, as well we may, we credit Sir Robert with the speech which Johnson gives to the Prime Minister's brother Horace. The passage represents, however, the kind of attack and counter-attack at which these participants apparently shone—the sort of thing which readers (and now television viewers) are thought to demand of their political favorites. This debate is notable especially for Pitt's ironic apology for "the atrocious crime of being a young man." Apparently invented by Johnson, that passage has been quoted again and again in characterizations of Pitt. The reader will observe also the realism with which Johnson, at the end of the debate, turns the parliamentary forms into a commentary on rhetoric, oratory, and parliamentary morals and manners.

Of this period Chauncey Goodrich wrote:

> Parliamentary speaking was literally "a keen encounter of the wits," in which
> the ball of debate was tossed to and fro between men of high talent, who per-
> fectly understood each other's motives, and showed infinite dexterity in twisting
> facts and arguments to serve a purpose. It was the maxim of the day, that every-
> thing was fair in politics.—The best speeches abounded in wit and sarcasm, in
> sly insinuations or cutting invective, all thrown off with a light, bold, confident
> air, in racy English, and without any apparent effort. The language of debate
> approached as near to that of actual conversation, as the nature of the topics, and
> the flow of continuous discourse, would permit. (*Select British Eloquence*, p. 30.)

There is evidence in the testimony of Lord Chesterfield and others that such
probably was the manner of parliamentary speaking at its best. Some of these
qualities are reflected in the debates written by Samuel Johnson. The wit, invective, and ingenuity of construction are there, but the style suggests the balanced phrasing of moral aphorisms in the periodical essays of Johnson and others,
rather than the "light, bold confident air . . . without any apparent effort."

∽

[FROM A] REMARKABLE DEBATE IN THE HOUSE OF CLINABS ON THE BILL FOR ENCOURAGING SEAMEN AND MANNING THE FLEET *

The Urg; [1] Ptit [Pitt] *spoke to the following Purport.*

S I R: It is common for those to have the greatest Regard to their own Interest
who discover [reveal] the least for that of others. I do not, therefore, despair
of recalling the Advocates of this Bill from the Prosecution of their favourite
Measures by Arguments of greater Efficacy than those which are founded on
Reason and Justice.

Nothing, Sir, is more evident, than that some Degree of Reputation is absolutely necessary to Men who have any Concern in the Administration of a Government like ours; they must either secure the Fidelity of their Adherents by the
Assistance of Wisdom, or of Virtue; their Enemies must either be awed by their
Honesty, or terrified by their Cunning. Mere artless Bribery will never gain a
sufficient Majority to set them entirely free from Apprehensions of Censure. To
different Tempers different Motives must be applied: Some, who place their
Felicity in being accounted Wise, are in very little Care to preserve the Character of Honesty; others may be persuaded to join in Measures which they easily
discover to be weak and ill-concerted, because they are convinced that the Authors
of them are not corrupt but mistaken, and are unwilling that any Man should be
punished for natural Defects or casual Ignorance.

I cannot say, Sir, which of these Motives influence the Advocates for the Bill

* The text is from *The Gentleman's Magazine*, XI (November 1741), 562–571. We
maintain the Lilliputian fiction as part of the idiom of the time. The anagrams of
the names are solved in brackets. This debate is included also in Benjamin B. Hoover,
Samuel Johnson's Parliamentary Reporting (1953), pp. 186–204.

[1] The designation *Urg* is the equivalent of *Mister* in "Lilliputian"; others, such as
Hurgolet and *Hurgolen*, apply to orders such as Knight and Baronet below *Hurgoes*
(Lords). The House of Clinabs is the House of Commons.

before us; a Bill in which such Cruelties are proposed as are yet unknown among the most savage Nations, such as Slavery has not yet borne, or Tyranny invented, such as cannot be heard without Resentment, nor thought of without Horror.

It is, Sir, perhaps, not unfortunate, that one more Expedient has been added rather ridiculous than shocking, and that these Tyrants of the Administration, who amuse themselves with oppressing their Fellow Subjects, who add without Reluctance one Hardship to another, invade the Liberty of those whom they have already overborn with Taxes, first plunder and then imprison, who take all Opportunities of Heightening the publick Distresses, and make the Miseries of War the Instruments of new Oppressions, are too ignorant to be formidable, and owe their Power not to their Abilities, but to casual Prosperity, or to the Influence of Money.[2]

The other Clauses of this Bill complicated at once with Cruelty and Folly, have been treated with becoming Indignation; but this may be considered with less Ardour of Resentment, and fewer Emotions of Zeal, because, tho' perhaps equally iniquitous, it will do no Harm; for a Law that can never be executed can never be felt.

That it will consume the Manufacture of Paper and swell the Books of Statutes, is all the Good or Hurt that can be hoped or fear'd from a Law like this; a Law which fixes what is in its own Nature mutable, which prescribes Rules to the Seasons and Limits to the Wind.

I am too well acquainted, Sir, with the Disposition of its two chief Supporters, to mention the Contempt with which this Law will be treated by Posterity, for they have already shewn abundantly their Disregard of succeeding Generations; but I will remind them, that they are now venturing their whole Interest at once, and hope they will recollect before it is too late that those who believe them to intend the Happiness of their Country will never be confirmed in their Opinion by open Cruelty and notorious Oppression; and that those who have only their own Interest in View, will be afraid of adhering to those Leaders, however old and practiced in Expedients, however strengthen'd by Corruption, or elated with Power, who have no reason to hope for Success from either their Virtue or Abilities.

The Urg; Brusttath [3] [Bathurst] *next spoke to this Effect.*

S I R: The Clause now under our Consideration is so inconsiderately drawn up, that it is impossible to read it in the most cursory Manner, without discovering the Necessity of numerous Amendments; no malicious Subtilities or artful Deductions are required in raising Objections to this Part of the Bill, they croud upon us without being sought, and instead of exercising our Sagacity, weary our Attention.

The first Error, or rather one Part of a general and complicated Error, is the Computation of Time not by Days but by Kalendar Months, which, as they are not equal one to another, may embarrass the Account between the Sailors and

[2] The highly abusive terms in which the speaker attacks Walpole and the administration are probably not exaggerated by the reporter. At this time the "Patriots" saw good prospects of achieving the downfall of Walpole.

[3] Probably Henry Bathurst (1714–1794). His father, the first Earl Bathurst, by this time sat in the House of Lords. Henry was a lawyer who later had a distinguished career at the bar and on the bench. In this speech he is made to take a lawyer's position.

those that employ them. In all Contracts of a short Duration, the Time is to be reckoned by Weeks and Days, by certain and regular Periods, which has been so constantly the Practice of the sea-faring Men, that perhaps many of them do not know the Meaning of a Kalendar Month: This indeed is a Neglect of no great Importance, because no Man can be deprived by it of more than the Wages due for the Labour of a few Days, but the other Part of this Clause is more seriously to be consider'd, as it threatens the Sailors with greater Injuries. For it is to be enacted, that all Contracts made for more Wages than are here allowed shall be totally void.

It cannot be denied to be possible, and in my Opinion it is very likely, that many Contracts will be made without the Knowledge of this Law, and consequently without any Design of violating it; but Ignorance, inevitable Ignorance, tho' it is a valid excuse for every other Man, is no Plea for the unhappy Sailor; he must suffer, tho' innocent, the Penalty of a Crime; must undergo Danger, Hardships, and Labour, without a Recompence, and at the End of a successful Voyage, after having enriched his Country by his Industry, return Home to a necessitous Family without being able to relieve them.

It is scarcely necessary, Sir, to raise any more Objections to a Clause in which nothing is Right; but to shew how its Imperfections multiply upon the slightest Consideration, I take the Opportunity to observe that there is no Provision made for regulating the Voyages performed in less Time than a Month, so that the greatest Part of the Abuses, which have been represented as the Occasion of this Clause, are yet without Remedy, and only those Sailors who venture far, and are exposed to the greatest Dangers, are restrain'd from receiving an adequate Reward.

Thus much, Sir, I have said upon the Supposition, that a Regulation of the Sailors Wages is either necessary or just, a Supposition of which I am very far from discovering the Truth. That it is just to oppress the most useful of our Fellow-Subjects, to load those Men with peculiar Hardships to whom we owe the Plenty that we enjoy, the Power that yet remains in the Nation, and which neither the Folly nor the Cowardice of Ministers have yet been able to destroy, and the Security in which we now sit and hold our Consultations; that it is just to lessen our Payments at a Time when we increase the Labour of those who are hired, and to expose Men to Danger without Recompence, will not easily be proved even by those who are most accustomed to Paradoxes, and are ready to undertake the Proof of any position which it is their Interest to find true.

Nor is it much more easy to shew the Necessity of this Expedient in our present State, in which it appears from the Title of the Bill, that our chief Endeavour should be the Increase and Encouragement of Sailors, and, I suppose, it has not often been discover'd, that by taking away the Profits of a Profession greater Numbers have been allured to it.

The high Wages, Sir, paid by Merchants are the chief Incitements that prevail upon the Ambitious, the Necessitous, or the Avaritious, to forsake the Ease and Security of the Land, to leave easy Trades, and healthful Employments, and expose themselves to an Element where they are not certain of an Hour's Safety. The Service of the Merchants is the Nursery in which Seamen are trained up for his Majesty's Navies, and from thence we must, in Time of Danger, expect those Forces by which alone we can be protected.

If, therefore, it is necessary to encourage Sailors, it is necessary to reject all

Measures that may terrify or disgust them; and as their Numbers must depend upon our Trade, let us not embarrass the Merchants with any other Difficulties than those which are inseparable from War, and which very little Care has been hitherto taken to alleviate.

The Urg; Heagh [4] *[Hay]* replied.

S I R: The Objections which have been urged with so much Ardour, and display'd with such Power of Eloquence, are not, in my Opinion, formidable enough to discourage us from prosecuting our Measures; some of them may be perhaps readily answered, and the rest easily removed.

The Computation of Time, as it now stands, is allow'd not to produce any formidable Evil, and therefore did not require so rhetorical a Censure, the Inconveniency of Kalendar Months may easily be removed by a little Candour in the contracting Parties, or that the Objection may not be repeated to the Interruption of the Debate, Weeks or Days may be substituted, and the usual reckoning of the Sailors be still continued.

That some Contracts may be annulled, and Inconveniencies or Delays of Payment arise, is too evident to be questioned; but in that Case the Sailor may have his Remedy provided, and be enabled to obtain by an easy Process, what he shall be judg'd to *have deserved;* for it must be allow'd reasonable, that every Man who labours in honest and useful Employments, should receive the Reward of his Diligence and Fidelity.

Thus, Sir, may the Clause, however loudly censured and violently opposed, be made useful and equitable, and the publick Service advanced without Injury to Individuals.

Sir Rub. Walelop *[Robert Walpole] next rose and spoke as follows.*

S I R: Every Law which extends its Influence to great Numbers in various Relations and Circumstances must produce some Consequences that were never foreseen or intended and is to be censured or applauded as the general Advantages or Inconveniencies are found to preponderate. Of this kind is the Law before us, a Law enforced by the Necessity of our Affairs and drawn up with no other Intention than to secure the publick Happiness and produce that Success which every Man's Interest must prompt him to desire.

If in the Execution of this Law, Sir, some Inconveniencies should arise, they are to be remedied as fast as they are discovered, or if not capable of a Remedy to be patiently born in Consideration of the general Advantage.

That some temporary Disturbances may be produced is not improbable; the Discontent of the Sailors may for a short Time rise high, and our Trade be suspended by their Obstinacy; but Obstinacy however determined must yield to Hunger, and when no higher Wages can be obtained they will cheerfully accept of those which are here allowed them. Short Voyages indeed are not comprehended in the Clause and therefore the Sailors will engage in them upon their own Terms, but this Objection can be of no weight with those that oppose the Clause, because, if it is unjust to limit the Wages of the Sailors, it is just to leave those Voyages without Restriction; and those that think the Expedient here proposed equitable and rational, may perhaps be willing to make some Concessions to those who are of a different Opinion.

[4] William Hay (1695–1755) was Commissioner for Victualling the Navy.

That the Bill will not remove every Obstacle to Success; nor add Weight to one Part of the Balance without making the other lighter; that it will not supply the Navy without incommoding the Merchants in some degree; that it may be sometimes evaded by Cunning, and sometimes abused by Malice, and that at last it will be less efficacious than is desired, may perhaps be proved; but it has not yet been proved that any other Measures are more eligible, or that we are not to promote the publick Service as far as we are able, though our Endeavours may not produce Effects equal to our Wishes.

The Hurgolet Branard [5] [Barnard] *then spoke to this Effect:*

S I R: I know not by what Fatality it is that Nothing can be urged in Defence of the Clause before us which does not tend to discover its Weakness and Inefficacy. The warmest Patrons of this Expedient are impelled by the mere Force of Conviction to such Concessions as invalidate all their Arguments, and leave their Opponents no Necessity of replying.

If short Voyages are not comprehended in this Provision what are we now controverting? what but the Expedience of a Law that will never be executed? The Sailors, however they are contemned by those who think them only worthy to be treated like Beasts of Burthen, are not yet so stupid but that they can easily find out, that to serve a Fortnight for greater Wages is more eligible than to toil a Month for less; and as the numerous Equipments that have been lately made have not left many more Sailors in the Service of the Merchants than may be employ'd in the Coasting Trade, those who traffick to remoter parts must shut up their Books and wait till the Expiration of this Act, for an Opportunity of renewing their Commerce.

To regulate the Wages for one Voyage, and to leave another without Limitation in time of Scarcity of Seamen, is absolutely to prohibit that Trade which is so restrained, and is doubtless a more effectual Embargo than has been yet invented.

Let any Man but suppose that the East *Idnian* [6] Company were obliged to give only half the Wages that other Traders allow, and consider how that part of our Commerce could be carried on; would not their Goods rot in their Warehouses, and their Ships lie forever in the Harbour? Would not the Sailors refuse to contract with them? or desert them after a Contract, upon the first prospect of more advantageous Employment?

But it is not requisite to multiply Arguments in a Question which may not only be decided without long Examination but in which we may determine our Conclusions by the Experience of our Ancestors. Scarcely any right or wrong Measures are without a Precedent, and amongst others this Expedient has been tried by the Wisdom of former times; a Law was once made for limiting the Wages of Tailors, and that it is totally ineffectual we are all convinced. Experience is a very safe Guide in political Enquiries, and often discovers what the most enlightened Reason failed to foresee.

Let us therefore improve the Errors of our Ancestors to our own Advantage, and whilst we neglect to imitate their Virtues, let us at least forbear to repeat their Follies.

[5] Sir John Barnard (1684–1764) was a merchant and politician in London, who sat in Parliament for the City. He was recognized as an authority on finance.

[6] The disguise on this name is very thin.

Macgya Peerur [7] [Perry] *Urg; spoke to this Purport.*

S I R: There is one Objection more which my Acquaintance with foreign Trade impresses too strongly upon my mind to suffer me to conceal it.

It is well known that the Condition of a Seaman subjects him to the Necessity of spending a great part of his Life at a Distance from his native Country, in places where he can neither hear of our Designs nor be instructed in our Laws, and therefore it is evident that no Law ought to affect him before a certain Period of Time in which he may reasonably be supposed to have been informed of it. For every Man ought to have it in his power to avoid Punishment, and to suffer only for Negligence or Obstinacy.

It is quite unnecessary, Sir, to observe to this Assembly, that there are now, as at all times, great Numbers of Sailors in every part of the World, and that they at least equally deserve our Regard with those who are under the more immediate Influence of the Government.

These Seamen have already contracted for the price of their Labour, and the Recompense of their Hazards, nor can we, in my Opinion, without manifest Injustice, dissolve a Contract founded upon Equity, and confirmed by Law.

It is, Sir, an undisputed Principle of Government, that no Persons should be punished without a Crime; but is it no Punishment to deprive a Man of what is due to him by a legal Stipulation, the Condition of which is on his part honestly fulfilled?

Nothing, Sir, can be imagined more calamitous than the Disappointment to which this Law Subjects the unhappy Men who are now promoting the Interest of their Country in distant Places amidst Dangers and Hardships, in unhealthy Climates and barbarous Nations, where they comfort themselves under the Fatigues of Labour and the Miseries of Sickness, with the Prospect of the Sum which they shall gain for the Relief of their Families, and the Respite which their Wages will enable them to Enjoy; but upon their Return they find their Hopes blasted and their Contracts dissolved by a Law made in their Absence.

No human Being, I think, can coolly and deliberately inflict a Hardship like this, and therefore I doubt not but those who have by Inadvertency given Room for this Objection will either remove it by an Amendment, or what is, in my Opinion, more eligible, reject the Clause as inexpedient, useless, and unjust.

The Hurgolen Yegon [8] [Yonge] *spoke next, to this Effect.*

S I R: This Debate has been protracted, not by any Difficulties arising from the Nature of the Questions which have been the Subject of it, but by a Neglect with which almost all the Opponents of the Bill may be justly charged, the Neglect of distinguishing between Measures eligible in themselves, and Measures preferable to Consequences which are apprehended from particular Conjunctures; between Laws made only to advance the publick happiness and Expedients of which the Benefit is merely occasional, and of which the sole Intention is to avert some national Calamity, and which are to cease with the Necessity that produced them.

Such are the Measures, Sir, which are now intended; Measures, which in Days

[7] Micajah Perry was a trader of London, who, like Barnard, sat in Parliament for the City. Like Barnard he usually opposed Walpole's financial and commercial measures. He was especially interested in the tobacco trade.

[8] Sir William Yonge (d. 1755), fourth Baronet Yonge, was a very active Whig politician and strong supporter of Walpole.

of Ease, Security, and Prosperity, it would be the highest Degree of Weakness to propose, but of which I cannot see the Absurdity in Times of Danger and Distress. Such Laws are the Medicines of a State, Useless and Nauseous in Health, but preferable to a lingering Disease, or to a miserable Death.

Even those Measures, Sir, which have been mentioned as most grossly absurd, and represented as parallel to the Provision made in this Clause only to expose it to Contempt and Ridicule, may in particular Circumstances be rational and just. To settle the Price of Corn in the Time of a Famine, may become the wisest State, and Multitudes might in Time of publick Misery, by the Benefit of temporary Laws, be preserved from Destruction. Even those Masts, to which with a prosperous Gale, the Ship owes its Usefulness and its Speed, are often cut down by the Sailors in the Fury of a Storm.

With regard to the Ships which are now in distant Places, whither no Knowledge of this Law can possibly be convey'd, it cannot be denied that their Crews ought to be secured from Injury by some particular Exception; for tho' it is evident in Competitions between public and private Interest, which ought to be preferred, yet we ought to remember that no unnecessary Injury is to be done to Individuals, even while we are providing for the Safety of the Nation.

The Urg; Fakazerly [9] [Fazakerly] spoke to this Effect.

S I R: Tho' I cannot be supposed to have much Acquaintance with Naval Affairs, and therefore may not perhaps discover the full Force of the Arguments that have been urged in Favour of the Clause now under Consideration, yet I cannot but think myself under an indispensible Obligation to examine it as far as I am able, and to make use of the Knowledge which I have acquired, however inferior to that of others.

The Argument, Sir, the only real Argument, which has been produced in Favour of the Restraint of Wages now proposed, appears to me by no Means Conclusive; nor can I believe that the meanest and most ignorant Seaman would, if it were proposed to him, hesitate a Moment for an Answer to it. Let me suppose, Sir, a Merchant urging it as a Charge against a Seaman, that he raises his Demand of Wages in Time of War, would not the Sailor readily reply, That harder Labour required larger Pay? Would he not ask, why the general Practice of Mankind is charged as a Crime upon him only? Enquire, says he, of the Workmen in the Docks, have they not double Wages for double Labour? And is not their Lot safe and easy in Comparison with mine, [who] at once encounter Danger and support Fatigue? carry on War and Commerce at the same Time, . . . conduct the Ship and oppose the enemy, and am equally exposed to Captivity and Shipwreck?

That this is in Reality the State of a Sailor in Time of War, I think, Sir, too evident to require Proof; nor do I see what Reply, can be made to the Sailor's artless Expostulation.

I know not why the Sailors alone should serve their Country to their Disadvantage, and be expected to encounter Danger without the Incitement of a Reward.

Nor will any Part of the Hardships of this Clause be alleviated by the Expedient suggested by an honourable Member, who spoke some Time ago, of granting, or

[9] Nicholas Fazakerly (d. 1767) was a lawyer and an authority on conveyancing.

allowing, to a Sailor, whose Contract shall be void, what our Courts of Law should adjudge him to deserve, a *Quantum meruit*.[10] For, according to the general Interpretation of our Statutes, it will be determined that he has forfeited his whole Claim by illegal Contract. To instance, Sir, the Statute of Usury. He that stipulates for higher Interest than is allowed, is not able to recover his legal Demand, but irrevocably forfeits the Whole.

Thus, Sir, an unhappy Sailor, who shall innocently transgress this Law, must lose all the Profit of his Voyage, and have nothing to relieve him after his Fatigues, but when he has by his Courage repell'd the Enemy, and by his Skill escaped Storms and Rocks, must suffer yet severer Hardships, in being subject to a Forfeiture where he expected Applause, Comfort, and Recompence.

The Attorney General [11] *spoke next to this Purport.*

S I R: The Clause before us cannot, in my Opinion, produce any such dreadful Consequences as the learned Gentleman appears to imagine: However, to remove all Difficulties, I have drawn up an Amendment, which I shall beg leave to propose, That the Contracts which may be affected as the Clause now stands, *shall be void only as to so much of the Wages as shall exceed the Sum to which the House shall agree to reduce the Seamen's Pay;* and as to the Forfeitures, they are not to be levied upon the Sailors, but upon the Merchants, or trading Companies, who employ them, and who are able to pay greater Sums without being involved in Poverty and Distress.

With regards, Sir, to the Reasons for introducing this Clause, they are, in my Judgment, valid and equitable. We have found it necessary to fix the Rate of Money at Interest, and the Rate of Labour in several Cases, and if we do not in this Case, what will be the Consequence? A second Embargo on Commerce, and perhaps a total Stop to all military Preparations. Is it reasonable that any Man should rate his Labour according to the immediate Necessities of those that employ him? Or that he should raise his own Fortune by the publick Calamities? If this has hitherto been a Practice, it is a Practice contrary to the general Happiness of Society, and ought to prevail no longer.

If the Sailor, Sir, is exposed to greater Dangers in Time of War, is not the Merchant's Trade carried on likewise at greater Hazard? Is not the Freight, equally with the Sailors, threatened at once by the Ocean and the Enemy? and is not the Owner's Fortune equally impaired, whether the Ship is dash'd upon a Rock, or seized by a Privateer?

The Merchant, therefore, has as much Reason for paying less Wages in Time of War as the Sailor for demanding more, and nothing remains but that the Legislative Power determine a Medium between their different Interests, with Justice, if possible, at least with Impartiality.

The Prime Minister's Brother,[12] *who had stood up Several Times, but was prevented by other Members, spoke next, to this Purport.*

S I R: I was unwilling to interrupt the Course of this Debate while it was

---

[10] An award of "as much as he should deserve."

[11] Sir Dudley Ryder (1691–1756) was a lawyer and later Chief Justice of the King's Bench. He was made Solicitor General in 1733 and Attorney General in 1737.

[12] Horatio (or Horace) Walpole (1678–1757), first Baron Walpole, was the younger brother of Sir Robert. He was a diplomatist, a member of Parliament for various con-

carried on with Calmness and Decency, by Men who do not suffer the Ardour of Opposition to cloud their Reason, or transport them to such Expressions as the Dignity of this Assembly does not admit. I have hitherto deferr'd to answer the Gentleman who declaimed against the Bill with such Fluency of Rhetoric, and such Vehemence of Gesture, who charged the Advocates for the Expedients now proposed, with having no Regard to any Interest but their own, and with making Laws only to consume Paper, and threatened them with the Defection of their Adherents, and the Loss of their Influence, upon this new Discovery of their Folly, and their Ignorance.

Nor, Sir, do I now answer him for any other purpose than to remind him how little the Clamours of Rage and Petulancy of Invectives, contribute to the Purposes for which this Assembly is called together; how little the Discovery of Truth is promoted, and the Security of the Nation established by pompous Diction, and theatrical Emotions.

Formidable Sounds, and furious Declamations, confident Assertions, and lofty Periods, may affect the young and inexperienced, and perhaps the Gentleman may have contracted his Habits of Oratory by conversing more with those of his own Age,[13] than with such as have had more Opportunities of acquiring Knowledge, and more successful Methods of communicating their Sentiments.

If the Heat of his Temper, Sir, would suffer him to attend to those whose Age and long Acquaintance with Business, give them an indisputable Right to Deference and Superiority, he would learn, in Time, to reason rather than declaim, and to prefer Justness of Argument, and an accurate Knowledge of Facts, to sounding Epithets and splendid Superlatives, which may disturb the Imagination for a Moment, but leave no lasting Impression on the Mind.

He will learn, Sir, that to accuse and prove are very different, and that Reproaches unsupported by Evidence, affect only the Character of him that utters them. Excursions of Fancy, and Flights of Oratory, are indeed pardonable in young Men, but in no other; and it would surely contribute more, even to the Purpose for which some Gentlemen appear to speak, that of depreciating the Conduct of the Administration, to prove the Inconveniences and Injustice of this Bill, than barely to assert them, with whatever Magnificence of Language, or Appearance of Zeal, Honesty, or Compassion.

The Urg; Ptit replied.

S I R: The atrocious Crime of being a young Man, which the honourable Gentleman has with such Spirit and Decency charged upon me, I shall neither attempt to palliate, nor deny, but content myself with wishing that I may be one of those whose Follies may cease with their Youth, and not of that Number, who are ignorant in spite of Experience.

Whether Youth can be imputed to any Man as a Reproach, I will not, Sir, assume the Province of determining; but surely Age may become justly contemptible, if the Opportunities which it brings have past away without Improvement, and Vice appears to prevail when the Passions have subsided. The Wretch

---

stituencies, and a holder of many offices. He is not to be confused with his more famous nephew, Sir Robert's son Horace, the man of letters, correspondent *par excellence,* and contemporary historian. The nephew later also sat in Parliament.

[13] Pitt was a "boy" of thirty-three at this time, Samuel Johnson a year younger.

that, after having seen the Consequences of a thousand Errors, continues still to blunder, and whose Age has only added Obstinacy to Stupidity, is surely the Object of either Abhorrence or Contempt, and deserves not that his grey Head should secure him from Insults.

Much more, Sir, is he to be abhorr'd, who, as he has advanced in Age, has receded from Virtue, and becomes more wicked with less Temptation; who prostitutes himself for Money which he cannot enjoy, and spends the Remains of his Life in the Ruin of his Country.

But Youth, Sir, is not my only Crime; I have been accused of acting a theatrical Part—A theatrical Part may either imply some Peculiarities of Gesture, or a Dissimulation of my real Sentiments, and an Adoption of the Opinions and Language of another Man.

In the first Sense, Sir, the Charge is too trifling to be confuted, and deserves only to be mentioned, that it may be despised. I am at Liberty, like every other Man, to use my own Language; and though I may perhaps have some Ambition to please this Gentleman, I shall not lay myself under any Restraint, nor very solicitously copy his Diction, or his Mien, however matured by Age, or modelled by Experience.

If any Man shall by charging me with theatrical Behavior imply, that I utter any Sentiments but my own, I shall treat him as a Calumniator, and a Villain; nor shall any Protection shelter him from the Treatment which he deserves. I shall, on such an Occasion, without Scruple, trample upon all those Forms with which Wealth and Dignity intrench themselves, nor shall any Thing but Age restrain my Resentment; Age, which always brings one Privilege, that of being insolent and supercilious without Punishment.

But, with Regard, Sir, to those whom I have offended, I am of Opinion, that if I had acted a borrowed Part, I should have avoided their Censure; the Heat that offended them is the Ardour of Conviction, and that Zeal for the Service of my Country, which neither Hope nor Fear shall influence me to suppress. I will not sit unconcerned while my Liberty is invaded, nor look in Silence upon publick Robbery.—I will exert my Endeavours at whatever Hazard, to repel the Aggressor, and drag the Thief to Justice, whoever may protect them in their Villainy, and whoever may partake of their Plunder.—And if the Honourable Gentleman—

Here the Urg; Wintinnong [14] *[Winnington] call'd to Order, and Urg; Ptit sitting down, he spoke thus.*

It is necessary, Sir, that the order of this Assembly be observed, and the Debate resumed without personal Altercations. Such Expressions as have been vented on this Occasion, become not an Assembly entrusted with the Liberty and Welfare of their Country. To interrupt the Debate on a Subject so important as that before us, is, in some measure to obstruct the publick Happiness, and violate our Trust: But much more heinous is the Crime of exposing our Determinations to Contempt, and inciting the People to Suspicion or Mutiny, by indecent Reflections, or unjust Insinuations.

---

[14] Thomas Winnington (1696–1746) was a supporter of Walpole. At this time he was Treasurer of the Navy. The expression "called to order" is the equivalent of "raised a point of order."

I do not, Sir, undertake to decide the Controversy between the two Gentlemen, but must be allowed to observe, that no Diversity of Opinion can justify the Violation of Decency, and the Use of rude and virulent Expressions; Expressions dictated only by Resentment, and uttered without Regard to—

Here the Urg; Ptit called to Order, and said.

S I R: If this be to preserve Order, there is no Danger of Indecency from the most licentious Tongue; for what Calumny can be more atrocious, or what Reproach more severe, than that of speaking with Regard to any thing but Truth. Order may sometimes be broken by Passion, or Inadvertency, but will hardly be re-establish'd by Monitors like this, who cannot govern his own Passion, whilst he is restraining the Impetuosity of others.

Happy, Sir, would it be for Mankind, if every one knew his own Province; we should not then see the same Man at once a Criminal and a Judge, nor would this Gentleman assume the Right of dictating to others what he has not learned himself.

That I may return in some Degree the Favour which he intends me, I will advise him never hereafter to exert himself on the Subject of Order; but whenever he finds himself inclined to speak on such Occasions, to remember how he has now succeeded, and condemn in Silence what his Censures will never reform.

The Urg; Wintinnong replied.

S I R: As I was hindered by the Gentleman's Ardour and Impetuosity from concluding my Sentence, none but myself can know the Equity or Partiality of my Intentions, and therefore as I cannot justly be condemn'd I ought to be supposed innocent; nor ought he to censure a Fault of which he cannot be certain that it would ever have been committed.

He has indeed exalted himself to a Degree of Authority never yet assumed by any Member of this House, that of condemning others to Silence. I am henceforward, by his inviolable Decree, to sit and hear his Harangues without daring to oppose him. How wide he may extend his Authority, or whom he will proceed to include in the same Sentence I shall not determine; having not yet arrived at the same Degree of Sagacity with himself, nor being able to foreknow what another is going to pronounce.

If, I had given Offense by any improper Sallies of Passion, I ought to have been censured by the concurrent Voice of the Assembly, or have received a Reprimand, Sir, from you [15] to which I should have submitted without Opposition; but I will not be doomed to Silence by one who has no Pretensions to Authority, and whose arbitrary Decisions can only tend to introduce Uproar, Discord and Confusion.

Hynrec Plemahm [16] [Henry Pelham] *Urg; next rose up and spoke to this Effect.*

S I R: When, in the Ardour of Controversy upon interesting Questions, the

[15] The Speaker of the House.

[16] Henry Pelham (1695–1754), brother of the Duke of Newcastle and one of Walpole's principal supporters. After the fall of Walpole, he and his brother were the leading politicians until the rise of Pitt.

Zeal of the Disputants hinders them from a nice Observation of Decency and Regularity, there is some Indulgence due to the common Weakness of our Nature; nor ought any Gentleman to affix to a negligent Expression a more offensive Sense than is necessarily implied by it.

To search deep, Sir, for Calumnies and Reproaches is no laudable nor beneficial Curiosity; it must always be troublesome to ourselves by alarming us with imaginary Injuries, and may often be unjust to others by charging them with Invectives which they never intended. General Candour and mutual Tenderness will best preserve our own Quiet and support that Dignity which has always been accounted essential to National Debates, and seldom infringed without dangerous Consequences.

Then the Urg; Lettyltno [17] [Lyttelton] *spoke as follows.*

S I R: No Man can be more zealous for Decency than myself, or more convinced of the Necessity of a methodical Prosecution of the Question before us. I am well convinced how near Indecency and Faction are to one another, and how inevitably Confusion produces Obscurity; but I hope it will always be remembered, that he who first infringes Decency, or deviates from Method, is to answer for all the Consequences that may arise from the Neglect of Senatorial Customs. For it is not to be expected that any Man will bear reproaches without Reply, or that he who wanders from the Question will not be followed in his Digressions and hunted through his Labyrinths.

It cannot, Sir, be denied, that some Insinuations were uttered, injurious to those whose Zeal may sometimes happen to prompt them to warm Declarations, or incite them to passionate Emotions. Whether I am of Importance enough to be included in the Censure, I despise it too much to enquire or consider, but cannot forbear to observe, that Zeal for the Right can never become reproachful, and that no Man can fall into Contempt but those who deserve it.

[The Clause was amended and agreed to.]

～

BIBLIOGRAPHICAL NOTE

The most authoritative life of Walpole and the best recent assessment is J. H. Plumb's (2 vols., 1956, 1960). An interesting brief characterization by Sir Richard Lodge appears in Dobrée's *From Anne to Victoria*. Lecky's estimate of Walpole, though old, is judicious. There have been no significant studies of his speaking. Johnson's *Debates* and the history and situation of parliamentary reporting are handled thoroughly in Benjamin B. Hoover, *Samuel Johnson's Parliamentary Reporting* (1953). See also Mary Ramsome, "The Reliability of the Contemporary Reporting of the House of Commons, 1727–1741," *Bulletin of the Institute of Historical Research*, XIX (May 1942), 67–79. For the later period see Peter D. G. Thomas, "The Beginning of Parliamentary Reporting in the Newspapers, 1768–1774," *English Historical Review*, LXXIV (1959), 623–36.

[17] George Lyttleton (1709–1773), later Baron Lyttelton, was an opponent of Walpole and with Pitt one of the so-called "Boy Patriots."

John Wesley

(1703–1791)

The Founder of Methodism, its organizer, its prime spokesman, and, with George Whitefield, one of the two great preachers of its first half-century, was John Wesley. While he was studying at Oxford, his disposition to strict, ascetic religious observance led him to the leadership of a society of young men, including his younger brother Charles, who were nicknamed "Methodists" because of the methodical way in which they pursued their religious devotions, took care of the sick, visited the prisons, and gave to the poor.

After coming under the influence of the good Moravians while doing missionary work in Georgia at the request of General Oglethorpe, Wesley in 1738 returned to preaching in England, declaring in his own country, as he said, "the glad tidings of salvation." From that mission, in speaking, in writing, and in action, he never relaxed for the rest of his long life.

The preaching of John Wesley and George Whitefield was one of the most important factors in the re-enlivening of religion which took place in this century. Wesley's, as Lecky wrote (*England in the Eighteenth Century,* II, 607), was "one of the most powerful and most active intellects in England"; Whitefield was the most eloquent and imaginative of popular orators. Together they furnished the principal impetus for that revival of living Christianity which, as Methodism, built a new dimension for evangelical Protestantism in Great Britain and America.

Wesley and his associates were at first not Dissenters. For as long as possible they stayed firmly within the Articles, the discipline, and the structure of the Church of England. They preached wherever they were admitted to pulpits, in churches often filled with ordinary folk little accustomed to attending, and with the curious. They sought first of all, however, to carry their message of simple piety and hope, of love and good works, of the new birth in Christ, and of justification by faith to the masses of the laboring poor and to the middle classes. They found that if they were to reach those who most needed their help—the coal miners of the West, the dock workers of London, the weavers of the Midlands—they would have to go outside the churches. Hence they took to preaching in the open air, wherever the crowds could be reached. This field preaching was their radical innovation.

The frequency with which Wesley and Whitefield preached, and the number to whom they spoke, are staggering. Wesley preached 800 times a year to audiences of a few to many thousands. Whitefield, who died twenty years before Wesley, preached 18,000 times in England and America to as many as 25,000 people at a time. The impact was commensurate with the effort.

Whitefield was perhaps more moving, more effective with the multitudes. "God's dramatist," as C. Harold King called him, sought first the heart of the sinner, his feelings, his affections, his yearnings. That was usually enough. He was impulsive, emotional, vivid, with a voice and delivery and a transparent goodness which themselves appeared to convey his message.

Within the limits of a more severe temperament, Wesley was hardly a less popular preacher than Whitefield; and he was besides an accomplished persuasive, instructional, and devotional writer. In preaching, Wesley was the master of orderliness, with perhaps an exaggerated passion for reasoning. His were the doctrinal sermons, adapted to the high or the lowly, to the learned or the ignorant. His also were the sermons on the conduct of the Christian life. He did not read his sermons, as most of his Anglican contemporaries did; his preaching was usually impromptu. He seldom planned a sermon in advance, and sometimes entered the pulpit without even knowing what his text was to be. Nevertheless, he was thoroughly in command of his message and his language, he understood his audiences, and his sense of orderliness imposed upon his sermons, as they grew, a transparent structure, a simple shapeliness.

In the Introduction to his first published sermons, Wesley wrote:

> The following sermons contain the substance of what I have been preaching for between eight and nine years last past. . . . Every serious man who peruses these, will therefore see, in the clearest manner, what these doctrines are which I embrace and teach as the essentials of true religion. . . . Nothing here appears in an elaborate, elegant, or oratorical dress. . . . I now write, as I generally speak, *ad populum*—to the bulk of mankind, to those who neither relish nor understand the art of speaking; but who, notwithstanding, are competent judges of those truths which are necessary to present and future happiness. . . . I design plain truth for plain people: Therefore . . . I abstain from all nice and philosophical speculations; from all perplexed and intricate reasonings. . . . I labour to avoid all words which are not easy to be understood, all which are not used in common life.

The sermon on *The Use of Money* does not show Wesley as the interpreter of the Christian mystery. For that side of him the reader should study, for example, the sermons on *Christian Perfection* and *The New Birth*. Nor does the preacher rise here to the spiritual elevation and eloquence of the sermon *On the Death of Mr. Whitefield*. Instead, this is practical Christian morality applied to one of the oldest and most persistent personal and social problems: "For what purpose are the goods of this world?" The sermon was published first in 1760. Wesley had preached on the same text often, beginning as early as 1744, and he continued to use it later as many Methodists grew rich and became more and more "lovers of this world."

∽

The Use of Money *

I say unto you, Make to yourselves friends of the mammon of unrighteousness; that, when ye fail, they may receive you into everlasting habitations. Luke 16:9.

1. Our Lord, having finished the beautiful parable of the Prodigal Son, which he had particularly addressed to those who murmured at his receiving publicans and sinners, adds another relation of a different kind, addressed rather to the children of God. "He said unto his disciples," not so much to the Scribes and

* The text is from *The Works of John Wesley* (London, 1872), VI, 124–36. It is Sermon L in *Sermons on Several Occasions: First Series*, 1771.

Pharisees to whom he had been speaking before,—"There was a certain rich man, who had a steward, and he was accused to him of wasting his goods. And calling him, he said, Give an account of thy stewardship, for thou canst be no longer steward." After reciting the method which the bad steward used to provide against the day of necessity, our Saviour adds, "His Lord commended the unjust steward"; namely, in this respect, that he used timely precaution; and subjoins this weighty reflection, "The children of this world are wiser in their generation than the children of light":[1] Those who seek no other portion than this world "are wiser" (not absolutely; for they are, one and all, the veriest fools, the most egregious madmen under heaven; but, "in their generation," in their own way; they are more consistent with themselves; they are truer to their acknowledged principles; they more steadily pursue their end) "than the children of light";—than they who see "the light of the glory of God in the face of Jesus Christ."[2] Then follow the words above recited: "And I,"—the only-begotten Son of God, the Creator, Lord, and Possessor of heaven and earth and all that is therein; the Judge of all, to whom ye are to "give an account of your stewardship," when ye "can be no longer stewards"; "I say unto you,"—learn in this respect, even of the unjust steward,—"make yourselves friends," by wise, timely precaution, "of the mammon of unrighteousness." "Mammon" means riches, or money. It is termed "the mammon of unrighteousness," because of the unrighteous manner wherein it is frequently procured, and wherein even that which was honestly procured is generally employed. "Make yourself friends" of this, by doing all possible good, particularly to the children of God; "that, when ye fail,"—when ye return to dust, when ye have no more place under the sun,—those of them who are gone before "may receive you," may welcome you, into the "everlasting habitations."

2. An excellent branch of Christian wisdom is here inculcated by our Lord on all his followers, namely, the right use of money;—a subject largely spoken of, after their manner, by men of the world; but not sufficiently considered by those whom God hath chosen out of the world. These, generally, do not consider, as the importance of the subject requires, the use of this excellent talent. Neither do they understand how to employ it to the greatest advantage; the introduction of which into the world is one admirable instance of the wise and gracious providence of God. It has, indeed, been the manner of poets, orators, and philosophers, in almost all ages and nations, to rail at this, as the grand corrupter of the world, the bane of virtue, the pest of human society. Hence nothing so commonly heard, as

> *Nocens, ferrum, ferroque nocentius aurum:*
> And gold, more mischievous than keenest steel.

Hence the lamentable complaint,

> *Effodiuntur opes, inritamenta malorum.*
> Wealth is dug up, incentive to all ill.

---

[1] The text and the quotations to this point are from Luke 16:1–9. Wesley does not always quote the Scriptures precisely but adapts the language to his immediate needs. The parable of the Prodigal Son is given in Luke 15:11–32.

[2] II Cor. 4:6.

Nay, one celebrated writer gravely exhorts his countrymen, in order to banish all vice at once, to "throw all their money into the sea":

> *In mare proximum,*
> *Summi materiem mali!* [3]

But is not all this mere empty rant? Is there any solid reason therein? By no means. For, let the world be as corrupt as it will, is gold or silver to blame? "The love of money," we know, "is the root of all evil"; [4] but not the thing itself. The fault does not lie in the money, but in them that use it. It may be used ill: And what may not? But it may likewise be used well: It is full as applicable to the best, as to the worst uses. It is of unspeakable service to all civilized nations, in all the common affairs of life: It is a most compendious instrument of transacting all manner of business, and (if we use it according to Christian wisdom) of doing all manner of good. It is true, were man in a state of innocence, or were all men "filled with the Holy Ghost," so that, like the infant Church at Jerusalem, "no man counted any thing he had his own," but "distribution was made to every one as he had need," [5] the use of it would be superseded; as we cannot conceive there is any thing of the kind among the inhabitants of heaven. But, in the present state of mankind, it is an excellent gift of God, answering the noblest ends. In the hands of his children, it is food for the hungry, drink for the thirsty, raiment for the naked: It gives to the traveller and the stranger where to lay his head. By it we may supply the place of an husband to the widow, and of a father to the fatherless. We may be a defence for the oppressed, a means of health to the sick, of ease to them that are in pain; it may be as eyes to the blind, as feet to the lame; yea, a lifter up from the gates of death!

3. It is, therefore, of the highest concern, that all who fear God know how to employ this valuable talent; that they be instructed how it may answer these glorious ends, and in the highest degree. And, perhaps, all the instructions which are necessary for this may be reduced to three plain rules, by the exact observance whereof we may approve ourselves faithful stewards of "the mammon of unrighteousness."

I. 1. The First of these is, (he that heareth, let him understand!) "Gain all you can." Here we may speak like the children of the world: We meet them on their own ground. And it is our bounden duty to do this: We ought to gain all we can gain, without buying gold too dear, without paying more for it than it is worth. But this it is certain we ought not to do; we ought not to gain money at the expense of life, nor (which is in effect the same thing) at the expense of our health. Therefore, no gain whatsoever should induce us to enter into, or to continue in, any employ, which is of such a kind, or is attended with so hard or so long labour, as to impair our constitution. Neither should we begin or continue in any business which necessarily deprives us of proper seasons for food and sleep, in such a proportion as our nature requires. Indeed, there is a great difference here. Some employments are absolutely and totally unhealthy; as those which imply the dealing much with arsenic, or other equally hurtful minerals, or the breathing an air tainted with steams of melting lead, which must at length

---

[3] Ovid *Metamorphoses* III. 141, 140; Horace *Odes* III.xxiv.47–49. Wesley selects and interprets lines freely to his purpose.

[4] I Tim. 6:10.

[5] Acts 4:31, 32, 35.

destroy the firmest constitution. Others may not be absolutely unhealthy, but only to persons of a weak constitution. Such are those which require many hours to be spent in writing; especially if a person write sitting, and lean upon his stomach, or remain long in an uneasy posture. But whatever it is which reason or experience shows to be destructive of health or strength, that we may not submit to; seeing "the life is more" valuable "than meat, and the body than raiment": [6] And, if we are already engaged in such an employ, we should exchange it, as soon as possible, for some which, if it lessen our gain, will, however, not lessen our health.

2. We are, Secondly, to gain all we can without hurting our mind, any more than our body. For neither may we hurt this: We must preserve, at all events, the spirit of an healthful mind. Therefore, we may not engage or continue in any sinful trade; any that is contrary to the law of God, or of our country. Such are all that necessarily imply our robbing or defrauding the king of his lawful customs. For it is, at least, as sinful to defraud the king of his right, as to rob our fellow-subjects: And the king has full as much right to his customs as we have to our houses and apparel. Other businesses [7] there are which, however innocent in themselves, cannot be followed with innocence now; at least, not in England; such, for instance, as will not afford a competent maintenance without cheating or lying, or conformity to some custom which is not consistent with a good conscience: These, likewise, are sacredly to be avoided, whatever gain they may be attended with, provided we follow the custom of the trade; for, to gain money, we must not lose our souls. There are yet others which many pursue with perfect innocence, without hurting either their body or mind; and yet, perhaps, you cannot: Either they may entangle you in that company which would destroy your soul; and by repeated experiments it may appear that you cannot separate the one from the other; or there may be an idiosyncrasy,—a peculiarity in your constitution of soul, (as there is in the bodily constitution of many), by reason whereof that employment is deadly to you, which another may safely follow. So I am convinced, from many experiments, I could not study, to any degree of perfection, either mathematics, arithmetic, or algebra, without being a Deist,[8] if not an Atheist: And yet others may study them all their lives without sustaining any inconvenience. None, therefore, can here determine for another; but every man must judge for himself, and abstain from whatever he in particular finds to be hurtful to his soul.

3. We are, Thirdly, to gain all we can, without hurting our neighbour. But this we may not, cannot do, if we love our neighbour as ourselves. We cannot, if we love every one as ourselves, hurt any one *in his substance*. We cannot devour the increase of his lands, and perhaps the lands and houses themselves, by gaming, by over-grown bills, (whether on account of physic, or law, or any thing else), or by requiring or taking such interest as even the laws of our country forbid. Hereby all pawn-broking is excluded: Seeing, whatever good we might

---

[6] Matt. 6:25.

[7] In the preceding and in what follows Wesley obviously has particular occupations in mind—smuggling, for example, and pawnbroking.

[8] The Deists professed a "natural religion." They believed in a Supreme Being as the origin of human existence, but they rejected divine revelation and the other supernatural doctrines of Christianity. Deism had been especially prevalent among intellectuals during the preceding century.

do thereby, all unprejudiced men see with grief to be abundantly over-balanced by the evil. And if it were otherwise, yet we are not allowed to "do evil that good may come." [9] We cannot, consistent with brotherly love, sell our goods below the market-price; we cannot study to ruin our neighbour's trade, in order to advance our own; much less can we entice away, or receive, any of his servants or workmen whom he has need of. None can gain by swallowing up his neighbour's substance, without gaining the damnation of hell!

4. Neither may we gain by hurting our neighbour *in his body*. Therefore we may not sell any thing which tends to impair health. Such is, eminently, all that liquid fire, commonly called drams, or spirituous liquors.[10] It is true, these may have a place in medicine; they may be of use in some bodily disorders; although there would rarely be occasion for them, were it not for the unskilfulness of the practitioner. Therefore, such as prepare and sell them only for this end may keep their conscience clear. But who are they? Who prepare them only for this end? Do you know ten such distillers in England? Then excuse these. But all who sell them in the common way, to any that will buy, are poisoners general. They murder His Majesty's subjects by wholesale, neither does their eye pity or spare. They drive them to hell like sheep. And what is their gain? Is it not the blood of these men? Who then would envy their large estates and sumptuous palaces? A curse is in the midst of them: The curse of God cleaves to the stones, the timber, the furniture of them! The curse of God is in their gardens, their walks, their groves; a fire that burns to the nethermost hell! Blood, blood is there: The foundation, the floor, the walls, the roof, are stained with blood! And canst thou hope, O thou man of blood, though thou art "clothed in scarlet and fine linen, and farest sumptuously every day"; [11] canst thou hope to deliver down thy *fields of blood* [12] to the third generation? Not so; for there is a God in heaven: Therefore, thy name shall soon be rooted out. Like as those whom thou hast destroyed, body and soul, "thy memorial shall perish with thee!" [13]

5. And are not they partakers of the same guilt, though in a lower degree, whether Surgeons, Apothecaries, or Physicians, who play with the lives or health of men, to enlarge their own gain? who purposely lengthen the pain or disease, which they are able to remove speedily? who protract the cure of their patient's body, in order to plunder his substance? Can any man be clear before God, who does not shorten every disorder "as much as he can," and remove all sickness and pain "as soon as he can"? He cannot: For nothing can be more clear, than that he does not "love his neighbour as himself"; [14] than that he does not "do unto others, as he would they should do unto himself." [15]

6. This is dear-bought gain. And so is whatever is procured by hurting our neighbour *in his soul*; by ministering, suppose, either directly or indirectly, to his unchastity, or intemperance; which certainly none can do, who has any fear of

[9] Rom. 3:8.

[10] See the Earl of Chesterfield's attack on the liquor traffic in his speech against licensing gin shops, 1743, in Goodrich, *Select British Eloquence,* pp. 46–52.

[11] Luke 16:19.

[12] Acts 1:19.

[13] Ps. 9:6.

[14] This requirement occurs in both the Old and New Testaments. See Lev. 19:18, Matt. 19:19 and 22:39, Rom. 13:9, Gal. 5:14, James 2:8.

[15] Luke 6:31, Matt. 7:12.

God, or any real desire of pleasing Him. It nearly concerns all those to consider this, who have anything to do with taverns, victualling-houses, opera-houses, play-houses, or any other places of public, fashionable diversion. If these profit the souls of men, you are clear; your employment is good, and your gain innocent; but if they are either sinful in themselves, or natural inlets to sin of various kinds, then, it is to be feared, you have a sad account to make. O beware, lest God say in that day, "These have perished in their iniquity, but their blood do I require at thy hands!" [16]

7. These cautions and restrictions being observed, it is the bounden duty of all who are engaged in worldly business to observe that first and great rule of Christian wisdom, with respect to money, "Gain all you can." Gain all you can by honest industry. Use all possible diligence in your calling. Lose no time. If you understand yourself, and your relation to God and man, you know you have none to spare. If you understand your particular calling, as you ought, you will have no time that hangs upon your hands. Every business will afford some employment sufficient for every day and every hour. That wherein you are placed, if you follow it in earnest, will leave you no leisure for silly, unprofitable diversions. You have always something better to do, something that will profit you, more or less. And "whatsoever thy hand findeth to do, do it with thy might." [17] Do it as soon as possible: No delay! No putting off from day to day, or from hour to hour! Never leave anything till to-morrow, which you can do to-day. And do it as well as possible. Do not sleep or yawn over it: Put your whole strength to the work. Spare no pains. Let nothing be done by halves, or in a slight and careless manner. Let nothing in your business be left undone, if it can be done by labour or patience.

8. Gain all you can, by common sense, by using in your business all the understanding which God has given you. It is amazing to observe, how few do this; how men run on in the same dull track with their forefathers. But whatever they do who know not God, this is no rule for you. It is a shame for a Christian not to improve upon *them,* in whatever he takes in hand. You should be continually learning, from the experience of others, or from your own experience, reading, and reflection, to do everything you have to do better to-day than you did yesterday. And see that you practise whatever you learn, that you may make the best of all that is in your hands.

II. 1. Having gained all you can, by honest wisdom, and unwearied diligence, the Second rule of Christian prudence is, "Save all you can." Do not throw the precious talent into the sea: Leave that folly to heathen philosophers. Do not throw it away in idle expenses, which is just the same as throwing it into the sea. Expend no part of it merely to gratify the desire of the flesh, the desire of the eye, or the pride of life.

2. Do not waste any part of so precious a talent, merely in gratifying the desires of the flesh; in procuring the pleasures of sense, of whatever kind; particularly, in enlarging the pleasure of tasting. I do not mean, avoid gluttony and drunkenness only: An honest Heathen would condemn these. But there is a regular, reputable kind of sensuality, an elegant epicurism, which does not immediately disorder the stomach, nor (sensibly at least) impair the understanding;

[16] Ezek. 3:18, 33:8.
[17] Eccl. 9:10.

and yet (to mention no other effects of it now) it cannot be maintained without considerable expense. Cut off all this expense! Despise delicacy and variety, and be content with what plain nature requires.

3. Do not waste any part of so precious a talent, merely in gratifying the desire of the eye, by superfluous or expensive apparel, or by needless ornaments. Waste no part of it in curiously adorning your houses; in superfluous or expensive furniture; in costly pictures, painting, gilding, books; in elegant rather than useful gardens. Let your neighbours, who know nothing better, do this: "Let the dead bury their dead." But "what is that to thee?" says our Lord: "Follow thou me." [18] Are you willing? Then you are able so to do!

4. Lay out nothing to gratify the pride of life, to gain the admiration or praise of men. This motive of expense is frequently interwoven with one or both of the former. Men are expensive in diet, or apparel, or furniture, not barely to please their appetite, or to gratify their eye, or their imagination, but their vanity too. "So long as thou doest well unto thyself, men will speak good of thee." [19] So long as thou art "clothed in purple and fine linen, and farest sumptuously every day," no doubt many will applaud thy elegance of taste, thy generosity and hospitality. But do not buy their applause so dear. Rather be content with the honour that cometh from God.

5. Who would expend anything in gratifying these desires, if he considered, that to gratify them is to increase them? Nothing can be more certain than this: Daily experience shows, the more they are indulged, they increase the more. Whenever, therefore, you expend anything to please your taste or other senses, you pay so much for sensuality. When you lay out money to please your eye, you give so much for an increase of curiosity,—for a stronger attachment to these pleasures which perish in the using. While you are purchasing anything which men use to applaud, you are purchasing more vanity. Had you not then enough of vanity, sensuality, curiosity, before? Was there need of any addition? And would you pay for it too? What manner of wisdom is this? Would not the literally throwing your money into the sea be a less mischievous folly?

6. And why should you throw away money upon your children, any more than upon yourself, in delicate food, in gay or costly apparel, in superfluities of any kind? Why should you purchase for them more pride or lust, more vanity, or foolish and hurtful desires? They do not want any more; they have enough already; nature has made ample provision for them: Why should you be at farther expense to increase their temptations and snares, and to pierce them through with more sorrows?

7. Do not leave it to them to throw away. If you have good reason to believe they would waste what is now in your possession, in gratifying, and thereby increasing, the desire of the flesh, the desire of the eye, or the pride of life; at the peril of theirs and your own soul, do not set these traps in their way. Do not offer your sons or your daughters unto Belial, any more than unto Moloch. [20] Have pity upon them, and remove out of their way what you may easily foresee would increase their sins, and consequently plunge them deeper into everlasting perdition! How amazing then is the infatuation of those parents who think they

[18] Put together from Matt. 8:22, Luke 9:60, John 21:22 and 23.

[19] Ps. 49:18.

[20] Do not tempt your children to wickedness any more than you would sacrifice them to false gods. See also Milton's *Paradise Lost* I, 490; II, 109; I, 392.

can never leave their children enough! What! cannot you leave them enough of arrows, firebrands, and death? not enough of foolish and hurtful desires? not enough of pride, lust, ambition, vanity? not enough of everlasting burnings? Poor wretch! thou fearest where no fear is. Surely both thou and they, when ye are lifting up your eyes in hell, will have enough both of "the worm that never dieth," and of "the fire that never shall be quenched!" [21]

8. "What then would you do, if you was in my case? if you had a considerable fortune to leave?" Whether I *would* do it or no, I know what I *ought* to do: This will admit of no reasonable question. If I had one child, elder or younger, who knew the value of money, one who, I believed, would put it to the true use, I should think it my absolute, indispensable duty, to leave that child the bulk of my fortune; and to the rest just so much as would enable them to live in the manner they had been accustomed to do. But what, if all your children were equally ignorant of the true use of money?" I ought then (hard saying! who can hear it?) to give each what would keep him above want; and to bestow all the rest in such a manner as I judged would be most for the glory of God.

III. 1. But let not any man imagine that he has done anything, barely by going thus far, by "gaining and saving all he can," if he were to stop here. All this is nothing, if a man go not forward, if he does not point all this at a farther end. Nor, indeed, can a man properly be said to save anything, if he only lays it up. You may as well throw your money into the sea, as bury it in the earth.[22] And you may as well bury it in the earth, as in your chest, or in the bank of England.[23] Not to use, is effectually to throw it away. If, therefore, you would indeed "make yourselves friends of the mammon of unrighteousness," add the Third rule to the two preceding. Having, First, gained all you can, and, Secondly, saved all you can, Then "give all you can."

2. In order to see the ground and reason of this, consider, when the Possessor of heaven and earth brought you into being, and placed you in this world, he placed you here, not as a proprietor, but a steward: As such he entrusted you, for a season, with goods of various kinds; but the sole property of these still rests in him, nor can ever be alienated from him. As you yourself are not your own, but his, such is, likewise, all that you enjoy. Such is your soul and your body, not your own, but God's. And so is your substance in particular. And he has told you, in the most clear and express terms, how you are to employ it for him, in such a manner, that it may be all an holy sacrifice, acceptable through Christ Jesus. And this light, easy service, he hath promised to reward with an eternal weight of glory.

3. The directions which God has given us, touching the use of our worldly substance, may be comprised in the following particulars. If you desire to be a faithful and a wise steward, out of that portion of your Lord's goods which he has for the present lodged in your hands, but with the right of resuming whenever it pleases him, First, provide things needful for yourself; food to eat, raiment to put on, whatever nature moderately requires for preserving the body in health and strength. Secondly, provide these for your wife, your children, your servants, or any others who pertain to your household. If, when this is done, there be an

---

[21] Is. 66:24; Mark 9:44, 46, 48.
[22] See the Parable of the Talents in Matt. 25:14–30.
[23] Wesley treats the Bank as a place for hiding money, not for putting it to use.

overplus left, then "do good to them that are of the household of faith." If there be an overplus still, "as you have opportunity, do good unto all men." [24] In so doing, you give all you can; nay, in a sound sense, all you have: For all that is laid out in this manner is really given to God. You "render unto God the things that are God's," [25] not only by what you give to the poor, but also by that which you expend in providing things needful for yourself and your household.

4. If, then, a doubt should at any time arise in your mind concerning what you are going to expend, either on yourself or any part of your family, you have an easy way to remove it. Calmly and seriously inquire, "(1.) In expending this, am I acting according to my character? Am I acting herein, not as a proprietor, but as a steward of my Lord's goods? (2.) Am I doing this in obedience to his word? In what scripture does he require me so to do? (3.) Can I offer up this action, this expense, as a sacrifice to God through Jesus Christ? (4.) Have I reason to believe, that for this very work I shall have a reward at the resurrection of the just?" You will seldom need anything more to remove any doubt which arises on this head; but, by this four-fold consideration, you will receive clear light as to the way wherein you should go.

5. If any doubt still remain, you may farther examine yourself by prayer, according to those heads of inquiry. Try whether you can say to the Searcher of hearts, your conscience not condemning you, "Lord, thou seest I am going to expend this sum on that food, apparel, furniture. And thou knowest, I act therein with a single eye, as a steward of thy goods, expending this portion of them thus, in pursuance of the design thou hadst in entrusting me with them. Thou knowest I do this in obedience to thy word, as thou commandest, and because thou commandest it. Let this, I beseech thee, be an holy sacrifice, acceptable through Jesus Christ! And give me a witness in myself, that for this labour of love I shall have a recompence when thou rewardest every man according to his works." Now, if your conscience bear you witness in the Holy Ghost, that this prayer is well-pleasing to God, then have you no reason to doubt but that expense is right and good, and such as will never make you ashamed.

6. You see, then, what it is to "make yourselves friends of the mammon of unrighteousness," and by what means you may procure, "that when ye fail, they may receive you into the everlasting habitations." You see the nature and extent of truly Christian prudence, so far as it relates to the use of that great talent, money. Gain all you can, without hurting either yourself or your neighbour, in soul or body, by applying hereto with unintermitted diligence, and with all the understanding which God has given you;—save all you can, by cutting off every expense which serves only to indulge foolish desire; to gratify either the desire of the flesh, the desire of the eye, or the pride of life; waste nothing, living or dying, on sin or folly, whether for yourself or your children;—and then, give all you can, or, in other words, give all you have to God. Do not stint yourself, like a Jew rather than a Christian, to this or that proportion. Render unto God, not a tenth,[26] not a third, not half, but all that is God's, be it more or less; by employing all on yourself, your household, the household of faith, and all mankind, in such a manner, that you may give a good account of your stewardship, when ye can

[24] Gal. 6:10.

[25] Matt. 22:21, Mark 12:17.

[26] A reference to *tithing*, the common principle of setting aside a tenth of one's income for God and the Church.

be no longer stewards; in such a manner as the oracles of God direct, both by general and particular precepts; in such a manner, that whatever ye do may be "a sacrifice of a sweet-smelling savour to God," [27] and that every act may be rewarded in that day, when the Lord cometh with all his saints.

7. Brethren, can we be either wise or faithful stewards, unless we thus manage our Lord's goods? We cannot, as not only the oracles of God, but our own conscience, beareth witness. Then why should we delay? Why should we confer any longer with flesh and blood, or men of the world? Our kingdom, our wisdom, is not of this world: Heathen custom is nothing to us. We follow no men any farther than they are followers of Christ. Hear ye him: Yea, to-day, while it is called to-day, hear and obey his voice! At this hour, and from this hour, do his will: Fulfil his word, in this and in all things! I entreat you, in the name of the Lord Jesus, act up to the dignity of your calling! No more sloth! Whatsoever your hand findeth to do, do it with your might! No more waste! Cut off every expense which fashion, caprice, or flesh and blood demand! No more covetousness! But employ whatever God has entrusted you with, in doing good, all possible good, in every possible kind and degree, to the household of faith, to all men! This is no small part of "the wisdom of the just." [28] Give all ye have, as well as all ye are, a spiritual sacrifice to Him who withheld not from you his Son, his only Son: So "laying up in store for yourselves a good foundation against the time to come, that ye may attain eternal life!" [29]

∾

Bibliographical Note

Publication on Wesley and Methodism is vast, as the catalogue of any good library will witness. The standard *Life* is that by Luke Tyerman (1872). John Telford's *Life of John Wesley* (1899) is also very good. The best source of information for the student of Wesley's speaking, however, will be his *Journals* (ed. by Nehemiah Curnock, 1938) and his *Letters* (ed. by Telford, 1931). Lecky (II, ch. ix) is especially good on Wesley, Whitefield, and Methodism. More recent, and excellent, is Maldwyn L. Edwards, *John Wesley and the Eighteenth Century* (1933). John Beresford's brief character essay in Bonamy Debrée's *Anne to Victoria* is also to be recommended. For a compact account of the state of the Church in the mid-eighteenth century, see N. Sykes, "The Church," in A. S. Turberville's *Johnson's England* (1933), I, ch. ii. Wesley's theory of public speaking and literature is presented in James L. Golden, "John Wesley on Rhetoric and Belles Lettres," *Speech Monographs*, XXVIII (1961), 250–64. The preaching of Wesley's friend and partner, George Whitefield, is treated by C. Harold King in "George Whitefield: Commoner Evangelist," *Historical Studies of Rhetoric and Rhetoricians* (ed. by Raymond F. Howes, 1961), pp. 253–70. See also Eugene E. White's articles on Whitefield in America: "Preaching of George Whitefield During the Great Awakening in America," *Speech Monographs*, XV (1948), 33–42; "The Great Awakener: George Whitefield," *Southern Speech Journal*, XI (January 1945), 6–15; "George Whitefield's Preaching in Massachusetts and Georgia: a Case Study in Persuasion," *Ibid.*, XV (May 1950), 249–62.

[27] Eph. 5:2.
[28] Luke 1:17.
[29] I Tim. 6:19.

William Pitt, the Elder, Earl of Chatham

(1708–1778)

Lord Chatham's best biographer called his subject "our greatest orator and our greatest war-minister." Perhaps still we need make no exception, even of Sir Winston Churchill. Pitt was educated for public life. At Eton and Oxford he cultivated the classics, literature, and rhetorical studies, not simply as the equipment of the cultivated gentleman, but as the source of eloquence, and hence of influence in politics. He enlarged his powers of mind and language, and he disciplined a naturally good voice and impressive appearance into instruments of formidable and fearsome oratory.

Pitt served in Parliament for over forty years, and as Chief Minister during the crisis of the Seven Years' War, he engineered victories in America, India, Germany, and the islands of the sea, which secured the Empire and were the astonishment and pride of all England. By such achievements, by eloquent denunciation of incompetence in government, and by grand expressions of devotion to the Constitution, the greatness of England, and the liberty of the people no matter how humble, he endeared himself to the public and was known as the "Great Commoner" even after he had risen to the House of Lords (1766).

Pitt, however, was a war minister, and when victory is assured, the cost of war quickly seems oppressive. In 1761 the new King George III sought peace short of the complete humiliation of France. Pitt thereupon resigned; and from then on, except for a very brief period, he fought in Opposition, where his distinctive qualities as orator always shone with conspicuous brilliance.

As William Pitt and as Lord Chatham he was the most formidable friend of America, and on the problems of America he made his most famous and most often quoted speeches. He argued for the repeal of the Stamp Act and the right of the Colonies to tax themselves (House of Commons, 14 January 1766: "I rejoice that America has resisted.") He demanded the removal of the troops from Boston (House of Lords, 20 January 1775: "I contend not for indulgence, but justice to America"). In the speech printed below, he pleaded for a final effort to restore the friendship of the Colonies before France should join in the war. These speeches are the passionate productions of a mature statesman, once the savior of his country, and still the idol of the people.

Chatham's was the oratory of indignation, harassment, invective—and grand appeals to liberty, patriotism, and the British Constitution. He was not notable for close or extended argument, but relied upon reiterated assertion of assumed authority, upon memorable sentences and figures of speech, and upon appeals to traditional British good sense. His scorn for concession and his arrogant independence enhanced his popular appeal. ("I am sure that I can save this country, and I am sure that no one else can.") He could not cooperate, he could only dominate. Hence the hostility of other leaders of Opposition, like Burke. Chatham's vanity insulted them; his theatrical manner they thought pompous fustian; and his frequent attacks of apparent madness they thought—madness.

Yet his position on every important question was awaited with eagerness or apprehension by friend and foe, and his speeches were listened to as few others were.

Even the "Great Commoner" was as little able as Burke and Fox to avert the war with the Colonies; and by November 1777 the defeat of Burgoyne at Saratoga (as yet unknown, but feared by Chatham) had brought the Americans close to an overt alliance with France. So catastrophic did the possibilities seem, and so misguided the determination of the government to prosecute the unfortunate war, that Chatham made a last, grand effort to avert the calamity.

Each year, at the opening of Parliament, all the aspects of public policy were open to discussion, as the Minister laid the Government's program before Parliament in the Speech from the Throne. In response, each house prepared an Address of Thanks, usually agreeing to perform what the Speech recommended, and thanking the king for his loving care for the nation. Opposition often sought to amend the Address so as to criticize the king's ministers and to advise His Majesty contrary to the recommendations of the Administration. So Lord Chatham on November 18, 1777, moved an amendment to the Address, urging the king to make all haste to reverse the policy of his ministers on America: to conclude an honest and happy peace before word of worse calamities should come from America and before France should openly come into the war on the side of the Colonies. The principal contentions were not new. They had been advanced by Chatham and the Opposition for a dozen years. To these contentions, once more, their most respected advocate gave uninhibited and, it is fair to say, eloquent expression. That speech is better reported than Chatham's usually were, and indeed is one of his most impressive. Three-quarters of a century later Chauncey Goodrich called it "a splendid blaze of genius, at once rapid, vigorous, and sublime" (*Select British Eloquence,* p. 134).

$\backsim$

ON RESTORING PEACE WITH AMERICA
(SPEECH ON HIS AMENDMENT TO THE ADDRESS OF THANKS) *

House of Lords
November 18, 1777

I rise, my Lords, to declare my sentiments on this most solemn and serious subject. It has imposed a load upon my mind, which, I fear, nothing can remove; but which impels me to endeavor its alleviation, by a free and unreserved communication of my sentiments.

---

* Chatham published none of his speeches. Most of our texts are erratic, partisan, condensed newspaper reports, or historical fictions like Johnson's (above, pp. 178, 186). A few texts of his later speeches, however, derive from contemporary first-hand notes and recollections by especially acute observers and reporters. These apparently come close to the language and qualities of his oratory, though usually abbreviated and hence heightened. The text used here is one of the best. It was published originally in 1779 by Hugh Boyd, a man of prodigious memory for language and an accomplished reproducer of parliamentary speeches. We have taken it from Francis Thackeray, *A History of the Right Honorable William Pitt, Earl of Chatham, Containing his Speeches in Parliament* . . . (London, 1827), II, 333–36.

In the first part of the Address, I have the honor of heartily concurring with the noble Earl who moved it.[1] No man feels sincerer joy than I do; none can offer more genuine congratulation on every accession of strength to the Protestant succession: I therefore join in every congratulation on the birth of another princess, and the happy recovery of her Majesty.[2] But I must stop here; my courtly complaisance will carry me no further: I will not join in congratulation on misfortune and disgrace: I cannot concur in a blind and servile address, which approves, and endeavors to sanctify, the monstrous measures that have heaped disgrace and misfortune upon us—that have brought ruin to our doors. This, my Lords, is a perilous and tremendous moment! It is no time for adulation. The smoothness of flattery cannot now avail—cannot save us in this rugged and awful crisis. It is now necessary to instruct the Throne in the language of truth. We must dispel the delusion and the darkness which envelope it; and display, in its full danger and true colors, the ruin that is brought to our doors.

This, my Lords, is our duty; it is the proper function of this noble assembly, sitting, as we do, upon our honors in this House, the hereditary council of the Crown: and *who* is the minister—*where* is the minister, that has dared to suggest to the Throne the contrary unconstitutional language, this day delivered from it? —The accustomed language from the Throne has been application to Parliament for advice, and a reliance on its constitutional advice and assistance: as it is the right of Parliament to give, so it is the duty of the Crown to ask it. But, on this day, and in this extreme momentous exigency no reliance is reposed on our constitutional counsels! no advice is asked from the sober and enlightened care of Parliament! But the Crown, from itself, and by itself, declares an unalterable determination to pursue measures—and what measures, my Lords?—The measures that have produced the imminent perils that threaten us; the measures that have brought ruin to our doors.

Can the minister of the day[3] now presume to expect a continuance of support, and in this ruinous infatuation? Can Parliament be so dead to its dignity and its duty as to be thus deluded into the loss of the one, and the violation of the other? —To give an unlimited credit and support for the *steady* perseverance in measures —that is the word and the conduct—proposed for our Parliamentary advice, but dictated and forced upon us—in measures, I say, my Lords, which have reduced this late flourishing empire to ruin and contempt!—*But yesterday, and* England *might have stood against the world: now none so poor to do her reverence.* I use the words of a poet;[4] but though it be poetry, it is no fiction. It is a shameful truth, that not only the power and strength of this country are wasting away and expiring; but her well-earned glories, her true honor, and substantial dignity, are sacrificed. France, my Lords, has insulted you; she has encouraged and sustained

---

[1] Earl Percy, son of the Duke of Northumberland.

[2] Princess Sophia, twelfth child of George III and Queen Charlotte, was born November 3, 1777.

[3] Lord North, who was Prime Minister from 1770 to 1782.

[4] Chatham adapts a portion of Antony's speech from Shakespeare's *Julius Caesar*, III, ii:

> But yesterday the word of Caesar might
> Have stood against the world; now lies he there,
> And none so poor to do him reverence.

He echoes the quotation later in the passage.

America; and whether America be wrong or right, the dignity of this country ought to spurn at the officious insult of French interference. The ministers and ambassadors of those who are called rebels and enemies are in Paris; in Paris they transact the reciprocal interests of America and France. Can there be a more mortifying insult? Can even our ministers sustain a more humiliating disgrace? Do they dare to resent it? Do they presume even to hint a vindication of their honor, and the dignity of the state, by requiring the dismissal of the plenipotentiaries of America? Such is the degradation to which they have reduced the glories of England! The people, whom they affect to call contemptible rebels, but whose growing power has at last obtained the name of enemies; the people with whom they have engaged this country in war, and against whom they now command our implicit support in every measure of desperate hostility: this people, despised as rebels, or acknowledged as enemies, are abetted against you, supplied with every military store, their interests consulted, and their ambassadors entertained, by your inveterate enemy! and our ministers dare not interpose with dignity or effect. Is this the honor of a great kingdom? Is this the indignant spirit of England, who, 'but yesterday,' gave law to the House of Bourbon? My Lords, the dignity of nations demands a decisive conduct in a situation like this. Even when the greatest Prince that perhaps this country ever saw, filled our throne, the requisition of a Spanish General, on a similar subject, was attended to, and complied with; for, on the spirited remonstrance of the Duke of Alva, Elizabeth found herself obliged to deny the Flemish exiles all countenance, support, or even entrance into her dominions; and the Count le Marque, with his few desperate followers, was expelled the kingdom. Happening to arrive at the Brille, and finding it weak in defence, they made themselves masters of the place: and this was the foundation of the United Provinces.[5]

My Lords, this ruinous and ignominious situation, where we cannot act with success, nor suffer with honor, calls upon us to remonstrate in the strongest and loudest language of truth, to rescue the ear of Majesty from the delusions which surround it. The desperate state of our arms abroad is in part known: no man thinks more highly of them than I do: I love and honor the English troops: [6] I know their virtues and their valor: I know they can achieve any thing except impossibilities; and I know that the conquest of English America *is an impossibility*. You cannot, I venture to say it, you CANNOT conquer America. Your armies last war effected every thing that could be effected; and what was it? It cost a numerous army, under the command of a most able general, now a noble Lord in this house, a long and laborious campaign, to expel five thousand Frenchmen from French America. My Lords, *you cannot conquer America*. What is your present situation there? We do not know the worst; but we know, that in three campaigns we have done nothing, and suffered much. Besides the sufferings, perhaps *total loss*, of the Northern force; the best appointed army that ever took the field commanded by Sir William Howe, has retired from the American lines; *he was obliged* to relinquish his attempt, and, with great delay and danger, to adopt

[5] The reference is to the bloody suppression by the Spanish Duke of Alva of the rebellion in the Spanish Netherlands, 1567–1573.

[6] A favorite theme with Chatham. The following sentences refer to the French and Indian War and to Chatham's commander in America, Sir Geoffrey Amherst, made Baron Amherst in 1776.

a new and distant plan of operations. We shall soon know, and in any event have reason to lament, what may have happened since. As to conquest, therefore, my Lords, I repeat, it is impossible.—You may swell every expence, and every effort, still more extravagantly; pile and accumulate every assistance you can buy or borrow; traffic and barter with every little pitiful German Prince,[7] that sells and sends his subjects to the shambles of a foreign Prince; your efforts are for ever vain and impotent—doubly so from this mercenary aid on which you rely; for it irritates, to an incurable resentment, the minds of your enemies—to overrun them with the mercenary sons of rapine and plunder; devoting them and their possessions to the rapacity of hireling cruelty! If I were an American, as I am an Englishman, while a foreign troop was landed in my country, I never would lay down my arms—never—never—never.

Your own army is infected with the contagion of these illiberal allies. The spirit of plunder and of rapine is gone forth among them. I know it—and notwithstanding what the noble Earl, who moved the address, has given as his opinion of our American army, I know from authentic information, and the *most experienced officers*, that our discipline is deeply wounded. Whilst this is notoriously our sinking situation, America grows and flourishes; whilst our strength and discipline are lowered, theirs are rising and improving.

But, my Lords, who is the man that, in addition to these disgraces and mischiefs of our army, has dared to authorize and associate to our arms the tomahawk and scalping-knife of the savage?[8] To call into civilized alliance the wild and inhuman savage of the woods; to delegate to the merciless Indian the defence of disputed rights, and to wage the horrors of his barbarous war against our brethren? My Lords, these enormities cry aloud for redress and punishment: unless thoroughly done away, it will be a stain on the national character—it is a violation of the constitution—I believe it is against law. It is not the least of our national misfortunes, that the strength and character of our army are thus impaired: infected with the mercenary spirit of robbery and rapine—familiarized to the horrid scenes of savage cruelty, it can no longer boast of the noble and generous principles which dignify a soldier; no longer sympathize with the dignity of the royal banner, nor feel the pride, pomp, and circumstance of glorious war, 'that make ambition virtue!' What makes ambition virtue?[9]—the sense of honor. But is the sense of honor consistent with a spirit of plunder, or the practice of murder? Can it flow from mercenary motives, or can it prompt to cruel deeds? Besides these murderers and plunderers, let me ask our ministers—what other allies have they acquired? What *other powers* have they associated to their cause? Have they entered into alliance with the *king of the gypsies*? Nothing, my Lords, is too low or too ludicrous to be consistent with their counsels.

The independent views of America have been stated and asserted as the foundation of this address. My Lords, no man wishes more for the due dependence of

---

[7] A reference to the employment of Hessian mercenaries and other foreign troops against the Americans.

[8] The employment of Indians against the Colonials drew from Opposition some of its most passionate protests, as, for example, Burke's, delivered later in this same session of Parliament (February 6, 1778).

[9] From a speech of Othello in Shakespeare's play (III, iii):

> Farewell the plumed troop, and the big wars,
> That make ambition virtue! O, farewell!

America on this country than I do: to preserve it, and not confirm that state of independence into which *your measures* hitherto have *driven* them, is the object which we ought to unite in attaining. The Americans, contending for their rights against arbitrary exactions, I love and admire; it is the struggle of free and virtuous patriots: but, contending for independency and total disconnection from England, as an Englishman, I cannot wish them success; for, in a due constitutional dependency, including the ancient supremacy of this country in regulating their commerce and navigation, consists the mutual happiness and prosperity both of England and America.[10] She derived assistance and protection from us, and we reaped from her the most important advantages: she was, indeed, the fountain of our wealth, the nerve of our strength, the nursery and basis of our naval power. It is our duty, therefore, my Lords, if we wish to save our country, most seriously to endeavour the recovery of these most beneficial subjects: and in this perilous crisis, perhaps the present moment may be the only one in which we can hope for success; for, in their negotiations with France, they have, or think they have, reason to complain: though it be notorious that they have received from that power important supplies and assistance of various kinds, yet it is certain they expected it in a more decisive and immediate degree. America is in ill humor with France, on some points that have not entirely answered her expectations: let us wisely take advantage of every possible moment of reconciliation. Besides, the natural disposition of America herself still leans towards England—to the old habits of connection and mutual interest that united both countries. This *was* the established sentiment of all the Continent; and still, my Lords, in the great and principal part—the sound part of America, this wise and affectionate disposition prevails; and there is a very considerable part of America yet sound—the middle and the southern provinces: some parts may be factious and blind to their true interests; but if we express a wise and benevolent disposition to communicate with them those immutable rights of nature, and those constitutional liberties, to which they are equally entitled with ourselves, by a conduct so just and humane, we shall confirm the favorable, and conciliate the adverse. I say, my Lords, the rights and liberties to which they are equally entitled with ourselves, but no more. I would participate to them every enjoyment and freedom which the colonizing subjects of a free state can possess, or wish to possess; and I do not see why they should not enjoy every fundamental right in their property, and every original substantial liberty, which Devonshire or Surrey, or the county I live in, or any other county in England, can claim; reserving always, as the sacred right of the mother-country, the due constitutional dependency of the Colonies. The inherent supremacy of the state, in regulating and protecting the navigation and commerce of all her subjects, is necessary for the mutual benefit and preservation of every part, to constitute and preserve the prosperous arrangement of the whole empire

   The sound parts of America, of which I have spoken, must be sensible of these great truths, and of their real interests. America is not in that state of desperate and contemptible rebellion which this country has been deluded to believe. It is not a wild and lawless banditti, who, having nothing to lose, might hope to snatch something from public convulsions; many of their leaders and great men have a great stake in this great contest:—the gentleman who conducts their armies, I am told, has an estate of four or five thousand pounds a year: and when I consider

---

[10] See Chatham's speech of January 14, 1766.

these things, I cannot but lament the inconsiderate violence of our penal acts—our declarations of treason and rebellion, with all the fatal effects of attainder and confiscation.

As to the disposition of foreign powers, which is asserted to be pacific and friendly, let us judge, my Lords, rather by their actions and the nature of things, than by interested assertions. The uniform assistance, supplied to America by France, suggests a different conclusion:—The most important interests of France, in aggrandizing and enriching herself with what she most wants, supplies of every naval store from America, must inspire her with different sentiments. The extraordinary preparations of the House of Bourbon, by land and by sea, from Dunkirk to the Streights,[11] equally ready and willing to overwhelm these defence-less islands, should rouse us to a sense of their real disposition, and our own danger. Not five thousand troops in England!—hardly three thousand in Ireland! What can we oppose to the combined force of our enemies?—Scarcely twenty ships of the line fully or sufficiently manned, that any Admiral's reputation would permit him to take the command of!—The river of Lisbon in the possession of our enemies![12]—The seas swept by American privateers!—Our channel torn to pieces by them! In this complicated crisis of danger, weakness at home, and calamity abroad, terrified and insulted by the neighbouring powers,—unable to act in America, or acting only to be destroyed;—where is the man with the forehead to promise or hope for success in such a situation? or, from perseverance in the measures that have driven us to it? Who has the forehead to do so? Where is that man? I should be glad to see his face.

You cannot *conciliate* America by your present measures—you cannot *subdue* her by your present, or by any measures. What, then, can you do? You cannot conquer, you cannot gain, but you can *address;* you can lull the fears and anxieties of the moment into an ignorance of the danger that should produce them. But, my Lords, the time demands the language of truth:—we must not now apply the flattering unction of servile compliance, or blind complaisance. In a just and necessary war, to maintain the rights or honor of my country, I would strip the shirt from my back to support it. But in such a war as this, unjust in its principle, impracticable in its means, and ruinous in its consequences, I would not contribute a single effort, nor a single shilling. I do not call for vengeance on the heads of those who have been guilty; I only recommend to them to make their retreat; let them walk off; and let them make haste, or they may be assured that speedy and condign punishment will overtake them.

My Lords, I have submitted to you, with the freedom and truth which I think my duty, my sentiments on your present awful situation. I have laid before you the ruin of your power, the disgrace of your reputation, the pollution of your discipline, the contamination of your morals, the complication of calamities, foreign and domestic, that overwhelm your sinking country. Your dearest interests, your own liberties, the constitution itself, totters to the foundation. All this disgraceful danger, this multitude of misery, is the monstrous offspring of this unnatural war. We have been deceived and deluded too long: let us now stop

[11] Gibraltar.

[12] England had long helped maintain the friendly Marquis de Pombal in political ascendency in Portugal, and thus secured the friendship and trade of that country. Early in 1777, however, the old King of Portugal died, Pombal fell from power, and a king hostile to England and friendly to Spain ruled the country.

short: this is the crisis—may be the only crisis, of time and situation, to give us a possibility of escape from the fatal effects of our delusions. But if in an obstinate and infatuated perseverance in folly, we meanly echo back the peremptory words this day presented to us, nothing can save this devoted country from complete and final ruin. We madly rush into multiplied miseries and 'confusion worse confounded.' [13]

Is it possible, can it be believed, that ministers are yet blind to this impending destruction?—I did hope, that instead of this false and empty vanity, this overweening pride, engendering high conceits, and presumptuous imaginations—that ministers would have humbled themselves in their errors, would have confessed and retracted them, and by an active, though a late repentance, have endeavored to redeem them. But, my Lords, since they had neither sagacity to foresee, nor justice nor humanity to shun, these oppressive calamities; since, not even severe experience can make them feel, nor the imminent ruin of their country awaken them from their stupefaction, the guardian care of Parliament must interpose. I shall therefore, my Lords, propose to you an amendment to the address to his Majesty, to be inserted immediately after the two first paragraphs of congratulation on the birth of a Princess: to recommend an immediate cessation of hostilities, and the commencement of a treaty to restore peace and liberty to America, strength and happiness to England, security and permanent prosperity to both countries.— This, my Lords, is yet in our power; and let not the wisdom and justice of your Lordships neglect the happy, and, perhaps the only opportunity. By the establishment of irrevocable law, founded on mutual rights, and ascertained by treaty, these glorious enjoyments may be firmly perpetuated. And let me repeat to your Lordships, that the strong bias of America, at least of the wise and sounder parts of it, naturally inclines to this happy and constitutional reconnection with you. Notwithstanding the temporary intrigues with France, we may still be assured of their ancient and confirmed partiality to us. America and France cannot be congenial; there is something decisive and confirmed in the honest American, that will not assimilate to the futility and levity of Frenchmen.

My Lords, to encourage and confirm that innate inclination to this country, founded on every principle of affection, as well as consideration of interest—to restore that favorable disposition into a permanent and powerful reunion with this country—to revive the mutual strength of the empire;—again, to awe the House of Bourbon, instead of meanly truckling, as our present calamities compel us, to every insult of French caprice, and Spanish punctilio—to re-establish our commerce—to re-assert our rights and our honor—to confirm our interests, and renew our glories for ever, (a consummation most devoutly to be endeavored! and which, I trust, may yet arise from reconciliation with America,)—I have the honor of submitting to you the following amendment; which I move to be inserted after the two first paragraphs of the address.

"And that this House does most humbly advise and supplicate His Majesty, to be pleased to cause the most speedy and effectual measures to be taken for restoring peace in America; and that no time may be lost in proposing an immediate

[13] Allusion to Milton's *Paradise Lost*, II, 996—the expulsion of the rebellious angels from Heaven:

> I saw and heard, for such a numerous host
> Fled not in silence through the frighted deep
> With ruin upon ruin, rout on rout,
> Confusion worse confounded.

cessation of hostilities there, in order to the opening a treaty for the final settlement of the tranquillity of these invaluable provinces, by a removal of the unhappy causes of this ruinous civil war; and by a just and adequate security against the return of the like calamities in times to come. And this House desire to offer the most dutiful assurances to His Majesty, that they will, in due time, cheerfully co-operate with the magnanimity and tender goodness of His Majesty for the preservation of his people, by such explicit and most solemn declarations, and provisions of fundamental and irrevocable laws, as may be judged necessary for the ascertaining and fixing for ever the respective rights of Great Britain and her Colonies."

[In the ensuing debate the Earl of Suffolk, one of the Secretaries of State, defended the use of Indians in the war as justified by policy and necessity, and on principle as well, because they were means that "God and nature had put into our hands." That argument brought Chatham to his feet once again.]

I am astonished! shocked! to hear such principles confessed—to hear them avowed in this House, or in this country:—principles equally unconstitutional, inhuman, and unchristian!

My Lords, I did not intend to have encroached again upon your attention; but I cannot repress my indignation—I feel myself impelled by every duty. My Lords, we are called upon as members of this House, as men, as Christian men, to protest against such notions standing near the throne, polluting the ear of Majesty. "That God and nature put into our hands!" I know not what ideas that Lord may entertain of God and nature; but I know, that such abominable principles are equally abhorrent to religion and humanity.—What! to attribute the sacred sanction of God and nature to the massacres of the Indian scalping-knife—to the cannibal savage torturing, murdering, roasting, and eating; literally, my Lords, *eating* the mangled victims of his barbarous battles! Such horrible notions shock every precept of religion, divine or natural, and every generous feeling of humanity. And, my Lords, they shock every sentiment of honor; they shock me as a lover of honorable war, and a detester of murderous barbarity.

These abominable principles, and this more abominable avowal of them, demand the most decisive indignation. I call upon that *Right Reverend* Bench, those holy ministers of the gospel, and pious pastors of our church; I conjure them to join in the holy work, and vindicate the religion of their God: I appeal to the wisdom and the law of *this learned* Bench to defend and support the justice of their country: I call upon the Bishops to interpose the unsullied sanctity of their lawn;—upon the learned Judges to interpose the purity of their ermine, to save us from this pollution: [14]—I call upon the honor of your Lordships, to reverence the dignity of your ancestors, and to maintain your own:—I call upon the spirit and humanity of my country, to vindicate the national character:—I invoke the genius of the constitution. From the tapestry that adorns these walls, the immortal ancestor of this noble Lord frowns with indignation at the disgrace of his country.[15] In vain he led your victorious fleets against the boasted Armada

[14] The bishops of the Church of England and the principal justices of the courts sat in the House of Lords.

[15] Chatham combines two of Suffolk's splendid ancestors: Thomas Howard (1561-1626), first Earl of Suffolk, who distinguished himself against the Armada; and Charles Howard (1536-1624), Baron Howard of Effingham, who commanded the fleet. This

of Spain; in vain he defended and established the honor, the liberties, the religion, the *Protestant religion,* of this country, against the arbitrary cruelties of Popery and the Inquisition, if these more than popish cruelties and inquisitorial practices are let loose among us; to turn forth into our setttlements, among our ancient connexions, friends, and relations, the merciless cannibal, thirsting for the blood of man, woman, and child! to send forth the infidel savage—against whom? against your Protestant brethren; to lay waste their country, to desolate their dwellings, and extirpate their race and name, with these horrible hell-hounds of savage war! —*hell-hounds, I say, of savage war!* Spain armed herself with blood-hounds to extirpate the wretched natives of America; and we improve on the inhuman example even of Spanish cruelty; we turn loose these savage hell-hounds against our brethren and countrymen in America, of the same language, laws, liberties, and religion; endeared to us by every tie that should sanctify humanity.

My Lords, this awful subject, so important to our honor, our constitution, and our religion, demands the most solemn and effectual enquiry. And I again call upon your Lordships, and the united powers of the state, to examine it thoroughly and decisively, and to stamp upon it an indelible stigma of the public abhorrence. And I again implore those holy prelates of our religion, to do away these iniquities from among us. Let them perform a lustration; let them purify this House and this country from this sin.

My Lords, I am old and weak, and at present unable to say more; but my feelings and indignation were too strong to have said less. I could not have slept this night in my bed, nor reposed my head on my pillow, without giving this vent to my eternal abhorrence to such preposterous and enormous principles.[16]

∽

Bibliographical Note

The standard authoritative biography of Chatham is Basil Williams' two-volume *William Pitt, Earl of Chatham* (1913). A good, recent, short biography is that by J. H. Plumb (1953). An interesting treatment of the two Pitts and the two Foxes is found in Erich Eyck's *Pitt versus Fox; Father and Son* (1950). The fullest criticisms of Chatham's speaking are to be found in the biographies, in such histories as Lecky's, and in Goodrich. Williams' brief essay on Chatham in Dobrée's *From Anne to Victoria* also treats the speeches. An interesting characterization of Chatham's speaking, by a contemporary admirer, is Henry Grattan's in *Memoirs of the Life and Times of Henry Grattan* (1839–46) by his son, I, 234–38, and reprinted in part by Goodrich, p. 398. Selections from the most significant speeches and writings on the American problem are collected and edited by Max Beloof in *The Debate on the American Revolution 1761–1783* (1949). Illuminating supplements to Chatham's speeches on America are Burke's of 1774 and 1775.

---

passage, to Henry Grattan, illustrated Chatham the "incomparable actor." "Had it not been so," wrote Grattan, "he would have appeared ridiculous. His address to the tapestry and to Lord Effingham's memory required an incomparable actor, and he was that actor." (See Bibliographical Note, below.)

[16] Chatham's amendment was defeated by a large majority, and the Address was passed.

Edmund Burke

(1729–1797)

An Irishman of mixed Protestant–Catholic parentage, Edmund Burke served in the British House of Commons from 1766 to 1794. Distinguished among his contemporaries because he was not only an eloquent speaker and an active politician, but a writer of extraordinary ability and a political philosopher, he was thinker-writer-speaker functioning as one in the public arena. For more than thirty years Burke helped shape most of the controversies which embroiled the British public, and he pressed his mark indelibly upon the interpretation of those controversies. Though he often had a lesser immediate impact than Chatham, or Fox, or the younger Pitt, his influence upon the thought of subsequent generations has far exceeded theirs. In fact, even today Burke is still a fertile subject and source of controversy, while his parliamentary contemporaries have passed quietly into history—or an occasional anthology.

Burke prepared many of his important speeches for publication shortly after they were given, not primarily as records for posterity but, like his writings, as contributions to the larger public debate on important issues: the taxation and government of America, the independence of Parliament, economy in administration, justice for the people of India, English-Irish relations, emancipation for Roman Catholics and the removal of disabilities from Protestant Dissenters, Jacobinism and the French Revolution. Because Burke himself published his speeches, and because, as we have said, writing and speaking for him were only different modes of the same kind of rhetorical endeavor, we have fuller and better texts of his than of any other contemporary speeches. Hence also the Burke of the pamphlets like *The Present Discontents* (1770), *Letter to the Sheriffs of Bristol* (1777), *Reflections on the Revolution in France* (1790), and *A Letter to a Noble Lord* (1796) is hardly distinguishable from the Burke of the speeches of the same periods.

When Burke entered politics under the Marquis of Rockingham in 1765, he had accumulated experience to equip him well for his new career and to give special characteristics to it. Educated in Ireland in a Quaker school and a Church-of-England college, he prepared for the bar in London but early turned to literature and political journalism. At college he had practiced oratory and debate and had engaged in public controversy and theatrical criticism. By his late twenties he had published an important book in aesthetics and criticism and had made his mark in political satire.[1] By that time also he had come to associate freely with

[1] In 1757 appeared his *Philosophical Enquiry into the Origin of our Ideas of the Sublime and Beautiful*, now edited with excellent introduction and notes by J. T. Boulton (1958). This work brought him to the attention of the literary world. Later, when he had become a speaker in Parliament, it provided his critics with the epithet "Sublime and Beautiful Burke." In 1756 he had published anonymously *A Vindication of Natural Society*, a satire on Lord Bolingbroke's doctrine of "natural" religion, which was mistaken at first for a posthumous work of Bolingbroke.

artists and men of letters: David Garrick, the actor; Arthur Murphy, the author and actor; Joshua Reynolds, the painter; and the lexicographer, essayist, and conversationalist, Samuel Johnson. Burke became one of the original members of Johnson's famous Club and its second greatest talker, and he remained the lifelong friend of the principal members. In 1758 he founded *The Annual Register*, a yearly volume of contemporary history, politics, and literature,[2] of which he was the sole author for seven or eight years thereafter.

Burke's first parliamentary assignment, and the occasion for his maiden speeches, was the repeal of the Stamp Act (1766); and from then on his efforts to heal the breach with America occupied his best talents for many years. His published speeches on *American Taxation* (1774) and *Conciliation with America* (1775) are perhaps his best known, especially in the United States. To these we should add the speech to the electors of Bristol in 1774, for the famous statement of the relation between members of Parliament and constituents, and the speeches on India opening the trial of Warren Hastings in 1788.

The speech which we include below comes at about the midpoint of Burke's career (1780). Most of the agitation over America was past; that over India and France was yet to come. Burke's fortunes and the fortunes of his party were still rising. He had just achieved special prominence for the efforts culminating in his speech on *Economical Reform*,[3] and he was concluding a six-year term as a member for Bristol, the second most important city in England.

The *Speech at the Guildhall in Bristol*, less known and less often reprinted than the American speeches, is an important political speech given outside Parliament, of which few good examples survive from that century. Furthermore, though campaign speaking as we have known it since the nineteenth century was virtually non-existent in Burke's time, this speech served a closely comparable function.

Burke is addressing his friends in the city government and other substantial citizens of Bristol. His speech is a review of the political faith which has governed him as member for Bristol, and is a manly defense of his position on the crucial questions of the past six years. He handles gently his steady opposition to those policies which had brought on and protracted the American Revolution, not wishing, as he says, unnecessarily to flaunt his wisdom before those whose trade was paralyzed by the war. Instead he gives most attention to the still resolvable problems of Ireland, the humanitarian treatment of debtors, and especially religious toleration.

He had supported increased freedom for Irish trade, but Ireland was a competitor of the Bristol traders, while America had been a customer. He had laid himself open to the assaults of certain banking and business interests by supporting humane and sensible treatment of debtors. And he had angered the rabid Protestants by supporting modification of the penal laws against Catholics. This latter measure had given rise to the Protestant Association and had set off anti-Catholic disturbances in Scotland the year before. During the terrifying three

---

[2] *The Annual Register*, continued by friends of Burke under his eye for many years, and still published, is a primary source for the study of the events, the politics, and the parliamentary activity of the period.

[3] See footnote 10, p. 218, below.

days of the Lord George Gordon riots in London that summer, Burke had been one of those proponents of toleration whose lives and property had been in danger.[4]

Under these circumstances, and because the political organization of his fellow member, Cruger, who had been elected with him in 1774, was working against him, Burke was in doubt whether to stand for re-election. He was characteristically not of a mind to modify his principles or his behavior in order to retain his seat, but he wished no misunderstanding to arise. He would give his supporters a full statement of his ideas before it was decided whether to chance the election, not, he said, "lest you censure me improperly, but lest you form improper opinions on matters of some moment to you." The result is one of Burke's best and most characteristic efforts, an impressive, passionate though moderate examination of political faith and practical public endeavor, which can stand with his *Letter to a Noble Lord* (1796) among the notable political apologias of history.

The distinguishing features of Burke's speaking were the largeness of view which it encompassed; the broad, deep knowledge which it exhibited; the fullness with which it developed particular problems in detail and in historical perspective; the clarity with which it related those problems to general principles of morality and human nature; and the happy fusion of emotion and reasoning which is the characteristic of eloquence and good literature. His imagination gives form and energy to the politics and the morality; his metaphoric expression does not merely decorate the thought, it incarnates the thought, it creates the idea. In his life and in his speaking and writing, Burke brought literature and politics into a union which had not been so close and so equal since Cicero.

These very qualities in Burke have caused critics in his own time and since to laud the writer and deplore the speaker, to compare him unfavorably with Fox, for example, as tedious and ineffective, as an extravagant orator rather than a parliamentary debater, as too long, lush, and literary.[5] Undeniably Burke was often more passionate, more excitable, more extreme in his language and less self-controlled than effective political leaders are expected to be. Perhaps that is why he never held high office even for the few months when he and his friends were in power. Perhaps the reasons were that he was an Irishman (an "adventurer" he was called) without fortune or distinguished family connection like Fox's and Pitt's, and that he chose the unpopular side on most great issues except the French Revolution. A comprehensive look at all the testimony and other evidence, nevertheless, reveals that at least until the French Revolution, Burke was indeed a consequential speaker who often commanded much attention in the House, even from those whose votes on the other side were to be taken for granted. In his later years, indeed, his writings on the French Revolution outstripped in importance even his speaking against Warren Hastings. It is those writings chiefly which still keep him in the midst of controversy.

∽

---

[4] When Gordon came to trial for instigating the riots, he was defended by Thomas Erskine (see below, pp. 294–96), the greatest courtroom speaker of the day.

[5] See note 1 above.

Burke to His Constituents *

The Guildhall, Bristol
September 6, 1780

Mr. Mayor, and Gentlemen: I am extremely pleased at the appearance of this large and respectable meeting. The steps I may be obliged to take will want the sanction of a considerable authority; and in explaining any thing which may appear doubtful in my public conduct, I must naturally desire a very full audience.

I have been backward to begin my canvass. The dissolution of the parliament was uncertain; and it did not become me, by an unseasonable importunity, to appear diffident of the fact of my six years' endeavours to please you. I had served the city of Bristol honourably, and the city of Bristol had no reason to think that the means of honourable service to the public were become indifferent to me.[1]

I found, on my arrival here, that three gentlemen had been long in eager pursuit of an object which but two of us can obtain.[2] I found that they had all met with encouragement. A contested election in such a city as this is no light thing.[3] I paused on the brink of the precipice. These three gentlemen, by various merits, and on various titles, I made no doubt were worthy of your favour. I shall never attempt to raise myself by depreciating the merits of my competitors. In the complexity and confusion of these cross pursuits, I wished to take the authentic public sense of my friends upon a business of so much delicacy. I wished to take your opinion along with me, that, if I should give up the contest at the very beginning, my surrender of my post may not seem the effect of inconstancy, or timidity, or anger, or disgust, or indolence, or any other temper unbecoming a man who has engaged in the public service. If, on the contrary, I should undertake the election, and fail of success, I was full as anxious that it should be manifest to the whole world that the peace of the city had not been broken by my rashness, presumption, or fond conceit of my own merit.

I am not come, by a false and counterfeit show of deference to your judgment, to seduce it in my favour. I ask it seriously and unaffectedly. If you wish that I should retire, I shall not consider that advice as a censure upon my conduct, or an alteration in your sentiments, but as a rational submission to the circumstances of affairs. If, on the contrary, you should think it proper for me to proceed on my

---

* We use the standard texts included in the *Works* (London, 1826, III, 353–434; Boston, 1894, II, 367–429).

[1] For special study of the circumstances of this speech see Burke's letters to the Duke of Portland, September 3, 1780, and to Rockingham, September 7 and 8, 1780, *Correspondence of Edmund Burke*, IV, ed. by John Woods (1963); G. E. Weare, *Edmund Burke's Connection with Bristol* (1894); I. R. Christie, "Henry Cruger and the End of Edmund Burke's Connection with Bristol," *Transactions of the Bristol and Gloucestershire Archeological Society*, LXXIV (1955), 157–70.

[2] Burke arrived on August 18. Besides his fellow Whig and colleague in Parliament, Henry Cruger, two Tories were campaigning hard: Matthew Brickdale, whom Burke had displaced in 1774, and Richard Combe.

[3] Especially because of expense. In Bristol there had usually been an agreement, therefore, that the Tories would choose one member and the Whigs one. In 1774 Burke and Cruger had upset that arrangement.

canvass, if you will risk the trouble on your part, I will risk it on mine. My pretensions are such as you cannot be ashamed of, whether they succeed or fail.

If you call upon me, I shall solicit the favour of the city upon manly ground. I come before you with the plain confidence of an honest servant in the equity of a candid and discerning master. I come to claim your approbation, not to amuse you with vain apologies, or with professions still more vain and senseless. I have lived too long to be served by apologies, or to stand in need of them. The part I have acted has been in open day; and to hold out to a conduct which stands in that clear and steady light for all its good and all its evil,—to hold out to that conduct the paltry winking tapers [candles] of excuses and promises,—I never will do it. They may obscure it with their smoke, but they never can illumine sunshine by such a flame as theirs.

I am sensible that no endeavours have been left untried to injure me in your opinion. But the use of character is to be a shield against calumny. I could wish undoubtedly (if idle wishes were not the most idle of all things) to make every part of my conduct agreeable to every one of my constituents. But in so great a city, and so greatly divided as this is, it is weak to expect it.[4]

In such a discordancy of sentiments it is better to look to the nature of things than to the humours of men. The very attempt towards pleasing every body discovers [reveals] a temper always flashy, and often false and insincere. Therefore, as I have proceeded straight onward in my conduct, so I will proceed in my account of those parts of it which have been most excepted to. But I must first beg leave just to hint to you that we may suffer very great detriment by being open to every talker. It is not to be imagined how much of service is lost from spirits full of activity and full of energy, who are pressing, who are rushing forward, to great and capital objects, when you oblige them to be continually looking back. Whilst they are defending one service, they defraud you of a hundred. Applaud us when we run; console us when we fall; cheer us when we recover: but let us pass on—for God's sake, let us pass on!

Do you think, gentlemen, that every public act in the six years since I stood in this place before you,—that all the arduous things which have been done in this eventful period, which has crowded into a few years' space the revolutions of an age,—can be opened to you on their fair grounds in half an hour's conversation?

But it is no reason, because there is a bad mode of inquiry, that there should be no examination at all. Most certainly it is our duty to examine; it is our interest too: but it must be with discretion; with an attention to all the circumstances, and to all the motives; like sound judges, and not like cavilling pettifoggers and quibbling pleaders, prying into flaws and hunting for exceptions. Look, gentlemen, to the *whole tenor* of your member's conduct. Try whether his ambition or his avarice have justled him out of the straight line of duty; or whether that grand foe of the offices of active life, that master-vice in men of business,—a degenerate and inglorious sloth,—has made him flag and languish in his course. This is the object of our inquiry. If our member's conduct can bear this touch, mark it for sterling. He may have fallen into errors: he must have faults; but our error is greater, and our fault is radically ruinous to ourselves, if we do not bear, if we do

[4] Burke's personal influence was, in fact, probably stronger than it had been in 1774. His friends controlled the Corporation, but the two Whig factions could not get together, nor would either yield.

not even applaud, the whole compound and mixed mass of such a character. Not to act thus is folly: I had almost said it is impiety. He censures God who quarrels with the imperfections of man.

Gentlemen, we must not be peevish with those who serve the people; for none will serve us, whilst there is a court to serve, but those who are of a nice and jealous honour. They who think every thing, in comparison of that honour, to be dust and ashes, will not bear to have it soiled and impaired by those for whose sake they make a thousand sacrifices to preserve it immaculate and whole. We shall either drive such men from the public stage, or we shall send them to the court for protection; where, if they must sacrifice their reputation, they will at least secure their interest. Depend upon it, that the lovers of freedom will be free. None will violate their conscience to please us, in order afterwards to discharge that conscience, which they have violated, by doing us faithful and affectionate service. If we degrade and deprave their minds by servility, it will be absurd to expect that they who are creeping and abject towards us, will ever be bold and incorruptible assertors of our freedom against the most seducing and the most formidable of all powers. No! human nature is not so formed; nor shall we improve the faculties or better the morals of public men by our possession of the most infallible receipt in the world for making cheats and hypocrites.

Let me say, with plainness, I who am no longer in a public character, that if by a fair, by an indulgent, by a gentlemanly behaviour to our representatives, we do not give confidence to their minds, and a liberal scope to their understandings; if we do not permit our members to act upon a *very* enlarged view of things, we shall at length infallibly degrade our national representation into a confused and scuffling bustle of local agency. When the popular member is narrowed in his ideas, and rendered timid in his proceedings, the service of the crown will be the sole nursery of statesmen. Among the frolics of the court it may at length take that of attending to its business. Then the monopoly of mental power will be added to the power of all other kinds it possesses. On the side of the people there will be nothing but impotence; for ignorance is impotence; narrowness of mind is impotence; timidity is itself impotence, and makes all other qualities that go along with it impotent and useless.

At present it is the plan of the court to make its servants insignificant. If the people should fall into the same humour, and should choose their servants on the same principles of mere obsequiousness, and flexibility, and total vacancy or indifference of opinion in all public matters, then no part of the state will be sound; and it will be in vain to think of saving it.[5]

I thought it very expedient at this time to give you this candid counsel; and with this counsel I would willingly close, if the matters which at various times have been objected to me in this city concerned only myself, and my own election. These charges, I think, are four in number;—my neglect of a due attention to my constituents, the not paying more frequent visits here;—my conduct on the affairs

[5] In the preceding passage and in what follows Burke echoes his belief in the duty of a member of Parliament to use his own best wisdom in legislative matters rather than to give in submissively to instructions from his constituents. He had asserted that principle explicitly in his speech following the election of 1774. It is the way of the Court, he says, to reward its servants for their submission. For an example of Burke's recent treatment of this same subject before the House of Commons, see his *Speech on a Bill for Shortening the Duration of Parliaments*, May 8, 1780.

of the first Irish trade acts;—my opinion and mode of proceeding on Lord Beauchamp's debtors' bills; and my votes on the late affairs of the Roman Catholics. All of these (except perhaps the first) relate to matters of very considerable public concern; and it is not lest you should censure me improperly, but lest you should form improper opinions on matters of some moment to you, that I trouble you at all upon the subject. My conduct is of small importance.

With regard to the first charge, my friends have spoken to me of it in the style of amicable expostulation; not so much blaming the thing, as lamenting the effects.[6]—Others, less partial to me, were less kind in assigning the motives. I admit, there is a decorum and propriety in a member of parliament's paying a respectful court to his constituents. If I were conscious to myself that pleasure or dissipation, or low unworthy occupations, had detained me from personal attendance on you, I would readily admit my fault, and quietly submit to the penalty. But, gentlemen, I live at an hundred miles' distance from Bristol;[7] and at the end of a session I come to my own house, fatigued in body and in mind, to a little repose, and to a very little attention to my family and my private concerns. A visit to Bristol is always a sort of canvass; else it will do more harm than good. To pass from the toils of a session to the toils of a canvass, is the furthest thing in the world from repose. I could hardly serve you *as I have done,* and court you too. Most of you have heard, that I do not very remarkably spare myself in *public* business; and in the *private* business of my constituents I have done very nearly as much as those who have nothing else to do. My canvass of you was not on the 'Change,[8] nor in the county meetings, nor in the clubs of this city: it was in the House of Commons; it was at the custom-house; it was at the council; it was at the treasury; it was at the admiralty. I canvassed you through your affairs, and not your persons. I was not only your representative as a body; I was the agent, the solicitor of individuals; I ran about wherever your affairs could call me; and in acting for you, I often appeared rather as a ship-broker, than as a member of parliament. There was nothing too laborious, or too low for me to undertake. The meanness of the business was raised by the dignity of the object. If some lesser matters have slipped through my fingers, it was because I filled my hands too full; and, in my eagerness to serve you, took in more than any hands could grasp. Several gentlemen stand round me who are my willing witnesses; and there are others who, if they were here, would be still better; because they would be unwilling witnesses to the same truth. It was in the middle of a summer residence in London, and in the middle of a negotiation at the admiralty for your trade, that I was called to Bristol; and this late visit, at this late day, has been possibly in prejudice to your affairs.[9]

Since I have touched upon this matter, let me say, gentlemen, that if I had a disposition, or a right to complain, I have some cause of complaint on my side. With a petition of this city in my hand, passed through the corporation without a dissenting voice, a petition in unison with almost the whole voice of the kingdom (with whose formal thanks I was covered over), while I laboured on no less

---

[6] He had not visited Bristol since August 1776, though he had carried on a considerable correspondence, both private and public, with his friends and supporters there.

[7] At Beaconsfield in Buckinghamshire.

[8] The exchange—where merchants meet to transact business.

[9] Burke's correspondence bears abundant witness to his activity in parliamentary committees and government agencies on behalf of citizens of Bristol.

than five bills for a public reform,[10] and fought against the opposition of great abilities, and of the greatest power, every clause, and every word of the largest of those bills, almost to the very last day of a very long session; all this time a canvass in Bristol was as calmly carried on as if I were dead. I was considered as a man wholly out of the question. Whilst I watched, and fasted, and sweated in the House of Commons—by the most easy and ordinary arts of election, by dinners and visits, by "How do you do's," and "My worthy friends," I was to be quietly moved out of my seat—and promises were made, and engagements entered into, without any exception or reserve, as if my laborious zeal in my duty had been a regular abdication of my trust.

To open my whole heart to you on this subject, I do confess, however, that there were other times besides the two years in which I did visit you, when I was not wholly without leisure for repeating that mark of my respect. But I could not bring my mind to see you. You remember, that in the beginning of this American war (that era of calamity, disgrace, and downfall, an era which no feeling mind will ever mention without a tear for England) you were greatly divided; and a very strong body, if not the strongest, opposed itself to the madness which every art and every power were employed to render popular, in order that the errors of the rulers might be lost in the general blindness of the nation. This opposition continued until after our great, but most unfortunate victory at Long Island.[11] Then all the mounds and banks of our constancy were borne down at once; and the frenzy of the American war broke in upon us like a deluge. This victory, which seemed to put an immediate end to all difficulties, perfected us in that spirit of domination which our unparalleled prosperity had but too long nurtured. We had been so very powerful, and so very prosperous, that even the humblest of us were degraded into the vices and follies of kings. We lost all measure between means and ends; and our headlong desires became our politics and our morals. All men who wished for peace, or retained any sentiments of moderation, were overborne or silenced; and this city was led by every artifice (and probably with the more management, because I was one of your members) to distinguish itself by its zeal for that fatal cause. In this temper of your and of my mind, I should have sooner fled to the extremities of the earth, than have shown myself here. I, who saw in every American victory [12] (for you have had a long series of these misfortunes) the germ and seed of the naval power of France and Spain, which all our heat and warmth against America was only hatching into life,—I should not have been a welcome visitant with the brow and the language of such feelings. When, afterwards, the other face of your calamity was turned upon you, and showed itself in defeat and distress, I shunned you full as

---

[10] His proposals for economy in administration, on which he had made his notable speech, *On Economical Reform*, February 11, 1780. He had received public congratulation and thanks from various parts of the country. Though always opposed to reforming the electoral structure and the basis of representation in Parliament, Burke presented the major proposals of the time for reforming the fiscal administration and reducing the sources of corruption.

[11] The defeat of Washington and the beginning of his retreat in August 1776. Many people in England thought that the colonies would soon be brought to terms.

[12] The defeat of Burgoyne at Saratoga is said to have clinched the alliance with France.

much. I felt sorely this variety in our wretchedness; and I did not wish to have the least appearance of insulting you with that show of superiority, which, though it may not be assumed, is generally suspected in a time of calamity, from those whose previous warnings have been despised. I could not bear to show you a representative whose face did not reflect that of his constituents; a face that could not joy in your joys, and sorrow in your sorrows. But time at length has made us all of one opinion; and we have all opened our eyes on the true nature of the American war, to the true nature of all its successes and all its failures.

In that public storm, too, I had my private feelings. I had seen blown down and prostrate on the ground several of those houses to whom I was chiefly indebted for the honour this city has done me. I confess, that, whilst the wounds of those I loved were yet green, I could not bear to show myself in pride and triumph in that place into which their partiality had brought me, and to appear at feasts and rejoicings, in the midst of the grief and calamity of my warm friends, my zealous supporters, my generous benefactors. This is a true, unvarnished, undisguised state of the affair. You will judge of it.

This is the only one of the charges in which I am personally concerned. As to the other matters objected against me, which in their turn I shall mention to you, remember once more I do not mean to extenuate or excuse. Why should I, when the things charged are among those upon which I found all my reputation? What would be left to me, if I myself was the man, who softened, and blended, and diluted, and weakened, all the distinguishing colours of my life, so as to leave nothing distinct and determinate in my whole conduct?

It has been said, and it is the second charge, that in the questions of the Irish trade, I did not consult the interest of my constituents; or, to speak out strongly, that I rather acted as a native of Ireland, than as an English member of parliament.

I certainly have very warm, good wishes for the place of my birth. But the sphere of my duties is my true country. It was, as a man attached to your interests, and zealous for the conservation of your power and dignity, that I acted on that occasion, and on all occasions. You were involved in the American war. A new world of policy was opened, to which it was necessary we should conform, whether we would or not; and my only thought was how to conform to our situation in such a manner as to unite to this kingdom, in prosperity and in affection, whatever remained of the empire. I was true to my old, standing, invariable principle, that all things, which came from Great Britain, should issue as a gift of her bounty and beneficence, rather than as claims recovered against a struggling litigant; or at least, that if your beneficence obtained no credit in your concessions, yet that they should appear the salutary provisions of your wisdom and foresight; not as things wrung from you with your blood by the cruel gripe of a rigid necessity. The first concessions, by being (much against my will) mangled and stripped of the parts which were necessary to make out their just correspondence and connexion in trade, were of no use. The next year a feeble attempt was made to bring the thing into better shape. This attempt (countenanced by the minister) on the very first appearance of some popular uneasiness, was, after a considerable progress through the House, thrown out by *him*.

What was the consequence? The whole kingdom of Ireland was instantly in a flame. Threatened by foreigners, and, as they thought, insulted by England, they resolved at once to resist the power of France, and to cast off yours. As for us, we were able neither to protect nor to restrain them. Forty thousand men were raised and disciplined without commission from the crown.[13] Two illegal armies were seen with banners displayed at the same time and in the same country. No executive magistrate, no judicature, in Ireland, would acknowledge the legality of the army which bore the king's commission; and no law, or appearance of law, authorized the army commissioned by itself. In this unexampled state of things, which the least error, the least trespass on the right or left, would have hurried down the precipice into an abyss of blood and confusion, the people of Ireland demand a freedom of trade with arms in their hands. They interdict all commerce between the two nations. They deny all new supply in the House of Commons, although in time of war. They stint the trust of the old revenue, given for two years to all the king's predecessors, to six months. The British parliament, in a former session, frightened into a limited concession by the menaces of Ireland, frightened out of it by the menaces of England, were now frightened back again, and made an universal surrender of all that had been thought the peculiar, reserved, uncommunicable rights of England;—the exclusive commerce of America, of Africa, of the West Indies—all the enumerations of the acts of navigation—all the manufactures—iron, glass, even the last pledge of jealousy and pride, the interest hid in the secret of our hearts, the inveterate prejudice moulded into the constitution of our frame, even the sacred fleece itself, all went together. No reserve; no exception; no debate; no discussion. A sudden light broke in upon us all. It broke in, not through well-contrived and well-disposed windows, but through flaws and breaches; through the yawning chasms of our ruin. We were taught wisdom by humiliation. No town in England presumed to have a prejudice; or dared to mutter a petition. What was worse, the whole parliament of England, which retained authority for nothing but surrenders, was despoiled of every shadow of its superintendence. It was, without any qualification, denied in theory, as it had been trampled upon in practice. This scene of shame and disgrace has, in a manner whilst I am speaking, ended by the perpetual establishment of a military power in the dominions of this crown, without consent of the British legislature,[14] contrary to the policy of the constitution, contrary to the declaration of right: and by this your liberties are swept away along with your supreme authority—and both, linked together from the beginning, have, I am afraid, both together perished, for ever.

What! gentlemen, was I not to foresee, or foreseeing, was I not to endeavour to save you from all these multiplied mischiefs and disgraces? Would the little, silly, canvass prattle of obeying instructions, and having no opinions but yours, and such idle senseless tales, which amuse the vacant ears of unthinking men, have saved you from "the pelting of that pitiless storm," [15] to which the loose improvidence, the cowardly rashness, of those who dare not look danger in the

---

[13] The Irish Volunteers. Burke's account of the vigor with which the Irish, under the leadership of Henry Grattan and Henry Flood, took advantage of England's perilous international situation is hardly exaggerated.

[14] The so-called Irish Perpetual Mutiny Act, by which the British conceded to Ireland the right to govern the military force in Ireland. Burke had opposed this concession and had become unpopular in Ireland on that account. See Grattan's speech, pp. 251–53 below.

[15] Poor naked wretches, wheresoe'er you are,
That bide the pelting of this pitiless storm.
King Lear, III, iv, 28–29.

face, so as to provide against it in time, and therefore throw themselves headlong into the midst of it, have exposed this degraded nation, beaten down and prostrate on the earth, unsheltered, unarmed, unresisting? Was I an Irishman on that day, that I boldly withstood our pride? or on the day that I hung down my head, and wept in shame and silence over the humiliation of Great Britain? I became unpopular in England for the one, and in Ireland for the other. What then? What obligation lay on me to be popular? I was bound to serve both kingdoms. To be pleased with my service, was their affair, not mine.

I was an Irishman in the Irish business, just as much as I was an American, when, on the same principles, I wished you to concede to America, at a time when she prayed concession at our feet. Just as much was I an American, when I wished parliament to offer terms in victory, and not to wait the well-chosen hour of defeat, for making good by weakness, and by supplication, a claim of prerogative, pre-eminence, and authority.

Instead of requiring it from me, as a point of duty, to kindle with your passions, had you all been as cool as I was, you would have been saved from disgraces and distresses that are unutterable. Do you remember our commission? We sent out a solemn embassy across the Atlantic ocean, to lay the crown, the peerage, the commons of Great Britain, at the feet of the American Congress.[16] That our disgrace might want no sort of brightening and burnishing, observe who they were that composed this famous embassy! My Lord Carlisle is among the first ranks of our nobility. He is the identical man who, but two years before, had been put forward, at the opening of a session in the House of Lords, as the mover of a haughty and rigorous address against America. He was put in the front of the embassy of submission. Mr. Eden was taken from the office of Lord Suffolk, to whom he was then under secretary of state; from the office of that Lord Suffolk, who but a few weeks before, in his place in parliament, did not deign to inquire where a congress of vagrants was to be found. This Lord Suffolk sent Mr. Eden to find these vagrants, without knowing where this king's generals were to be found, who were joined in the same commission of supplicating those whom they were sent to subdue. They enter the capital of America only to abandon it; and these assertors and representatives of the dignity of England, at the tail of a flying army, let fly their Parthian shafts of memorials and remonstrances at random behind them. Their promises and their offers, their flatteries and their menaces, were all despised; and we were saved from the disgrace of their formal reception, only because the congress scorned to receive them; whilst the state-house of independent Philadelphia opened her doors to the public entry of the ambassador of France. From war and blood we went to submission; and from submission plunged back again to war and blood; to desolate and be desolated, without measure, hope, or end. I am a Royalist, I blushed for this degradation of the crown. I am a Whig, I blushed for the dishonour of parliament. I am a true Englishman, I felt to the quick for the disgrace of England. I am a man, I felt for the melancholy reverse of human affairs, in the fall of the first power in the world.

To read what was approaching in Ireland, in the black and bloody characters of the American war, was a painful, but it was a necessary part of my public duty. For, gentlemen, it is not your fond desires or mine that can alter the nature of

---

[16] The conciliatory commission sent early in 1778. Its offers were too late and its honesty was distrusted. On May 4, the Congress ratified the alliance with France.

things; by contending against which, what have we got, or shall ever get, but defeat and shame? I did not obey your instructions: No. I conformed to the instructions of truth and nature, and maintained your interest, against your opinions, with a constancy that became me. A representative worthy of you ought to be a person of stability. I am to look, indeed, to your opinions; but to such opinions as you and I *must* have five years hence. I was not to look to the flash of the day. I knew that you chose me, in my place, along with others, to be a pillar of the state, and not a weathercock on the top of the edifice, exalted for my levity and versatility, and of no use but to indicate the shiftings of every fashionable gale. Would to God the value of my sentiments on Ireland and on America had been at this day a subject of doubt and discussion! No matter what my sufferings had been, so that this kingdom had kept the authority I wished it to maintain, by a grave foresight, and by an equitable temperance in the use of its power.

The next article of charge on my public conduct, and that which I find rather the most prevalent of all, is, Lord Beauchamp's bill.[17] I mean his bill of last session, for reforming the law-process concerning imprisonment. It is said, to aggravate the offence, that I treated the petition of this city with contempt even in presenting it to the House, and expressed myself in terms of marked disrespect. Had this latter part of the charge been true, no merits on the side of the question which I took could possibly excuse me. But I am incapable of treating this city with disrespect. Very fortunately, at this minute (if my bad eyesight does not deceive me) the worthy gentleman deputed on this business stands directly before me. To him I appeal, whether I did not, though it militated with my oldest and my most recent public opinions, deliver the petition with a strong, and more than usual recommendation to the consideration of the House, on account of the character and consequence of those who signed it. I believe the worthy gentleman will tell you, that, the very day I received it, I applied to the solicitor, now the attorney-general, to give it an immediate consideration; and he most obligingly and instantly consented to employ a great deal of his very valuable time to write an explanation of the bill. I attended the committee with all possible care and diligence, in order that every objection of yours might meet with a solution; or produce an alteration. I entreated your learned recorder[18] (always ready in business in which you take a concern) to attend. But what will you say to those who blame me for supporting Lord Beauchamp's bill, as a disrespectful treatment of your petition, when you hear, that out of respect to you, I myself was the cause of the loss of that very bill? For the noble lord who brought it in, and who, I must say, has much merit for this and some other measures, at my request consented to put it off for a week, which the speaker's illness lengthened to a fortnight; and then the frantic tumult about popery drove that and every rational

---

[17] This bill provided that if a man in prison for debt gave up all his property and declared upon oath that he was not worth five pounds, he might appear in court to be investigated, and the court might, if it chose, release him from imprisonment, but not from his debt. Bristol petitioned against the bill; Burke supported it.

[18] The "worthy gentleman" who brought the petition to London, and whom Burke calls to witness to his care with' the petition, is a merchant named Williams. "Your learned recorder" is John Dunning, a very able lawyer, of the Shelburne branch of Opposition in the House of Commons. The recorder in a city is a judicial magistrate.

business from the House.[19] So that if I chose to make a defence of myself, on the little principles of a culprit, pleading in his exculpation, I might not only secure my acquittal, but make merit with the opposers of the bill. But I shall do no such thing. The truth is, that I did occasion the loss of the bill, and by a delay caused by my respect to you. But such an event was never in my contemplation. And I am so far from taking credit for the defeat of that measure, that I cannot sufficiently lament my misfortune, if but one man, who ought to be at large, has passed a year in prison by my means. I am a debtor to the debtors. I confess judgment. I owe what, if ever it be in my power, I shall most certainly pay,—ample atonement and usurious amends to liberty and humanity for my unhappy lapse. For, gentlemen, Lord Beauchamp's bill was a law of justice and policy, as far as it went; I say as far as it went, for its fault was its being, in the remedial part, miserably defective.

There are two capital faults in our law with relation to civil debts. One is, that every man is presumed solvent. A presumption, in innumerable cases, directly against truth. Therefore the debtor is ordered, on a supposition of ability and fraud, to be coerced his liberty until he makes payment. By this means, in all cases of civil insolvency, without a pardon from his creditor, he is to be imprisoned for life:—and thus a miserable mistaken invention of artificial science operates to change a civil into a criminal judgment, and to scourge misfortune or indiscretion with a punishment which the law does not inflict on the greatest crimes.

The next fault is, that the inflicting of that punishment is not on the opinion of an equal and public judge; but is referred to the arbitrary discretion of a private, nay interested, and irritated, individual. He, who formally is, and substantially ought to be, the judge, is in reality no more than ministerial, a mere executive instrument of a private man, who is at once judge and party.[20] Every idea of judicial order is subverted by this procedure. If the insolvency be no crime, why is it punished with arbitrary imprisonment? If it be a crime, why is it delivered into private hands to pardon without discretion, or to punish without mercy and without measure?

To these faults, gross and cruel facts in our law, the excellent principle of Lord Beauchamp's bill applied some sort of remedy. I know that credit must be preserved; but equity must be preserved too; and it is impossible that any thing should be necessary to commerce, which is inconsistent with justice. The principle of credit was not weakened by that bill. God forbid! The enforcement of that credit was only put into the same public judicial hands on which we depend for our lives, and all that makes life dear to us. But, indeed, this business was taken up too warmly both here and elsewhere. The bill was extremely mistaken. It was supposed to enact what it never enacted; and complaints were made of clauses in it as novelties, which existed before the noble lord that brought in the bill was born. There was a fallacy that ran through the whole of the objections. The gentlemen who opposed the bill always argued, as if the option lay between that bill and the ancient law. But this is a grand mistake. For, practically, the option is between, not that bill and the old law, but between that bill and those occasional laws, called acts of grace. For the operation of the old law is so

---

[19] The Lord George Gordon riots, mentioned earlier.
[20] The debtor had to be committed to prison on complaint of the creditor.

savage, and so inconvenient to society, that for a long time past, once in every parliament, and lately twice, the legislature has been obliged to make a general arbitrary jail-delivery, and at once to set open, by its sovereign authority, all the prisons in England.

Gentlemen, I never relished acts of grace; nor ever submitted to them but from despair of better. They are a dishonourable invention, by which, not from humanity, not from policy, but merely because we have not room enough to hold these victims of the absurdity of our laws, we turn loose upon the public three or four thousand naked wretches, corrupted by the habits, debased by the ignominy, of a prison. If the creditor had a right to those carcases as a natural security for his property, I am sure we have no right to deprive him of that security. But if the few pounds of flesh were not necessary to his security, we had not a right to detain the unfortunate debtor, without any benefit at all to the person who confined him. Take it as you will, we commit injustice. Now Lord Beauchamp's bill intended to do deliberately, and with great caution and circumspection, upon each several case, and with all attention to the just claimant, what acts of grace do in a much greater measure, and with very little care, caution, or deliberation.

I suspect that here too, if we contrive to oppose this bill, we shall be found in a struggle against the nature of things. For as we grow enlightened, the public will not bear, for any length of time, to pay for the maintenance of whole armies of prisoners, nor, at their own expense, submit to keep jails as a sort of garrisons, merely to fortify the absurd principle of making men judges in their own cause. For credit has little or no concern in this cruelty. I speak in a commercial assembly. You know that credit is given, because capital *must* be employed; that men calculate the chances of insolvency; and they either withhold the credit, or make the debtor pay the risk in the price. The counting-house has no alliance with the jail. Holland understands trade as well as we, and she has done much more than this obnoxious bill intended to do. There was not, when Mr. Howard[21] visited Holland, more than one prisoner for debt in the great city of Rotterdam. Although Lord Beauchamp's act (which was previous to this bill, and intended to feel the way for it) has already preserved liberty to thousands; and though it is not three years since the last act of grace passed, yet by Mr. Howard's last account, there were near three thousand again in jail. I cannot name this gentleman without remarking that his labours and writings have done much to open the eyes and hearts of mankind. He has visited all Europe,—not to survey the sumptuousness of palaces, or the stateliness of temples; not to make accurate measurements of the remains of ancient grandeur, nor to form a scale of the curiosity of modern art; not to collect medals, or collate manuscripts:—but to dive into the depths of dungeons; to plunge into the infection of hospitals; to survey the mansions of sorrow and pain; to take the gauge and dimensions of misery, depression, and contempt; to remember the forgotten, to attend to the neglected, to visit the forsaken, and to compare and collate the distresses of all men in all countries. His plan is original; and it is as full of genius as it is of humanity. It was a voyage of discovery; a circumnavigation of charity. Already the benefit

---

[21] John Howard (1726?–1790), a philanthropist and reformer. He visited jails and prisons all over England and the Continent to arouse sentiment for reform of the deplorable conditions. In the next sentence Burke refers, perhaps, to Howard's *State of the Prisons* (1777) or his *Appendix to State of the Prisons* (1780).

of his labour is felt more or less in every country; I hope he will anticipate his final reward, by seeing all its effects fully realized in his own. He will receive, not by detail, but in gross, the reward of those who visit the prisoner; and he has so forestalled and monopolized this branch of charity, that there will be, I trust, little room to merit by such acts of benevolence hereafter.

Nothing now remains to trouble you with, but the fourth charge against me—the business of the Roman Catholics.[22] It is a business closely connected with the rest. They are all on one and the same principle. My little scheme of conduct, such as it is, is all arranged. I could do nothing but what I have done on this subject, without confounding the whole train of my ideas, and disturbing the whole order of my life. Gentlemen, I ought to apologize to you for seeming to think any thing at all necessary to be said upon this matter. The calumny is fitter to be scrawled with the midnight chalk of incendiaries, with "No popery," on walls and doors of devoted houses, than to be mentioned in any civilized company. I had heard, that the spirit of discontent on that subject was very prevalent here. With pleasure I find that I have been grossly misinformed. If it exists at all in this city, the laws have crushed its exertions, and our morals have shamed its appearance in daylight. I have pursued this spirit wherever I could trace it; but it still fled from me. It was a ghost which all had heard of, but none had seen. None would acknowledge that he thought the public proceeding with regard to our Catholic dissenters to be blamable; but several were sorry it had made an ill impression upon others, and that my interest was hurt by my share in the business.[23] I find with satisfaction and pride, that not above four or five in this city (and I dare say these misled by some gross misrepresentation) have signed that symbol of delusion and bond of sedition, that libel on the national religion and English character, the Protestant Association. It is therefore, gentlemen, not by way of cure, but of prevention, and lest the arts of wicked men may prevail over the integrity of any one amongst us, that I think it necessary to open to you the merits of this transaction pretty much at large; and I beg your patience upon it: for, although the reasonings that have been used to depreciate the act are of little force, and though the authority of the men concerned in this ill design is not very imposing; yet the audaciousness of these conspirators against the national honour, and the extensive wickedness of their attempts, have raised persons of little importance to a degree of evil eminence, and imparted a sort of sinister dignity to proceedings that had their origin in only the meanest and blindest malice.

In explaining to you the proceedings of parliament which have been complained of, I will state to you,—first, the thing that was done;—next, the persons

[22] Burke's account of the original penal act of William III's reign and of Sir George Savile's repeal bill are significant for understanding the situation. The reader may wish to go more fully into the great problem of emancipation of Catholics in connection with O'Connell's speech, below, pp. 358–70.

[23] Ever since Burke had entered politics his opponents had kept spreading the rumor that he was a Catholic and that he had been educated at the Jesuit College at St. Omers, France. This charge had been kept alive in Bristol to Burke's disadvantage. Burke was always a devoted Church of England Protestant, in Ireland and in England. His mother and sister were Catholics; he and his brother were brought up in their father's Protestant religion. Burke married the daughter of a Roman Catholic physician; his son was a Protestant.

who did it;—and lastly, the grounds and reasons upon which the legislature proceeded in this deliberate act of public justice and public prudence.

Gentlemen, the condition of our nature is such, that we buy our blessings at a price. The Reformation, one of the greatest periods of human improvement, was a time of trouble and confusion. The vast structure of superstition and tyranny, which had been for ages in rearing, and which was combined with the interest of the great and of the many, which was moulded into the laws, the manners, and civil institutions of nations, and blended with the frame and policy of states, could not be brought to the ground without a fearful struggle; nor could it fall without a violent concussion of itself and all about it. When this great revolution was attempted in a more regular mode by government, it was opposed by plots and seditions of the people; when by popular efforts, it was repressed as rebellion by the hand of power; and bloody executions (often bloodily returned) marked the whole of its progress through all its stages. The affairs of religion, which are no longer heard of in the tumult of our present contentions, made a principal ingredient in the wars and politics of that time; the enthusiasm of religion threw a gloom over the politics; and political interests poisoned and perverted the spirit of religion upon all sides. The Protestant religion in that violent struggle, infected, as the Popish had been before, by worldly interests and worldly passions, became a persecutor in its turn, sometimes of the new sects, which carried their own principles further than it was convenient to the original reformers; and always of the body from whom they parted: and this persecuting spirit arose, not only from the bitterness of retaliation, but from the merciless policy of fear.

It was long before the spirit of true piety and true wisdom, involved in the principles of the Reformation, could be depurated from the dregs and feculence of the contention with which it was carried through. However, until this be done, the Reformation is not complete; and those who think themselves good Protestants, from their animosity to others, are in that respect no Protestants at all. It was at first thought necessary, perhaps, to oppose to popery another popery, to get the better of it. Whatever was the cause, laws were made in many countries, and in this kingdom in particular, against Papists, which are as bloody as any of those which had been enacted by the popish princes and states; and where those laws were not bloody, in my opinion, they were worse; as they were slow, cruel outrages on our nature, and kept men alive only to insult in their persons every one of the rights and feelings of humanity. I pass those statutes, because I would spare your pious ears the repetition of such shocking things; and I come to that particular law, the repeal of which has produced so many unnatural and unexpected consequences.

A statute was fabricated in the year 1699, by which the saying mass (a church-service in the Latin tongue, not exactly the same as our liturgy, but very near it, and containing no offence whatsoever against the laws, or against good morals) was forged into a crime, punishable with perpetual imprisonment. The teaching school, an useful and virtuous occupation, even the teaching in a private family, was in every Catholic subjected to the same unproportioned punishment. Your industry, and the bread of your children, was taxed for a pecuniary reward to stimulate avarice to do what nature refused, to inform and prosecute on this law. Every Roman Catholic was, under the same act, to forfeit his estate to his nearest Protestant relation, until, through a profession of what he did not believe, he redeemed by his hypocrisy, what the law had transferred to the kinsman as the recompense of his profligacy. When thus turned out of doors from his paternal estate, he was disabled from acquiring any other by any industry, donation, or charity; but was rendered a foreigner in his native land, only because he retained the religion, along with the property, handed down to him from those who had been the old inhabitants of that land before him.

Does any one who hears me approve this scheme of things, or think there is common justice, common sense, or common honesty in any part of it? If any does, let him say it, and I am ready to discuss the point with temper and candour. But instead of approving, I perceive a virtuous indignation beginning to rise in your minds on the mere cold stating of the statute.

But what will you feel, when you know from history how this statute passed, and what were the motives, and what the mode of making it? A party in this nation, enemies to the system of the Revolution,[24] were in opposition to the government of King William. They knew that our glorious deliverer was an enemy to all persecution. They knew that he came to free us from slavery and popery, out of a country, where a third of the people are contented Catholics under a Protestant government. He came with a part of his army composed of those very Catholics, to overset the power of a popish prince. Such is the effect of a tolerating spirit: and so much is liberty served in every way, and by all persons, by a manly adherence to its own principles. Whilst freedom is true to itself, every thing becomes subject to it; and its very adversaries are an instrument in its hands.

The party I speak of (like some amongst us who would disparage the best friends of their country) resolved to make the king either violate his principles of toleration, or incur the odium of protecting Papists. They, therefore, brought in this bill, and made it purposely wicked and absurd that it might be rejected. The then court-party, discovering their game, turned the tables on them, and returned their bill to them stuffed with still greater absurdities, that its loss might lie upon its original authors. They, finding their own ball thrown back to them, kicked it back again to their adversaries. And thus this act, loaded with the double injustice of two parties, neither of whom intended to pass, what they hoped the other would be persuaded to reject, went through the legislature, contrary to the real wish of all parts of it, and of all the parties that composed it. In this manner these insolent and profligate factions, as if they were playing with balls and counters, made a sport of the fortunes and the liberties of their fellow creatures. Other acts of persecution have been acts of malice. This was a subversion of justice from wantonness and petulance. Look into the history of Bishop Burnet.[25] He is a witness without exception.

The effects of the act have been as mischievous, as its origin was ludicrous and shameful. From that time every person of that communion, lay and ecclesiastic,

[24] The "Glorious" Revolution of 1688, sometimes called the Whig Revolution, caused the removal of the Catholic-leaning Stuart, James II, and established the Protestant William of Orange and his wife Mary (a Stuart) on the throne. It also established Parliament as the principal power in the government. Modern parliamentary government is said to date from then.

[25] Gilbert Burnet (1643–1715), Bishop of Salisbury, was deeply involved with the politics and the religious controversy of the Restoration and the "Glorious" Revolution. He fell out of favor with both sides because of his advocacy of moderation in the treatment of Catholics. Burke refers to his *History of his own Times* (1723–24).

has been obliged to fly from the face of day. The clergy, concealed in garrets of private houses, or obliged to take a shelter (hardly safe to themselves, but infinitely dangerous to their country) under the privileges of foreign ministers, officiated as their servants, and under their protection. The whole body of the Catholics, condemned to beggary and to ignorance in their native land, have been obliged to learn the principles of letters, at the hazard of all their other principles, from the charity of your enemies. They have been taxed to their ruin at the pleasure of necessitous and profligate relations, and according to the measure of their necessity and profligacy. Examples of this are many and affecting. Some of them are known by a friend who stands near me in this hall. It is but six or seven years since a clergyman, of the name of Malony, a man of morals, neither guilty nor accused of any thing noxious to the state, was condemned to perpetual imprisonment for exercising the functions of his religion; and after lying in jail two or three years, was relieved by the mercy of government from perpetual imprisonment, on condition of perpetual banishment. A brother of the Earl of Shrewsbury, a Talbot, a name respectable in this country, whilst its glory is any part of its concern, was hauled to the bar of the Old Bailey,[26] among common felons, and only escaped the same doom, either by some error in the process, or that the wretch who brought him there could not correctly describe his person; I now forget which.—In short, the persecution would never have relented for a moment, if the judges, superseding (though with an ambiguous example) the strict rule of their artificial duty by the higher obligation of their conscience, did not constantly throw every difficulty in the way of such informers. But so ineffectual is the power of legal evasion against legal iniquity, that it was but the other day, that a lady of condition, beyond the middle of life, was on the point of being stripped of her whole fortune by a near relation, to whom she had been a friend and benefactor; and she must have been totally ruined, without a power of redress or mitigation from the courts of law, had not the legislature itself rushed in, and by a special act of parliament rescued her from the injustice of its own statutes. One of the acts authorizing such things was that which we in part repealed, knowing what our duty was; and doing that duty as men of honour and virtue, as good Protestants, and as good citizens. Let him stand forth that disapproves what we have done!

Gentlemen, bad laws are the worst sort of tyranny. In such a country as this they are of all bad things the worst, worse by far than any where else; and they derive a particular malignity even from the wisdom and soundness of the rest of our institutions. For very obvious reasons you cannot trust the crown with a dispensing power over any of your laws. However, a government, be it as bad as it may, will, in the exercise of a discretionary power, discriminate times and persons; and will not ordinarily pursue any man, when its own safety is not concerned. A mercenary informer knows no distinction. Under such a system, the obnoxious people are slaves, not only to the government, but they live at the mercy of every individual; they are at once the slaves of the whole community, and of every part of it; and the worst and most unmerciful men are those on whose goodness they most depend.

In this situation men not only shrink from the frowns of a stern magistrate; but they are obliged to fly from their very species. The seeds of destruction are sown

[26] The principal police court in old London.

in civil intercourse, in social habitudes. The blood of wholesome kindred is infected. Their tables and beds are surrounded with snares. All the means given by Providence to make life safe and comfortable are perverted into instruments of terror and torment. This species of universal subserviency, that makes the very servant who waits behind your chair the arbiter of your life and fortune, has such a tendency to degrade an abase mankind, and to deprive them of that assured and liberal state of mind, which alone can make us what we ought to be, that I vow to God I would sooner bring myself to put a man to immediate death for opinions I disliked, and so to get rid of the man and his opinions at once, than to fret him with a feverish being, tainted with the jail-distemper of a contagious servitude, to keep him above ground an animated mass of putrefaction, corrupted himself, and corrupting all about him.

The act repealed was of this direct tendency; and it was made in the manner which I have related to you. I will now tell you by whom the bill of repeal was brought into parliament. I find it has been industriously given out in this city (from kindness to me, unquestionably) that I was the mover or the seconder. The fact is, I did not once open my lips on the subject during the whole progress of the bill. I do not say this as disclaiming my share in that measure. Very far from it. I inform you of this fact, lest I should seem to arrogate to myself the merits which belong to others. To have been the man chosen out to redeem our fellow-citizens from slavery; to purify our laws from absurdity and injustice; and to cleanse our religion from the blot and stain of persecution, would be an honour and happiness to which my wishes would undoubtedly aspire; but to which nothing but my wishes could have possibly entitled me. That great work was in hands in every respect far better qualified than mine. The mover of the bill was Sir George Savile.[27]

When an act of great and signal humanity was to be done, and done with all the weight and authority that belonged to it, the world could cast its eyes upon none but him. I hope that few things which have a tendency to bless or to adorn life have wholly escaped my observation in my passage through it. I have sought the acquaintance of that gentleman, and have seen him in all situations. He is a true genius; with an understanding vigorous, and acute, and refined, and distinguishing even to excess; and illuminated with a most unbounded, peculiar, and original cast of imagination. With these he possesses many external and instrumental advantages; and he makes use of them all. His fortune is among the largest; a fortune which, wholly unincumbered, as it is, with one single charge from luxury, vanity, or excess, sinks under the benevolence of its dispenser. This private benevolence, expanding itself into patriotism, renders his whole being the estate of the public, in which he has not reserved a *peculium* for himself of profit, diversion, or relaxation. During the session, the first in, and the last out of the House of Commons; he passes from the senate to the camp; and seldom seeing the seat of his ancestors, he is always in the senate to serve his country, or in the

[27] Burke's praise of Sir George was indeed well merited. He came from one of the richest and most independent and at the same time most responsible families in Yorkshire, and was himself highly respected in and out of Parliament. Perhaps Burke's enthusiasm, however, is increased by Savile's close connection with the Rockinghams and hence with Burke. The strategy on this bill seems to have been good: give chief responsibility to a man known as unsympathetic to Catholicism; keep the known sympathizer quiet.

field to defend it. But in all well-wrought compositions, some particulars stand out more eminently than the rest; and the things which will carry his name to posterity, are his two bills; I mean that for a limitation of the claims of the crown upon landed estates,[28] and this for the relief of the Roman Catholics. By the former, he has emancipated property; by the latter he has quieted conscience; and by both he has taught that grand lesson to government and subject,—no longer to regard each other as adverse parties.

Such was the mover of the act that is complained of by men, who are not quite so good as he is; an act, most assuredly not brought in by him from any partiality to the sect which is the object of it. For, among his faults, I really cannot help reckoning a greater degree of prejudice against that people, than becomes so wise a man. I know that he inclines to a sort of disgust, mixed with a considerable degree of asperity, to the system; and he has few, or rather no habits with any of its professors. What he has done was on quite other motives. The motives were these, which he declared in his excellent speech on his motion for the bill; namely, his extreme zeal to the Protestant religion, which he thought utterly disgraced by the act of 1699; and his rooted hatred to all kind of oppression, under any colour, or upon any pretence whatsoever.

The seconder was worthy of the mover, and of the motion. I was not the seconder; it was Mr. Dunning, recorder of this city. I shall say the less of him, because his near relation to you makes you more particularly acquainted with his merits. But I should appear little acquainted with them, or little sensible of them, if I could utter his name on this occasion without expressing my esteem for his character. I am not afraid of offending a most learned body, and most jealous of its reputation for that learning, when I say he is the first of his profession. It is a point settled by those who settle every thing else; and I must add (what I am enabled to say from my own long and close observation) that there is not a man, of any profession, or in any situation, of a more erect and independent spirit; of a more proud honour; a more manly mind; a more firm and determined integrity. Assure yourselves, that the names of two such men will bear a great load of prejudice in the other scale before they can be entirely outweighed.[29]

With this mover, and this seconder, agreed the *whole* House of Commons; the *whole* House of Lords; the *whole* bench of bishops; the king; the ministry; the opposition; all the distinguished clergy of the establishment; all the eminent lights (for they were consulted) of the dissenting churches. This according voice of national wisdom ought to be listened to with reverence. To say that all these descriptions of Englishmen unanimously concurred in a scheme for introducing the Catholic religion, or that none of them understood the nature and effects of what they were doing so well as a few obscure clubs of people, whose names you never heard of, is shamelessly absurd. Surely it is paying a miserable compliment to the religion we profess, to suggest, that every thing eminent in the kingdom is indifferent, or even adverse to that religion, and that its security is wholly abandoned to the zeal of those, who have nothing but their zeal to distinguish them. In weighing this unanimous concurrence of whatever the nation has to boast of,

28 The Nullum Tempus Act of 1768–1769.

29 Burke often included character sketches, such as these of Savile and Dunning, in his speeches. See, for example, those of Townshend, Grenville, and Chatham in *American Taxation*.

I hope you will recollect, that all these concurring parties do by no means love one another enough to agree in any point, which was not, both evidently and importantly, right.

To prove this; to prove that the measure was both clearly and materially proper, I will next lay before you (as I promised) the political grounds and reasons for the repeal of that penal statute; and the motives to its repeal at that particular time.

Gentlemen, America—when the English nation seemed to be dangerously, if not irrecoverably divided; when one, and that the most growing branch, was torn from the parent stock, and ingrafted on the power of France, a great terror fell upon this kingdom. On a sudden we awakened from our dreams of conquest, and saw ourselves threatened with an immediate invasion; which we were at that time very ill prepared to resist.[30] You remember the cloud that gloomed over us all. In that hour of our dismay, from the bottom of the hiding-places, into which the indiscriminate rigour of our statutes had driven them, came out the body of the Roman Catholics. They appeared before the steps of a tottering throne, with one of the most sober, measured, steady, and dutiful addresses that was ever presented to the crown. It was no holiday ceremony; no anniversary compliment of parade and show. It was signed by almost every gentleman of that persuasion, of note or property in England. At such a crisis, nothing but a decided resolution to stand or fall with their country could have dictated such an address; the direct tendency of which was to cut off all retreat; and to render them peculiarly obnoxious to an invader of their own communion. The address showed what I long languished to see, that all the subjects of England had cast off all foreign views and connexions, and that every man looked for his relief from every grievance, at the hands only of his own natural government.

It was necessary, on our part, that the natural government should show itself worthy of that name. It was necessary, at the crisis I speak of, that the supreme power of the state should meet the conciliatory dispositions of the subject. To delay protection would be to reject allegiance. And why should it be rejected, or even coldly and suspiciously received? If any independent Catholic state should choose to take part with this kingdom in a war with France and Spain, that bigot (if such a bigot could be found) would be heard with little respect, who could dream of objecting his religion to an ally, whom the nation would not only receive with its freest thanks, but purchase with the last remains of its exhausted treasure. To such an ally we should not dare to whisper a single syllable of those base and invidious topics, upon which, some unhappy men would persuade the state, to reject the duty and allegiance of its own members. Is it then because foreigners are in a condition to set our malice at defiance, that with *them,* we are willing to contract engagements of friendship, and to keep them with fidelity and honour: but that, because we conceive some descriptions of our countrymen are not powerful enough to punish our malignity, we will not permit them to support our common interest? Is it on that ground, that our anger is to be kindled by their offered kindness? Is it on that ground, that they are to be subjected to penalties, because they are willing, by actual merit, to purge themselves from imputed crimes? Lest

[30] In the summer of 1779 England had been terrified at the prospect of an invasion from France. The French fleet controlled the Channel and stood off the south coast for weeks. England's fleet was helpless.

by an adherence to the cause of their country, they should acquire a title to fair and equitable treatment, are we resolved to furnish them with causes of eternal enmity; and rather supply them with just and founded motives to disaffection, than not to have that disaffection in existence to justify an oppression, which, not from policy but disposition, we have predetermined to exercise?

What shadow of reason could be assigned, why, at a time when the most Protestant part of this Protestant empire found it for its advantage to unite with the two principal Popish states, to unite itself in the closest bonds with France and Spain, for our destruction, that we should refuse to unite with our own Catholic countrymen for our own preservation? Ought we, like madmen, to tear off the plasters, that the lenient hand of prudence had spread over the wounds and gashes, which in our delirium of ambition we had given to our own body? No person ever reprobated the American war more than I did, and do, and ever shall. But I never will consent that we should lay additional, voluntary penalties on ourselves, for a fault which carries but too much of its own punishment in its own nature. For one, I was delighted with the proposal of internal peace. I accepted the blessing with thankfulness and transport; I was truly happy to find *one* good effect of our civil distractions, that they had put an end to all religious strife and heart-burning in our own bowels. What must be the sentiments of a man, who would wish to perpetuate domestic hostility, when the causes of dispute are at an end; and who, crying out for peace with one part of the nation on the most humiliating terms, should deny it to those, who offer friendship without any terms at all?

But if I was unable to reconcile such a denial to the contracted principles of local duty, what answer could I give to the broad claims of general humanity? I confess to you freely, that the sufferings and distresses of the people of America in this cruel war, have at times affected me more deeply than I can express. I felt every Gazette of triumph as a blow upon my heart, which has a hundred times sunk and fainted within me at all the mischiefs brought upon those who bear the whole brunt of war in the heart of their country. Yet the Americans are utter strangers to me; a nation among whom I am not sure that I have a single acquaintance. Was I to suffer my mind to be so unaccountably warped; was I to keep such iniquitous weights and measures of temper and of reason, as to sympathize with those who are in open rebellion against an authority which I respect, at war with a country which by every title ought to be, and is most dear to me; and yet to have no feeling at all for the hardships and indignities suffered by men, who, by their very vicinity, are bound up in a nearer relation to us; who contribute their share, and more than their share, to the common prosperity; who perform the common offices of social life, and who obey the laws to the full as well as I do? Gentlemen, the danger to the state being out of the question (of which, let me tell you, statesmen themselves are apt to have but too exquisite a sense), I could assign no one reason of justice, policy, or feeling, for not concurring most cordially, as most cordially I did concur, in softening some part of that shameful servitude, under which several of my worthy fellow-citizens were groaning.

Important effects followed this act of wisdom. They appeared at home and abroad, to the great benefit of this kingdom; and, let me hope, to the advantage of mankind at large. It betokened union among ourselves. It showed soundness, even on the part of the persecuted, which generally is the weak side of every community. But its most essential operation was not in England. The act was immediately, though very imperfectly, copied in Ireland; and this imperfect transcript of an imperfect act, this first faint sketch of toleration, which did little more than disclose a principle, and mark out a disposition, completed in a most wonderful manner the re-union to the state, of all the Catholics of that country. It made us what we ought always to have been, one family, one body, one heart and soul, against the family-combination, and all other combinations of our enemies. We have indeed obligations to that people, who received such small benefits with so much gratitude; and for which gratitude and attachment to us, I am afraid they have suffered not a little in other places.

I dare say you have all heard of the privileges indulged to the Irish Catholics residing in Spain. You have likewise heard with what circumstances of severity they have been lately expelled from the sea-ports of that kingdom; driven into the inland cities; and there detained as a sort of prisoners of state. I have good reason to believe, that it was the zeal to our government and our cause (somewhat indiscreetly expressed in one of the addresses of the Catholics of Ireland), which has thus drawn down on their heads the indignation of the court of Madrid; to the inexpressible loss of several individuals, and, in future, perhaps to the great detriment of the whole of their body. Now that our people should be persecuted in Spain for their attachment to this country, and persecuted in this country for their supposed enmity to us, is such a jarring reconciliation of contradictory distresses, is a thing at once so dreadful and ridiculous, that no malice short of diabolical would wish to continue any human creatures in such a situation. But honest men will not forget either their merit or their sufferings. There are men (and many, I trust, there are) who, out of love to their country and their kind, would torture their invention to find excuses for the mistakes of their brethren; and who, to stifle dissension, would construe even doubtful appearances with the utmost favour: such men will never persuade themselves to be ingenious and refined in discovering disaffection and treason in the manifest, palpable signs of suffering loyalty. Persecution is so unnatural to them, that they gladly snatch the very first opportunity of laying aside all the tricks and devices of penal politics; and of returning home, after all their irksome and vexatious wanderings, to our natural family mansion, to the grand social principle, that unites all men, in all descriptions, under the shadow of an equal and impartial justice.

Men of another sort, I mean the bigoted enemies to liberty, may, perhaps, in their politics, make no account of the good or ill affection of the Catholics of England, who are but a handful of people (enough to torment, but not enough to fear), perhaps not so many, of both sexes and of all ages, as fifty thousand. But, gentlemen, it is possible you may not know, that the people of that persuasion in Ireland amount at least to sixteen or seventeen hundred thousand souls. I do not at all exaggerate the number. A *nation* to be persecuted! Whilst we were masters of the sea, embodied with America, and in alliance with half the powers of the Continent, we might perhaps, in that remote corner of Europe, afford to tyrannize with impunity. But there is a revolution in our affairs, which makes it prudent to be just. In our late awkward contest with Ireland about trade, had religion been thrown in, to ferment and embitter the mass of discontents, the consequences might have been truly dreadful. But very happily, that cause of quarrel was previously quieted by the wisdom of the acts I am commending.

Even in England, where I admit the danger from the discontent of that persuasion to be less than in Ireland; yet even here, had we listened to the counsels of fanaticism and folly, we might have wounded ourselves very deeply; and wounded ourselves in a very tender part. You are apprized, that the Catholics of England consist mostly of our best manufacturers.[31] Had the legislature chosen, instead of returning their declarations of duty with correspondent good-will, to drive them to despair, there is a country at their very door, to which they would be invited; a country in all respects as good as ours, and with the finest cities in the world ready built to receive them. And thus the bigotry of a free country, and in an enlightened age, would have re-peopled the cities of Flanders, which, in the darkness of two hundred years ago, had been desolated by the superstition of a cruel tyrant. Our manufacturers were the growth of the persecutions in the Low Countries. What a spectacle would it be to Europe, to see us at this time of day, balancing the account of tyranny with those very countries, and by our persecutions, driving back trade and manufacture, as a sort of vagabonds, to their original settlement! But I trust we shall be saved this last of disgraces.

So far as to the effect of the act on the interests of this nation. With regard to the interests of mankind at large, I am sure the benefit was very considerable. Long before this act, indeed, the spirit of toleration began to gain ground in Europe. In Holland, the third part of the people are Catholics; they live at ease; and are a sound part of the state. In many parts of Germany, Protestants and Papists partake the same cities, the same councils, and even the same churches. The unbounded liberality of the King of Prussia's conduct on this occasion is known to all the world; and it is of a piece with the other grand maxims of his reign. The magnanimity of the imperial court, breaking through the narrow principles of its predecessors, has indulged its Protestant subjects, not only with property, with worship, with liberal education; but with honours and trusts, both civil and military. A worthy Protestant gentleman of this country now fills, and fills with credit, a high office in the Austrian Netherlands. Even the Lutheran obstinacy of Sweden has thawed at length, and opened a toleration to all religions. I know myself, that in France the Protestants begin to be at rest. The army, which in that country is every thing, is open to them; and some of the military rewards and decorations which the laws deny, are supplied by others, to make the service acceptable and honourable. The first minister of finance, in that country, is a Protestant.[32] Two years' war without a tax is among the first-fruits of their liberality. Tarnished as the glory of this nation is, and far as it has waded into the shades of an eclipse, some beams of its former illumination still play upon its surface; and what is done in England is still looked to, as argument, and as example. It is certainly true, that no law of this country ever met with such universal applause abroad, or was so likely to produce the perfection of that tolerating spirit, which, as I observed, has been long gaining ground in Europe; for abroad, it was universally thought that we had done, what, I am sorry to say, we had not; they thought we had granted a full toleration. That opinion was however so far from hurting the Protestant cause, that I declare, with the most serious solemnity, my firm belief, that no one thing done for these fifty years past was so likely to prove deeply beneficial to our religion at large as Sir George Savile's act. In its

---

[31] Meaning here handworkers, such as spinners, weavers, silversmiths, etc.

[32] Jacques Necker (1732–1804), well known for his financial reforms. Though dismissed for his Protestantism in 1781, he had to be reinstated in 1788 to help prevent the Revolution.

effects it was "an act for tolerating and protecting Protestantism throughout Europe": and I hope that those, who were taking steps for the quiet and settlement of our Protestant brethren in other countries, will, even yet, rather consider the steady equity of the greater and better part of the people of Great Britain, than the vanity and violence of a few.

I perceive, gentlemen, by the manner of all about me, that you look with horror on the wicked clamour which has been raised on this subject; and that instead of an apology for what was done, you rather demand from me an account, why the execution of the scheme of toleration was not made more answerable to the large and liberal grounds on which it was taken up? The question is natural and proper; and I remember that a great and learned magistrate,[33] distinguished for his strong and systematic understanding, and who at that time was a member of the House of Commons, made the same objection to the proceeding. The statutes, as they now stand, are, without doubt, perfectly absurd. But I beg leave to explain the cause of this gross imperfection, in the tolerating plan, as well and as shortly as I am able. It was universally thought that the session ought not to pass over without doing *something* in this business. To revise the whole body of the penal statutes was conceived to be an object too big for the time. The penal statute, therefore, which was chosen for repeal (chosen to show our disposition to conciliate, not to perfect a toleration) was this act of ludicrous cruelty, of which I have just given you the history. It is an act, which, though not by a great deal so fierce and bloody as some of the rest, was infinitely more ready in the execution. It was the act which gave the greatest encouragement to those pests of society, mercenary informers, and interested disturbers of household peace; and it was observed with truth, that the prosecutions, either carried to conviction or compounded for many years, had been all commenced upon that act. It was said, that, whilst we were deliberating on a more perfect scheme, the spirit of the age would never come up to the execution of the statutes which remained; especially as more steps, and a co-operation of more minds and powers, were required towards a mischievous use of them, than for the execution of the act to be repealed: that it was better to unravel this texture from below than from above, beginning with the latest, which, in general practice, is the severest evil. It was alleged, that this slow proceeding would be attended with the advantage of a progressive experience; and that the people would grow reconciled to toleration, when they should find by the effects, that justice was not so irreconcilable an enemy to convenience as they had imagined.

These, gentlemen, were the reasons why we left this good work in the rude, unfinished state, in which good works are commonly left, through the tame circumspection with which a timid prudence so frequently enervates beneficence. In doing good, we are generally cold, and languid, and sluggish; and of all things afraid of being too much in the right. But the works of malice and injustice are quite in another style. They are finished with a bold, masterly hand; touched as they are with the spirit of those vehement passions that call forth all our energies, whenever we oppress and persecute.

Thus this matter was left for the time, with a full determination in parliament not to suffer other and worse statutes to remain for the purpose of counteracting

---

[33] Edward Thurlow (1731–1806), made Lord Chancellor as Baron Thurlow in 1778.

the benefits proposed by the repeal of one penal law: for nobody then dreamed of defending what was done as a benefit, on the ground of its being no benefit at all. We were not then ripe for so mean a subterfuge.

I do not wish to go over the horrid scene that was afterwards acted.[34] Would to God it could be expunged for ever from the annals of this country! But since it must subsist for our shame, let it subsist for our instruction. In the year 1780, there were found in this nation men deluded enough (for I give the whole to their delusion) on pretences of zeal and piety, without any sort of provocation whatsoever, real or pretended, to make a desperate attempt, which would have consumed all the glory and power of this country in the flames of London; and buried all law, order, and religion, under the ruins of the metropolis of the Protestant world. Whether all this mischief done, or in the direct train of doing, was in their original scheme, I cannot say; I hope it was not: but this would have been the unavoidable consequence of their proceedings, had not the flames they had lighted up in their fury been extinguished in their blood.

All the time that this horrid scene was acting, or avenging, as well as for some time before, and ever since, the wicked instigators of this unhappy multitude, guilty, with every aggravation, of all their crimes, and screened in a cowardly darkness from their punishment, continued without interruption, pity, or remorse, to blow up the blind rage of the populace, with a continued blast of pestilential libels, which infected and poisoned the very air we breathed in.

The main drift of all the libels, and all the riots, was, to force parliament (to persuade us was hopeless) into an act of national perfidy, which has no example. For, gentlemen, it is proper you should all know what infamy we escaped by refusing that repeal, for a refusal of which, it seems, I, among others, stand somewhere or other accused. When we took away, on the motives which I had the honour of stating to you, a few of the innumerable penalties upon an oppressed and injured people; the relief was not absolute, but given on a stipulation and compact between them and us: for we bound down the Roman Catholics with the most solemn oaths, to bear true allegiance to this government; to abjure all sorts of temporal power in any other; and to renounce, under the same solemn obligations, the doctrines of systematic perfidy, with which they stood (I conceive very unjustly) charged. Now our modest petitioners came up to us, most humbly praying nothing more, than that we should break our faith, without any one cause whatsoever of forfeiture assigned; and when the subjects of this kingdom had, on their part, fully performed their engagement, we should refuse, on our part, the benefit we had stipulated on the performance of those very conditions that were prescribed by our own authority, and taken on the sanction of our public faith—that is to say, when we had inveigled them with fair promises within our door, we were to shut it on them; and, adding mockery to outrage—to tell them, "Now we have got you fast—your consciences are bound to a power resolved on your destruction. We have made you swear, that your religion obliges you to keep your faith: fools as you are! we will now let you see, that our religion enjoins us to keep no faith with you."—They who would advisedly call upon us to do such things must certainly have thought us not only a convention of treacherous tyrants, but a gang of the lowest and dirtiest wretches that ever disgraced humanity. Had we done

---

[34] Burke now comes to the calamitous Lord George Gordon riots of the previous summer. See above, pp. 212–13.

this, we should have indeed proved, that there were *some* in the world whom no faith could bind; and we should have *convicted* ourselves of that odious principle of which Papists stood *accused* by those very savages, who wished us, on that accusation, to deliver them over to their fury.

In this audacious tumult, when our very name and character as gentlemen was to be cancelled for ever along with the faith and honour of the nation, I, who had exerted myself very little on the quiet passing of the bill, thought it necessary then to come forward. I was not alone: but though some distinguished members on all sides, and particularly on ours, added much to their high reputation by the part they took on that day (a part which will be remembered as long as honour, spirit, and eloquence, have estimation in the world), I may and will value myself so far, that, yielding in abilities to many, I yielded in zeal to none. With warmth and with vigour, and animated with a just and natural indignation, I called forth every faculty that I possessed, and I directed it in every way in which I could possibly employ it. I laboured night and day. I laboured in parliament: I laboured out of parliament. If therefore the resolution of the House of Commons, refusing to commit this act of unmatched turpitude, be a crime, I am guilty among the foremost. But, indeed, whatever the faults of that House may have been, no one member was found hardy enough to propose so infamous a thing; and on full debate we passed the resolution against the petitions with as much unanimity, as we had formerly passed the law, of which these petitions demanded the repeal.

There was a circumstance (justice will not suffer me to pass it over) which, if any thing could enforce the reasons I have given, would fully justify the act of relief, and render a repeal, or any thing like a repeal, unnatural, impossible. It was the behaviour of the persecuted Roman Catholics under the acts of violence and brutal insolence, which they suffered. I suppose there are not in London less than four or five thousand of that persuasion from my country, who do a great deal of the most laborious works in the metropolis; and they chiefly inhabit those quarters, which were the principal theatre of the fury of the bigoted multitude. They are known to be men of strong arms, and quick feelings, and more remarkable for a determined resolution, than clear ideas, or much foresight. But though provoked by every thing that can stir the blood of men, their houses and chapels in flames, and with the most atrocious profanations of every thing which they hold sacred before their eyes, not a hand was moved to retaliate, or even to defend. Had a conflict once begun, the rage of their persecutors would have redoubled. Thus fury increasing by the reverberation of outrages, house being fired for house, and church for chapel, I am convinced, that no power under heaven could have prevented a general conflagration; and at this day London would have been a tale. But I am well informed, and the thing speaks it, that their clergy exerted their whole influence to keep their people in such a state of forbearance and quiet, as, when I look back, fills me with astonishment; but not with astonishment only. Their merits on that occasion ought not to be forgotten: nor will they, when Englishmen come to recollect themselves. I am sure it were far more proper to have called them forth, and given them the thanks of both houses of parliament, than to have suffered those worthy clergymen, and excellent citizens, to be hunted into holes and corners, whilst we are making low-minded inquisitions into the number of their people; as if a tolerating principle was never to prevail, unless we were very sure that only a few could possibly take advantage of it. But indeed we are not yet well recovered of our fright. Our reason, I trust, will return with our security; and this unfortunate temper will pass over like a cloud.

Gentlemen, I have now laid before you a few of the reasons for taking away the penalties of the act of 1699, and for refusing to establish them on the riotous requisition of 1780. Because I would not suffer any thing which may be for your satisfaction to escape, permit me just to touch on the objections urged against our act and our resolves, and intended as a justification of the violence offered to both Houses. "Parliament," they assert, "was too hasty, and they ought, in so essential and alarming a change, to have proceeded with a far greater degree of deliberation." The direct contrary. Parliament was too slow. They took fourscore years to deliberate on the repeal of an act which ought not to have survived a second session. When at length, after a procrastination of near a century, the business was taken up, it proceeded in the most public manner, by the ordinary stages, and as slowly as a law so evidently right as to be resisted by none would naturally advance. Had it been read three times in one day,[35] we should have shown only a becoming readiness to recognize, by protection, the undoubted dutiful behaviour of those whom we had but too long punished for offences of presumption or conjecture. But for what end was that bill to linger beyond the usual period of an unopposed measure? Was it to be delayed until a rabble in Edinburgh should dictate to the Church of England what measure of persecution was fitting for her safety? Was it to be adjourned until a fanatical force could be collected in London, sufficient to frighten us out of all our ideas of policy and justice? Were we to wait for the profound lectures on the reason of state, ecclesiastical and political, which the Protestant Association have since condescended to read to us? Or were we, seven hundred peers and commoners, the only persons ignorant of the ribald invectives which occupy the place of argument in those remonstrances, which every man of common observation had heard a thousand times over, and a thousand times over had despised? All men had before heard what they have to say; and all men at this day know what they dare to do; and I trust all honest men are equally influenced by the one, and by the other.

But they tell us, that those our fellow-citizens, whose chains we have a little relaxed, are enemies to liberty and our free constitution.—Not enemies, I presume, to their *own* liberty. And as to the constitution, until we give them some share in it, I do not know on what pretence we can examine into their opinions about a business in which they have no interest or concern. But after all, are we equally sure, that they are adverse to our constitution, as that our statutes are hostile and destructive to them? For my part, I have reason to believe their opinions and inclinations in that respect are various, exactly like those of other men: and if they lean more to the crown than I, and than many of you think *we* ought, we must remember, that he, who aims at another's life, is not to be surprised if he flies into any sanctuary that will receive him. The tenderness of the executive power is the natural asylum of those upon whom the laws have declared war: and to complain that men are inclined to favour the means of their own safety, is so absurd, that one forgets the injustice in the ridicule.

[35] A bill going through the House of Commons proceeded in three stages or "readings," at each of which it was open for debate and modification. These readings were usually spaced at intervals providing time for digesting and thinking-over between them.

I must fairly tell you, that, so far as my principles are concerned, (principles that I hope will only depart with my last breath), I have no idea of a liberty unconnected with honesty and justice. Nor do I believe, that any good constitutions of government, or of freedom, can find it necessary for their security to doom any part of the people to a permanent slavery. Such a constitution of freedom, if such can be, is in effect no more than another name for the tyranny of the strongest faction; and factions in republics have been, and are, full as capable as monarchs of the most cruel oppression and injustice. It is but too true, that the love, and even the very idea, of genuine liberty is extremely rare. It is but too true, that there are many, whose whole scheme of freedom is made up of pride, perverseness, and insolence. They feel themselves in a state of thraldom, they imagine that their souls are cooped and cabined in, unless they have some man, or some body of men, dependent on their mercy. This desire of having some one below them descends to those who are the very lowest of all,—and a Protestant cobbler, debased by his poverty, but exalted by his share of the ruling Church, feels a pride in knowing it is by his generosity alone, that the peer, whose footman's instep he measures, is able to keep his chaplain from a jail. This disposition is the true source of the passion, which many men, in very humble life, have taken to the American war. *Our* subjects in America; *our* colonies; *our* dependents. This lust of party-power is the liberty they hunger and thirst for; and this syren song of ambition has charmed ears, that one would have thought were never organized to that sort of music.

This way of *proscribing the citizens by denominations and general descriptions*, dignified by the name of reason of state, and security for constitutions and commonwealths, is nothing better at bottom, than the miserable invention of an ungenerous ambition which would fain hold the sacred trust of power, without any of the virtues or any of the energies that give a title to it: a receipt of policy, made up of a detestable compound of malice, cowardice, and sloth. They would govern men against their will; but in that government they would be discharged from the exercise of vigilance, providence, and fortitude; and therefore, that they may sleep on their watch, they consent to take some one division of the society into partnership of the tyranny over the rest. But let government, in what form it may be, comprehend the whole in its justice, and restrain the suspicious by its vigilance; let it keep watch and ward: let it discover by its sagacity, and punish by its firmness, all delinquency against its power, whenever delinquency exists in the overt acts; and then it will be as safe as ever God and nature intended it should be. Crimes are the acts of individuals, and not of denominations; and therefore arbitrarily to class men under general descriptions, in order to proscribe and punish them in the lump for a presumed delinquency, of which perhaps but a part, perhaps none at all, are guilty, is indeed a compendious method, and saves a world of trouble about proof: but such a method, instead of being law, is an act of unnatural rebellion against the legal dominion of reason and justice; and this vice, in any constitution that entertains it, at one time or other will certainly bring on its ruin.[36]

We are told that this is not a religious persecution; and its abettors are loud

---

[36] Compare the preceding sentences with Burke's famous sentence from the speech on *Conciliation with America*: "I do not know the method of drawing up an indictment against an whole people."

in disclaiming all severities on account of conscience. Very fine indeed! Then let it be so; they are not persecutors; they are only tyrants. With all my heart. I am perfectly indifferent concerning the pretexts upon which we torment one another; or whether it be for the constitution of the Church of England, or for the constitution of the state of England, that people choose to make their fellow-creatures wretched. When we were sent into a place of authority, you that sent us had yourselves but one commission to give. You could give us none to wrong or oppress, or even to suffer any kind of oppression or wrong, on any grounds whatsoever; not on political, as in the affairs of America; not on commercial, as in those of Ireland; not in civil, as in the laws for debt; not in religious, as in the statutes against Protestant or Catholic dissenters. The diversified but connected fabric of universal justice is well cramped and bolted together in all its parts: and depend upon it, I never have employed, and I never shall employ, any engine of power which may come into my hands, to wrench it asunder. All shall stand, if I can help it, and all shall stand connected. After all, to complete this work, much remains to be done; much in the East, much in the West. But, great as the work is, if our will be ready, our powers are not deficient.

Since you have suffered me to trouble you so much on this subject, permit me, gentlemen, to detain you a little longer. I am indeed most solicitous to give you perfect satisfaction. I find there are some of a better and softer nature than the persons with whom I have supposed myself in debate, who neither think ill of the act of relief, nor by any means desire the repeal; yet who, not accusing but lamenting what was done, on account of the consequences, have frequently expressed their wish, that the late act had never been made. Some of this description, and persons of worth, I have met with in this city. They conceive, that the prejudices, whatever they might be, of a large part of the people, ought not to have been shocked; that their opinions ought to have been previously taken, and much attended to; and that thereby the late horrid scenes might have been prevented.[37]

I confess, my notions are widely different; and I never was less sorry for any action of my life. I like the bill the better, on account of the events of all kinds that followed it. It relieved the real sufferers; it strengthened the state; and, by the disorders that ensued, we had clear evidence that there lurked a temper somewhere, which ought not to be fostered by the laws. No ill consequences whatever could be attributed to the act itself. We knew beforehand, or we were poorly instructed, that toleration is odious to the intolerant; freedom to oppressors; property to robbers; and all kinds and degrees of prosperity to the envious. We knew, that all these kinds of men would gladly gratify their evil dispositions under the sanction of law and religion, if they could: if they could not, yet, to make way to their objects, they would do their utmost to subvert all religion and all law. This we certainly knew. But knowing this, is there any reason, because thieves break in and steal, and thus bring detriment to you, and draw ruin on themselves, that I am to be sorry that you are in possession of shops, and of warehouses, and of wholesome laws to protect them? Are you to build no houses, because desperate men may pull them down upon their own heads? Or, if a malignant wretch will cut his own throat because he sees you give alms to the necessitous and deserving;

---

[37] The persistence of these arguments which Burke encountered, whenever it is proposed to remove public injustice, is worth the reader's consideration.

shall his destruction be attributed to your charity, and not to his own deplorable madness? If we repent of our good actions, what, I pray you, is left for our faults and follies? It is not the beneficence of the laws, it is the unnatural temper which beneficence can fret and sour, that is to be lamented. It is this temper which, by all rational means, ought to be sweetened and corrected. If froward men should refuse this cure, can they vitiate any thing but themselves? Does evil so react upon good, as not only to retard its motion, but to change its nature? If it can so operate, then good men will always be in the power of the bad; and virtue, by a dreadful reverse of order, must lie under perpetual subjection and bondage to vice.

As to the opinion of the people, which some think, in such cases, is to be implicitly obeyed; nearly two years' tranquillity, which followed the act, and its instant imitation in Ireland, proved abundantly, that the late horrible spirit was, in a great measure, the effect of insidious art, and perverse industry, and gross misrepresentation. But suppose that the dislike had been much more deliberate, and much more general than I am persuaded it was—when we know, that the opinions of even the greatest multitudes are the standard of rectitude, I shall think myself obliged to make those opinions the masters of my conscience. But if it may be doubted whether Omnipotence itself is competent to alter the essential constitution of right and wrong, sure I am, that such *things*, as they and I, are possessed of no such power. No man carries further than I do the policy of making government pleasing to the people. But the widest range of this politic complaisance is confined within the limits of justice. I would not only consult the interest of the people, but I would cheerfully gratify their humours. We are all a sort of children that must be soothed and managed. I think I am not austere or formal in my nature. I would bear, I would even myself play my part in, any innocent buffooneries, to divert them. But I never will act the tyrant for their amusement. If they will mix malice in their sports, I shall never consent to throw them any living, sentient creature whatsoever, no not so much as a kitling, to torment.

"But if I profess all this impolitic stubbornness, I may chance never to be elected into parliament." It is certainly not pleasing to be put out of the public service. But I wish to be a member of parliament, to have my share of doing good and resisting evil. It would therefore be absurd to renounce my objects, in order to obtain my seat. I deceive myself indeed most grossly, if I had not much rather pass the remainder of my life hidden in the recesses of the deepest obscurity, feeding my mind even with the visions and imaginations of such things, than to be placed on the most splendid throne of the universe, tantalized with a denial of the practice of all which can make the greatest situation any other than the greatest curse. Gentlemen, I have had my day. I can never sufficiently express my gratitude to you for having set me in a place, wherein I could lend the slightest help to great and laudable designs. If I have had my share in any measure giving quiet to private property, and private conscience; if by my vote I have aided in securing to families the best possession, peace; if I have joined in reconciling kings to their subjects, and subjects to their prince; if I have assisted to loosen the foreign holdings of the citizen, and taught him to look for his protection to the laws of his country, and for his comfort to the good-will of his countrymen;—if I have thus taken my part with the best of men in the best of their actions, I can shut the book;—I might wish to read a page or two more—but this is enough for my measure.—I have not lived in vain.

And now, gentlemen, on this serious day, when I come, as it were, to make up my account with you, let me take to myself some degree of honest pride on the nature of the charges that are against me. I do not here stand before you accused of venality, or of neglect of duty. It is not said, that, in the long period of my service, I have, in a single instance, sacrificed the slightest of your interests to my ambition, or to my fortune. It is not alleged, that to gratify any anger, or revenge of my own, or of my party, I have had a share in wronging or oppressing any description of men, or any one man in any description. No! the charges against me, are all of one kind, that I have pushed the principles of general justice and benevolence too far; further than a cautious policy would warrant; and further than the opinions of many would go along with me.—In every accident which may happen through life, in pain, in sorrow, in depression, and distress—I will call to mind this accusation; and be comforted.

Gentlemen, I submit the whole to your judgment. Mr. Mayor, I thank you for the trouble you have taken on this occasion: In your state of health, it is particularly obliging. If this company should think it advisable for me to withdraw, I shall respectfully retire; if you think otherwise, I shall go directly to the Council-house and to the 'Change, and, without a moment's delay, begin my canvass.

[The meeting then passed the following resolutions, and Burke undertook to run:

Resolved, That Mr. Burke, as a representative for this city, has done all possible honour to himself as a senator and a man, and that we do heartily and honestly approve of his conduct, as the result of an enlightened loyalty to his sovereign; a warm and zealous love to his country, through its widely-extended empire; a jealous and watchful care of the liberties of his fellow-subjects; an enlarged and liberal understanding of our commercial interest; a humane attention to the circumstances of even the lowest ranks of the community; and a truly wise, politic, and tolerant spirit, in supporting the national Church, with a reasonable indulgence to all who dissent from it; and we wish to express the most marked abhorrence of the base arts which have been employed, without regard to truth and reason, to misrepresent his eminent services to his country.

Resolved, That this resolution be copied out, and signed by the chairman, and be by him presented to Mr. Burke, as the fullest expression of the respectful and grateful sense we entertain of his merits and services, public and private, to the citizens of Bristol, as a man and a representative.

Resolved, That the thanks of this meeting be given to the right worshipful the Mayor, who so ably and worthily presided in this meeting.

Resolved, That it is the earnest request of this meeting to Mr. Burke, that he should again offer himself a candidate to represent this city in parliament; assuring him of that full and strenuous support which is due to the merits of so excellent a representative.

By September 9, however, one of the Tory candidates, Combe, had died, no agreement with the Cruger interests seemed possible, and Burke saw no hope of election. He, therefore, withdrew, with the following speech.]

～

Declining the Poll

Bristol
September 9, 1780

Gentlemen: I decline the election.—It has ever been my rule through life, to observe a proportion between my efforts and my objects. I have never been remarkable for a bold, active, and sanguine pursuit of advantages that are personal to myself.

I have not canvassed the whole of this city in form. But I have taken such a view of it as satisfies my own mind, that your choice will not ultimately fall upon me. Your city, gentlemen, is in a state of miserable distraction; and I am resolved to withdraw whatever share my pretensions may have had in its unhappy divisions. I have not been in haste; I have tried all prudent means; I have waited for the effect of all contingencies. If I were fond of a contest, by the partiality of my numerous friends (whom you know to be among the most weighty and respectable people of the city), I have the means of a sharp one in my hands. But I thought it far better with my strength unspent, and my reputation unimpaired, to do, early and from foresight, that which I might be obliged to do from necessity at last.

I am not in the least surprised, nor in the least angry at this view of things. I have read the book of life for a long time, and I have read other books a little. Nothing has happened to me, but what has happened to men much better than me, and in times and in nations full as good as the age and country that we live in. To say that I am no way concerned, would be neither decent nor true. The representation of *Bristol* was an object on many accounts dear to me; and I certainly should very far prefer it to any other in the kingdom. My habits are made to it; and it is in general more unpleasant to be rejected after long trial, than not to be chosen at all.

But, gentlemen, I will see nothing except your former kindness, and I will give way to no other sentiments than those of gratitude. From the bottom of my heart I thank you for what you have done for me. You have given me a long term, which is now expired. I have performed the conditions, and enjoyed all the profits to the full; and I now surrender your estate into your hands, without being in a single tile or a single stone impaired or wasted by my use. I have served the public for fifteen years. I have served you in particular for six. What is passed is well stored. It is safe, and out of the power of fortune. What is to come, is in wiser hands than ours: and He, in whose hands it is, best knows whether it is best for you and me that I should be in parliament, or even in the world.

Gentlemen, the melancholy event of yesterday reads to us an awful lesson against being too much troubled about any of the objects of ordinary ambition. The worthy gentleman, who has been snatched from us at the moment of the election, and in the middle of the contest, whilst his desires were as warm, and his hopes as eager as ours, has feelingly told us, what shadows we are, and what shadows we pursue.

It has been usual for a candidate who declines, to take his leave by a letter to the sheriffs; but I received your trust in the face of day: and in the face of day I accept your dismission. I am not,—I am not at all ashamed to look upon you; nor can my presence discompose the order of business here. I humbly and respectfully take my leave of the sheriffs, the candidates, and the electors, wishing heartily that the choice may be for the best, at a time which calls, if ever time did call, for service that is not nominal. It is no plaything you are about. I tremble when I consider the trust I have presumed to ask. I confided perhaps too much in my intentions. They were really fair and upright; and I am bold to say that I ask no ill thing for you, when on parting from this place I pray that whomever you choose to succeed me, he may resemble me exactly in all things, except in my abilities to serve, and my fortune to please you.

⌒

BIBLIOGRAPHICAL NOTE

The fullest and most recent biography drawing upon much new material is that by Carl B. Cone, *Burke and the Nature of Politics* (2 vols.; 1957–1964). Older biographies especially valuable are those by James Prior (5th ed., 1854) and John Morley ("English Men of Letters," 1882). The new *Correspondence of Edmund Burke* in ten volumes, edited by Thomas W. Copeland and others, is in the course of publication. It brings together for the first time all Burke's known letters and many of those to him, edited fully, so as to provide the primary source for the study of Burke. Writing about Burke has been very extensive and continues to be so. There is no complete bibliography, but recent studies are reviewed by Donald C. Bryant in "Edmund Burke: A Generation of Scholarship and Discovery," *Journal of British Studies*, II, 1 (November 1962), 91–114. No recent comprehensive study of Burke's speaking has been published. Those by Goodrich and by Lecky (III, 196 ff.) are excellent, though perhaps dated. Of more recent critics the most perceptive are W. J. Bate in the "Introduction" to *Selected Writings of Edmund Burke* ("Modern Library," 1960), Stephen Graubard in *Burke, Disraeli, and Churchill* (1961), and W. Somerset Maugham in *The Vagrant Mood* (1953). Useful also is Donald C. Bryant's "Contemporary Reception of Edmund Burke's Speaking," in *Historical Studies of Rhetoric and Rhetoricians* (ed. by Raymond F. Howes, 1961). Volumes of selections from Burke are always in print, of which the one by Bate is probably the best at present.

Henry Grattan

(1746–1820)

Ireland has sent such notable speakers to the British Parliament as Richard Brinsley Sheridan and Edmund Burke. From Ireland also there came to the House of Commons the formidable Colonel Isaac Barré, master of invective, ally of the earls of Chatham and Shelburne, and staunch friend of America. Ireland, however, retained some of the best of her orators for service at home, where a certain kind of passionate eloquence has often found more congenial climate than in England. Among these Henry Flood (1732–1791) and Henry Grattan enjoyed hardly less contemporary renown than the greatest in Westminster. Patriots, and at first close associates in the cause of Irish freedom, they remained patriots to the end, but became embittered foes.

Of the two, Grattan would be the more memorable speaker even if satisfactory texts of Flood's speeches had been preserved. Though Flood could produce as powerful an immediate impression as Grattan, Grattan's speaking had more substance and staying power. An unqualified admirer of Chatham, Grattan as a young man took the Great Commoner as the exemplar of the greatest oratory, and in his maturity he came in some measure to resemble his ideal. His speaking was clear, self-assured, dramatic with the force of conviction. He focused sharply upon a central idea or a central motive, and with massed evidence, striking examples, images, and memorable language, he gave life and impulse to his arguments and seemed to force them upon the minds and feelings of his audiences. In addition, like Burke, he had a talent for weaving his particular contentions into a fabric of general principles. His gesture and bodily movement in speaking, however, are said to have been extravagant, sometimes almost grotesque.

Well born, and educated to the law, Grattan entered the Irish House of Commons in 1775 under the influence of James Caulfield, Earl of Charlemont, the high-minded patriot and the friend of Burke, Fox, and the Opposition in England. He immediately assumed the place lately held by Flood as leader of the popular party, and he threw himself into the cause of Irish liberty.

The grievances of the Irish had to do with their government, their commerce, and their religion. Poynings' Law of 1495, reinforced by later acts of the British Parliament, gave the English Privy Council power to alter or suppress acts of the Irish Parliament. An act of 1718, known as the 6th of George I, declared Ireland a subordinate and dependent kingdom, permitted the English Parliament to make laws for Ireland, and denied the Irish House of Lords the right to act as a Court of Appeal. Besides all this, the Irish Parliament was managed by the English Administration through a group of agents known as "undertakers." As we have seen in connection with Burke's speech of 1780, Irish trade had been paralyzed by restrictions, including the 9th of William, which took away the woolen manufacture, measures obviously intended to prevent competition with English business. Of course the restrictive laws against Roman Catholics were more severe in Ireland, where the vast majority of the population was Catholic, than in England. (See Daniel O'Connell's speech, below, pages 358–70.)

The Irish resistance to English exploitation, familiar to students of literature through Jonathan Swift's pamphlets and his satiric *Modest Proposal* (see note 1, page 247), was raised to decisive proportions by Henry Grattan. As the war with the American colonies dragged on, the economic plight of the Irish, even more than that of Burke's Bristol friends, became worse and worse, and the reality of the danger of French invasion increased. To protect the country against the French and the American raider John Paul Jones, Grattan and Charlemont organized the Irish Volunteers, an armed force which served also as an association for the support of the campaign for freedom of trade. The more difficult England's international and domestic position became and the clearer the example of America, the greater the opportunity appeared for Ireland's success. In 1779, Lord North tried to quiet Ireland with commercial concessions, but the English traders intimidated him. Burke's support of these concessions, we have seen, contributed to his difficulties in Bristol. Grattan continued his demands, however; and in 1780, with the strength of the Volunteers behind him, he secured freedom of trade. That, however, was not enough. His famous speech in the Irish House of Commons on April 19, 1780, was a grand appeal to Irish patriotism and an uncompromising attack on British policy. He moved a declaration of the Irish right to complete equality with England under the Crown. The North Ministry was still in power, however, and the Irish Parliament, not ready for such a change, voted down the declaration. That speech of Grattan's should be studied as background to the one printed below.

The formation of the Rockingham Ministry in the spring of 1782 brought the effective support of Fox and Burke, and to Grattan the prospect of success. After a convention of the Irish Volunteers had declared that the British Parliament should not make laws for Ireland or interfere with Irish trade, Grattan reintroduced his Declaration of Irish Rights on February 22. Two months later, on April 16, following a triumphal procession to the House of Commons, in the speech printed here he proclaimed imminent independence as if it had already been won. He reasserted Irish rights and defiantly denied British authority. He congratulated the Volunteers, assured Parliament that they constituted no threat to the civilian government, and moved amendments to the Address to the Throne in a brief and eloquent paean of victory. In short order the Rockingham Ministry granted all that Ireland asked, and the grateful Irish bestowed upon Grattan an estate of £100,000, of which he accepted only £50,000.

The successes of 1782 were not well enough grounded, however, to clear up the problems of Ireland, and in the subsequent struggles Grattan and Flood parted company over what should be done to complete the reform of Irish government. One of the most frequently reprinted examples of Grattan's eloquence is his invective against Flood of October 28, 1783.

Grattan continued to be a leader in Irish affairs throughout Pitt's long ministry, during which discontent in Ireland grew more and more severe and violence increased to the point of peril (see Fox's speech, below, pages 260–61). Grattan campaigned against Pitt's proposed solution, the union of the British and Irish parliaments in the Imperial Parliament, which was finally realized in 1800, but he accepted election to the Imperial Parliament in 1805. There he spoke vigorously for Catholic emancipation, as he had done over the years in the Irish House of Commons. His speeches of February 22 and 27, 1793, on that subject are especially notable. He made his last trip to London, against his physician's advice, to reintroduce the Catholic question into Parliament. There he died in honor and was buried in Westminster Abbey.

∽

A Free People *

Irish House of Commons
April 16, 1782

I am now to address a free people: ages have passed away, and this is the first moment in which you could be distinguished by that appellation.

* Text is from *The Speeches of the Right Honourable Henry Grattan in the Irish and in the Imperial Parliament* (ed. by his son; 4 vols.; London, 1822), I, 123–30.

I have spoken on the subject of your liberty so often, that I have nothing to add, and have only to admire by what heaven-directed steps you have proceeded until the whole faculty of the nation is braced up to the act of her own deliverance.

I found Ireland on her knees, I watched over her with an eternal solicitude; I have traced her progress from injuries to arms, and from arms to liberty. Spirit of Swift! spirit of Molyneux![1] your genius has prevailed! Ireland is now a nation! in that new character I hail her! and bowing to her august presence, I say, *Esto perpetua!*[2]

She is no longer a wretched colony, returning thanks to her governor for his rapine, and to her king for his oppression; nor is she now a squabbling, fretful sectary, perplexing her little wits, and firing her furious statutes with bigotry, sophistry, disabilities, and death, to transmit to posterity insignificance and war.

Look to the rest of Europe, and contemplate yourself, and be satisfied. Holland lives on the memory of past achievement; Sweden has lost her liberty; England has sullied her great name by an attempt to enslave her colonies. You are the only people,—you, of the nations in Europe, are now the only people who excite admiration, and in your present conduct you not only exceed the present generation, but you equal the past. I am not afraid to turn back and look antiquity in the face: the revolution,—that great event, whether you call it ancient or modern I know not, was tarnished with bigotry: the great deliverer (for such I must ever call the Prince of Nassau,)[3] was blemished with oppression; he assented to, he was forced to assent to acts which deprived the Catholics of religious, and all the Irish of civil and commercial rights, though the Irish were the only subjects in these islands who had fought in his defence. But you have sought liberty on her own principle: see the Presbyterians of Bangor petition for the freedom of the Catholics of Munster. You, with difficulties innumerable, with dangers not a few, have done what your ancestors wished, but could not accomplish; and what your posterity may preserve, but will never equal: you have moulded the jarring elements of your country into a nation,[4] and have rivalled those great and ancient commonwealths, whom you were taught to admire, and among whom you are

[1] Jonathan Swift (1667–1745), the greatest of English satirists and the author of *Gulliver's Travels,* though an Englishman, lived much of his life in Ireland as rector of a country parish and as Dean of St. Patrick's (Anglican) Cathedral, Dublin. He espoused Irish causes and became a popular patriot. In 1720, he published a proposal for the universal use of Irish products; in his pseudonymous *Drapier's Letters* (1724) he argued Irish equality with England over the issue of copper coinage; and in 1729 he launched the grimmest of all his satires, *A Modest Proposal,* against English oppression of the ordinary people of Ireland. William Molyneux (1656–1698) published in 1698 a pamphlet asserting the legislative independence of the Irish Parliament, *The Case of Ireland's Being Bound by Acts of Parliament in England Stated.* A committee of the British Parliament declared the book dangerous.

[2] May she be that way forever.

[3] Henry Nassau (1641–1708), Count and Lord of Auverquerque, was a general who came to England with William of Orange at the time of the Revolution of 1688, and in 1690 helped defeat James II's attempt, with French support, to re-establish himself in Ireland. Nassau fought at the battle of the Boyne, 1 July 1690, and afterward occupied Dublin.

[4] Grattan, in the spirit of his triumph, proclaims what should be, as if it already were. Not for a century and a half did Ireland achieve the reconciliations which he declares as complete in 1780.

now to be recorded: in this proceeding you had not the advantages which were common to other great countries; no monuments, no trophies, none of those outward and visible signs of greatness, such as inspire mankind and connect the ambition of the age which is coming on with the example of that going off, and forms the descent and concatenation of glory: no; you have not had any great act recorded among all your misfortunes, nor have you one public tomb to assemble the crowd, and speak to the living the language of integrity and freedom.

Your historians did not supply the want of monuments; on the contrary, these narrators of your misfortunes, who should have felt for your wrongs, and have punished your oppressors with oppressions, natural scourges, the moral indignation of history, compromised with public villany and trembled; they excited your violence, they suppressed your provocation, and wrote in the chain which entrammelled their country.[5] I am come to break that chain, and I congratulate my country, who, without any of the advantages I speak of, going forth as it were with nothing but a stone and a sling, and what oppression could not take away, the favour of Heaven, accomplished her own redemption, and left you nothing to add and every thing to admire.

You want no trophy now; the records of Parliament are the evidence of your glory: I beg to observe, that the deliverance of Ireland has proceeded from her own right hand; I rejoice at it, for had the great requisition of your freedom proceeded from the bounty of England, that great work would have been defective both in renown and security: it was necessary that the soul of the country should have been exalted by the act of her own redemption, and that England should withdraw her claim by operation of treaty, and not of mere grace and condescension; a gratuitous act of parliament, however express, would have been revocable, but the repeal of her claim under operation of treaty is not: in that case, the legislature is put in covenant, and bound by the law of nations, the only law that can legally bind Parliament: never did this country stand so high; England and Ireland treat *ex æquo*.[6] Ireland transmits to the King her claim of right, and requires of the Parliament of England the repeal of her claim of power, which repeal the English Parliament is to make under the force of a treaty which depends on the law of nations,—a law which cannot be repealed by the Parliament of England.

I rejoice that the people are a party to this treaty, because they are bound to preserve it. There is not a man of forty shillings freehold[7] that is not associated in this our claim of right, and bound to die in its defence; cities, counties, assotions, Protestants and Catholics; it seems as if the people had joined in one great national sacrament; a flame has descended from heaven on the intellect of Ireland, plays round her head, and encompasses her understanding with a consecrated glory.

There are some who think, and a few who declare, that the associations to

[5] The idea that historians, as well as bards and playwrights, should sing a country's praises and justify her to posterity has always been popular: "When the history of these times is written . . . ."

[6] England and Ireland negotiate on a basis of equality. After the repeal of all the restrictive legislation, there was to be a treaty, freely negotiated, establishing the future relations between the two countries.

[7] The ownership of property on which a man paid as much as 40 shillings a year tax entitled him to vote. See Fox's speech, below, pp. 273–76.

which I refer are illegal: [8] come, then, let us try the charge, and state the grievance. And, first, I ask, What were the grievances? an army imposed on us by another country, that army rendered perpetual; the privy-council of both countries made a part of our legislature; our legislature deprived of its originating and propounding power; another country exercising over us supreme legislative authority; that country disposing of our property by its judgments, and prohibiting our trade by its statutes: these were not grievances, but spoliations, which left you nothing. When you contended against them, you contended for the whole of your condition; when the minister asked, by what right? we refer him to our Maker: we sought our privileges by the right which we have to defend our property against a robber, our life against a murderer, our country against an invader, whether coming with civil or military force,—a foreign army, or a foreign legislature. This is a case that wants no precedent; the *revolution* wanted no precedent: for such things arrive to reform a course of bad precedents, and, instead of being founded on precedent, become such: the gazing world, whom they come to save, begins by doubt and concludes by worship. Let other nations be deceived by the sophistry of courts. Ireland has studied politics in the lair of oppression, and, taught by suffering, comprehends the rights of subjects and the duty of kings. Let other nations imagine that subjects are made for the monarch, but we conceive that kings, and parliaments, like kings, are made for the subjects. The House of Commons, honourable and right honourable as it may be; the Lords, noble and illustrious as we pronounce them, are not original but derivative. Session after session they move their periodical orbit about the source of their being, the nation; even the King's Majesty must fulfil his due and tributary course round that great luminary; and created by its beam, and upheld by its attraction, must incline to that light, or go out of the system.

Ministers, we mean the ministers who have gone out,[9] (I rely on the good intentions of the present), former ministers, I say, have put questions to us; we beg to put questions to them. They desired to know by what authority this nation has acted. This nation desires to know by what authority they have acted. By what authority did Government enforce the articles of war? By what authority does Government establish the post-office? By what authority are our merchants bound by the charter of the East India Company? By what authority has Ireland, for near one hundred years been deprived of her export trade? By what authority are her peers deprived of their judicature? By what authority has that judicature been transferred to the peers of Great Britain, and our property in its last resort referred to the decision of a non-resident, unauthorised, and unconstitutional tribunal? Will ministers say it was the authority of the British Parliament? On what ground, then, do they place the question between the Government on one side, and the volunteer on the other? According to their own statement, the government has been occupied in superseding the lawgiver of the country; and the volunteers are here to restore him. The Government has contended for the

[8] The 80,000 Irish Volunteers, of course, had constituted one of Grattan's strongest arguments for independence.

[9] Lord North's Ministry had been replaced by that of the Marquis of Rockingham in March. In that ministry, Charles James Fox, Edmund Burke, the Earl of Shelburne, John Dunning, Colonel Barré, and the Duke of Portland were especially friendly to Ireland. The Duke had arrived in Dublin as Lord Lieutenant two days prior to Grattan's speech.

usurpation, and the people for the laws. His Majesty's late ministers imagined they had quelled the country when they had bought the newspapers; and they represented us as wild men, and our cause as visionary; and they pensioned a set of wretches to abuse both: but we took little account of them or their proceedings, and we waited and we watched, and we moved, as it were, on our native hills, with the minor remains of our parliamentary army, until that minority became Ireland. Let those ministers now go home, and congratulate their king on the redemption of his people. Did you imagine that those little parties whom three years ago you beheld in awkward squads parading in the streets, should have now arrived to such distinction and effect? What was the cause; for it was not the sword of the volunteer, nor his muster, nor his spirit, nor his promptitude to put down accidental disturbance or public disorder, nor his own unblamed and distinguished deportment. This was much; but there was more than this: the upper orders, the property, and the abilities of the country, formed with the volunteer; and the volunteer had sense enough to obey them. This united the Protestant with the Catholic, and the landed proprietor with the people. There was still more than this; there was a continence which confined the corps to limited and legitimate objects; there was a principle which preserved the corps from adultery with French politics; there was a good taste which guarded the corps from the affectation of such folly: this, all this, made them bold; for it kept them innocent, it kept them rational: no vulgar rant against England; no mysterious admiration of France; no crime to conceal,—no folly to be ashamed of. They were what they professed to be; and that was nothing less than the society asserting her liberty, according to the frame of the British constitution, her inheritance to be enjoyed in perpetual connection with the British empire.

I do not mean to say that there were not divers violent and unseemly resolutions; the immensity of the means was inseparable from the excess.

Such are the great works of nature: such is the sea; but, like the sea, the waste and excess were lost in the advantage: and now, having given a parliament to the people, the volunteers will, I doubt not, leave the people to Parliament, and thus close, specifically and majestically, a great work, which will place them above censure and above panegyric. These associations, like other institutions, will perish: they will perish with the occasion that gave them being, and the gratitude of their country will write their epitaph, and say, "This phenomenon, the departed volunteer, justified only by the occasion, the birth of spirit and grievances, with some alloy of public evil, did more public good to Ireland than all her institutions; he restored the liberties of his country, and thus from the grave he answers his enemies." [10] Connected by freedom as well as by allegiance, the two nations, Great Britain and Ireland, form a constitutional confederacy as well as one empire; the crown is one link, the constitution another; and, in my mind, the latter link is the most powerful.

You can get a king any where, but England is the only country with whom you can participate a free constitution. This makes England your natural connexion, and her king your natural as well as your legal sovereign: this is a connexion, not

---

[10] The original Volunteers did indeed disband, but not at once. They were succeeded, however, by other more radical and uncontrollable armed associations. See Fox's speech, below, pp. 260–61.

as Lord Coke has idly said, not as Judge Blackstone has foolishly said,[11] not as other judges have ignorantly said, by conquest; but as Molyneux has said, and as I now say, by compact; and that compact is a free constitution. Suffer me now to state some of the things essential to that free constitution; they are as follows: the independency of the Irish Parliament; the exclusion of the British Parliament from any authority in this realm; the restoration of the Irish judicature, and the exclusion of that of Great Britain. As to the perpetual mutiny bill, it must be more than limited; it must be effaced; that bill must fall, or the constitution cannot stand; that bill was originally limited by this House to two years, and it returned from England without the clause of limitation. What? a bill making the army independent of Parliament, and perpetual! I protested against it then, I have struggled with it since, and I am now come to destroy this great enemy of my country. The perpetual mutiny bill must vanish out of the statute book; the excellent tract of Molyneux was burned; it was not answered; and its flame illumined posterity. This evil paper shall be burned, but burned like a felon, that its execution may be a peace-offering to the people, and that a declaration of right may be planted on its guilty ashes; a new mutiny bill must be formed after the manner of England, and a declaration of right put in the front of it.[12]

As to the legislative powers of the Privy Councils, I conceive them to be utterly inadmissible against the constitution, against the privileges of Parliament, and against the dignity of the realm. Do not imagine such power to be theoretical; it is in a very high degree a practical evil. I have here an inventory of bills altered and injured by the interference of the Privy Councils; money bills originated by them, protests by the Crown in support of those money bills, prorogation following these protests. I have here a mutiny bill of 1780, altered by the Council, and made perpetual; a Catholic bill in 1778, where the Council struck out the clause repealing the test act; a militia bill, where the Council struck out the compulsory clause requiring the Crown to proceed to form a militia, and left it optional to His Majesty's minister whether there should be a militia, in Ireland. I have the money bill of 1775, where the Council struck out the clause enabling His Majesty to take a part of our troops for general service, and left it to the minister to withdraw the forces against act of parliament. I have to state the altered money bill of 1771, the altered money bill of 1775, the altered money bill of 1780; the day would expire before I could recount their ill-doings. I will never consent to have men (God knows whom), ecclesiastics, *etc. etc.*, men unknown to the constitution of Parliament, and only known to the minister, who has breathed into their nostrils an unconstitutional existence, steal to their dark divan to do mischief and make nonsense of bills, which their Lordships, the House of Lords, or we, the House of Commons, have thought good and fit for the people.

[11] Sir Edward Coke (1552–1634) and Sir William Blackstone (1723–1780) were the most renowned interpreters of the English constitution. Blackstone's *Commentaries* became the authoritative source of the meaning of English law. It has recently reappeared in paperback.

[12] The Mutiny Acts provided, usually a year at a time, for the maintenance of the army. Grattan's party had denied the validity of the English Mutiny Acts and had demanded an Irish Act. In 1780, however, the Irish Parliament submissively passed a Mutiny Bill without a time limit, thus making the army permanently independent of the Irish Parliament.

No; those men have no legislative qualifications; they shall have no legislative power.

1st. The repeal of the perpetual mutiny bill, and the dependency of the Irish army on the Irish Parliament.

2d. The abolition of the legislative power of the Council.

3d. The abrogation of the claim of England to make law for Ireland.

4th. The exclusion of the English House of Peers, and of the English King's Bench, from any judicial authority in this realm.

5th. The restoration of the Irish Peers to their final judicature. The independency of the Irish Parliament in its sole and exclusive legislature.

These are my terms. I will take nothing from the Crown.

[Mr. Grattan then moved, by way of amendment,] [13]

That an humble address be presented to His Majesty, to return His Majesty the thanks of this House for his most gracious message to this House, signified by His Grace the Lord-lieutenant.

To assure His Majesty of our unshaken attachment to His Majesty's person and government, and of our lively sense of his paternal care in thus taking the lead to administer content to His Majesty's subjects of Ireland.[14]

That, thus encouraged by his royal interposition, we shall beg leave, with all duty and affection, to lay before His Majesty the causes of our discontents and jealousies. To assure His Majesty that his subjects of Ireland are a free people. That the crown of Ireland is an imperial crown inseparably annexed to the crown of Great Britain, on which connection the interests and happiness of both nations essentially depend: but that the kingdom of Ireland is a distinct kingdom, with a parliament of her own—the sole legislature thereof. That there is no body of men competent to make laws to bind this nation except the King, Lords and Commons of Ireland; nor any other parliament which hath any authority or power of any sort whatsoever in this country save only the Parliament of Ireland. To assure His Majesty, that we humbly conceive that in this right the very essence of our liberties exists; a right which we, on the part of all the people of Ireland, do claim as their birthright, and which we cannot yield but with our lives.

To assure His Majesty, that we have seen with concern certain claims advanced by the Parliament of Great Britain, in an act entitled "An act for the better secur-

---

[13] Grattan is moving a substitute for the Address which is before the House. That Address is as follows: "That an humble address be presented to His Majesty, to return His Majesty the thanks of this House, for his most gracious message to this House, signified by his Grace the Lord-Lieutenant; that, in obedience to His Majesty's most gracious recommendation, this House will, without delay, take into their most serious consideration, the discontents and jealousies which have arisen in this kingdom; the causes whereof they will investigate with all convenient dispatch, and humbly submit to His Majesty's royal justice and wisdom."

[14] The message from the Throne had said: "His Majesty being concerned to find that discontents and jealousies are prevailing among his loyal subjects of this country, upon matters of great weight and importance, His Majesty recommends it to this House to take the same into their most serious consideration, in order to [recommend] such a final adjustment as may give mutual satisfaction to his kingdoms of Great Britain and Ireland."

ing the dependency of Ireland:"[15] an act containing matter entirely irreconcileable to the fundamental rights of this nation. That we conceive this act, and the claims it advances, to be the great and principal cause of the discontents and jealousies in this kingdom.

To assure His Majesty, that His Majesty's Commons of Ireland do most sincerely wish that all bills which become law in Ireland should receive the approbation of His Majesty under the seal of Great Britain; but that yet we do consider the practice of suppressing our bills in the council of Ireland, or altering the same any where, to be another just cause of discontent and jealousy.

To assure His Majesty, that an act, entitled "An act for the better accommodation of His Majesty's forces,"[16] being unlimited in duration, and defective in other instances, but passed in that shape from the particular circumstances of the times, is another just cause of discontent and jealousy in this kingdom.

That we have submitted these, the principal causes of the present discontent and jealousy of Ireland, and remain in humble expectation of redress.

That we have the greatest reliance on His Majesty's wisdom, the most sanguine expectations from his virtuous choice of a Chief Governor,[17] and great confidence in the wise, auspicious, and constitutional councils which we see, with satisfaction, His Majesty has adopted.

That we have, moreover, a high sense and veneration for the British character, and do therefore conceive that the proceedings of this country, founded as they were in right, and tempered by duty, must have excited the approbation and esteem instead of wounding the pride of the British nation.

And we beg leave to assure His Majesty, that we are the more confirmed in this hope, inasmuch as the people of this kingdom have never expressed a desire to share the freedom of England, without declaring a determination to share her fate likewise, standing and falling with the British nation.[18]

∽

BIBLIOGRAPHICAL NOTE

The history of Ireland for this period is covered amply in Lecky's *History of England in the Eighteenth Century* and exhaustively in his *History of Ireland in the Eighteenth Century* (rev. ed., 5 vols., 1892). A shorter general history is E. Curtis' *A History of Ireland* (1936). Stephen Gwynn's *Henry Grattan and his Times* (1939), written in a popular style, is reliable and judicious; the principal source for the biography of Grattan, however, is *Memoirs of the Life and Times of Henry Grattan* (5 vols., 1839–46) by his son, Henry Grattan, who also edited his father's *Miscellaneous Works* (1822) and *Speeches* (4 vols., 1822). A one-volume collection of Grattan's speeches, edited by D. O. Madden (2nd ed., 1854), is perhaps more likely to be available. Lecky's long essays on Grattan and Flood in the first volume of his *Leaders of Public Opinion in Ireland* (new ed., 1903) are to be recommended especially for analysis of their subjects' speaking. Goodrich's criticism, of course, is valuable, especially for Grattan's

[15] The Declaratory Act of 1718.

[16] The Perpetual Mutiny Act.

[17] The Marquis of Rockingham, the prime minister; or perhaps the compliment is intended for Portland, the Lord Lieutenant.

[18] The amendment passed unanimously.

early career. First-hand criticism may be found in Lord Brougham's *Historical Sketches of Statesmen of the Time of George III* (see below, page 323). Grattan's speech of April 19, 1780, on Irish Rights, is printed in *British Orations* (Everyman's Library No. 714), and in Goodrich's *Select British Eloquence*, which includes also the speech printed here, the invectives against Flood and Cory, and a portion of Grattan's critical sketch of Chatham.

Charles James Fox

(1749–1806)

Charles James Fox was bred to pleasure and politics. His father was Henry Fox, one of the most influential politicians of his day, who achieved a substantial fortune and a peerage (as Baron Holland) through political office. Charles, from his earliest years, was indulged beyond the aspirations of even a favorite son, and associated freely with his father's political colleagues and friends. Fortunately, the young man was intelligent, capable, and essentially good-natured, so that as he gave himself over to the pleasures of the rich man's son, with comparable energy and success he cultivated literature, history, the classics, and oratory—at home, at Eton, briefly at Oxford, on the Grand Tour, and in his abundant leisure.

When he entered the House of Commons at the age of twenty, therefore, he had already proved both his own talent for fast living and his father's capacity for paying his son's gambling debts. Almost at once, however, he began to show the other side of his genius: that aptitude for politics and the oratory of debate which made him for thirty years one of the first two or three speakers in the House. About 1774, after a brilliant parliamentary novitiate with Lord North, Fox turned to Burke and the Rockingham Whigs. Throughout the American Revolution, in close friendship and collaboration with them, he battled the Court and the North Administration. From 1783 he led the Opposition to the younger Pitt.

After Pitt's landslide in the election of 1784, Fox and his party were probably never in a position seriously to threaten Pitt's control of Parliament, and during the war against Revolutionary France their opposition faded to numerical impotence. Nevertheless, though denounced as Jacobin and traitor, Fox kept on attacking Pitt, exposing his measures as failures and charging him with desertion of those very principles of freedom and democracy which he himself had formerly advocated, and for which the war was being fought.

Though Fox was basically right as well as sentimental when in 1791 he confessed that he owed more of his political knowledge and nurture to Burke than to all other sources combined, his political temperament was significantly different from Burke's. The causes that attracted him most, though not more humanitarian, were frequently more popular. He and Burke were as one against the subjugation of the Americans, against the infringement of freedom of elections, and against the domination of Parliament by the Crown. Fox, however, gave his voice to proposals for electoral reform—for shortening the time between general elections, for correcting the notorious malapportionment of seats in the House of Commons, for reducing the patent injustices in the distribution of the right to vote. Burke resisted most such proposals. In the French Revolution, Fox saw a new dawn of freedom for an oppressed people and a salutary lesson for England, and he steadily opposed Pitt's policy of war against France. On that issue, he and Burke, the greatest rhetorical antagonist of the French Revolution, dissolved their long friendship. Other popular causes also found a friend in Fox. He joined Burke in defense of the exploited people of India through the trial of Warren Hastings; he supported the campaign in which Pitt himself and Wilberforce were prime movers, for the abolition of the slave trade; and he denounced the encroachments on civil liberties to which Pitt resorted during the French war. In fact, Fox's popularity with the English is probably attributable, after his general fairness and good nature, to his defense of political liberty—freedom of speech, freedom of assembly, freedom from religious restrictions.

One of Fox's best speeches from the long debate with Pitt, and one for which we have a reasonably good text, is that given below, on his friend Charles Grey's motion for reform of the House of Commons and the franchise. This was the Foxites' last futile effort against Pitt before they seceded from the House for many months—their last declaration, in effect, that "if you will not return to fundamental liberties, we cannot help you save the country." In principle, as Fox says, the proposal had been advanced many times before, notably by Pitt. The particular provisions may be gathered from the speech. In brief they would have reapportioned among the counties the seats from decayed boroughs, and would have enlarged the electorate to include all borough householders.

In this speech, Fox displayed his finest talents and his most conspicuous characteristics. He was speaking in reply, a position in which he was happiest, and he was on the offensive. In viewing his opponent's case he exhibited that special talent which had been commented on from the very beginning of his career, his extraordinary ability to analyze argument and get directly to its weaknesses. He pointed at once to the soft spots, the inconsistencies, and the duplicity in the case and conduct of Pitt. For the foundation of his arguments he appealed to reason and good sense, to love of country and the constitution, to justice, liberty, and the welfare of the people. His language was commonplace, copious, easy to follow, and for the most part unadorned. His delivery, we may suppose, displayed the naturalness and earnestness most often ascribed to him by his contempories. They noted especially his unpretentiousness, the absence of studied effects such as Sheridan sometimes exhibited.

The reception of the speech in the press was little short of enthusiastic. *The True Briton* (May 27), which had been critical of Fox, found in it "unparalleled brilliance and force"; *The St. James's Chronicle* (May 27–30) thought it "one of the most masterly pieces of reasoning, and one of the most profound political disquisitions" heard in the House in twenty years; *The Oracle* (May 27) called it "one of the most brilliant and animated speeches ever delivered by this distinguished orator"; and *The Times,* a paper which supported the Government, confessed (May 29): "We must do justice to Mr. Fox, in saying that his speech was a *chef d'oeuvre* of eloquence, of sound reasoning, and of mature reflection. It is acknowledged by everyone that he never spoke with greater ability in his life." In the debate, concludes the historian, J. Steven Watson (*The Reign of George III*, p. 362): "Fox soared and Pitt sat heavily upon the ground." Pitt, however, commanded 256 votes, the Opposition only 91; and the Foxites seceded from both Houses.

Reform, of course, though defeated again, was not dead. It remained an issue through most of the nineteenth century; profitable comparison may be made, for example, between the arguments, sanctions, and tactics employed by Fox in 1797 and by Lord Brougham thirty-five years later. Brougham's speech in support of the Reform Bill of 1832, the successful bill also sponsored by Fox's friend Charles Grey, by then Lord Grey and Prime Minister, is included in this volume.

Besides the speech on Grey's Motion, the study of Fox should include at least the following: "On the Westminster Scrutiny," June 8, 1784, in which Fox defends his career and lashes back at his enemies; "On the Russian Armament," March 1, 1792, probably as sharp and bitter an attack on Pitt and his foreign policy as Fox ever delivered; and "On Bonaparte's Overtures for Peace," February 3, 1800, Fox's share of a famous night of debate with Pitt, in which he made one of the great attacks on chauvinism and one of the most eloquent pleas for peace.

∽

On Electoral Reform *

House of Commons
May 26, 1797

Much and often, Sir, as this question has been discussed, and late as the hour is, I feel it my duty to deliver my opinion on a measure of high importance at all times, but which, at the present period, is become infinitely more interesting than ever. I fear, however, that my conviction on this subject is not common to the House: I fear that we are not likely to be agreed as to the importance of the measure, nor as to the necessity; since by the manner in which it has been discussed this night, I foresee that, so far from being unanimous on the proposition, we shall not be agreed as to the situation and circumstances of the country itself, much less as to the nature of the measures which, in my mind, that situation and those circumstances imperiously demand. I cannot suppress my astonishment at the tone and manner of gentlemen this day. The arguments that have been used would lead the mind to believe that we are in a state of peace and tranquillity, and that we have no provocation to any steps for improving the benefits we enjoy, or retrieving any misfortune that we have incurred.[1] To persons who feel this to

* *The Speeches of the Right Honourable Charles James Fox in the House of Commons* (6 vols.; London, 1815), VI, 339–70. Fox did not publish his speeches, and he seldom wrote out even parts of a speech. The texts, therefore, depend on reporters, usually those employed by the newspapers. This collection was made by J. Wright, who had compiled much of the *Parliamentary History*. Fox spoke last in the debate. The chief speakers for the motion had been Grey, Erskine, and Sheridan. Pitt and Hawkesbury had been the principal opponents.

[1] Pitt had belittled the strength of the French, and though admitting reverses in the war, he insisted that they were less severe for England than they would have been for a country with a different sort of government. See this debate in the *Parliamentary History*, XXXIII, 644–735, especially 676.

be our situation, every proposition tending to meliorate the condition of the country must be subject of jealousy and alarm: and if we really differ so widely in sentiment as to the state of the country, I see no probability of an agreement in any measure that is proposed. All that part of the argument against reform which relates to the danger of innovation,[2] is strangely misplaced by those who think with me, that, so far from procuring the mere chance of practical benefits by a reform, it is only by a reform that we can have a chance of rescuing ourselves from a state of extreme peril and distress. Such is my view of our situation. I think it so perilous, so imminent, that, though I do not feel conscious of despair, an emotion which the heart ought not to admit, yet it comes near to that state of hazard, when the sentiment of despair, rather than of hope, may be supposed to take possession of the mind. I feel myself to be the member of a community, in which the boldest man, without any imputation of cowardice, may dread that we are not merely approaching to a state of extreme peril, but of absolute dissolution; and with this conviction impressed upon my mind, gentlemen will not believe that I disregard all the general arguments that have been used against the motion on the score of the danger of innovation, from any disrespect to the honourable members who have urged them, or to the ingenuity with which they have been pressed; but because I am firmly persuaded that they are totally inapplicable to the circumstances under which we come to the discussion. With the ideas that I entertain, I cannot listen for a moment to suggestions that are applicable only to other situations, and to other times; for unless we are resolved pusillanimously to wait the approach of our doom, to lie down and die, we must take bold and decisive measures for our deliverance.[3] We must not be deterred by meaner apprehensions. We must combine all our strength, fortify one another by the communion of our courage; and by a seasonable exertion of national wisdom, patriotism, and vigour, take measures for the chance of salvation, and encounter with unappalled hearts, all the enemies, foreign and internal, all the dangers and calamities of every kind which press so heavily upon us. Such is my view of our present emergency; and under this impression, I cannot for a moment listen to the argument of danger arising from innovation, since our ruin is inevitable if we pursue the course which has brought us to the brink of the precipice.

But before I enter on the subject of the proposition that has been made to us, I must take notice of an insinuation that has again and again been flung out by gentlemen on the other side of the House, on party feelings, in which they affect to deplore the existence of a spirit injurious to the welfare of the public. I suspect, by the frequent repetition of this insinuation, that they are desirous of making it be believed, or that they understand themselves by the word party feelings, an unprincipled combination of men for the pursuit of office and its emoluments, the eagerness after which leads them to act upon feelings of personal enmity, ill-will, and opposition to his majesty's ministers. If such be their interpretation of party feelings, I must say, that I am utterly unconscious of any such feeling, and I am sure that I can speak with confidence for my friends, that they are actuated by no motives of so debasing a nature. But if they understand by party feelings, that men of honour, who entertain similar principles, conceive that those principles

---

[2] *Innovation* was a scare word, especially since the French Revolution. *Reform* might be good; *innovation* could not be. Fox liked to repeat his strong words like *reform*.

[3] Most of England's allies had melted away and she was everywhere on the defensive.

may be more beneficially and successfully pursued by the force of mutual support, harmony, and confidential connexion, then I adopt the interpretation, and have no scruple in saying, that it is an advantage to the country; an advantage to the cause of truth and the constitution; an advantage to freedom and humanity; an advantage to whatever honourable object they may be engaged in, that men pursue it with the united force of party feeling; that is to say, pursue it with the confidence, zeal, and spirit, which the communion of just confidence is likely to inspire.[4] And if the honourable gentlemen apply this description of party feeling to the pursuit in which we are engaged, I am equally ready to say, that the disastrous condition of the empire ought to animate and invigorate the union of all those who feel it to be their duty to check and arrest a career that threatens us with such inevitable ruin. For, surely, those who think that party is a good thing for ordinary occasions, must admit that it is peculiarly so on emergencies like the present; it is peculiarly incumbent upon men who feel the value of united exertion to combine all their strength to extricate the vessel when in danger of being stranded.

But gentlemen seem to insinuate, that this union of action is directed more against persons than measures, and that allusions ought not to be made to the conduct of particular men. It is not easy to analyse this sort of imputation, for it is not easy to disjoin the measure from its author, nor to examine the origin and progress of any evil without also inquiring into and scrutinising the motives and the conduct of the persons who gave rise to it. How, for instance, is it possible for us to enter into the discussion of the particular question now before the House, without a certain mixture of personal allusion? We complain that the representation of the people in parliament is defective. How does this complaint originate? From the conduct of the majorities in parliament. Does not this naturally lead us to inquire whether there is not something fundamentally erroneous in election, or something incidentally vicious in the treatment of those majorities? We surely must be permitted to inquire whether the fault and calamity of which we complain is inherent in the institution, in which nothing personal is to be ascribed to ministers, as it will operate in a more or less degree in all the circumstances in which we may find ourselves; or whether it is not an occasional abuse of the original institution, applicable only to these times and to these men, in which they are peculiarly guilty, but from which system representation itself ought to stand absolved.

I put the question in this way, in order to shew that a certain degree of personality is inseparable from the discussion, and that gentlemen cannot with justice ascribe to the bitterness of party feelings, what flows out of the principle of free inquiry. Indeed, this is a pregnant example of there being nothing peculiarly hostile to persons in this subject; it is not a thing now taken up for the first time, meditated and conceived in particular hostility to the right honourable the chancellor of the exchequer.[5] Be it remembered, that he himself has again and again introduced and patronized the same subject, and that on all the occasions on which he has brought it forward it has invariably received my approbation and support. When he brought it forward first in the year 1782, in a time of war, and

---

[4] Fox echoes the idea of party which he probably heard first from Burke or read in Burke's *Cause of the Present Discontents* (1770).

[5] Pitt. The first minister usually presided over the treasury.

of severe public calamity, I gave to the proposition my feeble support. Again, when he brought it forward in 1783,[6] at a time when I was in an office high in his majesty's service, I gave it my support. Again, in 1785, when the right honourable gentleman himself was in place, and renewed his proposition, it had my countenance and support. I have invariably declared myself a friend to parliamentary reform by whomsoever proposed; and though in all the discussions that have taken place, I have had occasion to express my doubt as to the efficacy of the particular mode, I have never hesitated to say, that the principle itself was beneficial; and that though not called for with the urgency which some persons, and, among others, the right honourable gentleman, declared to exist, I constantly was of opinion that it ought not to be discouraged. Now, however, that all doubt upon the subject is removed by the pressure of our calamities, and the dreadful alternative seems to be, whether we shall sink into the most abject thraldom, or continue in the same course until we are driven into the horrors of anarchy, I can have no hesitation in saying, that the plan of recurring to the principle of melioration which the constitution points out, is become a *desideratum* to the people of Great Britain. Between the alternatives of base and degraded slavery on the one side, or of tumultuous, though, probably, short-lived anarchy on the other, though no man would hesitate to make his choice, yet, if there be a course obvious and practicable, which, without either violence or innovation, may lead us back to the vigour we have lost, to the energy that has been stifled, to the independence that has been undermined, and yet preserve every thing in its place, a moment ought not to be lost in embracing the chance which this fortunate provision of the British system has made for British safety.

This is my opinion, and it is not an opinion merely founded upon theory, but upon actual observation of what is passing in the world. I conceive, that if we are not resolved to shut our eyes to the instructive lessons of the times, we must be convinced of the propriety of seasonable concession. I see nothing in what is called the lamentable example of France to prove to me that timely acquiescence with the desires of the people is more dangerous than obstinate resistance to their demands; but the situations of Great Britain and France are so essentially different, there is so little in common between the character of England at this day, and the character of France at the commencement of the Revolution, that it is impossible to reason upon them from parity of circumstances or of character. It is not necessary for me, I am sure, to enter into any analysis of the essential difference between the character of a people that had been kept for ages in the barbarism of servitude, and a people who have enjoyed for so long a time the light of freedom.[7] But we have no occasion to go to France for example; another country nearer to our hearts, with which we are better acquainted, opens to us a book so legible and clear, that he must be blind indeed who is not able to draw from it warning and instruction; it holds forth a lesson which is intelligible to dulness itself. Let us look to Ireland, and see how remarkably the arguments and reasoning of this day tally with the arguments and reasoning that unfortunately prevailed in the sister kingdom, and by which the king's ministers were fatally able to overpower the voice of reason and patriotism, and stifle all attention to the

---

[6] During the Fox–North Coalition.

[7] Here Fox avoids the suggestion that the situation of the English people is anything like that of the French before the Revolution. He turns to Ireland for his analogy.

prayers and applications of the people. It is impossible for any coincidence to be more perfect. We are told, that there are in England, as it is said there were in Ireland, a small number of persons desirous of throwing the country into confusion, and of alienating the affections of the people from the established government.

Permit me, Mr. Speaker, in passing to observe, that the right honourable the chancellor of the Exchequer did not represent my learned friend [8] quite correctly, when he stated that my learned friend admitted the existence of such men. On the contrary, the argument of my learned friend was hypothetical; he said, if it be true, as it is so industriously asserted, that such and such men do exist in the country, then surely in wisdom you ought to prevent their number from increasing by timely conciliation of the body of moderate men, who desire only reform. In this opinion I perfectly acquiesce with my learned friend. I believe that the number of persons who are discontented with the government of the country, and who desire to overthrow it, is very few, indeed. But the right honourable gentleman says, that the friends of moderate reform are few, and that no advantage is to be gained by conceding to this very small body what will not satisfy the violent, which he contends is more numerous; and he vehemently demands to know whom he is to divide, whom to separate, and what benefit he is to obtain from this surrender? To this I answer, that if there be two bodies, it is wisdom, it is policy, to prevent the one from falling into the other, by granting to the moderate what is just and reasonable. If the argument of the right honourable gentleman be correct, the necessity for concession is more imperious; it is only by these means that you can check the spirit of proselytism, and prevent a conversion that by and by will be too formidable for you to resist.

Mark this, and see how it applies to the precedent of Ireland. In the report that has been made by the parliament of that kingdom on the present disorders, it is said, that so long ago as the year 1791, there existed some societies in that country, who harboured the desire of separation from England, and who wished to set up a republican form of government.[9] The report does not state what was the precise number of those societies in 1791; it declares, however, that the number was small and insignificant. From small beginnings, however, they have increased to the alarming number of 100,000 men in the province of Ulster only. By what means have they so increased, and who are the proselytes that swell their numbers to so gigantic a size? Obviously the men who had no such design originally; obviously the persons who had no other object in view in all the petitions which they presented, than Catholic emancipation and reform of parliament. This is also admitted by the report. The spirit of reform spread over the country; they made humble, earnest, and repeated applications to the Castle [10] for redress; but there

[8] Thomas Erskine, the great lawyer and one of Fox's principal adherents in the House of Commons. Erskine as a legal pleader is represented in this volume.

[9] The society of the United Irishmen was founded in 1791 by Wolfe Tone to unite Dissenters and Roman Catholics against the British government. The organization was broken up in 1794 when a plot was discovered to promote a French invasion of Ireland. Tone had left the organization and was allowed to escape to America. Later he joined the French army for invasion of Ireland in 1796 to support the United Irishmen. The expedition was disabled by a storm.

[10] Dublin Castle, the residence of the Lord Lieutenant and the seat of the British Administration in Ireland.

they found a fixed determination to resist every claim, and a rooted aversion to every thing that bore even the colour of reform. They made their applications to all the considerable characters in the country, who had on former occasions distinguished themselves by exertions in the popular cause; and of these justly eminent men I desire to speak as I feel, with the utmost respect for their talents and virtues. But, unfortunately, they were so alarmed by the French Revolution, and by the cry which had been so artfully set up by ministers of the danger of infection, that they could not listen to the complaint. What was the consequence? These bodies of men, who found it vain to expect it from the government at the castle, or from the parliament, and having no where else to recur for redress, joined the societies, whom the report accuses of cherishing the desire of separation from England; and became converts to all those notions of extravagant and frantic ambition, which the report lays to their charge, and which threatens consequences so dreadful and alarming, that no man can contemplate them without horror and dismay.

What, then, is the lesson to be derived from this example, but that the comparatively small societies of 1791 became strong and formidable by the accession of the many who had nothing in common with them in the outset? I wish it were possible for us to draw the line more accurately between the small number that the report describes to have had mischievous objects originally in view, and the numerous bodies who were made converts by the neglect of their petition for constitutional rights. Is it improbable that the original few were not more than ten or twenty thousand in number? What, then, do I learn from this? That the impolitic and unjust refusal of government, to attend to the applications of the moderate, made 80 or 90,000 proselytes from moderation to violence. This is the lesson which the book of Ireland exhibits! Can you refuse your assent to the moral? Will any man argue, that if reform had been conceded to the 80 or 90,000 moderate petitioners, you would have this day to deplore the union of 100,000 men, bent on objects so extensive, so alarming, so calamitous? I wish to warn you by this example. Every argument that you have heard used this day was used at Dublin. In the short-sighted pride and obstinacy of the government, they turned a deaf ear to the supplicant; they have now, perhaps, in the open field to brave the assertor.[11] Unwarned, untutored by example, are you still to go on with the same contemptuous and stubborn pride?

I by no means think that Great Britain is at this moment in the same situation as Ireland. I by no means think that the discontents of this country have risen to such a height as to make us fear for the general peace of the country; but I deprecate the course which has been pursued in Ireland. What England is now, Ireland was in 1791. What was said of the few, they have now applied to the many; and as there are discontents in this country, which we can neither dissemble nor conceal, let us not, by an unwise and criminal disdain, irritate and fret them into violence and disorder. The discontents may happily subside; but a man must be sanguine indeed in his temper, or dull in his intellect, if he would leave to the operation of chance what he might more certainly obtain by the exercise of reason. Every thing that is dear and urgent to the minds of Englishmen presses upon us; in the critical moment at which I now address you, a day, an hour, ought not to elapse, without giving to ourselves the chance of this recovery. When

---

[11] They may have an open rebellion on their hands.

government is daily presenting itself in the shape of weakness that borders on dissolution—unequal to all the functions of useful strength, and formidable only in pernicious corruption—weak in power, and strong only in influence [12]—am I to be told that such a state of things can go on with safety to any branch of the constitution? If men think that, under the impression of such a system, we can go on without a recurrence to first principles, they argue in direct opposition to all theory and all practice. These discontents cannot, in their nature, subside under detected weakness and exposed incapacity. In their progress and increase, (and increase they must,) who shall say that direction can be given to the torrent, or that, having broken its bounds, it can be kept from overwhelming the country? Sir, it is not the part of statesmen, it is not the part of rational beings, to amuse ourselves with such fallacious dreams; we must not sit down and lament over our hapless situation; we must not deliver ourselves up to an imbecile despondency that would animate the approach of danger; but by a seasonable and vigorous measure of wisdom, meet it with a sufficient and a seasonable remedy. We may be disappointed. We may fail in the application, for no man can be certain of his footing on ground that is unexplored; but we shall at least have a chance for success—we shall at least do what belong to legislators, and to rational beings on the occasion, and I have confidence that our efforts would not be in vain. I say that we should give ourselves a chance, and, I may add, the best chance, for deliverance; since it would exhibit to the country a proof that we had conquered the first great difficulty that stood in the way of bettering our condition—that we had conquered ourselves. We had given a generous triumph to reason over prejudice; we had given a death-blow to those miserable distinctions of whig and tory, under which the warfare had been maintained between pride and privilege; and through the contention of our rival jealousies, the genuine rights of the many had been gradually undermined, and frittered away. I say, that this would be giving us the best chance; because, seeing every thing go on from bad to worse—seeing the progress of the most scandalous waste countenanced by the most criminal confidence, and that the effrontery of corruption no longer requires the mask of concealment—seeing liberty daily infringed, and the vital springs of the nation insufficient for the extravagance of a dissipated government, I must believe, that, unless the people are mad or stupid, they will suspect that there is something fundamentally vicious in our system, and which no reform would be equal to correct. Then, to prevent all this, and to try if we can effect a reform without touching the main pillars of the constitution, without changing its forms, or disturbing the harmony of its parts, without putting any thing out of its place, or affecting the securities which we justly hold to be so sacred, is, I say, the only chance which we have for retrieving our misfortunes by the road of quiet and tranquillity, and by which national strength may be recovered without disturbing the property of a single individual.[13]

It has been said, that the House possesses the confidence of the country as much as ever. This, in truth, is as much as to say, that his majesty's ministers possess the confidence of the country in the same degree as ever, since the majority

[12] In Pitt's ability to stay in office.

[13] Fox represents Grey's bill as corrective, not upsetting, to the basic, inherited system—"reform without overturning," a necessary condition in view of the fear of an English revolution like the French.

of the House support and applaud the measures of the government, and give their countenance to all the evils which we are doomed to endure. I was very much surprized to hear any proposition so unaccountable advanced by any person connected with ministers, particularly as the noble lord [14] had, but a sentence or two before, acknowledged that there had been, to be sure, a number of petitions presented to his majesty for the dismission of his ministers. The one assertion is utterly incompatible with the other, unless he means to assert, that the petitions which have been presented to the throne are of no importance. The noble lord can hardly, I think, speak in this contemptuous manner of the petitions of Middlesex, London, Westminster, Surrey, Hampshire, York, Edinburgh, Glasgow, and many other places, unless he means to insinuate that they are proofs only of our very great industry, and that they are not the genuine sense of the districts from which they come. If the noble lord ascribes them to our industry, he gives us credit for much more merit of that kind than we are entitled to. It certainly is not the peculiar characteristic of the present opposition, that they are very industrious in agitating the public mind. But, grant to the noble lord his position—be it to our industry that all these petitions are to be ascribed. If industry could procure them, was it our moderation, our good will and forbearance, that have made us for fourteen years relax from this industry, and never bring forward these petitions until now? No, Sir, it is not to our industry that they are to be ascribed now, nor to our forbearance that they did not come before. The noble lord will not give us credit for this forbearance; and the consequence is, that he must own, upon his imputation of industry, that the present is the first time when we were sure of the people, and that these petitions are a proof that at length the confidence of the people in ministers is shaken. That it is so, it is in vain for the noble lord to deny. They who in former times were eager to shew their confidence by addresses, have now been as eager to express their disapprobation in petitions for their removal. How, then, can we say that the confidence of the people is not shaken? Is confidence to be always against the people, and never for them?

It is a notable argument, that because we do not find, at the general election, very material changes in the representation, the sentiments of the people continue the same, in favour of the war, and in favour of his majesty's ministers. The very ground of the present discussion gives the answer to this argument. Why do we agitate the question of parliamentary reform? Why, but because a general election does not afford to the people the means of expressing their voice; because this House is not a sufficient representative of the people? Gentlemen are fond of arguing in this circle. When we contend that ministers have not the confidence of the people, they tell us that parliament is the faithful representative of the sense of the country. When we assert that the representation is defective, and shew, from the petitions to the throne, that the House does not speak the voice of the people, they turn to the general election, and say, that at this period they had an opportunity of choosing faithful organs of their opinion; and because very little or no change has taken place in the representation, the sense of the people must be the same. Sir, it is in vain for gentlemen to shelter themselves by this mode of reasoning. We assert, that under the present form and practice of elections, we cannot expect to see any remarkable change produced by a general election.

[14] Robert Jenkinson, Lord Hawkesbury, a member of Pitt's government.

We must argue from experience. Let us look back to the period of the American war. It will not be denied by the right honourable gentleman, that towards the end of that war, it became extremely unpopular, and that the king's ministers lost the confidence of the nation. In the year 1780 a dissolution [15] took place, and then it was naturally imagined by superficial observers, who did not examine the real state of representation, that the people would have returned a parliament that would have unequivocally spoken their sentiments on the occasion. What was the case? I am able to speak with considerable precision. At that time I was much more than I am at present in the way of knowing personally the individuals returned, and of making an accurate estimate of the accession gained to the popular side by that election. I can take upon me to say, that the change was very small indeed: not more than three or four persons were added to the number of those who had from the beginning opposed the disastrous career of the ministers in that war. I remember that, upon that occasion, Lord North made use of precisely the same argument as is now brought forward: "What!" said he, "can you contend the war is unpopular, after the declaration in its favour that the people have made by their choice of representatives? The general election is the proof that the war continues to be the war of the people of England." Such was the argument of Lord North, and yet it was notoriously otherwise; so notoriously otherwise, that the right honourable gentleman, the present chancellor of the exchequer, made a just and striking use of it, to demonstrate the necessity of a parliamentary reform. He referred to this event as to a demonstration of this doctrine. "You see," said he, "that so defective, so inadequate, is the present practice, at least of the elective franchise, that no impression of national calamity, no conviction of ministerial error, no abhorrence of disastrous war, is sufficient to stand against that corrupt influence which has mixed itself with election, and which drowns and stifles the popular voice." Upon this statement, and upon this unanswerable argument, the right honourable gentleman acted in the year 1782. When he proposed a parliamentary reform, he did it expressly on the ground of the experience of 1780, and he made an explicit declaration, that we had no other security by which to guard ourselves against the return of the same evils. He repeated this warning in 1783 and in 1785. It was the leading principle of his conduct. "Without a reform," said he, "the nation cannot be safe; this war may be put an end to, but what will protect you against another? as certainly as the spirit which engendered the present war actuates the secret councils of the crown, will you, under the influence of a defective representation, be involved again in new wars, and in similar calamities." This was his argument in 1782, this was his prophecy, and the right honourable gentleman was a true prophet.

Precisely as he pronounced it, the event happened; another war took place, and I am sure it will not be considered as an aggravation of its character, that it is at least equal in disaster to the war of which the right honourable gentleman complained. "The defect of representation," he said, "is the national disease; and unless you apply a remedy directly to that disease, you must inevitably take the consequences with which it is pregnant." With such an authority, can any man deny that I reason right? Did not the right honourable gentleman demonstrate his case? Good God! what a fate is that of the right honourable gentleman, and in what a state of whimsical contradiction does he stand! During the whole

---

[15] The House of Commons was dissolved and a new election called.

course of his administration, and particularly during the course of the present war, every prediction that he has made, every hope that he has held out, every prophecy that he has hazarded, has failed; he has disappointed the expectations that he has raised; and every promise that he has given, has proved to be fallacious. Yet, for these very declarations, and notwithstanding these failures, we have called him a wise minister. We have given him our confidence on account of his predictions, and have continued it upon their failure. The only instance in which he really predicted what has come to pass, we treated with stubborn incredulity. In 1785, he pronounced the awful prophecy, "Without a parliamentary reform the nation will be plunged into new wars; without a parliamentary reform you cannot be safe against bad ministers, nor can even good ministers be of use to you." Such was his prediction; and it has come upon us. It would seem as if the whole life of the right honourable gentleman, from that period, had been destined by Providence for the illustration of his warning. If I were disposed to consider him as a real enthusiast, and a bigot in divination, we might be apt to think that he had himself taken measures for the verification of his prophecy. For he might now exclaim to us, with the proud fervour of success, "You see the consequence of not listening to the oracle. I told you what would happen; it is true that your destruction is complete; I have plunged you into a new war; I have exhausted you as a people; I have brought you to the brink of ruin, but I told you before hand what would happen; I told you, that without a reform in the representation of the people, no minister, however wise, could save you; you denied me my means, and you take the consequence!" [16]

But a reform in the representation, say gentlemen on the opposite side of the House, is not called for by the country; and though meetings have been held in various parts of the kingdom, and petitions have come up for the dismissal of ministers, they have not expressed a wish for reform. In answer to this argument it is only necessary to observe, that the restrictions which have been recently laid on meetings of the people and on popular discussion,[17] may serve to account for the question of reform not being mixed with that which was the subject of their immediate consideration. The purpose of the meeting is necessarily specified in the requisition to the sheriff; and if any other business were attempted to be brought forward, the sheriff would have the power of dispersing the meeting. Their silence, therefore, upon the subject is no proof either way. But granting even the fact, that the country does not now call for this reform—a fact which, however, I deny—is the country in such a situation as to make it improbable that the universal demand of a parliamentary reform, which has burst from the people of Ireland, will not be speedily communicated by sympathy to the people of England? When I see that the treatment which the people of Ireland have received upon this subject, has exasperated their minds to such a degree as to throw the whole of that kingdom into confusion, and that we have daily to dread the danger of actual insurrection, shall I not take measures to prevent the rise of a passion that may swell into equal tumult? The nearness of the two countries, the sympathetic interests, the similarity of language, of constitution, and almost of suffer-

[16] In the preceding passage Fox demonstrates his great talent for exposing the contradictions and inconsistencies in his opponent's position.

[17] Pitt's Seditious Meetings Act (1794) prohibited meetings of more than fifty persons without the permission and supervision of the local magistrates. Only three days before the present debate Fox had unsuccessfully supported repeal of that act.

ing, make it probable that the one nation will catch the disease of the other, unless we interpose a seasonable cure. Is it not wisdom, is it not prudence, to erect a standard around which all the patriotism and moderation of the kingdom may rally, and the government be strengthened against the violence of the few by the countenance and support of the many?

The right honourable gentleman speaks, Sir, of the strength of government. But what symptom of strength does it exhibit? [18] Is it the cordiality of all the branches of the national force? Is it the harmony that happily reigns in all the departments of the executive power? Is it the reciprocal affection that subsists between the government and the people? Is it in the energy with which the people are eager to carry into execution the measures of the administration, from the heart-felt conviction that they are founded in wisdom, favourable to their own freedom, and calculated for national happiness? Is it because our resources are flourishing and untouched, because our vigour is undiminished, because our spirit is animated by success, and our courage by our glory? Is it because government have in a perilous situation, when they have been obliged to call upon the country for sacrifices, shewn a conciliating tenderness and regard for the rights of the people, as well as a marked disinterestedness and forbearance on their own parts, by which they have, in an exemplary manner, made their own economy to keep pace with the increased demands for the public service? Are these the sources of the strength of government? I forbear, Sir, to push the inquiry. I forbear to allude more particularly to symptoms which no man can contemplate at this moment without grief and dismay. It is not the declarations of right honourable gentlemen that constitute the strength of a government. That government is alone strong that possesses the hearts of the people; and will any man contend that we should not be more likely to add strength to the state, if we were to extend the basis of the popular representation? [19] Would not a House of Commons, freely elected, be more likely to conciliate the support of the people? If this be true in the abstract, it is certainly our peculiar duty to look for this support in the hour of difficulty. What man who foresees a hurricane is not desirous of strengthening his house? Shall nations alone be blind to the dictates of reason? Let us not, Sir, be deterred from this act of prudence by the false representations that are made to us. France is the phantom that is constantly held out to terrify us from our purpose. Look at France; it will not be denied but that she stands on the broad basis of free representation. Whatever other views the government of France may exhibit, and which may afford just alarm to other nations, it cannot be denied that her representative system has proved itself capable of vigorous exertion.

Now, Sir, though I do not wish you to imitate France, and though I am persuaded you have no necessity for any terror of such imitation being forced upon you, yet I say that you ought to be as ready to adopt the virtues, as you are steady in averting from the country, the vices of France. If it is clearly demonstrated, that genuine representation alone can give solid power, and that in order to make government strong, the people must make the government; you ought to act on

---

[18] Each of the following questions reminds the audience of recent trouble, beginning with a mutiny in the fleet. Listing is a frequent method of Fox's for heightening impact.

[19] This is the central proposition of the positive side of Fox's case.

this grand maxim of political wisdom thus demonstrated, and call in the people, according to the original principles of your system, to the strength of your government. In doing this you will not innovate, you will not imitate. In making the people of England a constituent part of the government of England, you do no more than restore the genuine edifice designed and framed by our ancestors.

An honourable baronet spoke of the instability of democracies, and says, that history does not give us the example of one that has lasted eighty years. Sir, I am not speaking of pure democracies, and therefore his allusion does not apply to my argument. Eighty years, however, of peace and repose would be pretty well for any people to enjoy, and would be no bad recommendation of a pure democracy. I am ready, however, to agree with the honourable baronet, that, according to the experience of history, the ancient democracies of the world were vicious and objectionable on many accounts; their instability, their injustice, and many other vices, cannot be overlooked; but, surely, when we turn to the ancient democracies of Greece, when we see them in all the splendour of arts and of arms, when we see to what an elevation they carried the powers of man, it cannot be denied that, however vicious on the score of ingratitude or of injustice, they were, at least, the pregnant source of national strength, and that in particular they brought forth this strength in a peculiar manner in the moment of difficulty and distress. When we look at the democracies of the ancient world, we are compelled to acknowledge their oppressions to their dependencies, their horrible acts of injustice and of ingratitude to their own citizens; but they compel us also to admiration by their vigour, their constancy, their spirit, and their exertions in every great emergency in which they are called upon to act. We are compelled to own, that it gives a power, of which no other form of government is capable. Why? Because it incorporates every man with the state, because it arouses every thing that belongs to the soul, as well as to the body of man: because it makes every individual feel that he is fighting for himself, and not for another; that it is his own cause, his own safety, his own concern, his own dignity on the face of the earth, and his own interest on the identical soil which he has to maintain, and accordingly we find that whatever may be objected to them on account of the turbulency of the passions which they engender, their short duration, and their disgusting vices, they have exacted from the common suffrage of mankind the palm of strength and vigour. Who that reads the history of the Persian war—what boy, whose heart is warmed by the grand and sublime actions which the democratic spirit produced, does not find in this principle the key to all the wonders which were achieved at Thermopylæ and elsewhere, and of which the recent and marvellous acts of the French people are pregnant examples? He sees that the principle of liberty only could create the sublime and irresistible emotion; and it is in vain to deny, from the striking illustration that our own times have given, that the principle is eternal, and that it belongs to the heart of man. Shall we, then, refuse to take the benefit of this invigorating principle? Shall we refuse to take the benefit which the wisdom of our ancestors resolved that it should confer on the British constitution? With the knowledge that it can be reinfused into our system without violence, without disturbing any one of its parts, are we become so inert, so terrified, or so stupid, as to hesitate for one hour to restore ourselves to the health which it would be sure to give? When we see the giant power that it confers upon others, we ought not to withhold it from Great Britain.

How long is it since we were told in this House, that France was a blank in the map of Europe, and that she lay an easy prey to any power that might be disposed to divide and plunder her? Yet we see that, by the mere force and spirit of this principle, France has brought all Europe at her feet. Without disguising the vices of France, without overlooking the horrors that have been committed, and that have tarnished the glory of the Revolution, it cannot be denied that they have exemplified the doctrine, that if you wish for power you must look to liberty.[20] If ever there was a moment when this maxim ought to be dear to us, it is the present. We have tried all other means; we have had recourse to every stratagem that artifice, that influence, that cunning could suggest; we have addressed ourselves to all the base passions of the nation; we have addressed ourselves to pride, to avarice, to fear; we have awakened all the interested emotions; we have employed every thing that flattery, every thing that address, every thing that privilege could effect; we have tried to terrify them [the British people] into exertion, and all has been unequal to our emergency. Let us try them by the only means which experience demonstrates to be invincible; let us address ourselves to their love; let us identify them with ourselves: let us make it their own cause as well as ours! To induce them to come forward in support of the state, let us make them a part of the state,[21] and this they become the very instant you give them a House of Commons that is the faithful organ of their will. Then, Sir, when you have made them believe and feel that there can be but one interest in the country, you will never call upon them in vain for exertion. Can this be the case as the House of Commons is now constituted? Can they think so if they review the administration of the right honourable gentleman, every part of which must convince them, that the present representation is a mockery and a shadow?

I shall not, Sir, go over the whole of that series of disastrous measures which has forced upon the country the impression that the House of Commons has lost its efficacy in the system of government. But let us look back to the very singular circumstances under which the right honourable gentleman came into power: from this we shall see in what estimation the House of Commons is held, even by government itself, when it does not suit their purpose to extol it as the representative of the people. The right honourable gentleman came into power against the sense of the majority of the then House of Commons; and, armed with all the corrupt power of the crown, he stood, and successfully resisted the power of the House of Commons. He declared, that it was not the representative of the people, that it did not speak the sense of the nation, and he derided its weakness and inefficiency. What is the doctrine that this conduct in 1784 promulgated? That the House of Commons, so long as it obeys the will of the minister, so long as it grants every thing which he demands, so long as it supports every measure which he brings forward, is the genuine representative of the country—so long it is powerful and omnipotent: but, the moment that a House of Commons presumes to be the censor of government, the moment that it assumes the character of defiance and opposition, from that instant it ceases to have power or authority in the kingdom—it then becomes a straw which the minister can puff away with a

---

[20] If Fox were looking at the revolutions of the twentieth century, he might reverse his opinion of liberty as the source of power.

[21] Compare this argument with Burke's remarks about freedom for Catholics, above, p. 238.

breath. This he did in 1784, and completed his triumph.[22] Since that time, who will say that the corrupt influence of the crown has not made enormous strides in destroying the power of election? Since that time, four-fifths of the elective franchises of Scotland, and Cornwall particularly, have passed into the hands of government; and the prediction which Mr. Burke then made upon the occasion has been literally fulfilled—no House of Commons has been since found strong enough to oppose the ministers of the crown. It has been said, that that period was not proper to be taken as a test of the public spirit on the subject of representation; that it was a moment of national prosperity, and that nothing can be decided for or against representation by that precedent. It was, however, in that moment that the seeds of rottenness and dissolution were sown. I thought I saw them at the time, and I have been confirmed in my observation by every thing that has occurred since. I pass over all the period between that time up to the present war, not because it is not fruitful of examples, but because I do not wish to trespass upon your time. The present war, say ministers, was popular in its commencement; the same was said of the commencement of the American war. I will not stop to inquire into the truth of the assertion, though it is at least doubtful. I will not deny that, through the artful machinations of government, a clamour was excited of the interested, which ministers called the voice of the nation. Whatever may have been the case, however, in the outset of the two wars, the progress in the public opinion has been the same in both; and I aver, that as in the American war the public opinion had changed, though no change was produced by the general election of 1780, so now, for the last two years, the present war has been universally unpopular in England, though it has not made its voice to be heard in the choice of representatives. Though the [recent] general election has not produced a change of men, yet he must be a dull observer of the public mind who says that the general election did not afford a striking proof of a change in the sentiments of the people. For what was the conduct of the candidates in populous places on the two sides? We boasted of having opposed the war; we made it our claim and our appeal to the confidence of the people, that we had resisted every one of the measures by which the government has brought us into our present condition. What was the conduct of the candidates on the other side? It consisted of apologies for their past offence of supporting the war; it consisted of whining and canting explanations, in descriptions of alarms, and not unfrequently in misrepresentations of facts. Such was the feeling conveyed by the general election. It served to convince every observing man, that if the representative system had been perfect, or the practice pure, the new parliament would have decidedly voted against the continuance of the war. Seeing, then, the conduct they have pursued, can the people have confidence in this House? Can they have confidence in a House that has given their countenance to misrepresentation through the whole course of the war? Suppose the people were to look for the history of the events that have happened in this war, and for the

---

[22] There was and is sufficient evidence to give force to Fox's argument; whether the election of 1784 was a popular endorsement of Pitt or a thoroughly managed electoral victory is still a question with historians. Fox's personal unpopularity, because of the coalition with North and the India Bill, probably had much to do with the outcome of the election of 1784. Fox's argument, in any case, is an orthodox Opposition view of the strength of the party in power, especially when that party has been in power a long time.

condition of the country, to the king's speeches from the throne, and to the addresses of the two Houses of parliament; they would see that almost in every instance his majesty has declared from the throne, and the House of Commons has replied in humble addresses, that our prospects were improved, and that the country was flourishing and prosperous. Look at all the king's speeches and addresses since the year 1793, and you will find that this is their general tone and language. And yet, this is the House of Commons in which the people of England are to have confidence! Amidst all the failures and sufferings which they have had to deplore, and in their present condition of dreadful and unparalleled calamity, they are called upon to trust to a House of Commons, that assures them their prospects and situation have been gradually improving since the year 1793!

There has been, at different times, a great deal of dispute about virtual representation.[23] Sir, I am no great advocate for these nice subtleties and special pleadings on the constitution: much depends upon appearance as well as reality. I know well that a popular body of 558 gentlemen, if truly independent of the crown, would be a strong barrier to the people; but the House of Commons should not only be, but appear to be, the representatives of the people; the system should satisfy the prejudices and the pride, as well as the reason of the people; and you never can expect to give the just impression which a House of Commons ought to make on the people, until you derive it unequivocally from them. It is asked, why gentlemen who were against a parliamentary reform on former occasions should vote for it now? Ten years ago men might reasonably object to any reform of the system, who ought now, in my opinion, to be governed by motives that are irresistible in its favour. They might look back with something like satisfaction and triumph to former parliaments, and console themselves with the reflection, that though in moments of an ordinary kind, in the common course of human events, parliament might abate from its vigilance, and give a greater degree of confidence than was strictly conformable with representative duty—yet there was a point beyond which no artifice of power, no influence of corruption, could carry them; that there were barriers in the British constitution over which the House of Commons never would leap, and that the moment of danger and alarm would be the signal for the return of parliament to its post. Such might have been the reasoning of gentlemen on the experience of former parliaments; and with this rooted trust in the latent efficacy of parliament, they might have objected to any attempt that should cherish hopes of a change in the system itself. But what will the same gentlemen say after the experience of the last and the present parliament? What reliance can they have for any one vestige of the constitution that is yet left to us? Or rather, what privilege, what right, what security, has not been already violated?—"*quid intactum nefasti liquimus?*" [24] And, seeing that in no one instance have they hesitated to go the full length of every outrage that was conceived by the minister—that they have been touched by no scruples—deterred by no sense of duty—corrected by no experience of calamity—checked by no admonition or remonstrance—that they have never made out a single case of inquiry—that they have never interposed a single restraint upon abuse, may not gentlemen consistently

[23] It was argued before the American Revolution, for example, that the colonies were *virtually* represented in Parliament.
[24] Horace *Odes* I.xxxv.35: "What iniquity have we left untouched?"

feel that the reform which they previously thought unnecessary is now indispensable?

We have heard to-day, Sir, all the old arguments about honour on the one side being as likely as honour on the other; that there are good men on both sides of the House; that a man may be a member for a close borough [25] upon the one side of the House as well as upon the other; and that he may be a good man, sit where he may. All this, Sir, is very idle language: it is not the question at issue. No man disputes the existence of private and individual integrity; but, Sir, this is not representation: if a man comes here as the proprietor of a burgage tenure,[26] he does not come here as the representative of the pople. The whole of this system, as it is now carried on, is as outrageous to morality, as it is pernicious to just government; it gives a scandal to our character, which not merely degrades the House of Commons in the eyes of the people; it does more, it undermines the very principles of integrity in their hearts, and gives a fashion to dishonesty and imposture. They hear of a person giving or receiving four or five thousand pounds as the purchase money of a seat for a close borough; and they hear the very man, who received and put into his pocket the money, make a vehement speech in this House against bribery; and they see him move for the commitment to prison of a poor, unfortunate wretch at your bar, who has been convicted in taking a single guinea for his vote in the very borough, perhaps, where he had publicly and unblushingly sold his influence, though that miserable guinea was necessary to save a family from starving, under the horrors of a war which he had contributed to bring upon the country.[27]

Sir, these are the things that paralyse you to the heart; these are the things that vitiate the whole system, that spread degeneracy, hypocrisy, and sordid fraud, over the country, and take from us the energies of virtue, and sap the foundations of patriotism and spirit. The system that encourages so much vice ought to be put an end to; and it is no argument that, because it lasted a long time without mischief, it ought now to be continued, when it is found to be pernicious; it has arisen to a height that defeats the very end of government; it must sink under its own weakness. And this, Sir, is not a case peculiar to itself, but inseparable from all human institutions. All the writers of eminence upon forms of government have said, that in order to preserve them, frequent recurrence must be had to their original principle. This is the opinion of Montesquieu, as well as of Machiavel.[28] Gentlemen will not be inclined to dispute the authority of the latter on this point at least; and he says, that without this recurrence they grow out of shape, and deviate from their general form. It is only by recurring to former principles that any government can be kept pure and unabused.

But, say gentlemen, if any abuses have crept into our system, have we not a

[25] An election district, formerly a borough (or town) but now containing few voters or none, controlled by a private landowner or the Crown.

[26] Burgage tenure was the holding of property in the ancient municipal corporations directly from the Crown. If a man held a seat from such a "borough" of which he was the proprietor (or owner) he hardly represented anyone but himself.

[27] Fox packs a great deal of accusation into this example.

[28] The eighteenth-century French author of *The Spirit of the Laws* (1748), and the Renaissance Italian author of *The Prince* (1513) would be known to many in Fox's audience as writers on government.

corrective, whose efficacy has been proved, and of which every body approves? Have we not Mr. Grenville's bill [29] as an amendment to the constitution? An amendment it is; an amendment which acknowledges the deficiency. It is an avowal of a defective practice. It is a strong argument for a reform, because it would not be necessary if the plan of representation were sufficient.

But, Sir, there is a lumping consideration, if I may be allowed the phrase, which now more than ever ought to make every man a convert to parliamentary reform; there is an annual revenue of twenty-three millions sterling collected by the executive government from the people. Here, Sir, is the despot of election; here is the new power that has grown up to a magnitude, that bears down before it every defensive barrier established by our ancestors for the protection of the people. They had no such tyrant to controul; they had no such enemy to oppose. Against every thing that was known, against every thing that was seen, they did provide; but it did not enter into the contemplation of those who established the checks and barriers of our system, that they would ever have to stand against a revenue of twenty-three millions a year. The whole landed rental of the kingdom is not estimated at more than twenty-five millions a year, and this rental is divided and dispersed over a large body, who cannot be supposed to act in concert, or to give to their power the force of combination and unity. But it is said, that though the government is in the receipt of a revenue of twenty-three millions a year, it has not the expenditure of that sum, and that its influence ought not to be calculated from what it receives, but what it has to pay away. I submit, however, to the good sense and to the personal experience of gentlemen who hear me, if it be not a manifest truth that influence depends almost as much upon what they have to receive, as upon what they have to pay? And if this be true, of the influence which individuals derive from the rentals of their estates, and from the expenditure of that rental, how much more so is it true of government, who, both in the receipt and expenditure of this enormous revenue, are actuated by one invariable principle, that of extending or withholding favour in exact proportion to the submission or resistance to their measures which the individuals make? Compare this revenue, then, with that against which our ancestors were so anxious to protect us, and compare this revenue with all the bulwarks of our constitution in preceding times, and you must acknowledge, that though those bulwarks were sufficient to protect us in the days of King William and Queen Anne,[30] they are not equal to the enemy we have now to resist.

But it is said, what will this reform do for us? Will it be a talisman sufficient to retrieve all the misfortunes which we have incurred? I am free to say, that it would not be sufficient, unless it led to reforms of substantial expence, and of all the abuses that have crept into our government. But at the same time I think it would do this, I think it would give us the chance, as I said before, of recovery. It would give us, in the first place, a parliament vigilant and scrupulous, and that would insure to us a government active and economical. It would prepare the way for every rational improvement, of which, without disturbing the parts, our constitution is susceptible. It would do more; it would open the way for exertions

---

[29] A plan proposed by George Grenville and passed in 1770, to settle disputed elections by a more judicious and objective method than a party vote in the House.

[30] A century earlier.

infinitely more extensive than all that we have hitherto made. The right honourable gentleman says, that we have made exertions. True. But what are they in comparison to our necessity? The right honourable gentleman says, that when we consider our situation compared with that of countries which have taken another line of conduct, we ought to rejoice. I confess, Sir, that I am at a loss to conceive what country the right honourable gentleman has in view in this comparison. Does he mean to assert, that the nations who preferred the line of neutrality to that of war have fallen into a severer calamity than ourselves? Does he mean to say, that Sweden, or that Denmark, has suffered more by observing an imprudent neutrality, than England or Austria by wisely plunging themselves into a war? Or does he mean to insinuate that Prussia has been the victim of its impolicy, in getting out of the conflict on the first occasion? If this be the interpretation of the right honourable gentleman's argument, I do not believe that he will get many persons to subscribe to the justice of his comparison. But probably he alludes to the fate of Holland: [31] if this be the object to which he wishes to turn our eyes, he does it unjustly. Holland acted under the despotic mandate of that right honourable gentleman; and Holland, whatever she has suffered, whatever may be her present situation, lays her calamities to the charge of England. I cannot, then, admit of the argument, that our situation is comparatively better than that of the nations who altogether kept out of the war, or, being drawn into it in the first instance, corrected their error, and restored to themselves the blessings of peace.

I come now to consider the specific proposition of my honourable friend, and the arguments that have been brought against it. Let me premise, that however averse gentlemen may be to any specific proposition of reform, if they are friendly to the principle, they ought to vote for the present question, because it is merely a motion for leave to bring in a bill.[32] An opposition to such a motion comes with a very ill grace from the right honourable gentleman, and contradicts the policy for which he strenuously argued. In 1785 he moved for leave to bring in a bill on a specific plan, and he fairly called for the support of all those who approved of the principle of reform, whatever might be the latitude of their ideas on the subject; whether they wished for more or less than his proposition, he thought that they should agree to the introduction of the bill, that it might be freely discussed in the committee,[33] in hopes that the united wisdom of the House might shape out something that would be generally acceptable. Upon this candid argument I, for one, acted. I did not approve of his specific proposition, and yet I voted with him for leave to bring in the bill. And this, Sir, has generally happened to me on all the former occasions, when propositions have been made. Though I have constantly been a friend to the principle, I have never before seen a specific plan that had my cordial approbation. That which came nearest, and of which I the least disapproved, was the plan of an honourable gentleman

---

[31] Holland had been the field of much fighting and devastation as a British army retreated before the French. She made a separate peace in May 1795.

[32] A stage in consideration prior to the first reading, often the critical stage for a proposal by Opposition.

[33] The Committee of the Whole House, a parliamentary device for permitting the fullest of unrestricted debate and amendment, within the structure of rigid parliamentary forms.

who is now no more: [34] he was the first person who suggested the idea of extending what might be proper to add to representation, to house-keepers, as to a description of persons the best calculated to give efficacy to the representative system. My honourable friend's plan, built upon this idea, is an improvement of it, since it is not an attempt even to vary the form and outline, much less to new-model the representation of the people; it keeps every thing in its place; it neither varies the number, nor changes the name, nor diverts the course of any part of our system; it corrects without change; it extends without destruction of any established right; it restores simply what has been injured by abuse, and reinstates what time has mouldered away; no man can have a right to complain of genuine property assailed; no habit even, no mode of thinking, no prejudice, will be wounded; it traces back the path of the constitution from which we have wandered, but it runs out into no new direction.

A noble lord says, that the county representation must be good, that it must be approved of; be it so: this proposes to leave the county representation where it is; I wish so to leave it. I think that representation ought to be of a compound nature.[35] The counties may be considered as territorial representation, as contradistinguished from popular; but, in order to embrace all that I think necessary, I certainly would not approve of any farther extension of this branch of the representation. It has been asked, whether the rights of corporations [36] ought not to be maintained? That is a matter for farther discussion. I have no hesitation in saying, that my opinion leads the other way; but if it should be thought so, it may be so modified in the bill. There is no reasonable objection to its introduction on account of our not now agreeing with all its parts. My honourable friend, with all his abilities and all the industry with which he has digested his proposition, does not presume to offer it as a perfect plan. He does not call upon you to adopt all his notions, nor does he think that every part of his plan will be found to quadrate with the abstract principles of representation. He looks to what is practicable in the condition in which we are placed, not to what a new people might be tempted to hazard. My opinion, however unimportant it may be, goes with my honourable friend. I think there is enough of enterprize and vigour in the plan to restore us to health, and not enough to run us into disorder. I agree with him, because I am firmly of opinion with all the philosophical writers on the subject, that when a country is sunk into a situation of apathy and abuse, it can only be recovered by recurring to first principles.

Now, Sir, I think, that acting on this footing, to extend the right of election to house-keepers,[37] is the best and most advisable plan of reform. I think also, that it is the most perfect recurrence to first principles; I do not mean to the first principles of society, nor the abstract principles of representation, but to the first known and recorded principles of our constitution. According to the early history

[34] Henry Flood (1732–1791), Irish reformer associated with Grattan in obtaining the independence of the Irish Parliament. Sat in the British Parliament after 1783, and introduced his reform bill in 1790.

[35] This issue is very much alive in many states of the United States today.

[36] Quasi-public organizations are referred to, such as municipal corporations, not private businesses.

[37] A house-keeper was one who occupied a house with his family. If he was not a property owner, he could not qualify for the vote. Grey's bill would grant him a vote, even though a renter.

of England, and the highest authorities on our parliamentary constitution, I find this to be the case. It is the opinion of the celebrated Glanville,[38] that in all cases where no particular right intervenes, the common-law right of paying scot and lot was the right of election in the land. This, Sir, was the opinion of Serjeant Glanville, and of one of the most celebrated committees of which our parliamentary history has to boast; and this, in my opinion, is the safest line of conduct you can adopt. But it is said, that extending the right of voting to house-keepers may, in some respects, be compared to universal suffrage. I have always deprecated universal suffrage, not so much on account of the confusion to which it would lead, as because I think that we should in reality lose the very object which we desire to obtain; because I think it would in its nature embarrass, and prevent the deliberative voice of the country from being heard. I do not think that you augment the deliberative body of the people by counting all the heads, but that in truth you confer on individuals, by this means, the power of drawing forth numbers, who, without deliberation, would implicitly act upon their will. My opinion is, that the best plan of representation is that which shall bring into activity the greatest number of independent voters, and that that is defective which would bring forth those whose situation and condition take from them the power of deliberation. I can have no conception of that being a good plan of election which should enable individuals to bring regiments to the poll.

I hope gentlemen will not smile if I endeavour to illustrate my position by referring to the example of the other sex. In all the theories and projects of the most absurd speculation, it has never been suggested that it would be advisable to extend the elective suffrage to the female sex; and yet, justly respecting, as we must do, the mental powers, the acquirements, the discrimination, and the talents of the women of England, in the present improved state of society—knowing the opportunities which they have for acquiring knowledge—that they have interests as dear and as important as our own, it must be the genuine feeling of every gentleman who hears me, that all the superior classes of the female sex of England must be more capable of exercising the elective suffrage with deliberation and propriety, than the uninformed individuals of the lowest class of men to whom the advocates of universal suffrage would extend it. And yet, why has it never been imagined that the right of election should be extended to women? Why! but because by the law of nations, and perhaps also by the law of nature, that sex is dependent on ours; and because, therefore, their voices would be governed by the relation in which they stand in society. Therefore it is, Sir, that with the exceptions of companies, in which the right of voting merely affects property, it has never been in the contemplation of the most absurd theorists to extend the elective franchise to the other sex.

The desideratum to be obtained, is independent voters, and that, I say, would be a defective system that should bring regiments of soldiers, of servants, and of persons whose low condition necessarily curbed the independence of their minds. That, then, I take to be the most perfect system which shall include the greatest number of independent electors, and exclude the greatest number of those who are necessarily by their condition dependent. I think that the plan of my honourable

---

[38] Sir John Glanville, the younger (1586–1661), lawyer and member of Parliament, distinguished for his opposition to the Stuart despotism. "Scot and lot" was the name for a parish tax which was levied according to ability to pay.

friend draws this line as discreetly as it can be drawn, and it by no means approaches to universal suffrage. It would neither admit, except in particular instances, soldiers nor servants. Universal suffrage would extend the right to three millions of men, but there are not more than 700,000 houses that would come within the plan of my honourable friend; and when it is considered, that out of these some are the property of minors, and that some persons have two or more houses, it would fix the number of voters for Great Britain at about 600,000; and I call upon gentlemen to say, whether this would not be sufficiently extensive for deliberation on the one hand, and yet sufficiently limited for order on the other. This has no similarity with universal suffrage; and yet, taking the number of representatives as they now stand, it would give to every member about 1500 constituents.

But it is said, would even this plan of reform protect us against the consequences of bribery and corruption? I do not affect to say that it would; I do not believe that in the present state of society we can be altogether free from this evil; no laws will be found sufficient to eradicate an evil, which example has so banefully established. We have for a course of years habituated the people to the sordid vice, and we certainly cannot wonder that a poor man should not scruple to take five guineas for his vote, when he knows that the noble lord in his neighbourhood took four or five thousand. But, it is to be hoped, that when this baneful encouragement is removed, the regulations that would be introduced would tend to diminish, if not altogether remove the evil. Among those regulations, that of shortening the duration of parliaments would be one strong corrective;[39] and this, I think, might be done with great convenience and facility by the plan upon which the elections would be made.

It has often been a question, both within and without these walls, how far representatives ought to be bound by the instructions of their constituents. It is a question upon which my mind is not altogether made up, though I own I lean to the opinion, that having to legislate for the empire, they ought not to be altogether guided by instructions that may be dictated by local interests.[40] I cannot, however, approve of the very ungracious manner in which I sometimes hear expressions of contempt for the opinion of constituents. They are made with a very bad grace in the first session of a septennial parliament, particularly if they should come from individuals, who in the concluding session of a former parliament did not scruple to court the favour of the very same constituents, by declaring that they voted against their conscience in compliance with their desire, as was the case of an honourable alderman of the city of London. But, Sir, there is one class of constituents whose instructions it is considered as the implicit duty of members to obey. When gentlemen represent populous towns and cities, then it is a disputed point, whether they ought to obey their voice, or follow the dictates of their own conscience; but, if they represent a noble lord, or a noble duke, then it becomes no longer a question of doubt; and he is not considered as a man of honour who does not implicitly obey the orders of his single constituent.

[39] Reducing the time between elections had been a favorite of the reformers for many years. The radicals wanted annual elections; some moderates were for returning to three-year-terms; opponents like Burke saw no harm in the prevailing seven-year limit.

[40] Fox is retaining the position announced by Burke in his speech after the election at Bristol in 1774.

He is to have no conscience, no liberty, no discretion of his own, he is sent here by my lord this, or the duke of that, and if he does not obey the instructions he receives, he is not to be considered as a man of honour and a gentleman. Such is the mode of reasoning that prevails in this House. Is this fair? Is there any reciprocity in this conduct? Is a gentleman to be permitted, without dishonour, to act in opposition to the sentiments of the city of London, of the city of Westminster, or of Bristol; but if he dares to disagree with the duke, or lord, or baronet, whose representative he is, that he must be considered as unfit for the society of men of honour?

This, Sir, is the chicane and tyranny of corruption; and this, at the same time, is called representation. In a very great degree the county members are held in the same sort of thraldrom. A number of peers possess an overweening interest in the county, and a gentleman is no longer permitted to hold his situation than as he acts agreeably to the dictates of those powerful families. Let us see how the whole of this stream of corruption has been diverted from the side of the people to that of the crown; with what constant, persevering art, every man who is possessed of influence in counties, corporations, or boroughs, that will yield to the solicitations of the court, is drawn over to that phalanx which is opposed to the small remnant of popular election. I have looked, Sir, to the machinations of the present minister in this way, and I find that, including the number of additional titles, the right honourable gentleman has made no fewer than 115 peers in the course of his administration; that is to say, he has bestowed no fewer than 115 titles, including new creations and elevations from one rank to another. How many of these are to be ascribed to national services, and how many to parliamentary interest, I leave the House to inquire. The country is not blind to these arts of influence, and it is impossible that we can expect them to continue to endure them.

A noble lord has quoted a most able book on the subject of the French Revolution, the work of Mr. Mackintosh,[41] and I rejoice to see that gentlemen begin to acknowledge the merits of that eminent writer, and that the impression that it made upon me at the time is now felt and acknowledged even by those who disputed its authority. The noble lord has quoted Mr. Mackintosh's book on account of the observation which he made on the article which relates to the French elections: he thought that their plan would lead to the evil of universal suffrage. I have not forgotten the sarcasms that were flung out on my approbation of this celebrated work; that I was told of my "new library stuffed with the jargon of the Rights of Man"; it now appears, however, that I did not greatly over-rate this performance, and that those persons now quote Mr. Mackintosh as an authority, who before treated him with splenetic scorn. Now, Sir, with all my sincere admiration of this book, I think the weakest and most objectionable passage in it, is that which the noble lord has quoted; I think it is that which the learned author would himself be the most desirous to correct. Without descending to minute and equivocal theories, and without inquiring farther into the Rights of Man than what is necessary to our purpose, there is one position in which we shall all agree —that man has the right to be well governed. Now, it is obvious, that no people can be satisfied with a government from the constituent parts of which they are

---

[41] Sir James Mackintosh's *Vindiciae Gallicae* (1791) was a defense of the French Revolution and its English friends against Burke. Lord Hawkesbury had paraphrased a few arguments from the book. By the date of this speech, Mackintosh had changed his mind and had become an admirer of Burke.

excluded. When we look to the kingdom of Scotland, we see a state of representation so monstrous and absurd, so ridiculous and revolting, that it is good for nothing, except, perhaps, to be placed by the side of the English, in order to set off our defective system, by the comparison of one still more defective. In Scotland there is no shadow even of representation; there is neither a representation of property for the counties, nor of population for the towns. It is not what we understand in England by freeholders, who elect in the counties; the right is vested in what are called the superiorities; and it might so happen that all the members for the counties of Scotland might come here without having the vote of a single person who had a foot of property in the land. This is an extreme case, but it is within the limits of their system. In the boroughs their magistrates are self-elected, and therefore the members have nothing to do with the population of the towns.

Now, Sir, having shewn this to be the state of our representation, I ask what remedy there can be other than reform? What can we expect, as the necessary result of a system so defective and vicious in all its parts, but increasing calamities, until we shall be driven to a convulsion that would overthrow every thing? If we do not apply this remedy in time, our fate is inevitable. Our most illustrious patriots, the men whose memories are the dearest to Englishmen, have long ago pointed out to us parliamentary reform as the only means of redressing national grievance. I need not inform you, that Sir George Savile [42] was its most strenuous advocate; I need not tell you that the venerable and illustrious Camden [43] was through life a steady adviser of seasonable reform; nay, Sir, to a certain degree we have the authority of Mr. Burke himself for the propriety of correcting the abuses of our system; for gentlemen will remember the memorable answer which he gave to the argument that was used for our right of taxing America, on the score of their being virtually represented, and that they were in the same situation as Manchester, Birmingham, and Sheffield.—"What!" said Mr. Burke, "when the people of America look up to you with the eyes of filial love and affection, will you turn to them the shameful parts of the constitution?" [44] With the concurring testimony of so many authorities for correcting our abuses, why do we hesitate? Can we do any harm by experiment? Can we possibly put ourselves into a worse condition than we are? What advantages we shall gain I know not. I think we shall gain many. I think we shall gain at least the chance of warding off the evil of confusion, growing out of accumulated discontent. I think we shall save ourselves from the evil that has fallen upon Ireland. I think we shall satisfy the moderate, and take even from the violent, if any such there be, the power of increasing their numbers, and of making converts to their schemes. This, Sir, is my solemn opinion, and upon this ground it is that I recommend with earnestness and solicitude the proposition of my honourable friend.

And now, Sir, before I sit down, allow me to make a single observation with

---

[42] See note 27, p. 229, above.

[43] Charles Pratt, Earl Camden (1713–1793), one of the great lawyers and judges of the century, very closely associated with Pitt's father, Chatham.

[44] "On American Taxation," *Works* (Boston, 1894), II, 74. The sentence in the published speech is: "When this child of ours wishes to assimilate to its parent, and to reflect with a true filial resemblance the beauteous countenance of British liberty, are we to turn to them the shameful parts of our constitution?" Fox seeks to bring Burke's authority, "to a certain degree," to the support of a principle to which Burke was always opposed.

respect to the character and conduct of those who have, in conjunction with myself, felt it their duty to oppose the progress of this disastrous war. I hear it said, "You do nothing but mischief when you are here; and yet we should be sorry to see you away." I do not know how we shall be able to satisfy the gentlemen who feel towards us in this way. If we can neither do our duty without mischief, nor please them with doing nothing, I know but of one way by which we can give them content, and that is, by putting an end to our existence. With respect to myself, and I believe I can also speak for others, I do not feel it consistent with my duty totally to secede from this House. I have no such intention; but, Sir, I have no hesitation in saying, that after seeing the conduct of this House, after seeing them give to ministers their confidence and support, upon convicted failure, imposition, and incapacity; after seeing them deaf and blind to the consequences of a career that penetrates the hearts of all other men with alarm, and that neither reason, experience, nor duty, are sufficiently powerful to influence them to oppose the conduct of government, I certainly do think that I may devote more of my time to my private pursuits, and to the retirement which I love, than I have hitherto done; I certainly think I need not devote much of it to fruitless exertions, and to idle talk, in this House. Whenever it shall appear that my efforts may contribute in any degree to restore us to the situation from which the confidence of this House in a desperate system and an incapable administration, has so suddenly reduced us, I shall be found ready to discharge my duty.[45]

Sir, I have done. I have given my advice. I propose the remedy, and fatal will it be for England if pride and prejudice much longer continue to oppose it. The remedy which is proposed is simple, easy, and practicable; it does not touch the vitals of the constitution; and I sincerely believe it will restore us to peace and harmony. Do you not think that you must come to parliamentary reform soon; and is it not better to come to it now when you have the power of deliberation, than when, perhaps, it may be extorted from you by convulsion? There is as yet time to frame it with freedom and discussion; it will even yet go to the people with the grace and favour of a spontaneous act. What will it be when it is extorted from you with indignation and violence? God forbid that this should be the case! but now is the moment to prevent it; and now, I say, wisdom and policy recommend it to you, when you may enter into all the considerations to which it leads, rather than to postpone it to a time when you will have nothing to consider but the number and the force of those who demand it. It is asked, whether liberty has not gained much of late years, and whether the popular branch ought not, therefore, to be content? To this I answer, that if liberty has gained much, power has gained more. Power has been indefatigable and unwearied in its encroachments. Every thing has run in that direction through the whole course of the present reign. This was the opinion of Sir George Savile, of the Marquis of Rockingham, and of all the virtuous men who, in their public life, proved themselves to be advocates for the rights of the people.[46] They saw and deplored the tendency of the court; they saw that there was a determined spirit in the secret advisers of the

[45] After the defeat of Grey's motion, 256 to 91, Fox and most of his friends did, in fact, stay away from Parliament. Fox, for the most part, kept away from London at his seat at St. Anne's Hill. In December he and Sheridan came to the House, and Fox spoke on the Assessed Taxes Bill. His next recorded speech is the famous one of February 3, 1800, on the proposal of peace with Napoleon.

[46] Fox's old colleagues in opposition to Lord North in the years of the American Revolution.

crown to advance its power, and to encourage no administration that should not bend itself to that pursuit. Accordingly, through the whole reign, no administration which cherished notions of a different kind has been permitted to last, and nothing, therefore, or next to nothing, has been gained to the side of the people, but every thing to the crown in the course of the reign. During the whole of this period we have had no more than three administrations, one for twelve months, one for nine, and one for three months, that acted upon the popular principles of the early part of this century:[47] nothing, therefore, I say, has been gained to the people, while the constant current has run towards the crown; and God knows what is to be the consequence, both to the crown and country! I believe that we are come to the last moment of possible remedy. I believe that at this moment the enemies of both are few; but I firmly believe, that what has been seen in Ireland will be experienced also here; and that if we are to go on in the same career with convention bills and acts of exasperation of all kinds,[48] the few will soon become the many, and that we shall have to pay a severe retribution for our present pride. What a noble lord said some time ago of France, may be applicable to this very subject—"What!" said he, "negociate with France? With men whose hands are reeking with the blood of their sovereign? What, shall we degrade ourselves by going to Paris, and there asking in humble, diplomatic language, to be on a good understanding with them?"[49] Gentlemen will remember these lofty words; and yet we have come to this humiliation; we have negociated with France; and I should not be surprised to see the noble lord himself going to Paris, not at the head of his regiment, but on a diplomatic mission to those very regicides, to pray to be upon a good understanding with them. Shall we, then, be blind to the lessons which the events of the world exhibit to our view? Pride, obstinacy, and insult, must end in concessions, and those concessions must be humble in proportion to our unbecoming pride. Now is the moment to prevent all these degradations; the monarchy, the aristocracy, the people themselves, may now be saved; it is only necessary, at this moment, to conquer our own passions. Let those ministers, whose evil genius has brought us to our present condition, retire from the post to which they are unequal. I have no hesitation in saying, that the present administration neither can nor ought to remain in place; let them retire from his majesty's councils, and then let us, with an earnest desire of recovering the country, pursue this moderate scheme of reform, under the auspices of men who are likely to conciliate the opinion of the people.

I do not speak this, Sir, from personal ambition. A new administration ought to be formed: I have no desire, no wish, to make a part of any such administration; and I am sure that such an arrangement is feasible, and that it is capable of being done without me. My first and chief desire is to see this great end accomplished. I have no wish to be the person, or to be one of the persons, to do it; but though my inclination is for retirement, I shall always be ready to give my free and firm

[47] The first Rockingham administration (1765–1766); the Fox–North Coalition (1783); the second Rockingham administration (1782).

[48] Such as the Seditious Meetings Act and the Treasonable Practices Act of 1794. There is allusion also, perhaps, to the suppression of the convention of Delegates of the People "Associated to Obtain Universal Suffrage and Annual Parliaments" in Edinburgh in 1793.

[49] Hawkesbury (Robert Jenkinson, later second Earl of Liverpool) is quoted more or less thus in a debate on December 15, 1792 (*Parliamentary History*, XXX, 90).

support to any administration that shall restore to the country its outraged rights, and re-establish its strength upon the basis of free representation; and therefore, Sir, I shall certainly give my vote for the proposition of my honourable friend.

⌒

Bibliographical Note

An adequate modern biography of Fox is yet to be written. The least deficient is perhaps that by E. P. C. Lascelles (1936). Those by John Drinkwater (1928) and Christopher Hobhouse (1935) are quite readable. *The Early History of Charles James Fox* (1880) by George Otto Trevelyan is a fine piece of biographical writing, but it brings Fox only to 1774. The standard and best source is still Lord John Russell's *Memorials and Correspondence of Charles James Fox* (4 vols., 1853–1857). Erich Eyck, a strong partisan of Fox, often draws interesting comparisons in *Pitt Versus Fox: Father and Son 1735–1806* (1950). Aside from Goodrich's and that found in the biographies and histories, critical analysis of Fox's speaking is scarce. The most extensive is Loren D. Reid's published dissertation, *Charles James Fox* (Iowa City, 1932). Various more recent articles by Professor Reid illumine particular aspects of Fox, especially "The Education of Charles Fox," *Quarterly Journal of Speech*, XLIII (1957), 357–64. Hobhouse develops the traditional contrast between the orator and the debater in "Burke and Fox," in Bonamy Dobrée's *Anne to Victoria*. W. F. Rae, in *Wilkes, Sheridan, Fox; the Opposition under George III* (1874), offers interesting insights into Fox's speaking.

William Pitt, the Younger

(1759–1806)

The favorite son of the Earl of Chatham, and his successor in political and oratorical renown, William Pitt entered politics at the age of twenty-two with immense advantages of education, position, and example. In his short life of less than forty-seven years, he showed himself worthy of those initial advantages. He was prime minister for over twenty years, including the era of the French Revolution, the rise of Napoleon, serious troubles in Ireland, and the union of the English and Irish parliaments. Against the formidable phalanx of Burke, Fox, Sheridan, and others, he maintained a control over Parliament and a secure place in the favor of the public unequalled even by Sir Robert Walpole. It would appear that the conflict between Pitt and Fox was the most stable fact of British politics from 1782 until the common year of their death.

Young Pitt was educated under his father's care specifically for the public arena, and at Cambridge he applied himself especially to the style of the classical writers and the detailed comparison of speeches on opposing sides of the same questions. In London, he listened to the speakers with whom he was to contend during much of the rest of his life, studying how to refute the arguments he heard and how *he* might have made a better case had *he* been the speaker. By the time he reached public position, he had at the tip of his tongue resources of distinguished and elegant language, a spontaneous command of the structure and rhythms of oral prose, and a fund of available arguments on persistent public questions, which impressed all who heard him.

With legal study and some practice behind him, Pitt came into Parliament in 1781 on the side of Burke, Fox, and their friends, the Rockingham Whigs. He took up the popular causes: the defeat of Lord North; peace with America; resistance to the political influence of the crown; fiscal, economic, and electoral reform. At the death of the Marquis of Rockingham in July 1782, he cast his fortunes with his father's old associate, the Earl of Shelburne, who made him Chancellor of the Exchequer at the age of twenty-two. There began his great contest with Fox, and in late 1783 the king chose Pitt to lead the government— the youngest prime minister in history, but by this time far from a novice.

Pitt conducted his administration in the spirit of the economical, reforming liberalism with which he had entered Parliament, until the French Revolution frightened England into reaction. He extended the economic reforms begun by Burke; he improved fiscal efficiency; he provided for the responsible government of India; he supported Wilberforce's assault on the slave trade; and as we have seen in our discussion of Fox, he twice brought forward plans for making the House of Commons more justly representative.

In short, in a very few years he established himself as the personification of a new kind of businesslike, economical government, which seemed a happy reconciliation of the royal will with the popular power. His success for so long in getting his measures accepted by great majorities in Parliament and the public, in spite of calamitous blunders and repeated reverses in the war with France, attests to the confidence which the people of England maintained in him.

Though the Foxites could never seriously threaten Pitt's measures, they could harass him, and the attacks of Opposition drew from him many of his most powerful speeches. Such is that of June 1799, on the French war, which we print here. Through these regular parliamentary debates, Pitt undertook to give the English people the fullest possible reason for hating the enemy, for encouraging (and paying) England's allies and discounting their weaknesses, and for sustaining the ancient English devotion to freedom and security and orderly government—in short, for supporting his conduct of the war. The speech on the "Deliverance of Europe" is the most forthright and devastating of Pitt's condemnations of the government of Revolutionary France.

For the war against France, Pitt put together at great expense subsidized coalitions, only to have them collapse without victory. In 1799 he wanted the second coalition, including Austria and Russia (under the new Czar Paul, Catherine's successor), to invade and "liberate" Holland. The Czar was willing to provide troops for an adequate consideration. Consequently on June 7, 1799, Pitt asked Parliament for £825,000 with which to subsidize Russian troops.

He introduced the motion in a brief speech in which he referred to the money as "destined for the deliverance of Europe." George Tierney immediately opposed the motion on the ground that its purpose was vague. He seized upon the phrase "the deliverance of Europe" and demanded clarification and reassurance.

Tierney (1761–1830), a barrister, had entered Parliament in 1788 and had been re-elected from a different constituency in 1796 as an opponent of Pitt. He deeply offended his Foxite colleagues by refusing to secede with them in 1797. In the House of Commons he maintained his opposition to Pitt so persistently and undiscriminatingly that Pitt at length accused him of obstructionism and fought a duel with him. Tierney later served in the governments of Addington and Canning and became the leader of his party. In Tierney's part of the present debate we may discern both his grim oppositionism and his Fox-like talent for hitting the weak spot in Pitt's argument.

Pitt's reply to Tierney's initial attack, once interrupted by another speech from Tierney, is a complete condemnation of the French system and a vivid justification of the war—"we are at war with armed opinions." Though the available texts, of course, are abbreviated in the reporting, the reader may easily perceive in this speech the qualities most frequently noticed in Pitt's speaking—complete self-possession and a patronizing or contemptuous treatment of his opponent; a fine fluency of dignified and sonorous language; strong logical analysis and clear, lucid organization; pointed reply to an argument or plausible sidestepping; calculated and formidable invective supported by sarcasm rather than wit; absence of vivid imagery and of brilliant and memorable expression such as pervaded his father's eloquence. Pitt, like his father, had a fine voice and an impressive delivery; his pronunciation was clear and elegant; and these resources, brought to the service of his fluent and abundant language, no doubt help to account for the favorable impression which his speaking made on educated people over many years and on many subjects.

If Pitt, as one reads him, often seems pompous and wordy, one should consider that a man in his position, unlike his opponents, is often required to speak when there is nothing to say, or nothing which can be said safely or properly. He must speak even when to reveal his plans prematurely, or to be "candid with the public" in the way demanded by the Opposition, might well be disastrous to his political effectiveness or even hazardous to the country. When such a speaker has Pitt's talents for language and verbal architecture, the plausible outpouring of fine, reassuring oratory may be far more fitting to the needs of the occasion than silence or crabbed brevity.

Probably the central impression which Pitt left with his audiences is the following, in the words of the historian Lecky: "The young minister, in the moments of his most vehement declamation, was always essentially calm and collected." For that reason, no doubt, his opponents, and some of his later critics, declared that he had no strong feelings about anything. Lecky is probably more nearly right in concluding that "his complete mastery over himself was one of the greatest secrets of his influence over others" (*England in the Eighteenth Century*, V, 10).

Further study of Pitt's speeches should include his masterpiece on Wilberforce's motion against the slave trade, April 2, 1792; his explanation of the rupture of peace negotiations with France, November 10, 1797; his justification of refusal to negotiate with Napoleon (directly answered by Fox the same night), February 3, 1800; and his speech on the Act of Union of the British and Irish parliaments, April 21, 1800.

The Deliverance of Europe *

House of Commons
June 7, 1799

PITT: Considerable as is the augmentation of expense which a compliance with the recommendation in his majesty's message will occasion, I do not think it will be necessary to detain you with much argument in its support. I am persuaded that in proposing to adopt such resolutions as will enable his Majesty to carry into effect the intention which the auspicious situation of affairs promises to conduct to so happy a conclusion, I rather meet than lead the feelings of all who cherish those sentiments of manly resistance to the destructive principles which have so long scattered dismay and ruin over so large a portion of the civilized world: sentiments here never extinguished, and now so fortunately reviving in Europe.[1] I congratulate the House upon the glorious success which has marked the magnanimous efforts of that power, for whom the supply is destined for the deliverance of Europe. Embracing with joy the extensive views of enlarged benefit to Europe and to society, looking at the period as not far distant when we shall see the just balance of power restored, and ancient principles and lawful government again recognized, while you enjoy the pure triumph of having contributed so essentially in stemming the torrent which threatened to desolate society, I trust that you will not be so overjoyed at the favourable change, as to relax in the least degree from that deliberate resolution to maintain your own honour and independence, by your own exertions, which has already proved your salvation, and which can give you the best title and chance to be instrumental in the deliverance of Europe. That spirit, and those exertions, can alone qualify you to promote the welfare of others, and to secure your own rights. Even were the common cause to be again abandoned by your allies, were you again to see yourselves called upon to rely upon your own exertions, you will never forget that in the moment of difficulty and danger, you found safety where it is only to be found, in your own resolution, firmness and conduct. In this moment of exultation, while you embrace the interest of others with your own you will resolve to meet every danger rather than submit to any compromise with a power, the existence of which, with the character that belongs to it, and the principles by which it is actuated, is as incompatible with that of legitimate government in other states, as it is with happiness in the people who are subjected to its authority.

[Pitt then moved, "That a sum not exceeding 825,000l. be granted to his Majesty towards enabling his Majesty to make good such engagements with the emperor of Russia as may be best adapted to the exigency of affairs."]

TIERNEY: Sir, I admit the necessity of bringing the war to a speedy conclusion;

* Pitt's opening speech and Tierney's speeches are taken from the *Parliamentary History*, XXXIV, 1043–50. Pitt's main speeches are from the standard collection: *The Speeches of the Right Honourable William Pitt in the House of Commons*, ed. by W. S. Hathaway (4 vols.; London, 1806), III, 413–24.

[1] Pitt's expression of confidence in the new coalition could be supported by Czar Paul's apparent enthusiasm in helping organize it, his active participation in the revival of the war, especially in the Mediterranean, and the success of the Russians and Austrians in Italy in 1798–1799.

but in the mode by which it is proposed to be done, we hear of a common cause and a common understanding. Now, before I give my consent to vote away English money, I must know what the common cause is for which I do it. I do not know what this deliverance of Europe means. If it means to rescue other nations from the power and oppression of France, and to drive her from those countries which she has over-run, to such a plan I readily subscribe my mite of approbation. But if it is still to remain a principle undefined, I must pause before I give my consent. I would therefore wish to understand what this common cause is. Does it consist in repelling France within her ancient limits, and seeking an honourable peace upon the *status quo*? If so, I have no objection to a foreign subsidy, because I think money might be more economically applied abroad, than by raising forces at home; and because I wish, if more blood is to be shed, it should be any other than English blood. But if a subsidy is to be given for an indefinite object, what security have I for its application? How do I know that the views of Russia are in unison with our own?[2] How do I know that Russia will not apply it to the furtherance of her own interests without any regard to ours; that she has not views of ambition and aggrandizement herself; and may not think Europe delivered but by stripping France of her conquests, and decorating herself with the spoils? I own, Sir, this sum seems to me to be voted under very extraordinary circumstances, and leading to conclusions which I cannot easily reconcile. The deliverance of Europe must be equally dear to Russia as to England. Why then does not Russia contribute to the success of her own cause; and why is England to pay for the deliverance of Russia? Has Russia exhausted herself by the exertions which she has already made? As yet I know of nothing which she has contributed, except manifestoes and proclamations. Sir, I am anxious for the hour of peace; but however great my solicitude for its arrival, I would not wish, whenever that period shall happen, to look back and see, in the efforts made to attain it, any thing left undone, which might be cause for regret or mortification. To any expense or effort for this purpose, I give my cordial assent; but at no hazard can I give it to that system which I have uniformly reprobated; that system by which war has been protracted from day to day; millions have been expended upon millions, and blood has flowed upon blood, in the pursuit of an indefinite object. Sir, I hope and trust that, whatever differences may have hitherto subsisted, ministers now have but one opinion, and that they are all agreed that the safety of England should be the main object. Deeply impressed with this truth, I will not vote any sum for a purpose I do not understand, and in aid of a power whose object I do not know, which may be appropriated to her own views exclusively, and to the injury instead of the welfare of England.

PITT: I wish, Sir, to offer such an explanation on some of the topics dwelt upon by the honourable gentleman who just sat down, as will, I think, satisfy the committee[3] and the honourable gentleman. The nature of the engagement to which

[2] Englishmen had long been used to the principle of hiring mercenary armies and subsidizing allied armies. Pitt's father, for example, had both hired and subsidized extensively for the Seven Years' War; and the use of Hessians and other Germans against the American Colonies is well known. On the other hand, Tierney had plenty of plausible foundation in England's late experience with Catherine the Great for casting doubt on the motives of Russia. Czar Paul, however, seemed more amenable to England's leadership.

[3] The whole House acting as the Committee of Supply.

the message would pledge the house is simply, that, 1st, for the purpose of setting the Russian army in motion, we shall advance to that country 225,000*l.*, part of which by instalments, to accompany the subsidy to be paid when the army is in actual service. And I believe no one, who has been the least attentive to the progress of affairs in the world, who can appreciate worth, and admire superior zeal and activity, will doubt the sincerity of the sovereign of Russia, or make a question of his integrity in any compact. The 2d head of distribution is 75,000*l.* per month, to be paid at the expiration of every succeeding month of service; and, lastly, a subsidy of 37,500*l.* to be paid after the war, on the conclusion of a peace by common consent. Now, I think it strange that the honourable gentleman should charge us with want of prudence, while it cannot be unknown to him that the principal subsidies are not to be paid until the service has been performed, and that in one remarkable instance the present subsidy differs from every other, in as much as a part of it is not to be paid until after the conclusion of a peace by common consent.

I think gentlemen would act more consistently if they would openly give their opposition on the principle that they cannot support the war under any circumstances of the country and of Europe, than in this equivocal and cold manner to embarrass our deliberations, and throw obstacles in the way of all vigorous cooperation. There is no reason, no ground to fear that that magnanimous prince will act with infidelity in a cause in which he is so sincerely engaged, and which he knows to be the cause of all good government, of religion and humanity, against a monstrous medley of tyranny, injustice, vanity, irreligion, ignorance, and folly. Of such an ally there can be no reason to be jealous; and least of all have the honourable gentlemen opposite me grounds of jealousy, considering the nature and circumstances of our engagements with that monarch. As to the sum itself, I think no man can find fault with it. In fact, it is comparatively small. We take into our pay 45,000 of the troops of Russia, and I believe, if any gentleman will look to all former subsidies, the result will be, that never was so large a body of men subsidized for so small a sum. This fact cannot be considered without feeling that this magnanimous and powerful prince has undertaken to supply at a very trifling expense a most essential force, and that for *the deliverance of Europe.* I still must use this phrase, notwithstanding the sneers of the honourable gentleman. Does it not promise the deliverance of Europe, when we find the armies of our allies rapidly advancing in a career of victory at once the most brilliant and auspicious that perhaps ever signalized the exertions of any combination? Will it be regarded with apathy, that that wise and vigorous and exalted prince has already, by his promptness and decision, given a turn to the affairs of the continent? Is the House to be called upon to refuse succours to our ally, who, by his prowess, and the bravery of his arms, has attracted so much of the attention and admiration of Europe?

The honourable gentleman says he wishes for peace, and that he approved more of what I said on this subject towards the close of my speech, than of the opening. Now what I said was, that if by powerfully seconding the efforts of our allies, we could only look for peace with any prospect of realizing our hopes, whatever would enable us to do so promptly and effectually would be true economy. I must, indeed, be much misunderstood, if generally it was not perceived that I meant, that whether the period which is to carry us to peace be shorter or longer, what we have to look to is not so much when we make peace, as whether we shall derive from it complete and solid security; and that whatever other nations may do, whether they shall persevere in the contest, or untimely abandon it, we have to look to ourselves for the means of defence, we are to look to the means to secure our constitution, preserve our character, and maintain our independence, in the virtue and perseverance of the people. There is a high-spirited pride, an elevated loyalty, a generous warmth of heart, a nobleness of spirit, a hearty, manly gaiety, which distinguish our nation, in which we are to look for the best pledges of general safety, and of that security against an aggressing usurpation, which other nations in their weakness or in their folly have yet no where found.

With respect to that which appears so much to embarrass certain gentlemen—the deliverance of Europe—I will not say particularly what it is. Whether it is to be its deliverance from that under which it suffers, or that from which it is in danger; whether from the infection of false principles, the corroding cares of a period of distraction and dismay, or that dissolution of all governments, and that death of religion and social order which are to signalize the triumph of the French republic, if unfortunately for mankind she should, in spite of all opposition, prevail in the contest;—from whichsoever of these Europe is to be delivered, it will not be difficult to prove, that what she suffers, and what is her danger, are the power and existence of the French government. If any man says that the government is not a tyranny, he miserably mistakes the character of that body. It is an insupportable and odious tyranny, holding within its grasp the lives, the characters, and the fortunes of all who are forced to own its sway, and only holding these that it may at will measure out of each the portion, which from time to time it sacrifices to its avarice, its cruelty, and injustice. The French republic is dyked and fenced round with crime, and owes much of its present security to its being regarded with a horror which appals men in their approaches to its impious battlements.

The honourable gentleman says, that he does not know whether the Emperor of Russia understands what we mean by the deliverance of Europe. I do not think it proper here to dwell much at length on this curious doubt. But whatever may be the meaning which that august personage attaches to our phrase "the deliverance of Europe," at least he has shewn that he is no stranger to the condition of the world; that whatever be the specific object of the contest, he has learnt rightly to consider the character of the common enemy, and shews by his public proceedings that he is determined to take measures of more than ordinary precaution against the common disturbers of Europe, and the common enemy of man.

Will the honourable gentleman continue in his state of doubt? Let him look to the conduct of that prince during what has passed of the present campaign. If in such conduct there be not unfolded some solicitude for the deliverance of Europe from the tyranny of France, I know not, Sir, in what we are to look for it. But the honourable gentleman seems to think no alliance can long be preserved against France. I do not deny that unfortunately some of the nations of Europe have shamefully crouched to that power, and receded from the common cause, at a moment when it was due to their own dignity, to what they owed to that civilized community of which they are still a part, to persevere in the struggle, to reanimate their legions with that spirit of just detestation and vengeance which such inhumanity and cruelty might so well provoke. I do not say that the powers of Europe have not acted improperly in many other instances; and Russia in her turn; for, during a period of infinite peril to this country, she saw our danger advance upon us, and four different treaties entered into of offensive alliance against us, without comment, and without a single expression of its disapprobation. This was the conduct of that power in former times. The conduct of his present Majesty raises quite other emotions, and excites altogether a different interest. His Majesty, since his accession, has unequivocally declared his attachment to Great Britain, and, abandoning those projects of ambition which formed the occupation of his predecessor, he chose rather to join in the cause of religion and order against France, than to pursue the plan marked out for him to humble and destroy a power, which he was taught to consider as his common enemy. He turned aside from all hostility against the Ottoman Porte,[4] and united his force to the power of that prince, the more effectually to check the progress of the common enemy. Will, then, gentlemen continue to regard with suspicion the conduct of that prince? Has he not sufficiently shewn his devotion to the cause in which we are engaged, by the kind, and number, and value of his sacrifices, ultimately to prevail in the struggle against a tyranny which, in changing our point of vision, we every where find accompanied in its desolating progress by degradation, misery, and nakedness, to the unhappy victims of its power—a tyranny which has magnified and strengthened its powers to do mischief, in the proportion that the legitimate and venerable fabrics of civilized and polished society have declined from the meridian of their glory, and lost the power of doing good—a tyranny which strides across the ill-fated domain of France, its foot armed with the scythe of oppression and indiscriminate proscription, that touches only to blight, and rests only to destroy; the reproach and the curse of the infatuated people who still continue to acknowledge it. When we consider that it is against this monster the Emperor of Russia has sent down his legions, shall we say that he is not entitled to our confidence?

But what is the constitutional state of the question? It is competent, undoubtedly, to any gentleman to make the character of an ally the subject of consideration; but in this case it is not to the Emperor of Russia we vote a subsidy, but to his Majesty. The question, therefore, is, whether his Majesty's government affix any undue object to the message, whether they draw any undue inference from the deliverance of Europe. The honourable gentleman has told us, that his deliverance of Europe is the driving of France within her ancient limits—that he is not indifferent to the restoration of the other states of Europe to independence, as connected with the independence of this country; but it is assumed by the honourable gentleman, that we are not content with wishing to drive France within her ancient limits, that, on the contrary, we seek to overthrow the government of France; and he would make us say, that we never will treat with it as a republic.

Now I neither meant any thing like this, nor expressed myself so as to lead to such inferences. Whatever I may in the abstract think of the kind of government called a republic, whatever may be its fitness to the nation where it prevails, there may be times when it would not be dangerous to exist in its vicinity. But while the spirit of France remains what at present it is, its government despotic,

---

[4] England had resisted Catherine's encroachments on Turkey. Russia and Turkey were now allies in the coalition.

vindictive, unjust, with a temper untamed, a character unchanged, if its power
to do wrong at all remains, there does not exist any security for this country or
Europe.[5] In my view of security, every object of ambition and aggrandizement
is abandoned. Our simple object is security, just security, with a little mixture of
indemnification. These are the legitimate objects of war at all times; and when
we have attained that end, we are in a condition to derive from peace its benef-
icent advantages; but until then, our duty and our interest require that we should
persevere unappalled in the struggle to which we were provoked. We shall not
be satisfied with a false security. War, with all its evils, is better than a peace in
which there is nothing to be seen but usurpation and injustice, dwelling with
savage delight on the humble, prostrate condition of some timid suppliant people.
It is not to be dissembled, that in the changes and chances to which the fortunes
of individuals, as well as of states, are continually subject, we may have the misfortune, and great it would be, of seeing our allies decline the contest. I hope
this will not happen. I hope it is not reserved for us to behold the mortifying
spectacle of two mighty nations abandoning a contest, in which they have sacrificed so much, and made such brilliant progress.

In the application of this principle, I have no doubt but the honourable gentleman admits the security of the country to be the legitimate object of the contest;
and I must think I am sufficiently intelligible on this topic. But wishing to be
fully understood, I answer the honourable gentleman when he asks, "Does the
right honourable gentleman mean to prosecute the war until the French republic
is overthrown? Is it his determination not to treat with France while it continues
a republic?"—I answer, I do not confine my views to the territorial limits of France;
I contemplate the principles, character, and conduct of France; I consider what
these are; I see in them the issues of distraction, of infamy and ruin, to every state
in her alliance; and therefore I say, that until the aspect of that mighty mass of
iniquity and folly is entirely changed;—until the character of the government is
totally reversed;—until, by the common consent of the general voice of all men, I
can with truth tell parliament, France is no longer terrible for her contempt of the
rights of every other nation—she no longer avows schemes of universal empire—
she has settled into a state whose government can maintain those relations in their
integrity, in which alone civilized communities are to find their security, and
from which they are to derive their distinction and their glory;—until in the situation of France we have exhibited to us those features of a wise, a just, and a
liberal policy, I cannot treat with her. The time to come to the discussion of a
peace can only be the time when you can look with confidence to an honourable
issue; to such a peace as shall at once restore to Europe her settled and balanced
constitution of general polity, and to every negotiating power in particular, that
weight in the scale of general empire which has ever been found the best guarantee and pledge of local independence and general security.

Such are my sentiments. I am not afraid to avow them. I commit them to the
thinking part of mankind; and if they have not been poisoned by the stream of
French sophistry, and prejudiced by her falsehood, I am sure they will approve
of the determination I have avowed, for those grave and mature reasons on which

---

[5] Napoleon was about to seize supreme power in France. Pitt, however, is speaking
of the revolutionary governments of the previous ten years.

I found it. I earnestly pray that all the powers engaged in the contest may think as I do, and particularly the Emperor of Russia, which, indeed, I do not doubt; and therefore I do contend, that with that power it is fit that the house should enter into the engagement recommended in his Majesty's message.

TIERNEY: I have received an answer, and it does carry the conviction, that we are now about to embark in a seventh year of the war, aiming at an indefinite object, warring against system, and fighting with English blood and English treasure, against French abstract principles, without the smallest regard to the burthened state of the country. The right hon. gentleman has spoken out. It is not merely against the power of France he struggles, but her system; not merely to repel her within her ancient limits, but to drive her back from her present to her ancient opinions—to such a style of thinking as may effect the deliverance of Europe. The result is, that we are to go on until the government of France is overthrown. The right hon. gentleman admits, that the republic may be placed in a situation in which it will not be dangerous to the liberty of Europe: and when a peace may be concluded with it in safety, but it is not until the mode of thinking on which the republic is founded shall be overthrown.

It is impossible to connect France and liberty together. No man more detests her than I do. I feel the greatest indignation at her perfidy and deceit, her pretence of delivering surrounding nations from tyranny, and ruling them, when in her power, like the most ferocious despot. With these sentiments, I am not afraid of being suspected of partiality for France. Sir, liberty has suffered much from the extravagant friends of it. I own I loved the principle of the revolution in its commencement, and therefore I may be allowed to lament the more the direction which its progress has taken. The question is not, I admit, whether this or that boundary shall be the limit of the country, but what shall most contribute to peace and tranquillity. My opinion then is, that France, driven back to any thing like her ancient limits, will not be any thing like what she was in strength and power. I believe the case of France is like that of all other bad governments. I believe, left to prey upon herself, France would be more in danger from internal discontent and dissention than from all the troops and armies that can be sent against them. But, admitting we are to wait until opinion shall be overthrown in France, how will the right hon. gentleman be able to ascertain the arrival of that period? I know some gentlemen enter sanguine expectations of overthrowing the government of France. My whole object, on the contrary, in the present state, is to contend for England, and England alone. I do not mean to say that she must be a disinterested observer of what is passing in the world; but I think the real interests of England would be found more in the exercise of her own virtue and perseverance. To this I would add another attribute, her good sound sense. I believe this will soon show itself. I believe the good sense of the people of England will not be willing to engage them in every attempt in which the right hon. gentleman is about to engage. It is not the spirit of this country to impose a government on France; and there is no good sense in engaging in a crusade against the rights and liberties of others. I know it will be said, they are not rights, but extravagant and dangerous principles. Here, then, the right hon. gentleman and they are at issue. May they not entertain the same ideas of a government which they understand fosters designs hostile to the liberty of others? and if so, who is to be the arbiter between them? For my part, I know of no security but the limited relative power of nations. In the crippled state of her marine, France has lost much of her power.[6] The wisdom which I wish to see displayed is, that which consists in knowing where to stop, and when France is sufficiently reduced. If the object of the minister had been to unite the other powers of Europe in confederacy for the purpose of diminishing the extensive and overgrown power of France, I do believe an extraordinary effort might have produced that effect; but now that we are confessedly at war against undefined principles and opinions,[7] what security have I that voting a sum of money will facilitate the attainment of the end proposed. At the efforts of Austria in Switzerland I rejoice; and I hope the Emperor will not, in rescuing it from France, purloin for himself. But does the right hon. gentleman believe, that when the Austrian arms have advanced to France, they will not find the French soldier very different on his own ground from what he was on a conquered soil? Does he not believe, that the moment a French foot is placed on this soil, all party and all difference will subside, and one unanimous wish alone fill every breast to rally round the government, and repel the invader? I do think a prospect is now opened to our view, which may be followed up with infinite advantage. The French by pillage and tyranny, have so disgusted all nations, that it might be very practicable to drive them back within their ancient limits. If that were the right hon. gentleman's view, I should readily support him; but that is not the case. The right hon. gentleman has disappointed my hopes: I thank him for his explanation; but having heard it, I cannot vote any subsidy for foreign service.

Pitt: Sir, I cannot agree to the interpretation the honourable gentleman has thought proper to give to parts of my speech. He has supposed that I said, we persevere in the war, and increase our activity, and extend our alliances, to impose a government on another country, and to restore monarchy to France. I never once uttered any such intention. What I said was, and the house must be in the recollection of it, that the France which now exists, affords no promise of security against aggression and injustice in peace, and is destitute of all justice and integrity in war. I observed also, and I think the honourable gentleman must agree with me when I repeat it, that the character and conduct of that government must enter into the calculation of security to other governments against wrong, and for the due and liberal observance of political engagements. The honourable gentleman says, that he has too much good sense, and that every man must have too much good sense, to suppose that territorial limits can, of themselves, be made to constitute the security of states. He does well to add his sanction to a doctrine that is as old as political society itself. In the civilized and regular community, states find their mutual security against wrong, not in territory only; they have the guarantee of fleets, of armies, of acknowledged integrity, and tried good faith; it is to be judged of by the character, the talents, and the virtues of the men who guide the councils of states, who are the advisers of princes: but what is it in the situation of the French republic, on which can be founded a confidence which is to be in itself some proof that she can afford security against wrong? She has

---

[6] In the summer of 1798 Nelson had destroyed the French Mediterranean fleet at the Battle of the Nile, and Napoleon had had to abandon his victorious army in Egypt.

[7] Pitt seized upon this statement for one of his strongest pieces of refutation. See below.

territory, she has the remains of a navy, she has armies; but what is her character as a moral being? who is there to testify her integrity? The Swiss nation! [8]—Who bears testimony to her good faith? The states she has plundered, under the delusive but captivating masks of deliverers from tyranny!—What is the character of her advisers? what the aspect of her councils? They are the authors of all that misery, the fountain-head of all those calamities, which, marching by the side of an unblushing tyranny, have saddened and obscured the fairest and the gayest portions of Europe, which have deformed the face of nature wherever their pestiferous genius has acquired an ascendancy. In fine, we are to look for security from a government which is constantly making professions of different kinds of sentiments, and is constantly receding from every thing it professes;—a government that has professed, and in its general conduct still manifests, enmity to every institution and state in Europe, and particularly to this country, the best regulated in its government, the happiest in itself, of all the empires that form that great community.

Having said thus much on those matters, I shall now shortly notice a continued confusion in the honourable gentleman's ideas. On another occasion he could not understand what I meant by the deliverance of Europe; and in this second effort of his inquisitive mind he is not more happy. He tells us, he cannot see any thing in the present principles of France but mere abstract metaphysical dogmas. What are those principles which guided the arms of France in their unprincipled attack on the independence of Switzerland, which the honourable gentleman has reprobated? Was the degradation, without trial, of the members of the assemblies of France—were, in short, those excesses, and that wickedness, in the contemplation of which the honourable gentleman says he first learnt to regard France as an odious tyranny—will he class the principles which could lead to all these things with the mere metaphysical obstructions of heated, over-zealous theorists? He will still persist, at least he has given the promise of considerable resistance to all arguments to the contrary, in saying that we have an intention to wage war against opinion. It is not so. We are not in arms against the opinions of the closet, nor the speculations of the school. We are at war with armed opinions; we are at war with those opinions which the sword of audacious, unprincipled, and impious innovation [9] seeks to propagate amidst the ruins of empires, the demolition of the altars of all religion, the destruction of every venerable, and good, and liberal institution, under whatever form of polity they have been raised; and this, in spite of the dissenting reason of men, in contempt of that lawful authority which, in the settled order, superior talents and superior virtues attain, crying out to them not to enter on holy ground, nor to pollute the stream of eternal justice;—admonishing them of their danger, whilst, like the genius of evil, they mimic their voice, and, having succeeded in drawing upon them the ridicule of the vulgar, close their day of wickedness and savage triumph with the massacre and waste of whatever is amiable, learned, and pious, in the districts they have over-run. Whilst the principles avowed by France, and acted upon so wildly, held their legitimate place, confined to the circles of a few ingenious

---

[8] On the pretext of supporting a people's equalitarian movement among certain of the Swiss, French armies had occupied the country in 1798 and treated Switzerland as conquered territory administered from Paris by the Directory.

[9] See note on "innovation," above, p. 257.

and learned men;—whilst these men continued to occupy those heights which vulgar minds could not mount;—whilst they contented themselves with abstract inquiries concerning the laws of matter or the progress of mind, it was pleasing to regard them with respect; for, while the simplicity of the man of genius is preserved untouched, if we will not pay homage to his eccentricity, there is, at least, much in it to be admired.[10] Whilst these principles were confined in that way, and had not yet bounded over the common sense and reason of mankind, we saw nothing in them to alarm, nothing to terrify; but their appearance in arms changed their character. We will not leave the monster to prowl the world unopposed. He must cease to annoy the abode of peaceful men. If he retire into the cell, whether of solitude or repentance, thither we will not pursue him; but we cannot leave him on the throne of power.

I shall now give some farther instances of the confusion of the honourable gentleman's ideas. He says, that the French republic and liberty cannot exist together: therefore, as a friend to liberty, he cannot be a friend to France. Yet he tells us almost in the same breath, that he will not vote for any thing that does not tend to secure the liberties of that country, though, to give him the benefit of his own proposition, not to wish the overthrow of France is not to wish for the preservation of English liberty. Indeed, he says, he will vote nothing for the purpose of overthrowing that tyranny, or, as he very strangely adds, the rights and liberties of others—the rights and liberties of France! But how will the gentleman maintain his character for consistency, while he will not vote for any measure that seeks to overthrow the power of a government, in the contemplation of which he has discovered a gulf in his mind between the ideas of its existence and the existence of liberty? It never, however, entered his mind to say that he made the overthrow of the French republic the *sine qua non.*

Here another example arises of that confusion of ideas into which, contrary to his usual custom, the honourable gentleman has fallen this evening:—he says he is one of those who think, that a republic in France is not contrary to the safety of other countries, and not incongruous to the state of France itself. How strange is this! whilst we have it from the honourable gentleman, that liberty and the French republic cannot exist together. I am ready to say, that if the republican regimen was characterized by the sobriety of reason, affording nourishment, strength, and health to the members of the community; if the government was just and unambitious, as wisdom and sound policy dictate; if order reigned in her senates, morals in the private walk of life, and in their public places there were to be found the temples of their God, supported in dignity, and resorted to with pious awe and strengthening veneration by the people, there would be in France the reality of a well-regulated state, under whatever denomination, but *obruit male partum, male retentum, male gestum imperium.*[11] Whilst republican France continues what it is, then I make war against republican France; but if I should see any chance of the return of a government that did not threaten to

---

[10] Pitt refers to Rousseau and to the so-called *"philosophes"* of the early part of the century, who promulgated the doctrine of the "rights of man" and other theories about society and government which were taken up by the engineers of the Revolution.

[11] Pitt adapted the quotation from the Roman historian Livy (ix.34.2–3): "quam obruerent eum male parta, male gesta, male retenta imperia," which is translated, "until he was overwhelmed by his ill-gotten, ill-administered, and ill-continued powers" (trans. B. O. Foster, Loeb Classical Library ed., IV, 290).

endanger the existence of other governments, far be it from me to breathe hostility to it. I must first see this change of fortune to France and to Europe make its progress with rapid and certain steps, before I relax in the assertion of those rights, which, dearer to Britons than all the world, because by them better understood and more fully enjoyed, are the common property, the links of union of the regular governments of Europe. I must regard as an enemy, and treat as such, a government which is founded on those principles of universal anarchy, and frightful injustice, which, sometimes awkwardly dissembled, and sometimes insolently avowed, but always destructive, distinguish it from every other government of Europe.

[The motion passed without a division.]

～

BIBLIOGRAPHICAL NOTE

Earl Stanhope's *Life of the Right Honourable William Pitt* (4 vols., 1861–1862; 3rd ed., 3 vols., 1879) is a primary biographical resource based on the correspondence. The standard biography, in two parts, is that by J. Holland Rose: *William Pitt and the National Revival* (1911) and *William Pitt and the Great War* (1911). The biography by Lord Roseberry (1904) is also valuable. A more recent work of sharp penetration is D. G. Barnes's *George III and William Pitt 1783–1806* (1939). Erick Eyck in *Pitt Versus Fox: Father and Son 1735–1806* shows strong partisanship for Fox. Goodrich's is still the most comprehensive criticism of Pitt's speaking, but see Lloyd Watkins, "After Goodrich: . . . William Pitt," *Quarterly Journal of Speech*, XLVIII (1962), 7–10. For a brief character miniature see P. H. M. Bryant's essay in Bonamy Dobrée's *Anne to Victoria*. A minor but important aspect of Pitt's achievement is treated in Alan M. Rees, "Pitt and the Achievement of Abolition," *Journal of Negro History*, XXXIX (1954), 167–84.

Lord Thomas Erskine

(1794–1823)

The English jurist, William Norman Lord Birkett, spoke in 1961 of Lord Erskine's place in history:

> Thomas Erskine was the greatest advocate who ever practised at the English Bar. I cannot help regretting that he ever entered the House of Commons, or that he left the Bar to become Lord Chancellor. In Parliament he was a failure, and Romilly, the great legal reformer, voiced the general view of Erskine as Lord Chancellor, when he said: "His incapacity for the office was too forcibly and generally felt." From 1778, when he made his first speech before the great Lord Mansfield, to the day, twenty-eight years later, when he took his seat on the Woolsack, he had no rival and no challenger.

It is even doubtful that Erskine has ever had a peer among all English-speaking advocates.

Erskine's courtroom delivery was more animated and direct than was common among pleaders of his day. His manner was quick, considerate, and, for the time, informal. But his unique strength as a legal pleader derived from his total devotion to the interests of each client, his astute identification of the most advantageous point for adjudication in each case, and his unequalled powers of extemporaneous composition. Under his management, all forces of communication were made to clarify and to render inviting some just and expedient rule for decision making. Few attorneys have achieved comparable mastery over thought, feeling, language, and behavior in unswerving service of immediate persuasion.

The effects of Erskine's phenomenal successes with judges and jurors were sometimes historic. In defending Lord George Gordon he won a judgment that established *intent* as an essential criterion in determining the guilt of defendants charged with high treason. His defense of James Hadfield introduced humane and realistic considerations into legal judgments of the criminally insane. Though he lost his case in behalf of William Shipley, Dean of Asaph, charged with seditious libel, his arguments furnished content and justifications for the Libel Act of 1792, which established the rights of juries to judge the quality of alleged libel as well as the fact of its publication. And it was Erskine for the defense who, in a succession of treason trials involving Thomas Walker, Thomas Hardy, John Horne Tooke, and James Thelwall, broke the repression of speech and press with which William Pitt's government sought in 1794 to strangle reformist movements.

Erskine was twenty-eight when called to the English Bar in 1778. He had served as an enlisted sailor and as an officer in the First Royal Regiment of Foot and spent three years in concurrent enrollment at Lincoln's Inn and Trinity College, Cambridge. Of the quality of his education, little is known beyond the fact that he studied his profession under Sir Francis Buller and Sir George Wood, both able pleaders, that he participated in debates at Coachmakers' Hall in London, and that he acquired a wide knowledge of English literature. Somewhere, too, he learned the art of great pleading. A mere five months after he was admitted to the Bar, a speech on behalf of Captain Thomas Baillie established his reputation and assured his immediate professional success. That he was credited with winning Captain Baillie's acquittal on charges of libel is the more remarkable since he was but a junior counsellor in the case and was not expected to speak at all.

Published accounts of court actions indicate that from 1778 to 1795 Erskine appeared in court at an average rate of twice a week. His specialties became damage suits against persons charged with criminal conversation (adultery) and the defense of persons charged with libel; on occasion, he accepted briefs for the defense in adultery cases and for the prosecution in libel cases. There are tolerably reliable records of his greatest forensic arguments: his defenses in the court-martial of Admiral Keppel (1779) and the libel cases of the Dean of Asaph (1784), John Stockdale (1789), Thomas Paine (1792), and the *Morning Chronicle* (1793); his pleas in defense of Lord George Gordon (1781), John Frost (1793), Thomas Hardy (1794), and James Thelwall (1794) against charges of treason; his defense of Richard Bingham (1794) against charges of criminal conversation and his prosecution of John Fawcett (1802) on the same charge; his prosecution of Thomas Williams for blasphemous libel against the Christian religion through publishing Paine's *Age of Reason*, Part II (1797);

and his defense of Hadfield (1800). Each is a superior example of forensic art.

Erskine entered the House of Commons in 1783 as a supporter of Charles James Fox. He was never a leader in the House, nor is his name associated with any great legislative decision except the enactment of Fox's Libel Act of 1792. In 1806, he became Lord Chancellor for the brief tenure of Grenville's All-the-Talents Ministry. Whatever the merits of his service in the Chancellorship, none can deny that the final third of Erskine's life, spent in office and in the House of Lords, compared feebly with the eventful, constructive years in which he served as an advocate.

The defense of James Hadfield was the last of Erskine's major pleas in a great state trial. On the night of May 15, 1800, Hadfield discharged a pistol loaded with two slugs at King George III, as the king stepped forward in his box just before a command performance of Cibber's *She Would and She Would Not* at Drury Lane Theater. The shots missed the king. Hadfield was taken from his place in the second row of the pit to be questioned in the "music room" beneath the stage before being imprisoned. His trial was held in a small, crowded courtroom in Westminster Hall.

〜

In Behalf of Hadfield *

Court of King's Bench
June 26, 1800

Gentlemen of the Jury: The scene which we are engaged in, and the duty which I am not merely *privileged*, but *appointed* by the authority of the court to perform, exhibits to the whole civilized world a perpetual monument of our national justice.[1]

The transaction, indeed, in every part of it, as it stands recorded in the evidence already before us, places our country, and its government, and its inhabitants, upon the highest pinnacle of human elevation. It appears that, upon the 15th day of May last, his Majesty, after a reign of forty years, not merely in sovereign power, but spontaneously in the very hearts of his people, was openly shot at (or to all appearance shot at) in a public theater [Drury Lane], in the center of his capital, and amid the loyal plaudits of his subjects, *yet not a hair of the head of the supposed assassin was touched*. In this unparalleled scene of calm forbear-

---

* *Rex. v. Hadfield*; Lord Kenyon presiding, assisted by Justices Grose, Laurence, and LeBlanc. Attorney General Sir John Mitford headed the Crown Counsel. Counsel assigned to the prisoner: Thomas Erskine and Serjeant William Draper Best. The record of the trial appears in *State Trials*, comp. T. B. and Thomas J. Howell (38–40 Geo. III) (London, 1820), XXVII, 1281–1356. The text printed here was recorded by Gurney, the ablest shorthand writer of the day. It was probably edited by Erskine, and was published in *State Trials, ibid.*, 1307–30. Goodrich later reprinted the text with modernized punctuation and critical notes in *Select British Eloquence* (pp. 766–77). We present Goodrich's text with additional notes.

[1] Goodrich draws attention to the felicity of these remarks on the judicial system. Ironically, the special protections Erskine praises were repealed soon after this trial. Those charged with treason were thereafter treated as persons charged with murder.

ance, the King himself, though he stood first in personal interest and feeling, as well as in command, was a singular and fortunate example. The least appearance of emotion on the part of that august personage must unavoidably have produced a scene quite different, and far less honorable than the court is now witnessing. But his Majesty remained unmoved, and the person *apparently* offending was only secured, without injury or reproach, for the business of this day.

Gentlemen, I agree with the Attorney General[2] (indeed, there can be no possible doubt) that if the same pistol had been maliciously fired by the prisoner, in the same theater, at the meanest man within its walls, he would have been brought to immediate trial, and, if guilty, to immediate execution. He would have heard the charge against him for the first time when the indictment was read upon his arraignment. He would have been a stranger to the names, and even to the existence, of those who were to sit in judgment upon him, and of those who were to be the witnesses against him. But upon the charge of even this murderous attack upon the King himself, he is covered all over with the armor of the law.[3] He has been provided with counsel by the King's own judges, and not of *their* choice, but of *his own*.[4] He has had a copy of the indictment ten days before his trial. He has had the names, descriptions, and abodes of all the jurors returned to the court; and the highest privilege of peremptory challenges derived from, and safely directed by that indulgence.[5] He has had the same description of every witness who could be received to accuse him; and there must at this hour be *twice* the testimony against him which would be legally competent to establish his guilt on a similar prosecution by [in behalf of] the meanest and most helpless of mankind.

Gentlemen, when this melancholy catastrophe happened, and the prisoner was arraigned for trial, I remember to have said to some now present, that it was, at first view, difficult to bring those indulgent exceptions to the general rules of trial within the principle which dictated them to our humane ancestors in cases of treasons against the political government, or of *rebellious* conspiracy against the person of the King. In these cases, the passions and interests of great bodies of powerful men being engaged and agitated, a counterpoise became necessary to give composure and impartiality to criminal tribunals; but a *mere murderous* attack upon the King's person, not at all connected with his political character, seemed a case to be ranged and dealt with like a similar attack upon any private man.

But the wisdom of the law is greater than any man's wisdom; how much more, therefore, than mine! An attack upon the King is considered to be parricide against the state, and the jury and the witnesses, and even the judges, are the

[2] Sir John Mitford, afterward Lord Redesdale, and Lord Chancellor of Ireland. (Goodrich.)

[3] Only those charged with high treason were so protected.

[4] By 7 William III, cap. 3, sec. 1, a person charged with high treason is allowed to make his defense by counsel, not exceeding two in number, to be selected by himself and assigned by the court. (Goodrich.) At his preliminary hearing, Hadfield had requested Erskine and Best as counsel.

[5] On a trial for high treason, the prisoner is allowed a peremptory challenge of thirty-five jurors; that is, one under the number of three full juries. This is the effect of 1 and 2 Philip and Mary, cap. 10, sec. 7. (Goodrich.) Erskine used twenty challenges in this case.

children. It is fit, on that account, that there should be a solemn pause before we rush to judgment; and what can be a more sublime spectacle of justice than to see a statutable disqualification of a whole nation for a limited period, a fifteen days' *quarantine* before trial, lest the mind should be subject to the contagion of partial affections!

From a prisoner so protected by the benevolence of our institutions, the utmost good faith would, on his part, be due to the public if he had consciousness and reason to reflect upon the obligation. The duty, therefore, devolves on *me*; and, *upon my honor,* it shall be fulfilled. I will employ no artifices of speech. I claim only the strictest protection of the law for the unhappy man before you. I should, indeed, be ashamed if I were to say any thing of the rule *in the abstract* by which he is to be judged, which I did not honestly feel; I am sorry, therefore, that the subject is so difficult to handle with brevity and precision. Indeed, if it could be brought to a clear and simple criterion, which could admit of a dry admission or contradiction, there might be very little difference, *perhaps none at all,* between the Attorney General and myself, upon the principles which ought to govern your verdict. But this is not possible, and I am, therefore, under the necessity of submitting to you, and to the judges, for their direction (and at greater length than I wish), how I understand this difficult and momentous subject.

The law, as it regards this most unfortunate infirmity of the human mind, like the law in all its branches, aims at the utmost degree of precision; but there are some subjects, as I have just observed to you, and the present is one of them, upon which it is extremely difficult to be precise. The general principle is clear, but the application is most difficult.

It is agreed by all jurists, and is established by the law of this and every other country, that it is the *reason of man* which makes him accountable for his actions; and that the deprivation of reason acquits him of crime. This principle is indisputable; yet so fearfully and wonderfully are we made, so infinitely subtle is the spiritual part of our being, so difficult is it to trace with accuracy the effect of diseased intellect upon human action, that I may appeal to all who hear me, whether there are any causes more difficult, or which, indeed, so often confound the learning of the judges themselves, as when insanity, or the effects and consequences of insanity, become the subjects of legal consideration and judgment. I shall pursue the subject as the Attorney General has properly discussed it. I shall consider insanity, as it annuls a man's dominion over property, as it dissolves his contracts, and other acts, which otherwise would be binding, and as it takes away his responsibility for crimes. If I could draw the line in a moment between these two views of the subject, I am sure the judges will do me the justice to believe that I would fairly and candidly do so; but great difficulties press upon my mind, which oblige me to take a different course.

I agree with the Attorney General, that the law, in neither civil nor criminal cases, will measure the degrees of men's understandings. A *weak* man, however much below the ordinary standard of human intellect, is not only responsible for crimes, but is bound by his contracts, and may exercise dominion over his property. Sir Joseph Jekyll, in the Duchess of Cleveland's case, took the clear, legal distinction, when he said, "The law will not measure the sizes of men's capacities, so as they be *compos mentis.*" [6]

[6] Mitford's contention was traditional: a defendant must be unable "to form a judgement of that which he proposed to do, of that which he did, and of that which he had designed," else he was responsible for his crimes.

Lord Coke, in speaking of the expression *non compos mentis*, says, "Many times (as here) the Latin word expresses the true sense, and calleth him not *amens*, *demens*, *furiosus*, *lunaticus*, *fatuus*, *stultus*, or the like, for *non compos mentis* is the most sure and legal." He then says, "*Non compos mentis* is of four sorts: first, *ideota* [an idiot], which from his nativity, by a perpetual infirmity, is *non compos mentis*; secondly, he that by sickness, grief, or other accident, wholly loses his memory and understanding; thirdly, a lunatic that hath sometimes his understanding, and sometimes not; *aliquando gaudet lucidis intervallis* [has sometimes lucid intervals]; and, therefore, he is called *non compos mentis* so long as he hath not understanding."

But notwithstanding the precision with which this great author points out the different kinds of this unhappy malady, the nature of his work, in this part of it, did not open to any illustration which it can now be useful to consider. In his fourth Institute he is more particular; but the admirable work of Lord Chief Justice Hale, in which he refers to Lord Coke's pleas of the Crown, renders all other authorities unnecessary.

Lord Hale says, "There is a partial insanity of mind, and a total insanity. The former is either in respect to things, *quoad hoc vel illud insanire* [to be insane as to this or that]. Some persons that have a competent use of reason in respect of some subjects, are yet under a particular *dementia* [deprivation of reason] in respect of some particular discourses, subjects, or applications; or else it is partial in respect of *degrees*; and this is the condition of very many, especially melancholy persons, who for the most part discover their defect in excessive fears and griefs, and yet are not wholly destitute of the use of reason; and this partial insanity seems not to excuse them in the committing of any offense for its matter capital. For, doubtless, most persons that are felons of themselves and others, are under a degree of partial insanity when they commit these offenses. It is very difficult to define the invisible line that divides perfect and partial insanity; but it must rest upon circumstances duly to be weighed and considered both by judge and jury, lest on the one side there be a kind of inhumanity toward the defects of human nature; or, on the other side, too great an indulgence given to great crimes."

Nothing, gentlemen, can be more accurately nor more humanely expressed; but the application of the rule is often most difficult. I am bound, besides, to admit that there is a wide distinction between civil and criminal cases. If, in the former, a man appears, upon the evidence, to be *non compos mentis,* the law avoids his act, though it can not be traced or connected with the morbid imagination which constitutes his disease, and which may be extremely partial in its influence upon conduct; but to deliver a man from responsibility for *crimes,* above all, for crimes of great atrocity and wickedness, I am by no means prepared to apply this rule, however well established when property only is concerned.

In the very recent instance of Mr. Greenwood (which must be fresh in his Lordship's recollection), the rule in civil cases was considered to be settled. That gentleman, while insane, took up an idea that a most affectionate brother had administered poison to him. Indeed, it was the prominent feature of his insanity. In a few months he recovered his senses. He returned to his profession as an advocate; was sound and eminent in his practice, and in all respects a most intelligent and useful member of society; but he could never dislodge from his mind the morbid delusion which disturbed it; and under the pressure, no doubt, of that diseased prepossession, he disinherited his brother. The cause to avoid this will was tried here. We are not now upon the evidence, but upon the principle adopted as the law. The noble and learned judge, who presides upon this trial, and who presided upon that, told the jury, that if they believed Mr. Greenwood, when he made the will, to have been *insane,* the will could not be supported, whether it had disinherited his brother or not; that the act, no doubt, strongly confirmed the existence of the false idea which, if believed by the jury to amount to *madness,* would equally have affected his testament, if the brother, instead of being disinherited, had been in his grave; and that, on the other hand, if the unfounded notion did not amount to madness, its influence could not vacate the devise.[7] This principle of law appears to be sound and reasonable, as it applies to civil cases, from the extreme difficulty of tracing with precision the secret motions of a mind, deprived by disease of its soundness and strength.

Whenever, therefore, a person may be considered *non compos mentis,* all his *civil* acts are void, whether they can be referred or not, to the morbid impulse of his malady, or even though, to all *visible appearances,* totally separated from it. But I agree with Mr. Justice Tracey, that it is not every man of an idle, frantic appearance and behavior, who is to be considered as a lunatic, either as it regards obligations or crimes; but that he must appear to the jury to be *non compos mentis,* in the legal acceptation of the term; and that, not at any anterior period, which can have no bearing upon any case whatsoever, but at *the moment* when the contract was entered into, or the crime committed.

The Attorney General, standing undoubtedly upon the most revered authorities of the law, has laid it down that to protect a man from *criminal* responsibility, there must be a *TOTAL deprivation of memory and understanding.* I admit that this is the very expression used, both by Lord Coke and by Lord Hale; but the true interpretation of it deserves the utmost attention and consideration of the court. If a total deprivation of memory was intended by these great lawyers to be taken in the *literal* sense of the words; if it was meant, that, to protect a man from punishment, he must be in such a state of prostrated intellect as not to know his name, nor his condition, nor his relation toward others—that if a husband, he should not know he was married; or, if a father, could not remember that he had children, nor know the road to his house, nor his property in it—then no such madness ever existed in the world. It is *IDIOCY* alone which places a man in this helpless condition; where, from an *original* mal-organization, there is the human frame alone without the human capacity; and which, indeed, meets the very definition of Lord Hale himself, when, referring to Fitzherbert, he says, "Idiocy, or fatuity *a nativitate, vel dementia naturalis,* is such a one as described by Fitzherbert, who knows not to tell twenty shillings, nor knows his own age, or who was his father." But in all the cases which have filled Westminster Hall with the most complicated considerations [8]—the lunatics, and other insane persons who have been the subjects of them, have not only had memory, in my sense of the expression—they have not only had the most perfect knowledge and recollections of all the relations they stood in toward others, and of the acts and circumstances of their lives, but have, in general, been remarkable for subtlety and acuteness. Defects in their reasonings have seldom been traceable—the disease consisting in the delusive sources of thought; all their deductions within the scope of

---

[7] The jury in that case found for the will; but after a contrary verdict in the Common Pleas, a compromise took place. (Goodrich.)

[8] The Courts of Common Pleas and of Exchequer also sat in Westminster Hall.

the malady being founded upon the *immovable* assumption of matters as *realities*, either without any foundation whatsoever, or so distorted and disfigured by fancy as to be almost nearly the same thing as their creation. It is true, indeed, that in some, perhaps in many cases, the human mind is stormed in its citadel, and laid prostrate under the stroke of frenzy; these unhappy sufferers, however, are not so much considered, by physicians, as maniacs, but to be in a state of delirium as if from fever. There, indeed, all the ideas are overwhelmed—for reason is not merely disturbed, *but driven wholly from her seat.* Such unhappy patients are unconscious, therefore, except at short intervals, even of external objects; or, at least, are wholly incapable of considering their relations. Such persons, *and such persons alone* (except idiots), *are wholly deprived of their UNDERSTAND-INGS,* in the Attorney General's seeming sense of that expression. But these cases are not only extremely rare, but never can become the subjects of judicial difficulty. There can be but one judgment concerning them. In other cases, reason is not driven from her seat, but distraction sits down upon it along with her, holds her, trembling, upon it, and frightens her from her propriety.[9] Such patients are victims to delusions of the most alarming description, which so over-power the faculties, and usurp so firmly the place of realities, as not to be dis-lodged and shaken by the organs of perception and sense: in such cases the images frequently vary, but in the same subject are generally of the same terrific char-acter. Here, too, no judicial difficulties can present themselves; for who could balance upon the judgment to be pronounced in cases of such extreme disease? Another class, branching out into almost infinite subdivisions, under which, in-deed, the former, and every case of insanity, may be classed, is, where the delu-sions are not of that frightful character, but infinitely various and often extremely *circumscribed;* yet where imagination (*within the bounds of the malady*) still holds the most uncontrollable dominion over reality and fact. These are the cases which frequently mock the wisdom of the wisest in judicial trials; because such persons often reason with a subtlety which puts in the shade the ordinary con-ceptions of mankind. Their conclusions are just, and frequently profound; but the premises from which they reason, *when within the range of the malady,* are uniformly false—not false from any defect of knowledge or judgment, but be-cause a delusive image, the inseparable companion of real insanity, is thrust upon the subjugated understanding, incapable of resistance, because unconscious of attack.

Delusion, therefore, where there is no frenzy or raving madness, is the true character of insanity. Where it can not be predicated of a man standing for life or death for a crime, he ought not, in my opinion, to be acquitted; and if courts of law were to be governed by any other principle, every departure from sober, rational conduct would be an emancipation from criminal justice. I shall place my claim to your verdict upon no such dangerous foundation. I must convince you, not only that the unhappy prisoner was a lunatic, within my own definition of lunacy, but that the act in question was the *immediate, unqualified offspring of the disease.* In *civil* cases, as I have already said, the law avoids every act of the lunatic during the period of the lunacy, although the delusion may be ex-

---

[9] "And *frights* the isle from her *propriety.*" *Othello,* II, 3. The reader cannot fail to remark the strength and beauty of the images used here, and in other passages above and below to describe the different kinds of madness. (Goodrich.)

tremely circumscribed; although the mind may be quite sound in all that is not within the shades of the very partial eclipse; and although the act to be avoided can in no way be connected with the influence of the insanity—but to deliver a lunatic from responsibility to *criminal* justice, above all in a case of such atrocity as the present, the relation between the disease and the act should be apparent. Where the connection is doubtful, the judgment should certainly be most indulgent, from the great difficulty of diving into the secret sources of a disordered mind; but still, I think that, as a doctrine of law, *the delusion and the act should be connected.*[10]

You perceive, therefore, gentlemen, that the prisoner, in naming me for his counsel, has not obtained the assistance of a person who is disposed to carry the doctrine of insanity in his defense so far as even books would warrant me in carrying it. Some of the cases—that of Lord Ferrers,[11] for instance—which I shall consider hereafter, as distinguished from the present—would not, in my mind, bear the shadow of an argument, as a defense against an indictment for murder. I can not allow the protection of insanity to a man who only exhibits violent passions and malignant resentments, acting upon *real circumstances;* who is impelled to evil by no morbid delusions; but who proceeds upon the ordinary perceptions of the mind. I can not consider such a man as falling within the protection which the law gives, and is bound to give, to those whom it has pleased God, for mysterious causes, to visit with this most afflicting calamity.

He alone can be so emancipated, whose disease (call it what you will) consists, not merely in seeing with a prejudiced eye, or with odd and absurd particularities, differing, in many respects, from the contemplations of sober sense, upon the actual existence of things; but *he only,* whose reasoning and corresponding conduct, though governed by the ordinary dictates of reason, proceed upon something which has no foundation or existence.

Gentlemen, it has pleased God so to visit the unhappy man before you; to shake his reason in its citadel; to cause him to build up as realities the most impossible phantoms of the mind, and to be impelled by them as motives *irresistible:* the whole fabric being nothing but the unhappy vision of his disease—existing nowhere else—having no foundation whatsoever in the very nature of things.

Gentlemen, it has been stated by the Attorney General, and established by evidence which I am in no condition to contradict, nor have, indeed, any interest in contradicting, that, when the prisoner bought the pistol which he discharged at or *toward* his Majesty, he was well acquainted with the nature and use of it; that, as a soldier, he could not but know, that in his hands it was a sure instrument of death; that, when he bought the gunpowder, he knew it would prepare the pistol for its use; that, when he went to the playhouse, he knew he was going there, and knew every thing connected with the scene, as perfectly as any other person. I freely admit all this; I admit, also, that every person who listened to his conversation, and observed his deportment upon his apprehension, must have given precisely the evidence delivered by his Royal Highness the Duke of York, and

[10] Erskine defines his task with seeming rigidity but adopts a standard of sufficiency in proof far more favorable to the prisoner than traditional interpretations of insanity allowed.

[11] The Attorney General had cited this precedent as proof that any "competent degree of reason" in a criminal rendered him subject to the full force of law.

that nothing like insanity appeared to those who examined him.[12] But what then? I conceive, gentlemen, that *I* am more in the habit of examination than either that illustrious person or the witnesses from whom you have heard this account. Yet I well remember (indeed, I never can forget it), that since the noble and learned Judge has presided in this court, I examined, for the greater part of a day, in this very place, an unfortunate gentleman, who had indicted a most affectionate brother, together with the keeper of a mad-house at Hoxton [Dr. Sims], for having imprisoned him as a lunatic, while, according to his evidence, he was in his perfect senses. I was, unfortunately, not instructed in what his lunacy consisted, although my instructions left me no doubt of the fact; but, not having the clue, he completely foiled me in every attempt to expose his infirmity. You may believe that I left no means unemployed which long experience dictated, but without the smallest effect. The day was wasted, and the prosecutor, by the most affecting history of unmerited suffering, appeared to the judge and jury, and to a humane English audience, as the victim of the most wanton and barbarous oppression. At last Dr. Sims came into court, who had been prevented, by business, from an earlier attendance, and whose name, by-the-by, I observe to-day in the list of the witnesses for the Crown. From Dr. Sims I soon learned that the very man whom I had been above an hour examining, and with every possible effort which counsel are so much in the habit of exerting, believed himself to be *the Lord and Savior of mankind*; not merely at the time of his confinement, which was alone necessary for my defense, but during the whole time that he had been triumphing over every attempt to surprise him in the concealment of his disease! I then affected to lament the indecency of my ignorant examination, when he expressed his forgiveness, and said, with the utmost gravity and emphasis in the face of the whole court, *"I am the Christ"*; and so the cause ended. Gentlemen, this is not the only instance of the power of concealing this malady. I could consume the day if I were to enumerate them; but there is one so extremely remarkable, that I can not help stating it.

Being engaged to attend the assizes at Chester upon a question of lunacy, and having been told that there had been a memorable case tried before Lord Mansfield [13] in this place, I was anxious to procure a report of it. From that great man himself (who, within these walls, will ever be reverenced, being then retired, in his extreme old age, to his seat near London, in my own neighborhood) I obtained the following account of it: "A man of the name of Wood," said Lord Mansfield, "had indicted Dr. Monro for keeping him as a prisoner (I believe in the same mad-house at Hoxton) when he was sane. He underwent the most severe examination by the defendant's counsel without exposing his complaint; but Dr. Battye, having come upon the bench by me, and having desired me to ask him what was become of the PRINCESS whom he had corresponded with in cherry-juice, he showed in a moment what he was. He answered, that there was

---

[12] Witnesses for the Crown were interrogated after Mitford's address and before Erskine spoke. These witnesses had testified that Hadfield had intelligently discussed his pistol, gunpowder, and his plan to attend a play—all on the day of the shooting. Neither Erskine nor Best challenged the Crown's emphasis on Hadfield's seeming rationality. Erskine did draw from the Duke of York testimony that the prisoner had said he wished to die and sought death through threatening the king.

[13] William Murray, first Earl of Mansfield; Lord Chief Justice, 1756–1788; said to have encouraged Erskine to enter law.

nothing at all in that, because, having been (as every body knew) imprisoned in a high tower, and being debarred the use of ink, he had no other means of correspondence but by writing his letters in cherry-juice, and throwing them into the river which surrounded the tower, where the Princess received them in a boat. There existed, of course, no tower, no imprisonment, no writing in cherry-juice, no river, no boat; but the whole the inveterate phantom of a morbid imagination. I immediately," continued Lord Mansfield, "directed Dr. Monro to be acquitted. But this man, Wood, being a merchant in Philpot Lane, and having been carried through the City in his way to the mad-house, he indicted Dr. Monro over again, for the trespass and imprisonment *in London,* knowing that he had lost his cause by speaking of the Princess at Westminster. And such," said Lord Mansfield, "is the extraordinary subtlety and cunning of madmen, that when he was cross-examined on the trial in London, as he had successfully been before, in order to expose his madness, all the ingenuity of the bar, and all the authority of the court, could not make him say a syllable upon that topic, which had put an end to the indictment before, although he still had the same indelible impression upon his mind, as he signified to those who were near him; but, conscious that the delusion had occasioned his defeat at Westminster, he obstinately persisted in holding it back." [14]

Now, gentlemen, let us look to the application of these cases. I am not examining, for the present, whether either of these persons ought to have been acquitted, if they had stood in the place of the prisoner now before you. That is quite a distinct consideration, which we shall come to hereafter. The direct application of them is only this, that if I bring before you such evidence of the prisoner's insanity as, *if believed to have really existed,* shall, in the opinion of the court, as the rule for your verdict in point of law, be sufficient for his deliverance, then that you ought not to be shaken in giving full credit to such evidence, notwithstanding the report of those who were present at his apprehension, who describe him as discovering no symptom whatever of mental incapacity or disorder. For I have shown you that insane persons frequently appear in the utmost state of ability and composure, even in the highest paroxysms of insanity, except when frenzy is the characteristic of the disease.[15] In this respect, the cases I have cited to you have the most decided application, because they apply to the overthrow of the whole of the evidence (admitting, at the same time, the truth of it), by which the prisoner's case can alone be encountered.

But it is said that whatever delusions may overshadow the mind, every person ought to be responsible for crimes *who has the knowledge of good and evil.*[16] I think I can presently convince you, that there is something too general in this mode of considering the subject; and you do not, therefore, find any such proposition in the language of the celebrated writer alluded to by the Attorney General in his speech. Let me suppose that the character of an insane delusion consisted in the belief that some given person was any brute animal, or an inanimate being (and such cases have existed), and that upon the trial of such a lunatic for murder, you firmly, upon your oaths, were convinced, upon the uncontradicted evi-

[14] The evidence at Westminster was then proved against him by the shorthand writer. (Goodrich.)

[15] Two physicians, examined after Erskine's address, corroborated Erskine's generalization and called Hadfield's such a case.

[16] The Attorney General had made much of this principle.

dence of a hundred persons, that he believed the man he had destroyed to have been a potter's vessel. Suppose it was quite impossible to doubt that fact, *although to all other intents and purposes he was sane;* conversing, reasoning, and acting, as men not in any manner tainted with insanity, converse, and reason, and conduct themselves. Let me suppose further, that he believed the man whom he destroyed, but whom he destroyed as a potter's vessel, to be the property of another; and that he had malice against such supposed person, and that he meant to injure him, knowing the act he was doing to be malicious and injurious, and that, in short, he had full knowledge of all the principles of good and evil. Yet it would be possible to convict such a person of murder, if, from the influence of his disease, he was ignorant of the relation he stood in to the man he had destroyed, and was utterly *unconscious* that he had struck at the life of a human being. I only put this case, and many others might be brought as examples to illustrate that the knowledge of good and evil is too general a description.

I really think, however, that the Attorney General and myself do not, in substance, very materially differ. From the whole of his most able speech, taken together, his meaning may, I think, be thus collected; that where the act which is criminal, is done under the dominion of malicious mischief and wicked intention, although such insanity might exist in a corner of the mind, as might avoid the acts of the delinquent as a lunatic in a *civil* case, yet that he ought not to be protected, if malicious mischief, and not insanity, had impelled him to the act for which he was *criminally* to answer; because, in such a case, the act might be justly ascribed to malignant motives, and not to the dominion of disease. I am not disposed to dispute such a proposition, in a case which would apply to it, and I can well conceive such cases may exist. The question, therefore, which you will have to try, is this: Whether, when this unhappy man discharged the pistol in a direction which convinced, and ought to convince, every person that it was pointed at the person of the King, he meditated mischief and violence to his Majesty, or whether he came to the theater (*which it is my purpose to establish*) under the dominion of the most melancholy insanity that ever degraded and overpowered the faculties of man. I admit that when he bought the pistol, and the gunpowder to load it, and when he loaded it, and came with it to the theater, and lastly, when he discharged it; every one of these acts would be overt acts of compassing the King's death, if at all or *any* of these periods he was actuated by that *mind and intention,* which would have constituted murder in the case of an individual, supposing the individual had been actually killed. I admit, also, that the mischievous, and, in this case, traitorous intention must be inferred from all these acts, unless *I can rebut the inferences by proof.* If I were to fire a pistol toward you, gentlemen, where you are now sitting, the act would undoubtedly infer the malice. *The whole proof, therefore, is undoubtedly cast upon ME.*

In every case of treason, or murder, which are precisely the same, except that the unconsummated intention in the case of the King is the same as the actual murder of a private man, the jury must impute to the person whom they condemn by their verdict, *the motive* which constitutes the crime. And your province to-day will, therefore, be to decide whether the prisoner, when he did the act, was under the uncontrollable dominion of insanity, and was impelled to it by a *morbid delusion;* or whether it was the act of a man who, though occasionally mad, or even at the time not perfectly collected, was yet not actuated by the disease, but by the suggestion of a wicked and malignant disposition.

I admit, therefore, freely, that if, after you have heard the evidence which I hasten to lay before you, of the state of the prisoner's mind,[17] and close up to the very time of this catastrophe, you shall still not feel yourselves clearly justified in negativing the wicked motives imputed by this indictment, I shall leave you in the hands of the learned judges to declare to you the law of the land, and shall not seek to place society in a state of uncertainty by any appeal addressed only to your compassion. I am appointed by the court to claim for the prisoner the full protection of the law, but not to misrepresent it in his protection.

Gentlemen, the facts of this melancholy case lie within a narrow compass.

The unfortunate person before you was a soldier. He became so, I believe, in the year 1793—and is now about twenty-nine years of age. He served in Flanders, under the Duke of York, as appears by his Royal Highness's evidence; and being a most approved soldier, he was one of those singled out as an orderly man to attend upon the person of the Commander-in-Chief. You have been witnesses, gentlemen, to the calmness with which the prisoner has sitten in his place during the trial. There was but one exception to it. You saw the emotion which overpowered him when the illustrious person now in court took his seat upon the bench. Can you then believe, from the evidence, for I do not ask you to judge as physiognomists, or to give the rein to compassionate fancy; but can there be any doubt that it was the generous emotion of the mind, on seeing the Prince, under whom he had served with so much bravery and honor? Every man, certainly, must judge for himself. I am counsel, not a witness, in the cause. But it is a most striking circumstance, as you find from the Crown's evidence, that when he was dragged through the orchestra under the stage, and charged with an act for which he considered his life as forfeited, he addressed the Duke of York with the same enthusiasm which has marked the demeanor I am adverting to. Mr. Richardson,[18] who showed no disposition in his evidence to help the prisoner, but who spoke with the calmness and circumspection of truth, and who had no idea that the person he was examining was a lunatic, has given you the account of the burst of affection on his first seeing the Duke of York, against whose father and sovereign he was supposed to have had the consciousness of treason. The King himself, whom he was supposed to have so malignantly attacked, never had a more gallant, loyal, or suffering soldier. His gallantry and loyalty will be proved; his sufferings speak for themselves.

About five miles from Lisle, upon the attack made on the British army, this unfortunate soldier was in the fifteenth light dragoons, in the thickest of the ranks, exposing his life for his Prince, whom he is supposed to-day to have sought to murder. The first wound he received is most materially connected with the subject we are considering; you may see the effect of it now.[19] The point of a sword was impelled against him with all the force of a man urging his horse in battle. When the court put the prisoner under my protection, I thought it my

[17] Defense witnesses later testified that Hadfield had talked and acted wildly between May 11 and 14, but appeared rational on May 15.

[18] John Richardson had been present at Hadfield's interrogation in the theater. He testified for the Crown.

[19] Mr. Erskine put his hand on the prisoner's head, who stood by him at the bar of the court. (Goodrich.)

duty to bring Mr. Cline [20] to inspect him in Newgate. It will appear by the evidence of that excellent and conscientious person, who is known to be one of the first anatomists in the world, that from this wound one of two things must have happened: either, that by the immediate operation of surgery the displaced part of the skull must have been taken away, or been forced inward on the brain. The second stroke, also, speaks for itself: you may now see its effects. [Here Mr. Erskine touched the head of the prisoner.] He was cut across all the nerves which give sensibility and animation to the body, and his head hung down almost dissevered, until by the act of surgery it was placed in the position you now see it. But thus, almost destroyed, he still recollected his duty, and continued to maintain the glory of his country, when a sword divided the membrane of his neck where it terminates in the head; yet he still kept his place, though his helmet had been thrown off by the blow which I secondly described, when by another sword he was cut into the very brain—you may now see its membrane uncovered. Mr. Cline will tell you that he examined these wounds, and he can better describe them. I have myself seen them, but am no surgeon; from his evidence you will have to consider their consequences. It may be said that many soldiers receive grievous wounds without their producing insanity. So they may, undoubtedly; but we are upon *the fact*. There was a discussion the other day, whether a man who had been seemingly hurt by a fall beyond remedy could get up and walk. The people around said it was impossible; but he did get up and walk, and so there was an end to the impossibility. The effects of the prisoner's wounds were known by the *immediate* event of insanity, and Mr. Cline will tell you that it would have been strange, indeed, if any other event had followed. We are not here upon a case of insanity arising from the spiritual part of man, as it may be affected by hereditary taint, by intemperance, or by violent passions, the operations of which are various and uncertain; but we have to deal with a species of insanity more resembling what has been described as idiocy, proceeding from original malorganization. *There* the disease is, from its very nature, *incurable;* and so where a man (like the prisoner) has become insane from *violence to the brain, which permanently affects its structure,* however such a man may appear occasionally to others, his disease is *immovable.* If the prisoner, therefore, were to live a thousand years, he *never* could recover from the consequence of that day.

But this is not all. Another blow was still aimed at him, which he held up his arm to avoid, when his hand was cut into the bone. It is an afflicting subject, gentlemen, and better to be spoken of by those who understand it; and, to end all further description, he was then thrust almost through and through the body with a bayonet, and left in a ditch among the slain.

He was afterward carried to a hospital, where he was known by his tongue to one of his countrymen, who will be examined as a witness, who found him, not merely as a wounded soldier deprived of the powers of his body, but bereft of his senses forever.

He was affected from the very beginning with that species of madness which, from violent agitation, fills the mind with the most inconceivable imaginations,

---

[20] Henry Cline, a well-known surgeon, later testified that though Hadfield's wounds could produce recurring periods of insanity, the prisoner might sometimes seem "in every respect rational" during those periods.

wholly unfitting it for all dealing with human affairs, according to the sober estimate and standard of reason. He imagined that he had constant intercourse with the Almighty Author of all things; that the world was coming to a conclusion; and that, like our blessed Savior, he was to *sacrifice himself for its salvation*. So obstinately did this morbid image continue, that you will be convinced he went to the theater to perform, as he imagined, that blessed sacrifice; and, because he would not be guilty of suicide, though called upon by the imperious voice of Heaven, he wished that by the appearance of crime his life might be taken away from him by others. This bewildered, extravagant species of madness appeared immediately after his wounds, on his first entering the hospital; and on the very same account he was discharged from the army on his return to England, which the Attorney General very honorably and candidly seemed to intimate.

To proceed with the proofs of his insanity *down to the very period of his supposed guilt*. This unfortunate man before you is the father of an infant of eight months; and I have no doubt, that if the boy had been brought into court (but this is a grave place for the consideration of justice, and not a theater for stage effect)—I say, I have no doubt whatever, that if this poor infant had been brought into court, you would have seen the unhappy father wrung with all the emotions of parental affection. Yet, upon the Tuesday preceding the Thursday when he went to the playhouse, you will find his disease still urging him forward, with the impression *that the time was come* when he must be destroyed for the benefit of mankind; and in the confusion, or, rather, delirium of this wild conception, he came to the bed of the mother, who had this infant in her arms, and endeavored to dash out its brains against the wall. The family was alarmed; and the neighbors being called in, the child was, with difficulty, rescued from the unhappy parent, who, in his madness, would have destroyed it.[21]

Now let me, for a moment, suppose that he had succeeded in the accomplishment of his insane purpose; and the question had been, whether he was guilty of murder. Surely, the affection for this infant, up to the very moment of his distracted violence, would have been conclusive in his favor. But not more so than his loyalty to the King, and his attachment to the Duke of York, as applicable to the case before us; yet at that very period, even of extreme distraction, he conversed as rationally on all other subjects as he did with the Duke of York at the theater. The prisoner knew perfectly that he was the husband of the woman and the father of the child. The tears of affection ran down his face at the very moment that he was about to accomplish its destruction. During the whole of this scene of horror, he was not at all deprived of memory, in the Attorney General's sense of the expression; he could have communicated, at that moment, every circumstance of his past life, and every thing connected with his present condition, *except only the quality of the act he was meditating*. In *that*, he was under the overruling dominion of a morbid imagination, and conceived that he was acting against the dictates of nature in obedience to the superior commands of Heaven, which had told him, that the moment he was dead, and the infant with him, all nature was to be changed, and all mankind were to be redeemed by his dissolution. There was not an idea in his mind, from the beginning to the end, of the destruction of the King. On the contrary, he always maintained his

---

[21] An army surgeon, fellow soldiers, and members of Hadfield's family later corroborated the details of this and preceding paragraphs.

loyalty—lamented that he could not go again to fight his battles in the field; and it will be proved, that only a few days before the period in question, being present when a song was sung, indecent, as it regarded the person and condition of his Majesty, he left the room with loud expressions of indignation, and immediately sang "God save the King," with all the enthusiasm of an old soldier, who had bled in the service of his country.

I confess to you, gentlemen, that this last circumstance, which may, to some, appear insignificant, is, in my mind, most momentous testimony. For if this man had been in the habit of associating with persons inimical to the government of our country, so that mischief might have been fairly argued to have mixed itself with madness (which, by-the-by, it frequently does); if it could in any way have been collected that, from his disorder, more easily inflamed and worked upon, he had been led away by disaffected persons to become the instrument of wickedness; if it could have been established that such had been his companions and his habits, I should have been ashamed to lift up my voice in his defense.[22] I should have felt that, however his mind might have been weak and disordered, yet if his understanding sufficiently existed to be methodically acted upon as an instrument of malice, I could not have asked for an acquittal. But you find, on the contrary, in the case before you, that, notwithstanding the opportunity which the Crown has had, and which, upon all such occasions, it justly employs to detect treason, either against the person of the King or against his government, *not one witness* has been able to fix upon the prisoner before you any one companion, of even a doubtful description, or any one expression from which disloyalty could be inferred, while the whole history of his life repels the imputation. His courage in defense of the King and his dominions, and his affection for his son, in such unanswerable evidence, all speak aloud against the presumption that he went to the theater with a mischievous intention.

To recur again to the evidence of Mr. Richardson, who delivered most honorable and impartial testimony. I certainly am obliged to admit, that what a prisoner says for himself, when coupled at the very time with an overt act of wickedness, is no evidence whatever to alter the obvious quality of the act he has committed. If, for instance, I, who am now addressing you, had fired the same pistol toward the box of the King, and, having been dragged under the orchestra and secured for criminal justice, I had said that I had no intention to kill the King, but was weary of my life, and meant to be condemned as guilty; would any man, who was not himself insane, consider that as a defense? Certainly not: because it would be without the whole foundation of the prisoner's previous condition, part of which it is even difficult to apply closely and directly by strict evidence, without taking his undoubted insanity into consideration, because it is his unquestionable insanity which alone stamps the effusions of his mind with sincerity and truth.

The idea which had impressed itself, but in most confused images, upon this unfortunate man, was, *that he must be destroyed, but ought not to destroy himself.* He once had the idea of firing over the King's carriage in the street; but then he

---

[22] The Crown did not charge Hadfield with revolutionary intentions, but the first newspaper and magazine reports of the shooting had suggested there might be a revolutionary conspiracy. Erskine therefore needed to absolve his client of association with any "treasonous" groups.

imagined he should be immediately killed, which was not the mode of propitiation for the world. And as our Savior, before his passion, had gone into the garden to pray, this fallen and afflicted being, after he had taken the infant out of bed to destroy it, returned also to the garden, saying, as he afterward said to the Duke of York, "that all was not over—that a great work was to be finished"; and there he remained in prayer, the victim of the same melancholy visitation.

Gentlemen, these are the facts, freed from even the possibility of artifice or disguise; because the testimony to support them will be beyond all doubt. In contemplating the law of the country, and the precedents of its justice to which they must be applied, I find nothing to challenge or question. I approve of them throughout. I subscribe to all that is written by Lord Hale. I agree with all the authorities cited by the Attorney General, from Lord Coke; but above all, I do most cordially agree in the instance of convictions by which he illustrated them in his able address.[23] I have now lying before me the case of Earl Ferrers: unquestionably there could not be a shadow of doubt, and none appears to have been entertained, of his guilt. I wish, indeed, nothing more than to contrast the two cases; and so far am I from disputing either the principle of that condemnation, or the evidence that was the foundation of it, that I invite you to examine whether any two instances in the whole body of the criminal law are more diametrically opposite to each other than the case of Earl Ferrers and that now before you. Lord Ferrers was divorced from his wife by act of Parliament; and a person of the name of Johnson, who had been his steward, had taken part with the lady in that proceeding, and had conducted the business in carrying the act through the two Houses. Lord Ferrers consequently wished to turn him out of a farm which he occupied under him; but his estate being in trust, Johnson was supported by the trustees in his possession. There were, also, some differences respecting coal-mines; and in consequence of both transactions, Lord Ferrers took up the most violent resentment against him. Let me here observe, gentlemen, that this was not a resentment founded upon any *illusion;* not a resentment forced upon a distempered mind by fallacious images, but depending upon *actual circumstances and real facts;* and, acting like any other man under the influence of malignant passions, he repeatedly declared that he would be revenged on Mr. Johnson, particularly for the part he had taken in depriving him of a contract respecting the mines.

Now, suppose Lord Ferrers could have showed that no difference with Mr. Johnson had ever existed regarding his wife at all—that Mr. Johnson had never been his steward—and that he had only, from delusion, believed so when his situation in life was quite different. Suppose, further, that an *illusive imagination* had *alone* suggested to him that he had been thwarted by Johnson in his contract for these coal-mines, there never having been any contract at all for coal-mines—in short, that the whole basis of his enmity was without any foundation in nature, and had been shown to have been a *morbid image* imperiously fastened upon his mind. Such a case as that would have exhibited a character of insanity

---

[23] The reader will remark, that in the cases which Mr. Erskine goes on to consider, the statement of the facts is not only clear and beautiful in itself, but is shaped throughout with a particular reference to the case of Hadfield, so as to bring out the points of contrast in strong relief, and thus open the way for the distinctions which follow. This kind of *preparation* is one of Mr. Erskine's greatest excellences. (Goodrich.)

in Lord Ferrers extremely different from that in which it was presented by the evidence to his peers. Before them, he only appeared as a man of turbulent passions, whose mind was disturbed by no fallacious images of things without existence; whose quarrel with Johnson was founded *upon no illusions,* but upon existing facts; whose resentment proceeded to the fatal consummation with all the ordinary indications of mischief and malice; and who conducted his own defense with the greatest dexterity and skill. *Who, then, could doubt that Lord Ferrers was a murderer?* When the act was done, he said, "I am glad I have done it. He was a villain, and I am revenged." But when he afterward saw that the wound was probably mortal, and that it involved consequences fatal to himself, he desired the surgeon to take all possible care of his patient; and, conscious of his crime, kept at bay the men who came with arms to arrest him: showing, from the beginning to the end, nothing that does not generally accompany the crime for which he was condemned. He was proved, to be sure, to be a man subject to unreasonable prejudices, addicted to absurd practices, and agitated by violent passions. But the act was not done under the dominion of uncontrollable disease; and whether the mischief and malice were substantive, or marked in the mind of a man whose passions bordered upon, or even amounted to insanity, it did not convince the Lords that, under all the circumstances of the case, he was not a fit object of criminal justice.

In the same manner, Arnold,[24] who shot at Lord Onslow, and who was tried at Kingston soon after the Black Act[25] passed on the accession of George I. Lord Onslow having been very vigilant as a magistrate in suppressing clubs, which were supposed to be set on foot to disturb the new government, Arnold had frequently been heard to declare that Lord Onslow would ruin his country; and although he appeared from the evidence to be a man of most wild and turbulent manners, yet the people round Guildford, who knew him, did not, in general, consider him to be insane. His counsel could not show that any morbid *delusion* had ever overshadowed his understanding. They could not show, as I shall, that just before he shot at Lord Onslow, he had endeavored to destroy his own beloved child. It was a case of *human resentment.*

I might instance, also, the case of Oliver, who was indicted for the murder of Mr. Wood, a potter, in Staffordshire. Mr. Wood had refused his daughter to this man in marriage. My friend, Mr. Milles, was counsel for him at the assizes. He had been employed as a surgeon and apothecary by the father, who forbid him his house, and desired him to bring in his bill for payment; when, in the agony of disappointment, and brooding over the injury he had suffered, on his being admitted to Mr. Wood to receive payment, he shot him upon the spot. The trial occupied great part of the day; yet, for my own part, I can not conceive that there was any thing in the case for a jury to deliberate on. He was a man acting upon *existing facts,* and upon *human resentments* connected with them.

[24] In the Edward Arnold (1724) case which Mitford had cited it was held that to be acquitted on the ground of insanity "a prisoner must be a madman . . . totally deprived of his understanding and memory," knowing no more "than an infant, than a brute, or a wild beast." W. C. J. Meredith, *Insanity as a Criminal Defence* (Montreal, 1931), p. 118.

[25] The Black Act (1722) was aimed at poachers who blackened their faces or otherwise disguised themselves; nonetheless, Arnold, who was not disguised, was tried under this Act for trying to kill Lord Onslow.

He was at the very time carrying on his business, which required learning and reflection, and, indeed, a reach of mind beyond the ordinary standard, being trusted by all who knew him as a practitioner in medicine. Neither did he go to Mr. Wood's under the influence of *illusion;* but he went to destroy the life of a man who was placed exactly in the circumstances [in] which the mind of the criminal represented him. He went to execute vengeance on him for refusing his daughter. In such a case there might, no doubt, be passion approaching to frenzy; but there wanted that characteristic of madness to emancipate him from criminal justice.

There was another instance of this description in the case of a most unhappy woman, who was tried, in Essex, for the murder of Mr. Errington, who had seduced and abandoned her and the children she had borne to him. It must be a consolation to those who prosecuted her, that she was acquitted, as she is at this time in a most undoubted and deplorable state of insanity. But I confess, if I had been upon the jury who tried her, I should have entertained great doubts and difficulties; for, although the unhappy woman had before exhibited strong marks of insanity, arising from grief and disappointment, yet she acted upon *facts* and *circumstances* which had an *existence,* and which were calculated, upon the ordinary principles of human action, to produce the most violent resentment. Mr. Errington having just cast her off, and married another woman, or taken his [her?] under his protection, her jealousy was excited to such a pitch as occasionally to overpower her understanding; but when she went to Mr. Errington's house, where she shot him, she went with the express and deliberate purpose of shooting him. That fact was unquestionable. She went there with a resentment long rankling in her bosom, bottomed on an existing foundation. She did not act under a *delusion,* that he had deserted her when he had not, but took revenge upon him for an actual desertion. But still the jury, in the humane consideration of her sufferings, pronounced the insanity to be predominant over resentment, and they acquitted her.

But let me suppose (which would liken it to the case before us) that she had never cohabited with Mr. Errington; that she never had had children by him, and, consequently, that he neither had, nor could possibly have deserted or injured her. Let me suppose, in short, that she had never seen him in her life, but that her resentment had been founded on the morbid delusion that Mr. Errington, who had never seen her, had been the author of all her wrongs and sorrows; and that, under that *diseased* impression, she had shot him. If that had been the case, gentlemen, she would have been acquitted upon the opening, and no judge would have sat to try such a cause. The *act itself* would have been decisively characteristic of madness, because, being founded upon nothing existing, it could not have proceeded from malice, which the law requires to be charged and proved, in every case of murder, as the foundation of a conviction.

Let us now recur to the cause we are engaged in, and examine it upon those principles by which I am ready to stand or fall, in the judgment of the court. You have a man before you who will appear, upon the evidence, to have received those almost deadly wounds which I described to you, producing the immediate and immovable effects which the eminent surgeon, whose name I have mentioned, will prove that they could not but have produced. It will appear that, from that period, he was visited by the severest paroxysms of madness, and was repeatedly confined with all the coercion which it is necessary to practice upon lunatics; yet, what is quite decisive against the imputation of treason against the person of the King, his loyalty never forsook him. Sane or insane, it was his very characteristic to love his Sovereign and his country, although the delusions which distracted him were sometimes, *in other respects,* as contradictory as they were violent.

Of this inconsistency, there was a most striking instance on only the Tuesday before the Thursday in question, when it will be proved that he went to see one Truelet,[26] who had been committed by the Duke of Portland as a lunatic. This man had taken up an idea that our Savior's second advent, and the dissolution of all human beings, were at hand; and conversed in this strain of madness. This mixing itself with the insane delusion of the prisoner, he immediately broke out upon the subject of his own propitiation and sacrifice for mankind, although only the day before he had exclaimed that the Virgin Mary was a whore; that Christ was a bastard; that God was a thief; and that he and this Truelet were to live with him at White Conduit House, and there to be enthroned together. His mind, in short, was overpowered and overwhelmed with distraction.

The charge against the prisoner is the overt act of compassing the death of the King, in firing a pistol at his Majesty—an act which only differs from murder, inasmuch as the bare compassing is equal to the accomplishment of the malignant purpose; and it will be *your* office, under the advice of the judge, to decide by your verdict to which of the two impulses of the mind you refer the act in question. You will have to decide, whether you attribute it wholly to mischief and malice, or wholly to insanity, or to the one mixing itself with the other. If you find it attributable to mischief and malice *only, LET THE MAN DIE.* The law demands his death for the public safety. If you consider it as conscious malice and mischief mixing itself with insanity, I leave him in the hands of the court, to say how he is to be dealt with; it is a question too difficult for me. I do not stand here to disturb the order of society, or to bring confusion upon my country. But if you find that the act was committed wholly under the dominion of insanity; if you are satisfied that he went to the theater contemplating his own destruction only; and that, when he fired the pistol, he did not *maliciously* aim at the person of the King—you will then be bound, even upon the principle which the Attorney General himself humanely and honorably stated to you, to acquit this most unhappy prisoner.

If, in bringing these considerations hereafter to the standard of the evidence, any doubts should occur to you on the subject, the question for your decision will then be, which of the two alternatives is the most probable—a duty which you will perform in the exercise of that reason of which, for wise purposes, it has pleased God to deprive the unfortunate man whom you are trying. Your sound understandings will easily enable you to distinguish *infirmities,* which are misfortunes, from *motives,* which are crimes. Before the day ends, the evidence will be decisive upon this subject.

There is, however, another consideration, which I ought distinctly to present to you; because I think that more turns upon it than any view of the subject; namely, whether the prisoner's defense can be impeached for artifice or fraud. I admit, that if, at the moment when he was apprehended, there can be fairly imputed to him any pretense or counterfeit of insanity, it would taint the whole case, and leave him without protection. But for such a suspicion there is

---

[26] This mad cobbler is called Truelock in the trial record.

not even a shadow of foundation. It is repelled by the whole history and character of his disease, as well as of his life, independent of it. If you were trying a man, under the Black Act, for shooting at another, and there was a doubt upon the question of malice, would it not be important, or rather decisive evidence, that the prisoner had no resentment against the prosecutor; but that, on the contrary, he was a man whom he had always loved and served? Now the prisoner was maimed, cut down, and destroyed, in the service of the King.

Gentlemen, another reflection presses very strongly on my mind, which I find it difficult to suppress. In every state there are political differences and parties, and individuals disaffected to the system of government under which they live as subjects. There are not many such, I trust, in this country. But whether there are many or any of such persons, there is one circumstance which has peculiarly distinguished his Majesty's life and reign, and which is in itself as a host in the prisoner's defense, since, amid all the treasons and all the seditions which have been charged on reformers of government as conspiracies to disturb it, no hand or voice has been lifted up against the person of the King. There have, indeed, been unhappy lunatics who, from ideas too often mixing themselves with insanity, have intruded themselves into the palace, but no malicious attack has ever been made upon the King to be settled by a trial. His Majesty's character and conduct have been a safer shield than guards, or than laws. Gentlemen, I wish to continue to that sacred life that best of all securities. I seek to continue it under that protection where it has been so long protected. We are not to do evil that good may come of it; we are not to stretch the laws to hedge round the life of the King with a greater security than that which the Divine Providence has so happily realized.

Perhaps there is no principle of religion more strongly inculcated by the sacred scriptures than that beautiful and encouraging lesson of our Savior himself upon confidence in the Divine protection: "Take no heed for your life, what ye shall eat, or what ye shall drink, or wherewithal ye shall be clothed; but seek ye first the kingdom of God, and all these things shall be added unto you." By which it is undoubtedly not intended that we are to disregard the conservation of life, or to neglect the means necessary for its sustentation; nor that we are to be careless of whatever may contribute to our comfort and happiness; but that we should be contented to receive them as they are given to us, and not seek them in the violation of the rule and order appointed for the government of the world. On this principle, nothing can more tend to the security of his Majesty and his government, than the scene which this day exhibits in the calm, humane, and impartial administration of justice; and if, in my part of this solemn duty, I have in any manner trespassed upon the just security provided for the public happiness, I wish to be corrected. I declare to you, solemnly, that my only aim has been to secure for the prisoner at the bar, whose life and death are in the balance, that he should be judged rigidly by the evidence and the law. I have made no appeal to your passions—you have no right to exercise them. This is not even a case in which, if the prisoner be found guilty, the royal mercy should be counseled to interfere. He is either an accountable being, or not accountable. If he was *unconscious* of the mischief he was engaged in, the law is a corollary, and he is not guilty. But if, when the evidence closes, you think he was conscious, and maliciously meditated the treason he is charged with, it is impossible to conceive a crime more vile and detestable; and I should consider the King's life to be ill attended to, indeed, if not protected by the full vigor of the laws, which are watchful over the security of the meanest of his subjects. It is a most important consideration, both as it regards the prisoner, and the community of which he is a member. Gentlemen, I leave it with you.[27]

∽

BIBLIOGRAPHICAL NOTE

There are two significant, modern biographies of Erskine: J. A. Lovat-Fraser's *Erskine* (1932) and Lloyd Paul Stryker's *For the Defense* (1947). The first is the more reliable in matters of fact. Neither work assesses the qualities of Erskine's speaking or examines the sources of his success in private cases. Lord James Campbell's *Lives of the Lord Chancellors* contains a biographical account in which much that is valuable is mingled with opinion and legend. Two critical essays by Lord Brougham have considerable merit. Both bear the title "English Orators—Lord Erskine"; they originally appeared in the *Edinburgh Review* (April 1810, and February 1812) and were reprinted in Brougham's *Contributions to the Edinburgh Review* (1856). The only recently published study of Erskine's rhetoric is Carroll C. Arnold's "Lord Erskine: Modern Advocate," *Quarterly Journal of Speech*, XLIV (1958), 17–30.

---

[27] When Erskine had presented more than a dozen witnesses, Lord Kenyon asked if he were nearing the close of his evidence. Erskine replied that he had twenty more witnesses, at which Kenyon asked Mitford if the Crown could contradict the facts so far offered in defense. Mitford said he could not, adding also that he had "no reason to imagine that this is a coloured case." There being no precedent to cover the situation, judges and attorneys conferred at length and finally agreed to instruct the jury to return the verdict: "Not Guilty; he being under the influence of insanity at the time the act was committed." It was also agreed that Hadfield be kept in custody in an asylum, even though no existing law authorized detention of an acquitted person. In consequence of this case, Parliament enacted legislation authorizing detention of criminal lunatics (40 Geo. III, cap. 94). The "delusion rule" that Erskine promulgated and the judges accepted was supplanted twelve years later by a rule of "ability to distinguish right from wrong." Erskine's speech did not "make law" in a technical sense, but it destroyed the ancient, absolutist doctrines on criminal insanity.

IV

The Nineteenth Century

Introduction

The years between the Battle of Waterloo (1815) and Queen Victoria's death in 1901 have historical unity at least in the sense that the interrelationships among God, Man, and the State furnished the crucial issues for discourse and action. Whatever men and monarchs thought, it was, as Esmé Wingfield-Stratford has said, the spirit of nationality that triumphed over Napoleon.[1] For the greater part of the nineteenth century the spirit and the "mission" of the modern British nation were in process of being defined.

It is a special mark of this era that the nature of God and of Man's relation to God were ubiquitous questions in the early Victorian years and that Britain's relations with societies beyond her shores produced the great popular issues of the last decades of the period. Equally important but less unique to the nineteenth century was the pervasiveness of controversy concerning the nature of the State and of the British citizen's relation to it. The dialogue in which these questions were at stake ultimately defined Great Britain as a democratic, secular society governed by popular representation through a regulatory State. Her "mission" was to extend political control and material well-being to whatever underdeveloped portions of the planet could be brought under her influence. Thus was the die cast while Victoria reigned.

Only George Canning[2] and Henry Brougham showed exceptional talent as parliamentary and hustings speakers in the years immediately following the Battle of Waterloo, when aristocracy ruled and the State repressed popular demands for change. Daniel O'Connell and Richard Lalor Sheil entered Parliament in 1829, fresh from the first successful popular agitation of the century. O'Connell's Catholic Emancipation movement in Ireland had at last brought the unreformed Parliament to grant Catholics political privileges comparable to those of other

---

[1] *The History of British Civilization* (rev. ed., London, 1948), p. 871.

[2] (1770–1827). Tory leader of the House of Commons from 1822 until his death. Selected speeches by Canning are conveniently available in Goodrich, *Select British Eloquence*, and in *British Orations*, Everyman's Library, No. 714, rev. ed.

Christian groups.[3] In 1830, Thomas Babington Macaulay took his seat in the House of Commons.[4] Thus, when Earl Grey[5] brought forward the first Parliamentary Reform Bill in 1831, the superior rhetorical skills of Macaulay and O'Connell were joined with Lord Brougham's in behalf of the measure. Macaulay's speech of March 2, 1831 and Brougham's on October 7 were accounted the outstanding addresses of these debates on parliamentary representation.[6] Sir Robert Peel was perhaps the ablest spokesman for the Tory Opposition.[7]

Debates on utilitarian economics and humanitarian reform were almost continuous between 1840 and the second Parliamentary Reform Act, passed in 1867. On behalf of economic policies calculated to make Britain the "workshop of the world," Peel, William E. Gladstone, Richard Cobden,[8] and John Bright were outstanding speakers. Against them Benjamin Disraeli argued year after year, the only debater of first rank among those who disbelieved the economic "laws" so confidently propounded by philosophers and politicians who traced their inspiration to Jeremy Bentham and David Ricardo.[9] Henry John Temple, third Viscount Palmerston, was often in disfavor with his parliamentary colleagues but remained popular with his countrymen. At his best he outshone all opponents in debates on foreign policy.[10] The leading advocate of humanitarian legislation was Lord Shaftesbury (Anthony Ashley Cooper), who successfully advanced measures regulating working conditions in factories, care of the insane, maintenance of lower-class dwellings, sanitation, and education.[11]

By Disraeli's Reform Act of 1867, suffrage was extended to the working class; by Gladstone's Reform Act of 1884, manhood suffrage was virtually achieved.

[3] Sheil and O'Connell were the outstanding orators of the Catholic Emancipation movement. Sheil's early difficulty in adapting to the requirements of parliamentary speaking limited his contribution to support of the reform bills of 1831–1832. In time he curbed his discursiveness and earned favor with the parliamentary audience.

[4] See Margaret Wood, "Lord Macaulay, Parliamentary Speaker: His Leading Ideas," Quarterly Journal of Speech, XLIV (1958), 375–84.

[5] Charles Grey, Second Earl Grey (1764–1845). As Prime Minister (1830–1834), Grey introduced the first Reform Bill and was second only to Brougham among those speakers who argued on behalf of the measure in the House of Lords.

[6] Macaulay's speech is available in British Orations; the complete text of Brougham's address appears in Goodrich, Select British Eloquence; a slightly abridged version is printed in this volume, pp. 325–58.

[7] Peel (1788–1850) was an able parliamentary debater but never a brilliant one. His later address on repeal of the Corn Laws is reprinted in British Orations.

[8] Cobden (1804–1865) was, like John Bright, a manufacturer-statesman. In the Anti-Corn Law movement his greatest strength lay in pamphleteering and popular speaking. He entered the House of Commons in 1841. See John Morley's Richard Cobden (1908). Cobden's speech on "The War with Russia," December 22, 1854, appears in British Orations.

[9] Bentham (1748–1832) was the chief philosopher of utilitarianism; Ricardo (1772–1823) published Principles of Political Economy and Taxation (1817), which became a basic authority for later utilitarians.

[10] Palmerston (1784–1865) was an individualist—colorful, with an un-English gaiety. He was a "bad speaker" by nineteenth-century standards of oratory, yet when hardest pressed in debate he displayed cogency, realism, and directness of statement that opponents could scarcely assail and the populace instinctively admired.

[11] Shaftesbury (1801–1885) devoted his public life to philanthropy and improving the conditions of the underprivileged.

out pay, at meeting rooms and in public squares on behalf of the "improving societies." Few men of note with a gift for speaking felt no obligations to such audiences. Henry ("Orator") Hunt,[21] Richard Oastler,[22] Lord Brougham, Dr. Thomas Arnold,[23] Canon Charles Kingsley, Charles Dickens,[24] Lord Shaftesbury, Thomas Huxley,[25] John Ruskin,[26] William Morris, and George Bernard Shaw are but representative of the many who acquitted themselves successfully in this branch of occasional speaking.

"The sermon was the standard vehicle of serious truth" in the early Victorian years,[27] yet the nineteenth century produced strikingly few great, popular preachers. The following is a representative list of those who were thought exceptional by their contemporaries and who published sermons that still suggest the sources of the preacher's influence: Thomas Chalmers (1780–1847), a Scotch Presbyterian; the two best preachers of the Oxford Movement, gracious John Henry Newman (1801–1890), who left the Anglican for the Roman Church, and the eloquent Henry P. Liddon (1829–1890); Alexander MacLaren (1826–1910), a Baptist pulpit-teacher of Manchester; Frederick William Robertson (1816–1853), whose small collection of sermons received unusual praise and circulation when published; and the internationally famous Baptist evangelist, Charles Haddon Spurgeon (1834–1892). That theological argumentation stood higher than affective preaching in the minds of most clergymen and churchgoers is probably the chief reason so few preachers of the period rose above the parochial in sermonic discourse.

William Wordsworth closed his "Ode to Duty" (1805) with these lines:

> Give unto me, made lowly wise,
> The spirit of self-sacrifice;
> The confidence of reason give;
> And in the light of truth thy Bondman let me live!

In 1896, A. E. Housman imagined a Grecian statue issuing counsel drawn from centuries of observations upon the role of Man:

> Courage, lad, 'tis not for long:
> Stand, quit you like stone, be strong.[28]

[21] Hunt (1773–1835) was the chief speaker at St. Peter's Fields, Manchester, when a crowd disturbance led to the "Peterloo Massacre." See Charles W. Lomas, "Orator Hunt at Peterloo and Smithfield," *Quarterly Journal of Speech*, XLVIII (1962), 400–5.

[22] Oastler (1789–1861) agitated against child labor and brutalizing working conditions.

[23] Arnold (1795–1842), Headmaster of Rugby, had deep reservations concerning mechanics' institutes because of their neglect of religion; nonetheless, he lectured at the Rugby and other institutes and published some of these lectures with a view toward "Christianizing" education for the lower classes.

[24] Dickens (1812–1870) appeared chiefly as a ceremonial speaker. Some 115 of his speeches have been accounted for by K. J. Fielding, whose edition of *The Speeches of Charles Dickens* (New York, 1960) contains the best texts available.

[25] Huxley's (1825–1895) "On a Piece of Chalk" and "The Method of Scientific Investigation" are among the best known of his many lectures to working men.

[26] Ruskin (1819–1900) is commonly remembered for his lectures on art and esthetics, but he spoke also on education, economics, and sociology.

[27] G. M. Young, *op. cit.*, p. 30.

[28] From *A Shropshire Lad*, LI.

The spiritual, intellectual, and practical problems that marked out the steps from Wordsworth's confident submission before a transcendent "duty" to Housman's agnostic stoicism constituted the themes that successive British speakers struggled to master for at least the moments in which they possessed the platforms and their fellows the seats. Nineteenth-century orators made little literature and little philosophy in these moments; nonetheless, they were primary agents in transforming an aristocratic society into a democracy without revolution, in substituting religious tolerance for religious intolerance, in rendering compassionate a neglectful State, in creating administrative machinery essential to an urban and industrial society, and in softening an imperial habit with the spirit of commonwealth.

The general history of the period is covered authoritatively in two volumes in the *Oxford History of England*: E. L. Woodward's *The Age of Reform (1815–1870)* (1938) and R. C. K. Ensor's *England, 1870–1914* (1936). In his history of politics and culture Woodward includes an unusual number of judicious personality sketches. Ensor's first ten chapters provide an excellent survey of the final third of the century. Brief and excellent on the intellectual outlook and social and political changes of the period is David Thomson's volume in the Penguin series, *England in the Nineteenth Century (1815–1914)* (1950). Book IV of Esmé Wingfield–Stratford's *The History of British Civilization* (second rev. ed., 1930) is an excellent, comprehensive treatment of nineteenth-century politics and culture. Brilliant, but perhaps difficult for those not already familiar with the facts of Victorian England, is G. M. Young's *Victorian England: Portrait of an Age* (1953). Besides Goodrich (for the early years), *British Orations,* and the *Parliamentary Debates* (Hansard), two works may be found useful for texts and criticism. Lord George Nathaniel Curzon's Rede Lecture (1911), published as *Modern Parliamentary Eloquence* (1913), assesses speakers and speeches with a clearer sense of the critical function than most comparable commentaries. *The Greville Memoirs, 1814–1860,* edited by Lytton Strachey and Roger Fulford (7 vols., 1938), contains the diaries of Charles C. F. Greville, clerk of the Council in Ordinary and acquaintance of leading Whigs and Liberals. It offers some of the best available accounts of parliamentary debates. Greville's partisanship must be remembered when the work is used.

Henry Lord Brougham

(1778–1868)

It was recently said that Lord Brougham (pronounced *broom*) demands "a polymath for a biographer."[1] He was versatile to a fault and observed the canons of no orthodoxy. To every school of thought he seemed a gifted nonconformist; hence, the unfortunate label *eccentric* became his "tag" in life and in history. We shall come nearer truth by calling him a brilliant, incorrigibly independent activist—a man possessed by those yearnings for knowledge and intelligent action

[1] R. K. Webb, review of Chester W. New's *Life of Henry Brougham* (Oxford, 1961), *Journal of Modern History,* XXXIV (1962), 447–48.

more often associated with life in the Renaissance than in nineteenth-century England.

Brougham was born in Edinburgh and educated at the Edinburgh High School and at Edinburgh University. By the age of twenty-five he had taken his university degree; written papers on mathematics and optics that attracted attention in Britain and on the Continent; been admitted to the Scottish Bar and elected Fellow of the Royal Academy; taken a leading role in founding the *Edinburgh Review*; published a two-volume work on the colonial policy of European powers. Education, science, law, politics, and literature remained his consuming interests throughout a long life.

In 1810, Brougham entered Parliament as a Whig, representing a closed borough. He immediately interested himself in questions that often seemed unimportant or positively dangerous to his fellow Whigs. Public education for the middle and working classes and legal reforms were matters for which he constantly spoke, wrote, and acted. He also urged Parliament to enforce slave-trading laws and ultimately to prohibit the slave trade, to curb military floggings, to repeal the Orders in Council, to maintain the Navigation Laws, to improve marriage and divorce laws, to amend the Poor Laws, and to reform parliamentary representation. Meanwhile, he busied himself with courtroom defenses of freedom of speech and press and, as the Queen's Attorney General, defended Queen Caroline against charges of immorality. He was unsuccessful in organizing Whig support for a coherent reform *program* partly because of his indifference to the sensibilities and prejudices of others, but especially because his views were usually in advance of his time.

Chauncey A. Goodrich's comment that Brougham's speeches reflect a life "spent in *beating down*" [2] seems somewhat unjust. Brougham and such essentially non-parliamentary friends as Francis Place, James Mill, Jeremy Bentham, Sir Samuel Romilly, Thomas Denman, and Sidney Smith were prepared with constructive alternatives to practices they deplored. It was not open to Brougham, however, to lead in the ultimate enactments of such alternatives, for after accepting the seals of the Lord Chancellor in 1830, he was constitutionally removed from the creative life of Parliament and the courtroom. Nonetheless, England inherited three historic monuments to his creative energies: the *Edinburgh Review*, the Society for the Diffusion of Useful Knowledge, and London University. In the founding of each he had a leading role.

Brougham was both orator and critic of oratory. He published at least five major essays on ancient and modern oratory.[3] His *Historical Sketches of Statesmen of the Time of George III* contains perceptive comment on the speaking of that period. He devoted his inaugural discourse as Lord Rector of the University of Glasgow to "the study of the Rhetorical Art, by which useful truths are promulgated with effect, and the purposes to which a proficiency in this art should be subservient." Demosthenes was Brougham's ideal orator, superior to Cicero by virtue of "the rigid steadiness with which the Greek orator keeps the object of all eloquence perpetually in view, never speaking for mere speaking's sake."

---

[2] Goodrich, *Select British Eloquence*, p. 887.
[3] Lloyd I. Watkins, "Lord Brougham's Authorship of Rhetorical Articles in the *Edinburgh Review*," *Quarterly Journal of Speech*, XLII (1956), 55–63.

In an era when three-hour speeches were commonplace, Brougham spoke at length; and he tended "to crowd an entire system of thought into a single statement."[4] He did not achieve the economy he so admired in Demosthenes, yet for the most part he avoided the faults he found in Roman and British orators: repetition and diffuseness. In Brougham's major addresses, ideas and language churn inexorably toward carefully predetermined conclusions. Here, perhaps, is the reason contemporaries so often applied the adjectives "powerful" and "terrible" to his speaking.

Two speeches in the parliamentary reform debates of 1831–1832 were immediately recognized as outstanding: Thomas Babington Macaulay's address in the House of Commons (March 2, 1831)[5] and Brougham's in the House of Lords (October 7, 1831). At issue before the Lords when Brougham spoke was the second reading of the "Second Reform Bill." Lord Grey and Brougham were the chief defenders of the bill, but their views of the political-rhetorical situation differed. Grey hoped by conciliation, cajolery, and pressure to eke out a favorable decision. Brougham was satisfied that only creation of new Peers, or the threat thereof, could force the bill through the upper house.

The Lord Chancellor spoke on the fifth and last night of debate.[6] His, says J. R. M. Butler, was "the great defense of the bill" in a debate "held at the time to have excelled all the displays in the Commons."[7] *The Times* said Brougham "eclipsed every effort of oratory made within the walls of Parliament in the memory of the living generation . . . but to produce its full effect, it must have been heard from the lips of the transcendent orator himself, for no report can do it justice. Even if we could give his words entire, where are the expressive looks, the commanding gestures,—above all, the emphasis, the sublime intonation of his various voice?"[8] *The Times* was ardently reformist, but even the speaker's opponents agreed he surpassed all his previous efforts in deliberative argument.

~

[4] Goodrich, p. 888.

[5] Macaulay's speech is conveniently available in *British Orations* (Everyman's Library, No. 714).

[6] Although the Lord Chancellor is Speaker of the House of Lords, he may participate in debate without relinquishing his role as presiding officer.

[7] *The Passing of the Great Reform Bill* (London, 1914), p. 284. Butler's further remark that Brougham's address "owed something of its force and fire to a bottle of mulled port" derives from Lord Campbell's *Lives of the Chancellors* and has been classed as "legend" by Brougham's later biographers.

[8] Editorial comment, October 8, 1831.

Speech on Parliamentary Reform *

Delivered in the House of Lords
October 7, 1831

My Lords,—I feel that I owe some apology to your lordships for standing in the way of any noble lords [1] who wish to address you: but after much deliberation, and after consulting with several of my noble friends on both sides of the House, it did appear to us, as I am sure it will to your lordships, desirable, on many grounds, that the debate should be brought to a close this night; [2] and I thought I could not better contribute to that end than by taking the present opportunity of addressing you. Indeed, I had scarcely any choice. I am urged on by the anxiety I feel on this mighty subject, which is so great, that I should hardly have been able to delay the expression of my opinion much longer; if I had, I feel assured that I must have lost the power to address you. This solicitude is not, I can assure your lordships, diminished by my recollection of the great talents and brilliant exertions of those by whom I have been preceded in the discussion, and the consciousness of the difficulties with which I have to contend in following such men. It is a deep sense of these difficulties that induces me to call for your patient indulgence. For although not unused to meet public bodies, nay, constantly in the habit, during many years, of presenting myself before great assemblies of various kinds, yet I do solemnly assure you, that I never, until this moment, felt what deep responsibility may rest on a member of the legislature in addressing either of its houses. And if I, now standing with your lordships on the brink of the most momentous decision that ever human assembly came to, at any period of the world, and seeking to arrest you, whilst it is yet time, in that position, could, by any divination of the future, have foreseen in my earliest years, that I should live to appear here, and to act as your adviser, on a question of such awful importance, not only to yourselves, but to your remotest posterity, I should have devoted every day and every hour of that life to preparing myself for the task which I now almost sink under,—gathering from the monuments of ancient experience the lessons of wisdom which might guide our course at the present

---

* We present here an abridgment of the "corrected text" of Brougham's address originally published by Ridgway and, later, in Hansard's *Parliamentary Debates* and Brougham's edition of his speeches. Reactions of the audience, as reported by *The Times*, October 8, 1831, and explanatory notes by Brougham, Goodrich, and the editors of this volume have been added. The "corrected text" is a slightly condensed and not always verbatim record of Brougham's address. *The Times'* account is less useful since it alternates between first- and third-person reporting. We have therefore chosen to rely on the traditional text and to indicate in footnotes the most prominent differences between the two basic sources. Where we have deleted portions of the traditional text, the omissions are plainly noted and summaries of the omitted material are supplied.

[1] The Marquis of Cleveland and several others had risen and given way. (Brougham.)

[2] At about six o'clock on the morning of October 8, 1831, the Lords divided on the second reading of the bill. A majority of forty-one voted in the negative. Parliament was prorogued October 20, 1831. Under threat that new Peers would be created if necessary, the Lords finally passed a third reform bill, June 4, 1832.

hour,—looking abroad on our own times, and these not uneventful, to check, by practice, the application of those lessons,—chastening myself, and sinking within me every infirmity of temper, every waywardness of disposition, which might by possibility impede the discharge of this most solemn duty:—but, above all, eradicating from my mind everything that, by any accident, could interrupt the most perfect candour and impartiality of judgment. (Cheers.) I advance thus anxious and thus humbled to the task before me; but cheered, on the other hand, with the intimate and absolute persuasion that I have no personal interest to serve,—no sinister views to resist,—that there is nothing, in my nature, or in my situation, which can cast even the shadow of a shade across the broad path, I will not say of legislative, but of judicial duty, in which I am now to accompany your lordships.

I have listened, my lords, with the most profound attention to the debate on this question, which has lasted during the five past days; and having heard a vast variety of objections brought against this measure, and having also attended to the arguments which have been urged to repel those objections, I, careless whether I give offence in any quarter or no, must, in common fairness, say, on the one hand, that I am so far moved by some of the things which I have heard urged, as to be inclined towards the reconsideration of several matters on which I had conceived my mind to be fully made up; and, on the other, that in the great majority of the objections which have been ingeniously raised against this bill, I can by no means concur; but viewing them as calmly and dispassionately as ever man listened to the arguments advanced for and against any measure, I am bound by a sense of duty to say, that those objections have left my mind entirely unchanged as to the bulk of the principles upon which the bill is framed. (Cheers.) If I presumed to go through those objections, or even through the majority of them, in detail, I should be entering upon a tedious, and also a superfluous, work: so many of them have been removed by the admirable speeches which you have already heard, that I should only be wasting your time were I once more to refute them; I should only be doing worse what my precursors have already done far better. I will begin, however, with what fell from a noble Earl,[3] with whose display I was far less struck than others, because I was more accustomed to it— who, viewing this bill from a remote eminence, and not coming close, or even approaching near, made a *reconnoissance* of it too far off to see even its outworks (cheers and laughter)—who, indulging in a vein of playful and elegant pleasantry, to which no man listens in private with more delight than myself, knowing how well it becomes the leisure hours and familiar moments of my noble friend, delivered with the utmost purity of diction, and the most felicitous aptness of allusion— I was going to say a discourse—but it was an exercise, or essay—of the highest merit, which had only this fault—that it was an essay, or exercitation, on some other thesis, and not on this bill. (Cheers and laughter.) It was as if some one had set to my noble friend, whose accomplishments I know—whose varied talents I admire, but in whom I certainly desiderate soundness of judgment and closeness of argument, a theme *de rebus publicis*, or *de motû civium*, or *de novarum rerum cupiditate*,[4]—on change, on democracies, on republicanism, on anarchy; and on these interesting but somewhat trite and even threadbare subjects, my noble friend

---

[3] Earl Dudley.

[4] On public affairs, or on popular uprising, or on love of new things.

made one of the most lucid, most terse, most classical, and, as far as such efforts will admit of eloquence, most eloquent exercitations, that ever proceeded from mortal pen. (Loud cries of "hear" from the ministerial benches.) [5] My noble friend proceeded altogether on a false assumption; it was on a fiction of his own brain—on a device of his own imagination, that he spoke throughout. He first assumed that the bill meant change and revolution, and on change and revolution he predicted voluminously and successfully. (Laughter.) So much for the critical merits of his performance; but, practically viewed—regarded as an argument on the question before us—it is to be wholly left out of view; it was quite beside the matter. If this bill be change, and be revolution, there is no resisting the conclusions of my noble friend. But on that point I am at issue with him; and he begins by taking the thing in dispute for granted. I deny that this bill is change in the bad sense of the word; nor does it lead to, nor has it any connection with, revolution, except so far as it has a direct tendency to prevent revolution. (Great cheering.)

My noble friend, in the course of his essay, talked to you of this administration as one prone to change; he told you that its whole system was a system of changes; and he selected as the first change on which he would ring a loud peal, that which he said we had made in our system of finance. If he is so averse to our making alterations in our scheme of finance the very first year we have been in office, what does he think, I ask, of Mr. Pitt's budgets, of which never one passed without undergoing changes in almost every one tax, beside those altogether abandoned? If our budget had been carried as it was originally brought in, with a remission of the timber duty, and the candle duty, and the coal duty, it would have been distinguished beyond all others only as having given substantial relief to the people on those very trivial and unnecessary articles, I suppose, of human life—fire, and light, and lodging. (Cheers from the ministerial benches.) Then, our law reform [6] is another change which my noble friend charged the government with being madly bent on effecting. Scarcely had the Lord President of the Council risen to answer the objection raised against us on this score, than up started my noble friend to assert that he had not pressed any such objection into his service. My lords, I am not in the habit of taking a note of what falls from any noble lord in debate—it is not my practice—but by some fatality it did so happen that, whilst my noble friend was speaking, I took a note of his observations, of which I will take the liberty of reading you the very first line. "Change and revolution; all is change; among the first—law." I took that note, because I was somewhat surprised at the observation, knowing, as I did, that this Law Reform had met with the approbation of my noble friend himself; and, what was yet more satisfactory to my mind, it had received the sanction of your lordships, and had been passed through all its stages without even a division. (Cheers.) My noble friend then told us, still reconnoitering our position at a distance, or, at most, partaking in an occasional skirmish, but holding himself aloof from the main

[5] Rhetorical analysis frequently provided the grounds for praise or refutation in Brougham's addresses.

[6] Law reform was a cause especially dear to Brougham. He had delivered a major address on "The Present State of the Law" in the House of Commons in 1828 and another on "Local Courts" in 1830. In 1831, he had introduced in the House of Lords a bill for reform of local courts, but the matter was referred to the Common Law Commissioners for study.

battle,—he told us that this bill came recommended neither by the weight of ancient authority, nor by the spirit of modern refinement; that this attack on our present system was not supported by the experience of the past, nor sanctioned by any appearance of the great mind of the master genius of our precursors in later times. As to the weight of ancient authority, skilled as my noble friend is in every branch of literary history, I am obliged to tell him he is inaccurate; and, because it may afford him some consolation in this his day of discomfiture and anguish, I will supply the defect which exists in his historical recollections; for an author, the first of satirists in any age—Dean Swift, with whom my noble friend must have some sympathy, since he closely imitates him in this respect, that as the Dean satirized, under the name of man, a being who had no existence save in his own imagination, so my noble friend attacks, under the name of the bill, a fancy of his own, a creature of his fertile brain, and which has no earthly connection with the real ink and parchment bill before you—Dean Swift, who was never yet represented as a man prone to change, who was not a Radical, who was not a Jacobin, (for, indeed, those terms were in his day unknown); Dean Swift, who was not even a Whig, but, in the language of the times, a regular, staunch, thick-and-thin Tory (cheers),—while enumerating the absurdities in our system, which required an adequate and efficient remedy, says:—"It is absurd that the boroughs, which are decayed, and destitute both of trade and population, are not extinguished"; (or, as we should say, in the language of the bill, which was as unknown to Dean Swift as it is now to my noble friend, put into schedule A[7]), "because," adds the Dean, "they return members who represent nobody at all"; so here he adopts the first branch of the measure; and next he approves of the other great limb; for the second grand absurdity which he remarks is, "that several large towns are not represented, though they are filled with those who increase mightily the trade of the realm." (Great cheers from the ministerial benches.) Then as to shortening the duration of Parliaments, on which we have not introduced a single provision into the bill—if we had, what a cry should we have heard about the statesmen in Queen Anne's day, the great men who lived in the days of Blenheim, and during the period sung of by my noble friend, from Blenheim to Waterloo; how we should have been taunted with the Somerses and Godolphins, and their contemporaries, the Swifts and the Addisons! What would *they* have said of such a change? Yet what did the same Dean Swift, the contemporary of Somers and Godolphin, the friend of Addison, who sang the glories of Blenheim, the origin of my noble friend's period,—what did the Dean, inspired by all the wisdom of ancient times, say to shortening the duration of Parliaments? "I have a strong love for the good old fashion of Gothic Parliaments, which were only of one year's duration." (Cheers.) Such is the ground, such the vouchers, upon the authority of which my noble friend, in good set phrase, sets the weight of ancient wisdom against the errors of the reformers, and triumphs in the round denial that we have anything in our favour like the sanction of authority (hear! hear!); and it turns out, after all, that the wise men of the olden time promulgated their opinions on the subject in such clear, and decisive, and vigorous terms, that if they were living in our days, and giving utterance to the same sentiments, they would be set down rather for determined radicals than for enemies of reform. (Hear! Hear!)

[7] Schedule A was the list of boroughs to lose both House of Commons representatives under the Grey Ministry's bill.

Then my noble friend, advancing from former times to our own, asked who and what they are that form the cabinet of the day? To such questions it would be unbecoming in me to hazard a reply. I do not find fault with my noble friend for asking them; I admit that it is fair to ask who are they that propound any measure, especially when it comes in the shape of a great change. The noble earl then complained of our poverty of genius—absence of commanding talents—want of master minds—and even our destitution of eloquence, a topic probably suggested by my noble friend's [8] display, who opened the debate, and whose efforts in that kind are certainly very different from those which the noble earl seems to admire. (Great cheering.) But if it be a wise rule to ask by whom a measure is propounded before you give it implicit confidence, it certainly cannot be an unwise rule to ask, on the other hand, who and what be they by whom that measure is resisted (cheers), before you finally reject it on their bare authority. Nor can I agree with a noble friend of mine,[9] who spoke last night, and who laid down one doctrine on this subject, at which I marvelled greatly. It was one of his many allegories—for they were not metaphors, nor yet similes—some of them, indeed, were endless, especially when my noble friend took to the water, and embarked us on board of his ship—for want of steam, I thought we should never have got to the end of our voyage. (Cheers and laughter.) When we reply to their arguments against our measure, by asking what reform they have got of their own to offer, he compares us to some host, who, having placed before his friends an uneatable dinner, which they naturally found fault with, should say, "Gentlemen, you are very hard to please: I have set a number of dishes before you, which you cannot eat—now, what dishes can you dress yourselves?" My noble friend says, that such an answer would be very unreasonable—for he asks, ingeniously enough, how *can* the guests dress a dinner, especially when they have not possession of the kitchen? But did it never strike him that the present is not the case of guests called upon to eat a dinner—it is one of rival cooks who want to get into our kitchen? (Roars of laughter.) We are here all on every side cooks—a synod of cooks, to use Dr. Johnson's phrase (laughter continued), and nothing but cooks; for it is the very condition of our being—the bond of our employment, under a common master—that none of us shall ever taste the dishes we are dressing. The Commons House may taste it; but can the Lords?—we have nothing to do but prepare the viands. (Great cheering and laughter continued.) It is therefore of primary importance, when the authority of the two classes of rival artists is the main question, to inquire what are our feats severally in our common calling. I ought perhaps to ask your lordships' pardon for pursuing my noble friend's allegory; but I saw that it produced an impression by the cheers it excited, and I was desirous to show that it was in a most extraordinary degree inapplicable to the question, to illustrate which it was fetched from afar off. (Hear! Hear!) I therefore must think myself entitled to ask who and what be they that oppose us, and what dish they are likely to cook for us, when once again they get possession of the kitchen? I appeal to any candid man who now hears me, and I ask him whether, it being fair to consider who are the authors of the bill, it is not equally fair to consider from whom the objections come? I therefore trust that any impartial man, unconnected with either class of statesmen, when called upon

[8] Lord Grey.
[9] Lord Caernarvon.

to consider our claims to confidence, before he adopts our measures, should, before he repudiates us in favour of our adversaries, inquire—Are they likely to cure the evils, and remedy the defects, of which they admit the existence in our system? —and are their motives such as ought to win the confidence of judicious and calmly reflecting men? (Great cheering.)

One noble lord[10] there is whose judgment we are called upon implicitly to trust, and who expressed himself with much indignation, and yet with entire honesty of purpose, against this measure. No man is, in my opinion, more single-hearted; no man more incorruptible. But in his present enmity to this bill, which he describes as pregnant with much mischief to the constitution, he gives me reason to doubt the soundness of the resolution which would take him as a guide, from the fact of his having been not more than five or six months ago most friendly to its provisions, and expressed the most unbounded confidence in the government which proposed it. (Cheers.) Ought not this to make us pause before we place our consciences in his keeping—before we surrender up our judgment to his prudence—before we believe in his cry that the bill is revolution, and the destruction of the empire,—when we find the same man delivered diametrically opposite opinions only six months ago?

[The Earl of Winchelsea here shouted out "No."]

Then I have been practised upon, if it is not so: and the noble earl's assertion should be of itself sufficient to convince me that I have been practised on. But I can assure the noble earl that this has been handed to me as an extract from a speech which he made to a meeting of the county of Kent, held at Maidstone, on the 24th of last March:—"They have not got reform yet; but when the measure does come, as I am persuaded it will come, into the law of the land—" (a loud cry of "No," from the opposition lords).—Then if noble lords will not let me proceed quietly, I must begin again, and this time I will go further back. The speech represents the noble earl to have said, "His Majesty's government is entitled to the thanks of the country. (Great cheering from the ministerial benches.) Earl Grey, with his distinguished talents, unites a political honesty not to be surpassed (cheering continued), and leaves behind him, at an immeasurable distance, those who have abandoned their principles and deceived their friends. (Cheering continued.) The noble lord is entitled to the eternal gratitude of his country, for the manner in which he has brought forward this question. (Cheering continued.) I maintain, that he deserves the support of the country at large." And, my lords, the way in which I was practised on to believe that all this praise was not referable to the timber duties, but to reform, I shall now explain. It is in the next passage of the same speech:—"They have not got reform yet; but when the measure does come, as I am persuaded it will come, into the law of the land, it will consolidate, establish, and strengthen our glorious constitution (cheers); and not only operate for the general welfare and happiness of the country, but will also render an act of justice to the great and influential body of the people. (Great cheering.) The measure has not yet been introduced to that House of which I am a member." (Lord Winchelsea and his friends here cheered loudly.) Ay, but it had been

[10] Lord Winchelsea.

debated in the House of Commons for near a month—it had been published in all books, pamphlets, and newspapers—it had been discussed in all companies and societies—and I will undertake to assert, that there was not one single man in the county of Kent, who did not know that Lord John Russell's bill [11] was a bill for Parliamentary reform. (Hear! Hear!) The speech thus concludes:—"When the bill is brought forward in that House of which I am a member, I shall be at my post, ready to give it my most hearty and cordial"—opposition?—no,—"support." (Great cheering from the ministerial benches.) But why do I allude to this speech at all? Merely to show, that if those who oppose the bill say to us, "Who are you that propound it?" and make our previous conduct a ground for rejecting it, through distrust of its authors, we have a right to reply to them with another question, and to ask, "Who are you that resist it, and what were your previous opinions regarding it?" (Great cheering.)

Another noble lord [12] has argued this question with great ability and show of learning; and if we are to take him as our guide, we must also look at the panacea which he provides for us in case of rejection. That noble lord, looking around him on all sides—surveying what had occurred in the last forty or fifty years—glancing above him and below him, around him and behind him—watching every circumstance of the past—anticipating every circumstance of the future—scanning every sign of the times—taking into his account all the considerations upon which a lawgiver ought to reckon—regarding also the wishes, the vehement desires, not to say absolute demands, of the whole country for some immediate reform—concentrates all his wisdom in this proposition—the result, the *practical result* of all his deliberations, and all his lookings about, and all his scannings of circumstances—the whole produce of his thoughts, by the value of which you are to try the safety of his counsels—namely, that you should suspend all your operations on this bill for two years, and, I suppose, two days, to give the people—what? breathing time. (Cheers and roars of laughter.) The noble lord takes a leaf out of the book of the noble duke near him—a leaf, which I believe the noble duke himself would now wish cancelled. The noble duke,[13] shortly before he proposed the great measure of Catholic emancipation, had said—"Before I can support that measure, I should wish that the whole question might sink into oblivion." But the proposition of the noble earl, though based on the same idea, goes still further. "Bury," says he, "this measure of reform in oblivion for two years and two days, and then see, good people, what I will do for you." And then what will the noble lord do for the good people?—Why, nothing—neither more nor less than nothing. (Cheers.) We, innocents that we were, fancied that the noble lord must, after all his promises, really mean to do something; and thought he had said somewhat of bribery—of doing a little about bribery—which was his expression; but when we mentioned our supposition, that he really meant to go as far as to support a bill for the more effectual prevention of bribery at elections, the noble lord told us he would do no such thing.

[The Earl of Mansfield.—I gave no opinion on the point.]

[11] Lord John Russell had taken the lead in drafting the reform bill and introduced it in the House of Commons.

[12] Lord Mansfield.

[13] The Duke of Wellington.

Exactly so. The noble lord reserves his opinion as to whether he would put down bribery for two years and two days; and when they are expired, he, peradventure, may inform us whether he will give us leave to bring in a bill to prevent bribery; not all kinds of bribery—that would be radical work—but as far as the giving away of ribands goes, leaving beer untouched, and agreeably to the venerable practice of the olden time. (Cheers.)

Another noble lord,[14] a friend of mine, whose honesty and frankness stamp all he says with still greater value than it derives from mere talent, would have you believe that all the petitions, under which your table now groans, are indeed for reform, but not for this bill, which he actually says the people dislike. Now is not this a droll way for the people to act, if we are to take my noble friend's statement as true? First of all, it is an odd time they have taken to petition for reform, if they do not like this bill. I should say that if they petition for reform, whilst this particular measure is passing through the House, it is proof that the bill contains the reform they want. Surely, when I see the good men of this country—the intelligent and industrious classes of the community—now coming forward, not by thousands but by hundreds of thousands, I can infer nothing from their conduct, but that this is the bill, and the only bill, for which they petition. (Cheers.) But if they really want some other than the bill proposes, is it not still more unaccountable that they should one and all petition, not for that other reform, but for this very measure? The proposition of my noble friend is, that they love reform in general, but hate this particular plan; and the proof of it is this, that their petitions all pray earnestly for this particular plan, and say not a word of general reform. Highly as I prize the integrity of my noble friend—much as I admire his good sense on other occasions—I must say, that on this occasion I descry not his better judgment, and I estimate how far he is a safe guide either as a witness to facts, or as a judge of measures, by his success in the present instance; in either capacity, I cannot hesitate in recommending your lordships not to follow him. As a witness to facts, never was failure more complete. The bill, said he, has no friends anywhere; and he mentioned Bond-street as one of his walks, where he could not enter a shop without finding its enemies abound. No sooner had Bond-street escaped his lips than up comes a petition to your lordships from nearly all its shopkeepers, affirming that their sentiments have been misrepresented, for they are all champions of the bill. My noble friend then says, "Oh, I did not mean the shopkeepers of Bond-street in particular; I might have said any other street, as St. James's equally." No sooner does that unfortunate declaration get abroad, than the shopkeepers of St. James's-street are up in arms, and forth comes a petition similar to that from Bond-street. My noble friend is described moving through Regent-street, and away scamper all the inhabitants, fancying that he is in quest of anti-reformers—sign a requisition to the churchwardens—and the householders, one and all, declare themselves friendly to the bill. Whither shall he go—what street shall he enter, in what alley shall he take refuge—since the inhabitants of every street, and lane, and alley, feel it necessary, in self-defence, to become signers and petitioners, as soon as he makes his appearance among them? (Cheers and laughter.) If harassed by reformers on land, my noble friend goes down to the water,[15] the thousand reformers greet him, whose petition I this day

[14] Lord Wharncliffe, who endorsed the bill in principle but opposed the extent of its enfranchising provisions.
[15] Lambeth.

presented to your lordships. If he were to get into a hackney coach, the very coachmen and their attendants would feel it their duty to assemble and petition. Wherever there is a street, an alley, a passage, nay, a river, a wherry, or a hackney coach, these, because inhabited, become forbidden and *tabooed* to my noble friend. (Cheers and laughter.) I may meet him not on "the accustomed hill," for Hayhill, though short, has some houses on its slope, but on the south side of Berkeleysquare, wandering "remote, unfriended, melancholy, slow,"—for there he finds a street without a single inhabitant, and therefore, without a single friend of the bill. If, in despair, he shall flee from the town to seek the solitude of the country, still will he be pursued by cries of "Petition, petition! The bill, the bill!" (Laughter.) His flight will be through villages placarded with "The Bill"[16]— his repose at inns holden by landlords who will present him with the bill—he will be served by reformers in the guise of waiters—pay tribute at gates where petitions lie for signing—and plunge into his own domains to be overwhelmed with the Sheffield petition, signed by 10,400 friends of the bill.

> Me miserable! which way shall I fly
> Infinite wrath and infinite despair?
> Which way I fly, Reform—myself Reform!

(cheers and laughter) for this is the most serious part of the whole—my noble friend is himself, after all, a reformer. (Cheers.) I mention this to show that he is not more a safe guide on matters of opinion than on matters of fact. He is a reformer—he is not even a bit-by-bit reformer—not even a gradual reformer—but that which at any other time than the present would be called a wholesale, and even a radical reformer. He deems that no shadowy unsubstantial reform—that nothing but an effectual remedy of acknowledged abuses, will satisfy the people of England and Scotland; and this is a fact to which I entreat the earnest and unremitting attention of every man who wishes to know what guides are safe to follow on this subject. (Cheers.) Many now follow men who say that reform is necessary, and yet object to this bill as being too large; that is, too efficient. This may be very incorrect; but it is worse; it is mixed up with a gross delusion, which can never deceive the country; for I will now say, once for all, that every one argument which has been urged by those leaders is as good against moderate reform as it is against this bill. (Cheers from ministerial benches.) Not a single reason they give, not a topic they handle, not an illustration they resort to, not a figure of speech they use, not even a flower they fling about, that does not prove or illustrate the position of *"no reform."* All their speeches, from beginning to end, are railing against the smallest as against the greatest change, and yet all the while they call themselves reformers! Are they then safe guides for any man who is prepared to allow any reform, however moderate, of any abuse, however glaring? Of another noble earl,[17] whose arguments, well selected and ably put, were yet

---

[16] *The Times'* report reads as follows from this point to the end of the paragraph: "At the inns on the road he will be served by landlords, who will present him with the bill (*cheers and laughter*); he will be followed by waiters and attendants in the shape of reformers; and even when he retires within his own princely domain, if the birds of heaven do not disturb his slumbers with their bill, the ten thousand petitioners from Sheffield will make him hear something of theirs. (*Cheers and laughter.*)"

[17] Lord Harrowby, associated with Lord Wharncliffe in attempts to moderate the bill.

received with such exaggerated admiration by his friends as plainly showed how pressing were their demands for a tolerable defender, we have heard it said, again and again, that no answer whatever has been given to his speech. I am sure I mean no disrespect to that noble earl, when I venture to remark the infinite superiority in all things, but especially in argument, of such speeches as those of the noble marquis [18] and the noble viscount.[19] The former, in his most masterly answer, left but little of the speech for any other antagonist to destroy. The latter, while he charmed us with the fine eloquence that pervaded his discourse, and fixed our thoughts by the wisdom and depth of reflection that informed it, won all hearers by his candour and sincerity. Little, indeed, have they left for me to demolish; yet if anything remain, it may be as well we should take it to pieces. But I am first considering the noble earl in the light of one professing to be a safe guide for your lordships. What then are his claims to the praise of calmness and impartiality? For the constant cry against the government is, "You are hasty, rash, intemperate men. You know not what you do; your adversaries are the true state physicians; look at their considerate deportment; imitate their solemn caution." This is the sort of thing we hear in private as well as public. "See such an one—*he* is a man of prudence, and a discreet (the olden times called such a *sad*) man; he is not averse to all innovation, but dislikes precipitancy; he is calm; just to all sides alike; never gives a hasty opinion; a safe one to follow; look how *he* votes." I have done this on the present occasion; and, understanding the noble earl might be the sort of personage intended, I have watched him. Common consistency was of course to be at all events expected in this safe model—some connection between the premises and conclusion, the speech and the vote. I listened to the speech, and also, with many others, expected that an avowal of all, or nearly all, the principles of the bill would have ended in a vote for the second reading, which might suffer the committee to discuss its details, the only subject of controversy with the noble earl. But no such thing; he is a reformer, approves the principle, objecting to the details, and, therefore, he votes against it in the lump, details, principle and all. But soon after his own speech closed, he interrupted another, that of my noble and learned friend,[20] to give us a marvellous sample of calm and impartial judgment. What do you think of the cool head—the unruffled temper—the unbiassed mind of that man—most candid and most acute as he is, when not under the domination of alarm—who could listen without even a gesture of disapprobation to the speech of one noble lord,[21] professedly not extemporaneous, for he, with becoming, though unnecessary modesty, disclaims the faculty of speaking off-hand, but elaborately prepared, in answer to a member of the other House, and in further answer to a quarto volume, published by him—silent and unmoved, could hear another speech, made up of extracts from the House of Commons' debates—could listen and make no sign when a noble marquis [22] referred to the House of Commons' speeches of my noble friend by his House of Commons' name, again and again calling him Charles Grey without even the prefix of Mr.; nay, could *himself* repeatedly comment upon those very speeches of the other House—what will your lordships say of the fatal effects of

[18] Marquis of Lansdowne.
[19] Viscount Melbourne.
[20] Lord Plunkett.
[21] Lord Mansfield.
[22] Marquis of Londonderry.

present fear, in warping and distorting a naturally just mind, when you find this same noble earl interrupt the chancellor of Ireland, because he most regularly, most orderly, referred to the public conduct of a right honourable baronet,[23] exhibited in a former Parliament, and now become a matter of history? (Loud cries of "Hear!" from the ministerial benches.) Surely, surely, nothing more is wanted to show that all the rashness—all the heedlessness, all the unreflecting precipitancy, is not to be found upon the right hand of the woolsack (loud cheers from the ministerial benches); and that they who have hurried across the sea, in breathless impatience, to throw out the bill, might probably, had they been at home, and allowed themselves time for sober reflection, have been found among the friends of a measure which they now so acrimoniously oppose! So much for the qualifications of the noble lords to act safely as our guides, according to the general view of the question as one of mere authority, taken by my noble friend.[24] But I am quite willing to rest the subject upon a higher ground, and to take it upon reason, and not upon authority. I will therefore follow the noble earl somewhat more closely through his argument, the boast of our antagonists.[25]

He began with historical matter, and gave a very fair and manly explanation of his family's connection with the Borough of Tiverton. This, he said, would set him *rectus in curiâ*, as he phrased it. If by this he meant that he should thence appear to have no interest in opposing the Bill, I cannot agree with him; but certainly his narrative, coupled with a few additions by way of reference, which may be made to it, throws considerable light upon the system of rotten boroughs. The influence by which his family have so long returned the two members, is, it seems, personal, and in no way connected with property. This may be very true; for certainly the noble lord has no property within a hundred miles of the place; yet, if it is true, what becomes of the cry, raised by his lordship, about property? But let that pass—the influence then is personal—ay, but it may be personal, and yet be *official* also. The family of the noble earl has for a long series of years been in high office, ever since the time when its founder also laid the foundations of the borough connection, as Solicitor-General. By some accident or other, they have always been connected with the government, as well as the borough. I venture to suspect that the matter of patronage may have had some share in cementing the attachment of the men of Tiverton to the house of Ryder. I take leave to suggest the bare possibility of many such men having always held local and other places—of the voters and their families having always got on in the world through that patronage. If it should turn out that I am right, there may be no very peculiar blame imputable to the noble earl and his Tiverton supporters; but it adds one to the numberless proofs that the borough system affords endless temptations to barter political patronage for Parliamentary power—to use official influence for the purpose of obtaining seats in the Commons, and, by means of those seats, to retain that influence.

The noble earl complained that the Reform Bill shut the doors of Parliament against the eldest sons of Peers, and thus deprived our successors of the best kind of political education. My lords, I freely admit the justice of his panegyric upon

---

[23] Sir Robert Peel.
[24] Lord Dudley.
[25] Lord Harrowby. The report of *The Times* indicates that the section of Brougham's address represented by this paragraph was slightly abridged in the corrected text.

this constitutional training, by far the most useful which a statesman can receive; but I deny that the measure proposed will affect it—will obstruct the passage to the House of Commons; it will rather clear and widen it to all, who, like your lordships' sons, ought there to come. (Hear! Hear!) My noble friend,[26] who so admirably answered the noble earl, in a speech distinguished by the most attractive eloquence, and which went home to every heart from the honest warmth of feeling, so characteristic of his nature, that breathed through it—has already destroyed this topic by referring to the most notorious facts, by simply enumerating the open counties represented by Peers' eldest sons. But I had rather take one instance for illustration, because an individual case always strikes into the imagination, and rivets itself deep in the memory. I have the happiness of knowing a young nobleman—whom to know is highly to esteem—a more virtuous, a more accomplished I do not know—nor have any of your lordships, rich as you are in such blessings, any arrow in all your quivers of which you have more reason to be proud. He sat for a nomination borough; formed his own opinion; decided for the bill; differed with his family—they excluded him from Parliament, closing against him, at least that avenue to a statesman's best education, and an heir-apparent's most valued preparation for discharging the duties of the Peerage. How did this worthy scion of a noble stock seek to re-open the door thus closed, and resume his political schooling, thus interrupted by the borough patrons? Did he resort to another close borough, to find an avenue like that which he had lost under the present system, and long before the wicked bill had prevented young lords from duly finishing their Parliamentary studies? No such thing. He threw himself upon a large community—canvassed a populous city—and started as a candidate for the suffrages of thousands, on the only ground which was open to such solicitation—he avowed himself a friend of the bill. (Cheers.) *Mutato nomine de te.*[27] The borough that rejected him was Tiverton—the young nobleman was the heir of the house of Ryder—the patron was the noble earl, and the place to which the ejected member resorted for the means of completing his political education in one house, that he might one day be the ornament of the other, was no small, rotten, nomination borough, but the great town of Liverpool. (Cheers.)

[Lord Harrowby begged to set the noble and learned lord right. He was himself abroad at the time, fifteen hundred miles off; and his family had nothing to do with the transaction. His son was not returned, because he did not offer himself. (Cries of Hear!)]

I hope the noble lords will themselves follow the course their cries seem to recommend, and endeavour to *hear*. Excess of noise may possibly deter some speakers from performing their duty; but my political education (of which we are now speaking) has been in the House of Commons; my habits were formed there; and no noise will stop me. I say so in tenderness to the noble persons who are so clamorous; and that, thus warned, they may spare their own lungs those

---

[26] Lord Goderich.

[27] *Mutato nomine de te*
    Fabula narratur.
Horace, *Satires*, Book 1, Sat. i., lines 69–70. Hubert Wetmore Wells' translation: "Change names and the story fits *you*." Horace, *Works,* ed. by C. J. Kraemer, Jr. (New York, 1936), p. 5.

exertions which can have no effect except on my ears, and perhaps to make me more tedious.[28] As to the noble earl's statement, by way of setting me right, it is wholly unnecessary, for I knew he was abroad—I had represented him as being abroad, and I had never charged him with turning out his son. The family, however, must have done it. (Lord Harrowby said, *No*.) Then so much the better for my argument against the system, for then the borough itself had flung him out, and prevented him from having access to the political school. I believe the statement that the family had nothing to do with it, because the noble earl makes it; but it would take a great deal of statement to make me believe that neither the patron nor the electors had anything to do with the exclusion, and that the member had voluntarily given up his seat, and indeed his office with his seat, beside abandoning his political studies, when he could have continued them as representative of his father's borough.

But the next argument of the noble earl I am, above all, anxious to grapple with, because it brings me at once to a direct issue with him, upon the great principle of the measure. The grand charge iterated by him, and re-echoed by his friends is, that population, not property, is assumed, by the bill, as the basis of representation. Now, this is a mere fallacy, and a gross fallacy. I will not call it a wilful misstatement; but I will demonstrate that two perfectly different things are, in different parts of this short proposition, carefully confounded, and described under the same equivocal name. If, by basis of representation is meant the ground upon which it was deemed right, by the framers of the bill, that some places should send members to Parliament, and others not, then I admit that there is some foundation for the assertion; but then it only applies to the new towns, and also it has no bearing whatever upon the question. For the objection—and I think the sound objection—to taking mere population as a criterion in giving the elective franchise, is, that such a criterion gives you electors without a qualification, and is, in fact, universal suffrage. And herein, my lords, consists the grievous unfairness of the statement I am sifting; it purposely mixes together different matters, and clothes them with an ambiguous covering, in order, by means of the confusion and the disguise, to insinuate that universal suffrage is at the root of the bill. Let us strip off this false garb. Is there in the bill anything resembling universal suffrage? Is it not framed upon the very opposite principles? In the counties, the existing qualification by freehold is retained in its fullest extent; but the franchise is extended to the other kinds of property, copyhold and leasehold. It is true that tenants at will are also to enjoy it, and their estate is so feeble, in contemplation of law, that one can scarce call it property. But whose fault is that? Not the authors of the bill, for they deemed that terms of years alone should give a vote; but they were opposed and defeated in this by the son of my noble friend [29] near me, and his fellow labourers against the measure. Let us now look to the borough qualification.

[28] From the opening of the Parliamentary Session, Opposition Lords had harassed Brougham and other supporters of the Ministry with obstructive points of order and disruptive behavior. As a new Lord and inexperienced presiding officer, Brougham suffered many moments of frustration before the time of this address. The notes of defiance in the speech doubtless reflect Brougham's impulsiveness, as Goodrich suggested, but given the behavior of the Opposition and Brougham's conviction that his cause was already lost, his bluntness seems less significant than Goodrich believed.

[29] The Duke of Buckingham.

[*Some noise from conversation here took place. Lord Brougham paused for a few seconds.*]

Noble lords must be aware that the chancellor, in addressing your lordships, stands in a peculiar situation. He alone speaks among his adversaries.[30] Other peers are at least secure against being interrupted by the conversation of those in their immediate neighbourhood. And for myself, I had far rather confront any distant cheers, however hostile, than be harassed by the talk of those close by. No practice in the House of Commons can ever accustom a person to this mode of annoyance, and I expect it, in fairness, to cease.

To resume the subject where I was forced to break off.—I utterly deny that population is the test, and property disregarded, in arranging the borough representation. The franchise is conferred upon householders only. Is not this a restriction? Even if the right of voting had been given to all householders, still the suffrage would not have been universal; it would have depended on property, not on numbers; and it would have been a gross misrepresentation to call population the basis of the bill. But its framers restricted that generality, and determined that property, to a certain considerable amount, should alone entitle to elect. It is true they did not take freehold tenure of land, as that qualification is inconsistent with town rights—nor did they take a certain amount of capital as the test—for that, beside its manifest inconvenience, would be a far more startling novelty than any the measure can be charged with. But the renting a £10 house is plainly a criterion both of property and respectability. It is said, indeed, that we have pitched this qualification too low—but are we not now debating on the principle of the bill? And is not the committee the place for discussing whether that principle should be carried into effect by a qualification of £10, or a higher? I have no objection, however, to consider this mere matter of detail here; and if I can satisfy the noble earl, that all over England, except in London and a few other great towns, £10 is not too low, I may expect his vote after all. Now, in small towns—I speak in the hearing of noble lords who are well acquainted with the inhabitants of them—persons living in £10 houses are in easy circumstances. This is undeniably the general case. In fact, the adoption of that sum was not a matter of choice. We had originally preferred £20, but, when we came to inquire, it appeared that very large places had a most inconsiderable number of such houses. One town, for instance, with 17,000 or 18,000 inhabitants, had not twenty who rented houses rated at £20 a-year. (Cheers.) Were we to destroy one set of close boroughs, the Old Sarums and Gattons, which had at least possession to plead for their title, in order to create another new set of boroughs just as close, though better peopled? In the large town I have alluded to, there were not three hundred persons rated at £10. (Hear!) Occupiers of such houses, in some country towns, fill the station of inferior shopkeepers—in some, of the better kind of tradesmen—here they are foremen of workshops—there, artisans earning good wages—sometimes, but seldom, labourers in full work: generally speaking, they are a class above want, having comfortable houses over their heads, and families and homes to which they are attached. An opinion has been broached, that the qualification might be varied in different places, raised in the larger

---

[30] The Chancellor spoke from his position toward the end of the House, with Opposition and Government benches on either side and the "cross-benches" for members of non-party views immediately before him.

towns, and lowered in the smaller. To this I myself, at one time, leant very strongly; I deemed it a great improvement of the measure. If I have since yielded to the objections which were urged, and the authorities brought to bear against me, this I can very confidently affirm, that if any one shall propound it in the committee, he will find in me, I will not say a supporter, but certainly an ample security, that the doctrine, which I deem important, shall undergo a full and candid and scrutinizing discussion. I speak for myself only—I will not even for myself say, that were the committee so to modify the bill, I would accept it thus changed. Candour prevents me from holding out any such prospect; but I do not feel called upon to give any decisive opinion now upon this branch of the details, not deeply affecting the principle; only, I repeat emphatically, that I shall favour its abundant consideration in the proper place—the committee. (Hear! Hear!)

My lords, I have admitted that there is some truth in the assertion of population being made the criterion of title in towns to send representatives, though it has no application to the present controversy. Some criterion we were forced to take; for nobody holds that each place should choose members severally. A line must be drawn somewhere, and how could we find a better guide than the population? That is the general test of wealth, extent, importance; and therefore substantially, though not in name, it is really the test of property. Thus, after all, by taking population as the criterion of what towns shall send members, we get at property by almost the only possible road, and property becomes substantially the basis of the title to send representatives; as it confessedly is, in name as well as in substance, the only title to concur in the election of them. The whole foundation of the measure, therefore, and on which all its parts rest, is property alone, and not at all population.

But then, says the noble earl, the population of a town containing 4000 souls, may, for any provision to the contrary in the bill, be all paupers! Good God! Did ever man tax his ingenuity so hard to find an absurdly extreme case? (Hear! and a laugh.) What! a town of 4000 paupers! 4000 inhabitants, and all quartered on the rates! (Much laughter.) Then who is to pay the rates? But if extreme cases are to be put on the one side, why may not I put one on the other? What say you to close boroughs coming, by barter or sale, into the hands of Jew jobbers, gambling loan-contractors, and scheming attorneys, for the materials of extreme cases? What security do these afford against the machinations of aliens—ay, and of alien enemies? (Hear! Hear!) What against a nabob of Arcot's Parliamentary and financial speculations? What against that truly British potentate naming eighteen or twenty of his tools members of the British House of Commons?[31] (Hear! Hear!) But is this an extreme case, one that stands on the outermost verge of possibility, and beyond all reach of probable calculation? Why, it once happened; the Nabob Wallajah Cawn Bahauder[32] had actually his eighteen or

[31] Mahomet Ali, Subah of Deccan in India, was alleged to have made collusive financial and political arrangements with agents of the East India Company. See Edmund Burke's speeches, "On the East India Bill," December 1, 1783, and "On the Nabob of Arcot's Debts," February 20, 1785.

[32] Member of a Mogul dynastic family of Hindustan in whose affairs the East India Company was deeply involved. Here, as in reference to the Nabob of Arcot, Brougham attributes to a foreign prince influence that was in fact exercised by Englishmen through the Company.

twenty members bought with a price, and sent to look after his pecuniary interests, as honest and independent members of Parliament. Talk now of the principle of property—the natural influence of great families—the sacred rights of the aristocracy—the endearing ties of neighbourhood—the paramount claims of the landed interest! Talk of British duties to discharge—British trusts to hold—British rights to exercise! Behold the sovereign of the Carnatic,[33] who regards nor land, nor rank, nor connection, nor open country, nor populous city; but his eye fastens on the time-honoured relics of departed greatness and extinct population—the walls of Sarum and Gatton; he arms his right hand with their venerable parchments, and, pointing with his left to a heap of star pagodas too massive to be carried along, lays siege to the citadel of the constitution, the Commons House of Parliament, and its gates fly open to receive his well disciplined band. (Cheers.) Am I right in the assertion, that a foreign prince obtaining votes in Parliament, under the present system, is no extreme case? Am I wrong in treating with scorn the noble earl's violent supposition of a town with 4000 souls, and all receiving parish relief?

[Lord Brougham next attacked as inconsistent those who opposed the reform bill on grounds it was inimical to the representation of property but who, at the same time, defended the *status quo* under which property-less freemen held voting rights.]

Certain it is, that the honours of the peerage have been bestowed before now upon right voters in right places. While I am on this subject, I cannot but advert to the remarks of my noble and learned friend [34] who was elevated from the bench to this House, and who greatly censured the ministers for creating some peers who happened to agree with them in politics. The coronation was, as all men know, forced upon us; nothing could be more against our will; but the opposition absolutely insisted on having one, to show their loyalty; a creation of peers was the necessary consequence, and the self same number were made as at the last coronation, ten years ago. But we did not make our adversaries peers—we did not bring in a dozen men to oppose us—that is my noble friend's complaint; and we did not choose our peers for such merits as alone, according to his view, have always caused men to be ennobled. Merit, no doubt, has opened to many the doors of this House. To have bled for their country—to have administered the highest offices of the state—to have dispensed justice on the bench—to have improved mankind by arts invented, or enlightened them by science extended—to have adorned the world by letters, or won the more imperishable renown of virtue—these, no doubt, are the highest and the purest claims to public honours; and from some of these sources are derived the titles of some among us—to others, the purest of all, none can trace their nobility—and upon not any of them can one single peer in a score rest the foundation of his seat in this place. Service without a scar in the political campaign—constant presence in the field of battle at St. Stephen's chapel—absence from all other fights, from "Blenheim down to Waterloo"—but above all, steady discipline—right votes in right places—these are the precious, but happily, not rare qualities, which have generally raised men to the

[33] The southeastern regions of India.
[34] Lord Wynford.

peerage. For these qualities the gratitude of Mr. Pitt showered down his baronies by the score, and I do not suppose he ever once so much as dreamt of ennobling a man who had ever been known to give one vote against him.

My lords, I have been speaking of the manner in which owners of boroughs traffic, and exercise the right of sending members to Parliament. I have dwelt on no extreme cases; I have adverted to what passes every day before my eyes. See now the fruits of the system, also by every day's experience. The Crown is stript of its just weight in the government of the country, by the masters of rotten boroughs;—they may combine; they do combine, and their union enables them to dictate their own terms. The people are stript of their most precious rights by the masters of rotten boroughs—for they have usurped the elective franchise, and thus gained an influence in Parliament which enables them to prevent its restoration. The best interests of the country are sacrificed by the masters of rotten boroughs (Hear! Hear!)—for their nominees must vote according to the interest not of the nation at large, whom they affect to represent, but of a few individuals, whom alone they represent in reality. (Hear! Hear!) But so perverted have men's minds become by the gross abuse to which they have been long habituated, that the grand topic of the noble earl,[35] and other debaters—the master-key which instantly unlocked all the sluices of indignation in this quarter of the House against the measure—which never failed, how often soever used, to let loose the wildest cheers, has been—that our reform will open the right of voting to vast numbers, and interfere with the monopoly of the few; while we invade, as it is pleasantly called, the property of the peers and other borough-holders. Why, say they, it absolutely amounts to representation! And wherefore should it not, I say? and what else ought it to be? (Hear! Hear!) Are we not upon the question of representation and none other? (Hear!) Are we not dealing with the subject of a representative body for the people? The question is, how we may best make the people's House of Parliament represent the people: and, in answer to the plan proposed, we hear nothing but the exclamations—"Why, this scheme of yours is a rank representation! (Cheers and laughter.) It is downright election! It is nothing more nor less than giving the people a voice in the choice of their own representatives! It is absolutely that most strange—unheard of—unimagined—and most abominable—intolerable—incredibly inconsistent and utterly pernicious novelty, that the members chosen should have electors, and that the constitutents should have something to do with returning the members!" (Loud cheers and laughter.)

But we are asked, at what time of our history any such system as we propose to establish was ever known in England, and this appeal, always confidently made, was never more pointedly addressed than by my noble and learned friend[36] to me. Now, I need not remind your lordships, that the present distribution of the right to send members, is anything rather than very ancient; still less has it been unchanged. Henry VIII created twenty boroughs—Edward VI made twelve—good Queen Elizabeth created one hundred and twenty, revived forty-eight; and in all there were created and revived two hundred down to the Restoration. I need only read the words of Mr. Prynne upon the remote antiquity of our borough system. He enumerates sixty-four boroughs—fourteen in Cornwall alone—as all

[35] Lord Harrowby.
[36] Lord Wynford.

new; and, he adds, "for the most part, the Universities excepted, very mean, poor, inconsiderable boroughs, set up by the late returns, practices of sheriffs, or ambitious gentlemen desiring to serve them, courting, bribing, feasting them for their voices, not by prescription or charter (some few excepted), since the reign of Edward IV, before whose reign they never elected or returned members to any English Parliament, as now they do."

Such then is the old and venerable distribution of representation time out of mind, had and enjoyed in Cornwall and in England at large. (Hear! Hear!) Falmouth and Bossiney, Lostwithiel and Grampound, may, it seems, be enfranchised, and welcome, by the mere power of the Crown. But let it be proposed to give Birmingham and Manchester, Leeds and Sheffield, members by an act of the legislature, and the air resounds with cries of revolution!

But I am challenged to prove that the present system, as regards the elective franchise, is not the ancient Parliamentary constitution of the country—upon pain, says my noble and learned friend, of judgment going against me if I remain silent. My lords, I will not keep silence, neither will I answer in my own person, but I will refer you to a higher authority, the highest known in the law, and in its best days, when the greatest lawyers were the greatest patriots. Here is the memorable report of the committee of the Commons, in 1623–4, of which committee Mr. Sergeant Glanville was the chairman, of which report he was the author. Among its members were the most celebrated names in the law—Coke, and Selden, and Finch, and Noy, afterwards Attorney-General, and of known monarchical principles. The first resolution is this:—

"There being no certain custom, nor prescription, who should be electors, and who not, we must have recourse to common right, which, to this purpose, was held to be, that more than the freeholders only ought to have voices in the election; namely, all men inhabitants, householders, resiants [residents] within the borough." (Hear! Hear!)

What then becomes of the doctrine that our bill is a mere innovation—that by the old law of England, inhabitant householders had no right to vote—that owners of burgage tenements, and freemen of corporations, have in all times exclusively had the franchise? Burgage tenants, it is true, of old had the right, but in the way I have already described—not as now, the nominal and fictitious holders for an hour merely for election purposes, but the owners of each—the real and actual proprietors of the tenement. Freemen never had it at all, till they usurped upon the inhabitants and thrust them out. But every householder voted in the towns without regard to value, as before the 8th of Henry VI every freeholder voted without regard to value in the counties—not merely £10 householders, as we propose to restrict the right, but the holder of a house worth a shilling, as much as he whose house was worth a thousand pounds. (Hear! Hear!) But I have been appealed to; and I will take upon me to affirm, that if the Crown were to issue a writ to the sheriff, commanding him to send his precept to Birmingham or Manchester, requiring those towns to send burgesses to Parliament, the votes of all inhabitant householders must needs be taken, according to the exigency of the writ and precept, the right of voting at common law, and independent of any usurpation upon it, belonging to every resident householder. (Hear! Hear!) Are, then, the King's ministers innovators—revolutionists—wild projectors—idle dreamers of dreams and feigners of fancies, when they restore the ancient common law right, but not in its ancient common law extent, for they limit, fix, and contract it? (Hear! Hear!) They add a qualification of £10 to restrain it, as our forefathers, in the fifteenth century, restrained the county franchise by the freehold qualification.

But then we hear much against the qualification adopted—that is, the particular sum fixed upon—and the noble earl [37] thinks it will only give us a set of constituents busied in gaining their daily bread, and having no time to study, and instruct themselves on state affairs. My noble friend too,[38] who lives near Birmingham, and may therefore be supposed to know his own neighbours better than we can, sneers at the statesmen of Birmingham and at the philosophers of Manchester. He will live—I tell him he will live to learn a lesson of practical wisdom from the statesmen of Birmingham, and a lesson of forbearance from the philosophers of Manchester. (Hear! Hear!) My noble friend was ill-advised, when he thought of displaying his talent for sarcasm upon 120,000 people in the one place, and 180,000 in the other. (Hear! Hear! Hear!) He did little, by such exhibitions, towards gaining a stock of credit for the order he belongs to—little towards conciliating for the aristocracy which he adorns, by pointing his little epigrams against such mighty masses of the people. Instead of meeting their exemplary moderation, their respectful demeanour, their affectionate attachment, their humble confidence, evinced in every one of the petitions, wherewithal they have in myriads approached the House, with a return of kindness—of courtesy—even of common civility;—he has thought it becoming and discreet to draw himself up in the pride of hexameter and pentameter verse,—skill in classic authors,—the knack of turning fine sentences,—and to look down with derision upon the knowledge of his unrepresented fellow-countrymen in the weightier matters of practical legislation. For myself, I too know where they are defective; I have no desire ever to hear them read a Latin line, or hit off in the mother tongue any epigram, whether in prose or in numerous verse. In these qualities they and I freely yield the palm to others. I, as their representative, yield it.—I once stood as such elsewhere, because they had none of their own; and though a noble earl [39] thinks they suffer nothing by the want, I can tell him they did severely suffer in the greatest mercantile question of the day, the Orders in Council, when they were fain to have a professional advocate for their representative, and were only thus allowed to make known their complaints to Parliament. Again representing them here, for them I bow to my noble friend's immeasurable superiority in all things, classical or critical. In book lore—in purity of diction—in correct prosody—even in elegance of personal demeanour, I and they, in his presence, hide, as well we may, our diminished heads. (Cheers and laughter.) But to say that I will take my noble friend's judgment on any grave practical subject,—on anything touching the great interests of our commercial country,—or any of those manly questions which engage the statesman, the philosopher in practice;—to say that I could ever dream of putting the noble earl's opinions, ay, or his knowledge, in any comparison with the bold, rational, judicious, reflecting, natural, and because natural, the trustworthy opinions of those honest men, who always give their strong natural sense fair play, having no affections to warp their judgment—to dream of any such comparison as this, would be, on my part, a flattery far too gross for any courtesy— or a blindness which no habits of friendship could excuse! (Cheers.)

[37] Lord Harrowby.
[38] Lord Dudley.
[39] Lord Harrowby.

[The speaker here enlarged on the common sense "of the manufacturers and artisans." *The Times'* account indicates that he treated this subject at greater length than is represented in the corrected text of the speech.]

The noble earl behind [40] addressed one observation to your lordships, which I must in fairness confess I do not think is so easily answered as those I have been dealing with. To the crown, he says, belongs the undoubted right, by the constitution, of appointing its ministers and the other public servants; and it ought to have a free choice, among the whole community, of the men fittest to perform the varied offices of the executive government. But, he adds, it may so happen, that the choice having fallen on the most worthy, his constituents, when he vacates his seat, may not re-elect him, or he may not be in Parliament at the time of his promotion; in either case he is excluded till a general election; and even at a general election, a discharge of unpopular, but necessary duties, may exclude him from a seat through an unjust and passing, and, possibly, a local disfavour with the electors. I have frankly acknowledged that I feel the difficulty of meeting this inconvenience with an apt and safe remedy, without a great innovation upon the elective principle. In the committee, others may be able to discover some safe means of supplying the defect. The matter deserves fuller consideration, and I shall be most ready to receive any suggestion upon it. But one thing I have no difficulty in stating, even should the evil be found remedyless, and that I have only the choice between taking the reform with this inconvenience, or perpetuating that most corrupt portion of our system, condemned from the time of Swift down to this day, and which even the most moderate and bit-by-bit reformers have now abandoned to its fate—my mind is made up, and I cheerfully prefer the reform. (Hear! Hear!)

The noble earl has told my noble friend at the head of the government [41] that he might have occupied a most enviable position, had he only abstained from meddling with Parliamentary Reform. He might have secured the support, and met the wishes, of all parties. "He stood," says the noble earl, "between the living and the dead." [42] All the benefit of this influence, and this following, it seems, my noble friend has forfeited by the measure of reform. My lords, I implicitly believe the noble lord's assertion, as far as regards himself. I know him to be sincere in these expressions, not only because he tells me so, which is enough, but because facts are within my knowledge, thoroughly confirming the statement. His support, and that of one or two respectable persons around him, we should certainly have had. [43] Believe me, my lords, we fully appreciated the value of the sacrifice we made; it was not without a bitter pang that we made up our minds to forego this advantage. But I cannot so far flatter those noble persons, as to say that their support would have made the government sufficiently strong in the last Parliament. (Hear! Hear!) Honest, and useful, and creditable as it would have been, it never could have enabled us to go on for a night without the support of the people. (Hear! Hear!) I do not mean the populace—the mob (hear!

[40] Lord Harrowby.

[41] Lord Grey.

[42] This is a misapplication, apparently, of the noble allusion of one of our greatest orators (Mr. Wilberforce), who said of Mr. Pitt and Revolution—"He stood between the living and the dead, and the plague was stayed." (Brougham.)

[43] See footnotes 14 and 17 above.

hear!): I never have bowed to them, though I never have testified any unbecoming contempt of them. Where is the man who has yielded less to their demands than he who now addresses you? Have I not opposed their wishes again and again? Have I not disengaged myself from them on their most favourite subject, and pronounced a demonstration, as I deemed it, of the absurdity and delusion of the ballot? [44] (Hear! Hear!) Even in the most troublous times of party, who has gone less out of his course to pay them court, or less submitted his judgment to theirs? But if there is the mob, there is the people also. (Cheers.) I speak now of the middle classes—of those hundreds of thousands of respectable persons —the most numerous, and by far the most wealthy order in the community; for if all your lordship's castles, manors, rights of warren and rights of chase, with all your broad acres, were brought to the hammer, and sold at fifty years' purchase, the price would fly up and kick the beam when counterpoised by the vast and solid riches of those middle classes, who are also the genuine depositaries of sober, rational, intelligent, and honest English feeling. (Cheers.) Unable though they be to round a period, or point an epigram, they are solid, right-judging men, and above all, not given to change. If they have a fault, it is that error on the right side, a suspicion of state quacks—a dogged love of existing institutions—a perfect contempt of all political nostrums. (Hear! Hear!) They will neither be led astray by false reasoning, nor deluded by impudent flattery: but so neither will they be scared by classical quotations, or browbeaten by fine sentences; and as for an epigram, they care as little for it as they do for a cannon-ball. (Hear! Hear!) Grave—intelligent—rational—fond of thinking for themselves—they consider a subject long before they make up their minds on it (hear! hear!); and the opinions they are thus slow to form they are not swift to abandon. It is an egregious folly to fancy that the popular clamour for reform, or whatever name you please to give it, could have been silenced by a mere change of ministers. The body of the people, such as I have distinguished and described them, had weighed the matter well, and they looked to the government and to the Parliament for an effectual reform. Doubtless they are not the only classes who so felt; at their backs were the humbler and numerous orders of the state; and may God of his infinite mercy avert any occasion for rousing the might which in peaceful times slumbers in their arms! To the people, then, it was necessary, and it was most fit, that the government should look steadily for support; not to save this or that administration; but because, in my conscience, I do believe that no man out of the precincts of Bethlem Hospital—nay, no thinking man, not certainly the noble duke, a most sagacious and reflecting man—can, in these times, dream of carrying on any government in despite of those middle orders of the state. (Cheers!) Their support must be sought, if the government would endure—the support of the people, as distinguished from the populace, but connected with that populace, who look up to them as their kind and natural protectors. (Hear!) The middle class, indeed, forms the link which connects the upper and the lower orders, and binds even your lordships with the populace, whom some of you are wont to despise. (Hear! Hear!) This necessary support of the country it was our duty to seek (and I trust we have not sought it in vain), by salutary reforms, not merely in the

---

[44] Brougham had disagreed with his Radical friends concerning the ballot as early as 1812; he also held out against including a section on the ballot in the Grey Ministry's reform bill.

representation, but in all the branches of our financial, our commercial, and our legal polity. But when the noble earl talks of the government being able to sustain itself by the support of himself and his friends, does he recollect the strong excitement which prevailed last winter? Could we have steered the vessel of the state safely through that excitement, either within doors or without, backed by no other support? (Hear! Hear!) I believe he was then on the Bay of Naples, and he possibly thought all England was slumbering like that peaceful lake— when its state was more like the slumbers of the mountain upon its margin. Stand between the living and the dead, indeed! Possibly we might; for we found our supporters among the latter class, and our bitter assailants among the former. (Hear! Hear!) True it is, the noble earl would have given us his honest support; *his* acts would have tallied with his professions. But can this be said of others? Did they, who used nearly the same language, and avowed the same feelings, give anything to the government, but the most factious opposition? Has the noble earl never heard of their conduct upon the timber duties, when, to thwart the administration, they actually voted against measures devised by themselves—ay, and threw them out by their division? Exceptions there were, no doubt, and never to be mentioned without honour to their names, some of the most noble that this House, or indeed any country of Europe can boast. They would not, for spiteful purposes, suffer themselves to be dragged through the mire of such vile proceedings, and conscientiously refused to join in defeating the measures themselves had planned. (Hear! Hear!) These were solitary exceptions; the rest, little scrupulous, gave up all to wreak their vengeance on the men who had committed the grave offence, by politicians not to be forgiven, of succeeding them in their offices. I do not then think that in making our election to prefer the favours of the country to those of the noble earl, we acted unwisely, independent of all considerations of duty and of consistency; and I fear I can claim for our conduct no praise of disinterestedness.[45]

My lords, I have followed the noble earl as closely as I could through his arguments, and I will not answer those who supported him with equal minuteness, because, in answering him, I have really answered all the arguments against the bill. One noble lord [46] seems to think he has destroyed it, when he pronounces, again and again, that the members chosen under it will be delegates. What if they were delegates? What should a representative be but the delegate of his constituents? But a man may be the delegate of a single person, as well as of a city or a town; he may be just as much a delegate when he has one constituent as when he has 5000—with this material difference, that under a single constituent, who can turn him off in a moment, he is sure to follow the orders he receives implicitly, and that the service he performs will be for the benefit of one man, and not of many. The giving a name to the thing, and crying out Delegate! Delegate! proves nothing, for it only raises the question, who should be the delegator of this public trust—the people or the borough-holders? (Hear! Hear!) Another noble lord,[47] professing to wish well to the great unrepresented towns, complained of the bill on their behalf, because, he said, the first thing it does is

[45] *The Times* indicates that Brougham said considerably more than is embodied in this paragraph and the paragraph immediately following.

[46] Lord Falmouth.

[47] Lord Caernarvon.

to close up the access which they at present possess to Parliament, by the purchase of seats for mercantile men, who may represent the different trading interests in general. Did ever mortal man contrive a subtlety so absurd, so nonsensical, as this? (Hear! Hear!) What! Is it better for Birmingham to subscribe, and raise £5000, for a seat at Old Sarum, than to have the right of openly and honestly choosing its own representative, and sending him direct to Parliament? (Hear! Hear!) Such horror have some men of the straight, open, highway of the constitution, that they would, rather than travel upon it, sneak into their seats by the dirty, winding, by-ways of rotten boroughs. (Cheers.)

But the noble earl behind [48] professed much kindness for the great towns—he had no objection to give Birmingham, Manchester, and Sheffield representatives as vacancies might occur, by the occasional disfranchisement of boroughs for crimes. Was there ever anything so fantastical as this plan of reform? (Hear! Hear!) In the first place, these great towns either ought to have members, or they ought not. If they ought, why hang up the possession of their just rights upon the event of some other place committing an offence? Am I not to have my right till another does a wrong? Suppose a man wrongfully keeps possession of my close; I apply to him, and say, "Mr. Johnson, give me up my property, and save me and yourself an action of ejectment." Should not I have some cause to be surprised, if he answered, "Oh no, I can't let you have it till Mr. Thomson embezzles £10,000, and then I may get a share of it, and that will enable me to buy more land, and then I'll give you up your field." (Laughter.)—"But I want the field, and have a right to get it; not because Thomson has committed a crime, but because it is my field, and not yours,—and I should be as great a fool as you are a knave, were I to wait till Thomson became as bad as yourself." (Great laughter.) I am really ashamed to detain your lordships with exposing such wretched trifling. (Hear! Hear!)

A speech, my lords, was delivered by my noble friend under the opposite gallery,[49] which has disposed of much that remains of my task. I had purposed to show the mighty change which has been wrought in later times upon the opinions, the habits, and the intelligence of the people, by the universal diffusion of knowledge. But this has been done by my noble friend with an accuracy of statement, and a power of language, which I should in vain attempt to follow; and there glowed through his admirable oration, a natural warmth of feeling to which every heart instinctively responded. (Hear! Hear!) I have, however, lived to hear that great speech talked of in the language of contempt. A noble lord,[50] in the fulness of his ignorance of its vast subject, in the maturity of his incapacity to comprehend its merits, described it as an amusing—a droll speech; and in this profound criticism a noble earl [51] seemed to concur, whom I should have thought capable of making a more correct appreciation. Comparisons are proverbially invidious; yet I cannot help contrasting that speech with another which I heard not very long ago, and of which my noble friend [52] knows something; one not certainly much resembling the luminous speech in question, but a kind of chaos of dark, disjointed figures, in which soft professions of regard for friends fought with

[48] Lord Harrowby.
[49] Lord Radnor.
[50] Lord Falmouth.
[51] Lord Caernarvon.
[52] Lord Caernarvon.

hard censures on their conduct, frigid conceptions with fiery execution, and the lightness of the materials with the heaviness of the workmanship—

> Frigida pugnabant calidis, humentia siccis,
> Mollia cum duris, sine pondere habentia pondus.[53]

A droll and amusing speech, indeed! It was worthy of the same speaker, of whom both Mr. Windham and Mr. Canning upon one occasion said, that he had made the finest they ever heard. It was a lesson deeply impregnated with the best wisdom of the nineteenth century, but full also of the profoundest maxims of the seventeenth. There was not a word of that speech—not one proposition in its luminous context—one sentence of solemn admonition or of touching regret—fell from my noble friend—not a severe reproof of the selfishness—nor an indignant exclamation upon the folly of setting yourselves against the necessary course of events, and refusing the rights of civilization to those whom you have suffered to become civilized—not a sentiment, not a topic, which the immortal eloquence and imperishable wisdom of Lord Bacon did not justify, sanction, and prefix.

[Lord Brougham next contended that the bill would not subvert the traditions of the Constitution as charged. The essence of the argument here omitted is expressed in the first four sentences of the paragraph immediately below.]

"Stand by the whole of the old constitution!" is the cry of our enemies. I have disposed of the issue of fact, and shown that what we attack is anything but the old constitution. But suppose, for argument's sake, the question had been decided against us—that Selden, Coke, Noy, Glanville, Prynne, were all wrong—that their doctrine and mine was a mere illusion, and rotten boroughs the ancient order of things—that it was a fundamental principle of the old constitution to have members without constituents, boroughs without members, and a representative Parliament without electors. Suppose this to be the nature of the old, and much admired, and more bepraised, government of England. All this I will assume for the sake of the argument; and I solicit the attention of the noble lords who maintain that argument, while I show them its utter absurdity. Since the early times of which they speak, has there been no change in the very nature of a seat in Parliament? Is there no difference between our days and those when the electors eschewed the right of voting, and a seat in Parliament, as well as the elective franchise, was esteemed a burthen? Will the same principles apply to that age and to ours, when all the people of the three kingdoms are more eager for the power of voting than for any other earthly possession; and the chance of sitting in the House of Commons is become the object of all men's wishes? Even as late as the union of the Crowns, we have instances of informations filed in the courts of law to compel Parliament men to attend their duty, or punish them for the neglect—so ill was privilege then understood. But somewhat earlier, we find boroughs petitioning to be relieved from the expense of sending members, and members supported by their constituents as long as they continued their attendance. Is it not clear that the Parliamentary law applicable to that state of things cannot be applied to the present circumstances, without in some respects making

---

[53] The cold and hot contended—dry and wet—
Things hard and soft—those with weight and without it.
Ovid, Metamp. (Chaos), Bk. i., 1. 19. (Goodrich.)

a violent revolution? But so it is in the progress of all those changes which time is perpetually working in the condition of human affairs. They are really the authors of change, who resist the alterations which are required to adjust the system, and adapt it to new circumstances;—who forcibly arrest the progress of one portion amidst the general advancement. Take, as an illustration, the state of our jurisprudence. The old law ordained that a debtor's property should be taken in execution. But in early times there were no public funds, no paper securities, no accounts at bankers; land and goods formed the property of all; and those were allowed to be taken in satisfaction of debts. The law, therefore, which only said, let land and goods be taken, excluded the recourse against stock and credits, although it plainly meant that all the property should be liable, and would clearly have attached stock and credits, had they then been known. But when nine-tenths of the property of our richest men consist of stock and credits, to exempt these under pretence of standing by the old law, is manifestly altering the substance for the sake of adhering to the letter; and substituting for the old law, that all the debtor's property should be liable, a new and totally different law, that a small part only of his property should be liable. Yet in no part of our system has there been a greater change than in the estimated value attached to the franchise, and to a seat in Parliament, from the times when one class of the community anxiously shunned the cost of electing, and another as cautiously avoided being returned, to those when both classes are alike anxious to obtain these privileges. Then, can any reasonable man argue, that the same law should be applied to two states of things so diametrically opposite? Thus much I thought fit to say, in order to guard your lordships against a favourite topic, one sedulously urged by the adversaries of reform, who lead men astray by constantly harping upon the string of change, innovation, and revolution.

But it is said, and this is a still more favourite argument, the system works well. How does it work well? Has it any pretensions to the character of working well? What say you to a town of five or six thousand inhabitants, not one of whom has any more to do with the choice of its representatives than any of your lordships sitting round that table—indeed, a great deal less—for I see my noble friend [54] is there? It works well, does it? How works well? It would work well for the noble duke, if he chose to carry his votes to market! Higher rank, indeed, he could not purchase than he has; but he has many connections, and he might gain a title for every one that bears his name. But he has always acted in a manner far more worthy of his own high character, and of the illustrious race of patriots from whom he descends, the founders of our liberties, and of the throne which our sovereign's exalted house fills; and his family have deemed that name a more precious inheritance than any title for which it could be exchanged. But let us see how the system works for the borough itself, and its thousands of honest, industrious inhabitants. My lords, I once had the fortune to represent it [55] for a few weeks; at the time when I received the highest honour of my life, the pride

[54] *The Times'* reporter recorded at this point: "(A laugh: the Duke of Devonshire was sitting at one of the angles of the table.)"

[55] The Duke of Devonshire offered Brougham the seat for the closed borough of Knaresborough. Brougham was "elected" early in 1830 but soon vacated the post upon his election in the county of York. "My return for the great county of York was my greatest victory, my most unsullied success," he wrote late in life. See *Life and Times of Henry Lord Brougham* (New York, 1872), III, 34.

and exultation of which can never be eradicated from my mind but by death, nor in the least degree allayed by any lapse of time—the most splendid distinction which any subjects can confer upon a fellow-citizen—to be freely elected for Yorkshire, upon public grounds, and being unconnected with the county. From having been at the borough the day of the election, I can give your lordships some idea how well the system works there. You may be returned for the place, but it is at your peril that you show yourself among the inhabitants. (A laugh.) There is a sort of polling; that is, five or six of my noble friend's tenants ride over from another part of the country—receive their burgage qualifications—vote, as the enemies of the bill call it, "in right of property," that is, of the duke's property— render up their title-deeds—dine, and return home before night. Being detained in court at York longer than I had expected on the day of this elective proceeding, I arrived too late for the chairing, and therefore did not assist at that awful solemnity. (A laugh.) Seeing a gentleman with a black patch, somewhere about the size of a sergeant's coif, I expressed my regret at his apparent ailment; he said, "It is for a blow I had the honour to receive in representing you at the ceremony." (Laughter.) Certainly no constituent ever owed more to his representative than I to mine; but the blow was severe, and might well have proved fatal. I understand this is the common lot of the members, as my noble friend,[56] who once sat for the place, I believe, knows; though there is some variety, as he is aware, in the mode of proceeding, the convenient neighbourhood of a river with a rocky channel sometimes suggesting operations of another kind. I am very far, of course, from approving such marks of public indignation; but I am equally far from wondering that it should seek a vent; for I confess, that if the thousands of persons whom the well working of the present system insults with the farce of the Knaresborough election (and whom the bill restores to their rights) were to bear so cruel a mockery with patience, I should deem them degraded indeed.

It works well, does it? For whom? For the constitution? No such thing. For borough proprietors it works well, who can sell seats, or traffic in influence, and pocket the gains. Upon the constitution it is the foulest stain, and eats into its very core.

It works well? For the people of England? For the people, of whom the many excluded electors are parcel, and for whom alone the few actual electors ought to exercise their franchise as a trust! No such thing. As long as a member of Parliament really represents any body of his countrymen, be they freeholders, or copyholders, or leaseholders—as long as he represents the householders in any considerable town—and is in either way deputed to watch over the interests of a portion of the community, and is always answerable to those who delegate him— so long has he a participation in the interests of the whole state, whereof his constituents form a portion; so long may he justly act as representing the whole community, having, with his particular electors, only a general coincidence of views upon national questions, and a rigorous coincidence where their special interests are concerned. But if he is delegated by a single man, and not by a county or a town, he does not represent the people of England; he is a jobber, sent to Parliament to do his own or his patron's work. (Cheers.) But then we are told, and with singular exultation, how many great men have found their way into the House of Commons by this channel. My lords, are we, because the only road

[56] Lord Tankerville.

to a place is unclean, not to travel it? If I cannot get into Parliament, where I may render the state good service, by any other means, I will go that way, defiling myself as little as I can, either by the filth of the passage, or the indifferent company I may travel with. I won't bribe; I won't job, to get in; but if it be the only path open, I will use it for the public good. But those who indulge in this argument about great men securing seats, do not, I remark, take any account of the far greater numbers of very little men who thus find their way into Parliament, to do all manner of public mischief. A few are, no doubt, independent; but many are as docile, as disciplined in the evolutions of debate, as any troops the noble duke had at Waterloo. One borough proprietor is well remembered, who would display his forces, command them in person, carry them over from one flank to the other, or draw them off altogether, and send them to take the field against the larks at Dunstable, that he might testify his displeasure. When conflicting bodies are pretty nearly matched, the evolutions of such a corps decide the fate of the day. The noble duke remembers how doubtful even the event at Waterloo might have been had Grouchy come up in time. Accordingly, the fortunate leader of that parliamentary force raised himself to an earldom and two lord lieutenancies, and obtained titles and blue ribands for others of his family, who now fill most respectable stations in this House.

[Here Brougham discussed historic misfortunes that might have been averted or mitigated if Parliament had been more representative of the people: loss of the American colonies, continuation of the war with Napoleon, etc.]

But it works well! Then why does the table groan with the petitions against it, of all that people, for whose interests there is any use in it working at all? Why did the country, at the last election, without exception, wherever they had the franchise, return members commissioned to complain of it, and amend it? (Hear!) Why were its own produce, the men chosen under it, found voting against it by unexampled majorities? Of eighty-two English county members, seventy six have pronounced sentence upon it, and they are joined by all the representatives of cities and of great towns.

It works well! Whence, then, the phenomenon of Political Unions,—of the people everywhere forming themselves into associations to put down a system which you say well serves their interests? Whence the congregating of 150,000 men in one place, the whole adult male population of two or three counties, to speak the language of discontent, and refuse the payment of taxes? [57] I am one who never have either used the language of intimidation, or will ever suffer it to be used towards me; but I also am one who regard those indications with unspeakable anxiety. With all respect for those assemblages, and for the honesty of the opinions they entertain, I feel myself bound to declare, as an honest man, as a minister of the crown, as a magistrate, nay, as standing, by virtue of my office, at the head of the magistracy, that a resolution not to pay the King's taxes is unlawful. (Hear! Hear!) When I contemplate the fact, I am assured that not above a few thousands of those nearest the chairman could know for what it was they held up their hands. (Hear!) At the same time there is too much reason

---

[57] The reference is to a recent mass meeting in Birmingham at which the crowd voted to withhold tax payments unless a reform bill were passed.

to think that the rest would have acted as they did, had they heard all that passed. My hope and trust is, that these men and their leaders will maturely reconsider the subject. There are no bounds to the application of such a power; the difficulty of counteracting it is extreme; and as it may be exerted on whatever question has the leading interest, and every question in succession is felt as of exclusive importance, the use of the power I am alluding to, really threatens to resolve all government, and even society itself, into its elements. I know the risk I run of giving offence by what I am saying. To me, accused of worshipping the democracy, here is indeed a tempting occasion, if in that charge there were the shadow of truth. Before the great idol, the Juggernaut, with his 150,000 priests, I might prostrate myself advantageously. But I am bound to do my duty, and speak the truth; of such an assembly I cannot approve; even its numbers obstruct discussion, and tend to put the peace in danger,—coupled with such a combination against payment of taxes, it is illegal; it is intolerable under any form of government; and as a sincere well-wisher to the people themselves, and devoted to the cause which brought them together, I feel solicitous, on every account, to bring such proceedings to an end.

But, my lords, it is for us to ponder these things well; they are material facts in our present inquiry. Under a system of real representation, in a country where the people possessed the only safe and legitimate channel for making known their wishes and their complaints, a Parliament of their own choosing, such combinations would be useless. Indeed, they must always be mere *brutum fulmen*,[58] unless where they are very general; and where they are general, they both indicate the universality of the grievance and the determination to have redress. Where no safety-valve is provided for popular discontent, to prevent an explosion that may shiver the machine in pieces—where the people—and by the people, I repeat, I mean the middle classes, the wealth and intelligence of the country, the glory of the British name—where this most important order of the community are without a regular and systematic communication with the legislature—where they are denied the constitution which is their birthright, and refused a voice in naming those who are to make the laws they must obey—impose the taxes they must pay,— and control, without appeal, their persons as well as properties—where they feel the load of such grievances, and feel too the power they possess, moral, intellectual, and, let me add, without the imputation of a threat, physical—then, and only then, are their combinations formidable; when they are armed by their wrongs, far more formidable than any physical force—then, and only then, they become invincible. (Hear! Hear!)

Do you ask what, in these circumstances, we ought to do? I answer, simply our duty. (Hear! Hear!) If there were no such combinations in existence—no symptom of popular excitement—if not a man had lifted up his voice against the existing system, we should be bound to seek and to seize any means of furthering the best interests of the people, with kindness, with consideration, with the firmness, certainly, but with the prudence also, of statesmen. How much more are we bound to conciliate a great nation, anxiously panting for their rights—to hear respectfully their prayers—to entertain the measure of their choice with an honest inclination to do it justice; and if, while we approve its principle, we yet dislike some of its details, and deem them susceptible of modification, surely we ought, at

---

[58] Meaningless flashes.

any rate, not to reject their prayers for it with insult. (Loud cries of "Hear!")
God forbid we should so treat the people's desire; but I do fear that a determination is taken not to entertain it with calmness and impartiality. (Cries of *No!*
No! from the opposition.) I am glad to have been in error; I am rejoiced to hear
this disclaimer, for I infer from it that the people's prayers are to be granted.
(Hear!) You will listen, I trust, to the advice of my noble and learned friend,[59]
who, with his wonted sagacity, recommended you to do as you would be done by.
This wise and Christian maxim will not, I do hope, be forgotten. Apply it, my
lords, to the case before you.

[Brougham next applied the golden rule to legislation, supposing the House
of Commons to have before it a bill originating with the Lords and exclusively concerned with affairs of their House. He concluded this hypothetical analogy with:
"Will you not extend an equal courtesy to the bill of the Commons and of the
people?"]

I am asked what great practical benefits are to be expected from this measure?
And is it no benefit to have the government strike its roots into the hearts of the
people? Is it no benefit to have a calm and deliberative, but a real organ of the
public opinion, by which its course may be known, and its influence exerted upon
state affairs regularly and temperately, instead of acting convulsively, and as it
were by starts and shocks? I will only appeal to one advantage, which is as certain
to result from this salutary improvement of our system, as it is certain that I am
addressing your lordships. A noble earl[60] inveighed strongly against the licentiousness of the press; complained of its insolence; and asserted that there was no
tyranny more intolerable than that which its conductors now exercised.[61] It is
most true, that the press has great influence, but equally true, that it derives this
influence from expressing, more or less correctly, the opinion of the country. Let
it run counter to the prevailing course, and its power is at an end. (Hear! Hear!)
But I will also admit that, going in the same general direction with public opinion,
the press is oftentimes armed with too much power in particular instances; and
such power is always liable to be abused. But I will tell the noble earl upon what
foundation this overgrown power is built. The press is now the only organ of
public opinion. This title it assumes; but it is not by usurpation: it is rendered
legitimate by the defects of your Parliamentary constitution; it is erected upon
the ruins of real representation. The periodical press is the rival of the House of
Commons; and it is, and it will be, the successful rival, as long as that House does
not represent the people—but not one day longer. If ever I felt confident in any
prediction, it is in this, that the restoration of Parliament to its legitimate office of
representing truly the public opinion will overthrow the tyranny of which noble
lords are so ready to complain, who, by keeping out the lawful sovereign, in truth
support the usurper. It is you who have placed this unlawful authority on a

---

[59] Lord Plunkett.

[60] Lord Winchelsea.

[61] What follows concerning the press and Irish affairs appears, from *The Times'* report, to have been considerably abridged in the corrected text. The traditional text
retains all basic ideas and reproduces language reported by *The Times,* but extended
amplifications and some vigorously phrased applications were apparently deleted in
revision.

rock: pass the bill, it is built on a quicksand. (Hear! Hear!) Let but the country have a full and free representation, and to that will men look for the expression of public opinion, and the press will no more be able to dictate, as now, when none else can speak the sense of the people. Will its influence wholly cease? God forbid! Its just influence will continue, but confined within safe and proper bounds. It will continue, long may it continue, to watch the conduct of public men—to watch the proceedings even of a reformed legislature—to watch the people themselves—a safe, an innoxious, a useful instrument, to enlighten and improve mankind! But its overgrown power—its assumption to speak in the name of the nation—its pretension to dictate and to command, will cease with the abuse upon which alone it is founded, and will be swept away, together with the other creatures of the same abuse, which now "fright our isle from its propriety." (Loud cries of "Hear!")

Those portentous appearances, the growth of later times, those figures that stalk abroad, of unknown stature, and strange form—unions of leagues, and musterings of men in myriads, and conspiracies against the exchequer; whence do they spring, and how come they to haunt our shores? What power engendered those uncouth shapes, what multiplied the monstrous births till they people the land? Trust me, the same power which called into frightful existence, and armed with resistless force, the Irish volunteers of 1782—the same power which rent in twain your empire, and raised up thirteen republics—the same power which created the Catholic Association, and gave it Ireland for a portion. What power is that? Justice denied—rights withheld—wrongs perpetrated—the force which common injuries lend to millions—the wickedness of using the sacred trust of government as a means of indulging private caprice—the idiotcy of treating Englishmen like the children of the South Sea Islands (hear!)—the phrensy of believing, or making believe, that the adults of the nineteenth century can be led like children, or driven like barbarians! (Hear! Hear!) This it is that has conjured up the strange sights at which we now stand aghast! And shall we persist in the fatal error of combating the giant progeny, instead of extirpating the execrable parent? Good God! Will men never learn wisdom, even from their own experience? Will they never believe, till it be too late, that the surest way to prevent immoderate desires being formed, ay, and unjust demands enforced, is to grant in due season the moderate requests of justice? You stand, my lords, on the brink of a great event; you are in the crisis of a whole nation's hopes and fears. An awful importance hangs over your decision. Pause, ere you plunge! There may not be any retreat! It behoves you to shape your conduct by the mighty occasion. They tell you not to be afraid of personal consequences in discharging your duty. I too would ask you to banish all fears; but, above all, that most mischievous, most despicable fear—the fear of being thought afraid. (Loud cheers!) If you won't take counsel from me, take example from the statesmanlike conduct of the noble duke,[62] while you also look back, as you may, with satisfaction upon your own. He was told, and you were told, that the impatience of Ireland for equality of civil rights was partial, the clamour transient, likely to pass away with its temporary occasion, and that yielding to it would be conceding to intimidation. I recollect hearing this topic urged within this hall in July 1828; less regularly I heard it than I have now done, for I belonged not to your number—but I heard it urged in the self-same

---

[62] The Duke of Wellington.

terms. The burthen of the cry was—It is no time for concession; the people are turbulent, and the Association dangerous. That summer passed, and the ferment subsided not; autumn came, but brought not the precious fruit of peace—on the contrary, all Ireland was convulsed with the unprecedented conflict which returned the great chief of the Catholics to sit in a Protestant Parliament; winter bound the earth in chains, but it controlled not the popular fury, whose surge, more deafening than the tempest, lashed the frail bulwarks of law founded upon injustice. (Hear! Hear!) Spring came; but no etherial mildness was its harbinger, or followed in its train; the Catholics became stronger by every month's delay, displayed a deadlier resolution, and proclaimed their wrongs in a tone of louder defiance than before. And what course did you, at this moment of greatest excitement, and peril, and menace, deem it most fitting to pursue? Eight months before, you had been told how unworthy it would be to yield when men clamoured and threatened. No change had happened in the interval, save that the clamours were become far more deafening, and the threats, beyond comparison, more overbearing. What, nevertheless, did your lordships do? Your duty; for you despised the cuckoo-note of the season, "be not intimidated." You granted all that the Irish demanded, and you saved your country. (Cheers.) Was there in April a single argument advanced, which had not held good in July? None, absolutely none, except the new height to which the dangers of longer delay had risen, and the increased vehemence with which justice was demanded; and yet the appeal to your pride, which had prevailed in July, was in vain made in April, and you wisely and patriotically granted what was asked, and ran the risk of being supposed to yield through fear.

But the history of the Catholic Claims conveys another important lesson. Though in right and policy and justice, the measure of relief could not be too ample, half as much as was received with little gratitude when so late wrung from you, would have been hailed twenty years before with delight (loud cries of "hear!"); and, even the July preceding, the measure would have been received as a boon freely given, which, I fear, was taken with but sullen satisfaction in April, as a right long withheld. (Hear! Hear!) Yet, blessed be God, the debt of justice, though tardily, was at length paid, and the noble duke won by it civic honours which rival his warlike achievements in lasting brightness—than which there can be no higher praise. (Cheers.) What, if he had still listened to the topics of intimidation and inconsistency which had scared his predecessors? He might have proved his obstinacy, and Ireland would have been the sacrifice. (Hear! Hear!)

Apply now this lesson of recent history—I may say of our own experience to the measure before us. We stand in a truly critical position. If we reject the bill, through fear of being thought to be intimidated, we may lead the life of retirement and quiet, but the hearts of the millions of our fellow-citizens are gone for ever; their affections are estranged; we and our order and its privileges are the objects of the people's hatred, as the only obstacles which stand between them and the gratification of their most passionate desire. (Loud cries of "hear!") The whole body of the aristocracy must expect to share this fate, and be exposed to feelings such as these. For I hear it constantly said, that the bill is rejected by all the aristocracy. Favour, and a good number of supporters, our adversaries allow it has among the people; the ministers, too, are for it; but the aristocracy, say they, is strenuously opposed to it. I broadly deny this silly, thoughtless assertion. What, my lords! the aristocracy set themselves in a mass against the people—they who sprang from the people—are inseparably connected with the people—are supported by the people—are the natural chiefs of the people! (Hear! Hear!) *They* set themselves against the people, for whom peers are ennobled—bishops consecrated—Kings anointed—the people to serve whom Parliament itself has an existence, and the Monarchy and all its institutions are constituted, and without whom none of them could exist for an hour! (Cheers.) The assertion of unreflecting men is too monstrous to be endured—as a member of this House, I deny it with indignation. I repel it with scorn, as a calumny upon us all. (Continued cheers.) And yet are there those who even within these walls speak of the bill augmenting so much the strength of the democracy, as to endanger the other orders of the state; and so they charge its authors with promoting anarchy and rapine. Why, my lords, have its authors nothing to fear from democratic spoliation? (Hear! Hear!) The fact is, that there are members of the present cabinet, who possess, one or two of them alone, far more property than any two administrations within my recollection; and all of them have ample wealth. I need hardly say, I include not myself, who have little or none. But even of myself I will say, that whatever I have depends on the stability of existing institutions; and it is as dear to me as the princely possessions of any amongst you. (Loud cries of "hear!") Permit me to say, that, in becoming a member of your House, I staked my all on the aristocratic institutions of the state. I abandoned certain wealth, a large income, and much real power in the state, for an office of great trouble, heavy responsibility, and very uncertain duration. I say, I gave up substantial power for the shadow of it, and for distinction depending upon accident. I quitted the elevated station of representative for Yorkshire, and a leading member of the Commons. I descended from a position quite lofty enough to gratify any man's ambition; and my lot became bound up in the stability of this House. Then, have I not a right to throw myself on your justice, and to desire that you will not put in jeopardy all I have now left? (Cheers.)

But the populace only, the rabble, the ignoble vulgar, are for the Bill! Then what is the Duke of Norfolk, Earl Marshal of England? What the Duke of Devonshire? What the Duke of Bedford? (Cries of *"Order"* from the Opposition.) I am aware it is irregular in any noble lord that is a friend to the measure; its adversaries are patiently suffered to call Peers even by their Christian and surnames. Then I shall be as regular as they were, and ask, does my friend John Russell (cheers and laughter), my friend William Cavendish (cheers and laughter), my friend Harry Vane, belong to the mob, or to the aristocracy? Have they no possessions? Are they modern names? Are they wanting in Norman blood, or whatever else you pride yourselves on? (Cheers and laughter.) The idea is too ludicrous to be seriously refuted;—that the bill is only a favourite with the democracy, is a delusion so wild as to point a man's destiny towards St. Luke's. (Cheers and laughter.) Yet many, both here and elsewhere, by dint of constantly repeating the same cry, or hearing it repeated, have almost made themselves believe that none of the nobility are for the measure. A noble friend of mine has had the curiosity to examine the list of Peers, opposing and supporting it, with respect to the dates of their creation, and the result is somewhat remarkable.[63] A large majority of the

---

[63] *The Times* reports that Brougham discussed the division of opinion among Peers at much greater length than the corrected text indicates. He also said, according to *The Times,* "We have not abused the discretion placed in every ministry with reference to the augmentation of the peerage."

Peers, created before Mr. Pitt's time, are for the Bill; the bulk of those against it are of recent creation (hear! hear!); and if you divide the whole into two classes, those ennobled before the reign of George III and those since, of the former, fifty-six are friends, and only twenty-one enemies of the reform. So much for the vain and saucy boast, that the real nobility of the country are against reform. I have dwelt upon this matter more than its intrinsic importance deserves, only through my desire to set right the fact, and to vindicate the ancient aristocracy from a most groundless imputation.

My lords, I do not disguise the intense solicitude which I feel for the event of this debate, because I know full well that the peace of the country is involved in the issue. I cannot look without dismay at the rejection of the measure. But grievous as may be the consequences of a temporary defeat—temporary it can only be; for its ultimate, and even speedy success, is certain. Nothing can now stop it. Do not suffer yourselves to be persuaded, that even if the present ministers were driven from the helm, any one could steer you through the troubles which surround you without reform. But our successors would take up the task in circumstances far less auspicious. Under them, you would be fain to grant a bill, compared with which, the one we now proffer you is moderate indeed. (Loud cries of "hear!") Hear the parable of the Sybil; for it conveys a wise and wholesome moral. (Hear! Hear!) She now appears at your gate, and offers you mildly the volumes—the precious volumes—of wisdom and peace. The price she asks is reasonable; to restore the franchise, which, without any bargain, you ought voluntarily to give: you refuse her terms—her moderate terms—she darkens the porch no longer. But soon, for you cannot do without her wares, you call her back;—again she comes, but with diminished treasures; the leaves of the book are in part torn away by lawless hands,—in part defaced with characters of blood. But the prophetic maid has risen in her demands—it is Parliaments by the Year—it is Vote by the Ballot—it is suffrage by the million! (Hear!) From this you turn away indignant, and for the second time she departs. Beware of her third coming; for the treasure you must have; and what price she may next demand, who shall tell? It may even be the mace which rests upon that woolsack. What may follow your course of obstinacy, if persisted in, I cannot take upon me to predict, nor do I wish to conjecture. But this I know full well, that, as sure as man is mortal, and to err is human, justice deferred enhances the price at which you must purchase safety and peace (hear! hear!);—nor can you expect to gather in another crop than they did who went before you, if you persevere in their utterly abominable husbandry, of sowing injustice and reaping rebellion.

But among the awful considerations that now bow down my mind, there is one which stands pre-eminent above the rest. You are the highest judicature in the realm; you sit here as judges, and decide all causes, civil and criminal, without appeal. It is a judge's first duty never to pronounce sentence, in the most trifling case, without hearing. (Hear!) Will you make this the exception? Are you really prepared to determine, but not to hear the mighty cause upon which a nation's hopes and fears hang? (Cheers.) You are. Then beware of your decision! Rouse not, I beseech you, a peace-loving, but a resolute people; alienate not from your body the affections of a whole empire. As your friend, as the friend of my order, as the friend of my country, as the faithful servant of my sovereign, I counsel you to assist with your uttermost efforts in preserving the peace, and upholding and perpetuating the constitution. (Cheers.) Therefore, I pray and exhort you not to reject this measure. (Cheers.) By all you hold most dear—by all the ties that bind every one of us to our common order and our common country, I solemnly adjure you—I warn you—I implore you—yea, on my bended knees,[64] I supplicate you—reject not this bill! (Loud cheering which lasted for a considerable time.)

༄

Bibliographical Note

There is but one definitive biographical study of Lord Brougham, Chester W. New's *Life of Henry Brougham to 1830* (1961). No other work is based upon the full range of primary source materials now available. Of the biographies and sketches treating the whole of Brougham's life, *Lord Brougham* (1935) by G. T. Garratt is probably the best. Brougham's relationships with his party are reliably treated in Arthur Aspinall's *Lord Brougham and the Whig Party* (1927). Most published criticism of his speaking is largely anecdotal and often rendered unreliable by partisan purposes. Goodrich's analysis is superior, though written without the advantage of historical perspective.

Daniel O'Connell

(1775–1847)

The most distinguished successor of Henry Grattan as an apostle of Irish liberty, Daniel O'Connell commanded the energies of his countrymen for almost half a century on the seemingly paradoxical principle that power may be wrested from one group by another without violence. He won a bloodless struggle in 1829 for the freedom of Irish Catholics, and he directed the peaceful demonstrations of 1843 for the dissolution of the parliamentary union of England and Ireland. His speech at Tara was the greatest in that latter campaign.

In moral, not physical, force O'Connell placed his life-long faith.[1] Typical is this declaration from his speech at the last monster meeting held on October 1, 1843, at Mullaghmast, following the speech at Tara:

[Here, as at Tara, I find] the same resolution not to violate the peace—not to be guilty of the slightest outrage—not to give the enemy powers by committing a crime, but peacefully and manfully to stand together in the open day—to protest before man, and in the presence of God, against the iniquity of continuing the Union [loud cheers].[2]

[64] *The Times* records: "Here Lord Brougham slightly bent his knee on the woolsack."

[1] Only once, in "The Mallow Defiance" in the spring of 1843, did he allow himself to explode into warlike language. See the passage quoted in Sean O'Faolain, *King of the Beggars* (New York, 1938), pp. 300–1.

[2] Quoted from the text appearing in William E. White, "Daniel O'Connell's Oratory on Repeal" (unpublished Ph.D. dissertation, Department of Speech, University of Wisconsin, 1954), p. 345.

O'Connell was not a doctrinaire, not a philosopher, not even a sound scholar. He did not elevate his belief in moral force to the level of a profound theory. Rather, he found the idea expedient because Ireland could scarcely cope with the military might of Britain; he found it workable because with it he achieved Catholic emancipation in 1829; and he found it psychologically right because he believed that human beings, if shown a choice, would abandon error and accept justice.

A demagogue to his enemies, but the "Liberator" to his friends, this man began his life in 1775 in County Kerry, Ireland. Early in childhood, he was adopted by an uncle whose prosperity arose from his success in the smuggling trade. By various stratagems, the uncle, defying the penal laws which forbade the establishment of Catholic schools, succeeded in having Daniel educated as a Catholic in Ireland until he was sixteen. Then after three years of schooling in France, Daniel took up the study of law in London in 1794, and in 1798 was admitted to the Irish Bar.

Inevitably, O'Connell's career in law, so successful that it netted him £8,000 in 1828, gave way to his interest in politics. He received national attention from a speech to a Catholic meeting in Dublin attacking the Act of Union which nonetheless was passed in 1800; he became the leader of the Irish masses in 1813 after his speech in defense of Magee, which he changed from a defense of freedom of the press into a prosecution of England for her governance of Ireland. These two speeches, the first on freedom in religion and the second on freedom in politics, epitomized O'Connell's philosophy and foreshadowed his future.

The two movements for freedom were separate but O'Connell pursued in each a common method of agitation. That agitation was to be total; consequently he invented every conceivable device to unite in one voice all of Ireland—the priest and the peasant, the rich and the poor, the urban and the rural, the Protestant and the Catholic. The agitation was to be peaceable; accordingly, he shunned the military and fostered pacific resolution. The agitation was to be constant; so he sent orators about the land, distributed pamphlets, formed associations, staged demonstrations, presented petitions, filed lawsuits, arranged thousands of meetings.

As director, symbol, and spokesman for the agitation, O'Connell looked and lived the part. People remembered him for his curly flame-colored hair, his six feet of height, his powerful torso. He had the strength, grace, and energy of an athlete. The testimony concerning the clarity, range, power, melody, and flexibility of his voice suggests that he was as prodigiously endowed for speech as Caruso was for song. He learned to adapt his delivery to subject, audience, and occasion whether in the courtroom, the House of Commons, or the mass meeting.[3] Gladstone considered O'Connell the "greatest popular leader the world has ever seen"; Balzac called him the "incarnation of the people"; Wendell Phillips maintained that O'Connell was "Clay, Corwin, Choate, Everett, and Webster in one." [4]

His physical stamina enabled him, even at the age of sixty-eight, in 1843, to lead

[3] To one observer, Monsieur Duvergier, a Frenchman who toured Ireland in 1826, it all sounded spontaneous. Translations of some of Duvergier's letters appear in the appendix of Thomas Wyse, *Historical Sketch of the late Catholic Association* (London, 1829). See especially Wyse, II, lxxi. In Letters II and III, there are revealing contrasts between O'Connell and Sheil, another Catholic orator.

[4] Denis Gwynn, *Daniel O'Connell* (Cork, 1947), pp. 1–2 for the first two comments; for the third, "Daniel O'Connell," an oration by Wendell Phillips in *Speeches, Lectures, and Letters*, second series (Boston, 1894), p. 415.

the greatest of all his political agitations for repeal of the Union. Between April 19 and October 1 he spoke at thirty-two "monster meetings." No other speaker in history has ever gathered such large audiences.

The most celebrated of these monster meetings, for which nearly a million people were assembled, was held at Tara on Tuesday, August 15. The place and the date were carefully chosen, the arrangements skillfully executed. Tara was an Irish shrine. It had been the seat of the early High Kings of Ireland; there the Ark of the Covenant and Jacob's stone were said to be buried; at Tara, Saint Patrick had converted the Irish kings to Christianity, using a shamrock to explain the Trinity; at Tara in 1798 a band of Irish revolutionaries had been killed by the British and buried in a common grave.[5]

Geographically, Tara was perfect. As its Gaelic name implies, Tara is a hill, a place that commands a prospect. Near its summit, O'Connell had erected a platform accommodating a thousand dignitaries and commanding a view of a plain that sloped gently and evenly to the west—limited only by the horizon.

The date was chosen because it is the holyday of the Feast of the Assumption of the Blessed Virgin, a day when Catholics are obliged to attend Mass and refrain from manual labor. Priests led entire congregations to Tara, saying Masses at shrines along the way.

Processions started from four different points of the compass: from Navan, fifteen miles to the northwest; from Slane, twelve miles northeast; from Dunshaughlin on the southeast; from Trim on the southwest. O'Connell himself set out at eight o'clock in the morning from Dunshaughlin in a decorated carriage, escorted by bands and horsemen; for the last three miles he rode under archways of banners to the beat of forty bands and the acclaim of thousands. At one-thirty, he bowed his head at the grave of the revolutionaries, then mounted the platform and addressed the audience.

How many of the million actually could have heard him? We cannot say. Perhaps 63,000 people could follow his words. Years later, romantic recollections were reported. Said a man who had been there, "You could hear his voice a mile away and it sounded as if it was coming through honey." Another claimed that O'Connell told those around the platform to repeat his words and to tell those who heard to repeat in turn until, like the ripples dispatched by the dropping of a pebble in a pond, his words would be carried to the edges of the crowd.

But the Liberator's strength could not last forever. During 1844, after being jailed from May until September on a charge of treason to England, he declined in body and mind. By 1846 he had lost control of the repeal movement; early in 1847 he made his last speech in the House of Commons; in May, 1847, he died in Genoa while on a pilgrimage to Rome.

∽

[5] R. A. S. Macalister, *Tara: A Pagan Sanctuary of Ancient Ireland* (London, 1931), *passim.*

THE SPEECH AT TARA *

August 15, 1843

It would be the extreme [of] affectation in me to suggest that I have not some claims to be the leader of this majestic meeting (loud cheers). It would be worse than affectation—it would be drivelling folly—if I were not to feel the awful responsibility that the part I have taken in this majestic movement imposes upon me (hear, hear). I feel responsibility to my country and especially to my Creator (hear). Yes, I feel the tremulous nature of that responsibility. Ireland is aroused, is aroused from one end to another. Her multitudinous population has but one expression and one wish, and that is the extinction of the Union—the restoration of her nationality (cheers).

(A voice: There will be no compromise.)

Who is it that talks of compromise (cheers)?

I am not here for the purpose of making anything like a schoolboy's attempt at declamatory eloquence. I am not here to revive in your recollection any of those poetic imaginings respecting the spot on which we stand (hear, hear), and which have really become as familiar as household words. I am not here to exaggerate the historical importance of the spot on which we are congregated—but it is impossible to deny that Tara has historical recollections that give to it an importance, relatively, to other portions of the land.

It deserves to be so considered by every person who comes to it for political purposes (hear), for it has an elevation and point of impression in the public mind that no other part of Ireland can possibly have.

History may be tarnished by exaggeration, but the fact is undoubted that we are at Tara of the Kings (cheers). We are on the spot where the monarchs of Ireland were elected, and where the chieftains of Ireland bound themselves by the sacred pledge of honor and the tie of religion to stand by their native land against the Danes, or any other stranger (cheers).

This is emphatically the spot from which emanated the social power—the legal authority—the right to dominion over the furthest extremes of the island, and the power of concentrating the force of the entire nation for the purpose of national defense (cheers).

On this important spot I have an important duty to perform. I here protest in the face of my country, in the face of my Creator—in the face of Ireland and our God—against the continuance of the unfounded and unjust Union (cheers).

My proposition to Ireland is that the Union is not binding upon us—it is not binding, I mean, upon conscience. It is void in principle; it is void as matter of right; and it is void in constitutional law (hear, hear, hear and cheers). I protest

---

* For a mass meeting, O'Connell would not have used a manuscript; nor does an original text for Tara exist. What purports to be a complete text is published in *The Nation* of August 19, 1843; a shorter version appeared two days earlier in *The Times;* and a text whose length falls between the first two has been published by T. M. Kettle, who does not reveal his source, in *Irish Orators and Oratory.* Our text, prepared by William E. White, is a collation of these three sources. It appears in the appendix of his unpublished dissertation, *Daniel O'Connell's Oratory on Repeal* (University of Wisconsin, 1954).

by everything that is sacred, without being profane, to the truth of my assertion [that] there is really no union between the two countries.

My proposition is that there was no authority vested in any person to pass the Act of Union. I deny the authority of the act; I deny the competency of the two legislatures to pass that act. The English Legislature had no such competency —that must be admitted by every person. The Irish Legislature had no such competency. I arraign the Union, therefore, on the ground of incompetency of the bodies that passed it. No authority could render it binding but the authority of the Irish people, consulted individually through the counties, cities, towns, and villages. If the people of Ireland called for the Union, then it was binding on them, but there was no other authority that could make it binding.

The Irish Parliament had no such authority; they were elected to make laws and not legislatures. It had no right to the authority which alone belonged to the people of Ireland. The trustee might as well usurp the right of the person who trusts him; the servant might as well usurp the power of the master. The [members of the] Irish Parliament were but our servants; and they had no right to transfer us to any other power on the face of the earth.

This doctrine is manifest, and would be admitted by every person if it were applied to England. Would any person venture to assert that the Parliament of England should have the power to transfer its privileges to make laws from England to the legislative chamber of France? Would any persons be so insane as to admit it? Such insanity would not be mitigated even if they were allowed to send over their representatives to France. Yes, every person would admit in that case that the Union was void.

I have no higher affection for England than for France; they are both foreign authorities to me. The highest legal authority in England[1] has declared us aliens in blood, aliens in religion, and aliens in language from the English (groans).

Let no person groan him. I thank him for the honesty of the expression. I never heard of any other act of honesty on his part, and the fact of his having committed one act of honesty ought to recommend him to your good graces (laughter).

I can refer you to the principle of constitutional law, and to Locke on government, to show that the Irish Parliament had no power or authority to convey itself away (hear, hear, hear).[2] I will only detain you on that point by citing the words of Lord Chancellor Plunket. He declared in the Irish House of Commons that they had no right to transfer the power of legislation from the country.[3] He called upon them to have his words taken down, and he defied the power of Lord Castlereagh[4] to have him censured for this expression on limiting the authority of

[1] Henry Brougham, Lord Chancellor from 1830 to 1834.

[2] Chapter XIX, "Of the Dissolution of Government," in *The Second Treatise of Civil Government,* contains several statements referring to the conception that Americans call the "consent of the governed." See paragraphs numbered 217, 221, 222, 223, 227. *Two Treatises of Government,* ed. by Thomas I. Cook (New York, 1947), pp. 228–47.

[3] William C. Plunket, Chancellor of Ireland, 1830–1841, provided the major opposition to the passage of the Act of Union in a speech before the Irish House of Commons on January 15, 1800.

[4] Lord Robert Castlereagh, British foreign minister in 1800, supported the Act of Union.

parliament. He said to them that they could not transfer their authority—that the maniacal suicide might as well imagine that the blow by which he destroyed his miserable body could annihilate the soul of Ireland, her constitutional right (hear, hear, and loud cheers).

I am here the representative of the Irish nation; and in the name of that great, that virtuous, that moral, temperate, brave, and religious nation, I proclaim the Union a nullity (hear and loud cheers) for it is a nullity in point of right!

Mr. Saurin,[5] who for twenty years was attorney-general to the Tories, made the declaration and distinction. He said, "You have no right to pass the Union. You may make it law, but it will be void in principle. No man's conscience will be bound by it; and it will be the duty of the Irish people to take the first favorable opportunity to repeal the Union, and to restore the nationality of Ireland" (hear, hear, and loud cheers).

I agree with Saurin that they have power to enforce the law, but they have no power to alter the right (hear, hear).

Never was any measure carried by such iniquitous means as the Union was carried (hear, hear). The first thing that taints it in its origin, and makes it, even if it were a compact, utterly void, was the fraud committed in fomenting discord in the country, and encouraging the rebellion until it broke out—and in making that rebellion, and the necessity for crushing it, the means of taking from Ireland her constitution and her liberties.

There was this second fraud committed on her; that at the time of the passing of the Act of Union, Ireland had no legal protection. The habeas corpus was suspended, martial law was proclaimed, trial by jury was at an end, and the lives and liberties of all the King's subjects in Ireland were at the mercy of the courts martial. Those among you who were old enough at the time remember when the shriek from the triangle [6] was heard from every village and town, and when the troops would march out from Trim [7] and lay desolate the country for nine or ten miles around. Military law was established in all its horrors throughout every district of the country and the people were trampled in the dust under the feet of yeomanry, army, and fencibles.

The next fraudulent device to which England had recourse in order to carry this infamous measure, and to promote her own prosperity on the ruins of Irish nationality, was to take the most effective means in order to prevent the Irish people from meeting to remonstrate against the insult and the injury which was about to be inflicted upon them. The Union was void no less from the utter incompetency of the contracting parties to enter into any such contract, than [it was] by reason of the fact that it was carried into operation by measures most iniquitous, atrocious and illegal.

The habeas corpus act was suspended. Torture, flogging, pitch caps, and imprisonment were the congenial agencies whereby England endeavored to carry her infamous designs. Executions upon the gallows, for no other crime than that

[5] William Saurin opposed the Act of Union in 1800. His views having changed, he held a British appointment as Attorney-General of Ireland from 1807 to 1822.

[6] A triangle is a frame formed of three poles stuck in the ground and bound together at the top and used to bind persons undergoing physical punishment.

[7] Trim was a fortified town about ten miles southwest of Tara. On this day, it was one of four points where people assembled to form the great processions that marched to Tara.

of being suspected of being suspicious, were of daily occurrence in every part of the kingdom. Thus it was that they endeavored to crush the expression of the people's feelings, whom they resolved to plunder and degrade.

The people were not permitted to assemble together for the purpose of remonstrating against the Union. Meetings, convened by the officers of justice—by the high sheriffs of counties—were dispersed at the point of bayonet. The people were not permitted to meet together for remonstrance, but they got up petitions in every direction, to testify their feelings upon the subject. Although no less than 707,000 signatures were signed to petitions against the Union—despite all the corrupt influence of the Government—more than three thousand wretches could not be found to sign a petition in favor of the measure.

The next impeachment which I bring against the Union is that it was brought about not only by physical force, but by bribery the most unblushing and corruption the most profligate.

One million two hundred seventy-five thousand pounds were expended upon the purchase of rotten boroughs alone, and no less a sum than two millions of money was lavished upon peculation unparalleled, and bribery the most enormous and most palpable that ever yet disgraced the annals of humanity. There was not an office, civil, military, or ecclesiastical in the country, which was not flung open to the Unionist as the price and wages of his depravity. Six or seven judges bought their seats upon the bench by giving their adhesion to the Union, having no claim to wear the ermine other than that which was to be derived from the fact of their being recreants to their country. They continued, in right of this, during their lives to inflict the effects of their iniquity upon the people whom they betrayed.

Twelve bishops obtained their sees by voting for the Union, for the spirit of corruption spared nothing. Men were made prelates, generals, admirals, commissioners, for supporting the ministry in this infamous design, and every office in the revenue and customs was placed at the disposal of those who were base enough to sell their country for a mess of pottage. In fact, corruption was never known to have been carried before or since to such excess in any country of the world.[8]

[8] On the charge of corruption, see Stephen Gwynn, *The History of Ireland* (New York, 1923), p. 415; Edmund Curtis, *A History of Ireland* (London, 1942), pp. 350–51; James O'Connor, *History of Ireland, 1797–1942* (London, 1925) who gives a balanced view on p. 117 of Vol. I: "That Pitt corrupted the Irish Parliament is beyond controversy. . . . Under the Union eighty-three boroughs were abolished, and compensation amounting to about £15,000 was paid to each owner. . . . Each borough owner was paid whether he voted for the Union or against it. A great number of offices were abolished, and pensions were paid to the office holders. Thus Lord Clare, Speaker of the House of Lords and an advocate of the Union, got a pension of £3,987 a year; Foster, Speaker of the House of Commons, who opposed it, got a pension of £5,038 a year.

"At the same time, there was considerable undisguised corruption. Forty-six promotions in the peerage were made; twenty ecclesiastical jobs, and twelve legal jobs were provided; twelve pensions and four titular honours were dispensed. Making every due allowance for the fact that some of the payments were, legitimately enough, recompense for the extinguished boroughs, and for the practice, then more extensively followed than now, of recompensing political adherents by honours, the scale of this corruption staggers modern conceptions. . . .

If such a contract, if contract it would be called, is to be binding on the Irish nation, there is no longer any use for honesty or justice in the world.

Strong as was the influence on the human mind, the victory which the English ministry achieved was slow, and by no means easy of accomplishment. Intimidation to the death upon one hand, and bribery on the other, were impotent to procure a majority in the Irish House of Commons in the first session when the bill was introduced. On the contrary, when the first attempt was made to prostrate our liberties, there was a majority of eleven against the Union bill.

But the despoiler was not easy to be foiled, nor was he apt to be disheartened by a single failure. The work of corruption was set on foot with redoubled energy, and the wretches who were not so utterly abandoned as to suffer themselves to be bribed for the direct and positive purpose of giving their vote for the Union, accepted bribes on the condition of withdrawing from the house altogether. Accordingly, they vacated their seats, and in their places stepped Englishmen and Scotchmen who knew nothing of Ireland, and who were not impeded by any conscientious scruple whatever from giving their unqualified sanction to any plot of the English, how infamous soever, to oppress and plunder the country.

By these accumulated means the Union was carried, and the fate of Ireland sealed (hear, hear). But in the name of the great Irish nation I proclaim it a nullity (loud cheers).

But the monster evil of the Union is the financial robbery which by its means was practised upon Ireland. The scandalous injustice thus inflicted would be in itself sufficient even in the absence of other arguments—even if other arguments were wanting—to render the Union void and of no effect.

At the passing of that fatal act—badge of our ruin and disgrace—Ireland owed only twenty millions, England owed 446 millions. The equitable terms upon which the contract was based whereby both countries were to be allied and identified—identified, indeed!—were these: that England was generously to undertake the liability of one-half of our national debt, on condition that we would undertake the responsibility of one-half of hers!

This is not a befitting time nor season to enter into minute details relative to the particulars of this particular financial swindle; but I may be permitted to direct your attention to this very obvious fact: that whereas England has only doubled her debt since the passing of the Union, the increase of the national debt of Ireland during the same period cannot with justice be estimated on a different ratio. Consequently, Ireland, at the very highest calculation, cannot in reality, and as of her own account, owe a larger sum than forty millions. And I will tell you, my friends, that never will we consent to pay one shilling more of a national debt than that (cheers, and cries of "never").

I say it in the name and on behalf of the Irish nation (loud cheers). But I will tell you this as a secret, and you may rely upon it as the truth, that in point of fact we do not owe one farthing more than thirty millions. In proof of the truth of this assertion, I beg leave to refer to you a work published by a very near and

---

"The opponents of the Union were not behind in their attempts at bribery. A subscription list, which it was intended to bring up to £100,000, was opened for the purchase of seats. A member named Whaley, who, in 1799, had voted for the Union and had spent £4,000 on his election, voted against it on being paid £4,000 out of the fund."

dear relative of mine—my third son, the member for Kilkenny—who, by the most accurate statistical calculations, and by a process of argument intelligible to the humblest intellect, has made the fact apparent to the world that according to the terms of honest and equitable dealing, as between both countries, Ireland's proportion of the national debt cannot be set down at a larger sum than I state—thirty millions (hear, hear, and loud cheers for Mr. John O'Connell).[9]

I am proud that there is a son of mine who, after the Repeal shall have been carried, will be able to meet the cleverest English financier of them all foot to foot and hand to hand, and prove, by arguments the most incontestable, how grievous and intolerable is the injustice which was inflicted upon our country in this respect by the Union.

The project of robbing Ireland by joining her legislatively with England was no new scheme, which entered the minds of the English for the first time about the year 1800 (hear, hear and loud cheering). It was a project which was a favorite theme of dissertation with all the English essayists for years previous to the period when it was carried into practical effect. The policy towards Ireland, which their literary men were continually urging upon the English people for their adoption, was similar to that of the avaricious housewife, who killed the goose who laid her golden eggs (laughter). Yes, such was the course they pursued towards Ireland, and you will deserve the reputation of being the lineal descent of that goose if you be such ganders as not to declare in a voice of thunder that no longer shall this system of plunder be permitted to continue (hear).

My next impeachment of the Union is founded upon the disastrous effects which have resulted therefrom to our commercial and manufacturing interests, as well as to our general national interests.

Previous to the Union, the County Meath was filled with seats of noblemen and gentlemen. What a contrast does its present state present! I yesterday read at the association a list of the deserted mansions which are now to be found ruined and desolate in your country. Even the spot where the Duke of Wellington —famed the world over for his detestation of his country—drew his first breath, instead of bearing a noble castle or splendid mansion, presented the aspect of ruin and desolation, and briars and nettles adequately marked the place that produced him (hear).[10]

The County of Meath was at one time studded thickly with manufactories in every direction, and an enormous sum was expended yearly in wages; but here, as in every other district of the country, the eye is continually shocked with sights which evidence with but too great eloquence the lamentable decay which has been entailed upon our country by the Union.

The linen trade at one time kept all Ulster in a state of affluence and prosperity (hear, hear). Kilkenny was for ages celebrated for its extensive blanket manufactures. In Cork, also in Carrick-on-Suir and in a thousand other localities, too numerous to mention, thousands were kept in constant and lucrative employment,

[9] John O'Connell wrote "The Commercial Injustices," which appeared in the *Report to the Repeal Association on the General Case of Ireland for a Repeal of the Legislative Union* (Dublin, 1843), and "The Taxation Injustice," printed separately. Both are carried in the appendices to *An Argument for Ireland* (Dublin, 1844). John was the heir apparent for the leadership of the repeal movement, but he lacked the personal force necessary to command such an undertaking.

[10] The Duke of Wellington was born at Dangan Castle, County Meath, Ireland.

at various branches of national industry, from year's end to year's end, before the passing of the Union.

But this is no longer the case, and one man is not now kept in employment for a thousand who were employed before the Union. The report of the English commissioners themselves has declared this appalling fact to the world—that one-third of our population is in a state of actual destitution!

Yet in the face of all this, men may be found who, claiming to themselves the character of political honesty, stand up and declare themselves in favor of the continuance of the Union!

It was no bargain—it was a base swindle. Had it, indeed, been a fair bargain, the Irish would have continued faithful to their contracts; whereas England never yet made a promise which she did not violate, nor ever entered into a contract which she did not shamelessly and scandalously outrage (hear, hear, hear). Even the Union itself, beneficial as it is to England, is but a living lie to Ireland. Everybody now admits the mischief that the Union has produced to Ireland.

The very fact of its not being a compact is alone sufficient to nullify the Union; and on that ground I here proclaim, in the name of the Irish nation, that it is null and void (loud cheers). It is no nation at all. It is a union of legislators, not a union of nations.

Are you and I one bit more Englishmen now than we were twenty or forty years ago (cheers and laughter)? If we had a union, would not Ireland have the same parliamentary franchise that is enjoyed by England?

England, calling it a union [continues] the singular extreme of fraud, and injustice, and iniquity; and no nation on the face of the earth ever committed so much of injustice, fraud, and iniquity, as England. But calling it a union, could anything be more unjust on the part of England than to give her own people a higher and more extensive grade of franchise, and to the Irish people a more limited and an extinguishing and perishing franchise?

She has given to her people an extended municipal reform, and to Ireland a wretched and perishing municipal reform. Even within the last week a plan was brought forward by Lord Eliot [11] and the sneaking Attorney-General Smith [12] that will have the effect of depriving one-third of those Irishmen who now enjoy the franchise of its possession.

No, the Union is void. But it is more peremptorily void on the ground of the ecclesiastical revenues of the country being left to support a church of a small portion of the people. In England the ecclesiastical revenues of the country are given to the clergy that the majority of the people believe to teach the truth. In Scotland the ecclesiastical revenues are, or at least were up to a late period, paid to the majority of the people. But the Irish people are compelled to pay the clergy of a small minority, not amounting to more than the one-tenth of the people of the entire island (great cheering).

The Union was effected against all constitutional principle—by the most atrocious fraud—by the most violent and most iniquitous exercise of force—by the most abominable corruption and bribery—by the shifting of Irish members out of their seats and the putting of Englishmen and Scotchmen into their places. That was followed by the destruction of our commerce, by the annihilation of our

---

[11] Lord Edward Eliot became Chief Secretary to Ireland in 1841.
[12] Thomas Berry Cusack Smith became Attorney-General late in 1842.

manufactures and by the depreciation of our farmers. You know I speak the truth when I talk of the depression of the farming interests by financial robbery —on an extensive scale to be sure, but a robbery on that every account only the more iniquitous, fiendish, and harsh.

I contend, therefore, that the Union is a nullity.

But do I, on that account, advise you to turn out against it? No such thing—I advise you to act quietly and peaceably, and in no other way.

(A voice: Any way you like it.)

Remember that my doctrine is that, "the man who commits a crime gives strength to the enemy," and you should not act in any manner that would strengthen the enemies of your country (hear, hear).

You should act peaceably and quietly, but firmly and determinedly. You may be certain that your cheers today will be conveyed to England (the vast assemblage here commenced cheering for several minutes in the most deafening and enthusiastic manner, and the distant lines of human beings that on the walls and hedges marked the limits of the immense assemblage might be seen waving their hats and handkerchiefs in response). Yes, the overwhelming opinion of your multitude will be taken to England, and will have its effect there.

He[13] talked of civil war, but he does not say a single word of that now (hear, hear, and laughter). He is now getting eyelit holes made in the old barracks; and only think of any old general doing such a thing—just as if we were going to break our heads against stone walls (laughter). I am glad to find that a great quantity of brandy and biscuits has been latterly imported, and I hope the poor soldiers get some of them. The Duke of Wellington is not now talking of attacking us, and I am glad of it; but I tell him this—I mean no disrespect to the brave, the gallant, and the good-conducted soldiers that compose the Queen's Army and all of them that we have in this country are exceedingly well-conducted (hear, hear, and cheers). There is not one of you that has a single complaint to make against any of them (cries of "not one"). They are the bravest army in the world, and therefore I do not mean to disparage them at all; but I feel it to be a fact, that Ireland roused as she is at the present moment would, if they made war upon us, furnish enough women to beat the entire of the Queen's force (great cheers).

At the last fight for Ireland [the Irish] were betrayed by having confided in England's honor.[14] But oh! English honor will never again betray our land, for the man would deserve to be betrayed who would confide again in England!

I would as soon think of confiding in the cousin-german of a certain personage having two horns and a hoof (laughter).[15]

At that last battle, the Irish soldiers, after three days' fighting, being attacked by fresh troops, faltered and gave way, and 1,500 of the British army entered the breach. The Irish soldiers were fainting and retiring when the women of Limerick threw themselves between the contending forces, and actually stayed the progress of the advancing enemy. I am stating matters of history to you, and the words I use are not mine, but those of Parson Story, the chaplain of King William who describes the siege, and who admits that the Limerick women drove

---

[13] The Duke of Wellington.

[14] The First Siege of Limerick in 1690.

[15] That is to say, in someone related by descent from a common ancestor, the Devil.

back the English soldiers from fifteen to thirty paces. Several of the women were killed, when a shriek of horror resounded from the ranks of the Irish. They cried out, "Let us rather die to the last man than that our women should be injured." They then threw themselves forward, and, made doubly valiant by the bravery of the women, they scattered the Saxon and the Dane before them (loud applause).[16]

Yes, I have women enough in Ireland to beat them if necessary; but, my friends, it is idle to imagine that any statesman ever existed who could resist the cry that Ireland makes for justice (cheers).

There is one thing that I wish to caution you against. I have ascertained that some scoundrel Ribbon Society swearers [17] are endeavoring to delude the people. I have traced their progress from Manchester, and I have ascertained that some of them even had the audacity to state that they are in my confidence.

This [18] is a holy festival in the Roman Catholic Church. It is the anniversary of the blessed day when the Mother of our Redeemer ascended from earth to meet her Son, and reign with him for ever. Oh! on such a day I would not tell you a falsehood. I hope I am under her protection. I hope that our sacred cause has her prayers for its success (loud cheers). The church within the last year offered prayers throughout the Christian world for the cause of religion in Spain, and against the sacrilegious plunderers of the church in that country, and what happened? The minion of these plunderers has fallen from power, and nobody knows why.[19] He made no effort to return, and nobody can tell why. It seems as if he had been bewildered in his course from on high; and the tyrant of Spain has fallen from his power and station.

Well, by the solemnity of this day, I conjure you to lay hold of any of these followers [20] you can meet with, and take them to the police-office. You will very

[16] The reference is to George Story, *A True and Impartial History of the Most Material Occurrences in Ireland* (London, 1693). Participation by the women in defense of the city is frequently mentioned in older histories, although the accounts quote only Story as authority. Walter Harris, in *The History of the Life and Reign of William-Henry* (Dublin, 1746), says that the British force breached the ramparts of Limerick and attacked the Irish defenders who retreated into the town, "but, observing that few of the *English* had entered the town, they rallied, and killed many of them. Elated with this success, they ventured again upon the breach, and the resolution of their women was so great, that they incessantly pelted the besiegers with stones, and so inspired the men by their example, that, after three hours unequal fighting, the *English* were forced to retire to their trenches" (p. 288). John Ryan in the *Life of William the Third* (Dublin, 1836) concludes his account with these words: "It is related, that on this occasion, some of the women of the city, with a boldness strangely in discordance with the gentleness generally appointed to the sex, assisted the military, and with stones and other missiles did no small execution on the besiegers. These amazons were, however, of the lower orders" (p. 227).

[17] The Irish nationalists who advocated armed revolution.

[18] August 15, 1843, which fell on a Tuesday (not on a Sunday as Bowers says), is a holiday of the Roman Catholic Church called the Feast of the Assumption of the Blessed Virgin. Devotion to the Mother of God being particularly strong in Ireland, August 15 is known as "Lady Day."

[19] General Baldomero Esparteo, regent for the young Queen Isabella II after 1841, adopted a policy of persecution of Catholics; he was removed from power by a military uprising in 1843.

[20] Followers of the Ribbon Societies.

probably find some of the stipendiary magistrates that they [21] send here very sorry to see their friend in trouble (laughter and loud cries of hear, hear). I tell you again that I am afraid of nothing but the establishment of Ribbonism (hear, hear).

I told you that the Union did not deprive the people of the right or take away the authority to have self-legislation. It has not lessened the prerogatives of the crown, or taken away the rights of the sovereign. Amongst them is the right to call her parliament wherever the people are entitled to it—(cheers)! The Queen has only tomorrow to issue her writs and get the Chancellor to seal them, and if Sir Edward Sugden [22] does not sign them she will soon get an Irishman that will revive the Irish Parliament.

Remember, I pronounce the Union to be null—to be obeyed, as an injustice must be obeyed, when it is supported by law, until we have the royal authority to set the matter right, and substitute our own parliament.

I delight at having this day presided over such an assemblage on Tara Hill (cheers). Those shouts that burst from you were enough to recall to life the kings and chiefs of Ireland. I almost fancy that the spirit of the mighty dead are hovering over us; that the ancient kings and chiefs of Ireland are from yonder clouds listening to us.

Oh, what a joyous and cheering sound is conveyed in the chirrup for Old Ireland! It is the most beautiful—the most fertile—the most abundant—the most productive country on the face of the earth. It is a lovely land—indented with noble harbors, intersected with transcendent translucent streams, divided by mighty estuaries. Its harbors are open at every hour for every tide, and are sheltered from every storm that can blow from any quarter of heaven. Oh yes, it is a lovely land, and where is the coward that would not dare to die for it?

Yes, our country exhibits the extreme of civilization. Your majestic movement is already the admiration of the civilized world. No other country could produce such an amount of physical force, coupled with so much decorum and propriety of conduct. Many thousands of persons assembled together, and, though they have forces sufficient to carry any battle that ever was fought, they separate with the tranquility of schoolboys breaking up in the afternoon (hear).

I wish you could read my heart, to see how deeply the love of Ireland is engraven upon it. Let the people of Ireland, who stood by me so long, stand by me a little longer, and Ireland shall be a nation again (cheers).

∽

BIBLIOGRAPHICAL NOTE

The most extensive analysis of O'Connell's oratory is contained in White's dissertation. W. E. H. Lecky in *Leaders of Public Opinion in Ireland: Swift, Flood, Grattan, O'Connell* (new ed., 2 vols., 1903) is particularly acute in contrasting O'Connell with another Irish orator, Richard Lalor Sheil. Claude G. Bowers' essay on O'Connell in *The Irish Orators* (1916) is slight but interesting. Best of the many contemporary accounts is William J. O. Daunt's *Personal Recollections of the Late Daniel O'Connell, M.P.* (2 vols., 1848). Although not the first major biography to appear

[21] "They" refers to the government of England.
[22] Appointed by Peel, Edward Sugden was Lord Chancellor of Ireland from 1841 to 1846.

after O'Connell's death, the earliest one that is still useful is Mary Frances Cusack's *The Liberator: His Life and Times, Political and Social* (2 vols., Dublin, n.d.). Virtually all of O'Connell's biographers are critics of his oratory as well as chroniclers of the events of his life. Among the best of them is Denis Gwynn in his *Daniel O'Connell* (1947), which is concerned more with emancipation than with repeal. More sensational is Sean O'Faolain's *King of the Beggars* (1938). Angus Macintyre's *The Liberator* (1965), being an examination of the Irish Party, sometimes called the O'Connellite Party, is perforce also a biographical account of O'Connell in his last seventeen years. Michael Tierney has edited a book of nine essays entitled *Daniel O'Connell* (1949), of which the last by John J. Horgan, "O'Connell—The Man," is a scholarly assessment of O'Connell's beliefs. Although incomplete, the best general source for O'Connell's speeches is Mary Frances Cusack's *The Speeches and Public Letters of the Liberator* (2 vols., 1875). More likely to be available in college and university libraries, however, is *The Select Speeches of Daniel O'Connell*, edited by his son John (1854, reprinted several times). Histories of Ireland have earned a reputation in the past for a notorious deficiency in objectivity, but at least one modern account appears to be a sound historical document: Edmund Curtis's *A History of Ireland* (4th ed., 1942).

Benjamin Disraeli, Lord Beaconsfield

(1804–1881)

In the long list of British Prime Ministers there is but one professional novelist and but one man of purely Jewish descent: Benjamin Disraeli, First Earl of Beaconsfield. "Dizzy," as he was first condescendingly and later affectionately called, seemed to nineteenth-century Englishmen uniquely able and disconcertingly inscrutable. Sir Robert Peel, Lord John Russell, and William Gladstone were among Disraeli's chief opponents in politics. For all their differences of personality, these men seemed predictable, understandable leaders, as Disraeli did not. His most distinguished biographer was led to write:

> I have sometimes been asked if my book would at last dispel the mystery that surrounds Disraeli; and my answer has invariably been that, unless the mystery remained when I had finished my labours, I should have failed in my task of portraiture.[1]

Nor is the "mystery" dispelled by J. A. Froude's remark at the conclusion of his *Life of the Earl of Beaconsfield*: "He was English only by adoption, and he never completely identified himself with the country which he ruled."

Almost by accident, it seems, Disraeli was baptized in the Anglican faith, thus attaining the right to political leadership. The future Minister lacked even that standard British preparation for high office, a university degree. In childhood he studied at nonconformist private schools; then the library of his father, a literary historian, became his "college." At twenty-two he published a financially

---

[1] W. F. Monypenny and G. E. Buckle, *The Life of Benjamin Disraeli, Earl of Beaconsfield* (New York, 1913–1920), VI, 640. Monypenny's statement.

successful novel; in later years he completed and published eleven more novels, a variety of short literary pieces, a bad epic poem, a closet drama, a political biography of Lord George Bentinck, and many political essays and reviews. From youth to old age he found self-expression through fiction as vital an experience as self-realization through politics. Victorians were prone to ask whether the novelist or the statesman-debater-essayist was the true Disraeli.

Though in his youth he had thought of himself as a Radical, Disraeli entered Parliament in 1837 as a Tory. He supported Sir Robert Peel's Conservative Ministry of 1841 until he began to suspect Peel's loyalty to the Protectionist system. Then began his campaign of opposition against the Minister whom he described as devoid of imagination but "the greatest Member of Parliament that ever lived." Disraeli believed, and historians agree, that his philippics of 1845 and 1846 welded the Protectionists into an active political force and destroyed Peel's capacity ever to lead again after he secured repeal of the Corn Laws. Imaginativeness and an exceptional alertness to the power of symbolic acts and phrases were, indeed, the qualities of mind that most dramatically set Disraeli apart from Sir Robert, the very model of intelligent, practical, safe, English statesmanship.

As an officer of government, Disraeli served as Chancellor of the Exchequer under Lord Derby for three relatively brief periods (1852, 1858–1859, 1866–1868) and as Prime Minister during 1868 and 1874–1880. In 1876, Queen Victoria was "happy to call him up to the other House, where the fatigue would be *far less* and where he would be able to *direct* everything." [2] Among the legislative and other public achievements in which he had a leading part were the transfer of authority over India from the East India Company to the Crown, designation of the Queen as Empress of India, the Canadian Federation Act which joined the provinces of Canada, the Reform Act of 1867 which opened suffrage to the working classes, a variety of acts to improve and regulate sanitation and factory conditions, and acquisition of control over the Suez Canal. Perhaps, however, Disraeli's efforts to "educate" the Conservative Party should stand above his other achievements. Beset by *laissez-faire* liberalism on one side and parochial agrarianism on the other, he steadily and successfully supplied ideas, strategies, and language to speed the evolution of a socially conscious conservatism not unlike that of which he had written in his condition-of-England novels: *Sybil* and *Coningsby*.

Disraeli failed dramatically in his maiden parliamentary speech, but in time he learned the arts of debate so well that on the floor of the House of Commons he shared eminence only with Gladstone. His political principles tended to be procedural. He insisted that responsible political parties and responsible leaders, not "laws" of human calculus, were the key assurances of constructive political change. The nation and the empire could only be unified, he thought, if their parts shared allegiance to stable institutions—institutions that governments in each generation must conserve, perfect, and sometimes create for the next. Understandably, Disraeli could affirm and illustrate such ideas more successfully through novels than through propositional discourse. He was not, in fact, gifted in exposition and amplification; in these Gladstone was his master. It was in dissecting

---

[2] Queen Victoria to Disraeli, June 5, 1876. Monypenny and Buckle, V, 491. Italics the Queen's.

divisive, unimaginative, or doctrinaire ideas and actions that Disraeli had no peer among the orators of Victoria's reign.

Disraeli's major addresses were prepared with care, often rehearsed in part, and delivered somewhat impassively with the least possible reference to notes or other papers. However, laborious preparation did not impair his capacity to meet the unexpected in debate. It was in the style of the advocate that Disraeli excelled; at his best he was clear, intellectual rather than sensuous in imagery, didactic but often brilliantly satiric, and always more than a little aloof. Few of his addresses illustrate these features of his speaking as well as the final philippic against Peel and the doctrine of free trade, in the last few pages of the speech reprinted below. The bulk of that speech represents excellently the kind of statistical, evidential argument which those who looked to the House of Commons for the high eloquence of another day referred to contemptuously as the oratory of the countinghouse and the eloquence of the bookkeeper.

$\backsim$

Third Reading of the Corn Importation Bill *

May 15, 1846

Sir, the Secretary of State,[1] in the speech he made on the first night of this discussion, reminded gentlemen sitting on these benches, and professing opinions favourable to the protection of the industry of their country, that in the various and prolonged discussions which during late years have occurred with regard to great commercial changes they have, nevertheless, found it necessary to abandon many of the opinions they professed, and to give up many of those dogmas which they previously upheld. Sir, I acknowledge the fact. I believe that to be the necessary result of all discussion: nor can I understand the use of public discussion at all, if it be not to correct erroneous impressions, or if at the conclusion both parties are to take refuge in the cry that they have not changed a single opinion which they held before the question came under debate.

Sir, I do not claim for myself, and I think I may venture to say none of my friends around me claim, an infallibility in argument. We listen with attention and respect to every argument brought against the opinions which we advocate; and if we find that any argument thus advanced cannot be satisfactorily answered, we feel the necessity of no longer maintaining an opposite and untenable conclusion. But if this rule applies to our party, I think I could without difficulty show to the Secretary of State that it is a quality not peculiar to us. I rather

---

* The text is from Hansard, *Parliamentary Debates,* third series, LXXXVI, 651–77. It appears to be a slightly condensed version of the actual three-hour speech and it undoubtedly received some editorial "improvement." There are minor differences between this and the text published in *The Times,* May 16, 1846, but the Hansard version may be taken as a substantially true account of what Disraeli said. Disraeli spoke on the third and last night of debate on the Third Reading of the Corn Importation Bill. Sir Robert Peel's reply is available in *British Orations* (Everyman's Library, No. 714). Peel's bill passed by a vote of 327 to 229, thus effectively ending the most hotly contested controversy on public policy since enactment of Parliamentary Reform.

[1] Sir James Graham, Home Secretary in Peel's Government.

imagine that some opinions loudly advocated and long ably maintained by honourable gentlemen opposite—I still address myself to honourable gentlemen opposite, for though this discussion was commenced by Her Majesty's Government, I always remember who were really the originators of the ideas [2]—I say, I think that some of the opinions formerly advocated by honourable gentlemen opposite, are now no longer upheld, and are therefore to be placed in that category of abandonment to which the Secretary of State referred.

I might begin with cheap bread. We heard a minister of the Crown, a member of the Cabinet, even in this year, in this important session when all the opinions of Her Majesty's Government must doubtless be so well matured and so well considered, with all the advantages of four Cabinet meetings in a week—we heard a member of Her Majesty's Government announce that the clap-trap cry of cheap bread was given up by all parties. The right honourable gentleman seemed to hold it, as his noble colleague, the Secretary for Ireland, did a few years back, as "the fugitive cry of a dying faction." Even the honourable member for Stockport,[3] the highest authority on this point, announced that the cry of cheap bread had never been his. Well, then, that is one great opinion abandoned. We shall presently find that there are others in the same predicament.

I believe it is no longer maintained that our Corn Laws are productive of extraordinary fluctuations in the price of corn. And yet that was an opinion which was once very industriously disseminated in this country, one perpetually introduced into the discussions of this House, and which has unquestionably influenced the existing public opinion on the main question; yet I believe it is now admitted that the tendency neither of the present nor even of the late Corn Laws has been to produce extraordinary fluctuations in price. Well, that is another great opinion that has been abandoned.

Then we were told that these same Corn Laws were the bane of agriculture. That opinion is certainly given up. We have shown you—and you have admitted the facts—from the evidence of the best authorities, the most intelligent valuers under the Tithe Commutation Act, and the most skilful land-agents in the country —we have shown you that in England the average produce of an acre is twenty-eight bushels of wheat. We know by a report prepared by a public commissioner that the average produce per acre in Russia is sixteen bushels; while we have evidence that the average amount in France is fifteen bushels. But I have got a document here which is very much at the service of honourable members opposite. It is the Report in 1845 of the Agricultural Society of New York, giving the average produce of sixty-nine counties in that State, and it appears from this report that the average produce of wheat per acre in the United States is fourteen bushels. Does it, then, appear from these figures that protection is indeed the bane of agriculture? These statements show that England produces more corn per acre in a great degree than any other country.

This, then, is a third opinion that has been abandoned. Again, there is another opinion which has been put forward with much pertinacity. It has been

---

[2] The allusion is to utilitarian economists and politicians generally, but Disraeli probably intended hearers to think particularly of Richard Cobden. Peel had privately justified his own assumption of leadership in repealing the Corn Laws as the only alternative to a Cobden Government.

[3] Cobden.

long loudly and diligently asserted that the population in this country increases in a greater ratio than its production. That opinion has been given up. You came down to the House and told us always that the population was increasing a thousand a day, or 365,000 a year, and after your fashion you assumed the country could not feed the people. We have shown you—or rather you have shown us, for it has been one of the circumstances adduced by the minister in favour of his measure—that the price of wheat for years has regularly declined. If we divide the current century into three equal portions of fifteen years each, you will find the price of wheat lowest in the last division; so that while the population has been increasing in the ratio you allege, the means of production have been increasing in a still greater ratio: the population has been increasing in this degree, and at the same time the price of the necessaries of life has been decreasing.

There is another dogma which has also much influenced public opinion; and that is, that our Corn Laws have produced hostile tariffs. This opinion also is, I believe, now abandoned. Every day's experience assures us, whatever may be the policy of the Government of this country, that continental nations and manufacturing countries are not to be influenced by it. But, according to the new school of philosophy we need not dwell on this; it does not signify whether other nations are influenced by our liberal policy or not, we are quite independent of all such considerations.

There is yet another opinion which I have observed frequently advanced in speeches out of this House; and speeches out of this House, be it remembered, have had much influence on conduct within it. It has often been urged at public meetings by the honourable member for Stockport, whose speeches I always read with attention, that the amount of freight alone would be a sufficient protection to land. The honourable member has been in the habit of assuring his audience that the average rate of freight was 10s. 6d. per quarter of corn, and that to this extent a protection was afforded to agriculture. I believe honourable gentlemen have even made the same declaration in this House; and I believe, had it been made in this House a year ago, we should all of us have believed it. Now, I doubt whether there is any freight which amounts to 10s. 6d. I doubt whether at present we pay 10s. 6d. per quarter even from Odessa. But, generally speaking, it is now universally admitted that freight is no protection at all, for it is just as expensive to transport a quarter of corn from one English port to another as to bring it from any of the contiguous foreign ports from which your chief supply is anticipated.

I will say one word on a topic which I have already touched upon lightly, because I heard a cheer from an honourable member opposite when I mentioned that the tendency of the present Corn Laws was not to produce great fluctuations in price. I do not mention these topics merely in retort to the Secretary of State, but because I think it not an inconvenient mode to clear the course of all collateral topics before I address myself to the main question. We maintain, then, with regard to the present and even the late Corn Laws, that they have not produced extraordinary fluctuation in price; on the contrary, we maintain that the fluctuation in price in England has been less than in any other country in the world. I will establish this fact on data that are incontrovertible. Understand, I lay this down as a fact, that every country, rich or poor, in Europe or America, has in respect of the important necessary of life, grain, been subject to much greater fluctuation in price than England. Mr. Secretary Gladstone recently moved for an important return—a return which I observe is never alluded to by honourable gentlemen opposite. It is a return, from 1834 to 1840 inclusive, of the highest and lowest weekly prices of wheat per imperial quarter in most of the principal capitals of the United States. Now, I take one of these capitals, Philadelphia, because the peculiar circumstances of that capital tell the least for my argument. Philadelphia is the capital of one of the wealthiest and most populous States of the American union; and it has this peculiarity, that it is a State that does not commonly produce sufficient corn for the supply of its inhabitants. It should be observed that little or no corn or flour was imported from America into England during the first five years of this period, and that the importation in 1839 and 1840 tended to raise the low prices of these years, and so to diminish the extreme limits of their fluctuation. Philadelphia, too, is a great mart of commerce, communicating freely with every region of the world, and its corn trade is free, being subject only to a moderate fixed duty—a moderate fixed duty of 8s. 8d. per quarter. Now, Sir, what are the facts? It appears by this return of Mr. Secretary Gladstone that the average annual difference between the highest and lowest prices of wheat in Philadelphia is 47 per cent, while during the corresponding period in England it was only 33 per cent; and while the extreme difference between the highest and lowest prices of wheat in this septennial period was 270 per cent in Philadelphia, it was only 227 in England. And yet no septennial period could have been chosen which would have exhibited, under the operation of the Corn Laws, such extensive fluctuation of prices.

It may be objected to this return that it only gives the extreme weekly prices of wheat, and it may be possible that local and peculiar causes may have had an effect on those prices. Well, then, here is a return of the average annual prices of wheat in Philadelphia from 1830 to 1838 inclusive, and I find the difference between the highest and lowest price of wheat at Philadelphia to be 121 per cent, while the corresponding difference during the same period in England is only 69 per cent. The reports from every considerable port and corn market in Europe have been analysed, and the result I find to be of exactly the same character. But it will be urged that the prices of corn abroad are disturbed by the action of our Corn Laws, and that we cannot form a correct idea of the price of grain when trade flows in its natural course. But this will not impair our argument. The noble lord the member for Lynn [4] has anticipated this objection, and he says: —"I will take rye, because that is the food of the continental people, and cannot be influenced by our Corn Laws; and I will show you equal fluctuations in the price of rye." Now, Sir, I also have a return of the prices of rye at Warsaw and at Dantzic. We have been told to-night that Dantzic is in favour of a fluctuating scale, but that at Warsaw they are devoted to free trade. Yet the difference in the annual price of rye, during the years from 1834 to 1839, in the market at Warsaw sometimes amounted to 149 per cent, whereas in Dantzic the difference was only 65 per cent. In all the great Prussian markets the difference during the same period between the annual prices of rye was 100 per cent. I think, therefore, we may fairly conclude that the objection urged against the system of graduated protection with regard to its producing fluctuation in prices is no longer an argument for this House. But I must remind the House that the instances which I

---

[4] Lord George Bentinck, member for King's Lynn and formal leader of the Protectionists.

have adduced, and the inferences which I have drawn from these instances, are under the influence of the late law, a law much more tending to fluctuation than the present. The scale of the late law was originally well devised. It was planned by Mr. Canning, but altered for the worse, let it always be remembered, altered for the worse by the present First Minister.[5] If I had taken the experience of the present scale, the result would have been still more favourable; but, the result being favourable enough, I am content with the former scale.

It seems, therefore, that some arguments have been abandoned by honourable gentlemen opposite as well as by us. It is possible that both sides may have abandoned many important opinions without losing faith in the principles on which their respective systems are upheld. But I defy gentlemen opposite, who have had for years such free warren of sarcasm against the advocates of protection, to bring forward a catalogue of renounced opinions on the subject which can compete with the one I have sketched, and yet left imperfect, before the House. What, then, are we to do with these opinions, these exhausted arguments, these exploded fallacies? Our great poet conceived the existence of a Limbo [6] for exploded systems and the phantasies of the schools. I think we ought to invent a limbo for political economists, where we might hang up all those arguments that have served their purpose and which have turned out to be sophistries. Yes, but these are the arguments that have agitated a nation and have converted a ministry. It is all very well to say, after six or seven years' discussion, "We have discovered them to be false and there is not a single gentleman opposite prepared to maintain them"; but these are the agencies by which a certain amount of public opinion has been brought to bear on great economical questions; that public opinion has changed the policy of a Government, and according to our belief is perilling the destinies of a great people.

Now, Sir, I must fairly acknowledge that one of these fallacies must be resuscitated by myself. Notwithstanding the high authority of the Secretary at War,[7] notwithstanding the influential adhesion to his opinion of the still higher authority of the member for Stockport, I must raise on this occasion the cry of "cheap bread." I do believe the effect of the present Corn Laws is to raise the price of the necessaries of life to the community. That is my opinion. But I believe, and I think I can show, that they increase in an infinitely greater ratio the purchasing powers by the community of the necessaries of life. I hope I am meeting the argument fairly. The Secretary of State did me the honour to say that I had on another occasion fairly expressed the question at issue, and I wish strictly to address myself to it. Now, how am I to prove my proposition? The first witness I shall call is a high authority. It is a work circulated under the immediate influence of that great commercial confederation, the power of which is acknowledged, written, I believe, by a gentleman who was once a member of this House, and, I believe I may add, who would have been a member of this House now if I had not had the pleasure of beating him in the first election I won

---

[5] Sir Robert Peel.

[6] Probably Milton's "Lymbo of Vanity"; *Paradise Lost*, Bk. III, lines 487–97. *The Times'* report reads from this point: "I think we should invent a limbo for political economists where we should bind up all these arguments that have turned out to be sophistries."

[7] Sidney Herbert, member for South Wiltshire and Secretary at War in Peel's Government.

—Colonel Thompson.[8] In his "Corn Law Catechism" it is maintained that the Corn Law is a tax upon the community, because, assuming a certain number of quarters of corn are produced every year in this country—say, for instance, fifty millions of quarters—the Corn Law, by artificially raising the price of that corn 8s. or 10s. per quarter, on an average, acts as a tax on the community, we will say, of 20,000,000l. Another economist, an equally celebrated and more successful free trader, has fallen foul of the calculations of this work, which is a great authority with the Anti-Corn-Law League, and he has shown the gallant calculator that he has omitted to deduct the number of quarters that are required for seed, for the sustenance of the agriculturists themselves, for the support of their horses; and so at once the critic cuts down the estimate of the Colonel to a tax of nine or ten millions on the public. But I will give, as is my custom, an advantage to my opponents, and take the first calculation. The conclusion of the Colonel, and of the school of which he is so distinguished a champion, is, that it is better for England not to raise a single quarter of corn, and then the whole of this tax might thus be saved. You will say this is an extreme statement; but the statement is not mine, and an extreme case tests the truth of a principle. Let us suppose, then, that England imports fifty millions of quarters of corn: let us suppose that she thus saves ten or twenty millions of taxation. We will admit it for the purpose of discussion. But you cannot deny that England has lost the wages of labour that would have produced those fifty millions of quarters; you cannot deny that England has lost the profits of the capital that would have been invested in the production of those fifty millions of quarters; you cannot deny that England has lost the rent that this cultivation would have afforded after paying these wages of labour and furnishing these profits of capital. What is their united amount? It would be a light estimate to place it at twenty times that of the imaginary tax. In the proportion that united amount bears to the assumed tax the purchasing power of the community created by the law exceeds the tax on the community alleged to be occasioned by the law.

I am ready to acknowledge that the honourable member for Stockport never addressed any public assembly with these opinions. He is a practical man: he knows very well there is no chance of changing the laws of England with abstract doctrines, and he says very properly, "I don't admit your conclusion. We don't suppose any land will be thrown out of cultivation; there may be a reduction of price or not; but what we say is, you are creating that artificial price for the first necessaries of life in the country, and you are creating that artificial price for the benefit of a class; and therefore the reduction of price is, at the worst, the destruction of rent." That is the position he takes up. Now, for my own part, I will admit that I see no difference between a territorial class and the handloom weavers. If you show me that there is a law kept up merely to give a revenue to any class in this country, and that by putting an end to that law the great body of the people can be fed better and be as well employed, I cannot imagine anything like a Corn Law can be maintained. Well, then, we are brought to the gist of the question. Will this change occasion a great displacement of labour? And if so, can you supply new employment for those who are displaced? It seems to me, Sir, impossible to arrive at any conclusion on this head, unless we form some estimate

---

[8] Colonel Perronet Thompson, Radical, editor of the *Westminster Review*. He was defeated by Wyndham Lewis and Disraeli in the 1837 election at Maidstone.

of the probable price of corn in this country after the measures of the ministers have fairly come into play. It is vain to make this inquiry of the right honourable gentleman, and therefore we must be thrown on our own elements of calculation.

If we can show to you that for the future the price of corn must necessarily be such as to render it impossible in the greater part of this country to cultivate wheat or other grain with a profit, you must acknowledge there will be a great displacement of labour. We will endeavour to meet you with facts, and protest against your answering us with assumptions. I will not trouble the House by referring to those countries whose names have been so long familiar in these debates; if I allude to them it is only because I do not wish the House to suppose that I depreciate the productive power of these countries.

My honourable friend the member for Somersetshire [9] said that the surplus produce of Russia was 28,000,000 quarters of corn; whereupon the Secretary of State rose to express his incredulity, amid the sympathising derision of gentlemen opposite. Why, Sir, the authority for that statement is the officer of the Government—(loud cheers)—the functionary who is employed by you to analyse the tariffs and resources of foreign countries, and probably the Secretary of State is the minister who laid his Report on the Table of the House. The authority is Mr. M'Gregor. I allude to it in passing—not that I value the authority of Mr. M'Gregor a rush—but it is right that it should be known that the statement of my honourable friend was derived from your own Blue Books,[10] and prepared by one of your own officers. What is the object of publishing these Blue Books except to furnish us with the elements of opinion?

I will not, however, enter into the empire of all the Russias: I know that it contains about twenty principalities, that more than one of them has an area greater than the United Kingdom, and that every one produces corn. I cannot forget the rich valley of the Volga, or the exuberant plains of the Ukraine. I won't take you to the valley of the Mississippi, though I have a statement here made by a high authority on this subject, who declares that its produce may be indefinitely extended, and that its wheat can be supplied, with a high estimate for freight in London at 30s. per quarter. But what I wish to bring before the notice of the House are the markets that are never mentioned, but which I believe will exercise a great influence on the price of corn. There is one market which has never been mentioned in the course of these discussions, and that is Hungary. Hungary is a plain which consists of 36,000 English square miles. It is the richest soil in the world; the soil of a garden, varying in depth from one foot to seven feet. You may go hundreds of miles together and not find a stone in it. If you deduct one-third of that area for morasses, there are 24,000 square miles of the most fertile soil in the world under the influence of a climate admirably adapted to the growth of corn. I have had a return sent to me of the production of one province in 1844—12,000,000 bushels: in Croatia the produce was 1,500,000 quarters. Yet thousands upon thousands of acres are uncultivated. But honourable gentlemen will say, how are we to get this corn from Hungary? That is what I am going to tell you.

[9] William Miles, Conservative member for East Somersetshire, cited this figure from MacGregor's *Tables* in a speech on May 11.

[10] A "Blue Book" is any official publication bulky enough to be given a standard set of (blue) covers.

Here is a letter from the greatest corn-merchant in Hungary. He lives at Sissek on the Saave, the great depot of the corn trade of that country. I will not give you the prices of this year, which is a year of scarcity, but I will give you the average of the last five years. An English quarter of Hungarian wheat—which, it should be remembered, ranks with the highest classes of Dantzic wheats, costs in English money from 18s. to 20s. per quarter. It is sent from Sissek by the river Kulpa to Carlstadt for 4d. per quarter, and from Carlstadt by land to Fiume for 1s. 8d. per quarter. The person who gives me this information is a practical man. He says, "Only give me a regular trade with England and I will send you from Sissek 500,000 quarters in the first year." I will soon show you what is the effect of a steady market on increased supply and decreased price.

I will take another market, a very interesting one—that of the Danubian provinces. In the year 1842 at the two ports of the Danube, Galatz and Ibrail, there were 1,350 ships laden with the produce of those countries, and only eight of them were English. That is a remarkable fact. We are the greatest commercial country in the world, and yet, in an active scene of commerce where an almost absolute freedom of trade is enjoyed, it appears by a return dated since the accession of the present Government to office, that out of 1,350 merchant ships laden in the two ports of the Danube, only eight were English. A house at Galatz has written to a house in England on the subject of supplying this country with corn, and the writer says: "I will undertake to lay down, if secured a price of 18s. per quarter, in any English port 200,000 quarters of wheat from this particular district, at 28s. to 30s.; but if you will secure me a certain market, I will double that quantity next year." From the same place another house asserts that if you will ensure a regular trade they can supply 1,000,000 quarters of wheat at 18s. per quarter; and if this measure passes, they undertake at the end of seven years that that quantity shall be doubled and sent to England at a reduced price. I speak of mercantile letters, and can give honourable gentlemen opposite the names of the firms.

I feel I must not dwell too long on this point: but yet, under the head of unenumerated markets, which have not been the subject of discussion in the House, I may mention Spain—which will act greatly on this country—Egypt, and Sicily. Each of these countries, when the new measures are fairly in play, will be able, I believe, to furnish this country with as much corn as they have required in years of deficiency. My opinion is that in exact proportion as your demand for wheat and for various kinds of grain increases, in the same proportion the price will diminish. I believe it may be laid down as a principle of commerce, that where an article can be progressively produced to an indefinite extent, precisely as the demand increases the price will decrease. I am aware that that is exactly contrary to the opinion of honourable gentlemen opposite, and to the opinion of the Government. We have had it announced from the hustings that exactly as you import a million of quarters of wheat from continental markets, prices abroad will rise 10s. per quarter. That which was announced by a great authority is only the echo of the Manchester school,[11] and has been accepted by the Government. The honourable member for Montrose[12] stated the other night that the

---

[11] Cobden credited Disraeli with having invented this phrase, which was widely applied to utilitarian philosophers, economists, and any advocates of free trade.

[12] Joseph Hume, Radical member for Montrose, Scotland.

result of those contemplated changes was only to equalise prices—we shall equalise prices by the demand, but we shall not lower prices. The gist of the question is the accuracy of this opinion. Is it true? The question whether England can maintain her character as an agricultural country—the question whether her people can be employed as they have been—the question whether there will be a great displacement of labour depends upon the accuracy of this opinion.

I referred on a former occasion to the instance of tea. I said, in that case, that an increased demand had decreased the price. That intimation was received—rather incredulously. It was not met by any argument or decided fact; but subsequently it was contradicted, and in a very unsatisfactory manner. I will now show the House how far I was justified in that statement. I wrote to a mercantile house which is more largely connected with the China trade than any other house in the country. I placed before them the assertion I had made, and the reply it had met. What was the answer I received? Here it is:—"I hand you enclosed the prices per pound of sound common Congou tea, which is the kind most consumed in this country, from which you will be able to observe that there has been a great fall in the price since the year 1831." What, then, was that fall in price per pound of Congou tea—the sort most consumed in this country? In the year 1831 Congou tea was 2s. 2d. per pound; in the year 1846 it is 9d. per pound. I know very well that the price of tea in 1831 was to a certain degree artificial. The mercantile influence of the East India Company still prevailed, and the supply was limited. But that influence was not greater than that of the China War, and, it will be observed, those disturbances only affected the market for a couple of years. In 1832, tea was 2s. 1½d.; in 1833, 1s. 11d.; 1834, 1s. 7¼d.; 1835, 1s. 4d.; 1836, 1s. 1d.; 1837, 1s. 7d.; 1838, 1s. 2d. And then we come to the disorders in China, which had the effect of raising the price in 1839 to 2s. 5d.; it then fell in 1842 to 1s. 3½d.; 1843, to 11d.; 1844, to 10d.; 1845, to 9½d.; until in 1846 we find it reduced to 9d. per pound; and all this time the import of tea from that country, which, from its being solely produced there, enjoys a quasi-monopoly, was increasing by millions of pounds. And then, Sir, I am told that by the last accounts from Canton the price of tea is rising; and that is called an answer. Why, Sir, if by the last accounts from Canton the price of tea had been falling, I should not have adduced that as an argument in favour of the principle I am upholding. The price of tea will fall and will rise according to the circumstances of the market: there must always be undulation in price. But the question is what, if I may use the expression, is the gradient of price—what the inevitable and unmistakeable tendency of price during a series of years?

The next instance I shall take is one which is more favourable to our case, but at the same time strictly legitimate. It is one which bears more analogy to corn— namely, cotton. The price of cotton upland per pound in the year 1836 was 10⅛d.; in 1837, 8d.; 1838, 8¼d.; 1839, 6¾d.; 1840, 6⅛d.; 1841, 5⅝d.; 1842, 5¼d.; 1843, 5⅛d.; 1844, 4⅛d.; and in 1845, from 4d. to 4¼d., per pound; and in these ten years of progressive fall in price the import of cotton into England had risen from 350,000,000 pounds to 597,000,000 pounds, while during the same period of a falling price, other manufacturing countries, including the United States, had increased their consumption of that article from 282,000,000 pounds to 439,000,000 pounds.

It seems, therefore, to be demonstrable that where there is no natural or artificial cause to check the progress of production, prices will proportionately fall.

Now, in the article I am about to refer to there are these causes in operation, and the whole state of the sugar trade is so anomalous that I might fairly have omitted it from the application of the test. But it occurred to me that it might be tried with reference to the production of East India sugar since the duties were equalised. What is the result? At the end of the year 1841, the price of brown Bengal sugar was 47s. to 52s.; 1842, 45s. to 51s.; 1843, 47s. to 55s.; 1844, 39s. to 49s.; 1845, 38s. to 42s.; 1846, 37s. to 42s.; and with that falling price the amount imported increased from 24,000 tons in the first year to 62,000 tons in the last year. With respect to the finest kinds of the same sugar the price fell from 69s. to 74s. down to 52s. to 56s. during the same period. Therefore, the instance of sugar is in perfect harmony with the general and ruling principle I have laid down.

The case of coffee I find to be still more satisfactory. I must apply my rule again to East India production in this case, owing to the anomalous state of our West India colonies. Let us, then, take Ceylon coffee, and we shall find that the importation has greatly increased. The price of that article in 1840 was, per bag, 90s. to 91s.; in 1846, it fell to 44s.; and in the first year the quantity imported was 53,000 bags; in the last year, 133,000 bags. Then take the case of Mysore coffee during the same time. In the first year the price was 70s. to 80s. per cask; in the last year, 36s. to 48s. per cask; the quantity imported in the former year being 48,000 casks, in the latter, 63,530. There are many other important articles which it would be wearisome to refer to in detail, but which I mention that gentlemen may have an opportunity of investigating this important principle. Look at the instances of indigo, salt, iron, coal, and fruits, ever since the alteration of the law, and you will find this principle is invariably observed, universally demonstrated.

Well, Sir, is it, then, unreasonable for me to ask what there is in corn to make it an exception to this general rule? I want that question to be answered. It is a fair question. Why, I repeat, is corn to be an exception to this rule? Is it because corn is produced in every country and under every clime? I want to know where it is you will not produce corn. We have had by late arrivals accounts of the price of wheat in Persia, where we find it is at present 5s. per quarter. True, you can't very easily import corn from Persia; but there are countries lying at each point of the compass from Persia where you may purchase corn at from 10s. to 20s. per quarter. The rest is an affair of the cost of transport in an age when the principle of locomotion is bringing all articles to a level. Now, Sir, before I estimate the consequences of these proposed changes, I will first advert to the parallel which has been so often drawn between the importation of foreign corn and foreign cattle, in order to show how ill-founded may be our fears. It does not appear to me that there is much analogy between these two instances which are always treated as the same. In the first place continental countries have been corn-growing countries long before England became so. But they have never been to any extent cattle-feeding countries. The very fact of the prevalence in them of the Roman Catholic religion, which prevented the consumption of meat to the same extent as in Protestant countries, alone has discouraged it. Besides, the pastures of England have always, even in old days, been unrivalled. Nor should we forget the difficulties and dangers of transport in the commerce of live stock. It appears, therefore, that the analogy between these cases is very imperfect.

I say, then, assuming, as I have given you reason to assume, that the price of wheat when this system is established ranges in England at 35s. per quarter, and other grain in proportion, this is not a question of rent, but it is a question of displacing the labour of England that produces corn, in order, on an extensive and even universal scale, to permit the entrance into this country of foreign corn produced by foreign labour! Will that displaced labour find new employment? The Secretary of State says that England is no longer an agricultural but a commercial and manufacturing country, and the right honourable gentleman, when reminded by the noble lord the member for Gloucestershire of his words, said, "No, I did not say that; but I said that England was no longer exclusively an agricultural country." [13] Why, Sir, the commerce of England is not a creation of yesterday; it is more ancient than that of any other existing country. This is a novel assumption on the part of the Government, to tell us that England has hitherto been a strictly agricultural country, and that now there is a change and that it is passing into a commercial and manufacturing country. I doubt whether, in the first place, England is a greater commercial country now than she has been at other periods of her history. I do not mean to say that she has not now more commercial transactions, but that with reference to her population, and the population of the world, her commerce is not now greater than at other periods of her history: for example, when she had her great Levantine trade; when the riches of the world collected in the Mediterranean; when she had her great Turkey merchants, her flourishing Antilles, and her profitable though in some degree surreptitious trade with the Spanish main. But then it is also said that England has become a great manufacturing country. I believe, Sir, if you look to the general distribution of labour in England, you will find she may be less of a manufacturing country now than she has been.[14] Well, I give you my argument: answer it if you can. I say, looking to the employment of the people, manufacturing industry was more scattered over the country a hundred years ago than it is now. Honourable gentlemen have laid hold of a word uttered in the heat of speaking. I say, manufacturing industry was more dispersed over the country then than now: there were more counties in which manufactures flourished then than at the present moment. For instance, in the west of England manufactures were more flourishing, and your woollen manufacture bore a greater ratio in importance to the industrial skill of Europe 300 years ago than it does to the aggregate industry of Europe at the present moment. That manufacture might not have been absolutely more important; but as a development of the national industry it bore a greater relative importance to the industry of Europe then than at the present moment. You had then considerable manufactures in various counties—manufactures a hundred years ago which are now obsolete or but partially pursued. You have, no doubt, now a gigantic development of manufacturing skill in a particular county which is unprecedented. It is one of those developments which confer the greatest honour on this country; which has been a great source of public wealth—a development of which Englishmen should be justly proud—but, generally speaking, it is confined to one county. And now ministers tell us we must change our whole system, because, forsooth, England has ceased to be an agricultural country, and has become a commercial and manufacturing one. That is to say, that we must change

[13] Sir James Graham made the original statement on May 11. On May 15, he interrupted when the Marquess of Worcester said Graham "avowed his opinion that this country is no longer to be considered as an agricultural country."

[14] At this moment there was a laugh, then another at the end of Disraeli's next pair of sentences.

our whole system in favour of one particular county. Sir, that is an extremely dangerous principle to introduce. I have heard of a repeal of the Union, but we may live to hear of a revival of the Heptarchy [15] if Her Majesty's ministers pursue this policy—if those portions of the country which are agricultural or suffering under the remains of an old obsolete manufacturing population are to be told that we must change our whole system because one county, where there is a peculiar development of one branch of industry, demands it. But what are the resources of this kind of industry to employ and support the people, supposing the great depression in agricultural produce occur which is feared: that this great revolution, as it has appropriately been called, takes place—that we cease to be an agricultural people—what are the resources that would furnish employment to two-thirds of the subverted agricultural population, in fact from 3,500,000 to 4,000,000 of people? Assume that the workshop-of-the-world principle is carried into effect; assume that the attempt is made to maintain your system both financial and domestic, on the resources of the cotton trade; assume that, in spite of hostile tariffs, that already gigantic industry is doubled—a bold assumption, even if there be no further improvements in machinery, further reducing the necessity of manual labour—you would only find increased employment for 300,000 of your population. Perhaps mechanical invention may reduce the number half, and those only women and children. What must be the consequence? I think we have pretty good grounds for anticipating social misery and political disaster.

But then, I am told, immense things are to be done for the agriculturist by the application of capital and skill. Let us test the soundness of this doctrine. When a man lends his capital, he looks to the security he is to have and to what is to pay the interest. Is the complexion of these measures such as to render men more ready to lend money on landed estates? The mortgagee, when he advances money on land, looks to the margin in the shape of rent for his security. Will any man rise and maintain that the tendency of these measures is to increase that margin? But you are not only diminishing the opportunity of obtaining loans upon your own estates, but you are creating for capital an investment which will be more profitable for it in the estates of the foreigner. Look at the relations in which you will place the foreign merchant with his London correspondent. He has no longer to fear the capricious effects of the sliding scale; [16] he has got a certain market; he goes to his London banker with an increased security for an advance; he obtains his loan with ease; he makes his advances to the country dealers on the Continent as he makes his advance of English capital now in the foreign wool trade between the clip and the great fairs; and thus while you diminish the security of the landed proprietor, you are offering to the English capitalist a better and securer investment.

But then you tell us of the aid to be had by the agriculturist from skill. It is not easy to argue on a phrase so indefinite as skill, but I think I can show you that the English agriculturist is far more advanced in respect to skill than even the English manufacturer. I don't mean to say that there are not English farmers who might cultivate their lands better and with more economy than they do; but the same may surely be said in their respective pursuits of many a manufac-

---

[15] The seven kingdoms of Anglo-Saxon England: Northumbria, East Anglia, Mercia, Essex, Sussex, Wessex, and Kent.

[16] Under the Corn Laws, import duties declined as grain prices rose, and vice versa.

turer and many a miner; but what I mean to say is, that an English farmer produces more effectively and wastes less, is more intelligent and more industrious, than the manufacturer. I will prove this by the evidence of a member of the Anti-Corn-Law League—Mr. Greg. Mr. Greg says that the competition is so severe that he almost doubts the possibility of the English manufacturer long maintaining that competition with the Continental or American manufacturer, who approach them nearer every day in the completeness of their fabrics and the economy of their productions. But no such thing can be said of the English agriculturist who, I have shown you, can produce much more per acre than the French, Russian, or American agriculturist. So much, then, for the argument with respect to skill.

There is one argument, or rather appeal, which I know has influenced opinion out of this House, and also within it. You bring before us the condition of the English peasant. It is too often a miserable condition. My honourable friend the member for Shaftesbury has gained and deserves great credit for investigating the condition of the Dorsetshire labourer.[17] He has introduced it into this discussion. Now, the condition of the Dorsetshire labourer is one of the reasons which induce me to support this law. It is very easy to say that the condition of the agricultural labourer, when compared with the general state of our civilisation, is a miserable and depressed one, and that protection has produced it. If I cannot offer you reasons which may induce you to believe that protection has had nothing to do with it, I shall be perfectly ready to go to-night into the same lobby with Her Majesty's ministers. I asked you the other night, if protection has produced the Dorsetshire labourer at 7s. per week, how is it that protection has produced the Lincolnshire labourer with double that sum? I do not say that is an argument: it is a suggestive question which I will endeavour to follow up.

Mr. Huskisson[18] made an observation in conversation with an acquaintance of mine which has always struck me very forcibly. When Mr. Huskisson first settled in Sussex, his attention was naturally drawn to the extraordinary state of pauperism in that county, and after giving the subject all the meditation of his acute mind, he said that he traced it to the fact that Sussex had formerly been the seat of a great iron trade, and that agriculture had never been able to absorb the manufacturing population. Now, apply that principle to the western counties, and don't you think it will throw some light upon their condition? They also have been the seats of manufactures, many of them obsolete, and many of them now only partially pursued. There, too, you will find that the manufacturing population has never been absorbed by the agricultural—that is, agriculture does not bear its ratio in its means of support to the amount of the population which it has to sustain, but which it did not create.

And now go to Lincolnshire. I will rest our case on Lincolnshire. It is a new county; it is a protected county. Lincolnshire is to agriculture what Lancashire is to manufactures. The population there is produced by land and supported by land in the same manner that the population of Lancashire has been produced and is supported by manufactures. Let us picture to ourselves for a moment that

---

[17] Richard Brinsley Sheridan, member for Shaftesbury, had offered evidence that wages of Dorsetshire agricultural workers had not risen as grain prices rose.
[18] William Huskisson (1770–1830) held various ministerial offices and was leader of the House of Commons in 1827–1828.

celebrated tower that looks over that city which my gallant friend [19] and his ancestors have represented since the time of the last Stuart. Let us picture him for a moment placing the archfiend of political economy in that befitting niche, and calling his attention to the surrounding landscape. To the north, extending to the Humber, an endless tract of wolds rescued from the rabbits, once covered with furze and whins, and now with exuberant crops of grain; to the south, stretching for miles, is what was once Lincoln Heath, where in the memory of living men there used to be a lighthouse for the traveller, and which—even in the recollection of the middle-aged was let to the warrener at 2s. 6d. an acre—now one of the best farmed and most productive corn districts in the kingdom. Then, turning from the wolds and the heaths eastward, reaching to the sea, he might behold a region of fens, the small ones drained by the steam engine, with the East and West and Wildmere fens, once more than half of the year under water, now cleared by large canals, and bearing magnificent wheat and oats; with the great Witham and Black Sluice drainage-districts, one extending over 60,000 and the other over 90,000 acres, admirably reclaimed and drained, and bearing and creating, and well sustaining a large and industrious and thriving population. And all under the faith of protective Acts of Parliament. I am told that it is the contiguity of manufactures that makes Lincolnshire so prosperous. But, Sir, the frontiers of Wilts are nearer that great manufacturing district of which Birmingham is the centre than those of Lincolnshire are to Lancashire. Now, see what Lincolnshire has produced under protection: there you see the protective system fairly tested. But when you find the labourers in the western counties wretched and miserable, do not say that protection has been the cause of it, when protection is perhaps the reason why they exist at all; but see if you cannot find other causes for their poverty, and means to counteract it. I must say that nothing astonished me more than when the noble lord the member for Falkirk [20] asked the farmers in Newark market, "What has protection done for you?" Why, that market is supplied with the wheat of Lincoln Heath, the intrinsic poverty of whose soil is only sustained by the annual application of artificial manures, but which produces the finest corn in the kingdom. What has protection done for them? Why, if protection had never existed, Lincolnshire might still have been a wild wold, a barren heath, a plashy marsh.

There are one or two points to which I could have wished to call the attention of the House, but which time will only permit me to glance at; I will not presume to discuss them. But you cannot decide this question without looking to your colonies. I am not one of those who think it the inevitable lot of the people of Canada to become annexed to the United States. Canada has all the elements of a great and independent country, and is destined, I sometimes believe, to be the Russia of the New World. The honourable and learned member for Bath,[21] in answering the speech of the noble lord the member for Lynn,[22] last night treated our commerce with Canada very lightly, rather as a smuggling traffic than legitimate commerce. That is an argument for keeping the Canadas. I have no desire to see a smuggling trade if we can have any other. But I will ask the gentlemen

[19] Colonel C. D. W. Sibthorp, Conservative member for the city of Lincoln.

[20] Henry Pelham Clinton, Lord Lincoln and later Fifth Duke of Newcastle. A staunch Peelite and close friend of Gladstone.

[21] John Arthur Roebuck, Radical member for Bath.

[22] Lord George Bentinck.

of Manchester to consider what may become of the transatlantic market for their manufactures if the whole of that continent belong to one Power? But I must not dwell on the colonies, and I shall scarcely touch the case of Ireland: it is too terrible, especially if there be truth in the opinion of the noble lord, whose conversion has been so much a matter of congratulation to the Government,[23] that their measure must be fatal to small farmers. Why, Ireland is a nation of small farmers. There was, however, one observation made with respect to Ireland by the honourable member for Stockport, which, considering the effect it has had, I cannot help noticing. The honourable gentleman says, "Ireland an argument in favour of the Corn Laws! Of all countries in the world, I never should have supposed that Ireland would have been brought forward in support of the Corn Laws!" That is a saucy and gallant sally; but is it an argument? What does it prove? The population is reduced to the lowest sources of subsistence. Admitted: but how do they gain even their potatoes except by cultivating the soil, and by producing that wheat and those oats which they send to England? I should be very glad if that wheat and those oats remained in Ireland; but I ask, what will be the state of Ireland if the effect of this measure on your markets be such as I have assumed? You say that capital will flow into the country and that manufactures will be established. What length of time will elapse before these manufactures are established? Perhaps before that time the iron trade will revive in Sussex, or we shall see the drooping energies of the Dorsetshire labourer revived by his receiving the same wages as are paid at Rochdale and Stockport.[24]

Believing that this measure would be fatal to our agricultural interests; believing that its tendency is to sap the elements and springs of our manufacturing prosperity; believing that in a merely financial point of view it will occasion a new distribution of the precious metals, which must induce the utmost social suffering in every class, I am obliged to ask myself, if the measure be so perilous, why is it produced? Sir, I need not ask what so many gentlemen, both in and out of this House, have already asked, what was there in the circumstances of this country to authorise the change? If we are only a commercial and manufacturing people, all must admit that commerce was thriving and that manufactures flourished. Agriculture was also content, and even had it been suffering and depressed, what does it signify, since England has ceased to be an agricultural country? Obliged, then, to discover some cause for this social revolution, I find that a body of men have risen in this country, eminent for their eloquence, distinguished for their energy, but more distinguished, in my humble opinion, for their energy and their eloquence than for their knowledge of human nature or for the extent of their political information. Sir, I am not one of those who here or elsewhere, in public or in private, have spoken with that disrespect which some have done of that great commercial confederation which now exercises so great an influence in this country. Though I disapprove of their doctrines, though I believe from the bottom of my heart that their practice will eventually be as pernicious to the manufacturing interest as to the agricultural interests of this country, still I admire men of abilities, who, convinced of a great truth and proud of their energies, band

[23] Probably Lord Heytesbury, Lord Lieutenant of Ireland. Peel had quoted Lord Heytesbury's reports on the failure of the Irish potato crop.

[24] Rochdale was John Bright's birthplace and the seat of his cotton milling enterprises; Richard Cobden, who had built a fortune in printing calico, represented the important cotton manufacturing center of Stockport.

themselves together for the purpose of supporting it, and come forward devoting their lives to what they consider to be a great cause. Sir, this country can only exist by free discussion. If it is once supposed that opinions are to be put down by any other means, then, whatever may be our political forms, liberty vanishes. If we think the opinions of the Anti-Corn-Law League are dangerous; if we think their system is founded on error and must lead to confusion, it is open in a free country like England for men who hold opposite ideas to resist them with the same earnestness, by all legitimate means—by the same active organisation, and by all the intellectual power they command. But what happens in this country? A body of gentlemen,[25] able and adroit men, come forward and profess contrary doctrines to those of these new economists. They place themselves at the head of that great popular party who are adverse to the new ideas, and professing their opinions, they climb and clamber into power by having accepted, or rather by having eagerly sought, the trust. It follows that the body whom they represent, trusting in their leaders, not unnaturally, slumber at their posts. They conclude that their opinions are represented in the State. It was not for us or the millions out of the House to come forward and organize a power in order to meet the hostile movements of the honourable member for Stockport. No, we trusted to others—to one who, by accepting, or rather by seizing, that post, obtained the greatest place in the country, and at this moment governs England. Well, Sir, what happens? The right honourable gentleman, the First Minister, told his friends that he had given them very significant hints of the change of his opinions. He said that even last year Lord Grey had found him out, and he was surprised that we could have been so long deluded.[26]

Sir, none of the observations of the right honourable gentleman applied to me. More than a year ago, I rose in my place and said that it appeared to me that protection was in about the same state as Protestantism was in 1828.[27] I remember my friends were very indignant with me for that assertion, but they have since been so kind as to observe that instead of being a calumny it was only a prophecy. But I am bound to say, from personal experience, that, with the very humble exception to which I have referred, I think the right honourable baronet may congratulate himself on his complete success in having entirely deceived his party, for even the noble lord the member for Lynn, himself, in a moment of frank conversation, assured me that he had not till the very last moment the slightest doubt of the right honourable gentleman. The noble lord, I suppose, like many others, thought that the right honourable gentleman was, to use a very favourite phrase on these benches in 1842, "only making the best bargain for them."[28] I remember when the Whig budget was rejected and the right honourable gentleman was installed into office, the changes which he proposed at the time created some suspicion; but all suspicion was hushed at the moment, because the right honourable gentleman was looked upon as the man who could make the "best bargain" for the party. I want to know what gentlemen think of their best bargain now. Suddenly, absolute as was the confidence in the right honourable

[25] The reference is to Peel's Conservative Ministry of 1841.

[26] Peel discussed his changed views on January 22, 1846.

[27] The reference is to Disraeli's speech on agricultural distress, March 17, 1845. In 1828, Peel reversed himself on Catholic Emancipation and assisted in passing the Act of 1829.

[28] The next sentence does not appear in *The Times*.

gentleman, the announcement was made that there was to be another change: that that was to occur, under his auspices, which only a few months before he had aptly described as a "social revolution." And how was that announcement made? Were honourable gentlemen called together, or had the influential members of either House any intimation given to them of the nature of it? No, Sir. It was announced through the columns of a journal [29] which is always careful never to insert important information except on the highest authority. Conceive the effect of that announcement on foreign countries and on foreign ministers. I can bear witness to it: I happened to be absent from England at the time, and I know of great potentates sending for English ambassadors and demanding an explanation; and of English ambassadors waiting on great potentates and officially declaring that there was not the slightest truth in the announcement. And all this time, too, members of the Government—I have some of them in my eye—were calling on other newspapers devoted to the Government and instructing them to announce that the whole was an "infamous fabrication." [30] How ingenious was the conduct of Her Majesty's Government—or of that minister who formed the omnipotent minority of the Cabinet, I leave the House to decide. But was it not strange that, after so much agitation, after all these schemes, after all these Machiavellian manouevres, when the minister at last met the House and his party, he acted as if we had deserted him instead of his having left us? Who can forget those tones? Who can forget that indignant glance?

> Vectabor humeris tunc ego inimicis eques:
> Meæque terra cedet insolentiæ: [31]

which means to say, "I, a protectionist minister, mean to govern England by the aid of the Anti-Corn-Law League; and as for the country gentlemen, why, I snap my fingers in their face."

Yet even then the right honourable gentleman had no cause to complain of his party. It is very true that on a subsequent occasion 240 gentlemen recorded their sense of his conduct.[32] But then he might have remembered the considerable section of converts that he obtained even in the last hour. Why, what a compliment to a minister—not only to vote for him, but to vote for him against your opinions and in favour of opinions which he had always drilled you to distrust! That was a scene, I believe, unprecedented in the House of Commons. Indeed, I recollect nothing equal to it unless it be the conversion of the Saxons by Charlemagne, which is the only historical incident that bears any parallel to that illustrious occasion. Ranged on the banks of the Rhine, the Saxons determined to resist any further movement on the part of the great Caesar; but when the Emperor appeared, instead of conquering he converted them. How were they

[29] The Times, December 4, 1845, announced editorially: "The decision of the Cabinet is no longer a secret. . . . The Royal Speech . . . will recommend an immediate consideration of the Corn Laws preparatory to their total repeal."

[30] The Standard, December 5, 1845. (Kebbel.)

[31] "Then as a horseman I'll ride upon thy hated shoulders, and the earth shall give way before my unexampled might." Horace, Epode XVII. Horace, trans. by C. E. Bennett (Cambridge, 1952), p. 413.

[32] On February 27, 1846, 231 Conservatives and 11 Liberals voted to postpone action on the government's tariff proposals. Disraeli is pointing out that of some 343 Conservatives, Peel commanded support from only 112; his government continued, thanks to non-Conservatives.

converted? In battalions—the old chronicler informs us they were converted in battalions, and baptised in platoons. It was utterly impossible to bring these individuals from a state of reprobation to a state of grace with a celerity sufficiently quick. When I saw the hundred and twelve fall into rank and file, I was irresistibly reminded of that memorable incident on the banks of the Rhine.

And now, Sir, I must say in vindication of the right honourable gentleman that I think great injustice has been done to him throughout these debates. A perhaps justifiable misconception has universally prevailed. Sir, the right honourable gentleman has been accused of foregone treachery—of long-mediated deception—of a desire unworthy of a great statesman, even if an unprincipled one—of always having intended to abandon the opinions by professing which he rose to power. Sir, I entirely acquit the right honourable gentleman of any such intention. I do it for this reason, that when I examine the career of this minister, which has now filled a great space in the Parliamentary history of this country, I find that for between thirty and forty years, from the days of Mr. Horner to the days of the honourable member for Stockport, that right honourable gentleman has traded on the ideas and intelligence of others. His life has been one great Appropriation Clause. He is a burglar of others' intellect. Search the Index of Beatson [33] from the days of the Conquerer to the termination of the last reign, there is no statesman who has committed political petty larceny on so great a scale. I believe, therefore, when the right honourable gentleman undertook our cause on either side of the House, that he was perfectly sincere in his advocacy; but as in the course of discussion the conventionalisms which he received from us crumbled away in his grasp, feeling no creative power to sustain him with new arguments, feeling no spontaneous sentiments to force upon him conviction, the right honourable gentleman—reduced at last to defending the noblest cause, one based on the most high and solemn principles, upon "the burdens peculiar to agriculture" [34]— the right honourable gentleman, faithful to the law of his nature, imbibed the new doctrines, the more vigorous, bustling, popular and progressive doctrines, as he had imbibed the doctrines of Mr. Horner—as he had imbibed the doctrines of every leading man in this country for thirty or forty years, with the exception of the doctrine of Parliamentary Reform which the Whigs very wisely led the country upon and did not allow to grow sufficiently mature to fall into the mouth of the right honourable gentleman. [35]

Sir, the right honourable gentleman tells us that he does not feel humiliated. Sir, it is impossible for anyone to know what are the feelings of another. Feeling depends upon temperament; it depends upon the idiosyncrasy of the individual; it depends upon the organisation of the animal that feels. But this I will tell the right honourable gentleman, that, though he may not feel humiliated, his country ought to feel humiliated. Is it so pleasing to the self-complacency of a great nation, is it so grateful to the pride of England, that one who from the position he has contrived to occupy must rank as her foremost citizen, is one of whom it may be said, as Dean Swift said of another minister, that "he is a gentleman who has

[33] Robert Beatson, *A Political Index to the Histories of Great Britain and Ireland; or, a Complete Register of the Hereditary Honors, Public Offices, and Persons in Office*, etc.

[34] The words in inverted commas were uttered in a tone of sarcasm which elicited very great laughter. (Kebbel.)

[35] Peel had opposed Lord Grey's reform bills in 1832–1833.

the perpetual misfortune to be mistaken"? And, Sir, even now, in this last scene of the drama, when the party whom he unintentionally betrayed is to be unintentionally annihilated—even now, in this the last scene, the right honourable gentleman, faithful to the law of his being, is going to pass a project which I believe it is matter of notoriety is not of his own invention. It is one which may have been modified, but which I believe has been offered to another Government and by that Government has been wisely rejected. Why, Sir, these are matters of general notoriety. After the day that the right honourable gentleman made his first exposition of his scheme, a gentleman well known in this House, and learned in all the political secrets behind the scenes, met me and said, "Well, what do you think of your chief's plan?" Not knowing exactly what to say, but taking up a phrase which has been much used in the House, I observed, "Well, I suppose it is a 'great and comprehensive' plan." "Oh!" he replied, "we know all about it; it was offered to us! It is not his plan; it's Popkins's plan."[36] And is England to be governed by Popkins's plan? Will he go to the country with it? Will he go with it to that ancient and famous England that once was governed by statesmen—by Burleighs and by Walsinghams; by Bolingbrokes and by Walpoles; by a Chatham and a Canning—will he go to it with this fantastic scheming of some presumptuous pedant? I won't believe it: I have that confidence in the common sense, I will say the common spirit, of our countrymen, that I believe they will not long endure this huckstering tyranny of the Treasury Bench—these political pedlars that bought their party in the cheapest market and sold us in the dearest.

I know, Sir, that there are many who believe that the time is gone by when one can appeal to those high and honest impulses that were once the mainstay and the main element of the English character. I know, Sir, that we appeal to a people debauched by public gambling—stimulated and encouraged by an inefficient and shortsighted minister. I know that the public mind is polluted with economic fancies, a depraved desire that the rich may become richer without the interference of industry and toil. I know, Sir, that all confidence in public men is lost. But, Sir, I have faith in the primitive and enduring elements of the English character. It may be vain now, in the midnight of their intoxication, to tell them that there will be an awakening of bitterness; it may be idle now, in the springtide of their economic frenzy, to warn them that there may be an ebb of trouble. But the dark and inevitable hour will arrive. Then, when their spirit is softened by misfortune, they will recur to those principles that made England great, and which, in our belief, can alone keep England great. Then, too, perchance they may remember, not with unkindness, those who, betrayed and deserted, were neither ashamed nor afraid to struggle for the "good old cause"—the cause with which are associated principles the most popular, sentiments the most entirely national, the cause of labour, the cause of the people—the cause of England.[37]

❧

[36] Monypenny and Buckle report "peals of laughter from all parts of the House" at this point and great cheering at each of Disraeli's subsequent sallies. (*Life*, II, 386.)

[37] *The Times* reported: "The hon. member resumed his seat amidst applause which lasted fully two minutes." The newspaper endorsed repeal of the Corn Laws editorially, but added that Disraeli's was the only Protectionist speech of the final night recognizing there was no more to say; hence, "with literary zeal and tact" Disraeli "produced something like a table of contents of the debate."

BIBLIOGRAPHICAL NOTE

Of the nearly two dozen book-length studies of Disraeli, only the six-volume *Life* begun by W. F. Monypenny and completed by G. E. Buckle is definitive. The best one-volume biographies are George M. C. Brandes' *Lord Beaconsfield* (translated by Mrs. George Sturge, 1880), J. A. Froude's *Life of the Earl of Beaconsfield* (1890), and Hesketh Pearson's *Dizzy: The Life and Personality of Benjamin Disraeli, Earl of Beaconsfield* (1951). Robert Blake's *Disraeli* (1967) adds new detail on Disraeli's personal life, especially his youth. The substance of Disraeli's addresses is carefully reviewed in the *Life* by Monypenny and Buckle. For analyses of Disraeli's rhetoric see Carroll C. Arnold, "Invention in the Parliamentary Speaking of Benjamin Disraeli, 1842–1852," *Speech Monographs*, XIV (1947), 66–80; and "The Speech Style of Benjamin Disraeli," *Quarterly Journal of Speech*, XXXIII (1947), 427–36. The only available collection of Disraeli's speeches is the two-volume *Selected Speeches of Lord Beaconsfield* (1882) edited by Thomas E. Kebbel.

Charles Kingsley

(1819–1875)

Charles Kingsley was one of Queen Victoria's favorite preachers, yet like her favorite Prime Minister, Disraeli, he little resembled the stereotyped "Victorian" that later generations created in imagination. Kingsley was a gentle radical who resisted complacency and doctrinaire reform in social and religious life with exceptional energy and verbal skill. "As a parson, he seemed like a layman in disguise; as a reformer, like a half-trained pugilist; as an author, like an enthusiastic amateur." [1] On public platforms he seemed a gentlemanly missionary.

Kingsley's life-long interest in the forces of nature emerged during his youth in the maritime county of Devonshire. He was formally educated in private preparatory schools, at King's College, London, and at Magdalene College, Cambridge. He became curate, then rector, of Eversley parish, Hampshire (Hants) and made that parish his permanent home, though in later years he served as Chaplain-in-Ordinary to the Queen, Regius Professor of Modern History at Cambridge (1860–1869), Canon of Chester (1869–1873), and Canon of Westminster (1873–1875). He died at Eversley on January 28, 1875, soon after completing a highly successful lecture tour of the United States.

Canon Kingsley's was not a profound influence, but he was an effective, prolific popularizer of religious and social causes important in his day. In his lifetime he published one play, six novels, four books for children, scores of essays and reviews (chiefly as "Parson Lot" in *Politics for the People* and as contributor to *The Christian Socialist* and *Fraser's Magazine*), eleven book-length collections of sermons, two books of lectures, twenty pamphlets containing one to four sermons, and eighteen pamphlets of one or two lectures and occasional speeches. In the history of imaginative literature, he stands with Disraeli and Mrs. Elizabeth

[1] Una Pope-Hennessy, *Canon Charles Kingsley* (New York, 1949), p. 286.

Gaskell as one of the century's three most successful authors of social or "condition-of-England" novels. His *Yeast, Alton Locke, Hypatia,* and *Two Years Ago* belong to this genre. A vigorous anti-Catholic, he challenged John Henry Newman's intellectual integrity. The charge was ill-advised, but it caused Newman to write his famous *Apologia pro Vita Sua.*

Stuttering disturbed Kingsley's informal talk, but his hesitation diminished or disappeared when, manuscript in hand, he rose to address an audience. He read carefully to repress his stutter, yet listeners uniformly felt his messages were distinctively adapted to their needs and delivered with warmth and personal power. He seems to have been far less polemical in speaking than in writing. On the platform he was sometimes colloquial, often playfully humorous or gently ironic, but, for the most part, earnest without being factious or sombre. A tall, athletic, but slightly awkward man, Kingsley was in all respects unpretentious.

Social rather than political issues interested Kingsley when he commented on secular matters. He chided the Chartists for "fancying that *legislative* reform is *social* reform."[2] The "Christian Socialism" that he and Frederick D. Maurice and others promulgated was actually "associationism"—co-operation among workers for self-education and for production and distribution of goods. When this movement floundered, Kingsley intensified his efforts to promote "the art of health," an enterprise that had occupied his attention since he entered the ministry. In 1857, he wrote to a friend:

> I see one work to be done ere I die, in which (men are beginning to discover) Nature must be counteracted, lest she prove a curse and a destroyer, not a blessing and a mother; and that is Sanitary Reform. . . . If I can help to save the lives of a few thousand working people and their children, I may earn the blessing of God.[3]

The cholera epidemics of 1849 and 1854 and the primitive state of sanitation in England fully justified the high priority Kingsley and others gave to what seems, now, a routine concern in civilized nations.

The address below was delivered to, and later published by, the Ladies' National Association for the Diffusion of Sanitary Knowledge, meeting for its first annual session in Willis's Rooms, King Street, St. James's, London. Lord Shaftesbury (Anthony Ashley Cooper) presided; he and Dr. Thomas Southwood Smith also addressed the meeting. In Shaftesbury, the upper-class audience heard the leading parliamentary advocate for public health reforms; in Dr. Smith, the leading physician associated with these programs; in Kingsley, the leading author-lecturer on the subject.

∽

---

[2] "Parson Lot," *Politics for the People,* No. 2, May 13, 1848.
[3] Frances Kingsley, *Charles Kingsley, His Letters and Memories of His Life* (London, 1882), II, 67. Letter to John Bullar, November 26, 1857.

The Massacre of the Innocents *

1859

Let me begin by asking the ladies who are interesting themselves in this good work, whether they have really considered what they are about to do in carrying out their own plans? Are they aware that if their Society really succeeds, they will produce a very serious, some would think a very dangerous, change in the state of this nation? Are they aware that they would probably save the lives of some thirty or forty per cent. of the children who are born in England, and that therefore they would cause the subjects of Queen Victoria to increase at a very far more rapid rate than they do now? And are they aware that some very wise men inform us that England is already over-peopled, and that it is an exceedingly puzzling question where we shall soon be able to find work or food for our masses, so rapidly do they increase already, in spite of the thirty or forty per cent. which kind Nature carries off yearly before they are five years old? Have they considered what they are to do with all those children whom they are going to save alive? That has to be thought of; and if they really do believe, with some political economists, that over-population is a possibility to a country which has the greatest colonial empire that the world has ever seen; then I think they had better stop in their course, and let the children die, as they have been in the habit of dying.[1]

But if, on the other hand, it seems to them, as I confess it does to me, that the most precious thing in the world is a human being; that the lowest, and poorest, and the most degraded of human beings is better than all the dumb animals in the world; that there is an infinite, priceless capability in that creature, fallen as it may be; a capability of virtue, and of social and industrial use, which, if it is taken in time, may be developed up to a pitch, of which at first sight the child gives no hint whatsoever; if they believe again, that of all races upon earth now, the English race is probably the finest, and that it gives not the slightest sign whatever of exhaustion; that it seems to be on the whole a young race, and to have very great capabilities in it which have not yet been developed, and above all, the most marvellous capability of adapting itself to every sort of climate and every form of life, which any race, except the old Roman, ever has had in the world; if they consider with me that it is worth the while of political economists and social philosophers to look at the map, and see that about four-fifths of the globe cannot be said as yet to be in anywise inhabited or cultivated, or in the state into which men could put it by a fair supply of population, and industry, and human intellect: then, perhaps, they may think with me that it is a duty, one of the noblest

---

* This text was published by Kingsley in *New Miscellanies* (1861) under the title, "Speech in Behalf of the Ladies' Sanitary Association, 1859." The title used here is that adopted by the Ladies' National Association when the speech was first published and by the editors of Charles Kingsley, *Sanitary and Social Lectures and Essays* (1880).

[1] The irony reflects Kingsley's usual impatience with doctrinaire social theories. In his original edition of *An Essay on the Principle of Population* (1798), Thomas Robert Malthus accepted only war, famine, and disease as effective population controls. He later qualified his position, but the simpler, more absolute doctrine was the "Malthusian theory" most widely known.

of duties to help the increase of the English race as much as possible, and to see that every child that is born into this great nation of England be developed to the highest pitch to which we can develop him in physical strength and in beauty, as well as in intellect and in virtue. And then, in that light, it does seem to me, that this Institution—small now, but I do hope some day to become great and to become the mother institution of many and valuable children—is one of the noblest, most right-minded, straightforward, and practical conceptions that I have come across for some years.

We all know the difficulties of sanitary legislation. One looks at them at times almost with despair. I have my own reasons, with which I will not trouble this meeting, for looking on them with more despair than ever: not on account of the government of the time, or any possible government that could come to England, but on account of the peculiar class of persons in whom the ownership of the small houses has become more and more vested, and who are becoming more and more, I had almost said, the arbiters of the popular opinion, and of every election of Parliament.[2] However, that is no business of ours here; that must be settled somewhere else; and a fearfully long time, it seems to me, it will be before it is settled. But, in the meantime, what legislation cannot do, I believe private help, and, above all, woman's help, can do even better.[3] It can do this; it can improve the condition of the working man: and not only of him; I must speak also of the middle classes, of the men who own the house in which the working man lives. I must speak, too, of the wealthy tradesman; I must speak—it is a sad thing to have to say it—of our own class as well as of others. Sanitary reform, as it is called, or, in plain English, the art of health, is so very recent a discovery, as all true physical science is, that we ourselves and our own class know very little about it, and practise it very little. And this society, I do hope, will bear in mind that it is not simply to seek the working man, not only to go into the foul alley: but it is to go to the door of the farmer, to the door of the shopkeeper, aye, to the door of ladies and gentlemen of the same rank as ourselves. Women can do in that work what men cannot do. The private correspondence, private conversation, private example, of ladies, above all of married women, of mothers of families, may do what no legislation can do. I am struck more and more with the amount of disease and death I see around me in all classes, which no sanitary legislation whatsoever could touch, unless you had a complete house-to-house visitation by some government officer, with powers to enter every dwelling, to drain it, and ventilate it; and not only that, but to regulate the clothes and the diet of every inhabitant, and that among all ranks. I can conceive of nothing short of that, which would be absurd and impossible, and would also be most harmful morally, which would stop the present amount of disease and death which I see around me, without some such private exertion on the part of women, above all of mothers, as I do hope will spring from this institution more and more.

I see this, that three persons out of every four are utterly unaware of the general causes of their own ill-health, and of the ill-health of their children. They talk of their "afflictions," and their "misfortunes"; and, if they be pious people, they talk of "the will of God," and of "the visitation of God." I do not like to trench

---

[2] Kingsley deplored utilitarian doctrines which minimized the need for collective action and reform.

[3] The nobility of Woman and her special role as teacher of mankind were common themes in Kingsley's speaking and writing.

upon those matters here; but when I read in my book and in your book, "that it is not the will of our Father in Heaven that one of these little ones should perish," it has come to my mind sometimes with very great strength that that may have a physical application as well as a spiritual one; and that the Father in Heaven who does not wish the child's soul to die, may possibly have created that child's body for the purpose of its not dying except in a good old age. For not only in the lower class, but in the middle and upper classes, when one sees an unhealthy family, then in three cases out of four, if one will take time, trouble, and care enough, one can, with the help of the doctor, who has been attending them, run the evil home to a very different cause than the will of God; and that is, to stupid neglect, stupid ignorance, or what is just as bad, stupid indulgence.

Now, I do believe that if those tracts which you are publishing, which I have read and of which I cannot speak too highly, are spread over the length and breadth of the land, and if women—clergymen's wives, the wives of manufacturers and of great employers, district visitors and schoolmistresses, have these books put into their hands, and are persuaded to spread them, and to enforce them, by their own example and by their own counsel—that then, in the course of a few years, this system being thoroughly carried out, you would see a sensible and large increase in the rate of population. When you have saved your children alive, then you must settle what to do with them. But a living dog is better than a dead lion; I would rather have the living child, and let it take its chance, than let it return to God—wasted. O! it is a distressing thing to see children die. God gives the most beautiful and precious thing that earth can have, and we just take it and cast it away; we toss our pearls upon the dunghill and leave them. A dying child is to me one of the most dreadful sights in the world. A dying man, a man dying on the field of battle—that is a small sight; he has taken his chance; he is doing his duty; he has had his excitement; he has had his glory, if that will be any consolation to him; if he is a wise man, he has the feeling that he is dying for his country and his queen: and that is, and ought to be, enough for him. I am not horrified or shocked at the sight of the man who dies on the field of battle; let him die so. It does not horrify or shock me, again, to see a man dying in a good old age, even though the last struggle be painful, as it too often is. But it does shock me, it does make me feel that the world is indeed out of joint, to see a child die. I believe it to be a priceless boon to the child to have lived for a week, or a day: but oh, what has God given to this thankless earth, and what has the earth thrown away; and in nine cases out of ten, from its own neglect and carelessness! What that boy might have been, what he might have done as an Englishman, if he could have lived and grown up healthy and strong! And I entreat you to bear this in mind, that it is not as if our lower or our middle classes were not worth saving: bear in mind that the physical beauty, strength, intellectual power of the middle classes—the shopkeeping class, the farming class, down to the lowest working class—whenever you give them a fair chance, whenever you give them fair food and air, and physical education of any kind, prove them to be the finest race in Europe. Not merely the aristocracy, splendid race as they are, but down and down and down to the lowest labouring man, to the navigator—why, there is not such a body of men in Europe as our navigators; and no body of men perhaps have had a worse chance of growing to be what they are; and yet see what they have done! See the magnificent men they become, in spite of all that is against them, dragging them down, tending to give them rickets and consumption, and all the miserable diseases which children contract; see what men they are, and then conceive what they might be! It has been said, again and again, that there are no more beautiful race of women in Europe than the wives and daughters of our London shopkeepers; and yet there are few races of people who lead a life more in opposition to all rules of hygiene.[4] But, in spite of all that, so wonderful is the vitality of the English race, they are what they are; and therefore we have the finest material to work upon that people ever had. And, therefore, again, we have the less excuse if we do allow English people to grow up puny, stunted, and diseased.

Let me refer again to that word that I used; death—the amount of death. I really believe there are hundreds of good and kind people who would take up this subject with their whole heart and soul if they were aware of the magnitude of the evil. Lord Shaftesbury told you just now that there were one hundred thousand preventable deaths in England every year. So it is. We talk of the loss of human life in war. We are the fools of smoke and noise; because there are cannon-balls, forsooth, and swords and red coats; and because it costs a great deal of money, and makes a great deal of talk in the papers, we think: What so terrible as war? I will tell you what is ten times, and ten thousand times, more terrible than war, and that is—outraged Nature. War, we are discovering now, is the clumsiest and most expensive of all games; we are finding that if you wish to commit an act of cruelty and folly, the most costly one that you can commit is to contrive to shoot your fellow-men in war. So it is; and thank God that so it is; but Nature, insidious, inexpensive, silent, sends no roar of cannon, no glitter of arms to do her work; she gives no warning note of preparation; she has no protocols, nor any diplomatic advances, whereby she warns her enemy that war is coming. Silently, I say, and insidiously she goes forth; no! she does not even go forth; she does not step out of her path; but quietly, by the very same means by which she makes alive, she puts to death; and so avenges herself of those who have rebelled against her. By the very same laws by which every blade of grass grows, and every insect springs to life in the sunbeam, she kills, and kills, and kills, and is never tired of killing; till she has taught man the terrible lesson he is so slow to learn, that Nature is only conquered by obeying her.[5]

And bear in mind one thing more. Man has his courtesies of war, and his chivalries of war; he does not strike the unarmed man; he spares the woman and the child. But Nature is as fierce when she is offended, as she is bounteous and kind when she is obeyed. She spares neither woman nor child. She has no pity; for some awful, but most good reason, she is not allowed to have any pity. Silently she strikes the sleeping babe, with as little remorse as she would strike the strong man, with the spade or the musket in his hand. Ah! would to God that some man had the pictorial eloquence to put before the mothers of England the mass of preventable suffering, the mass of preventable agony of mind and body, which exists in England year after year; and would that some man had the logical

[4] In Kingsley's view, even the fashions of the time conspired against the well-being of women. The corset, with its confining stays, he thought an outrage against the "art of health."

[5] Note that this and the following paragraph are elaborations of that view of Nature which Kingsley expressed to John Bullar in private correspondence. See p. 393 above. Compare this passage with Thomas Henry Huxley's analogy between the laws of nature and the rules of chess, in his address, "A Liberal Education, Where to Find It."

cloquence to make them understand that it is in their power, in the power of the mothers and wives of the higher class, I will not say to stop it all—God only knows that—but to stop, as I believe, three-fourths of it.

It is in the power, I believe, of any woman in this room to save three or four lives—human lives—during the next six months. It is in your power, ladies; and it is so easy. You might save several lives apiece, if you choose, without, I believe, interfering with your daily business, or with your daily pleasure; or, if you choose, with your daily frivolities, in any way whatsoever. Let me ask, then, those who are here, and who have not yet laid these things to heart: Will you let this meeting to-day be a mere passing matter of two or three hours' interest, which you may go away and forget for the next book or the next amusement? Or will you be in earnest? Will you learn—I say it openly—from the noble chairman, how easy it is to be in earnest in life; how every one of you, amid all the artificial complications of English society in the nineteenth century, can find a work to do, a noble work to do, a chivalrous work to do—just as chivalrous as if you lived in any old magic land, such as Spenser talked of in his "Faërie Queene"; how you can be as true a knight-errant or lady-errant in the present century, as if you had lived far away in the dark ages of violence and rapine? Will you, I ask, learn this? Will you learn to be in earnest; and to use the position, and the station, and the talent that God has given you to save alive those who should live? And will you remember that it is not the will of your Father that is in Heaven that one little one that plays in the kennel [gutter] outside should perish, either in body or in soul?

∽

Bibliographical Note

The best published bibliography of Kingsley's literary and rhetorical works is in Margaret F. Thorp's *Charles Kingsley* (1937). This literary study and Una Pope-Hennessy's *Canon Charles Kingsley* (1949) are biographies of considerable value. The two-volume *Charles Kingsley, His Letters and Memories of His Life* (1882), edited by his wife, is adulatory and selective, but it remains the chief published source for original materials concerning Kingsley's career. Thomas Hughes' "Prefatory Memoir," published in the Eversley Edition of *Alton Locke,* contains the most intimate account of Kingsley's association with the Christian Socialist movement. Although his other literary achievements have been extensively studied, Canon Kingsley's preaching and lecturing have received little scholarly attention.

John Bright

(1811–1889)

John Bright's life provides a case study for the examination of the human being as a functioning moral unity. Born in Rochdale, one of eleven children of a moderately prosperous textile manufacturer, Bright was a Quaker, a businessman, a politician, and a reformer. In each of these roles he was active; in each, his actions took their premises from moral principle. Like most moralists, Bright could be as strong in denunciation of the evils he observed as he was warm in support of the truth as he saw it. Said Lord George Bentinck, "If Bright had not been a Quaker he would have been a prizefighter." [1]

Bright took to the rostrum at an early age to express his convictions, making his first public speech at nineteen on the subject of temperance. He got through a second speech but broke down in his third. The Reverend John Aldis thereupon advised him to give up memorizing and to speak extemporaneously.[2] The clergyman's memory of this advice became clearer the farther Bright's fame as an orator spread, while Bright's grew correspondingly dimmer.

In 1833, Bright presided over the first meeting of the Rochdale Literary and Philosophical Society, a debating society which he often addressed in the next four years. It was the hall of this same society that he used, along with his own bedroom, as a classroom in which to extend the scanty formal education he had received in Quaker schools between the ages of ten and fifteen. For politics, history, and economics, his textbooks were the newspapers, which he read devotedly for the rest of his life. For philosophy, ethics, and literary style, he went to the Bible and the well-known poets, especially Milton. His knowledge of commerce and his later technical skill in the handling of statistics he acquired in the living experience obtained in his father's business, which he joined shortly after his fifteenth birthday, and from which he derived a substantial income all his life.

Beginning in 1838, Bright spoke frequently for the Anti-Corn Law League in the environs of Rochdale. After the death of his wife in 1841, he accepted the invitation of Richard Cobden, the moving force of the League, to join him in fighting for the repeal of the tariff laws. His first speech in London, delivered in late 1841, marks the beginning of a career of agitation and reform that lasted until his death, but that was most distinguished in the twenty-six years from 1841 to 1867 when he participated in arguing four great issues of the period.

The first of these was the anti-Corn Law agitation, a great propaganda movement that employed the talents of thousands of people as writers, researchers, and fund raisers, and of Cobden and Bright as its leading platform spokesmen. It culminated in the repeal of the Corn Laws in 1846.

The second was peace. Bright deplored war, opposed the theory of the balance of power, and resisted the practice of intervention in the affairs of foreign nations. Two of his most compelling speeches, noted for their unstudied pathos as well as for their logic, he delivered as a member of the House of Commons in opposition to the Crimean War. In 1854, speaking of the reports of the war dead, he said, "The Angel of Death has been abroad throughout the land; you may almost hear the beating of his wings." After this speech, so it is reported, Cobden said to Bright, "You went very near that time. If you had said 'flapping' instead of 'beating of his wings,' the House would have laughed." [3] But Bright could

---

[1] Quoted in C. A. Vince, *John Bright*, p. 232.

[2] William Robertson, *Life and Times of the Right Hon. John Bright*, pp. 52–53. For Bright's thoughts on extemporaneity as well as other rhetorical topics, see two letters quoted by Joseph O. Baylen in "John Bright as Speaker and Student of Speaking," *Quarterly Journal of Speech*, XLI (1955), 159 ff. See also Bright's *Diaries*, ed. by R. A. J. Walling, p. 52.

[3] George M. Trevelyan, *The Life of John Bright*, p. 385.

never have introduced such a false note; in his speaking, the words *are* the idea.

On the issue of the American Civil War, in the Commons and in the large cities, Bright spoke of his admiration of the United States, of his hatred of slavery, and of his support for the North. His reply to Gladstone's statement that the North would not prevail in the Civil War ends with a vision of the United States that is Websterian in tone and idea: "I see one vast confederation . . . one people, and one language, and one law, and one faith, and over all that wide continent the home of freedom and a refuge for the oppressed of every race and of every clime."[4]

The fourth great movement with which Bright was connected most of his life was the extension of suffrage. In a day when only sixteen males in every hundred could vote, he scorned the aristocracy for their failure in the governance of the nation, and he made the vote for the working man the basis for his proposals for parliamentary reform. He saw many of his principles enacted into law in the Reform Bill of 1867, which Disraeli called the "leap in the dark." Although Bright was a champion of democracy and a stalwart logician on the need for extended suffrage, he could not bring himself to support the vote for women. His brother Jacob could and did.

Bright was a humanist, believing in the freedom and the dignity of man and hating the forces that destroyed human rights. His philosophy was whole; his principles and values, in order; his application of them to an immediate proposal in hand, almost always right. Bright "entangles his conscience in his intellect," Cobden wrote.[5] He supported efforts to provide cheap and abundant food for the working man and his family; to enfranchise the people; to admit Jews to membership in Parliament; to increase educational opportunities for all. He denounced forced payments for the support of churches, the abuse of power by the Irish landlords, the institution of slavery, and the moral squalor of war.

Perhaps he lacked intellectual complexity. He refused to support Lord Shaftesbury on factory reform, or to encourage legislation to limit the hours of work for adult laborers, because he believed that the contrary policy of laissez-faire preserved the independence of human beings. This belief arose from his basic conception of the free man and not from his vested interests as the owner of a cotton-spinning factory. He was vehement, it will be remembered, in his denunciation of the South in the Civil War, even though his six factories were closed for lack of imported raw cotton. Bright was in favor of general education, but against compulsory education. To have been right all of the time, Bright would have needed a complexity as profound as his simplicity and a power to see beyond the horizons of his middle-class Victorian world.

Bright was as successful with a popular audience as he was with the House of Commons. About five feet nine inches in height, he had a robust frame, mobile facial features, a fringe of whiskers encircling his jaw, but no beard to obscure the play of his mouth. His voice was strong, his inflectional patterns intricately shaped, his rate relatively slow, his enunciation perfect. Like many orators gifted with extraordinary voices, he used gestures sparingly. Just as style is the man, so

[4] Speech at Birmingham, December 18, 1862.

[5] From a letter written by Richard Cobden to Rev. Henry Richard. British Museum, Add. MS. 43,658; f. 251. Bright's nephew, Charles McLaren, called his speeches "political sermons"; see his article, "Reminiscences of John Bright," *The North American Review*, CLV (September 1892), 323.

is delivery. A man who had heard him often said that "he always spoke as if living continually in the presence of the Deity." [6]

No single speech is representative of every important characteristic of an orator. The speech against capital punishment printed in this volume is more typical of Bright's use of evidence than it is of his ability to introduce pathos, sentiment, ridicule, or humor into his speaking, even though the subject matter invites rather than resists their use. Like all of Bright's speeches, this speech lacks tight organizational patterning; it falls midway in the firmness of its topical handling between his loosely organized anti-Corn Law speeches delivered early in his speaking career, and his more artfully constructed speeches on home rule delivered toward the close of his life. The speech conveys those qualities of earnestness, simplicity, and directness that were typical of all of his compositions.

Bright delivered this speech in the House of Commons in support of a motion by Mr. Ewart to abolish the death penalty. The subject arose because two cases involving capital punishment had brought the Home Secretary under attack.[7]

∽

On Punishment of Death [*]

May 3, 1864

Sir, I shall not, after the discussion which has taken place, and which has been, I think, almost on one side, take up the time of the House by making a speech. But the right hon. Gentleman [1] has said something which I am obliged to contest to some extent. He has quoted the opinion of Judges upon this question, and he has laid, I think, more stress upon these opinions than they generally deserve. I think, if there is one thing more certain than another, it is this— that every amelioration of the criminal code of this country has been carried against the opinion of the majority of the Judges. And I may on this point quote the opinion of an eminent Irish Judge, who, I believe, is still living, and with whom

[6] Quoted in Vince, p. 23.

[7] Under date of May 3, 1864, Bright recorded in his Diary: "House: Capital Punishment. I spoke at some length and with evident effect on the House. Discussion very good. Mr. Denman and Lord Henry Lennox made good speeches. The question has advanced greatly, and has never before received so much attention in the House."

[*] This text of Bright's speech is taken from Hansard with paragraphing inserted. The text in *The Times*, May 4, 1864, is slightly shorter, the difference in length being almost solely attributable to an editorial tightening of the composition. At two points, noted below, the Hansard text contains material not carried in the *Times* text. The other sentences in both texts are the same in sense but different in wording or syntax more often than not. In three places, noted below, readings in the *Times* text suggest that the Hansard text is in error. The Hansard text contains certain specificities of statement, certain conventionalized parliamentary wordings, and certain habitual syntactical forms characteristic of Bright's speaking, which indicate that this text represents more nearly than the *Times* text what Bright said on May 3, 1864.

[1] Sir George Grey (1799–1882), Secretary of State for Home Affairs intermittently from 1846 to 1866, to whom criminal cases involving the death penalty could be referred for clemency.

I had some conversation in Ireland some fifteen years ago. The conversation turned on this very question. He said, "Beware of the Judges. If Parliament had acted on the opinion of the Judges we should have been hanging now for forgery, for horse stealing, and for I know not how many other offences for which capital punishment has long been abolished." [2]

Now the right hon. Gentleman proposes to have a Commission, as I understand, instead of a Committee. [3] There was an inconsistency in his speech I thought, on that point; for at first he seemed to say that the question, whether capital punishment should be continued or be abolished, was not one which a Committee of this House was fitted to consider; but towards the close of his speech he moderated that by admitting that some of the points referred to in the Amendment, which is, I suppose, to be agreed to, might be considered by a Committee.

I will undertake to say that if he were to inquire in every civilized country in the world where there is a representative legislative assembly, he would find that the changes which had been made in their laws have been made invariably in consequence of inquiries instituted by those Chambers and carried on by means of Committees formed amongst their members. I admit that the bulk of the Committees of this House are not fairly constituted. I served very assiduously on Committees for the first ten or fifteen years after I became a Member of this House, and I did not find out till about the year 1850 or 1853 that a Committee was generally of no use; and from that time to this I have avoided, in nine cases out of ten, when I have been applied to, sitting upon a Committee. But that observation refers principally to questions where political interests are concerned. When, however, you come to a question of this nature, where we should necessarily take the opinion of Judges, to whom the right hon. Gentleman pays so much attention, and of those men of whose great authority he has spoken, and of a great many other men who are not wedded to existing systems, and of men who could give us the facts with regard to other countries, I say that a Committee of this House, so far at any rate as obtaining evidence is concerned, I think would be equal to any tribunal, or any court of inquiry, which the right hon. Gentleman could establish.

The right hon. Gentleman has led the House away a little from the main question. The main question proposed by my hon. Friend the Member for Dumfries [4] is whether capital punishment should be retained or abolished. The

---

[2] Bright's diary for September 7, 1849, gives the following version: "Dined at Thos. Hutton's, Elm Park. . . . I sat next to Judge Perrin, a pleasant and most sensible man. Against Capital Punishment: 'Judges should not be consulted on these points, for if Judges' opinions had been acted upon, sheep stealers would have been hanged still.'" (*The Diaries of John Bright*, p. 106.)

[3] A select committee, composed of Members of Parliament, expired with the particular session of Parliament in which it was formed. If the work of the committee was not finished, it had to be re-appointed in the following session. On the other hand, a Royal Commission was composed of members of both the Lords and Commons, as well as experts on the subject under inquiry. For a prolonged inquiry, it was usual to employ a commission rather than a committee since the mandate of a commission did not expire until the investigation was complete. (Montgomery and Cambray, *Dictionary of Political Phrases and Allusions*, p. 72.)

[4] William Ewart (1798–1869), Member of Parliament from Dumfries from 1841 to 1868. He frequently spoke in Parliament on various liberal causes, especially on re-

right hon. Gentleman has led the House into a discussion of a question somewhat personal to himself—in connection with recent cases.[5] I know the right hon. Gentleman was justified in what he said in reference to the position which he holds in the performance of his painful duties with regard to the execution of the criminal law. But that is not exactly what is wanted—this Motion was not brought forward for that purpose.

I think the House would agree with great unanimity if the right hon. Gentleman would introduce a Bill proposing certain changes at which he has hinted. This country has always been the most barbarous of all civilized nations in its punishments; and at this moment is the most barbarous still, notwithstanding what the right hon. Gentleman said about the punishment of death being inflicted only for the crime of murder. But did he not afterwards tell the House that this crime of murder is a net which includes cases as different in their quality as in their guilt and in their consequences to society, as the difference between the lowest class of murder which the law now includes and the pettiest larceny which is punishable before a single magistrate. Yet all these are part of the same list of crimes, and if a jury does its duty—that is what is always said, as if a jury had no other duty but inexorably to send a man to the scaffold—if a jury will find a verdict of guilty, the punishment is death, unless the right hon. Gentleman, importuned by a number of persons, or having examined into the case himself, will interfere to save the unfortunate wretch from the gallows.

There can be no doubt whatever that if capital punishment be retained, and if it be absolutely necessary that there should be a crime called murder to which capital punishment attaches, it is no less necessary that there should be, as there are in some other countries, three or four degrees of manslaughter, and that for the highest degree of manslaughter there should be the highest kind of secondary punishment, and that the power should be placed in the hands of the jury of determining what should be the particular class in which the criminal should be placed.

There is no doubt that this is necessary to be done. I think Voltaire—who said a good many things that were worth remembering—remarked that the English were the only people who murdered by law.[6] And Mirabeau, when in this country, hearing of a number of persons who had been hanged on a certain morning, said, "The English nation is the most merciless of any that I have heard or read of." And at this very moment, when we have struck off within the last fifty years

---

form of criminal law, and was responsible for many reform bills on the practice of capital punishment. Bright's speech was in support of Ewart's motion "that a Select Committee be appointed to inquire into the expediency of maintaining the Punishment of Death." (Hansard, May, 1864, p. 2992.)

[5] See notes 1 and 7.

[6] "The members of the English Parliament are fond of comparing themselves to the old Romans. . . . Marius and Sylla, Caesar and Pompey, Anthony and Augustus, did not draw their swords and set the world in a blaze merely to determine whether the flamen should wear his shirt over his robe, or his robe over his shirt, or whether the sacred chickens should eat and drink, or eat only, in order to take the augury. The English have hanged one another by law, and cut one another to pieces in pitched battles, for quarrels of as trifling a nature." (Letters Concerning the English, IV, 1733, quoted in Desmond Flower, ed., Voltaire's England, p. 37.) Bright's use of the quotation was better than his memory of it.

at least a hundred offences which were then capital, we remain still in this matter the most merciless of Christian countries. If anybody wishes to satisfy himself upon this point let him take those late cases in which the right hon. Gentleman has had so much trouble. Take the case of Townley; take the case of Wright; take the case of Hall, of Warwick; [7] and I will take the liberty of repeating—what I said to the right hon. Gentleman when I was permitted to see him on the case of the convict Hall—that there is not a country in Europe, nor a State among the Free States of America, in which either of those criminals would have been punished with death. [8] Yet we have gone on leaving the law as it is; and the right hon. Gentleman, to my utter astonishment, every time this question has been discussed, has given us very much the same speech as he has addressed to us to-night: he has repeated the same arguments for continuing a law which drives him to distraction almost every time he has to administer it.

I am surprised that the right hon. Gentleman, who has had to face the suffering which has been brought on him by this law, has never had the courage to come to this House and ask it fairly to consider, in the light of the evidence which all other Governments and the laws of all other countries afford, whether the time has not come when this fearful punishment may be abolished. The right hon. Gentleman says the punishment is so terrible that it will deter offenders from the commission of crime. Of course it is terrible to one just standing upon the verge of the grave; but months before, when the crime is committed, when the passion is upon the criminal, the punishment is of no avail whatsoever. I do not

[7] (a) George Victor Townley was the self-confessed murderer of his former fiancée, Elizabeth Goodwin, on August 21, 1863. His counsel entered a plea of insanity for him, but he was convicted and sentenced to death on December 18, 1863. The presiding judge, Mr. Baron Martin, informed Sir George Grey that in his opinion the prisoner's sanity should be further investigated. This communication, plus appeals from four Justices of the Peace and two physicians, eventuated in a declaration of insanity, and Townley's death sentence was respited, but not commuted. On December 30, 1863, he was committed to the Criminal Lunatic Asylum in St. George's Fields, Surrey. When a subsequent medical report certified that Townley was sane, his sentence was commuted and he was sentenced to life imprisonment in Pentonville Prison in February, 1864.

(b) Samuel Wright was a Surrey working man who was accused of murdering his common-law wife, Maria Green, "with malice aforethought." Wright confessed to the murder, but said that Maria had threatened to run a knife into him. Wright was condemned to death in December, 1863. The Visiting Justices of Surrey County Gaol pleaded his case with the Home Secretary, who refused clemency, and Wright was executed.

(c) George Hall was convicted on March 3, 1864, of shooting his wife to death. Finding that his wife had provoked him by deserting him for another man, the jury recommended mercy. Hall's sentence was commuted to life imprisonment after a petition from his home town, Birmingham, containing thousands of signatures, including that of the mayor, was presented in his behalf.

[8] The *Times* report of Bright's speech differs in syntax at this point from that of Hansard, eliminating the ambiguity that makes Warwick appear to be a fourth case: "At this moment, when we have during the last 50 years struck out 100 offences which were punishable by death, we still remain the most merciless of all Christian countries in reference to this matter (hear, hear); and if any one wishes to satisfy himself upon this point he has only to refer to the late instances of Townley, Wright (hear, hear), and Hall at Warwick."

think it is possible to say too much against the argument that this is a dreadful punishment, and is very efficient to deter a criminal from the commission of crime.

As the right hon. Gentleman proposes to give a Commission, I shall not trouble the House with the observations that I had intended to make. There are, however, two or three cases which have not been mentioned and which I should like to bring under the notice of the House. My hon. Friend the Member for Dumfries referred to Russia. Russia is a country in which capital punishments have for almost a hundred years been unknown. I was reading yesterday a very remarkable Report of a Committee of the Legislature of the State of New York, written in the year 1841.[9] It states that the Empress Elizabeth determined that for twenty years there would be no capital punishments in Russia. The Empress Catherine, in giving her instructions for the new Grand Code, stated her opinion upon the subject in these words—

> Experience shows that the frequent repetition of capital punishment has never yet made men better. If, therefore, I can show that in the ordinary state of society the death of a citizen is neither useful nor necessary, I shall have pleaded the cause of humanity with success.

She then says what I think is worthy of hearing—

> When the laws bear quiet and peaceful sway, and under a form of government approved by the united voice of the nation, in such a state there can be no necessity for taking away the life of a citizen.[10]

The exception is in the case of some great political offender whose incarceration did not destroy his power to do mischief; and I believe that since the enactment of this law there have been only two cases of persons who have been put to death by law in Russia, and that these have been cases arising out of circumstances of a political and insurrectionary character.

Count Ségur, the French Ambassador at St. Petersburgh, states that the Empress Catherine said to him—

> We must punish crime without imitating it. The punishment of death is rarely anything but a useless barbarity.

[9] *The Times,* omitting this sentence, does not mention Bright's source. The full title is *Report of Select Committee on Capital Punishment,* New York State Assembly Document 249, 1841.

[10] "The Empress Elizabeth of Russia, on ascending the throne, pledged herself never to inflict the punishment of death; and throughout her reign, twenty years, she kept the noble pledge. And so satisfactory was found its operation, that her successor, the great Catherine, adopted it into her celebrated Code of Laws, with the exception of very rare cases of offences against the state. 'Experience demonstrates,' is the language of her 'Grand Instructions for framing a new code of laws for the Russian Empire,' Article 210, 'that the frequent repetition of capital punishments has never yet made men better. If, therefore, I can show that in the ordinary state of society the death of a citizen is neither useful nor necessary, I shall have pleaded the cause of humanity with success. I said, "in the ordinary state"; for the death of a citizen may be necessary in one particular case; I mean, when, though deprived of liberty, he has still means and power left to disturb the national repose; a case which can never happen, except when a people loses or recovers its liberty; or in times of anarchy, when disorder and confusion usurp the place of laws.'" (*Ibid.,* p. 99.)

In reporting this to the French Government, Count Ségur stated that under the mildness of the law murders were very rare in Russia.[11]

My hon. Friend the Member for Dumfries referred to the case of Tuscany,[12] where it is well known that for a lifetime capital punishment has never been inflicted. In the case of Belgium, to which reference was made by my hon. and learned Friend the Member for Tiverton,[13] as one of the most remarkable, I think the right hon. Gentleman was not successful in getting rid of his figures. It happens, as I understand, the law in Belgium does not prohibit capital punishments; but the result of omitting to inflict capital punishment has been so satisfactory that now the law is literally obsolete, and that capital punishment is never inflicted.

Take then the case of Bombay, which is of a very striking character. We have the evidence from the pen of Sir James Mackintosh,[14] who says—

> It will appear that the capital crimes committed during the last seven years (1804 and 1811) with no capital executions, have in proportion to the population not been much more than a third of those committed in the first seven years (1756 to 1763) when forty-seven persons suffered death.

He adds—

> The intermediate periods lead to the same results.

The House ought to bear in mind, that to us who have examined this question for many years, no fact is more clearly demonstrated than this—that there is no

---

[11] Louis Philippe, Comte de Ségur (1753–1830), French diplomat and historian, served in the American War of Independence in 1781 as a colonel, was minister plenipotentiary to the Court at St. Petersburgh, where he became friendly with Catherine II, even writing plays for her theatre. Bright's quotation comes from the New York State Assembly Document 249, p. 100: "The Count de Ségur, on his return from his embassy at St. Petersburgh, in a letter published in the *Moniteur,* in June, 1791, declared that Russia, under the operation of this law, was one of the countries in which the least number of murders was committed,—adding that Catherine herself had several times said to him: '*We must punish crime without imitating it; the punishment of death is rarely any thing but a useless barbarity.*'"

[12] The Grand Duke Leopold, upon ascending to the throne of Tuscany in 1765, abolished the punishment of death provisionally and experimentally. In 1786, proclaiming the experiment a success, he signed a law forever abolishing the punishment of death. (The New York State Assembly Document 249, pp. 103–7.)

[13] George Denman (1819–1896), lawyer, later judge of the Queen's Bench, 1872–1896. At the time of Bright's speech there had been no cases of capital punishment in Belgium since 1829.

[14] Bright takes this idea and quotation from the New York State Assembly Document 249. Sir James Mackintosh (1765–1832), Scottish essayist and Whig Member of Parliament, was president of the court in Bombay, India, from 1804 to 1811. In 1811, reviewing his administration of the law, he pointed out that the punishment of death had never been inflicted by his court which had a jurisdiction over 200,000 persons, and that no evil consequences had ensued. He compared the seven years from 1756 to 1763 when capital convictions were 141 and executions 47, with his seven years when there were 109 convictions and no executions. The last portion of the quotation used by Bright reads as follows in the original ". . . notwithstanding the infliction of death on *forty-seven* persons" (p. 102). Sir James reviews his presidency in a speech of 1811 contained in *The Miscellaneous Works of the Right Honourable Sir James Mackintosh,* ed. by R. J. Mackintosh.

country in the world, be it a great empire or be it a small state—where the law has been made milder, and capital punishment has been abolished, in which there is any proof that murders have been more frequent, and the security of life in the slightest degree endangered. If that be so—if I could convince every Member of this House that the abolition of capital punishment would not cause more murders than the average of the last ten years—if all that would be left would be that those ten or twelve wretches who are publicly strangled every year would be living in some prison, or engaged in some labour with a chance of penitence, and with life not suddenly cut off by law—is there a man in this House—I speak not of party, or to one side or the other—who durst demand that we should still continue these terrible punishments?

There used to be in this House a venerable old Gentleman who represented the University of Oxford, who in the discussion on this subject constantly quoted a certain verse of a certain chapter in the Book of Genesis.[15] I am delighted that in the seven or eight years that have elapsed since this question was last discussed, we have advanced so far that nobody has brought forward that argument. We have discussed it to-night by the light of proved experiments, of facts, and of reason.

Seeing what has been done in this country by the amelioration of the Criminal Code, and what has been done in all other countries, is there any man with one particle of sense or the power of reason who believes that human life in this country is made more secure because ten or twelve men are publicly put to death every year? The security of human life does not depend upon any such miserable and barbarous provision as that. The security for human life depends upon the reverence for human life; and unless you can inculcate in the minds of your people a veneration for that which God only has given, you do little by the most severe and barbarous penalties to preserve the safety of your citizens. If you could put down what it is that secures human life in figures and estimate it at 100, how much of it is to be attributed to your savage law, and how much of it to the reverence of human life implanted in the human soul? No doubt 5 or 10 per cent out of the 100 may be owing, for aught I know, to the influence of the law; but 90 or 95 per cent is owing to that feeling of reverence for human life.[16] Whenever you hang a man in the face of the public under the circumstances to which we are so accustomed in this country, if you do so in the slightest degree deter from crime by the shocking nature of the punishment, I will undertake to say that you by so much—nay, by much more—weaken that other and greater security which depends upon the reverence with which human life is regarded.

Since this notice of this Motion was given by my hon. Friend I took the liberty of writing to the Governors of three of the States of America in which capital punishment has for several years been abolished; and, with the permission of the House, I will read extracts from the answers which I have received. I think they are important in a discussion of this nature when we are attempting to persuade doubtful and timid people that we are not proposing a rash or dangerous change.

[15] Possibly Sir Robert Peel (1788–1850), Member of Parliament from 1818 to his death in 1850, during which time he was Prime Minister twice. As Home Secretary, from 1822 to 1827, he was instrumental in passing eight acts mitigating and consolidating criminal law, and in repealing in whole or in part, 250 obsolete criminal statutes. His three major Parliamentary speeches on criminal reform (21 May 1823; 9 March 1826; and 22 February 1827), however, contain no Biblical quotations.

[16] *The Times* omits the above two sentences, and drastically alters the beginning of this paragraph.

In the State of Rhode Island, one of the small States of America, with a population of not more than 200,000, capital punishment has been abolished. The Governor, the Hon. J. Pye Smith,[17] writing from the Executive Department, March 21, 1864, says—

> 1. The death penalty was abolished in this State in the year 1852. 2. I do not think its abolition has had any effect upon the security of life. 3. Is the law against the death penalty sustained by the public opinion of the State? Very decidedly. 4. Are convictions and punishments more certain than before the change was made? I think they are. 5. What is the punishment now inflicted on such criminals as were formerly punished with death? Imprisonment for life at hard labour. I have conversed with one supreme Judge, State attorney, and warden of the State prison, and they support my own established views upon the subject.

In a second letter, dated April 4, and which I received a few days ago, he says—

> Our present able Chief Justice says:—"Although [opposed] [18] to the present law when passed, I am equally opposed to a change in it until the experiment has been tried long enough to satisfy us that it has failed. I am clearly of opinion that the present state of the law is sustained by public opinion, and I believe it will continue to be until it is satisfactorily shown that crimes against life have been considerably increased in consequence of it. My observation fully justifies me in saying that conviction for murder is far more certain now in proper cases than when death was the punishment of it."

Here is the answer which I received from the Hon. Austin Blair, the Governor of the State of Michigan—[19]

> Executive Office, Lancing [Lansing], March 23, 1864.
> 1. The death penalty for murder was abolished March 1, 1847, when the revised statutes of 1846 went into effect. 2. Life is not considered less secure than before; murders are probably less frequent in proportion to population. Twenty years ago the population of the State was 300,000, and we have now a population of about 900,000. Then it was chiefly agricultural, and now we have mines of copper, iron, coal, etc., bringing into proximity dissimilar classes, and increasing the probabilities of frequent crime. Before the abolition of the death penalty murders were not unfrequent, but convictions were rarely or never obtained. It became the common belief that no jury could be found (the prisoner availing himself of the common law right of challenge) which would convict. Since the abolition there have been in seventeen years thirty-seven convictions. 3. There can be no doubt that public opinion sustains the present law and is against the restoration of the death penalty. 4. Conviction and punishment are now much more certain than before the change was made. Murder requires a greater amount of proof [20] than any other crime, and it is found practically that a trial for murder excites no very unusual interest.

[17] The Honorable J. Y. Smith (not J. Pye Smith as Hansard spells it) was Governor of Rhode Island from 1863 to 1866.
[18] Hansard: "disposed"; *Times*: "opposed."
[19] The Honorable Austin Blair was Governor of Michigan from 1861 to 1865.
[20] *Times*: "Murder requires no greater amount . . . ." The context suggests that Hansard is correct.

It, therefore, does not make a hero of the criminal. The letter proceeds—

5. The punishment now is solitary confinement at hard labour for life. Since 1861 this class of prisoners have been employed as other prisoners, as it was found difficult to keep them at work in cells without giving them tools, and there was danger of their becoming insane. The reform has been successfully tried, and is no longer an experiment.

The last letter is from the Hon. J. S. Lewis,[21] the Governor of Wisconsin, and is dated Madison, March 29, 1864—

The evil tendency of public executions, the great aversion of many to the taking of life rendering it almost impossible to obtain jurors from the more intelligent portion of the community, the liability of the innocent to suffer so extreme a penalty and be placed beyond the reach of the pardoning power, and the disposition of courts and juries not to convict, fearing the innocent might suffer, convinced me that this relic of barbarism should be abolished. The death penalty was repealed in 1853. No legislation has since re-established it, and the people find themselves equally secure, and the public more certain than before. The population in 1850 was 305,000; in 1860 it was 775,000. With this large increase of population we might expect a large increase of criminal cases, but this does not appear to be the case.

If you take those two last States of Wisconsin and Michigan which have been comparatively recently settled, you will see that it was highly probable, as they are on the outskirts of advancing civilization, that crimes of violence should not be uncommon. But here, with the abolition of this punishment, crimes and violence are not more common than before; people are just as secure, the law is upheld by public opinion, and the elected Governors of those three States, after the experience of these years, are enabled to write me letters like these, so satisfactory and so conclusive with regard to the effect of the experiment as it has been tried with them.

The special cases that have been mentioned to-night with regard to executions have not been by any means the most fearful that have occurred. There was a case last year at Chester of so revolting a nature that I should be afraid to state the details to the House.[22] I think it is hardly conceivable that a Christian gentleman, a governor of a gaol, and a clergyman, another Christian gentleman, should be concerned in such a dreadful catastrophe as then took place. Sir, if there be fiends below, how it must rejoice them to discover that, after the law of gentleness and love has been preached on earth for 1,800 years, such a scene as that should be enacted in our day in one of the most civilized and renowned cities of this country. Well, but these are cases which will happen again if this law remains; and all the difficulties which the right hon. Gentleman has alluded to to-night and on previous occasions are difficulties inseparable from the continuance of this punishment.

Now, the right hon. Gentleman has referred to one or two cases; the noble

[21] The Honorable J. T. Lewis (not J. S. Lewis as Hansard has it) was Governor of Wisconsin from 1864 to 1866.

[22] Possibly the case in which Alice Hewitt, a 27-year-old factory worker, poisoned her mother, presumably to obtain her insurance. She was sentenced to death at the Chester Winter Assizes, December, 1863. Her appeal for mercy was not granted and she was executed. (*The Times*, December 11, 1863, p. 10.)

Lord opposite [23] has likewise referred to one or two. Why, the case at Glasgow, the case at Derby, the recent case in London, and the recent case at Warwick,[24] are cases which move whole populations; and, if that be so, how can any man argue that this law is in a satisfactory state, or that this punishment can be wisely and beneficially administered and executed in this country? Why, Parliament, unfortunately—we need not disguise it, and I will not at any rate conceal it— Parliament has been very heedless upon this question. Secretaries of States have gone on from year to year hobbling, as it were, through the performance of their duties in connection [with this law] [25] with great pain to themselves, and yet they have never had the courage to ask Parliament to consider whether the system might not be entirely abolished. Does not every man now feel that it is in opposition to the sentiment of what I will call—and I think I may say without disparaging anybody—the most moral and religious portion of the population of this country—the men who have led the advance during the past century in every contest that we have had with ignorance, and crime, and cruelty, in whatsoever shape it has shown itself? And every day they are becoming more and more estranged from the spirit and operation of this law. Whenever there are paragraphs floating about in the newspapers that on the 15th or the 25th of such a month such a one is to meet his doom for some crime, however foul, there is in every city, in every parish, and in almost every house in this country where there is any regard to humanity and to Christianity, a feeling of doubt as to whether this law is right, and a feeling of disgust and horror amongst hundreds and thousands of the best portion of our people.

Now, merciful laws are, in my opinion, the very highest testimony to any Government, as I likewise think that they are the highest blessing a people can enjoy. I believe they give security to a Government, and they soften and humanise the people. Now, all the steps that have been taken in this direction have been so successful, that I wonder that even the late Lord Mayor of London [26] should not himself have come to the conclusion that after all [we] [27] would still sleep comfortably in our beds if men were not hanged; and that, if the law were gentle and merciful whilst it was just, he would find gradually growing up in the minds of all classes a greater dislike to crime and violence, and a greater reverence for human life. Benjamin Franklin, a great authority on matters of this nature, said that the virtues are all parts of a circle; that whatever is humane, is wise; whatever is wise, is just; and whatever is wise, just, and humane, will be found to be the true interests of states, whether criminals or foreign enemies are the objects of their legislation. Would any of us like to go back to the barbarism of that time when Charles Wesley wrote a note to the celebrated and excellent John Fletcher, the vicar of Madeley, in 1776? We were then trying to keep the empire together, and neglecting this great work at home. He says—

[23] Lord Henry Lennox (1821–1886), Conservative Member of Parliament for Chichester. He moved an amendment to Ewart's motion, namely, "That a select committee be appointed to inquire into the operation of the laws relating to capital punishment." (Hansard, Vol. 174, p. 2071.)

[24] Townley was tried at Derby and Hall at Warwick.

[25] *Times* text.

[26] William Anderson Rose who, both as Lord Mayor and as Member of Parliament, had opposed reform of the criminal code. (*The Times,* September 30, 1863, p. 6.)

[27] Hansard: "he"; *Times:* "we."

> A fortnight ago I preached a condemned sermon to about twenty criminals, and every one of them, I had good grounds to believe, died penitent. Twenty more must die next week.[28]

And there were then cases in which twenty were hanged, not one of whom had been convicted or found guilty of the crime of murder. Have not we from that time made great and salutary and satisfactory advances in this question? Is there any man who wants to turn back to the barbarism of that day? But if you turn back to the Secretaries of State of that day, or to the Judges of that day, or even to the Bishops of that day, you will find that they had just the same sort of arguments in favour of the barbarism in which they were then concerned that the right hon. Gentleman, I suppose forced by the necessities of his office, has offered to the House to-night. I confess I wonder that all the right hon. Gentleman has gone through in these painful cases has not driven him stark mad many times. At any rate, I wonder that it has not driven him to the table of this House to propose, under the solemn feelings with which he must often have been impressed, that the House should take into consideration whether this vast evil—as I believe it to be—might not be put an end to. Is the Englishman worse than another man? Is this nation worse than other nations? Cannot the lenient laws practised with perfect safety in every other—not every other, but in many nations of the world—be practised in this nation, and at the same time leave us perfectly secure—at least as much so as we are at present? I say we may wash vengeance and blood from our code without difficulty and without danger.

The right hon. Gentleman is going to appoint a Commission—he prefers it to a Committee, and I will not contest the point with him if the Commission be a fair Commission; but I should not like to see it a Commission of Judges. Mind I am not wishing to speak disrespectfully of Judges. I agree with what the right hon. Gentleman has said, that with the exception of a case or two, perhaps, in one's lifetime, we notice nothing on the bench but that which is honourable to the Judges of this country; and I would say that the Judges of this country may be compared with advantage probably with the Judges of any other country. But Judges are but men. Several of them, as a proof of that, have been Members of this House. And I am free to confess that the feelings I had when I was a schoolboy at York, and first went to an assize trial [29] and saw that venerable old gentleman in his wig, were those of utter awe and astonishment; but those feelings have been considerably modified by my experience of many of the present Judges when they were Members of this House. But we know that Judges are like other men in this—they have trodden a certain path which has led them to the honourable position which they hold. They are there, however, not to make law, but to administer it; and they have tempered its severity, as the noble Lord said, as their judgments are merciful or otherwise. But they adhere to the law, for it is that

---

[28] The original letter from which this quotation is taken is deposited in the library of the Wesley House in London, England, and is dated May 21, 1785, not 1776 as Bright says. The quotation reads as follows in the original: "A fortnight ago I preached the condemned sermon to above twenty criminals. Every one of them, I have good grounds to believe, died penitent. Twenty men must die next week." (Information on this quotation was provided by Louise A. Dygoski.)

[29] A sitting or session of a court, or the court itself; especially, one of the regular sessions of the judges of a superior court for the trial of cases by jury in any county of England or Wales, or the time and place of holding a court.

which they have to administer. Some of them are not desirous, perhaps, to express an opinion, like the noble Lord, the father of the hon. and learned Member for Tiverton.[30] They are strongly attached to that system which they have been administering; and, as I said at the beginning of the observations I have offered to the House, they have been in all past times—not all of them, but a majority of them—generally opposed to the amelioration of our Criminal Code. Although, therefore, I believe that at this moment there are more Judges on the bench who are in favour of the abolition of capital punishment, yet I should not like the right hon. Gentleman to leave the inquiry into this question entirely or even to a majority of the members of the bench. There is no reason to believe that a Judge is more competent to give an opinion on this question than any other intelligent, educated, and observing man; nor would I admit that the right hon. Gentleman himself, who is in his whole person the whole bench of Judges, is more capable of giving an opinion than any other Member of this House who has paid long and careful attention to this subject. Therefore, I hope that if the right hon. Gentleman does appoint a Commission he will put upon it—I do not say men who have not an opinion on one side or the other, for men who have no opinion at all are not likely to give any worth hearing—but men in whom the House and the country and those in the House who are against capital punishment shall have confidence, feeling that they would take evidence from every source whence it could be fairly offered to them, and that they would give to the House and the Government a fair opinion on that evidence in their Report.

If that be done I am quite certain that the result will be a great improvement of the law, although it may not carry it to the point which my hon. Friend the Member for Dumfries has so long desired to carry it. But I shall be very thankful if that much is accomplished; and if ever we come to that point, I have confidence too that even you Gentlemen opposite, who are so very timid, always fancying that the ice is going to break, will be induced to go further than you seem inclined to do now; and perhaps the ten or twelve who are now hanged annually may be brought down to three or four, and at last we may come unanimously to the opinion, that the security of public life in England does not depend upon the public strangling of three or four poor wretches every year.

This Parliament is about to expire, I suppose, before very long—though some say it is to endure during another Session; I should be glad indeed if it might be said of this Parliament at some future time, that it had dared to act upon the true lessons, and not upon the—what shall I say?—the superstitions of the past; and that this Parliament might be declared to be the Parliament which destroyed the scaffold and the gallows in order that it might teach the people that human life is sacred, and that on that principle alone can human life be secured.

∾

BIBLIOGRAPHICAL NOTE

The shortest and most readable biography of Bright is by Charles Anthony Vince, *John Bright* (1898); a longer, more fully documented, almost equally readable biography is George Macaulay Trevelyan's *The Life of John Bright*, new edition (1925);

[30] The first Lord Denman (1779–1854), Lord Chief Justice of England from 1832 to 1850, had been active in legal reform and the anti-slave-trade movement.

the longest and least readable is William Robertson's *Life and Times of the Right Hon. John Bright,* third edition (1912). John Morley's superb biography, *The Life of Richard Cobden* (1881), contains a detailed account of the Bright–Cobden partnership in politics and life. *Cartoons from the Collection of "Mr. Punch"* (1878) is a thin, quarto volume of cartoons dated 1846–1875, which may have been amusing in their day. J. E. Thorold Rogers had the "benefit" of Bright's personal revisions for his compilations, *The Speeches of the Right Honourable John Bright* (1869), in two volumes, and *Public Addresses by John Bright, M.P.* (1879), which contains speeches delivered outside Parliament only. Other collections are Ernest Rhys, *Selected Speeches of the Right Honourable John Bright, M.P. on Public Questions* (1907), and Frank Moore, *Speeches of John Bright, M.P. on the American Question* (1865). Bright personally supplied some notes to George B. Smith for his two volumes, *The Life and Speeches of the Right Honourable John Bright, M.P.* (1881). Smith does not print the texts of speeches but summarizes each major speech at that point where it falls in the chronological narrative of Bright's life. The British Museum holds a large collection of Bright's letters; there are some specialized published collections, but the only general one is H. J. Leech's *The Public Letters of the Right Honourable John Bright, M.P.* (1885). R. A. J. Walling edited *The Diaries of John Bright* (1931), covering the years 1837–1887, the diaries for the earlier years having been lost. Joseph O. Baylen's article "John Bright as Speaker and Student of Speaking" in *The Quarterly Journal of Speech,* XLI (1955), 159–68, is a thoroughly documented discussion of Bright's meager theory, but extensive practice, of speaking. Of the biographers, Vince is the most acute in his comments on Bright's speaking.

William Ewart Gladstone

(1809–1898)

In more than sixty years of public life William E. Gladstone proved himself one of the nineteenth century's most prolific and formidable controversialists in matters of religion and politics. Ultimately "the Grand Old Man" became the very personification of the English Liberal Party and of Protestant orthodoxy.

Gladstone was born in Liverpool, the youngest son of a wealthy merchant who had served briefly in Parliament. At Eton and Oxford (Christ Church) the young Gladstone excelled as a student. Having decided to enter politics rather than the Church, he was elected to Parliament as a Tory in 1833 and rose through minor posts to Cabinet rank in the Ministries of Sir Robert Peel. Following the fall of Peel's last government (see pages 372–73), Conservatives sought to draw Gladstone back into their party but he refused. Among his reasons were his admiration for Peel and his strong dislike for Benjamin Disraeli. By 1859, he was a recognized Liberal Party leader.

Trade and fiscal policies were Gladstone's specialties in parliamentary government and debate. On most other matters he lacked firm political principles. Intuition and fine-spun moral scruples usually determined his positions on social and foreign-policy questions.

Of the four Ministries Gladstone headed, the first two were most successful

(1868–1874, 1880–1885). He carried measures for civil service reform, vote by ballot, expansion of education, disestablishment of the Church of Ireland, improved Irish land policies, extension of suffrage, and court reorganization. His advocacy of home rule for Ireland caused defeat of his brief, third Ministry (1886), but as Prime Minister for the last time in 1892–1894 he guided a home rule bill through the House of Commons only to have it defeated in the House of Lords. He thereupon resigned the premiership to his friend and colleague, Lord Rosebery, but without reconstruction the Liberal Party could no longer lead the country. Gladstone's relative neglect of imperial and social problems and his commitment to Irish home rule temporarily broke his party as Sir Robert Peel's commitment to free trade had temporarily broken the Tory–Conservative Party in 1846.

Gladstone had "retired" from leadership once before, in 1875, but the period of that withdrawal proved brief. He soon satisfied himself that his continued good health and unimpaired speaking ability were divine indications that he should oppose "Beaconsfieldism," especially in foreign affairs. He therefore agreed, in 1878, to stand for the Scottish Midlothian seat in the House of Commons at the next election. Beaconsfield then stood at the pinnacle of his career; the "Peace with Honour" he had won by the Treaty of Berlin was overwhelmingly popular, but Beaconsfield delayed in calling an election. Within a year, Britain was entangled in war with Afghanistan and had suffered losses in defense of the newly annexed Transvaal. It was all too evident that imperialism was costly, that British representatives abroad had bungled, and that with rising deficits, Beaconsfield's government could not aid the depressed agricultural community by tax reductions. Given these circumstances, Gladstone and the Midlothian Liberals determined to begin their contest for the Conservatives' seat in Midlothian immediately. In November 1879, Gladstone launched England's first "whistle-stop" political campaign.

Most of Gladstone's themes in the Midlothian campaigns are enumerated in the speech below. He paid scant attention to Lord Dalkeith, incumbent holder of the seat. He mounted a massive charge that Beaconsfield's was an immoral government. In the words of one of his biographers, he "stumped the country invoking the wrath of Heaven like some ancient Hebrew prophet; and at the General Election of 1880, when he enjoyed his finest hour, he was wafted back to Downing Street . . . by the spirit of a nation which had never before been summoned from its depths by a call so heartfelt and so clear." [1] The man Beaconsfield privately called "the Impetuous Hypocrite" thus changed the character of political campaigning in England and won a last victory over the Conservative leader he privately considered an "infection."

The speech appearing here is unrepresentative of Gladstone's speaking in two respects: it is unusually brief, and the style is relatively uncomplicated. In other respects it depicts the speaker in characteristic form: messianically forensic, joyously in rapport with his audience, overflowing with his subject, fluent, vigorous, quick in audience adaptation. On the hustings as in the House of Commons, it was Gladstone's personality that translated even the most detailed content into human terms. Says one careful critic: "In his delivery the power of a vigorous and dynamic presentation combined with the *ethos* of the speaker to overcome a

---

[1] Philip Magnus, *Gladstone, A Biography* (New York, 1954), p. 255.

style of utterance whose weaknesses are apparent to all." [2] The force of his personality and physical communication was enhanced by his custom of speaking extemporaneously in all but the most formal and ceremonial situations.

Gladstone's special train arrived at Perth on December 1, 1879, the fifth day of his first swing through Midlothian. Earlier in the day he had spoken at other villages and towns. At Perth he delivered an essentially nonpolitical address to two or three thousand people at the city hall, then gave the speech below to between six and eight thousand people gathered at the railway station in the chilly afternoon. At the station he spoke for about a half-hour, was enthusiastically cheered, and then resumed his journey by rail to Taymouth Castle, where he was to rest.

~

Campaign Speech [*]

At the Railway Station, Perth
December 1, 1879

My Lord Provost, Sir James Ramsay, Ladies and Gentlemen,—Sir James Ramsay has not read, has not caused to be read, the county address out of consideration for the limited time which is at our disposal.[1] That was most considerate on his part, and I think that we do not lose a great deal on this account, for we can form some idea of what was in it. (Cheers.) I have had a varied experience during my short stay at Perth. In the City Hall just now I fell in with a Lord Provost Richardson who in the City Hall was no politician. Neither was I. (Laughter and cheers.) But I come here, and I find a Lord Provost Richardson [who is perfectly intelligible in his statements of public opinion] and I really believe he is the same man. (Renewed laughter and cheers.) My friend Mr. Parker spoke of the influence that this visit may have upon the city and county elections. But I am not here to interfere with your elections. You don't want any advice from me. Your city is a virgin city. It has never been stormed by the adversary (cheers), and I believe it never will be. (Cheers.) And as to the county, no doubt I am a spectator, a spectator only, but I am much mistaken if it does not, on the earliest occasion, follow the example of the city. I was very glad to hear the address of the city Liberals read, but the address of the city Liberals said that while it was pleasing to welcome me, their pleasure would be still greater if Scotland should make me one of her representatives. (Cheers.) Now, gentlemen, I want to get

[2] Albert A. Austen, "Gladstone's Characteristics as a Speaker," *The Quarterly Journal of Speech,* XLIV (October 1958), 254.

[*] This text is essentially that published by *The Times,* December 2, 1879, but the more satisfactory punctuation of the text appearing in the first volume of W. E. Gladstone, *Political Speeches in Scotland* (Edinburgh, 1879) has been adopted at many points. Some alternate readings taken from the latter, revised text are supplied in brackets and in notes to illustrate Gladstone's editorial practices and his second thoughts about this address.

[1] Both city and county Liberal Associations presented addresses, but only that from the city group was read aloud. For further details of the speech see *The Times,* December 2, 1879, p. 10.

rid of that "if." (Cheers.) You may depend upon it, except for the uncertainty of my life, or of human life, there is no "if" at all in the matter. (Cheers.) The county of Midlothian, if it has not spoken sufficiently already, has spoken in this last week in a manner [perfectly intelligible to us, and, depend upon it] perfectly well understood by those who are opposed to us. (Cheers.)

I came down here upon a very grave errand, and upon that errand I will say a few words, because that business is a common business, for us, for the men of Midlothian, and for you [all]. I came to advance a most serious indictment. The declarations that I have made have covered a very wide field; they have exposed a large open front. I have not been able, I admit, to read with perfect care all that has been written in the newspaper press of the country upon this interesting occasion. (Cheers.) But so far as I have read, or so far as friends have informed me, there is only one statement of fact,—and I have made a great many,—[there is only one] which has been seriously challenged. I stated in Edinburgh[2] that it was an established usage for a great length of time that the Parliaments of this country should only address themselves to the regular transaction of the business of six and not of seven sessions. (Cheers.) I wish here to repeat that statement, and to say that so far as the time of my own experience is concerned, [and I believe so far as an earlier experience is concerned]—but I will not now speak of that, because I have not had time to re-examine the whole of the facts,—but so far as the last half-century is concerned, I say that I will [hereafter] shatter to pieces the allegations of those who have impugned my statement. And the matter is of some importance; because my point is this. I have never said that the Parliament might not have grave cause to go through the regular business of a seventh session. I can conceive certain circumstances which would render it right and expedient, but the rule being that seven full sessions should not be taken, I [am entitled to] ask why it is that rule is to be departed from on the present occasion. This is a most instructive question for us, because there is but one answer. The Government do not like to dissolve, because they dare not dissolve. (Cheers.) They do not like to dissolve, because they naturally and [not dishonourably,] not culpably, wish to prolong their Ministerial existence. They think that they are conferring immense blessings on the country (laughter) and they very naturally desire that the flow of those blessings—which we may almost call a deluge—should not be arrested one day sooner than is necessary. (Laughter and cheers.) But the practical point of the whole discussion is this; I omit the investigation of the facts for the present, I will deal with it before I go out of Scotland, if life and breath are given [me]. But the practical question is this. They do not dissolve because they dare not dissolve; and the fact that they do not dissolve is and must be to you an additional incitement and an additional ground of confidence, because it amounts to a moral demonstration that we are those who now represent the mature convictions of the majority of the constituencies. (Cheers.)

Gentlemen, I came down here with a set of very ugly charges to sustain, for notwithstanding that, as I have said, Her Majesty's Government believe themselves to be the authors and parents of innumerable blessings and benefits to the country (laughter), we have the misfortune to believe exactly the reverse. (Renewed laughter.) In fact, gentlemen, their speeches could be made into speeches suitable for us by a very simple process and I will tell you what it is. If you

[2] First Midlothian Address, November 25, 1879.

would strike out the word "not" wherever they insert it, and if you would put it in wherever they don't use it (great laughter), their speeches, depend upon it, would in a great degree save us the trouble of making speeches for ourselves. (Renewed laughter.) I will read to you, gentlemen, because they are very short, the charges that I came to Scotland to sustain. I advanced them in a letter in which I accepted the offer of the Liberals of Midlothian, and I wish to be pinned to what I then said; it is a very good thing for public men to be so pinned. (Cheers.) I charged them, first, with the mismanagement of the finances; secondly, with an extravagant scale of expenditure; thirdly, with having allowed legislation, which is always in arrear in this country, through the necessary pressure of the concerns of so vast an Empire, with having allowed that legislation to go into such a state that its arrears are intolerable and almost hopeless. (Cheers.) I charged them with foreign policy which has gravely compromised the faith and honour of the country. (Cheers.) I charged them with having, both through their ruinous finance, and through their disturbing measures, broken up confidence in the commercial community, and thereby aggravated the public distress. I charged them with having contributed unjustly and wrongfully to the aggrandisement of Russia. I charged them with having made an unjust and dangerous war in Afghanistan, and I further charged them in these terms: I said that by their making use of the treaty- and war-making powers of the Crown, they have abridged the just rights of Parliament, and have presented prerogative to the nation under an unconstitutional aspect, which tends to make it insecure. (Cheers.) Now, gentlemen, I am very anxious to go about the concerns of this Midlothian contest, which is, in fact, in some degree a Scottish contest,—I am very anxious to go about it like a man of business; and I grieve to say that, so many are the counts of the indictment, and so heavy—so copious is the matter which it is necessary to bring out fully before the country in connection with the coming dissolution, that I have not yet discharged myself, though I have been pretty liberally heard (laughter) on various occasions, I have not yet discharged myself of all that requires to be said. And, therefore, with your permission, I will avail myself of the quarter of an hour that is at my disposal (cheers), before the time appointed for the departure of the train for the North, in order to explain to you one of the phrases that I have used in this letter to the electors of Midlothian.

I charged the Government with having abused the war-making power and the treaty-making power. Of the war-making power I will not now speak further than to say that I allude especially to the war in Afghanistan, on which I hope to have an opportunity of explaining myself more at length. To you I will speak, within the narrow limits I have described, of the treaty-making power; and, gentlemen, though you are a vast assembly, meeting here in circumstances of some inconvenience, and though the subject is one not free from difficulty, I have so much reliance on your intelligence, as well as upon your patience, that I am confident you will clearly understand what I want to convey to you. (Cheers.)

Consider, gentlemen, [I entreat you,] what is [meant by] this treaty-making power. It is a power under which the Crown of the United Kingdom is entitled to pledge the faith and honour of the country to any other State whatever, and for any purpose whatever [unless I except the payment of money, but the exception is more apparent than it is real]. Now that is a power so large, that it must be most dangerous unless [very] discreetly used. It is so large that at various times it has attracted the jealousy of patriotic men; and attempts have been made in Parliament to limit the action of that power, by requiring that treaties should be submitted to Parliament before they are finally concluded. (Cheers.) I do not wonder for a moment that you are disposed to receive with some favour a suggestion of that kind. The objections to that suggestion are not objections of principle. On the principle I do say it would be unsound. They are objections entirely, in my opinion, of practice, and they come to this, that the nature of negotiation with foreign States is frequently so complicated and so delicate that they can hardly be carried on except by a single agency [concentrated, like the agency of Ministers], and that agency invested with the exercise of a large discretion. (Cheers.) Now, my opinion is that the treaty-making power of the Crown, as it has been used by former Governments, was a safe and a useful power. Some time ago— I forget exactly how long ago—Mr. Rylands, a well-known member of Parliament, made a motion in the House of Commons to the effect that some control ought to be placed on this power. I opposed that motion, upon grounds which I wish to state to you. I said the Crown, and the Crown acting through its responsible Ministers, is by far the most effective agent for the conclusion of the difficult subjects that are necessarily involved in the making of treaties. (Cheers.) [But] then I said—no doubt you will object that it is a vast power which is thus placed in the hands of Ministers, and that it would be most dangerous if it were exercised without reference to the known convictions and desires of the nation; and, gentlemen, I stated my reply to the objection as, that after all the long years of my public life, I can hardly recollect a case in which any treaty has been made except in conformity with the well-understood national tendencies and convictions of the people. The subjects have usually been long before the public. It may not be known what the precise materials of the treaty are, but it is known within certain bounds what they must be, and any right-minded Government has no difficulty whatever—as I can say from practical experience—in so conducting itself in these delicate matters as to have a moral certainty that though they have had no formal communication with the Parliament or the people, yet it is truly expressing the convictions of the Parliament and the people.

I will not now trouble you with references to instances, but if, gentlemen, you were to go back to the time of the Crimean War, and the treaties at the close of that war,—if you were to take the treaty made in 1870 with respect to Belgium, or, in fact, a whole multitude of instances upon which we might go,—I do not hesitate to say that these treaties were instruments which [in each case] were agreeable to the national feeling at the time. Now, that was the express ground on which I defended the treaty-making power and I stated in Parliament that it was impossible to defend that power upon any other grounds. I want to tell you what then happened. Sir Stafford Northcote, as the leader of the Government in the House of Commons, and as the man who, upon the highest subjects, is entitled to speak the sense of the Government—Sir Stafford Northcote rose after me, and he said—I do not quote his words, but I quote their effect—he said, such was his concurrence with the opinions I had given as reasons for not entertaining the motion of Mr. Rylands, that it would save him the trouble of entering at length upon the subject. (Hear! Hear!) Therefore, gentlemen, I hold that the Government are bound, in making treaties to do nothing of importance except upon the principles to which Sir Stafford Northcote then assented. They are bound to make no treaties upon questions of a novel character and of vast importance with regard to which the country has had no opportunity of making up its mind. Now I want you to know what it was that happened a very short time after that debate. To the perfect astonishment alike of Tories and Liberals, it was announced, without almost the notice of a day, that Her Majesty's Government had contracted what is called the Anglo-Turkish Convention. (Laughter.) No human being had heard of the subject-matter of that Convention.[3] Neither Tories nor Liberals had had the slightest opportunity of considering it. We were told, one fine day, that we had become responsible for the good government of the whole of Turkey in Asia. Look at your map and see what that vast country is, seething, I am afraid, with all the consequences of bad government. And here we, whose own affairs properly belonging to us are beyond our power to deal with, so that they are constantly running into arrear, by the act of the Government, taken and done in the dark, were involved suddenly and without notice in the provisions of the Convention.

Now, what were those? I have given you one. We were to be responsible for the good government of the whole of Turkey in Asia. You are sometimes told it is Asia Minor. It is not Asia Minor peculiarly; it is all Syria, [all] Palestine, Assyria, and [Turkish] Arabia. The whole of those vast countries [are] placed under our responsibility; and if any functionary of the Turkish Empire misconducts himself in any of those countries, that is now your affair. (Laughter and cheers.) But that is not all. You have also undertaken by this treaty—made on a sudden [and] in the dark, while the Powers of Europe were assembled at Berlin, but without the knowledge of any of those Powers—[you have also undertaken] to defend the frontier of Armenia against the Russian arms. You, at a distance of three thousand miles, have undertaken to send your fleets and armies to that country to meet Russia on her own borders, and to repel her from [the] Turkish territory. And, moreover, you have made that covenant irrespectively of the goodness or badness of the case; for it does not say that you will defend Turkey against Russia on the Armenian frontier after convincing yourselves that she is in the right, but you are placed under an unconditional engagement. But then, along with all this, what other great provision is there? There is this great provision, that you have become practically the masters of the island of Cyprus. (Laughter and jeers.) Well I find this—I cannot name the island of Cyprus in any assembly of my fellow-countrymen without immediately drawing forth a flood of derisive laughter. But this is no laughing matter. [Hear! Hear!] You have undertaken responsibility for that island. You have undertaken the good government of that island. And what have you done? I have no doubt that in many matters of administration you will have to improve the government. (Laughter and cheers.)[4] [It would be very difficult indeed to take over any Turkish island and not to improve the government. But] I am sorry to say that we have imported some new scandals

[3] Under the Treaty of Berlin, Montenegro, Serbia, and Roumania became independent; Macedonia, Bulgaria, and Eastern Roumelia remained parts of Turkey but the last two were to be autonomous; Austria occupied Bosnia and Herzegovina; Russia retained Turkish Armenia which she had conquered, and gained Bessarabia from Roumania; Turkey was to cede Thessaly and part of Epirus to Greece. By the Anglo-Turkish or Cyprus Convention, Turkey granted Britain occupation rights in Cyprus in return for fees and guaranties of Turkish territories in Asia.

[4] Gladstone's revised text reads: "I have no doubt that in many matters of administration we may have improved the government." The Times' text more clearly accounts for the laughter and cheers noted by The Times' reporter.

into that island. I will tell you of two ordinances that have been passed by British authority. First of all, I ask you, was it a right or a proper thing, without the knowledge of the people of this country, to take over an island of that kind? I think it a very shabby trick to play the Turk. But, independent of that, was it right for you people, who were a free people, to take over that island and govern it despotically? You are governing that island despotically by the hands of military officers. Is that a proper position for a free people to be placed in without its knowledge as well as without its consent? But you have done these things [already]. Under the Turk, any man could buy land in the island of Cyprus and go and cultivate it. You in your wisdom—because it is the nation after all (cries of "No, no!"), this is a self-governed country,—I do not mean the people of Perth,— [not at all,] the people of Perth would not have done it (laughter),—but I mean the people of the country—we have passed an ordinance, under which no man is allowed to buy land in Cyprus unless he is either an English or a Turkish subject. Before Cyprus became ours, any Greek of the kingdom of Greece might have bought land in Cyprus; [and remember] Cyprus is inhabited by Greeks. Nothing could have been more natural and proper than the purchase of land by a Greek. That we have forbidden. But I will tell you what [else] we have done that is a great deal worse, and you will hardly believe it. Under the Government of this free nation, an ordinance has been passed, the effect of which is that authorities of the island, [who are] military authorities chiefly appointed by us, have power to banish from the island any man they please without putting him on trial for any offence. (Cries of "Shame.") Yes; you are justified in crying "Shame." It is a shame—it is a disgrace to this country (hear! hear!); it is a scandal before the world. (Hear! Hear!) Gentlemen, I have given you three leading points. I will not speak now upon the worthlessness of Cyprus for the purpose for which we were told it was to be so valuable, because time would forbid it.[5]

But now observe, I come to my practical conclusion—the treaty-making power has been abused. It has been used for purposes in themselves objectionable, and it has been so used in contempt, as I should say, of the moral title of Parliament and of the nation to be aware of the principles on which a Government is acting, and of the ends that it has in view. (Hear! Hear!) [That treaty-making power, in my opinion, is good while it is rightly and wisely used; it is evil and indefensible when used as it has been used by the present Administration.] On that account, gentlemen, I say that this in its effect, whatever its intention may be, is, on the part of the Government, a disloyal contract; because the effect of it is to prejudice the prerogatives of the Crown, and to impair their foundation by making them odious in the sight of the nation at large.[6] That is all I will now say, because [it is true that] our time is all but exhausted. But I wish you to see even from this brief exposition that I did not speak lightly when I said that prerogative had been presented to the country in a light which tended to make it insecure, and thereby to import organic disturbance among us,—among a people who love our institutions, among a people who desire only to turn them to the best account, and not to be brought into the condition of countries which, less fortunate than ourselves,

[5] The Beaconsfield Government contended that basing military and naval forces at Cyprus would maintain peace in Mediterranean areas and protect the route to India.

[6] The Times notes that Mrs. Gladstone here touched her husband's arm and reminded him of the train schedule. Gladstone replied, amid cheers and laughter, "No, I have five minutes."

are obliged to be considering from day to day in what manner they shall remake the Government of the land. I beg your pardon, I want to remake the Government of the land (hear! hear! and a laugh)—but by "remake the Government," I meant the institutions of the land.

This is, gentlemen, a small part of the whole case that is before you. It is a most grave case. Some portions of it, I think, I have been able in some degree to develop and explain in the county of Midlothian. (Cheers.) I very much doubt whether it will be again very confidently asserted by any Minister that finance is the strong point of the Government. That was so stated. That very word was used at the meeting in the Guildhall on the 10th of November;[7] and when I read it, I recollected the exclamation, "Oh that mine enemy would write a book!"[8] By a very slight change, I am disposed to alter that expression, and to say, "Oh that mine enemy would speak a speech!" (Great laughter.) He could not have done better. Gentlemen, I want you to understand that the claim of the Government is that finance is their strong point. (Hear!) Pray understand it when they produce their deficiencies; pray understand it when they propose their taxes; or pray understand it when they present to you figures which will measure the accumulation of debt upon the country. (Cheers.) Let us all do our best to make clear the issue that is to be brought before the nation. That issue is—Is this the way, or is this not the way, in which the people of the United Kingdom desire to be governed? [Gentlemen, I bid you a grateful farewell.]

∽

BIBLIOGRAPHICAL NOTE

The best biographies of Gladstone are John Morley's three-volume *Life of Gladstone* (1903) and Philip Magnus' *Gladstone: A Biography* (1954). The most detailed accounts of Gladstone's movements and speeches in the Midlothian region are found in *The Times* for November–December 1879 and March–April 1880. Robert Kelley's "Midlothian: A Study in Politics and Ideas," *Victorian Studies*, IV (December 1960), 119–40, is a valuable analysis of the issues discussed in this campaign. The two biographies cited above and the essay by Albert A. Austen quoted in the headnote to Gladstone's address at Perth contain superior evaluations of the orator's rhetorical practice. Gladstone, himself, wrote an essay of some merit on public speaking. It may be found in Loren Reid, "Gladstone's Essay on Public Speaking," *The Quarterly Journal of Speech*, XXXIX (October 1953), 265–72. A. Tilney Bassett's *Gladstone's Speeches* (1916) and *Speeches and Public Addresses of the Right Hon. W. E. Gladstone* edited by A. W. Hutton and H. J. Cohen, 10 vols. (1894), are the chief sources, aside from parliamentary records, for Gladstone's speeches.

[7] Beaconsfield spoke at the Guildhall, London, on November 10, 1879. Defending his policies as necessary in the existing world situation, he concluded: "One of the greatest of Romans, when asked what were his politics, replied, '*Imperium et Libertas.*' That would not make a bad programme for a British Ministry. It is one from which Her Majesty's advisers do not shrink." (W. F. Monypenny and G. E. Buckle, *The Life of Benjamin Disraeli* (New York, 1920), VI, 494–95.

[8] Gladstone's revised text reads: ". . . and when I read it, I recollected that there is a passage found in a book of highest authority, and commonly cited in these words, 'O that mine enemy would write a book!'"

William Morris

(1834–1896)

William Morris, although perhaps not a genius, was a man of great and varied talents. His twenty-year outpouring of poetry, which included *The Defence of Guenevere, The Life and Death of Jason,* and *The Earthly Paradise,* might have earned him the honor of the poet laureateship had he not refused to be a nominee. His scholarly achievements in literature—among them his translations of the *Aeneid,* the *Odyssey,* and some of the Icelandic sagas—and his close interest in Chaucer prompted the offer of a professorship from Oxford, which he refused. His pursuit of art took him from an early apprenticeship in architecture to painting, to the arts of decoration, and finally, to the producing of books in new typographies. His life in politics, intense in its dedication to the Socialism of the 1880's, was a direct outgrowth of his idealized conception of art, particularly of the "household" arts with which people have everyday contact. For Morris, these interests and activities were never disparate or compartmentalized; they led into or merged with one another.

From the age of four in 1838, when he read the Waverley novels, to his last days in 1896, when his Kelmscott Press published a magnificent edition of Chaucer, he was interested in things romantic, medieval, and mythological. At Oxford, he was a member of the "Brotherhood," a small group of attractive young men who met to study theology, medieval history, and poetry, and during holidays to tour the great cathedrals of England and the Continent. The cathedrals, Morris thought, were among the noblest monuments of man. His love of beauty, his reverence of medievalism, and his professional interest in architecture led him in 1877 to help found the Society for the Protection of Ancient Buildings, and to speak many times thereafter in its behalf.

Like Ruskin, Morris believed that Gothic architecture was great partially because it allowed self-expression on the part of the individual workman. Indeed, in most eras, he insisted, common men had been free to produce things, usually practical things, in forms and shapes that flowed from their own understanding, talent, and craftsmanship. The artistic spirit of the people expressed itself not only through single artists exercising rare genius, but also through the multitude of craftsmen working freely at commonplace tasks. The degree of skill that went into the making of everyday objects, he thought, spelled the difference between one civilization and another. If the England of the nineteenth century was not producing great art, Morris blamed its urbanized and industrialized society, which abused art by forbidding individualized effort by workmen inside the factories, and by denying them leisure and beauty outside the factories.

Morris' beliefs that the production and consumption of art were the prerogatives of all men, and that there was a direct relationship in any civilization between its standards of art and its strength, inevitably led him into politics. In contrast to Carlyle, Morris did not see the millennium as an age of heroes in which workers would worship their leaders; nor did he, like Arnold, envision an age in which the middle classes (and only the middle classes) would be allowed the same privileges as the upper classes. The idea of segregated classes within a living society disgusted Morris, whether the segregation had its basis in economics or in intellect.

Morris was convinced that it was only a matter of time before the common people would insist on their rightful place in society, and it was to expedite their uprising that he undertook his lecturing crusade.

Audiences were not hard to find. Speaking before such diverse groups as the Royal Institution, the Radical Working Men's Club of Clerkenwell, the Birmingham Society of Arts and School of Design, and the working men's clubs and the mechanics' institutes in every major city of England, he attempted on the one hand to inspire the working men to demand universal education, and on the other to prove to the wealthy that civilization and education are impossible unless art is the privilege of all. Whether he was representing the Society for the Protection of Ancient Buildings or the Socialist-inspired Democratic Federation, his goals were the same: art and education for the poor, beauty and joy for all. In "Art, Wealth, and Riches," one of the speeches used in this crusade, he argues that art is the index of a civilization's health, and that the upper classes—in this case those persons assembled at a Joint Conversazione of Manchester Societies—must support reform voluntarily while they still have the opportunity to do so.

Morris considered himself a revolutionary Socialist, and devoted much of his time, money, and energy to various Socialistic groups. Yet he remained politically naïve all his life. Although at times he was capable of sound administrative advice in party affairs, he substituted romantic idealism for theoretical subtlety in his political philosophy. He was impatient with Marxian economics and the notion of violent revolution, contending that economics was too narrow a base for Socialism, and that what was needed more than revolution was a change in attitude on the part of the wealthy:

> To speak quite frankly, I do not know what Marx's theory of value is, and I'm damned if I want to know! It's enough political economy for me to know that the idle class is rich and the working class is poor! And it doesn't matter a rap whether the robbery is accomplished by what is termed "surprise value" or by means of serfage or open brigandage!

This non-doctrinal approach to Socialism twice caused Morris to break away from Socialist groups and form his own.

Despite his inherited income of £900 per year, Morris was never a member of the "idle class." For his decorating firm (consisting of Morris and his friends—Edward Burne-Jones, the painter; Philip Webb, an architect; and Dante Gabriel Rossetti, the poet-painter, among others) he hired workmen, but considered them assistants rather than hirelings. He tried, in short, to put his principles into practice, establishing those conditions of freedom under which workers could find joy in their labor and the expression of it in their finished products.

On a wider front he tried, by writing and lecturing, to bring about the classless society that he believed in.

Art, Wealth, and Riches *

March 6, 1883

Art, Wealth, and Riches are the words I have written at the head of this paper. Some of you may think that the two latter words, wealth and riches, are tautologous; but I cannot admit it. In truth there are no real synonyms in any language, I mean unless in the case of words borrowed from another tongue; and in the early days of our own language no one would have thought of using the word rich as a synonym for wealthy. He would have understood a wealthy man to mean one who had plentiful livelihood, and a rich man one who had great dominion over his fellow-men. Alexander the Rich, Canute the Rich, Alfred the Rich; [1] these are familiar words enough in the early literature of the North; the adjective would scarcely be used except of a great king or chief, a man pre-eminent above other kings and chiefs. Now, without being a stickler for etymological accuracy, I must say that I think there are cases where modern languages have lost power by confusing two words into one meaning, and that this is one of them. I shall ask your leave therefore to use the words of wealth and riches somewhat in the way in which our forefathers did, and to understand wealth as signifying the means of living a decent life, and riches the means for exercising dominion over other people. Thus understood the words are widely different to my mind; yet, indeed, if you say that the difference is but one of degree I must needs admit it; just so it is between the shepherd's dog and the wolf. Their respective views on the subject of mutton differ only in degree.

Anyhow, I think the following question is an important one: Which shall art belong to, wealth or riches? Whose servant shall she be? or rather, Shall she be the slave of riches, or the friend and helpmate of wealth? Indeed, if I put the question in another form, and ask: Is art to be limited to a narrow class who only care for it in a very languid way, or is it to be the solace and pleasure of the whole people? the question finally comes to this: Are we to have art or the pretence of art? It is like enough that to many or even most of you the question will seem of no practical importance. To most people the present condition of art does seem in the main to be the only condition it could exist in among cultivated people, and they are (in a languid way as I said) content with its present

---

* Our text is that printed in *The Collected Works of William Morris*, with introductions by his daughter May Morris (24 vols.; London, 1910–1915), XXIII, 143–63.) The full title of the lecture is "Art, Wealth, and Riches: An Address Delivered at a Joint Conversazione of Manchester Societies at the Royal Institution, Manchester, 6th March 1883." The text of the lecture appeared first in *The Manchester Quarterly* for April 1883, and was reprinted later in pamphlet form (Manchester, 1883); it became part of a volume entitled *Architecture, Industry, and Wealth* (London, 1902). Apparently, all texts that appeared after April 1883, were taken from *The Manchester Quarterly*. A "conversazione" is a meeting that combines discussion of art, literature, or science with social recreation. In this instance the members of the Academy of Fine Arts and of the Literary Club of Manchester met jointly to hear Morris' lecture, to participate in a forum period, and to converse informally while refreshments were served.

[1] Probably refers to Alexander the Great (356–323 b.c.), King of Macedonia (336–323 b.c.); Canute (995–1035), King of England and Denmark (1017–1035); Alfred the Great (849–901), King of Wessex, England (871–901).

aims and tendencies. For myself, I am so discontented with the present conditions of art, and the matter seems to me so serious, that I am forced to try to make other people share my discontent, and am this evening risking the committal of a breach of good manners by standing before you, grievance in hand, on an occasion like this, when everybody present, I feel sure, is full of goodwill both towards the arts and towards the public. My only excuse is my belief in the sincerity of your wish to know any serious views that can be taken of a matter so important. So I will say that the question I have asked, whether art is to be the helpmate of wealth or the slave of riches, is of great practical import, if indeed art is important to the human race, which I suppose no one here will gainsay.

Now I will ask those who think art is in a normal and healthy condition to explain the meaning of the enthusiasm (which I am glad to learn the people of Manchester share) shown of late years for the foundation and extension of museums, a great part of whose contents is but fragments of the household goods of past ages. Why do cultivated, sober, reasonable people, not lacking in a due sense of the value of money, give large sums for scraps of figured cloth, pieces of roughly made pottery, worm-eaten carving, or battered metal work, and treasure them up in expensive public buildings under the official guardianship of learned experts? Well, we all know that these things are supposed to teach us something; they are educational. The type of all our museums, that at South Kensington, is distinctly an educational establishment.[2] Nor is what they are supposed to teach us mere dead history; these things are studied carefully and laboriously by men who intend making their living by the art of design. Ask any expert of any school of opinion as to art what he thinks of the desirability of those who are to make designs for the ornamental part of industrial art studying from these remains of past ages, and he will be certain to answer you that such study is indispensable to a designer. So you see this is what it comes to. It is not to the best works of our own time that a student is sent; no master or expert could honestly tell him that that would do him good, but to the mere wreckage of a bygone art, things which, when they were new, could be bought for the most part in every shop and market-place. Well, need one ask what sort of a figure the wreckage of our ornamental art would cut in a museum of the twenty-fourth century? The plain truth is that people who have studied these matters know that these remnants of the past give tokens of an art which fashioned goods not only better than we do now, but different in kind, and better because they are different in kind and were made in quite other ways than we make such things.

Before we ask why they were so much better, and why they differ in kind and not merely in degree of goodness, I want you to note specially once more that they were common wares, bought and sold in any market. I want you to note that, in spite of the tyranny and violence of the days when they were fashioned, the beauty of which they formed a part surrounded all life; that then, at all events, art was the helpmate of wealth and not the slave of riches. True it is that then as now rich men spent great sums of money in ornament of all kinds,

[2] Upon its establishment at Marlborough House in 1852, this museum was called the Museum of Ornamental Art; after its relocation on Cromwell Road in west London in 1857, it became unofficially known as the South Kensington Museum; in 1909, after the present facades were built, it was named the Victoria and Albert Museum. Its collection of applied arts, which may be the largest in the world, was originally established to provide models for study by craftsmen and manufacturers.

and no doubt the lower classes were wretchedly poor (as they are now); nevertheless, the art that rich men got differed only in abundance and splendour of
material from what other people could compass. The thing to remember is that
then everything which was made by man's hand was more or less beautiful.

Contrast that with the state of art at the present, and then say if my unman-
nerly discontent is not somewhat justified. So far from everything that is made
by man being beautiful, almost all ordinary wares that are made by civilized man
are shabbily and pretentiously ugly; made so (it would almost seem) by perverse
intent rather than by accident, when we consider how pleasant and tempting to
the inventive mind and the skilful hand are many of the processes of manufacture.
Take for example the familiar art of glass-making. I have been in a glass-house,
and seen the workmen in the process of their work bring the molten glass into the
most elegant and delicious forms. There were points of the manufacture when,
if the vessel they were making had been taken straight to the annealing house, the
result would have been something which would have rivalled the choicest pieces
of Venetian glass; but that could not be, they had to take their callipers and
moulds and reduce the fantastic elegance of the living metal to the due marketable
ugliness and vulgarity of some shape, designed most likely by a man who did not
in the least know or care how glass was made; and the experience is common
enough in other arts. I repeat that all manufactured goods are now divided into
two classes; one class vulgar and ugly, though often pretentious enough, with
work on it which it is a mockery to call ornamental, but which probably has some
wretched remains of tradition still clinging to it; that is for poor people, for the
uncultivated. The other class, made for some of the rich, intends to be beautiful,
is carefully and elaborately designed, but usually fails of its intent partly because
it is cast loose from tradition, partly because there is no co-operation in it between
the designer and the handicraftsman. Thus is our wealth injured, our wealth, the
means of living a decent life, and no one is the gainer; for while on the one hand
the lower classes have no real art of any kind about their houses, and have instead
to put up with shabby and ghastly pretences of it which quite destroy their capacity
for appreciating real art when they come across it in museums and picture-gal-
leries, so on the other hand, not all the superfluous money of the rich can buy
what they profess to want; the only real art they can have is that which is made
by unassisted individual genius, the laborious and painful work of men of rare
attainments and special culture, who, cumbered as they are by unromantic life
and hideous surroundings, do in spite of all manage now and then to break
through the hindrances and produce noble works of art, which only a very few
people even pretend to understand or be moved by. This art rich people can buy
and possess sometimes, but necessarily there is little enough of it; and if there
were tenfold what there is, I repeat it would not move the people one jot, for they
are deadened to all art by the hideousness and squalor that surround them. Nor
can I honestly say that the lack is wholly on their side, for the great artists I have
been speaking of are what they are in virtue of their being men of very peculiar
and especial gifts, and are mostly steeped in thoughts of history, wrapped up in
contemplation of the beauty of past time. If they were not so constituted, I say,
they would not in the teeth of all the difficulties in their way be able to produce
beauty at all. But note the result. Everyday life rejects and neglects them; they
cannot choose but let it go its way, and wrap themselves up in dreams of Greece
and Italy. The days of Pericles and the days of Dante are the days through which

they move, and the England of our own day with its millions of eager struggling people neither helps nor is helped by them: yet it may be they bide their time of usefulness, and in days to come will not be forgotten. Let us hope so.

That, I say, is the condition of art amongst us. Lest you doubt it, or think I exaggerate, let me ask you to note how it fares with that art which is above all others co-operative: the art of architecture, to wit. Now, none know better than I do what a vast amount of talent and knowledge there is amongst the first-rate designers of buildings nowadays; and here and there all about the country one sees the buildings they have planned, and is rejoiced by them. Yet little enough does that help us in these days when, if a man leaves England for a few years, he finds when he comes back half a county of bricks and mortar added to London. Can the greatest optimists say that the style of building in that half county has improved meanwhile? Is it not true, on the contrary, that it goes on getting worse, if that be possible? the last house being built always the vulgarest and ugliest, till one is beginning now to think with regret of the days of Gower Street,[3] and to look with some complacency on the queer little boxes of brown brick which stand with their trim gardens choked up amongst new squares and terraces in the suburbs of London? It is a matter of course that almost every new house shall be quite disgracefully and degradingly ugly, and if by chance we come across a new house that shows any signs of thoughtfulness in design and planning we are quite astonished, and want to know who built it, who owns it, who designed it, and all about it from beginning to end; whereas when architecture was alive every house built was more or less beautiful. The phrase which called the styles of the Middle Ages Ecclesiastical Architecture has been long set aside by increased knowledge, and we know now that in that time cottage and cathedral were built in the same style and had the same kind of ornaments about them; size and, in some cases, material were the only differences between the humble and the majestic building. And it will not be till this sort of beauty is beginning to be once more in our towns, that there will be a real school of architecture; till every little chandler's shop in our suburbs, every shed run up for mere convenience, is made without effort fit for its purpose and beautiful at one and the same time. Now just think what a contrast that makes with our present way of housing ourselves. It is not easy to imagine the beauty of a town all of whose houses are beautiful, at least unless you have seen (say) Rouen or Oxford thirty years ago. But what a strange state art must be in when we either won't or can't take any trouble to make our houses fit for reasonable human beings to live in! Cannot, I suppose: for once again, except in the rarest cases, rich men's houses are no better than common ones. Excuse an example of this, I beg you. I have lately seen Bournemouth, the watering place south-west of the New Forest.[4] It is a district (scarcely a town) of rich men's houses. There was every inducement there to make them decent, for the place, with its sandy hills and pine-trees, gave really a remarkable site. It would not have taken so very much to have made it romantic. Well,

[3] Located in the Bloomsbury district, Gower Street runs northwest from the British Museum. Some famous people of the nineteenth century lived on this short street, among them Charles Darwin, Mrs. Siddons, Sir Samuel Romilly, and Sir John Millais.

[4] Bournemouth, a fashionable resort on the coast of Hampshire about 25 miles south-west of Southampton, is noted for its temperate climate, its beaches, and its parks. New Forest is a national park; formerly a royal hunting ground, the area was afforested and called "new" in 1079 by William the Conqueror.

there stand these rich men's houses among the pine-trees and gardens, and not even the pine-trees and gardens can make them tolerable. They are (you must pardon me the word) simply blackguardly, and while I speak they are going on building them by the mile.

And now why cannot we amend all this? Why cannot we have, for instance, simple and beautiful dwellings fit for cultivated, well-mannered men and women, and not for ignorant, purse-proud digesting-machines? You may say because we don't wish for them, and that is true enough; but that only removes the question a step further, and we must ask: why don't we care about art? Why has civilized society in all that relates to the beauty of man's handiwork degenerated from the time of the barbarous, superstitious, unpeaceful Middle Ages? That is indeed a serious question to ask, involving questions still more serious, and the mere mention of which you may resent if I should be forced to speak of them.

I said that the relics of past art which we are driven to study nowadays are of a work which was not merely better than what we do now, but different in kind from it. Now this difference in kind explains our shortcomings so far, and leaves us only one more question to ask: How shall we remedy the fault? For the kind of the handiwork of former times down to at least the time of the Renaissance was intelligent work, whereas ours is unintelligent work, or the work of slaves; surely this is enough to account for the worsening of art, for it means the disappearance of popular art from civilization. Popular art, that is, the art which is made by the co-operation of many minds and hands varying in kind and degree of talent, but all doing their part in due subordination to a great whole, without any one losing his individuality—the loss of such an art is surely great, nay, inestimable. But hitherto I have only been speaking of the lack of popular art being a grievous loss as a part of wealth; I have been considering the loss of the thing itself, the loss of the humanizing influence which the daily sight of beautiful handiwork brings to bear upon people; but now, when we are considering the way in which that handicraft was done, and the way in which it is done, the matter becomes more serious still. For I say unhesitatingly that the intelligent work which produced real art was pleasant to do, was human work, not overburdensome or degrading; whereas the unintelligent work which produces sham art, is irksome to do, it is unhuman work, burdensome and degrading; so that it is but right and proper, that it should turn out nothing but ugly things. And the immediate cause of this degrading labour which oppresses so large a part of our people is the system of the organization of labour, which is the chief instrument of the great power of modern Europe, competitive commerce. That system has quite changed the way of working in all matters that can be considered as art, and the change is a very much greater one than people know or think of. In times past these handicrafts were done on a small, almost a domestic, scale by knots of workmen who mostly belonged to organized gilds, and were taught their work soundly, however limited their education was in other respects. There was little division of labour among them; the grades between master and man were not many; a man knew his work from end to end, and felt responsible for every stage of its progress. Such work was necessarily slow to do and expensive to buy; neither was it always finished to the nail; but it was always intelligent work; there was a man's mind in it always, and abundant tokens of human hopes and fears, the sum of which makes life for all of us.

Now think of any kind of manufacture which you are conversant with, and note how differently it is done nowadays; almost certainly the workmen are collected in huge factories, in which labour is divided and subdivided, till a workman is perfectly helpless in his craft if he finds himself without those above to feed his work, and those below to be fed by it. There is a regular hierarchy of masters over him; foreman, manager, clerk, and capitalist, every one of whom is more important than he who does the work. Not only is he not asked to put his individuality into his share of the work, but he is not allowed to. He is but part of a machine, and has but one unvarying set of tasks to do; and when he has once learned these, the more regularly and with the less thought he does them, the more valuable he is. The work turned out by this system is speedily done, and cheap to buy. No wonder, considering the marvellous perfection of the organization of labour that turns it out, and the energy with which it is carried through. Also, it has a certain high finish, and what I should call shop-counter look, quite peculiar to the wares of this century; but it is of necessity utterly unintelligent, and has no sign of humanity on it; not even so much as to show weariness here and there, which would imply that one part of it was pleasanter to do than another. Whatever art or semblance of art is on it has been doled out with due commercial care, and applied by a machine, human or otherwise, with exactly the same amount of interest in the doing it as went to the non-artistic parts of the work. Again I say that if such work were otherwise than ugly and despicable to look at one's sense of justice would be shocked; for the labour which went to the making of it was thankless and unpleasurable, little more than a mere oppression on the workman.

Must this sort of work last forever? As long as it lasts the mass of the people can have no share in art; the only handicraftsmen who are free are the artists, as we call them to-day, and even they are hindered and oppressed by the oppression of their fellows. Yet I know that this machine-organized labour is necessary to competitive commerce; that is to say, to the present constitution of society; and probably most of you think that speculation on a root and branch change in that is mere idle dreaming. I cannot help it; I can only say that change must come, or at least be on the way, before art can be made to touch the mass of the people. To some that may seem an unimportant matter. One must charitably hope that such people are blind on the side of art, which I imagine is by no means an uncommon thing; and that blindness will entirely prevent them from understanding what I have been saying as to the pleasure which a good workman takes in his handiwork. But all those who know what good art means will agree with me in asserting that pleasure is a necessary companion to the making of everything that can be called a work of art. To those, then, I appeal and ask them to consider if it is fair and just that only a few among the millions of civilization shall be partakers in a pleasure which is the surest and most constant of all pleasures, the unfailing solace of misfortune, happy and honourable work. Let us face the truth, and admit that a society which allows little other human and undegrading pleasure to the greater part of its toilers save the pleasure that comes of rest after the torment of weary work—that such a society should not be stable if it is; that it is but natural that such a society should be honeycombed with corruption and sick with oft-repeated sordid crimes.

Anyhow, dream or not as we may about the chances of a better kind of life which shall include a fair share of art for most people, it is no dream, but a certainty, that change is going on around us, though whitherward the change is leading us may be a matter of dispute. Most people though, I suppose, will be inclined to think that everything tends to favour the fullest development of competitive commerce and the utmost perfection of the system of labour which it depends upon. I think that it is likely enough, and that things will go on quicker and quicker till the last perfection of blind commercial war has been reached; and then? May the change come with as little violence and suffering as may be!

It is the business of all of us to do our best to that end of preparing for change, and so softening the shock of it; to leave as little as possible that must be destroyed to be destroyed suddenly and by violence of some sort or other. And in no direction, it seems to me, can we do more useful work in forestalling destructive revolution than in being beforehand with it in trying to fill up the gap that separates class from class. Here is a point surely where competitive commerce has disappointed our hopes; she has been ready enough to attack the privilege of feudality, and successful enough in doing it, but in levelling the distinctions between upper and middle classes, between gentleman and commoner, she has stopped as if enough had been done: for, alas, most men will be glad enough to level down to themselves, and then hold their hands obstinately enough. But note what stopping short here will do for us. It seems to me more than doubtful, if we go no further, whether we had better have gone as far; for the feudal and hierarchical system under which the old gild brethren whose work I have been praising lived, and which undoubtedly had something to do with the intelligence and single-heartedness of their work: this system, while it divided men rigorously into castes, did not actually busy itself to degrade them by forcing on them violent contrasts of cultivation and ignorance. The difference between lord and commoner, noble and burgher, was purely arbitrary; but how does it fare now with the distinction between class and class? Is it not the sad fact that the difference is no longer arbitrary but real? Down to a certain class, that of the educated gentleman, as he is called, there is indeed equality of manners and bearing, and if the commoners still choose to humble themselves and play the flunkey, that is their own affair; but below that class there is, as it were, the stroke of a knife, and gentlemen and non-gentlemen divide the world.

Just think of the significance of one fact; that here in England in the nineteenth century, among all the shouts of progress that have been raised for many years, the greater number of people are doomed by the accident of their birth to misplace their aitches; that there are two languages talked in England: gentleman's English and workman's English. I do not care who gainsays it, I say that this is barbarous and dangerous; and it goes step by step with the lack of art which the same classes are forced into; it is a token, in short, of that vulgarity, to use a hateful word, which was not in existence before modern times and the blossoming of competitive commerce.

Nor, on the other hand, does modern class-division really fall much short of the caste system of the Middle Ages. It is pretty much as exclusive as that was. Excuse an example: I was talking with a lady friend of mine the other day who was puzzled as to what to do with her growing son, and we discussed the possibility of his taking to one of the crafts, trades as we call them now: say cabinet-making. Now neither of us was much cumbered with social prejudices, both of us had a wholesome horror of increasing the army of London clerks, yet we were obliged to admit that unless a lad were of strong character and could take the step with his own eyes open and face the consequences on his own account, the thing could not be done; it would be making him either a sort of sloppy amateur or an involuntary martyr to principle. Well, really after that we do not seem to have quite cast off even the mere mediæval superstition founded, I take it, on the exclusiveness of Roman landlordism (for our Gothic forefathers were quite free from the twaddle), that handiwork is a degrading occupation. At first sight the thing seems so monstrous that one almost expects to wake up from a confused dream and find oneself in the reign of Henry the Eighth, with the whole paraphernalia in full blossom, from the divine right of kings downwards. Why in the name of patience should a carpenter be a worse gentleman than a lawyer? His craft is a much more useful one, much harder to learn, and at the very worst, even in these days, much pleasanter; and yet, you see, we gentlemen and ladies durst not set our sons to it unless we have found them to be enthusiasts or philosophers who can accept all consequences and despise the opinion of the world; in which case they will lie under the ban of that terrible adjective, eccentric.

Well, I have thought we might deduce part of this folly from a superstition of past ages, that it was partly a remnant of the accursed tyranny of ancient Rome; but there is another side to the question which puts a somewhat different face upon it. I bethink me that amongst other things the lady said to me: "You know, I wouldn't mind a lad being a cabinetmaker if he only made 'Art' furniture." Well, there you see! she naturally, as a matter of course, admitted what I have told you this evening is a fact, that even in a craft so intimately connected with fine art as cabinetmaking there could be two classes of goods, one the common one, quite without art; the other exceptional and having a sort of artificial art, so to say, tacked on to it. But furthermore, the thought that was in her mind went tolerably deep into the matter, and cleaves close to our subject; for in fact these crafts are so mechanical as they are now carried on, that they don't exercise the intellectual part of a man; no, scarcely at all; and perhaps after all, in these days, when privilege is on its deathbed, that has something to do with the low estimate that is made of them. You see, supposing a young man to enter the cabinetmaker's craft, for instance (one of the least mechanical, even at present): when he attained to more than average skill in it, his next ambition would be to better himself, as the phrase goes; that is, either to take some other occupation thought more gentlemanly, or to become, not a master cabinetmaker, but a capitalist employer of cabinetmakers. Thus the crafts lose their best men because they have not in themselves due reward for excellence. Beyond a certain point you cannot go, and that point is not set high enough. Understand, by reward I don't mean only money wages, but social position, leisure, and above all, the self-respect which comes of our having the opportunity of doing remarkable and individual work, useful for one's fellows to possess, and pleasant for oneself to do; work which at least deserves thanks, whether it gets them or not. Now, mind you, I know well enough that it is the custom of people when they speak in public to talk largely of the dignity of labour and the esteem in which they hold the working classes, and I suppose while they are speaking they believe what they say; but will their respect for the dignity of labour bear the test I have been speaking of? to wit, can they, being of the upper or middle classes, put their sons to this kind of labour? Do they think that, so doing, they will give their children a good prospect in life? It does not take long to answer that question, and I repeat that I consider it a test question; therefore I say that the crafts are distinctly marked as forming part of a lower class, and that this stupidity is partly the remnant of the prejudices of the hierarchical society of the Middle Ages, but also is partly the result of the reckless pursuit of riches, which is the main aim of competitive commerce. Moreover, this is the worst part of the folly, for the mere superstition would of itself wear away, and not very slowly either, before political and social progress; but the side of it which is fostered by competitive commerce is more enduring, for there is reality about it. The crafts really are degraded, and the classes that form them are only kept sweet by the good blood and innate good sense of the workmen as men out of their working hours, and by their strong political tendencies, which are wittingly or unwittingly at war with competitive commerce, and may, I hope, be trusted slowly to overthrow it. Meanwhile, I believe this degradation of craftsmanship to be necessary to the perfection and progress of competitive commerce: the degradation of craftsmanship, or, in other words, the extinction of art. That is such a heavy accusation to bring against the system, that, crazy as you may think me, I am bound to declare myself in open rebellion against it: against, I admit it, the mightiest power which the world has ever seen. Mighty, indeed, yet mainly to destroy, and therefore I believe short-lived; since all things which are destructive bear their own destruction with them.

And now I want to get back before I finish to my first three words, Art, Wealth, and Riches. I can conceive that many people would like to say to me: You declare yourself in rebellion against the system which creates wealth for the world. It is just that which I deny; it is the destruction of wealth of which I accuse competitive commerce. I say that wealth, or the material means for living a decent life, is created in spite of that system, not because of it. To my mind real wealth is of two kinds; the first kind, food, raiment, shelter, and the like; the second, matters of art and knowledge; that is, things good and necessary for the body, and things good and necessary for the mind. Many other things than these is competitive commerce busy about, some of them directly injurious to the life of man, some merely encumbrances to its honourable progress; meanwhile the first of these two kinds of real wealth she largely wastes, the second she largely destroys. She wastes the first by unjust and ill-managed distribution of the power of acquiring wealth, which we call shortly money; by urging people to the reckless multiplication of their kind, and by gathering population into unmanageable aggregations to satisfy her ruthless greed, without the least thought of their welfare.

As for the second kind of wealth, mental wealth, in many ways she destroys it; but the two ways which most concern our subject to-night are these: first, the reckless destruction of the natural beauty of the earth, which compels the great mass of the population, in this country at least, to live amidst ugliness and squalor so revolting and disgusting that we could not bear it unless habit had made us used to it; that is to say, unless we were far advanced on the road towards losing some of the highest and happiest qualities which have been given to men. But the second way by which competitive commerce destroys our mental wealth is yet worse: it is by the turning of almost all handicraftsmen into machines; that is to say, compelling them to work which is unintelligent and unhuman, a mere weariness to be borne for the greater part of the day; thus robbing men of the gain and victory which long ages of toil and thought have won from stern hard nature and necessity, man's pleasure and triumph in his daily work.

I tell you it is not wealth which our civilization has created, but riches, with its necessary companion poverty; for riches cannot exist without poverty, or in other words slavery. All rich men must have some one to do their dirty work, from the collecting of their unjust rents to the sifting of their ash heaps. Under the dominion of riches we are masters and slaves instead of fellow-workmen as we should be. If competitive commerce creates wealth, then should England surely be the wealthiest country in the world, as I suppose some people think it is, and as it is certainly the richest; but what shabbiness is this rich country driven into? I belong, for instance, to a harmless little society whose object is to preserve for the public now living and to come the wealth which England still possesses in historical and beautiful buildings; and I could give you a long and dismal list of buildings which England, with all her riches, has not been able to save from commercial greed in some form or another. "It's a matter of money" is supposed to be an unanswerable argument in these cases, and indeed we generally find that if we answer it our answer is cast on the winds. Why, to this day in England (in England only, I believe, amongst civilized countries) there is no law to prevent a madman or an ignoramus from pulling down a house which he chooses to call his private property, though it may be one of the treasures of the land for art and history.

Or again, of how many acres of common land has riches robbed the country, even in this century? a treasure irreplaceable, inestimable in these days of teeming population. Yet where is the man who dares to propose a measure for the reinstatement of the public in its rights in this matter? How often, once more, have railway companies been allowed for the benefit of the few to rob the public of treasures of beauty that can never be replaced, owing to the cowardly and anarchical maxims which seem always to be favoured by those who should be our guardians herein; but riches has no bowels except for riches. Or you of this part of the country, what have you done with Lancashire? It does not seem to be above ground. I think you must have been poor indeed to have been compelled to bury it. Were not the brown moors and the meadows, the clear streams and the sunny skies, wealth? Riches has made a strange home for you. Some of you, indeed, can sneak away from it sometimes to Wales, to Scotland, to Italy; some, but very few. I am sorry for you; and for myself too, for that matter, for down by the Thames-side there we are getting rid of the earth as fast as we can also; most of Middlesex, most of Surrey, and huge cantles of Essex and Kent are buried mountains deep under fantastic folly or hideous squalor; and no one has the courage to say: "Let us seek a remedy while any of our wealth in this kind is left us."

Or, lastly, if all these things may seem light matters to some of you, grievously heavy as they really are, no one can think lightly of those terrible stories we have been hearing lately of the housing of poor people in London; indeed and indeed no country which can bear to sit quiet under such grievances has any right to be called wealthy. Yet you know very well that it will be long indeed before any party or any Government will have the courage to face the subject, dangerous as they must needs know it is to shut their eyes to it.

And what is to amend these grievances? You must not press me too close on that point. I believe I am in such a very small minority on these matters that it is enough for me if I find here and there some one who admits the grievances; for my business herein is to spread discontent. I do not think that this is an unimportant office; for, as discontent spreads, the yearning for bettering the state of things spreads with it, and the longing of many people, when it has grown deep and strong, melts away resistance to change in a sure, steady, unaccountable manner. Yet I will, with your leave, tell the chief things which I really want to see changed, in case I have not spoken plainly enough hitherto, and lest I should seem to have nothing to bid you to but destruction, the destruction of a system by some thought to have been made to last forever. I want, then, all persons to be educated to their capacity, not according to the amount of money which their parents happen to have. I want all persons to have manners and breeding according to their innate goodness and kindness, and not according to the amount of money which their parents happen to have. As a consequence of these two things I want to be able to talk to any of my countrymen in his own tongue freely, and feeling sure that he will be able to understand my thoughts according to his innate capacity; and I also want to be able to sit at table with a person of any occupation without a feeling of awkwardness and constraint being present between us. I want no one to have any money except as due wages for work done; and, since I feel sure that those who do the most useful work will neither ask nor get the highest wages, I believe that this change will destroy that worship of a man for the sake of his money, which everybody admits is degrading, but which very few indeed can help sharing in. I want those who do the rough work of the world, sailors, miners, ploughmen, and the like, to be treated with consideration and respect, to be paid abundant money-wages, and to have plenty of leisure. I want modern science, which I believe to be capable of overcoming all material difficulties, to turn from such preposterous follies as the invention of anthracine colours [5] and monster cannon to the invention of machines for performing such labour as is revolting and destructive of self-respect to the men who now have to do it by hand. I want handicraftsmen proper, that is, those who make wares, to be in such a position that they may be able to refuse to make foolish and useless wares, or to make the cheap and nasty wares which are the mainstay of competitive commerce, and are indeed slave-wares, made by and for slaves. And in order that the workmen may be in this position, I want division of labour restricted within reasonable limits, and men taught to think over their work and take pleasure in it. I also want the wasteful system of middlemen restricted, so that workmen may be brought into contact with the public, who will thus learn something about their work, and so be able to give them due reward of praise for excellence.

Furthermore, I want the workmen to share the good fortunes of the business which they uphold, in due proportion to their skill and industry, as they must in any case share its bad fortunes. To which end it would be necessary that those who organize their labour should be paid no more than due wages for their work,

[5] Usually spelled "anthracene." In another speech Morris said, "The dyestuffs . . . which are the product of coal-tar, are brighter and stronger in colour than the old dyes, cheaper (much cheaper) in price, and . . . infinitely easier to use. No wonder, therefore, that they have almost altogether supplanted the older dyes except in a few cases: surely the invention seems a splendid one!

"Well, it is only marred by one fact, that being an invention for the benefit of an art whose very existence depends upon its producing beauty, it is on the road, and far advanced on it, towards destroying all beauty in the art. The fact is, that every one of these colours is hideous in itself, whereas all the old dyes are in themselves beautiful colours; only extreme perversity could make an ugly colour out of them." From "The Lesser Arts of Life" in *Architecture, Industry, and Wealth*.

and should be chosen for their skill and intelligence, and not because they happen to be the sons of money-bags. Also I want this, and, if men were living under the conditions I have just claimed for them, I should get it, that these islands which make the land we love should no longer be treated as here a cinder-heap, and there a game preserve, but as the fair green garden of Northern Europe, which no man on any pretence should be allowed to befoul or disfigure. Under all these conditions I should certainly get the last want accomplished which I am now going to name. I want all the works of man's hand to be beautiful, rising in fair and honourable gradation from the simplest household goods to the stately public building, adorned with the handiwork of the greatest masters of expression which that real new birth and the dayspring of hope come back will bring forth for us.

These are the foundations of my Utopia, a city in which riches and poverty will have been conquered by wealth; and however crazy you may think my aspirations for it, one thing at least I am sure of, that henceforward it will be no use looking for popular art except in such an Utopia, or at least on the road thither; a road which, in my belief, leads to peace and civilization, as the road away from it leads to discontent, corruption, tyranny, and confusion. Yet it may be we are more nearly on the road to it than many people think; and however that may be, I am cheered somewhat by thinking that the very small minority to which I belong is being helped by every one who is of goodwill in social matters. Every one who is pushing forward education helps us; for education, which seems such a small power to classes which have been used to some share of it for generations, when it reaches those who have grievances which they ought not to bear spreads deep discontent among them, and teaches them what to do to make their discontent fruitful. Every one who is striving to extinguish poverty is helping us; for one of the greatest causes of the dearth of popular art and the oppression of joyless labour is the necessity that is imposed on modern civilization for making miserable wares for miserable people, for the slaves of competitive commerce. All who assert public rights against private greed are helping us; every foil given to common-stealers, or railway-Philistines, or smoke-nuisance-breeders, is a victory scored to us. Every one who tries to keep alive traditions of art by gathering together relics of the art of bygone times, still more if he is so lucky as to be able to lead people by his own works to look through Manchester smoke and squalor to fair scenes of unspoiled nature or deeds of past history, is helping us. Every one who tries to bridge the gap between the classes, by helping the opening of museums and galleries and gardens and other pleasures which can be shared by all, is helping us. Every one who tries to stir up intelligence in their work in workmen, and more especially every one who gives them hope in their work and a sense of self-respect and responsibility to the public in it, by such means as industrial partnerships and the like, is helping the cause most thoroughly.

These, and such as these, are our helpers, and give us a kind of hope that the time may come when our views and aspirations will no longer be considered rebellious, and when competitive commerce will be lying in the same grave with chattel slavery, with serfdom, and with feudalism. Or rather, certainly the change will come, however long we shall have been dead by then; how, then, can we prevent its coming with violence and injustice that will breed other grievances in time, to be met by fresh discontent? Once again, how good it were to destroy all that must be destroyed gradually and with good grace!

Here in England, we have a fair house full of many good things, but cumbered also with pestilential rubbish. What duty can be more pressing than to carry out the rubbish piecemeal and burn it outside, lest some day there be no way of getting rid of it but by burning it up inside with the goods and house and all? [6]

∽

Bibliographical Note

No scholarly examination of Morris as a speaker has been published. Most of the writers responsible for the vast literature on Morris are critics more interested in poetry than in art or speeches. John Drinkwater is one such in his study, *William Morris* (1912). John W. Mackail is no exception, but his two-volume commissioned biography, *The Life of William Morris* (1899), is the standard work. A more recent biography, *A Victorian Rebel: The Life of William Morris* (1940), by Lloyd Wendell Eshleman [also published with the title *William Morris: Prophet of England's New Order* (1949) under the pseudonym Lloyd Eric Grey] uses material not available to Mackail, traces in detail the development of the socialist movement in the late nineteenth century, explains the evolution of Morris' thought, and provides an extensive bibliography of works published to 1937. *William Morris* (1934) by Paul Bloomfield is a mediocre biography, but it contains a few comments on Morris' speaking (pp. 211–56 *passim*). J. Bruce Glasier has written his reminiscences of Morris as a propagandist in *William Morris and the Early Days of the Socialist Movement* (1921), which includes eleven pages on "Characteristics: His Public Speaking" (pp. 142–52). May Morris, daughter of the artist, collaborated with Sir Sydney Cockerell in editing *The Collected Works of William Morris* in 24 volumes (1910–1915). She compiled also *William Morris: Artist, Writer, Socialist* (2 vols.; 1936), a collection of letters, lectures, and other writings. Volume II on Morris as a socialist is quite valuable for our purposes. Miss Morris' commentaries not only provide a semblance of narrative for the volume but also certain here-and-there references to Morris' speaking that contribute more to an understanding of his ideas than to a file of information about his experiences. George Bernard Shaw, a propagandist comrade of Morris on many a street corner, writes of him in *William Morris as I Knew Him* (1936). G. D. H. Cole's preface to his collection of stories, poems, and lectures entitled *William Morris* (1934) is a brief and objective essay on the theme that "if much of William Morris' work falls short of greatness, there is about the man something great." The fullest collection of letters is *The Letters of William Morris to his Family and Friends* (1950), edited with introduction and notes by Philip Henderson. Morris' relation to the socialist

---

[6] On March 14, 1883, Morris wrote a letter to the editors of *The Manchester Examiner* replying to one in which the author complained that Morris' lecture had raised "another question than one of mere art." The opening of Morris' letter reads as follows: "Sir,—It was the purpose of my lecture to raise another question than one of 'mere art.' I specially wished to point out that the question of popular art was a social question, involving the happiness or misery of the greater part of the community. The absence of popular art from modern times is more disquieting and grievous to bear for this reason than for any other, that it betokens that fatal division of men into the cultivated and the degraded classes which competitive commerce has bred and fosters; popular art has no chance of a healthy life, or, indeed, of a life at all, till we are on the way to fill up this terrible gulf between riches and poverty."

movement is described in many books. R. Page Arnot's *William Morris: The Man and the Myth* (1964) is recent, short, sharp, and polemical. Arnot maintains that Morris, "the whole man," was a great artist, a great craftsman, and a revolutionary socialist fighting for the overthrow of capitalism; in the latter part of the book he publishes some fifty hitherto "lost" letters of Morris on socialism, which contain some information on his lecturing.

V

The Twentieth Century

Introduction

Social and economic change in twentieth-century Great Britain is generally traceable to ideas generated by the Victorians. Economics remains queen of the social sciences. The new century has seen continued equalization of wealth, completion of the democratizing process, and extension of the tradition of free expression—despite economic crises and threats of invasion. Britons of the twentieth century have not had to establish as generalized social goods such goals as self-realization for men and states, domestic and international freedom within the bounds of order, or the legitimacy of collective action. Their forebears had woven these threads of value into the patterns called British tradition. Opinion and policy makers of the present century have had the task of implementing these principles by reshaping the machinery of society. In only one great sector of public life has twentieth-century Britain broken with its immediate past; events outside and conviction within the British Isles reduced the Empire to a Commonwealth of freely, almost informally associated nations. Thus, Anthony Hardy could write in 1963:

> The early 1960's have all the air of being a watershed in our history. Two great movements of reform have now reached their zenith and appear likely to be of diminishing importance in the foreseeable future. These are the establishment of the Welfare State society at home and the liquidation of the British colonial empire abroad.[1]

There remain the difficult, scarcely tangible task of defining the further aspirations, if any, of a stable and relatively affluent, regulated society, and the need to discover the international role of an island nation no longer the seat of empire.

The issues to which leading British speakers most often addressed themselves between 1900 and 1960 were, in a sense, largely procedural. Most of the society's broadest social, economic, and international goals were settled, at least in the abstract, by past commitments or by the course of uncontrollable events. Spokes-

[1] *A State of England* (New York, 1963), p. 12.

439

men for workers, for women, for the unemployed or aged or ill could claim succor under rights already admitted in principle; they were answered by arguments from degree, practicability, and convenience. Those who propounded alternative roads to peace or military victory were met by counterarguments from probability and feasibility. Even the emotional crisis produced by Edward VIII's decision to marry a divorcée was resolved by reference to the pragmatic principle that monarchy must abhor controversy or lose its symbolic usefulness. And for all the drama and violence that attended settlement of the "Irish question," the nineteenth-century doctrine of "home rule" was never severely questioned.

True to inherited tradition, even astute and charismatic speakers found it impossible to penetrate the citadels of ultimate power if their premises or proposals were markedly doctrinaire. The evolution of the Labour Party illustrates:

> . . . the great political parties in the country have identified themselves with the national rather than a partisan interest. Even the exceptions change. The early Labour Party was a class party. But as the position of the working class has changed for the better, the party has moved perceptibly away from its old positions as a one-class party. The heirs of Keir Hardie [1856–1915], the Attlees, Bevins, Morrisons, and Gaitskells, understand that Labour must appeal now to the whole people.[2]

Radicalism was common enough outside the established framework of politics in all decades of the century. Indeed, the most colorful speakers of the first thirty years were associated with radical causes or attacked representative causes radically. We have for this reason included among the speeches that follow one of Emmeline Pankhurst's popular pleas for women's suffrage and her defense of civil disobedience, one of George Bernard Shaw's many challenges to capitalism, and G. K. Chesterton's defense of an unorthodox, distributive capitalism. The undoubted vigor and skill of advocates such as these cannot, however, obliterate the facts that Mrs. Pankhurst's demands were but partially met in 1918 (and even then, not in response to civil disobedience) and fulfilled only in 1928, and that neither the Marxian socialism to which Shaw adhered nor Chesterton's primitive capitalism are leading features of the mixture of economic and social programs that is the modern British welfare state.

For reasons that are not entirely clear, the twentieth century has produced no great debates in which titans of rhetoric ranged against one another as in the revolutionary and Napoleonic eras, the anti-Corn Law agitation, or the periods of nineteenth-century parliamentary reform. The fortunate movement or political party of this century has been able, perhaps, to claim some single spokesman of marked rhetorical skill. Shaw could draw thousands when debating on economics; H. G. Wells and Sidney Webb, who were equally devoted to "the cause" and better informed than Shaw, could establish little rapport with audiences. The Liberal Party found in Herbert Asquith a skillful strategist who lost listeners in his extended parallelisms and qualifications; its voice was the all too unpredictable David Lloyd George, whose popular oratory is exemplified below. Labour Party speakers included the bluff Ernest Bevin; Sir Stafford Cripps, whose speeches seemed lectures; and Herbert Stanley Morrison, who achieved exceptional clarity and cogency. Only Aneurin Bevan could command audiences with skill sufficient to wring approval from both right and left wings of his divided party. Bevan,

[2] Drew Middleton, *The British* (London, 1957), pp. 40–41.

however, veered too far from the mainstream of British thought to reach the highest rung of Labour's leadership. No Conservative, probably no Englishman, approximated Sir Winston Churchill at his rhetorical best; even so, Stanley Baldwin's direct and unimpassioned speech making was the chief vehicle of Conservative expression for more than twenty years. There is little doubt that Churchill alone among the British political speakers of our period ranks with the best political orators of previous centuries; we have therefore represented him in two periods of greatness: as a minority critic of defense and foreign policies and as a wartime Prime Minister.

The street speech, so familiar in earlier times and still symbolized by Hyde Park oratory, was a prominent feature of public life at the beginning of the twentieth century but is no longer a major force save in periods of electioneering. Doubtless the coming of radio, and then television, contributed to its decline as, perhaps, these new media also hastened the general disappearance of formality, careful structure, and emotional force from British public address. Extensive partisan persuasion addressed to mass audiences is also less well known in Great Britain than elsewhere, since British broadcasting is required to observe the strictest impartiality in programming. Even during elections, candidates' access to the broadcasting media is closely regulated. Lectures, talks, interviews, and debates reflecting the widest variety of views and subjects have been features of broadcast programming since the British Broadcasting Corporation was created; however, it remains unclear whether such speaking, when not part of news coverage, is widely influential.[3]

The great seats of British political discussion are still the Houses of Parliament.[4] Unpredictably, the House of Lords has become the scene of leisurely but significant debates on questions of manners, morals, and privilege—issues sometimes too divisive for members of the House of Commons to handle initially. Debate in the House of Commons ventilates issues; speeches from the floor seldom aim at immediately influencing the votes of members; eloquence is rare. As in the legislatures of other highly developed states, committee rooms and lobbies are the sites of decision making. In consequence, "The present debates in the House of Commons in many ways seem to be cooperative ventures, motivated by a mutual desire on both sides to explore several aspects of a problem and thoroughly talk out a solution."[5]

Preaching and legal pleading have declining importance in British public discourse. The influence of dissenting churches has diminished, the number of Anglican ministers has declined, less than three per cent of all common-law cases are tried before juries, and the number of barristers is falling. It is not remark-

---

[3] Edgar E. Willis, "Broadcasting and the British," *The Quarterly Journal of Speech,* LI (1965), 268–75. See also Samuel L. Becker, "Broadcasting and Politics in Great Britain," *ibid.,* LIII (1967), 34–43.

[4] Anthony Sampson observes that the annual meeting of the Commissioners of the Church of Scotland has come "near to taking the place of a Scottish parliament" since adopting the policy of debating general questions. *Anatomy of Britain* (London, 1962), pp. 168–69.

[5] Waldo W. Braden, "Contemporary Debating in the House of Commons," *The Southern Speech Journal,* XXVII (Summer 1962), 271–72. Those unfamiliar with procedural details of modern debating in the House of Commons will find them clearly set forth in this essay.

able that the twentieth century can point to no Donne or Spurgeon, no Mansfield or Erskine. By contrast, lecturing has become a second profession, especially for literary men and journalists. The poet and critic T. S. Eliot devoted much of his time to the international lecture platform during the last twenty-five years of his life, and few literary lecturers have been more sought after than he.

It would be presumptuous to predict the course of British public address in the final third of the twentieth century; not even the leading issues, much less the qualities of that speaking, are discernible in the sixth decade.

BIBLIOGRAPHICAL NOTE

A definitive history of Britain in the twentieth century is, of course, a contradiction in terms. For the period 1900–1914, however, the histories by David Thomson and R. C. K. Ensor (above, page 322) may be recommended. Sir Winston S. Churchill's six-volume *The Second World War* (1961–1962) is a monumental contribution to our knowledge of those times. Volumes I and VI, *The Gathering Storm* and *Triumph and Tragedy,* provide comment on prewar and postwar years. Alfred F. Havighurst's *Twentieth-Century Britain* (1962) is a superior textbook history covering the years 1900–1961. For analysis of persons and classes wielding political power between 1832 and 1960, W. L. Guttsman's *The British Political Elite* (1963) is good. Robert T. McKenzie's *British Political Parties* (1955) has been called the most important and clearest treatment of the Conservative and Labour parties ever to appear. C. L. Mowat's *Britain Between the Wars* (1955) provides an especially valuable and just treatment of political questions.

Besides such obvious sources of current texts as Hansard and *The Times,* one should mention *The Listener,* a periodical published by the British Broadcasting Corporation. *Voices from Britain: Broadcast History, 1939–1945* (1947), edited by Henning Krabbe, is made up of selected talks made by British and other nationals on BBC during the Second World War. From March 1943 through June 1947, the British Information Services issued in New York five volumes of *British Speeches of the Day.* Some interesting observations on British speakers may be found in James Johnston's *Westminster Voices: Studies in Parliamentary Speech* (1928), and from time to time in *The Quarterly Journal of Speech.*

Emmeline G. Pankhurst

(1858–1928)

Mrs. Emmeline Pankhurst was forty-five years old when she and her daughter Christabel founded the militant Women's Social and Political Union to secure votes for women. At forty-seven, she approved the first act of feminine militancy; at fifty, she was jailed for the first time; by the age of fifty-six, when she declared a truce to suffrage hostilities during the World War of 1914–1918, she had been in prison more than a dozen times, usually being released on the point of collapse after hunger, thirst, and sleep strikes; in 1918 she saw the bill enfranchising most women pass so easily in Parliament that the action was almost anti-climactic;

in 1928, her seventieth year, she died while campaigning for a seat in Parliament.

Mrs. Pankhurst spent her entire life in an environment of political reform. Her childhood home, where her father entertained the reformers of his day, was as valuable a part of her education as were the formal schools of Manchester and those of Paris, which she attended until she was eighteen. At twenty-one she married Richard Marsden Pankhurst, a forty-three-year-old Manchester lawyer of brilliant accomplishments, best known as a reformer for drafting the Married Women's Property Act. For the twenty years of their marriage, they were devoted to each other, to their five children, and to suffrage. After the death of her husband in 1898, Mrs. Pankhurst earned a living for a time in the Civil Service, but it was as a propagandist and as a lecturer that she made her livelihood from 1907 until her death.

Mrs. Pankhurst was the leader of a continuous program of propaganda from 1903 to 1914. Her work included the directing of a large organization with a large budget; the management of a vast campaign of propaganda of the word through speeches, newspapers, and pamphlets; the devising of a constantly changing campaign of propaganda of the deed, involving mass meetings, demonstrations, marches, petitions, stone-throwing, arson, and ingenious acts of civil disobedience. At her command, women chained themselves to statues in Westminster Hall or to the railings in the House of Commons; broke windows at 10 Downing Street or along the length of Regent Street; created disturbances at the government's political meetings; suffered arrest, imprisonment, and the agony of forcible feeding when they persisted in hunger strikes.

The Women's Social and Political Union (WSPU) was the political arm of Mrs. Pankhurst and her daughter. They ran it as a military organization, wielding dictatorial control. Besides adhering to the principle of obtaining attention at any cost—even at the risk of death—and to that of rallying her followers at every opportunity, Mrs. Pankhurst also held firm to the principle of striking the opposition at the top. She took deadly aim at any unfriendly member of the government. She and the Suffragettes bore allegiance to no party, only to candidates who worked for the cause of woman. They vowed defeat for any government which would not make woman suffrage a governmental measure. They not only participated in general elections, but persistently and dramatically intervened in by-elections—a technique of organizational propaganda of which they may be accounted the originators. At Peckham, for example, on March 24, 1908, the day Mrs. Pankhurst delivered "The Importance of the Vote," the Suffragettes helped to defeat by 2,500 votes a man who had won his seat in the previous election by a majority of 2,000 votes.

For all her adamantine rigor and ready contentiousness, Mrs. Pankhurst was not a monster. She was, in fact, an appealingly feminine woman. Of medium height, she was straight and slender, her air of frailty belied by her appearance of youthfulness and health. She had the quality of serenity so assuring to followers and so maddening to enemies. An American called her beautiful and described her as "active as a bit of quicksilver, as glistening, as enticing." [1] She habitually spoke in even tones, holding her head high, and occasionally punctuating the rhythm of her discourse with short strokes of the lorgnette which she always wore. She had the physical courage that is part of the make-up of the martyr. Her own

---

[1] Mrs. Stanton Blatch, daughter of Mrs. Cady Stanton, a great American crusader for women's rights. Quoted by Christabel Pankhurst in *Unshackled*, p. 30.

heroine was Joan of Arc. When her daughter saw the statue of Joan in the Place St. Augustin in Paris, she said, "It is exactly Mother!"[2]

Two of Mrs. Pankhurst's speeches are included in this volume. "The Importance of the Vote" was delivered in the privately owned reception and meeting facilities called the Portman Rooms, located on Baker Street in London. From February to July of 1908, the Women's Social and Political Union held "At Homes" every Monday afternoon in these rooms, until the gatherings began to draw overflow crowds, and had to be moved to Queen's Hall, a much larger auditorium. The typical program included a summary of the week's activities by Christabel, a statement by the treasurer, possibly a speech by a Suffragette newly released from prison, or by an American visitor about the movement in the United States, or a report by an organizer from some outlying city or county. Frequently Mrs. Pankhurst spoke, usually informally and extemporaneously. Generally her remarks were recorded by a stenographer and published later in *Votes for Women*, the "newspaper" of the WSPU. We have no original text of this speech. Presumably it was recorded stenographically and edited, but not drastically. It was published as a separate pamphlet because the subject-matter virtually embodied the entire movement. The student may profitably compare this speech with those by Fox and Brougham on electoral reform (above, pages 256–81, 325–58).

The second speech was delivered in Bow Street Police Court about seven months after "The Importance of the Vote." The Suffragettes were determined to make a strong impression upon the Parliament which was to convene on October 12, 1908. On October 11, Mrs. Pankhurst, Mrs. Drummond, and Miss Christabel Pankhurst addressed a large meeting which they had called in Trafalgar Square. Suffragettes distributed a leaflet which proclaimed: "Men and Women: Help the Suffragettes to Rush the House of Commons on Tuesday Evening, 13th October, at 7:30." The magistrate of Bow Street Police Court ordered the arrest of the three women on October 13, charging that by using the word "rush" they were "guilty of conduct likely to provoke a breach of the peace." He jailed them overnight and opened the trial the next day. The defense then and later was conducted by Christabel, who very skillfully cross-questioned and discomfited David Lloyd George and Herbert Gladstone, the Home Secretary responsible for security. In her summation on October 24, Christabel scornfully compared Herbert to his famous father, even though the father had been opposed to votes for women: "The Gladstone of those days was less absurd, hesitating, and cowardly than the present Gladstone and his colleagues."[3]

Mrs. Pankhurst then addressed the court "in her voice of mournful melody." She spoke quietly, as she characteristically did, in marked contrast to Christabel's "lively arabesques." Christabel's subject was the trial; Mrs. Pankhurst's was her life, the trial being merely an event to be understood in that larger context. The full account of the trial is well worth reading.[4]

If the magistrate was moved, he recovered quickly. He sentenced Mrs. Pankhurst and Mrs. Drummond to a fine or three months' imprisonment, and Miss Pankhurst to a fine or 10 weeks' imprisonment. Of course they went to prison.

〰

[2] *Ibid.*, p. 17.

[3] Quoted in E. Sylvia Pankhurst, *The Suffragette Movement*, p. 291.

[4] See E. Sylvia Pankhurst, *The Suffragette*, pp. 263–321; and *The Times*, October 15, 22, 26, 1908.

The Importance of the Vote *

March 24, 1908

It seems to me a very strange thing that large numbers of women should have met together to-night to consider whether the vote is of importance, while all day long, across the water, in the Peckham Bye-election,[1] men, whether they realise the importance of the vote or not, have been exercising it, and in exercising it settling for women as well as for themselves great questions of public importance.

What, then, is this vote that we are hearing so much about just now, so much more than people have heard in discussion at least, for a great many years? I think we may give the vote a threefold description. We may describe the vote as, first of all, a symbol, secondly, a safeguard, and thirdly, an instrument. It is a symbol of freedom, a symbol of citizenship, a symbol of liberty. It is a safeguard of all those liberties which it symbolises. And in these later days it has come to be regarded more than anything else as an instrument, something with which you can get a great many more things than our forefathers who fought for the vote ever realised as possible to get with it. It seems to me that such a thing is worth fighting for, and women to-day are fighting very strenuously in order to get it.

Wherever masses of people are gathered together there must be government. Government without the vote is more or less a form of tyranny. Government with the vote is more or less representative according to the extent to which the vote is given. In this country they tell us we have representative government. So far as women are concerned, while you have representative government for men, you have despotic government for women. So it is in order that the government of the country may be made really representative, may represent not only all classes of the community, but both sexes of the community, that this struggle for the vote is going on on the part of women.

To-day, women are working very hard for it. And there is no doubt whatever that very, very soon the fight will be over, and victory will be won. Even a Liberal Government will be forced to give votes to women.[2] Gentlemen with Liberal principles have talked about those principles for a very long time, but it is only just lately that women have realised that so far as they are concerned, it began in talk and ended in talk, and that there was absolutely no intention of performance. To-day, we have taken off the mask, and we have made these gentlemen realise that,

---

* This text is taken from a twelve-page pamphlet entitled *The Importance of the Vote*, published by the Woman's Press, 156 Charing Cross Road, London. The author is identified as "Mrs. Pankhurst"; the source as "A Lecture delivered at the Portman Rooms on Tuesday, March 24th, 1908"; the price as one penny. There were at least seven editions of this pamphlet in 1908, the year of its issuance, and many printings thereafter.

[1] Peckham is a district of London in Surrey, across the Thames from Portman Mansions where this speech was delivered. By-election: an election in a single district to fill a vacancy that occurs in the House of Commons between general elections.

[2] The Liberal Government took office after the resignation of Balfour's Conservative Unionist Government on December 4, 1905. In the subsequent elections the Liberals won their first victory in ten years. Sir Henry Campbell-Bannerman, the Liberal Prime Minister, favored women's suffrage, although the Liberal Party itself was split over the issue. When Campbell-Bannerman resigned in April, 1908, because of poor health, he was succeeded by an opponent of the suffragist movement, Henry Asquith.

whether they like it or not, they will have to yield. People ask us, "Why force it on just now? Why give all this trouble to the Liberals, with their great and splendid programme of reform?" Well, we say, after all, they are just the people to whom we ought to give trouble, and who, if they are sincere, ought to be very glad that we are giving them trouble, and forcing them to put their great principles into practice.

To-night, it is not for me to talk to you very much about the agitation. I have to talk to you about what the vote will do for women, and what being deprived of the vote has caused women to suffer. And so I mean to devote most of the time at my disposal to this side of the question. What I am going to say to you to-night is not new. It is what we have been saying at every street corner, at every bye-election during the last eighteen months. It is perfectly well known to many members of my audience, but they will not mind if I repeat for the benefit of those who are here for the first time to-night, those arguments and illustrations with which many of us are so very familiar.

In the first place it is important that women should have the vote in order that in the government of the country the women's point of view should be put forward. It is important for women that in any legislation that affects women equally with men, those who make the laws should be responsible to women in order that they may be forced to consult women and learn women's views when they are contemplating the making or the altering of laws. Very little has been done by legislation for women for many years—for obvious reasons. More and more of the time of Members of Parliament is occupied by the claims which are made on behalf of the people who are organised in various ways in order to promote the interests of their industrial organisations or their political or social organisations. So the Member of Parliament, if he does dimly realise that women have needs, has no time to attend to them, no time to give to the consideration of those needs. His time is fully taken up by attending to the needs of the people who have sent him to Parliament. While a great deal has been done, and a great deal more has been talked about for the benefit of the workers who have votes, yet so far as women are concerned, legislation relating to them has been practically at a standstill. Yet it is not because women have no need, or because their need is not very urgent. There are many laws on the Statute-book to-day which are admittedly out of date, and call for reformation; laws which inflict very grave injustices on women. I want to call the attention of women who are here to-night to a few Acts on the Statute-book which press very hardly and very injuriously on women.

Men politicians are in the habit of talking to women as if there were no laws that affect women. "The fact is," they say, "the home is the place for women. Their interests are the rearing and training of children. These are the things that interest women. Politics have nothing to do with these things, and therefore politics do not concern women." Yet the laws decide how women are to live in marriage, how their children are to be trained and educated, and what the future of their children is to be. All that is decided by Act of Parliament. Let us take a few of these laws, and see what there is to say about them from the women's point of view.

First of all, let us take the marriage laws. They are made by men for women. Let us consider whether they are equal, whether they are just, whether they are wise. What security of maintenance has the married woman? Many a married woman having given up her economic independence in order to marry, how is she compensated for that loss? What security does she get in that marriage for which she gave up economic independence? Take the case of a woman who has been earning a good income. She is told that she ought to give up her employment when she becomes a wife and mother. What does she get in return? All that a married man is obliged by law to do for his wife is to provide for her shelter of some kind, food of some kind, and clothing of some kind. It is left to his good pleasure to decide what the shelter shall be, what the food shall be, what the clothing shall be. It is left to him to decide what money shall be spent on the home, and how it shall be spent; the wife has no voice legally in deciding any of these things. She has no legal claim upon any definite portion of his income. If he is a good man, a conscientious man, he does the right thing. If he is not, if he chooses almost to starve his wife, she has no remedy. What he thinks sufficient is what she has to be content with.

I quite agree, in all these illustrations, that the majority of men are considerably better than the law compels them to be, so the majority of women do not suffer as much as they might suffer if men were all as bad as they might be, but since there are some bad men, some unjust men, don't you agree with me that the law ought to be altered so that those men could be dealt with?[3]

Take what happens to the woman if her husband dies and leaves her a widow, sometimes with little children. If a man is so insensible to his duties as a husband and father when he makes his will, as to leave all his property away from his wife and children, the law allows him to do it. That will is a valid one. So you see that the married woman's position is not a very secure one. It depends entirely on her getting a good ticket in the lottery. If she has a good husband, well and good: if she has a bad one, she has to suffer, and she has no remedy. That is her position as a wife, and it is far from satisfactory.

Now let us look at her position if she has been very unfortunate in marriage, so unfortunate as to get a bad husband, an immoral husband, a vicious husband, a husband unfit to be the father of little children. We turn to the Divorce Court. How is she to get rid of such a man? If a man has got married to a bad wife, and he wants to get rid of her, he has but to prove against her one act of infidelity. But if a woman who is married to a vicious husband wants to get rid of him, not one act nor a thousand acts of infidelity entitle her to a divorce; she must prove either bigamy, desertion, or gross cruelty, in addition to immorality before she can get rid of that man.[4]

Let us consider her position as a mother. We have repeated this so often at our meetings that I think the echo of what we have said must have reached many. By English law no married woman exists as the mother of the child she brings into the world. In the eyes of the law she is not the parent of her child. The child, according to our marriage laws, has only one parent, who can decide the future of the child, who can decide where it shall live, how it shall live, how much shall be spent upon it, how it shall be educated, and what religion it shall profess. That parent is the father.

These are examples of some of the laws that men have made, laws that concern

[3] For a digest of property laws affecting women in England during the nineteenth century, see "Woman, Position in Society," *Encyclopaedia of the Social Sciences*, XV, 449.

[4] For a concise review of English marriage and divorce legislation from the mid-nineteenth century to our own time, see Sir Seymour Karminski, "Family Law," in Morris Ginsberg, ed., *Law and Opinion in England in the 20th Century*, pp. 286–95.

women. I ask you, if women had had the vote, should we have had such laws? If women had had the vote, as men have the vote, we should have had equal laws. We should have had equal laws for divorce, and the law would have said that as Nature has given the children two parents, so the law should recognise that they have two parents.

I have spoken to you about the position of the married woman who does not exist legally as a parent, the parent of her own child. In marriage, children have one parent. Out of marriage children have also one parent. That parent is the mother—the unfortunate mother. She alone is responsible for the future of her child; she alone is punished if her child is neglected and suffers from neglect. But let me give you one illustration. I was in Herefordshire [5] during the bye-election. While I was there, an unmarried mother was brought before the bench of magistrates charged with having neglected her illegitimate child. She was a domestic servant, and had put the child out to nurse. The magistrates—there were colonels and landowners on that bench—did not ask what wages the mother got; they did not ask who the father was or whether he contributed to the support of the child. They sent that woman to prison for three months for having neglected her child. I ask you women here to-night, if women had had some share in the making of laws, don't you think they would have found a way of making all fathers of such children equally responsible with the mothers for the welfare of those children?

Let us take the law of inheritance. Often in this agitation for the vote, we have been told by advanced members of the Liberal Party that to give votes to women on the same terms as those on which men now have the vote, would be to strengthen the influence of property, and to help to continue the existing laws of property.

When you look at the laws of inheritance in this country, it makes you smile to hear that argument. Men have taken very good care that women do not inherit until all male heirs are exhausted. So I do not think these democratic gentlemen are quite sincere in the fears they express lest the influence of property should be very much strengthened if women got the Parliamentary franchise. I do not think it is time yet for women to consider whether the law that the eldest son shall inherit the estate is a just law. I think we should put it in this way: if it is to be the eldest child, let it be the eldest child, whether that child is a man or a woman. [6] I am perfectly certain that if women had had the vote when that law was made, that that is how it would have been settled, if they had decided to have a law of primogeniture.

Well, one could go on giving you many more of these examples. I want now to deal with an objection which may be in the minds of some people here. They say, you are talking about laws made a long time ago. Laws would not now be made like that. If a new law were made, it would of course be equal between the sexes. But as a matter of fact, it seems almost impossible for men, when making new laws that will affect both sexes, to recognise that there is any woman's side at all. Let us take an illustration from the last session of Parliament. For many years we have been accustomed to see pass through the House of Commons and go up to the House of Lords that hardy evergreen, the Deceased Wife's Sister

[5] County in southwest England, bordering on Wales.
[6] See "Succession, Laws of," *Encyclopaedia of the Social Sciences*, XIV, 438–39.

Bill.[7] I used—it is many years since I began reading the debates on that measure—I used to read the speeches carefully through to see if I could find one speech from a man which showed any kind of realisation of the women's side of that Bill. You read eloquent appeals to make it possible for a man who had lost his wife to give to the children the best kind of step-mother that they could have. Who could make a better step-mother, it was asked, than the sister of their deceased mother? By natural ties, by old associations, by her knowledge of the children, she was better fitted than anybody else to take the mother's place. But you never heard of a man who thought there might be another side to the picture. So you have on the Statute-book a piece of legislation which gives relief to the widower who would like to provide a kind step-mother for his children, but does not give relief to the widow who would like to give a kind step-father to her children. I do not think it ever entered into the minds of these legislators that there might be a widow who would like to fulfil the behest of the Old Testament that the living brother should take up his deceased brother's burden and do his duty to his brother's family. So you see, even in this twentieth century, you have got the same spirit.

The man voter and the man legislator see the man's needs first, and do not see the woman's needs. And so it will be until women get the vote. It is well to remember that, in view of what we have been told of what is the value of women's influence. Woman's influence is only effective when men want to do the thing that her influence is supporting.

Now let us look a little to the future. If it ever was important for women to have the vote, it is ten times more important to-day, because you cannot take up a newspaper, you cannot go to a conference, you cannot even go to church, without hearing a great deal of talk about social reform and a demand for social legislation. Of course, it is obvious that that kind of legislation—and the Liberal Government tell us that if they remain in office long enough we are going to have a great deal of it—is of vital importance to women. If we have the right kind of social legislation it will be a very good thing for women and children. If we have the wrong kind of social legislation, we may have the worst kind of tyranny that women have ever known since the world began.

We are hearing about legislation to decide what kind of homes people are to live in. That surely is a question for women. Surely every woman, when she seriously thinks about it, will wonder how men by themselves can have the audacity to think that they can say what homes ought to be without consulting women. Then take education. Since 1870 men have been trying to find out how to educate children.[8] I think that they have not yet realised that if they are ever to find out how to educate children, they will have to take women into their confidence, and try to learn from women some of those lessons that the long experience of ages has taught to them. One cannot wonder that whole sessions of Parliament should be wasted on Education Bills. For, you see, it is only just

[7] The Deceased Wife's Sister Marriage Act was passed in 1907, making it lawful for a man to marry his deceased wife's sister. The Anglican High Church had opposed repeal of the old canon law's prohibition of such a marriage.

[8] The Education Act of 1870, a milestone in a national system of public education in Britain, set up locally elected school boards empowered to compel school attendance to the age of thirteen. It did not provide free education for all, fees being remitted for the children of poor parents only.

lately that men have begun to consider education, or to try to learn what the word means. So as we are going to have a great deal more time devoted to education, I think it will be a great economy of time if we get the vote, if only that we may have an opportunity of deciding how girls are to be trained, even in those domestic duties which gentlemen are so fond of reminding us we ought to attend to.

I suppose you all read your newspapers this morning. You saw that a great statesman was pouring out words of wisdom on a subject which one may think might well be regarded as women's business, and which they might at all events have some share in deciding.[9] How it makes one smile to hear a statesman comparing whisky and milk, and discussing whether babies should have natural mother's milk, or humanised milk, or sterilised milk, or what is a sufficient quantity of milk. All these things Cabinet Ministers have discovered that they are quite competent to decide without us. And when a few women ventured to make a small protest and suggested that perhaps it would be best to give to women, the mothers of the race, an opportunity of expressing themselves on the subject, they were characterised as disgraceful, and turned out of the meeting for daring to raise their voices in protest.

Well, we cannot wonder that they are deciding what sort of milk the babies are to have, for it is only a few months ago that they decided how babies should be brought into the world, and who should officiate on the occasion. The Midwives Act, owing to the extreme difficulty and slowness with which, during twelve years of ceaseless agitation, it was carried through Parliament, has made of the women who agitated for it convinced suffragists, since, if they had had votes the measure could have been passed in a couple of years.[10] Even when carried, it was at the expense of many concessions, which, had the women promoting the Bill possessed the franchise, they would certainly have been able to avoid. To this day the midwives have no direct representation on the Central Board which administers the Act. Still, in spite of legislation like that, we find politicians, responsible members of the Government, saying that women ought to have nothing to do with politics, and that they ought not to ask for the vote.

What limits are there to be to this? The same gentleman who thinks himself quite competent to say how babies ought to be fed tells us that he is going to interfere not only with babies, but with their mothers as well.[11] He is going to decide by Act of Parliament whether married women are to be allowed to earn an economic independence, or are to be prevented from doing so. He thinks married women who are earning their living are going to submit to a virtual repeal

[9] Mr. John Burns. Of working-class origin, and a Socialist of long standing, he was made president of the Local Government Board in 1906 and appointed to the Liberal Cabinet, an appointment designed to gain the support of the working class for the Liberal Party. According to *The Times* of March 24, 1908, Burns's address to the National Conference on Infantile Mortality dealt primarily with the types of milk which ought to be fed to infants.

[10] The Midwives Act, passed in 1902, provided for the improved training of midwives, required all midwives to be certified by approved institutions after January 1, 1905, and set up a Central Midwives Board to regulate the practices of midwives in England and Wales. The Act did not apply to Scotland and Ireland. [*Parliamentary Papers*, 1902 (10) III, 485–95.]

[11] In his speech, Mr. Burns suggested that a mother be required to stay at home from the time of the last few months of pregnancy until her new-born child became six months old.

of the Married Women's Property Act, and to leave it to their husbands to decide whether they shall have any money to spend as they please.[12] To deprive married women of the right to go out to work, to decide this for them without consulting women voters whether they are to earn wages or not, is an act of tyranny to which, I believe, women, patient and long-suffering as they are, will not submit. I hope that even the Liberal women will revolt when it comes to that. But I am not over hopeful about them, because, unfortunately for poor married women who know what it is to need to earn a living, those who decide what the policy of the Liberal women shall be are women who have never had to earn a living, and do not know what it is to have little children dependent upon them and liable to be starved if their mothers are prevented from going out to work. But fortunately the women who are going to be interfered with are not the kind of women who will submit to be interfered with quietly. Women who belong to the aristocracy of industry, women such as the cotton workers in the Lancashire [13] mills, are not likely to be driven into the ranks of the sweated without protest.

What is the reason for the proposal? We are told it is to set these women free, to let them stay at home. I do not see that Mr. John Burns proposes to compensate women for the loss of their earnings. I do not see that he proposes to compel husbands to give to their wives a definite portion of their income for house-keeping purposes. All he proposes is that women, who are earning from ten shillings to thirty shillings a week shall be prevented from earning that income for themselves. He does not propose if the husband is sick or weakly and unable to earn enough to keep the home, to supplement that income by a grant from the State. All he proposes to do is to take away from the married woman the right to earn an income for herself. This, he says, will stop infantile mortality and put an end to race degeneracy. Could you have a greater example of ignorance of the real facts of the situation? I come from Lancashire. I was born in Lancashire. I think I know more about Lancashire than Mr. John Burns. I can tell you this, that infantile mortality and physical degeneration are not found in the homes of the well-paid factory operatives, but they are found in the home of the slum-dweller, the home of the casual labourer, where the mother does not go out to work, but where there is never sufficient income to provide proper food for the child after it is born. That is where babies die—in those horrible slum districts, where families have to be maintained on incomes of from sixteen shillings to eighteen shillings per week, and where you have rents from five shillings to eight shillings per week to pay. What woman can feed her children on an income like that, even if her husband brings the whole of it home?

I know the cotton workers of Lancashire. Not long ago, we were in the Rossendale Valley, Mr. Harcourt's constituency.[14] In that constituency more women

12 The Married Women's Property Act of 1882, drawn up by Mr. Pankhurst, consolidated and expanded the previous acts of 1870 and 1874. It provided that the entire property of a married woman, both that which she possessed at the time of her marriage, and that which she acquired after marriage, should be recognized as her own. Four later statutes, in 1884, 1893, 1907, and 1908, completed the 1882 Act.

13 County in northwest England, containing Liverpool and Manchester. At the time of this speech it was the most populous county in England.

14 Rossendale is a district north of Manchester in Lancashire. Lewis Harcourt, first Commissioner of Works under Campbell-Bannerman, a devoted anti-suffragist, later became a direct target of suffragist agitation. See E. Sylvia Pankhurst, The Suffragette, pp. 178, 405, 463–64.

earn wages than men. You find daughters earning more money than their fathers. You find wives earning more money than their husbands. They do piece work, and they often earn better wages than the men. I was talking one day to one— a married woman worker whom I met in the train. She was going home from the mill. She had a child three or four years of age, well dressed, very blithe, and looking well fed. I asked her if she worked in the mill. She said, "Yes." I asked her what wages she earned. She said, "Thirty shillings a week." She told me she had other children. "Who looks after the children while you are at work?" "I have a housekeeper," she answered. I said to her, "You are not going to be allowed to work much longer. Mr. John Burns is going to make you stay at home and look after the children." And she said, "I don't know what we shall do then. I suppose we shall have to clem." I don't know whether you all know our Lancashire word "clem." When we say clem, we mean starve. In thousands of homes in Lancashire, if we get Mr. John Burns' proposal carried into law, little children, now well clothed and well fed and well cared for, will have clemmed before many months are over. These women say a shilling that they earn themselves is worth two shillings of their husbands' money, for it is their own. They know far better than their husbands how much money is needed for food, how much is needed to be spent on the home. I do not think there is a woman in Lancashire who does not realise that it is better to earn an income of her own than to be dependent on her husband. They realise it better than women of the upper classes who provide nurses and governesses for their children. I put it to you whether the woman of the working class, so long as she sees that her children are well fed and are well enough cared for, has not as much right as her well-off sister to provide a nurse for her children. We should like to say this to Mr. John Burns, that when women get the vote, they will take very much better care of babies than men have been able to do.

There may be many women in this room to-night who do not know much about the industrial women from practical experience. I want to say something about them. Here in London last year there was the Sweated Industries Exhibition.[15] That Exhibition went to Manchester. It went to Birmingham. The papers were full of it. After it was held there were conferences in the Guildhall, conferences in the large centres of population, and resolutions were carried demanding legislation to deal with the sweating evil. Nothing has come of it all. If any of you women are doubtful about the value of the vote to women, that example ought to be enough. Look at the Government's proposals. What do you get in the forefront of their programme? You get an eight hours' day for miners. But you get nothing for the sweated women. Why is the miner being attended to rather than the sweated worker? The miner is being attended to because he, the

[15] Sweating is the exacting of excessively long hours of toil for excessively low wages, frequently under unsanitary conditions in shops in slum areas or in the crowded room of a tenement that might be used for both living and working; hence the expression *sweat shops*. The system flourishes when labor is plentiful and unorganized; when the laws regulating wages and conditions are nonexistent; when simple, monotonous tasks can be performed by children, skilled work by women, and unskilled by men. The first inquiry into sweating was carried out by a select committee of the House of Lords which published its findings in 1890. The first of the Sweated Industries Exhibitions was arranged in 1906 by the *Daily News* to publicize the horrors of sweating. The exhibition to which Mrs. Pankhurst refers was opened in 1907 by Lord Milner.

miner, has got a vote. You see what the vote will do. You see what political power will do. If women had had the vote there would have been proposals to help the sweated woman worker in the Government programme of this session. I think that women, realising the horrible degradation of these workers, the degradation not only to themselves, but to all of us, caused by that evil of sweating, ought to be eager to get political freedom, in order that something may be done to get for the sweated woman labourer some kind of pay that would enable her to live at least a moral and a decent life.

Now let me say something on another point. Among those here are some professional women. You know what a long and a weary struggle it has been for women to get into the professions, some of which are now open to women. But you all know that the position of women in those professions is not what it ought to be, and is certainly not what it will be when women get the franchise. How difficult it is for women to get posts after they have qualified for them. I know this from practical experience on a public body. Every time we had applications from women for posts open to them, we had applications also from men. Usually the standing of the women was very much higher than that of the men. And yet the women did not get those appointments. The men got them. That would all be altered if we got political equality. It is the political key that is needed to unlock the door.

Again, in all grades of education, certainly in elementary education, women are better qualified for the work than the men. You get a better type of woman. Yet for work equal to that of men, she cannot get equal pay. If women teachers had the Parliamentary vote, those men who go to the House of Commons to represent the interests of teachers would have to represent the interests of women teachers as well as the interests of the men. I think that the gentleman who made the teachers the stepping-stone to office, and who talks at bye-elections about manhood suffrage would have taken up the interests of the women who have paid his wages if he felt that he was responsible to women voters.

Almost everywhere the well-paid posts are given to men. Take the College of Arts.[16] Women art students do quite as well as the men students. And yet after their training is over, women never get any of the posts. All the professorships, all the well-paid posts in the colleges and Universities are given to men. I knew the Head of one of the training colleges in one of our great cities. She said to me: "It makes me feel quite sad to see bright young girls expecting to get their living, and finding after their training is over that they can get nothing to do." The Parliamentary vote will settle that. There is no department of life that you can think of in which the possession of the Parliamentary vote will not make things easier for women than they are to-day.

Then there is the administrative side of public life. We want the vote not merely to get laws made. I think the possession of the Parliamentary vote is very important on the administrative side of politics. I have every reason to think that, because I have just come out of prison. We may congratulate ourselves that the Militant Suffragists, of whom I am one, have at least succeeded in forcing the Government to appoint the first woman inspector of prisons. Of course, it is a very small thing, but it means a very great deal. It means the beginning of prison reform, reform in prison discipline and prison treatment that have been needed

[16] Mrs. Pankhurst's daughter, Estelle Sylvia Pankhurst, was a student at the Royal College of Art, Kensington.

for a very long time. Well, when we get the vote, it won't take many years talking about things to get one woman inspector appointed. The immediate result of our getting the vote will be the appointment of many more women inspectors of factories. When I last made inquiries there was only one woman inspector of factories in all Ireland. Yet in Belfast alone, more women and girls are working in factories than men and boys. The need there for inspection is enormous in those linen and jute factories. It is perfectly obvious that when you have women and girls working in factories, if they are to be properly inspected, you must have women inspectors. We shall get them as soon as we are able to get women's interests properly attended to, which we shall only be able to do when we are in possession of the vote.

There is the same thing with regard to education. Women inspectors of schools are greatly needed. Moreover, there is not a single woman Poor Law inspector, nor a woman inspector of workhouses and workhouse hospitals. And yet it is to the workhouses and the workhouse hospitals that we send old people, sick people, and little children. We need to get women relieving officers [17] appointed. I cannot get away from Mr. John Burns. You would think that a working man by origin, and the son of working people, might have been able to realise that it would have been a good thing to have women as relieving officers. And yet when Mr. John Burns, shortly after his appointment, was asked whether he would sanction the appointment of a woman relieving officer in a large Union [18] in the North of England, he said it was not illegal, but it was a practice not to be encouraged. We shall get that position for women. We shall get it made possible for women to manage the business which men have always conceded is the business of women, the care of the sick, the care of the aged, the care of little children.

Well, I could go on giving you many, many more of these illustrations. In fact, the more one thinks about the importance of the vote for women, the more one realises how vital it is. We are finding out new reasons for the vote, new needs for the vote every day in carrying on our agitation.

I hope that there may be a few men and women here who will go away determined at least to give this question more consideration than they have in the past. They will see that we women who are doing so much to get the vote, want it because we realise how much good we can do with it when we have got it. We do not want it in order to boast of how much we have got. We do not want it because we want to imitate men or to be like men. We want it because without it we cannot do that work which it is necessary and right and proper that every man and woman should be ready and willing to undertake in the interests of the community of which they form a part. It has always been the business of women to care for these things, to think of these home questions. I assure you that no woman who enters into this agitation need feel that she has got to give up a single one of her woman's duties in the home. She learns to feel that she is attaching a larger meaning to those duties which have been woman's duties since the race began, and will be till the race has ceased to be. After all, home is a very, very big thing indeed. It is not just your own little home, with its four walls,

[17] A "relieving" officer is one appointed by a parish or union to administer relief to the poor.

[18] A "Union" is a number of parishes united under one Board of Guardians for the Administration of the poor laws. The "Poor House" or "Work House" administered by the Union is sometimes referred to as the "Union House."

and your own little private and personal interests that are looked after there. The home is the home of everybody of the nation. No nation can have a proper home unless women as well as men give their best to its building up and to making it what a home ought to be, a place where every single child born into it shall have a fair chance of growing up to be a fit, and a happy, and a useful member of the community.

⌒

SPEECH AT THE BOW STREET POLICE COURT *

October 24, 1908

Sir, I want to endorse what my daughter has said,[1] that in my opinion we are proceeded against in this Court by malice on the part of the Government. [She began quietly and firmly.] I want to protest as strongly as she has done. I want to put before you that the very nature of your duties in this Court—although I wish to say nothing disrespectful to you—make you perhaps unfitted to deal with a question which is a political question, as a body of jurymen could do. We are not women who would come into this Court as ordinary law-breakers,[2] and we feel that it is a great indignity—as have felt all the other women who have come into this Court—that for political offences we should come into the ordinary police-court. We do not object to that if from that degradation we shall ultimately succeed in winning political reform for the women of this country.

Mrs. Drummond here is a woman of very great public spirit; she is an admirable wife and mother; she has very great business ability, and she has maintained herself, although a married woman, for many years, and has acquired for herself the admiration and respect of all the people with whom she has had business relations.[3] I do not think I need speak about my daughter. Her abilities

---

* The text is that in The Trial of the Suffragette Leaders (1908?), a forty-eight-page pamphlet published, like The Importance of the Vote, by the Woman's Press, the organ of the Women's Social and Political Union. It contains verbatim reports of the speeches of the three women who were on trial—Mrs. Pankhurst (pp. 19–24), Mrs. Drummond, and Christabel Pankhurst—and of much of the questioning and testimony in the hearing. Versions of the speech, abbreviated and occasionally altered from the text in the pamphlet, are included in E. Sylvia Pankhurst's The Suffragette (1911), pp. 315–19, and in Christabel Pankhurst's Unshackled (1959), edited by Lord Pethick-Lawrence, pp. 110–12. For permission to reprint Mrs. Pankhurst's speeches, and for other help and encouragement, we are grateful to Miss Grace Roe, who was Mrs. Pankhurst's chief organizer in the closing years of the Militant Movement, and is Dame Christabel Pankhurst's executrix and President of the Suffragette Fellowship.

[1] Christabel Pankhurst, who had earned a law degree from Victoria University, Manchester, conducted the defense and spoke for two hours in summation.

[2] The reference is to women arrested on petty charges; for example, drunkenness. A police court with a magistrate presiding has jurisdiction over simple cases dealing with the behavior of the populace. Christabel failed in her effort to have the case tried before a jury.

[3] Mrs. Flora Gibson Drummond (1878–1949), called "The General," was a short, stout, pug-nosed woman, noted in the movement as an organizer, an audacious campaigner, and a speaker with a flair for the comic.

and earnestness of purpose are very well known to you. They are young women. I am not, sir. You and I are older, and have had very great and very wide experience of life under different conditions. Before you decide what is to be done with us, I should like you to hear from me a statement of what has brought me into this dock this morning.

I was brought up by a father who taught me that it was the duty of his children, boys and girls alike, to realise that they had a duty towards their country; they had to be good citizens. I married a man, whose wife I was, but also his comrade in all his public life. He was, as you know, a distinguished member of your own profession, but he felt it his duty, in addition, to do political work, to interest himself in the welfare of his fellow countrymen and countrywomen.[4] Throughout the whole of my marriage I was associated with him in his public work. In addition to that, as soon as my children were of an age to permit me to leave them, I took to public duties. I was for many years a Guardian of the Poor.[5] For many years I was a member of the School Board, and when that was abolished I was elected on to the Education Committee.[6] My experience in doing that work brought me in contact with many of my own sex, who in my opinion found themselves in deplorable positions because of the state of the English law as it affects women. You in this Court must have had experience of women who would never have come here if married women were afforded by law that claim for maintenance by their husbands which I think in justice should be given them when they give up their economic independence and are unable to earn a subsistence for themselves. You know how inadequate are the marriage laws to women. You must know, sir, as I have found out in my experience of public life, how abominable, atrocious, and unjust are the divorce laws as they affect women. You know very well that the married woman has no legal right of guardianship of her children. Then, too, the illegitimacy laws; you know that a woman sometimes commits the dreadful crime of infanticide, while her partner, the man who should share her punishment, gets off scot-free. I am afraid that great suffering is inflicted upon women because of these laws, and because of the impossibility that women have of getting legal redress. Because of these things I have tried, with other women, to get some reform of these laws. Women have petitioned members of Parliament, have tried for many, many years to persuade them to do something to alter these laws, to make them more equal, for they believe, as I do, that in the interests of men quite as much as of women it would be a good thing if laws were more equal between both sexes. I believe it would be better for men. I have a son myself, and I sometimes dread to think that my young son may be influenced

[4] For a sketch of Richard M. Pankhurst (1836–1898), an able and attractive man, see Chapter I, "Richard Marsden Pankhurst," of *The Suffragette Movement* by E. Sylvia Pankhurst.

[5] National laws governing the administration of relief for the poverty-stricken were first passed in the reign of Elizabeth I; by the amendments of 1834 and 1871, administrative control was vested in locally elected Boards of Guardians. In the twentieth century, schemes of social security have completely replaced the Poor Laws. Mrs. Pankhurst served as Guardian from 1894 to 1898.

[6] Members of the school boards had been elected directly until 1902, when membership became appointive. From about 1899 to 1902, Mrs. Pankhurst was elected as a member of the Manchester School Board; in 1902 and for a few years thereafter, she was appointed to the Board as the representative of the Trades Council.

in his behaviour to the other sex by the encouragement which the law of the land gives to men when they are tempted to take to an immoral life. I have seen, too, that men are encouraged by law to take advantage of the helplessness of women. Many women have thought as I have, and for many, many years women have tried by that influence we have so often been reminded of, to alter these laws, but we have found for many years that that influence counts for nothing. When we went to the House of Commons we used to be told, when we were persistent, that Members of Parliament were not responsible to women, they were responsible only to voters, and that their time was too fully occupied to reform those laws, although they agreed that they needed reforming.

Ever since my girlhood, a period of about thirty years, I have belonged to organizations to secure for women that political power which I have felt was essential to bringing about those reforms which women need. I have tried constitutional methods. I have been womanly. When you spoke to some of my colleagues the day before yesterday about their being unwomanly, I felt that bitterness which I know every one of them felt in their hearts. We have tried to be womanly, we have tried to use feminine influence, and we have seen that it is of no use. Men who have been impatient have invariably got reforms for their impatience. And they have not our excuse for being impatient.

You had before you in this Court yesterday a man who has a vote, a man who had been addressing other men with votes, and he advised action which we would never dream of advising.[7] But I want to say here and now, as a woman who has worked in the way you advised, that I wonder whether this womanly way is not a weakness that has been taken advantage of. I believe that Mr. Will Thorne was right when he said that no action would have been taken against him if his name had not been mentioned in this Court, because it is a very remarkable thing that the authorities are only proceeding against him when goaded to it by the observations which women made here.

Now, while I share in the feeling of indignation which has been expressed to you by my daughter, I have lived longer in the world than she has. Perhaps I can look round the whole question better than she can, but I want to say here, deliberately, to you, that we are here to-day because we are driven here. We have taken this action, because as women—and I want you to understand it is as women we have taken this action—it is because we realise that the condition of our sex is so deplorable that it is our duty even to break the law in order to call attention to the reasons why we do so.

I do not want to say anything which may seem disrespectful to you, or in any way give you offence, but I do want to say that I wish, sir, that you could put yourself into the place of women for a moment before you decide upon this case. My daughter referred to the way in which women are huddled into and out of these police-courts without a fair trial. I want you to realise what a poor hunted creature, without the advantages we have had, must feel.

I have been in prison. I was in Holloway Gaol for five weeks. I was in various parts of the prison. I was in the hospital, and in the ordinary part of the

[7] Mr. Will Thorne, M.P. During the trial, Christabel pointed out that Mr. Thorne had used the word "rush" in a speech in Trafalgar Square on October 4 in the same sense as that used by the Suffragettes. Brought into court and bound over, he claimed that no action would have been taken against him if the Pankhursts had not called attention to him.

prison, and I tell you, sir, with as much sense of responsibility as if I had taken the oath, that there were women there who have broken no law, who are there because they have been able to make no adequate statement.

You know that women have tried to do something to come to the aid of their own sex. Women are brought up for certain crimes, crimes which men do not understand—I am thinking especially of infanticide—they are brought before a man judge, before a jury of men, who are called upon to decide whether some poor, hunted woman is guilty of murder or not. I put it to you, sir, when we see in the papers, as we often do, a case similar to that of Daisy Lord,[8] for whom a great petition was got up in this country, I want you to realise how we women feel; because we are women, because we are not men, we need some legitimate influence to bear upon our law-makers.

Now, we have tried every way. We have presented larger petitions than were ever presented for any other reform, we have succeeded in holding greater public meetings than men have ever had for any reform, in spite of the difficulty which women have in throwing off their natural diffidence, that desire to escape publicity which we have inherited from generations of our foremothers; we have broken through that. We have faced hostile mobs at street corners, because we were told that we could not have that representation for our taxes which men have won unless we converted the whole of the country to our side. Because we have done this, we have been misrepresented, we have been ridiculed, we have had contempt poured upon us. The ignorant mob at the street corner has been incited to offer us violence, which we have faced unarmed and unprotected by the safeguards which Cabinet Ministers have. We know that we need the protection of the vote even more than men have needed it.

I am here to take upon myself now, sir, as I wish the prosecution had put upon me, the full responsibility for this agitation in its present phase. I want to address you as a woman who has performed the duties of a woman, and, in addition, has performed the duties which ordinary men have had to perform, by earning a living for her children, and educating them. In addition to that I have been a public officer. I enjoyed for ten years an official post under the Registrar, and I performed those duties to the satisfaction of the head of the department.[9] After my duty of taking the census was over, I was one of the few Registrars who qualified for a special bonus, and was specially praised for the way in which the work was conducted. Well, sir, I stand before you, having resigned that office when I was told that I must either do that or give up working for this movement.

I want to make you realise that it is a point of honour that if you decide—as

---

[8] A young woman convicted of murder and given the mandatory sentence of death for killing her illegitimate infant. Her appeal to have the sentence set aside was refused, and during the weeks prior to Mrs. Pankhurst's trial, a great stir had arisen over the case, generated in part by some of the Suffragettes. A mass meeting was held in mid-September, and petitions poured in on the Home Secretary, Herbert Gladstone, who undertook to exercise his authority to commute the sentence to life imprisonment, and announced his intention of seeking modification of the law. See *The Times,* August 15, 1908, p. 14, col. b; September 14, p. 10, col. d; September 16, p. 8, col. d; September 24, p. 4, col. e.

[9] Registrar of Births and Deaths, a post which she held from 1898 to 1907, when she chose to resign and forfeit her claim to a pension rather than cease her suffrage work.

I hope you will not decide—to bind us over,[10] that we shall not sign any under-taking, as the Member of Parliament did who was before you yesterday. Perhaps his reason for signing that undertaking may have been that the Prime Minister had given some assurance to the people he claimed to represent that something should be done for them. We have no such assurance. Mr. Birrell[11] told the woman who questioned him the other day that he could not say that anything would be done to give an assurance to the women that their claims should be con-ceded. So, sir, if you decide against us to-day, to prison we must go, because we feel that we should be going back to the hopeless condition this movement was in three years ago if we consented to be bound over to keep the peace which we have never broken. And so, sir, if you decide to bind us over, whether it is for three or six months, we shall submit to the treatment, the degrading treatment, that we have submitted to before.

Although the Government admitted that we are political offenders, and, there-fore, ought to be treated as political offenders are invariably treated, we shall be treated as pickpockets and drunkards; we shall be searched. I want you, if you can, as a man, to realise what it means to women like us. We are driven to do this, we are determined to go on with this agitation, because we feel in honour bound. Just as it was the duty of your forefathers, it is our duty to make this world a better place for women than it is to-day.

I was in the hospital at Holloway, and when I was there I heard from one of the beds near me the moans of a woman who was in the pangs of child-birth. I should like you to realise how women feel at helpless little infants breathing their first breath in the atmosphere of a prison. We believe that if we get the vote we will find some more humane way of dealing with women than that. It turned out that that woman was a remand prisoner. She was not guilty, because she was finally acquitted.

We believe that if we get the vote it will mean better conditions for our un-fortunate sisters. We know what the condition of the woman worker is. Her con-dition is very bad. Many women pass through this Court who I believe would not come before you if they were able to live morally and honestly. The average earnings of the women who earn their living in this country are only seven shil-lings and sixpence a week. There are women who have been driven to live an immoral life because they cannot earn enough to live decently.

We believe your work would be lightened if we got the vote. Some of us have worked, as I have told you, for many years to help our own sex, and we have been driven to the conclusion that only through legislation can any improvement be effected, and that that legislation can never be effected until we have the same power as men have to bring pressure to bear upon our representatives and upon Governments to give us the necessary legislation.

Now, sir, I do want to say this, that we have not wished to waste your time in any way; we have wished to make you realise that there is another side of the case than that put before you by the prosecution. We want you to use your power— I do not know what value there is in the legal claims that have been put before you as to your power to decide this case—but we want you, sir, if you will, to send

---

[10] To "bind over" means to place on probation, the accused agreeing to desist from his "unlawful" conduct for a stated period of time, usually a year.

[11] Augustine Birrell (1850–1933) is known chiefly as a literary essayist and biog-rapher. At the time he was a member of the Government as Chief Secretary for Ireland.

us to trial in some place more suitable for the trial of political offenders than an ordinary police-court. I do not know what you will do; I do not know what your powers are; but I do think, speaking as a woman to a man, I do say deliberately to you—I think your experience has been a large one—I come here not as an ordinary law-breaker. I should never be here if I had the same kind of power that the very meanest and commonest of men have—the same power that the wife-beater has, the same power that the drunkard has. I should never be here if I had that power, and I speak for all the women who have come before you and the other magistrates.

This is the only way we can get that power which every citizen should have of deciding how the taxes she contributes to should be spent, and how the laws she has to obey should be made, and until we get that power we shall be here— we are here to-day, and we shall come here over and over again. You must realise how futile it is to settle this question by binding us over to keep the peace. You have tried it; it has failed. Others have tried to do it, and have failed. If you had power to send us to prison, not for six months, but for six years, for sixteen years, or for the whole of our lives, the Government must not think that they can stop this agitation. It will go on.

I want to draw your attention to the self-restraint which was shown by our followers on the night of the 13th, after we had been arrested. It only shows that our influence over them is very great, because I think that if they had yielded to their natural impulses, there might have been a breach of the peace on the evening of the 13th. They were very indignant, but our words have always been, "be patient, exercise self-restraint, show our so-called superiors that the criticism of women being hysterical is not true; use no violence, offer yourselves to the violence of others." We are going to win. Our women have taken that advice; if we are in prison they will continue to take that advice.

Well, sir, that is all I have to say to you. We are here not because we are law-breakers; we are here in our efforts to become law-makers.

∽

BIBLIOGRAPHICAL NOTE

The important and fascinating story of women's suffrage has received comparatively little serious treatment. For general background on the social position of women in England, E. Halévy, *A History of the English People in the Nineteenth Century*, Vol. VI (rev. ed., 1952) is excellent. G. M. Young in his unrivalled *Victorian England: Portrait of an Age* (1936) recurs to the theme of the relationship between women and society. The best work on the suffrage movement in England is actually a vast work primarily on the American movement, *History of Woman Suffrage*, 6 vols. (1881– 1922), by E. C. Stanton, S. B. Anthony, M. J. Gap, and I. H. Harper. A recent, dignified, dispassionate treatment of the WSPU is Roger Fulford's *Votes for Women* (1957). Of those most intimately connected with the WSPU, E. Sylvia Pankhurst is the most scholarly and most prolific. She wrote *The Suffragette* (1911) when militancy was within a year of being at its height. In *The Suffragette Movement* (1931) she provides a completely new account, although it covers much of the same ground. In *The Life of Emmeline Pankhurst* (1935), she has written the longest and best biography of the leader of the militant movement. Mrs. Emmeline Pankhurst is credited as the author of *My Own Story* (1914), but it was really produced by Rhita Childe Dorr from her conversations with Mrs. Pankhurst and from Suffragette literature. In 1938 Christabel Pankhurst wrote *Unshackled,* a history of the WSPU and of her own role in the struggle; the book was seen through the press in 1958 after her death by Lord Pethick-Lawrence, a comrade in the militant days. Annie Kenny, a sturdy battler in the WSPU, has written *Memoirs of a Militant* (1924); Mary R. Richardson, in *Laugh a Defiance* (1953), provides some moderately interesting but scarcely valuable reminiscences. There are no collections of speeches by Mrs. Pankhurst in existence, no collected works, no collections of letters. There are some single speeches published in pamphlet form, and there are the pages of *Votes for Women* which contain countless references to her. After the franchise was won, the Suffrage Fellowship gathered together the papers of the WSPU and of other suffrage organizations, and deposited them in the London Museum. Fulford provides a good starting bibliography; O. R. McGregor has compiled and adroitly annotated a bibliography of which the militant movement is a small part, "The Social Position of Women in England, 1850–1914: A Bibliography," *British Journal of Sociology,* VI (1955), 48–60.

David Lloyd George

(1863–1945)

A Welshman of extraordinary vitality, fervor, eloquence, and devotion to the people, Lloyd George was the most conspicuous political figure in Britain from 1908 to 1922. He was Prime Minister during the latter half of World War I, and was the most striking, though perhaps not the most statesmanly, of the Big Four at the Peace Conference. Medium-to-short in stature, he exhibited a head of unruly greying hair, a shaggy moustache, and a roar which impelled cartoonists to draw him as the wily or the formidable British Lion, as they made Clemenceau the Tiger of France.

Before forcing Asquith out as Prime Minister in 1916, Lloyd George had demonstrated executive ability and leadership as Minister of Munitions and Secretary of State for War. In these offices he had borne, in addition, much of the responsibility for spurring England on to her war effort and for keeping peace with Labor. Like Churchill twenty-five years later, he supplanted his chief and became a vigorous war leader who could sustain the spirits of his countrymen and their allies with his oratory and his action.

Though never entirely trusted by the English middle classes, Lloyd George had built himself a strong popular position, especially during his six years as Chancellor of the Exchequer. By reforming the tax structure to remove unfair immunities from the very wealthy, and through vehement advocacy of welfare legislation for the laboring classes, he had established himself as a friend of the people who had not only the will to agitate (which he had been demonstrating since his youth) but the power to deliver. The speech below is one of the most characteristic and notable of his non-parliamentary speeches of that period. The only major cause for the relief of the deprived which even Lloyd George seems to have been unwilling to advocate was women's suffrage.

Lloyd George was born in Manchester, in the industrial Midlands, but because of his father's early death, he was reared mostly in his maternal uncle's home in Wales. The family had to live frugally, and it adhered to the strict moral code of the Protestant Dissenter tradition of Wales. David, nevertheless, was brought up in a thoroughly activist social and political climate and in an atmosphere of superb popular preaching. From his uncle, perhaps, he first acquired his respect for the Welsh social ideal, his pride in the Welsh national heritage, his hostility to the arrogance of privilege and to English domination. Then too began his experience with the problems of the common people and his sympathy with the needs of workers and farmers.

By the age of twenty-one, David had served five years in a law office, had been admitted to the Bar, and had set himself up in practice. By the following year he was firmly established as a local spokesman of the Liberals, and in 1890 he was elected to Parliament. His favorite topics, on which he lavished his growing talent for oratory, were access to land for the people, hostility toward game-preserving landlords, non-sectarian education, temperance, defense of non-conformity in religion, and Welsh nationalism.

Over a period of fifteen years in Parliament, Lloyd George grew in political stature and influence through his espousal of controversial causes and his brilliance in debate in and out of the House. Perhaps he gained only notoriety through his bitter personal attacks on Chamberlain during his opposition to the Boer War, but in 1905 he achieved cabinet rank as President of the Board of Trade. When Campbell-Bannerman died in April 1908 and was succeeded as Prime Minister by another Liberal, Herbert Asquith, Lloyd George moved into Asquith's place as Chancellor of the Exchequer. There he was responsible for tax legislation and the budget. He was replaced on the Board of Trade by Winston Churchill, then a Liberal.

The years 1909–1911 saw the Liberal Government, with Lloyd George in the forefront of the attack, make important changes in taxation to support new legislation which was a preview of the involvement of the government, in later decades, in social services. Furthermore, as a direct consequence of the budget of 1909, the Liberals abolished the power of the House of Lords effectively to block vital legislation.

The chief features of Lloyd George's budget are listed below in the notes to the speech. Needless to say, they aroused the vehement hostility of the moneyed interests and the large landowners. The Chancellor's speech introducing his budget in the Commons was apparently as long as some of Gladstone's and even more tedious. After the Lords had rejected the budget, however, and Lloyd George took the case to the people, he was vehement, he was violent, he was self-confident, he was folksy and amusing, he was sentimental; but he was not dull or tedious.

His Limehouse speech is part of that campaign and is characteristic of his techniques of popular persuasion. Under the auspices of a Liberal party affiliate known as the Budget League, Lloyd George, on the evening of July 30, 1909, harangued and delighted a mass meeting of 4,000 at a hall called the Edinburgh Castle in Limehouse, a lower-class district of East London along the Thames. Lacking today's loudspeaker systems, he repeated the principal parts of the speech before an overflow audience in an adjoining hall right after the main event. An interesting sidelight is that twelve persons, most of whom were Suffragettes, were arrested for trying to rush the meeting in the Edinburgh Castle (see above, Emmeline Pankhurst).

The speech was more overtly popular and demagogic than any other in this book, with the possible exception of O'Connell's Tara speech. Of it his brother wrote:

> It was, doubtless, a deliberately provocative speech in the course of which Dafydd hurtled all the artillery at his command by way of an overpowering frontal attack on the ramparts behind which the aristocracy had thrived whilst trampling on the common people for centuries.[1]

That is, of course, a brother's recollection, but apparently Lloyd George's partisans were indeed delighted, and the Tories enraged. Lloyd George wrote on August 3: "They are raging over Limehouse, but our fellows [are] most enthusiastic." And a month later he reported a *Times* editorial as saying, "Limehouse is read and quoted far and wide, and has swayed opinion." [2]

After the general election of 1910, Lloyd George's reforms were passed, but only because the King threatened to create enough new Peers to carry the vote. The consequence was the Parliament Act which destroyed the absolute veto of the House of Lords.

As a war leader, we have said, Lloyd George was popular and successful, and his public speaking was an important source of his popularity and success. Especially notable is his "Scrap of Paper" speech of 1914. Even before the peace, however, he was weakening at home. A union with Bonar Law preserved him in power in the general election of 1918, but Liberal strength was rapidly disappearing. At the Peace Conference he seemed at times more the politician mending his fences at home than the statesman facing the problems of the world. In 1921 he laid the basis for a solution of the troubles of Ireland, but in 1922, under many pressures, he resigned. Though he remained in Parliament in opposition, his influence was never again politically great. Perhaps he was justifying himself when he said of Lincoln in Springfield, Illinois, in 1923:

> The tenderest soul who ever ruled over men was . . . worried, harassed, encumbered, lassoed at every turn by the vanities, the jealousies, the factiousness and the wiles of swarms of little men. . . . There are the great men of the party, and the great men of creeds. There are the great men of their time and there are the great men of all time of their own native land; but Lincoln was a great man of all time, for all parties, for all lands and for all races of men.[3]

David Lloyd George was not a man for the ages, but in his own time and land he was a dynamic spokesman for the new socio-economic forces of the twentieth century.

∾

[1] William George, *My Brother and I,* p. 228.

[2] *Ibid.,* pp. 230–31.

[3] David Lloyd George, *Abraham Lincoln, An Address before the Midday Luncheon Club, Leland Hotel, Springfield, Illinois, Thursday, October 18, 1923* (Cleveland, 1924), pp. 9–10.

Speech at Limehouse *

July 30, 1909

A few months ago a meeting was held not far from this hall, in the heart of the City of London, demanding that the Government should launch out and run into enormous expenditure on the Navy. That meeting ended up with a resolution promising that those who passed that resolution would give financial support to the Government in their undertaking. There have been two or three meetings held in the City of London since (laughter and cheers), attended by the same class of people, but not ending up with a resolution promising to pay. (Laughter.) On the contrary, we are spending the money, but they won't pay. (Laughter.) What has happened since to alter their tone? Simply that we have sent in the bill. (Laughter and cheers.) We started our four Dreadnoughts.[1] They cost eight millions of money. We promised them four more; they cost another eight millions. Somebody has got to pay, and these gentlemen say, "Perfectly true; somebody has got to pay, but we would rather that somebody were somebody else." (Laughter.) We started building; we wanted money to pay for the building; so we sent the hat round. (Laughter.) We sent it round amongst the workmen (hear, hear), and the miners of Derbyshire (loud cheers) and Yorkshire, the weavers of High Peak (cheers), and the Scotchmen of Dumfries (cheers), who, like all their countrymen, know the value of money. (Laughter.) They all brought in their

---

* The text, taken from *The Times*, July 31, 1909, p. 9, is printed here with minor changes which are identified in the footnotes. It has been collated with the text appearing in *Better Times* (London, 1910) edited by the speaker himself, David Lloyd George. The text in *The Times* contains the interpolations of general audience reaction inserted in parentheses, such as (Cheers), and more specific audience participation such as calls from the crowd and the speaker's follow-up rallies. Other omissions in the text in *Better Times* are repetitions of the definite article modifying nouns in a series; nouns in apposition: "taxes that are fertile taxes [, taxes] that will bring forth fruit"; words used to express the future progressive tense rather than the present: "I [am going to] tell you"; conjunctions used to open sentences: "Now," "But"; additional clinching phrases when the topic has already been concluded: "There are no end of these cases." Other differences between the two texts may be classified as corrections, clarifications, completions, compositional changes, and transitions. Some of the readings from the text in *Better Times* have been incorporated in the text appearing here. These readings are set off in brackets, the deleted portions of *The Times* text being given in the footnotes. In the footnotes, the text in *The Times* is referred to by the initials *LT,* and the text in *Better Times,* by the initials *BT.*

[1] The Conservatives had demanded naval expansion to keep pace with the growth of the German Navy. Despite his opposition to expansion, Lloyd George promised funds for the construction of eight large battleships, popularly called Dreadnoughts, with four to be built immediately. He made it clear, however, that the wealthy would be made to pay for such expansion. Although the new graduated income tax would be the chief instrument for taxing the wealthy, the land taxes, it was hoped, would also provide some of the revenue required for the program. Because the land taxes were also being used to provide old age pensions, the 1909 budget provoked numerous protest meetings even among those who most strongly supported the Dreadnought building program.

coppers.[2] We went round Belgravia,[3] but there has been such a howl ever since that it has completely deafened us.

But they say, "It is not so much the Dreadnoughts we object to, it is the pensions." (Hear, hear.) If they object to pensions, why did they promise them? (Cheers.) They won elections on the strength of their promises. It is true they never carried them out. (Laughter.) Deception is always a pretty contemptible vice, but to deceive the poor is the meanest of all crimes. (Cheers.) But they say, "When we promised pensions we meant pensions at the expense of the people for whom they were provided. We simply meant to bring in a Bill to compel workmen to contribute to their own pensions." (Laughter.) If that is what they meant, why did they not say so? (Cheers.) The Budget, as your chairman has already so well reminded you, is introduced not merely for the purpose of raising barren taxes, but taxes that are fertile taxes, taxes that will bring forth fruit—the security of the country which is paramount in the minds of all. The provision for the aged and deserving poor—it was time it was done. (Cheers.) It is rather a shame for a rich country like ours—probably the richest country in the world, if not the richest the world has ever seen—that it should allow those who have toiled all their days to end in penury and possibly starvation. (Hear, hear.) It is rather hard that an old workman should have to find his way to the gates of the tomb, bleeding and footsore, through the brambles and thorns of poverty. (Cheers.) We cut a new path [for him][4] (cheers), an easier one, a pleasanter one, through the fields of waving corn. We are raising money to pay for the new road (cheers), aye, and to widen it so that 200,000 paupers shall be able to join in the march. (Cheers.) There are many in the country blessed by Providence with great wealth, and if there are amongst them men who grudge out of their riches a fair contribution towards the less fortunate of their fellow-countrymen they are shabby rich men. (Cheers.) We propose to do more by means of the Budget. We are raising money to provide against the evils and the sufferings that follow from unemployment. (Cheers.) We are raising money for the purpose of assisting our great friendly societies to provide for the sick and the widows and orphans.[5] We are providing money to enable us to develop the resources of our own land. (Cheers.) I do not believe any fair-minded man would challenge the justice and the fairness of the objects which we have in view in raising this money.

But there are some of [our critics][6] who say that the taxes themselves are unjust, unfair, unequal, oppressive—notably so the land taxes.[7] (Laughter.) They

[2] By-elections held at Derbyshire, Yorkshire, and Dumfries during July had all resulted in substantial support for the budget. (*Better Times*, p. 144n.)

[3] Belgravia is a district of London. In Lloyd George's time it was still the unchallenged home of the British aristocracy.

[4] *LT*: [through it].

[5] Friendly Societies, agencies for mutual insurance and personal saving, provided channels for voluntary service by supplying aid to their members in the times of misfortune. Later, Lloyd George's National Insurance Act of 1911 used approved Friendly Societies to administer national insurance benefits.

[6] *LT*: [them].

[7] By 1909, direct taxes were accounting for more than 50 per cent of the country's total revenue. Thus the budget, introducing four new Land Taxes which imposed additional burdens on those who paid direct taxes, aroused opposition. The new taxes were: (1) the undeveloped land and ungotten minerals tax of a halfpenny in the pound on the value of land which its owner did not cultivate or whose mineral wealth

are engaged, not merely in the House of Commons, but outside the House of Commons, in assailing these taxes with a concentrated and a sustained ferocity which will not allow even a comma to escape with its life. ("Good," and laughter.) How are they really so wicked? Let us examine them, because it is perfectly clear that the one part of the Budget that attracts all this hostility and animosity is that part which deals with the taxation of land.[8] Well, now let us examine it. I do not want you to consider merely abstract principles. [I want to invite your attention to a number of concrete cases; fair samples to show you how in these concrete illustrations our Budget proposals work.][9] Now let us take them. Let us take first of all the tax on undeveloped land and on increment.

Not far from here not so many years ago, between the Lea and the Thames, you had hundreds of acres of land which was not very useful even for agricultural purposes. In the main it was a sodden marsh. The commerce and the trade of London increased under free trade (loud cheers); the tonnage of your shipping went up by hundreds of thousands of tons and by millions, labour was attracted from all parts of the country to help with all the trade and business done here. What happened? There was no housing accommodation. This part of London [10] became overcrowded and the population overflowed. That was the opportunity of the owners of the marsh. All that land became valuable building land, and land which used to be rented at £2 or £3 an acre has been selling within the last few years at £2,000 an acre, £3,000 an acre, £6,000 an acre, £8,000 an acre. Who created that increment? (Cheers.) Who made that golden swamp? (More cheers.) Was it the landlord? (Cries of "No.") Was it his energy? Was it his brains (laughter and cheers), his forethought? It was purely the combined efforts of all the people engaged in the trade and commerce of that part of London—the trader, the merchant, the ship-owner, the dock labourer, the workman—everybody except the landlord. (Cheers.) Now you follow that transaction. The land worth £2 or £3 an acre ran up to thousands. During the time it was ripening the landlord was paying his rates [11] and his taxes not on £2 or £3 an acre. It was

---

he did not exploit; (2) "a tax of 20 per cent on the increment value obtained by the sale of land, where such increase was due, not to the owner's expenditure and enterprise, but to that of neighbours as a whole"; (3) a tax of 10 per cent on the increased value of property let out on lease, calculated at the renewal of the lease; and (4) a Mineral Rights Duty of one shilling in the pound on mineral royalties. In the speech, Lloyd George illustrates the application of each of these taxes.

[8] Although the Land Taxes provoked the greatest protests, they were not the only feature of the budget which met opposition. The budget called for a rise in income taxes, as well as increases in estates duties and duties on spirits and tobacco. There was also a Miners' Welfare Fund proposed, which was to come from the Mineral Rights Duty, for improving conditions in the mines; a Development Fund, for subsidizing land and water conservation; and a Road Fund, for improving highways, to be derived from the first taxes ever imposed on motor cars and gasoline.

[9] LT: [I want to invite your attention to a number of concrete cases and fair samples to show you how these concrete illustrations—how our budget proposals work.]

[10] BT: [Port].

[11] In England, the term rate means public money levied for local purposes; the term taxes means money for general national purposes. The money required for local administration in England is raised (when the ordinary revenues are insufficient) by assessments on lands and buildings based on their annual rental value. The local financial authority estimates what additional amount beyond revenue is required for the

agricultural land, and because it was agricultural land a munificent Tory Government (laughter) voted a sum of two millions to pay half the rates of those poor
distressed landlords. (Laughter, and cries of "Shame.") You and I had to pay
taxes in order to enable those landlords to pay half their rates on agricultural land,
while it was going up every year by hundreds of pounds from your efforts and the
efforts of your neighbours. Well, now that is coming to an end. (Loud and long-
continued cheering.) On the walls of Mr. Balfour's meeting last Friday were the
words, "We protest against fraud and folly." [12] (Laughter.) So do I. (Great
cheering.) These things I am going to tell you of have only been possible up to
the present through the fraud of the few and the folly of the million. (Cheers.)
[What is going to happen in the future?] In future those landlords will have to
contribute to the taxation of the country on the basis of the real value (more
cheers) only one-halfpenny in the pound! (Laughter.) And that is what all the
howling is about. But there is another little tax called the increment tax. For the
future what will happen? We mean to value all the land in the kingdom.
(Cheers.) And here you can draw no distinction between agricultural land and
other land, for the simple reason that East and West Ham [13] was agricultural land
a few years ago. And if land goes up in the future by hundreds and thousands
an acre through the efforts of the community the community will get 20 per cent.
of that increment. (Cheers.) What a misfortune it is that there was not a
Chancellor of the Exchequer who did this 30 years ago. (Cheers and cries of
"Better late than never.") Only 30 years ago and we should now have an abundant
revenue from this source. (Cheers.)

Now I have given you West Ham. Let me give you a few more cases. Take
a case like Golder's-green [13] and other cases of a similar kind where the value of
land has gone up in the course, perhaps, of a couple of years through a new
tramway or a new railway being opened. Golder's-green is a case in point. A few
years ago there was a plot of land there which was sold at £160. Last year I went
and opened a tube railway there. What was the result? That very piece of land
has been sold at £2,100 ("Shame"); £160 before the railway was opened—before
I went there (laughter); £2,100 now. So I am entitled to 20 per cent. on that.[14]
(Laughter.) Now there are many cases where landlords take advantage of the
exigencies of commerce and of industry—take advantage of the needs of munic-
ipalities and even of national needs and of the monopoly which they have got in
land in a particular neighbourhood in order to demand extortionate prices. Take
the very well-known case of the Duke of Northumberland (hear, hear), when a
county council wanted to buy a small plot of land as a site for a school to train
the children who in due course would become the men labouring on his property.
The rent was quite an insignificant thing; his contribution to the rates—I forget—

---

expenses of the administration, and levies a rate to meet it. *Ground rent* is the rent at
which land is let for the purpose of improvement by building; it is a rent charged for
the use of the land only, and not for the use of the buildings to be placed on it.

[12] Arthur James Balfour (1848–1930), Prime Minister from 1902 to 1905, and Conservative Member of Parliament from the City of London, opposed the budget of 1909.

[13] East and West Ham: county boroughs in Essex, 7–9 miles east of the center of
London. Golder's Green: an area in the borough of Hendon, in Middlesex, about 8
miles northwest of the center of London. These are areas which were becoming industrialized in the early years of the century.

[14] BT: [My budget demands 20 per cent. of that.]

I think on the basis of 30s. an acre. What did he demand for it for a school? £900 an acre. (Hear, hear, and "Shame.") Well all we say is this, Mr. Buxton [15] and I say—if it is worth £900, let him pay taxes on £900. (Cheers.)

Now there are several of these cases that I want to give to you. Take the town of Bootle, a town created very much in the same way as these towns in the east of London [, by the growth of a great port, in this case Liverpool.] [16] In 1879 the rates of Bootle were £9,000 a year—the ground-rents were £10,000—so that the landlord was receiving more from the industry of the community than all the rates derived by the municipality for the benefit of the town. In [1898] [17] the rates were £94,000 a year—for improving the place, constructing roads, laying out parks, and extending lighting and so on. But the ground landlord was receiving in ground-rent £100,000. It is time that he should pay for all this value. (Cheers.) A case was given me from Richmond which is very interesting. The Town Council of Richmond recently built some workmen's cottages under a housing scheme. The land appeared on the rate-book as of the value of £4, and being agricultural (laughter) the landlord only paid half the rates, and you and I paid the rest for him. (Laughter.) It is situated on the extreme edge of the borough, therefore it is not very accessible, and the town council thought they would get it cheap. (Laughter.) But they did not know their landlord. They had to pay £2,000 an acre for it. ("Shame.") The result is that instead of having a good housing scheme with plenty of gardens [and] open space,[18] plenty of breathing space, plenty of room for the workmen at the end of their days, 40 cottages had to be crowded into two acres. Now if the land had been valued at its true value that landlord would have been at any rate contributing his fair share of the public revenue, and it is just conceivable that he might have been driven to sell at a more reasonable price.

Now, I do not want to weary you with these cases. (Cries of "Go on!") I could give you many. I am a member of a Welsh county council, and landlords even in Wales are not more reasonable. (Laughter.) The police committee the other day wanted a site for a police station. Well, you might have imagined that if a landlord sold land cheaply for anything it would have been for a police station. (Laughter.) The housing of the working classes—that is a different matter. (Laughter.) But a police station means security to property. (Laughter and cheers.) Not at all. The total population of Carnarvonshire [19] is not as much—I am not sure it is as much—as the population of Limehouse alone. It is a scattered area, with no great crowded population. And yet they demanded for a piece of land which was contributing 2s. a year to the rates £2,500 an acre! All we say is, "If the land is as valuable as all that, let us have the same value on the assessment book (cheers) as it seems to possess in the auction room." (Cheers.) There are no end of these cases. There was a case at Greenock the other day. The Admiralty wanted a torpedo range. Here was an opportunity for patriotism! (Laughter.) These are the men who want an efficient navy to protect our shores, and the Admiralty state that one element in efficiency is straight shooting, and say, "We want a

---

[15] Sidney Charles Buxton (1853–1934), Postmaster General from 1905 to 1910, presided at the meeting.

[16] LT: [—Purely by the commerce of Bootle.] Bootle was a suburb of Liverpool.

[17] LT: [1900].

[18] LT: [of].

[19] Home county of Lloyd George, in northwest Wales.

range for practice for torpedoes on the [coast] [20] of Scotland." There was a piece of land there. It was rated at something like £11 2s. a year. They went to the landlord, and it was sold to the nation for £27,225. And there are the gentlemen who accuse us of robbery and spoliation! (Cheers.) Now, all we say is—"In future you must pay one-halfpenny in the pound on the real value of your land. In addition to that if the value goes up, not owing to your efforts—though if you spend money on improving it we will give you credit for it—but if it goes up owing to the industry and the energy of the people living in that locality one-fifth of that increment shall in future be taken as a toll by the State." (Cheers.) They say, "Why should you tax this increment on landlords and not on other classes of the community?" They say, "You are taxing the landlord because the value of his property is going up through the growth of population with the increased prosperity of the community. Does not the value of a doctor's business go up in the same way?" Ha! fancy comparing themselves for a moment. What is the landlord's increment? Who is the landlord? The landlord is a gentleman—I have not a word to say about him in his personal capacity—who does not earn his wealth. He does not even take the trouble to receive his wealth. (Laughter.) He has a host of agents and clerks that receive for him. He does not even take the trouble to spend his wealth. He has a host of people around him to do the actual spending for him. He never sees it until he comes to enjoy it. His sole function, his chief pride is stately consumption of wealth produced by others. (Cheers.) What about the doctor's income? How does the doctor earn his income? The doctor is a man who visits our homes when they are darkened with the shadow of death: his skill, his trained courage, his genius bring hope out of the grip of despair, win life out of the fangs of the Great Destroyer. (Cheers.) All blessings upon him and his divine art of healing that mends bruised bodies and anxious hearts. (Cheers.) To compare the reward which he gets for that labour with the wealth which pours into the pockets of the landlord purely owing to the possession of his monopoly is a piece of insolence which no intelligent community will tolerate. (Cheers.) So much for the halfpenny tax and the unearned increment.

Now I come to the reversion tax. What is the reversion tax? You have got a system in this country which is not tolerated in any other country in the world, except, I believe, Turkey (laughter)—the system whereby landlords take advantage of the fact that they have got complete control over the land, to let it for a term of years, spend money upon it in building, in developing. You improve the building and year by year the value passes into the pockets of the landlord, and at the end of 60, 70, 80 or 90 years the whole of it passes away to the pockets of the man who never spent a penny upon it. In Scotland they have a system of 999 years' lease. The Scotsmen have a very shrewd idea that at the end of 999 years there will probably be a better land system in existence (laughter and cheers), and they are prepared to take their chance of the millennium coming round by that time. But in this country we have 60 years' leases. I know [quarry] districts in Wales where a little bit of barren rock where you could not feed a goat, where the landlord could not get a shilling an acre of agricultural rent, is let to quarrymen for the purposes of building houses, where 30s. or £2 a house is charged for ground-rent. The quarryman builds his house. He goes to a building society to borrow money. He pays out of his hard-earned weekly wage [con-

---

[20] *LT*: [west].

tributions] to the building society for 10, 20, or 30 years. By the time he has become an old man he has cleared off the mortgage, and more than half the value of the house has passed into the pockets of the landlord. You have got cases in London here. (A voice—"Not half" and laughter.) There is the famous Gorringe case.[21] In that case advantage was taken of the fact that a man has built up a great business, and they say, "Here you are, you have built up a great business here; you cannot take it away; you cannot move to other premises because your trade and goodwill are here; your lease is coming to an end, and we decline to renew it except on the most oppressive terms." The Gorringe case is a very familiar case. It was the case of the Duke of Westminster. ("Oh, oh." Laughter and hisses.) Oh! these dukes (loud laughter), how they harass us. (More laughter.) Mr. Gorringe had got a lease of the premises at a few hundred pounds a year ground-rent. He built up a great business there. He was a very able business man, and when the end of the lease came he went to the Duke of Westminster, and he said, "Will you renew my lease? I want to carry on my business here." He said, "Oh, yes, I will, but I will do it on condition that the few hundreds a year you pay for ground-rent shall in the future be £4,000 a year." (Groans.) In addition to that he had to pay a fine—a fine, mind you!—of £50,000, and he had to build up huge premises at enormous expense according to plans submitted to the Duke of Westminster. ("Oh, oh.") All I can say is this—if it is confiscation and robbery for us to say to that duke that, being in need of money for public purposes, we will take 10 per cent. after all you have got for that purpose, what would you call his taking nine-tenths? (Cheers.) These are the cases we have got to deal with. Look at this leasehold system. A case like that is not business, it is blackmail.[22] (Loud cheers.) No doubt some of you have taken the trouble to peruse some of these leases. They are really worth reading, and I will guarantee that if you circulate copies of some of these building and mining leases at tariff reform meetings (hisses), and if you can get the workmen at these meetings and the business men to read them they will come away sadder and wiser men. (Cheers.) What are they? Ground-rent is a part of it—fines, fees; you are to make no alteration without somebody's consent. Who is that somebody? It is the agent of the landlord. [A fee to him.][23] You must submit the plans to the landlord's architect and get his consent. There is a fee to him. There is a fee to the surveyor, and then, of course, you cannot keep the lawyer out. (Laughter.) ("Set a lawyer to catch a lawyer," Mr. Lloyd George continued, pointing to one of his audience amidst laughter.) And a fee to him. Well, that is the system, and the landlords come to us in the House of Commons and they say:—"If you go on taxing reversions we will grant no more leases." Is not that horrible? (Loud laughter.) No more leases, no more kindly landlords. (Laughter.) With all their rich and good fare, with all their retinue of good fairies ready always to receive (laughter)—ground-rents, fees, premiums, fines, reversions—no more, never again. (Laughter.) They will not do it. You cannot persuade them. (Laughter.) They won't have it. (Renewed laughter.) The landlord has threatened us that if we proceed with the Budget he will take his sack (loud laughter) clean away from the cupboard

[21] Gorringe was the proprietor of one of the large fashionable west-end London shops exploited by his landlord, the Duke of Westminster.

[22] BT: [This system—it is the system I am attacking, not individuals—is not business, it is blackmail.]

[23] LT: [A fee to whom?]

and the grain which we are all grinding to our best to fill his sack will go into our own. Oh! I cannot believe it. There is a limit even to the wrath of an out-raged landlord. We must really appease them; we must offer some sacrifice to them. Supposing we offer the House of Lords to them. (Loud and prolonged cheers.) Well now you seem rather to agree with that. I will make the suggestion.

Now unless I am wearying you (loud cries of "No, no"), I have got just one other land tax, and that is a tax on royalties. The landlords are receiving eight millions a year by way of royalties. What for? They never deposited the coal there. (Laughter.) It was not they who planted [those] [24] great granite rocks in Wales, who laid the foundations of the mountains. Was it the landlord? (Laughter.) And yet he, by some Divine right, demands—for merely the right for men to risk their lives in hewing these rocks—eight millions a year! Take any coalfield. I went down to a coalfield the other day (cheers), and they pointed out to me many collieries there. They said:—"You see that colliery there. The first man who went there spent a quarter of a million in sinking shafts, in driving mains and levels. He never got coal. The second man who came spent £100,000—and he failed. The third man came along and he got the coal." But what was the landlord doing in the meantime? The first man failed; but the landlord got his royalties, the landlord got his dead-rents [—and a very good name for it]. The second man failed, but the landlord got his royalties. These capitalists put their money in. When the scheme failed, what did the landlord put in? [25] He simply put in the bailiffs. (Loud laughter.) The capitalist risks at any rate the whole of his money; the engineer puts his brains in, the miner risks his life. (Hear, hear.) Have you been down a coal mine? (Cries of "Yes.") Then you know. I was telling you I went down the other day. We sank down into a pit half a mile deep. We then walked underneath the mountain and we did about three-quarters of a mile with rock and shale about us. The earth seemed to be straining—around us and above us—to crush us in. You could see the pit-props bent and [twisted and sundered, their fibres split in resisting the pressure]. [26] Sometimes they give way, and then there is mutilation and death. Often a spark ignites, the whole pit is deluged in fire, and the breath of life is scorched out of hundreds of breasts by the consuming fire. In the very next colliery to the one I descended, just three years ago 300 people lost their lives in that way; and yet when the Prime Minister and I knock at the door of these great landlords and say to them:—"Here, you know these poor fellows have been digging up royalties at the risk of their lives, some of them are old, they have survived the perils of their trade, they are broken, they can earn no more. Won't you give something towards keeping them out of the work-house?" [they scowl at us. We say, "Only a ha'penny, just a copper." They retort,] [27] "You thieves." And they turn their dogs on to us, and every day you can hear their bark. (Loud laughter and cheers.) If this is an indication of the view taken by these great landlords of their responsibility to the people who, at the risk of life, create their wealth, then I say their day of reckoning is at hand. (Loud cheers.)

The other day, at the great Tory meeting held at the Cannon-street Hotel, they had blazoned on the walls, "We protest against the Budget in the name of de-

[24] LT: [these].
[25] BT: [, and I asked, "When the cash failed, what did the landlord put in?"]
[26] LT: [twisted and sundered until you saw their fibres split.]
[27] LT: [they scowl at you and we say, "Only a ha'penny, just a copper." They say,]

mocracy—(loud laughter)—liberty, and justice." Where does the democracy come in in this landed system? [Where is the liberty in our leasehold system?] Where is the [seat of] justice in all these transactions? We claim that the tax we impose on land is fair, just, and moderate. (Cheers.) They go on threatening that if we proceed they will cut down their benefactions and discharge labour. What kind of labour? (A voice, "Hard labour," and laughter.) What is the labour they are going to choose for dismissal? Are they going to threaten to devastate rural England, [by] [28] feeding themselves, and dressing themselves? Are they going to reduce their gamekeepers? That would be sad! (Laughter.) The agricultural labourer and the farmer might have some part of the game which they fatten with their labour. But what would happen to you in the season? No week-end shooting with the Duke of Norfolk for any of us! (Laughter.) But that is not the kind of labour that they are going to cut down. They are going to cut down productive labour—builders and gardeners—and they are going to ruin their property so that it shall not be taxed. All I can say is this—the ownership of land is not merely an enjoyment, it is a stewardship. (Cheers.) It has been reckoned as such in the past, and [if the owners cease to discharge their functions in seeing to the security and defence of the country, in looking after the broken in their villages and in their neighbourhoods the time will come to reconsider the conditions under which land is held in this country].[29] (Loud cheers.) No country, however rich, can permanently afford to have quartered upon its revenue a class which declines to do the duty which it was called upon to perform. (Hear, hear.) And, therefore, it is one of the prime duties of statesmanship to investigate those conditions. But I do not believe it. They have threatened and menaced like that before. They have seen it is not to their interest to carry out these futile menaces. They are now protesting against paying their fair share of the taxation of the land, and they are doing so by saying:—"You are burdening the community; you are putting burdens upon the people which they cannot bear." Ah! They are not thinking of themselves. (Laughter.) Noble souls! (Laughter.) It is not the great dukes they are feeling for, it is the market gardener (laughter), it is the builder, and it was, until recently, the small holder. (Hear, hear.) In every debate in the House of Commons they said:—"We are not worrying for ourselves. We can afford it with our broad acres; but just think of the little man who has only got a few acres"; and we were so very impressed with this tearful appeal that at last we said, "We will leave [the small holder] [30] out." (Cheers.) And I almost expected to see Mr. Pretyman [31] jump over the table [when I said it—fall on my neck and embrace me].[32] (Loud laughter.) Instead of that he stiffened up, his face wreathed with anger, and he said, "The Budget is more unjust than ever." (Laughter and cheers.) Oh! no. We are placing the burdens on the broad

---

[28] *LT:* [while]

[29] *LT:* [if they cease to discharge their functions, the security and defence of the country, looking after the broken in their villages and neighbourhoods—then those functions which are part of the traditional duties attached to the ownership of land and which have given it its title—if they cease to discharge those functions, the time will come to reconsider the conditions under which the land is held in this country.]

[30] *LT:* [him].

[31] Conservative Member of Parliament for Chelmsford, Essex, who supported the Dreadnought program, but opposed the new land taxes.

[32] *LT:* [and say—"Fall on my neck and embrace me."]

shoulders. (Cheers.) Why should I put burdens on the people? I am one of the children of the people. (Loud and prolonged cheering, and a voice, "Bravo, David; stand by the people and they will stand by you.") I was brought up amongst them. I know their trials; and God forbid that I should add one grain of trouble to the anxiety which they bear with such patience and fortitude. (Cheers.) When the Prime Minister did me the honour of inviting me to take charge of the National Exchequer (a voice, "He knew what he was about," and laughter) at a time of great difficulty, I made up my mind in framing the Budget which was in front of me, that at any rate no cupboard should be bared (loud cheers), no lot would be harder to bear.[33] (Cheers.) By that test, I challenge them to judge the Budget. (Loud and long-continued cheers, during which the right hon. gentleman resumed his seat.)

◇

BIBLIOGRAPHICAL NOTE

Writings about Lloyd George and his times are numerous and various, but the definitive biography has yet to be written. *David Lloyd George: The Official Biography,* by Malcolm Thomson with the assistance of the Lloyd George family, appeared in 1948. Other accounts from the family are his son Richard's *My Father, Lloyd George* (1961) and William George's *My Brother and I* (1958). The best life, and reasonably short, is Thomas Jones's *Lloyd George* (1951). Charles L. Mowat's brief sketch in "The Clarendon Biographies" (1964) is well stocked with photographs. Two recent studies suggesting possible lines of reassessment include Frank Owen, *Tempestuous Journey: Lloyd George, his Life and Times* (1955); and the hostile Donald McCormick, *The Mask of Merlin: A Critical Study of David Lloyd George* (1963). Brief and judicious is A. J. P. Taylor's lecture, *Lloyd George, Rise and Fall* (1961). For context and point of view, the student will find useful at least two books by Lord Beaverbrook, the famous newspaper publisher, who was a member of both Lloyd George's and Churchill's war cabinets: *Men and Power: 1917–1918* (1957) and *The Decline and Fall of Lloyd George* (1963).

Many of Lloyd George's speeches were published individually, and various of the war speeches were translated into French. There are few collections of whole speeches, however. For the period of the Limehouse speech, there is only *Better Times* (1910), edited by the speaker himself. Selections from the war speeches may be found in *Through Terror to Triumph* . . . (1915) and *The Great Crusade* . . . (1918). Lloyd George's reputation for wit and pungent comment promoted such as the following: *Slings and Arrows: Sayings Chosen from the Speeches of* . . . *David Lloyd George* (1929), edited by the historian Philip Guedalla; and *The Wit and Wisdom of Lloyd George* (1917), compiled and edited by Dan Rider.

---

[33] *BT:* [no cupboard should be barer, no lot should be harder.]

G. B. Shaw, G. K. Chesterton, and Hilaire Belloc

(1856–1953)

The friendly differences between George Bernard Shaw (1856–1950) and the two Catholic idealists, Gilbert Keith Chesterton (1874–1936) and Hilaire Belloc (1870–1953), were a source of satisfaction to the controversialists and of enlightening entertainment to a generation of English readers and listeners. Shaw is, of course, chiefly remembered as dramatist and critic; Chesterton as essayist and novelist; Belloc as historian and poet. It is often forgotten that each man was also an exceptionally active public speaker.

It has been estimated that Shaw delivered some two thousand speeches to a wide variety of audiences.[1] Chesterton and Belloc, whose constant association gave rise to Shaw's amalgam, "The Chesterbelloc," were likewise energetically engaged in lecturing and debating throughout their active careers. In addition, they collaborated in staging mock trials at which personages and concepts were "charged," "prosecuted," "defended," and "judged" in what were essentially rhetorical presentations. Of all these platform activities the Shaw *vs.* "Chesterbelloc" debates that recurred during almost twenty years were the most memorable. Frank Swinnerton remembered the participants and their clashes thus:

> [Shaw, Chesterton, and Belloc] . . . were as happy face to face as they were in column. Sometimes Shaw would debate with Chesterton, and sometimes with Belloc: once, I recall, he debated with Chesterton while Belloc took the chair and rang an infuriating bell; upon another occasion he met Belloc in the large Queen's Hall, when an audience of three thousand people heard these two discuss the question of whether a Democrat who was not also a Socialist could possibly be a Gentleman, and came away with the problem unsolved after two hours of resolute hard hitting. The admiration between these men was not that of the literary nest, but that of the battlefield or the ring.[2]

The announced questions for such debates were often preposterous, but the real issue was always the same: Were the socio-religious, anti-materialistic reforms advocated by Chesterton and Belloc preferable to the materialistic, state socialism advocated by Shaw?

Shaw, Chesterton, and Belloc shared an irrepressible urge to preach. Each embraced the role Shaw described as natural to the Critic:

> Criticism is not only medicinally salutary: it has positive popular attractions in its cruelty, its gladiatorship, and the gratification given to envy by its attacks on the great, and to enthusiasm by its praises. It may say things which many

---

[1] Dan H. Laurence, *Bernard Shaw: Platform and Pulpit* (New York, 1961), p. xiv.

[2] *The Georgian Scene* (New York, 1934), pp. 87–88. Swinnerton appears to mingle memories of a Shaw–Chesterton meeting at Memorial Hall, London, November 30, 1911, and a Shaw–Belloc clash at Queen's Hall, London, January 28, 1913. An abridged text of the former debate appears in Laurence, pp. 86–93.

would like to say, but dare not, and indeed for want of skill could not even if they durst. Its iconoclasms, seditions, and blasphemies, if well turned, tickle those whom they shock; so that the critic adds the privileges of the court jester to those of the confessor.[3]

Chesterton and Belloc assumed this role in the hope of prodding society back toward Catholic unity and economic decentralization; Shaw adopted it for the purpose of hectoring society into "sanity," defined as Shaw's way of viewing things. What Chesterton and Belloc usually debated with Shaw were the premises from which social reform ought to proceed.

On the platform, Shaw was ostensibly casual and undisciplined; in fact, he prepared himself with utmost care for extemporaneous discourse. It was, he said, only by failing often that he had learned the necessity of "letting your audience dictate to you, instead of [you] dictating to them—which they don't like, but I do."[4] Pitted against the lean, bearded Shaw, who gaily violated listeners' conclusions by extending their premises to the breaking point, Chesterton presented a striking and entertaining contrast. He was huge. With imperturbable good humor he disarmingly appealed from Shaw's logic-stretching to common sense. Belloc contrasted with Shaw in a different way. He "would look like John Bull if he did not look like a French parish priest," said Swinnerton. His wit was satiric where Shaw's was ironic; his argumentation was detailed, analytic, and refutative where Shaw's was clever and sweeping; his manner was aggressive where Shaw's was provocative. When Shaw met Chesterton or Belloc in debate, Londoners expected originality of conception and sparkling repartee. But there is perhaps a more significant explanation for these speakers' popularity. They posed what Esmé Wingfield-Stratford called the chief question of the twentieth century's "flight from Victorianism": "Whether . . . it was possible for mankind to level up its mental capacities to the demands of the environment that its own conquest of matter had created."[5]

The debate printed here grew out of G. K. Chesterton's interest in The Distributist League. In 1925, Chesterton published the first issue of G. K.'s Weekly, a journal of social and political opinion. The periodical gave rise to the League, of which Chesterton was the first president and Belloc an active leader. The objectives of this anti-Marxist association included: dissolution of trusts, abolition of giantism in all possible enterprises, and distribution of private ownership by granting special encouragement to small businesses and to small landholders. By late 1927, The Distributist League was nearing the height of its always limited influence, and G. K.'s Weekly arranged that Shaw should debate Chesterton during the League's annual general meeting.

_____

[3] George Bernard Shaw, "Preface" to 1898 edition of The Philanderer, Widowers' Houses, and Mrs Warren's Profession. Reprinted in his Nine Plays (New York, 1935), pp. vii–xxvi.

[4] Quoted in Laurence, p. xii.

[5] The History of British Civilization (rev. ed.; London, 1948), p. 1263.

Do We Agree? *

MR. BELLOC: I am here to take the chair in the debate between two men whom you desire to hear more than you could possibly desire to hear me. They will debate whether they agree or do not agree. From what I know of attempts at agreement between human beings there is a prospect of a very pretty fight. When men debate agreement between nations then you may be certain a disastrous war is on the horizon. I make an exception for the League of Nations, of which I know nothing. If the League of Nations could make a war it would be the only thing it ever has made.

I do not know what Mr. Chesterton is going to say. I do not know what Mr. Shaw is going to say. If I did I would not say it for them. I vaguely gather from what I have heard that they are going to try to discover a principle: whether men should be free to possess private means, as is Mr. Shaw, as is Mr. Chesterton; or should be, like myself, an embarrassed person, a publishers' hack. I could tell them; but my mouth is shut. I am not allowed to say what I think. At any rate, they are going to debate this sort of thing. I know not what more to say. They are about to debate. You are about to listen. I am about to sneer.

MR. SHAW: Mr. Belloc, Ladies and Gentlemen. Our subject this evening, "Do We Agree?" was an inspiration of Mr. Chesterton's. Some of you might reasonably wonder, if we agree, what we are going to debate about. But I suspect that you do not really care much what we debate about provided we entertain you by talking in our characteristic manners.

The reason for this, though you may not know it—and it is my business to tell you—is that Mr. Chesterton and I are two madmen. Instead of doing honest and respectable work and behaving ourselves as ordinary citizens, we go about the world possessed by a strange gift of tongues—in my own case almost exclusively confined to the English language—uttering all sorts of extraordinary opinions for no reason whatever.

Mr. Chesterton tells and prints the most extravagant lies. He takes ordinary incidents of human life—commonplace middle-class life—and gives them a monstrous and strange and gigantic outline. He fills suburban gardens with the most impossible murders; and not only does he invent the murders but also succeeds in discovering the murderer who never committed the murders. I do very much the same sort of thing. I promulgate lies in the shape of plays; but whereas Mr. Chesterton takes events which you think ordinary and makes them gigantic and colossal to reveal their essential miraculousness, I am rather inclined to take these

* This debate took place before a capacity audience at Kingsway Hall, London, on October 28, 1927. Desmond Gleeson asserted years later that the debate was broadcast by radio. See Maisie Ward, *Return to Chesterton* (New York, 1952). The text used here was first published by Cecil Palmer (London, 1928) and is, admittedly, an incomplete record. There are differences between the present text and another published in *G. K.'s Weekly*, VI (November 5, 1927), 725–30. Palmer's is unquestionably the more complete report, but at some points the editor appears to have sacrificed accuracy to brevity and literary polish. Where readings from the *Weekly* clarify a speaker's meaning or significantly restore the language of face-to-face debate, they are supplied in the notes that follow.

things in their utter commonplaceness, and yet to introduce among them outrageous ideas which scandalize the ordinary play-goer and send him away wondering whether he has been standing on his head all his life or whether I am standing on mine.

A man goes to see one of my plays and sits by his wife. Some apparently ordinary thing is said on the stage, and his wife says to him: "Aha! What do you think of that?" Two minutes later another apparently ordinary thing is said and the man turns to his wife and says to her: "Aha! What do *you* think of *that?*"

Curious, is it not, that we should go about doing these things and be tolerated and even largely admired for doing them? Of late years I might say that I have almost been reverenced for doing these things.

Obviously we are mad; and in the East we should be reverenced as madmen. The wisdom of the East says: "Let us listen to these men carefully; but let us not forget that they are madmen."

In this country they say, "Let us listen to these amusing chaps. They are perfectly sane, which we obviously are not." [1] Now there must be some reason for shewing us all this consideration. There must be some force in nature which . . .

[At this point the debate was interrupted by persistent knocking at the doors by ticket-holders who had, through some misunderstanding, been locked out. On the chairman's intervention the doors were opened, and order was restored. Mr. Shaw then proceeded.] [2]

Ladies and Gentlemen, I must go on because, as you see, if I don't begin to talk everybody else does. Now I was speaking of the curious respect in which mad people are held in the East and in this country. What I was leading up to is this, that it matters very little on what points they differ: they have all kinds of aberrations which rise out of their personal circumstances, out of their training, out of their knowledge or ignorance. But if you listen to them carefully and find that at certain points they agree, then you have some reason for supposing that here the spirit of the age is coming through, and giving you an inspired message. Reject all the contradictory things they say and concentrate your attention on the things upon which they agree, and you may be listening to the voice of revelation.

You will do well to-night to listen attentively, because probably what is urging us to these utterances is not personal to ourselves but some conclusion to which all mankind is moving either by reason or by inspiration. The mere fact that Mr. Chesterton and I may agree upon any point may not at all prevent us from debating it passionately. I find that the people who fight me generally hold the very ideas I am trying to express. I do not know if it is because they resent the liberty I am taking or because they do not like the words I use or the twist of my mind; but they are the people who quarrel most with me.

You have at this moment a typical debate raging in the Press. You have a very pretty controversy going on in the Church of England between the Archbishop of

[1] *G. K.'s Weekly* has "we" and "they" exactly transposed in this sentence.
[2] According to Desmond Gleeson the disturbance was provoked by one of Chesterton's friends who, like others who arrived late or were without tickets, found himself locked out of the hall when the broadcast began. See Ward, *Return to Chesterton*, pp. 271–72.

Canterbury and the Bishop of Birmingham.[3] I hope you have all read the admirable letter of the Archbishop of Canterbury. Everybody is pleased with that letter. It has the enormous virtue of being entirely good-humoured, of trying to make peace, of avoiding making mischief: a popular English virtue which is a credit to the English race. But it has another English quality which is a little more questionable, and that is the quality of being entirely anti-intellectual. The letter is a heartfelt appeal for ambiguity. You can imagine the Archbishop of Canterbury, if he were continuing the controversy in private, saying to the Bishop of Birmingham: "Now, my dear Barnes, let me recommend you to read that wonderful book, *The Pilgrim's Progress*. Read the history of the hero, Christian, no doubt a very splendid fellow, and from the literary point of view the only hero of romantic fiction resembling a real man. But he is always fighting. He is out of one trouble into another. He is leading a terrible life. How different to that great Peacemaker, Mr. Facing-Both-Ways! Mr. Facing-Both-Ways has no history. Happy is the country that has no history; and happy, you may say, is the man who has no history; and Mr. Facing-Both-Ways in *The Pilgrim's Progress* is that man."

Bunyan, by the way, does not even mention Mr. Facing-Both-Ways' extraordinary historical feat of drafting the Twenty-seventh Article of the Church of England.[4] There being some very troublesome people for Elizabeth to deal with—Catholics and Puritans, for instance, quarrelling about Transubstantiation—Mr. Facing-Both-Ways drafted an Article in two paragraphs. The first paragraph affirmed the doctrine of Transubstantiation. The second paragraph said it was an idle superstition. Then Queen Elizabeth was able to say, "Now you are all satisfied; and you must all attend the Church of England. If you don't I will send you to prison."

[3] On October 16, 1927, Dr. E. W. Barnes, Bishop of Birmingham, preached at St. Paul's Cathedral, London. Before he began to speak, Canon G. R. Bullock-Webster, rector of St. Michael, Paternoster Royal, "robed in cassock and surplice," walked up the transept, turned to the congregation, and denounced the Bishop for "false and heretical teaching." The Canon and his followers then withdrew and Bishop Barnes preached on "Man's Creation: Blind Mechanism or Divine Design?" In a public letter to the Archbishop of Canterbury, Bishop Barnes protested the Canon's intrusion and defended his own teaching. He specifically insisted that "we have no right to assume the existence of spiritual properties in an inanimate object [the bread and wine of the Holy Communion sacrament] unless they can be spiritually discerned—which no one can do." The Archbishop's reply was published October 24. It condemned the Canon's action, assured Bishop Barnes that no one "desires to drive you either to Rome or to Tennessee," declined to take issue with the Bishop's doctrine on Transubstantiation, but pointed out that the Bishop's language in previous sermons had offended many communicants by seeming to treat their different views contemptuously. These exchanges received extensive coverage and editorial comment in London newspapers the week before the Shaw–Chesterton debate.

[4] Either Shaw or the text is in error. The Article in question is Article XXVIII of The Thirty-Nine Articles of the Church of England. The first paragraph to which Shaw refers says in part, "the Bread which we break is a partaking of the Body of Christ; and likewise the cup of blessing is a partaking of the Blood of Christ." The second paragraph includes these words: "Transubstantiation . . . in the Supper of the Lord cannot be proved by Holy Writ; but it is repugnant to the plain words of Scripture, overthroweth the nature of a Sacrament, and hath given occasion to many superstitions." See E. J. Bicknell, *A Theological Introduction to the Thirty-Nine Articles of the Church of England* (3rd ed., Glasgow, 1955), pp. 382–83.

But I am not for one moment going to debate the doctrine of Transubstantiation. I mention it only to shew, by the controversy between the Archbishop and the Bishop, that in most debates you will find two types of mind playing with the same subject. There is one sort of mind that I think is my own sort. I sometimes call it the Irish mind, as distinct from the English mind. But that is only to make the English and Irish sit up and listen. Spengler talks not of Irish and English minds, but of the Greek, or Grecian mind, and the Gothic mind—the Faustian mind as he, being a German, calls it. And in this controversy you find that what is moving Bishop Barnes is a Grecian dislike of not knowing what it is he believes, and on the other side a Gothic instinctive feeling that it is perhaps just as well not to know too distinctly. I am not saying which is the better type of mind. I think on the whole both of them are pretty useful. But I always like to know what it is I am preaching. It gets me into trouble in England, where people say, "Why go into these matters? Why do you want to think so accurately and sharply?" I can only say that my head is built that way; but I protest that I do not claim any moral superiority because when I know what I mean the other people do not know what they mean, and very often do not know what I mean. And one subject on which I know what I mean is the opinion which has inevitably been growing up for the last hundred years or so, not so much an opinion as a revolt against the mis-distribution, the obviously monstrous and anomalous mis-distribution of wealth under what we call the capitalist system.

I have always, since I got clear on the subject of Socialism, said, Don't put in the foreground the nationalization of the means of production, distribution, and exchange: you will never get there if you begin with them. You have to begin with the question of the distribution of wealth.

The other day a man died and the Government took four and a half million pounds as death duty on his property. That man made all his money by the labour of men who received twenty-six shillings a week after years of qualifying for their work. Was that a reasonable distribution of wealth between them? We are all coming to the opinion that it was not reasonable. What does Mr. Chesterton think about it? I want to know, not only because of the public importance of his opinions, but because I have always followed Mr. Chesterton with extraordinary interest and enjoyment, and his assent to any view of mine is a great personal pleasure, because I am very fond of Mr. Chesterton.

Mr. Chesterton has rejected Socialism nominally, probably because it is a rather stupid word. But he is a Distributist, which means to-day a Redistributist. He has arrived by his own path at my own position. (Laughter.) I do not see why you should laugh: I cannot imagine anything more natural.

But now comes the question upon which I will ask Mr. Chesterton whether he agrees with me or not. The moment I made up my mind that the present distribution of wealth was wrong, the peculiar constitution of my brain obliged me to find out exactly how far it was wrong and what is the right distribution. I went through all the proposals ever made and through the arguments used in justification of the existing distribution; and I found they were utterly insensate and grotesque.

Eventually I was convinced that we ought to be tolerant of any sort of crime except unequal distribution of income. In organized society the question always arises at what point are we justified in killing for the good of the community. I should answer in this way. If you take two shillings as your share and another man wants two shillings and sixpence, kill him. Similarly, if a man accepts two shillings while you have two shillings and sixpence, kill him.

On the stroke of the hour, I ask Mr. Chesterton: "Do you agree with that?"

MR. CHESTERTON: Ladies and gentlemen. The answer is in the negative. I don't agree with it. Nor does Mr. Shaw. He does not think, any more than I do, that all the people in this hall, who have already created some confusion, should increase the confusion by killing each other and searching each other's pockets to see whether there is half-a-crown or two shillings in them. As regards the general question, what I want to say is this: I should like to say to begin with that I have no intention of following Mr. Shaw into a discussion which would be very improper on my part on the condition of the Church of England. But since he has definitely challenged me on the point I will say—he will not agree—that Mr. Shaw is indeed a peacemaker and has reconciled both sides. For if the Archbishop is anti-intellectual, there will be nobody to pretend that the Bishop is intellectual.

A VOICE: Yes he is.

MR. CHESTERTON: Now as to the much more interesting question, about a much more interesting person than Bishop Barnes—I mean Mr. Shaw—I should like to say that in a sense I can agree with him, in which case he can claim a complete victory. This is not a real controversy or debate. It is an enquiry, and I hope a profitable and interesting enquiry. Up to a point I quite agree with him, because I did start entirely by agreeing with him, as many years ago I began by being a Socialist, just as he was a Socialist. Barring some difference of age we were in the same position. We grew in beauty side by side. I will not say literally we filled one home with glee: but I do believe we have filled a fair number of homes with glee. Whether those homes included our own personal households it is for others to say. But up to a point I agreed with Mr. Shaw by being a Socialist, and I agreed upon grounds he has laid down with critical justice and lucidity, grounds which I can imagine nobody being such a fool as to deny: the distribution of property in the modern world is a monstrosity and a blasphemy. Thus I come to the important stage of the proceedings. I claim that I might agree with Mr. Shaw a step farther.

I have heard from nearly all the Socialists I have known, the phrase which Mr. Shaw has with characteristic artfulness avoided, a phrase which I think everyone will agree is common to collectivist philosophy, and the phrase is this: "that the means of production should be owned by the community." I ask you to note that phrase because it is really upon that that the whole question turns.

Now there is a sense in which I do agree with Mr. Bernard Shaw. There is a point up to which I would agree with that formula. So far as is possible under human conditions I should desire the community—or, as we used to call it in the old English language, the Commons—to own the means of production. So far, I say, you have Mr. Bernard Shaw and me walking in fact side by side in the flowery meads. But after that, alas! a change takes place. The change is owing to Mr. Shaw's vast superiority, to his powerful intellect. It is not my fault if he has remained young, while I have grown in comparison wrinkled and haggard, old and experienced, and acquainted with the elementary facts of human life.

Now the first thing I want to note is this. When you say the community ought to own the means of production, what do you mean? That is the whole point. There was a time when Mr. Shaw would probably have said in all sincerity that anything possessed by the State or the Government would be in fact possessed by the Commons: in other words, by the community. I do not wish to challenge Mr. Shaw about later remarks of his, but I doubt whether Mr. Shaw, in his eternal youth, still believes in democracy in that sense. I quite admit he has a more hopeful and hearty outlook in some respects, and he has even gone to the length of saying that if democracy will not do for mankind, perhaps it will do for some other creature different from mankind. He has almost proposed to invent a new animal, which might be supposed to live for 300 years. I am inclined to think that if Mr. Shaw lived for 300 years—and I heartily hope he will—I never knew a man more likely to do it—he would certainly agree with me. I would even undertake to prove it from the actual history of the last 300 years, but though I think it is probable I will not insist upon it. As a very profound philosopher has said, "You never can tell." And it may be that Mr. Shaw's immortal power of talking nonsense would survive even that 300 years and he would still be fixed in his unnatural theories in the matter.

Now I do not believe myself that Mr. Shaw thinks that the community, in the sense of that state which owns and rules, the thing that issues postage stamps and provides policemen, I do not believe he thinks that that community is now, at this moment, identical with the Commons, and I do not believe he really thinks that in his own socialistic state it would be identical. I am glad therefore that he has sufficient disordered common sense to perceive that, as a matter of fact, when you have vast systems, however just and however reasonably controlled, indirectly, by elaborate machinery of officials and other things, you do in fact find that those who rule are the few. It may be a good thing or a bad thing, but it is not true that all the people directly control. Collectivism has put all their eggs in one basket. I do not think that Mr. Shaw believes, or that anybody believes, that 12,000,000 men, say, carry the basket, or look after the basket, or have any real distributed control over the eggs in the basket. I believe that it is controlled from the centre by a few people. They may be quite right or quite necessary. A certain limit to that sort of control any sane man will recognize as necessary: it is not the same as the Commons controlling the means of production. It is a few oligarchs or a few officials who do in fact control all the means of production.

What Mr. Shaw means is not that all the people should control the means of production, but that the product should be distributed among the vast mass of the Commons, and that is quite a different thing. It is not controlling the means of production at all. If all the citizens had simply an equal share of the income of the State they would not have any control of the capital. That is where G. K. Chesterton differs from George Bernard Shaw. I begin at the other end. I do not think that a community arranged on the principles of Distributism and on nothing else would be a perfect community. All admit that the society that we propose is more a matter of proportion and arrangement than a perfectly clear system in which all production is pooled and the result given out in wages. But what I say is this: Let us, so far as is possible in the complicated affairs of humanity, put into the hands of the Commons the control of the means of production—and real control. The man who owns a piece of land controls it in a direct and real sense. He really owns the means of production. It is the same with a man who owns a piece of machinery. He can use it or not use it. Even a man who owns his own tools or works in his own workshop, to that extent owns and controls the means of production.

But if you establish right in the middle of the State one enormous machine, if you turn the handle of that machine, and somebody, who must be an official, and therefore a ruler, distributes to everybody equally the food or whatever else is produced by that machine, no single one of any of these people receiving more than any other single person, but all equal fragments: that fulfils a definite ideal of equality, yet no single one of those citizens has any control over the means of production. They have no control whatever—unless you think that the prospect of voting about once every five years for Mr. Vanboodle—then a Socialist member— with the prospect that he will or will not make a promise to a political assembly or that he will or will not promise to ask a certain question which may or may not be answered—unless you think that by this means they possess control.

I have used the metaphor of the Collectivists of having all your eggs in one basket. Now there are men whom we are pleased to call bad eggs. They are not all of them in politics. On the other hand there are men who deserve the encomium of "good egg." There are, in other words, a number of good men and a number of bad men scattered among the commonwealth.

To put the matter shortly, I might say that all this theory of absolutely equal mechanical distribution depends upon a sort of use of the passive mood. It is easy enough to say Property should be distributed, but who is, as it were, the subject of the verb? Who or what is to distribute? Now it is based on the idea that the central power which condescends to distribute will be permanently just, wise, sane, and representative of the conscience of the community which has created it.

That is what we doubt. We say there ought to be in the world a great mass of scattered powers, privileges, limits, points of resistance, so that the mass of the Commons may resist tyranny. And we say that there is a permanent possibility of that central direction, however much it may have been appointed to distribute money equally, becoming a tyranny. I do not think it would be difficult to suggest a way in which it could happen. As soon as any particular mob of people are behaving in some way which the governing group chooses to regard as anti-civic, supplies could be cut off easily with the approval of this governing group. You have only to call someone by some name like Bolshevist or Papist. You have only to tie some label on a set of people and the community will contentedly see these people starved into surrender.

We say the method to be adopted is the other method. We admit, frankly, that our method is in a sense imperfect, and only in that sense illogical. It is imperfect, or illogical, because it corresponds to the variety and differences of human life. Mr. Shaw is making abstract diagrams of triangles, squares, and circles; we are trying to paint a portrait, the portrait of a man. We are trying to make our lines and colours follow the characteristics of the real object. Man desires certain things. He likes a certain amount of liberty, certain kinds of ownership, certain kinds of local affection, and won't be happy without them.

There are a great many other things that might be said, but I think it will be clearer if I repeat some of the things we have already said.

I do in that sense accept the proposition that the community should own the means of production, but I say that the Commons should own the means of production, and the only way to do that is to keep actual hold upon land. Mr. Bernard Shaw proposes to distribute wealth. We propose to distribute power.

MR. SHAW: I cannot say that Mr. Chesterton has succeeded in forcing a difference of opinion on me. There are, I suppose, at least some people in this room who have heard me orating on this platform at lectures of the Fabian Society, and they must have been considerably amused at Mr. Chesterton's attempt to impress upon me what income is. My main activity as an economist of late has been to try to concentrate the attention of my party on the fact not only that they must distribute income, but that there is nothing else to distribute.[5]

We must be perfectly clear as to what capital is. I will tell you. Capital is spare money. And, of course, spare money means spare food. If I happen to have more of the means of subsistence than I can use, I may take that part that is unconsumed, and say to another man: "Let me feed you whilst you produce some kind of contraption that will facilitate my work in future." But when the man has produced it for me, the capital has all gone: there is nothing left for me or him to eat. If he has made me a spade I cannot eat that spade.

I have said I *may* employ my spare subsistence in this way; but I *must* employ it so because it will not keep: if nobody eats it, it will go rotten. The only thing to be done with it is to have it promptly consumed. All that remains of it then is a figure in a ledger. Some of my capital was employed in the late war; and this country has still my name written down as the proprietor of the capital they blew to pieces in that war.[6]

Having said that for your instruction, let us come down to facts. Mr. Chesterton has formed the Distributist League which organized this meeting.[7] What was the very first thing the League said must be done? It said the coal-mines must be nationalized. Instead of saying that the miner's means of production must be made his own property, it was forced to advocate making national property of the coal-mines. These coal-mines, when nationalized, will not be managed by the House of Commons: if they were you would very soon have no coal. But neither will they be managed by the miners. If you ask the man working in the mine to manage the mine he will say, "Not me, governor! That is your job."

I would like Mr. Chesterton to consider what he understands by the means of production. He has spoken of them in rather a nineteenth-century manner. He has been talking as though the means of production were machines. I submit to you that the real means of production in this country are men and women, and that consequently you always have the maximum control of the individual over the means of production, because it means self-control over his own person. But he must surrender that control to the manager of the mine because he does not know how to manage it himself. Under the present capitalistic system he has to surrender it to the manager appointed by the proprietors of the mine. Under

[5] G. K.'s Weekly adds a sentence here: "Control of capital in the sense of its being a distributable thing, and at the same time being identical with machinery is a complete delusion."

[6] G. K.'s Weekly reports two further sentences here: "Some of the Socialists make the same kind of mistake. Some of them, too, want to have their cake and eat it."

[7] From this point to the end of the paragraph the text in G. K.'s Weekly reads: "He has been explaining his notion of distributing property, which I want to abolish altogether. What was his first regular utterance on the subject? What was the very first thing the League said must be done? They said the coal-mines must be nationalized. Instead of saying Mr. Hodges's own garden must be made his own property, they were forced to advocate making national property of the coal-mines. No doubt these coal-mines, when nationalized, will not be controlled by the Commons: if they were, you would very soon have no coal. If you ask the man working in the mine to rule the mine he would say, 'No thanks, governor: that is your job.'"

Socialism he would have to surrender it to the manager appointed by the Coal-master-General. That would not prevent the product of the mine being equally distributed among the people.

There is no difficulty here. In a sense Mr. Chesterton really does not disagree with me in this matter, since he does see that in the matter of fuel in this country you have to come to nationalization. Fuel must be controlled equally for the benefit of all the people. Since we agreed upon that, I am not disposed to argue the matter further. Now that Mr. Chesterton agrees that the coal-mines will have to be nationalized he will be led by the same pressure of facts to agree to the nationalization of everything else.

I have to allow for the pressure of facts because, as a playwright, I think of all problems in terms of actual men and women. Mr. Chesterton lets himself idealize them sometimes as virtuous peasant proprietors and self-managing petty capitalists.[8]

The capitalist and the landlord have their own particular ways of robbing the poor; but their legal rights are quite different. It is a very direct way on the part of the landlord. He may do exactly what he likes with the land he owns. If I own a large part of Scotland I can turn the people off the land practically into the sea, or across the sea. I can take women in child-bearing and throw them into the snow and leave them there. That has been done. I can do it for no better reason than that I think it is better to shoot deer on the land than allow people to live on it. They might frighten the deer.

But now compare that with the ownership of my umbrella. As a matter of fact the umbrella I have to-night belongs to my wife; but I think she will permit me to call it mine for the purpose of the debate. Now I have a very limited legal right to the use of that umbrella. I cannot do as I like with it. For instance, certain passages in Mr. Chesterton's speech tempted me to get up and smite him over the head with my umbrella. I may presently feel inclined to smite Mr. Belloc. But should I abuse my right to do what I like with my property—with my umbrella—in this way I should soon be made aware—possibly by Mr. Belloc's fist—that I cannot treat my umbrella as my own property in the way in which a landlord can treat his land. I want to destroy ownership in order that possession and enjoyment may be raised to the highest point in every section of the community. That, I think, is perfectly simple.

There are points on which a landlord, even a Scottish landlord, and his tenant the crofter entirely agree. The landlord objects to being shot at sight. The Irish landlord used to object. His tenants sometimes took no notice of his objection; but all the same they had a very strong objection to being shot themselves. You have no objection to a State law being carried out vigorously that people shall not shoot one another. There is no difficulty in modern civilized States in having it carried out. If you could once convince the people that inequality of income is a greater social danger than murder, very few people would want to continue to commit it; and the State could suppress it with the assent of the community gen-

[8] An additional paragraph appears at this point in the *Weekly*:
"It is very difficult to get a trustworthy State. Under the capitalist system it is utterly impossible. If putting all your eggs into different baskets means breaking up property among many capitalists, to work as they like, you will never get your common property. The capitalist State is built up to represent and carry out the desires of the people only so long as those desires coincide with the desires of the capitalists who really control the State."

erally. We are always adding fresh crimes to the calendar. Why not enact that no person shall live in this community without pulling his weight in the social boat, without producing more than he consumes—because you have to provide for the accumulation of spare money as capital—who does not replace by his own labour what he takes out of the community, who attempts to live idly, as men are proud to live nowadays. Is there any greater difficulty in treating such a parasite as a malefactor, than in treating a murderer as a malefactor? [9]

Having said that much about the property part of the business, I think I have succeeded in establishing that Mr. Chesterton does not disagree with me. I should like to say I do not believe in Democracy. I do believe in Catholicism; but I hold that the Irish Episcopal Protestant Church, of which I was baptized a member, takes the name of Catholicism in vain; that the Roman Church has also taken it in vain; and so with the Greek Church and the rest. My Catholicism is really catholic Catholicism: that is what I believe in, as apart from this voting business and democracy. Does Mr. Chesterton agree with me on that?

MR. CHESTERTON: Among the bewildering welter of fallacies which Mr. Shaw has just given us, I prefer to deal first with the simplest. When Mr. Shaw refrains from hitting me over the head with his umbrella, the real reason—apart from his real kindness of heart, which makes him tolerant of the humblest of the creatures of God—is not because he does not own his umbrella, but because he does not own my head. As I am still in possession of that imperfect organ, I will proceed to use it to the confutation of some of his other fallacies.

I should like to say now what I ought perhaps to have said earlier in the evening, that we are enormously grateful to Mr. Shaw for his characteristic generosity in consenting to debate with a humble movement like our own. I am so conscious of that condescension on his part that I should feel it a very unfair return to ask him to read any of our potty little literature or cast his eye over our little weekly paper or become conscious of the facts we have stated a thousand times. One of these facts, with which every person who knows us is familiar, is our position with regard to the coal question. We have said again and again that in our human state of society there must be a class of things called exceptions. We admit that upon the whole in the very peculiar case of coal it is desirable and about the best way out of the difficulty that it should be controlled by the officials of the State, just in the same way as postage stamps are controlled. No one says anything else about postage stamps. I cannot imagine that anyone wants to have his own postage stamps, of perhaps more picturesque design and varied colours. I can assure you that Distributists are perfectly sensible and sane people, and they have always recognized that there are institutions in the State in which it is very difficult to apply the principle of individual property, and that one of these cases is the discovery under the earth of valuable minerals. Socialists are not alone in believing this. Charles I, who, I suppose, could not be called a Socialist, pointed out that certain kinds of minerals ought to belong to the State, that is, to the Commons. We have said over and over again that we support the nationalization of the coal-mines, not as a general example of Distribution but as a common-sense admission of an exception. The reason why we make it an exception is because

---

[9] G. K.'s Weekly adds two sentences here: "Mr. Chesterton is raising an unreal difficulty. These things can be done if you can once create public opinion enough to back them."

it is not very easy to see how the healthy principle of personal ownership can be applied. If it could we should apply it with the greatest pleasure. We consider personal ownership infinitely more healthy. If there were a way in which a miner could mark out one particular piece of coal and say, "This is mine, and I am proud of it," we should have made an enormous improvement upon State management. There are cases in which it is very difficult to apply the principle, and that is one of them. It is the reverse of the truth for Mr. Shaw to say that the logic of that fact will lead me to the application of the same principle to other cases, like the ownership of the land. One could not illustrate it better than by the case of coal. It may be true for all I know that if you ask a miner if he would like to manage the mine he would say, "I do not want to manage it; it is for my betters to manage it." I had not noticed that meek and simple manner among miners. I have even heard complaints of the opposite temper in that body. I defy Mr. Shaw to say if you went to the Irish farmers, or the French farmers, or the Serbian or the Dutch farmers, or any of the millions of peasant owners throughout the world, I defy him to say if you went to the farmer and said, "Who controls these farms?" he would say, "It is not for the likes of me to control a farm." Mr. Shaw knows perfectly well it is nonsense to suggest that peasants would talk that way anywhere. It is part of his complaints against peasants that they claim personal possessions. I am not likely to be led to the denial of property in land, for I know ordinary normal people who feel property in land to be normal. I fully agree with Mr. Shaw, and speak as strongly as he would speak, of the abomination and detestable foulness and sin of landlords who drove poor people from their land in Scotland and elsewhere. It is quite true that men in possession of land have committed these crimes; but I do not see why wicked officials under a socialistic state could not commit these crimes. But that has nothing to do with the principle of ownership in land. In fact these very Highland crofters, these very people thus abominably outraged and oppressed, if you asked them what they want would probably say, "I want to own my own croft; I want to own my own land."

Mr. Shaw's dislike of the landlord is not so much a denial of the right to private property, not so much that he owns the land, but that the landlord has swallowed up private property. In the face of these facts of millions and millions of ordinary human beings who have private property, who know what it is like to own property, I must confess that I am not overwhelmed and crushed by Mr. Shaw's claim that he knows all about men and women as they really are. I think Mr. Shaw knows something about certain kinds of men and women; though he sometimes makes them a little more amusing than they really are. But I cannot agree with his discovery that peasants do not like peasant property, because I know the reverse is the fact.

Then we come to the general point he raised about the State. He raised a very interesting question. He said that after all the State does command respect, that we all do accept laws even though they are issued by an official group. Up to a point I willingly accept his argument. The Distributist is certainly not an anarchist. He does not believe it would be a good thing if there were no such laws. But the reason why most of these laws are accepted is because they correspond with the common conscience of mankind. Mr. Shaw and Bishop Barnes might think it would be an inadequate way of explaining it, but we might call attention to an Hebraic code called the Ten Commandments. They do, I think, correspond pretty roughly to the moral code of every religion that is at all sane.

These all reverence certain ideas about "Thou shalt not kill." They all have a reverence for the commandment which says, "Thou shalt not covet thy neighbour's goods." They reverence the idea that you must not covet his house or his ox or his ass. It should be noted, too, that besides forbidding us to covet our neighbour's property, this commandment also implies that every man has a right to own some property.

MR. SHAW: I now want to ask Mr. Chesterton why he insists, on the point about the nationalization of the coal-mines—on which he agrees with me—that they are an exception. Are they an exception? In what way are the coal-mines an exception? What is the fundamental reason why you must nationalize your coal-mine? The reason is this. If you will go up to the constituency of Mr. Sidney Webb,[10] to the Sunderland coast, you will be able to pick up coal for nothing, absolutely nothing at all. You see people doing it there. You take a perambulator, or barrow, or simple sack, and when the tide goes out you go out on the foreshore and pick up excellent coal. If you go to other parts of England, like Whitehaven, you will find you have to go through workings driven out under the sea, which took 20 years to make, 20 years continual expenditure of capital before coal could be touched, where men going down the shaft have to travel sometimes two or three miles to their work. That is the reason at bottom why you cannot distribute your coal-mine. The reason you have to pay such monstrous prices for your coal is they are fixed by the cost of making the submarine mines. People who have mines like the Sunderland foreshore naturally make colossal fortunes. Everyone can see at once that in order to have any kind of equable dealing in coal, the only way is to charge the citizens the average cost for the total national supply. You cannot average the cost of putting your eggs into different baskets.[11] Now this is not the exception: it is the rule.[12] You have exactly the same difference in the case of the land. You have land worth absolutely nothing at all and land worth a million an acre or more. And the acre worth more than a million and the acre worth nothing are within half-an-hour's drive in a taxi.

You cannot say that the coal-mine is an exception. The coal-mine is only one instance. Mr. Chesterton in arriving at the necessity for the nationalization of the coal-mines has started on his journey towards the nationalization of all the industries. If he goes on to the land, and from the land to the factory, and from there to every other industrial department, he will find that every successive case is an exception; and eventually he will have to say to himself: "I think it will be better to call nationalization the rule rather than the exception."

I must deny that I ever said that the coal-miner says he wants to be ruled by his betters. I may not be a democrat; but I am not a snob. Intellectually I am a snob, and you will admit that I have good ground for that. Socially I am not a

[10] Sidney Webb and his wife, Beatrice, were central figures in the Fabian Society, which was formed to advance Socialism. Shaw was actively associated with the Society. Webb was elected to Parliament as a Labour Party member for Seaham Harbour in 1922.

[11] G. K.'s Weekly inserts the following at this point: "Mr. Chesterton says he knows it is impossible and he regrets that every man cannot go down and pick up his own scuttle of coals. I should like to see Mr. Chesterton do it. To come to the point."

[12] Here G. K.'s Weekly inserts: "Mr. Chesterton talks very little about the city worker, the urban worker. He is a different animal. You have exactly the same difference in the case of land."

snob. There is no question of betters at all in the matter.[13] The manager is not better than the executant, nor the executant better than the manager. Both are equally necessary and equally honorable. But if you ask the executant to manage he will refuse on the ground that it is not his job; and vice versa.

Mr. Chesterton says he does not see why State officials under a system which recognizes nationalization of land should not act as the old landlords acted. I should say, in the first place, they won't have the power. A State official does what he is instructed to do and paid to do, just as a landlord's agent does; and there is no more danger of the official making himself a landlord than there is now of the agent making himself one.

As to the instinct of owning—and you have it widely in the country—you have not got it in the towns. People are content to live in houses they do not own: when they possess them they often find them a great nuisance.[14] But you must not conclude that because a miner would refuse to manage a mine a farmer will refuse to manage his farm. The farmer is himself a manager.

How does this wonderful system of peasant proprietorship work? Do you realise that it has to be broken up every day? The reason is that when a man owning a farm has a family, each son, when the farmer dies, has a right to an equal part of the land. They find that this arrangement is entirely impossible, and they have to make some other arrangement, and some of the sons have to go off into the towns to work. It is unthinkable that all could remain on the land: you cannot split up the land and give every person a bit of property.

I have stolen two minutes from Mr. Chesterton, and I apologise.

MR. CHESTERTON: I am sure Mr. Shaw is very welcome to as many minutes as I can offer him, or anything else, for his kindness in entertaining us this evening. It is rather late now and there is not much time left for me. He has been rather slow in discovering what Distributism is and what the whole question is about. If this were the beginning of the discussion I could go over our system completely. I could tell him exactly what we think about property in towns. It is absurd to say it does not exist.

In rural ownership different problems have to be faced. We are not cutting a thing up into mathematical squares. We are trying to deal with human beings, creatures quite outside the purview of Mr. Shaw and his political philosophy. We know town people are a little different from country people; business of one kind is different from business of another kind; difficulties arise about family, and all the rest of it. We show [sic] man's irrepressible desire to own property and be-

---

[13] The remaining sentences of this paragraph do not appear in the *Weekly*. Instead, the following remarks are reported: "On the strength of this system of private property the State officials are instructed and employed to carry out these evictions from the land. When the landlord turns people out, he does not actually do it himself; he sends an official. The official does it because he is employed to do it, because he is paid to do it. For precisely the same reason he will do the other thing. For precisely the same reason he will call on the landlord and take from him the entire rent of the land."

[14] The remainder of this paragraph reads as follows in the *Weekly*: "Take this question of the peasant. There is no parallel between my case of a coal-miner refusing to manage the mine and my going to a farmer who is managing a farm and expecting to hear the same thing. I did not say if you went to the manager of a coal-mine he would say, 'Let the men manage it.' He will say at once they can't. When you go to the peasant proprietor he will say he can do it."

cause some landlords have been cruel, it is no use talking of abolishing, denying, and destroying property, saying no one shall have any property at all. It is characteristic of his school, of his age. The morality he represents is, above all, the morality of negations. Just as it says you must not drink wine at all as the only solution to a few people drinking too much: just as it would say you must not touch meat or smoke tobacco at all.[15] Let us always remember, therefore, that when Mr. Shaw says he can persuade all men to give up the sentiment of private property, it is in exactly the same hopeful spirit that he says he will get all of you to give up meat, tobacco, beer, and a vast number of other things. He will not do anything of the sort and I suspect he himself suspects by this time that he will not do it. It is quite false to say you must have a centralised machinery, even in towns. It is quite false to say that all forces must be used, as they are in monopolies, from the centre. It is absurd to say that because the wind is a central thing you cannot separate windmills. How am I to explain all that in five minutes? I could go through a vast number of fallacies into which he has fallen. He said, ironically, he would like to see me go down a mine. I have no difficulty in imagining myself sinking in such a fashion in any geological deposit.[16] I really should like to see him doing work on a farm, because he would find out about five hundred pieces of nonsense he has been speaking to be the nonsense they are.

It is absolutely fallacious to suggest that there is some sort of difficulty in peasantries whereby they are bound to disappear. The answer to that is that they have not disappeared. It is part of the very case against peasantry, among those who do not like them, that they are antiquated, covered with hoary superstition. Why have they remained through all these centuries, if they must immediately break up and become impossible? There is an answer to all that and I am quite prepared to give it at some greater length than five minutes. But at no time did I say that we must make the whole community a community of agricultural peasants. It is absurd. What I said was that a desire for property which is universal, everywhere, does appear in a perfect and working example in the ownership of land. It only remains for me to say one thing. Mr. Shaw said, in reference to the State owning the means of production, that men and women are the only means of production. I quite accept the parallel of the phrase. His proposition is that the government, the officials of the State, should own the men and women: in other words that the men and women should be slaves.

Mr. Belloc: I was told when I accepted this onerous office that I was to sum up. I shall do nothing of the sort. In a very few years from now this debate will be antiquated. I will now recite you a poem:

> Our civilization
> Is built upon coal.
> Let us chaunt in rotation
> Our civilization
> That lump of damnation
> Without any soul,
> Our civilization
> Is built upon coal.

---

[15] Among Shaw's many causes were vegetarianism and opposition to the use of tobacco.

[16] Chesterton was as ready as his friends to find humor in his own great girth.

> In a very few years
> It will float upon oil.
> Then give three hearty cheers,
> In a very few years
> We shall mop up our tears
> And have done with our toil.
> In a very few years
> It will float upon oil.

In I do not know how many years—five, ten, twenty—this debate will be as antiquated as crinolines are. I am surprised that neither of the two speakers pointed out that one of three things is going to happen. One of three things: not one of two. It is always one of three things. This industrial civilization which, thank God, oppresses only the small part of the world in which we are most inextricably bound up, will break down and therefore end from its monstrous wickedness, folly, ineptitude, leading to a restoration of sane, ordinary human affairs, complicated but based as a whole upon the freedom of the citizens. Or it will break down and lead to nothing but a desert. Or it will lead the mass of men to become contented slaves, with a few rich men controlling them. Take your choice. You will all be dead before any of the three things comes off. One of the three things is going to happen, or a mixture of two, or possibly a mixture of the three combined.

~

Bibliographical Note

Two volumes of Shaw's speeches have recently been published: *The Religious Speeches of Bernard Shaw*, edited by Warren S. Smith (1963), and *Bernard Shaw: Platform and Pulpit*, edited by Dan H. Laurence (1961). The introductions to these works and Marie Hochmuth Nichols' "George Bernard Shaw: Rhetorician and Public Speaker," which appears in her *Rhetoric and Criticism* (1963), are the best published critiques of Shaw as a speaker. The speeches of G. K. Chesterton and Hilaire Belloc have not been systematically studied.

In the vast literature on Shaw's career, Archibald Henderson's *George Bernard Shaw, Man of the Century* (1956) and Richard M. Ohmann's *Shaw: The Style and the Man* (1962) are especially valuable to the serious student. Hesketh Pearson's *Bernard Shaw: His Life and Personality* is probably the best popular biography.

G. K. Chesterton's speaking is treated incidentally in Maisie Ward's *Gilbert Keith Chesterton* (1943) and *Return to Chesterton* (1952). These works form the best biographical sources on Chesterton. Garry Wills' *Chesterton, Man and Mask* (1961) adds valuable literary and philosophical insights.

The best biography of Belloc is Robert Speaight's *Life of Hilaire Belloc* (1957). It gives passing attention to Belloc's platform activities.

The Abdication of Edward VIII
(December, 1936)

The abdication of Edward VIII on December 11, 1936, was the first and, to date, the only voluntary one in English history. The abdication itself, the events that led to it, the various issues raised, the personalities involved, all combined to produce a historical drama that was the more spectacular for being played against the somber backdrop of the Europe of 1936. Both the audience and the critics have supplied it with numerous and diverse interpretative subtitles which include among others: one of the world's great all-for-love stories; a personal melodrama; a constitutional crisis; a struggle between conservative tradition and liberal modernism; even "an event . . . perhaps partly responsible for the present [1953] plight of the world."[1] Whatever history's final appraisal of the whole performance may be, millions of people around the globe were able to make their own first-hand evaluation of its curtain speech. This speech was, of course, Edward's now famous farewell broadcast to his people.

The focal point of the dramatic conflict was the King's determination to marry Mrs. Wallis Simpson, an American whose second divorce was pending. The marriage was opposed by Prime Minister Stanley Baldwin and his Cabinet, who found a union involving such a record of divorce incompatible with the throne—a viewpoint shared and supported by the Church.

The royal romance, begun when Edward was still Prince of Wales, was practically unknown to the British public until December 2 or 3, because of the voluntary silence maintained by the newspapers until then. However, it had been for some time the subject of discussion in London court and political circles and in the American press, whose increasing coverage of it during the summer and fall of 1936 had been spreading into and alarming the British Dominions, especially Canada. It was this last fact and the imminence of the divorce proceedings, which began October 27, that brought the first official (though private) acknowledgment by the Prime Minister on October 20.[2] From then on, the situation developed from a serious into a critical one, and after December 2, into a public one as well.

Once made public, the crisis in all its intricate aspects sped to a climactic end. The King's proposal of legislation for a morganatic marriage was rejected by the Cabinet and the Dominion Governments; Mrs. Simpson fled to France; Baldwin for the first time publicly acknowledged the problem when he clarified the morganatic marriage issue in the House of Commons; the "Simpson Press"[3] took up the King's cause; references to a "King's party"[4] began to appear; a request from

[1] Iles Brody, *Gone with the Windsors*, p. 5.

[2] See Baldwin's speech, 318 *H. C. Deb.* 5s, 2178.

[3] Composed largely of the popular newspapers, notably those owned by Lord Rothermere and the weekly paper owned by Lady Houston.

[4] This was never an organized party as such. The term seems to have been loosely applied to any or all factions, however disparate, which supported the King and therefore offered the potential for a King's party. Among such factions, Robert Sencourt includes Churchill, the young people of England, the "two Press Lords [Beaverbrook and

the King to lay his case before the people via radio was refused by the Cabinet as unconstitutional; Lord Beaverbrook, the newspaper publisher, then Churchill urged the King to delay any decision, and each set about executing his own strategy to effect such delay; the Archbishop of Canterbury made a discreet official statement about the controversy and "at his request nothing was said of the crisis in Anglican pulpits—a good deal, however, was said in those of the Free Churches";[5] Mrs. Simpson issued a communiqué from Cannes that she was willing to withdraw if that would help to solve the problem—an announcement duly followed up by Baldwin;[6] witnesses asserted they would charge collusion in the divorce case;[7] the King decided to prepare for abdication; Baldwin's fellow ministers concluded they could not recommend passage of the so-called Simpson Bill which would have accompanied the Abdication Bill and which would have made the divorce absolute at the end of six weeks instead of six months. All this and more took place in the last ten feverish days. London was ablaze with headlines and tense with mounting feeling, and "gossip, comment and surmise, like the result of some portentous seismic convulsion, broiled through the country as from a chain of volcanoes which erupted from the bowels of the globe."[8]

In the midst of this explosive situation, the House of Commons gathered on Thursday, December 10, to hear the King's final decision.

We present below most of the ensuing debate, not only because of its intrinsic interest in the context of the unique constitutional crisis, but because it is a fair, though of course not typical, example of speaking in the House of Commons in the twentieth century prior to the Second World War. Here are speeches by Stanley Baldwin, perhaps the norm of Conservative speaking early in the century; by Clement Attlee, who was to lead the Labor Party after the war; and by Winston Churchill before his great triumphs as the wartime leader.

Baldwin's speech was the convincing last effort in what Churchill himself later

---

Rothermere] with their popular papers, backed too by Lady Houston, and by Sir Oswald Mosley [notorious leader of the British Fascists] with his blackshirts." (*The Reign of Edward VIII*, p. 170.) The King himself speaks of it as a curious phenomenon, "something that newspapers had begun to call the 'King's party.'" He says that he "was dubious of its motives and apprehensive of its consequences"; that the only visible evidence of it he could detect were the people touring city streets with signs and loudspeakers, crowds shouting "God Save the King—from Stanley Baldwin," and slogans chalked on walls; but that granted "the so-called King's party was only an idea in people's heads—a simple idea that their King should have justice and that they should have their King," it may well have "startled" Mr. Baldwin into his "abrupt moves." The King continues: "For no doubt there had by this time [December 4] emerged, in an inchoate form, many elements conducive to a popular movement in my favor. Had I made a move to encourage the growth of this movement, it might have grown. If I had made an appeal to the public, I might have persuaded a majority, and a large majority at that. I shall go further and say that had I remained passive while my friends acted the result might well have been the same. For there is no want of evidence that a multitude of the plain people stood waiting to be rallied to my side." (*A King's Story*, pp. 382–84.)

[5] Sencourt, *The Reign of Edward VIII*, p. 176.

[6] For an account of this episode, see *A King's Story*, pp. 393–97, 400–3; and Sencourt, pp. 181–85.

[7] Sencourt, p. 171. For other comments on the collusion factor, see pp. 118–19, 181.

[8] *Ibid.*, p. 169.

admitted was "his deft and skilful handling of the abdication issue [which] raised him in a fortnight from the depths to the pinnacle."[9] Instead of presenting arguments *per se* for accepting the abdication, Baldwin incorporated them almost imperceptibly into a subtly "simple," straight-from-the-heart narration of what had happened between him and the King and into a sympathetic portrayal of the King. There were some omissions in the story—the King's desire to broadcast his case to the people and the matter of the Simpson Bill, to name two—and a few inaccuracies, such as the assertion that there had been no kind of conflict. Sencourt in his discussion of the speech attributes them all to Baldwin's loyal and chivalrous endeavor to build a case to protect the King and the monarchy. It would seem only logical and natural, however, that in doing so—and he obviously had to shelter the throne as well as he could—Baldwin should also have given some consideration to strengthening his own position and that of his Ministry. No doubt he kept both in mind, working toward the ultimate objective of establishing unity of feeling about the abdication, not only in the House but in the nation and the Commonwealth. Whether the speech is viewed as a justification of his own actions and an answer to any criticism, or as "the truth appropriately chiselled and decked in graceful garments so as to shield the King and save the imperilled honour of his throne,"[10] or as both, it must be agreed that he left his audience with little to say in opposition.

Churchill's speech was in effect a giving in and a graceful retreat—carried out in the best Churchillian manner—from his advocated policy of delay and from his implications that the King had been forced into a hasty decision to abdicate by an ultimatum from the Ministry; for only the previous Saturday he had been giving vehement voice to both in the press, and as late as Monday had tried to urge his arguments on a hostile House, which had virtually shouted him down.[11]

Since Baldwin headed a "National Government" Coalition Cabinet, and has been generally conceded to have had backing throughout the crisis from a great part of the Labor and Liberal parties as well as from his own Conservative (Unionist) Party, it probably needed only his dexterous speech to win him the almost unanimous support he received from the House. Both Clement Attlee, leader of the Opposition and leader of the Labor Party, and Sir Archibald Sinclair, the Liberal leader, spoke in favor—although Attlee found reason to warn that, in his opinion, in order to survive, the monarchy must replace some of its pomp and its "unreal halo" with a simplicity that would provide a stronger, more realistic link with the people. What challenge there was came from a small group of Labor extremists and from the one Communist member of Commons, all of whom found in the abdication issue a heaven-sent opportunity to attack constitutional monarchy. Since, as they themselves pointed out, they had always seized every possible chance to advance their anti-monarchist views, neither Baldwin nor the House could have been surprised that they did so now. This time, however, the

---

[9] Sir Winston Churchill, *The Gathering Storm*, p. 218. "The depths," according to Churchill, had been reached in November when Baldwin had "shocked" the House by linking the rearmament issue to winning or losing elections (pp. 215–17). Baldwin had also previously lost some prestige during the Ethiopian affair.

[10] Sencourt, p. 192.

[11] As a result of this fiasco, Churchill's political career, already suffering from earlier defeats, was considered by many to be completely finished. (*The Gathering Storm*, pp. 218–19.)

chance itself spoke for them, and with force. As Hardie put it, "What has happened recently has done more for Republicanism than 50 years' propaganda could do." [12] Consequently their arguments took on a meaning and immediacy previously lacking. Even in their most wildly extravagant allegations there were a few barbed truths that must have found their mark and raised some uneasy doubts in the minds of the most conservative members present.

◇

Stanley Baldwin (1867–1947) and the Debate in the House of Commons [*]

December 10–11, 1936

The Prime Minister (Mr. Baldwin) at the Bar, acquainted the House that he had a Message from His Majesty the King to this House, signed by His Majesty's own hand. And he presented the same to the House, and it was read out by Mr. Speaker as followeth, all the Members of the House being uncovered:

> Fort Belvedere,
> Sunningdale,
> Berkshire.

Members of the House of Commons,

After long and anxious consideration, I have determined to renounce the Throne to which I succeeded on the death of My father, and I am now communicating this, My final and irrevocable decision. Realising as I do the gravity of this step, I can only hope that I shall have the understanding of My peoples in the decision I have taken and the reasons which have led Me to take it. I will not enter now into My private feelings, but I would beg that it should be remembered that the burden which constantly rests upon the shoulders of a Sovereign is so heavy that it can only be borne in circumstances different from those in which I now find Myself. I conceive that I am not overlooking the duty that rests on Me to place in the forefront the public interest, when I declare that I am conscious that I can no longer discharge this heavy task with efficiency or with satisfaction to Myself.

I have accordingly this morning executed an Instrument of Abdication in the terms following:—

"I, Edward VIII, of Great Britain, Ireland, and the British Dominions beyond the Seas, King, Emperor of India, do hereby declare My irrevocable determination to renounce the Throne for Myself and for My descendants, and My desire that effect should be given to this Instrument of Abdication immediately.

---

[12] 318 H. C. Deb. 5s, 2218.

[*] Except for abridgments made necessary in meeting space restrictions, the debate on the abdication in the House of Commons is given verbatim from Great Britain's official publication *House of Commons, Parliamentary Debates,* 5th Series, Vol. 318, comprising the period from Monday, November 23, to Friday, December 18, 1936; it is cited in footnotes as 318 *H. C. Debs.* 5s. These official reports are still often referred to and cited simply as *Hansard,* a title adopted from the name of their eighteenth- and nineteenth-century printers.

"In token whereof I have hereunto set My hand this tenth day of December, nineteen hundred and thirty-six, in the presence of the witnesses whose signatures are subscribed.

(Signed) EDWARD R.I."

My execution of this Instrument has been witnessed by My three brothers, Their Royal Highnesses the Duke of York, the Duke of Gloucester and the Duke of Kent.

I deeply appreciate the spirit which has actuated the appeals which have been made to Me to take a different decision, and I have, before reaching My final determination, most fully pondered over them. But My mind is made up. Moreover, further delay cannot but be most injurious to the peoples whom I have tried to serve as Prince of Wales and as King and whose future happiness and prosperity are the constant wish of My heart.

I take My leave of them in the confident hope that the course which I have thought it right to follow is that which is best for the stability of the Throne and Empire and the happiness of My peoples. I am deeply sensible of the consideration which they have always extended to Me both before and after My accession to the Throne and which I know they will extend in full measure to My successor.

I am most anxious that there should be no delay of any kind in giving effect to the Instrument which I have executed and that all necessary steps should be taken immediately to secure that My lawful successor, My brother, His Royal Highness the Duke of York, should ascend the Throne.[1]

EDWARD R.I.

THE PRIME MINISTER: I beg to move,
"That His Majesty's most Gracious Message be now considered."

No more grave message has ever been received by Parliament and no more difficult, I may almost say repugnant, task has ever been imposed upon a Prime Minister. I would ask the House, which I know will not be without sympathy for me in my position to-day, to remember that in this last week I have had but little time in which to compose a speech for delivery to-day, so I must tell what I have to tell truthfully, sincerely and plainly, with no attempt to dress up or to adorn. I shall have little or nothing to say in the way of comment or criticism, or of praise or of blame. I think my best course to-day, and the one that the House would desire, is to tell them, so far as I can, what has passed between His Majesty and myself and what led up to the present situation.

I should like to say at the start that His Majesty as Prince of Wales has honoured me for many years with a friendship which I value, and I know that he would agree with me in saying to you that it was not only a friendship, but, between man and man, a friendship of affection. I would like to tell the House that when we said "Good-bye" on Tuesday night at Fort Belvedere[2] we both knew and felt and said to each other that that friendship, so far from being im-

---

[1] Prepared by government legal officers and approved by the King, the Prime Minister, and other government officials. (*A King's Story*, p. 403; Sencourt, pp. 190–91.)

[2] Edward's private residence near Windsor and Sunningdale, about 25 miles from London. It had been a "Grace and Favour" house (one at the disposal of the sovereign) which he had asked his father for in 1930 and then reconditioned for his own.

paired by the discussions of this last week, bound us more closely together than ever and would last for life.

Now, Sir, the House will want to know how it was that I had my first interview with His Majesty. I may say that His Majesty has been most generous in allowing me to tell the House the pertinent parts of the discussions which took place between us. As the House is aware, I had been ordered in August and September a complete rest which, owing to the kindness of my staff and the consideration of all my colleagues, I was able to enjoy to the full, and when October came, although I had been ordered to take a rest in that month, I felt that I could not in fairness to my work take a further holiday, and I came, as it were, on half-time before the middle of October, and, for the first time since the beginning of August, was in a position to look into things.

There were two things that disquieted me at that moment. There was coming to my office a vast volume of correspondence, mainly at that time from British subjects and American citizens of British origin in the United States of America, from some of the Dominions and from this country, all expressing perturbation and uneasiness at what was then appearing in the American Press. I was aware also that there was in the near future a divorce case coming on, as a result of which, I realised that possibly a difficult situation might arise later, and I felt that it was essential that someone should see His Majesty and warn him of the difficult situation that might arise later if occasion was given for a continuation of this kind of gossip and of criticism, and the danger that might come if that gossip and that criticism spread from the other side of the Atlantic to this country. I felt that in the circumstances there was only one man who could speak to him and talk the matter over with him, and that man was the Prime Minister. I felt doubly bound to do it by my duty, as I conceived it, to the country and my duty to him not only as a counsellor, but as a friend. I consulted, I am ashamed to say—and they have forgiven me—none of my colleagues.

I happened to be staying in the neighbourhood of Fort Belvedere about the middle of October, and I ascertained that His Majesty was leaving his house on Sunday, 18th October, to entertain a small shooting party at Sandringham,[3] and that he was leaving on the Sunday afternoon. I telephoned from my friend's house on the Sunday morning and found that he had left earlier than was expected. In those circumstances, I communicated with him through his Secretary and stated that I desired to see him—this is the first and only occasion on which I was the one who asked for an interview—that I desired to see him, that the matter was urgent. I told him what it was. I expressed my willingness to come to Sandringham on Tuesday, the 20th, but I said that I thought it wiser, if His Majesty thought fit, to see me at Fort Belvedere, for I was anxious that no one at that time should know of my visit, and that at any rate our first talk should be in complete privacy. The reply came from His Majesty that he would motor back on the Monday, 19th October, to Fort Belevedere, and he would see me on the Tuesday morning. And on the Tuesday morning I saw him.

Sir, I may say, before I proceed to the details of the conversation, that an adviser to the Crown can be of no possible service to his master unless he tells him at all times the truth as he sees it, whether that truth be welcome or not. And let me say here, as I may say several times before I finish, that during those

---

[3] One of the royal family's estates; located in Norfolk.

talks, when I look back, there is nothing I have not told His Majesty of which I felt he ought to be aware—nothing. His Majesty's attitude all through has been—let me put it in this way: Never has he shown any sign of offence, of being hurt at anything I have said to him. The whole of our discussions have been carried out, as I have said, with an increase, if possible, of that mutual respect and regard in which we stood. I told His Majesty that I had two great anxieties— one the effect of a continuance of the kind of criticism that at that time was proceeding in the American Press, the effect it would have in the Dominions and particularly in Canada, where it was widespread, the effect it would have in this country.

That was the first anxiety. And then I reminded him of what I had often told him and his brothers in years past. The British Monarchy is a unique institution. The Crown in this country through the centuries has been deprived of many of its prerogatives, but to-day, while that is true, it stands for far more than it ever has done in its history. The importance of its integrity is, beyond all question, far greater than it has ever been, being as it is not only the last link of Empire that is left, but the guarantee in this country so long as it exists in that integrity, against many evils that have affected and afflicted other countries. There is no man in this country, to whatever party he may belong, who would not subscribe to that. But while this feeling largely depends on the respect that has grown up in the last three generations for the Monarchy, it might not take so long, in face of the kind of criticisms to which it was being exposed, to lose that power far more rapidly than it was built up, and once lost I doubt if anything could restore it.

That was the basis of my talk on that aspect, and I expressed my anxiety and desire, that such criticism should not have cause to go on. I said that in my view no popularity in the long run would weigh against the effect of such criticism. I told His Majesty that I for one had looked forward to his reign being a great reign in a new age—he has so many of the qualities necessary—and that I hoped we should be able to see our hopes realised. I told him I had come—naturally, I was his Prime Minister—but I wanted to talk it over with him as a friend to see if I could help him in this matter. Perhaps I am saying what I should not say here; I have not asked him whether I might say this, but I will say it because I do not think he would mind, and I think it illustrates the basis on which our talks proceeded. He said to me, not once, but many times during those many, many hours we have had together and especially towards the end, "You and I must settle this matter together; I will not have anyone interfering."

I then pointed out the danger of the divorce proceedings, that if a verdict was given in that case that left the matter in suspense for some time, that period of suspense might be dangerous, because then everyone would be talking, and when once the Press began, as it must begin some time in this country, a most difficult situation would arise for me, for him, and there might well be a danger which both he and I had seen all through this—I shall come to that later— and it was one of the reasons why he wanted to take this action quickly—that is, that there might be sides taken and factions grow up in this country in a matter where no faction ought ever to exist.

It was on that aspect of the question that we talked for an hour, and I went away glad that the ice had been broken, because I knew that it had to be broken. For some little time we had no further meetings. I begged His Majesty to consider all that I had said. I said that I pressed him for no kind of answer, but would he consider everything I had said? The next time I saw him was on Monday, 16th November. That was at Buckingham Palace. By that date the decree nisi had been pronounced in the divorce case. His Majesty had sent for me on that occasion. I had meant to see him later in the week, but he had sent for me first. I felt it my duty to begin the conversation, and I spoke to him for a quarter of an hour or 20 minutes on the question of marriage.

Again, we must remember that the Cabinet had not been in this at all—I had reported to about four of my senior colleagues the conversation at Fort Belvedere. I saw the King on Monday, 16th November, and I began by giving him my view of a possible marriage. I told him that I did not think that a particular marriage was one that would receive the approbation of the country. That marriage would have involved the lady becoming Queen. I did tell His Majesty once that I might be a remnant of the old Victorians, but that my worst enemy would not say of me that I did not know what the reaction of the English people would be to any particular course of action, and I told him that so far as they went I was certain that that would be impracticable. I cannot go further into the details, but that was the substance. I pointed out to him that the position of the King's wife was different from the position of the wife of any other citizen in the country; it was part of the price which the King has to pay. His wife becomes Queen; the Queen becomes the Queen of the country; and, therefore, in the choice of a Queen the voice of the people must be heard. It is the truth expressed in those lines that may come to your minds:

> His will is not his own;
> For he himself is subject to his birth,
> He may not, as unvalued persons do,
> Carve for himself; for on his choice depends
> The safety and the health of the whole State.[4]

Then His Majesty said to me—I have his permission to state this—that he wanted to tell me something that he had long wanted to tell me. He said, "I am going to marry Mrs. Simpson, and I am prepared to go." I said, "Sir, that is most grievous news and it is impossible for me to make any comment on it to-day." He told the Queen that night; he told the Duke of York and the Duke of Gloucester the next day, and the Duke of Kent, who was out of London, either on the Wednesday or the Thursday; and for the rest of the week, so far as I know, he was considering that point.

He sent for me again on Wednesday, 25th November. In the meantime a suggestion had been made to me that a possible compromise might be arranged to avoid those two possibilities that had been seen, first in the distance and then approaching nearer and nearer. The compromise was that the King should marry, that Parliament should pass an Act enabling the lady to be the King's wife without the position of Queen; and when I saw His Majesty on 25th November he asked me whether that proposition had been put to me, and I said yes. He asked me what I thought of it. I told him that I had not considered it. I said,

---

[4] Laertes' words to Ophelia about Hamlet. (*Hamlet*, I, iii, 17–21.) Sencourt says "[Sir John] Simon, when helping to prepare Baldwin's speech for the House of Commons, quoted [these lines] from Shakespeare. (*The Reign of Edward VIII*, p. 129.)

"I can give you no considered opinion." If he asked me my first reaction informally, my first reaction was that Parliament would never pass such a Bill. But I said that if he desired it I would examine it formally. He said he did so desire. Then I said, "It will mean my putting that formally before the whole Cabinet and communicating with the Prime Ministers of all the Dominions, and was that his wish?" He told me that it was. I said that I would do it.

On 2nd December the King asked me to go and see him. Again I had intended asking for an audience later that week, because such inquiries as I thought proper to make I had not completed. The inquiries had gone far enough to show that neither in the Dominions nor here would there be any prospect of such legislation being accepted. His Majesty asked me if I could answer his question. I gave him the reply that I was afraid it was impracticable for those reasons. I do want the House to realise this: His Majesty said he was not surprised at that answer. He took my answer with no question and he never recurred to it again. I want the House to realise—because if you can put yourself in His Majesty's place and you know what His Majesty's feelings are, and you know how glad you would have been had this been possible—that he behaved there as a great gentleman; he said no more about it. The matter was closed. I never heard another word about it from him. That decision was, of course, a formal decision, and that was the only formal decision of any kind taken by the Cabinet until I come to the history of yesterday. When we had finished that conversation, I pointed out that the possible alternatives had been narrowed, and that it really had brought him into the position that he would be placed in a grievous situation between two conflicting loyalties in his own heart—either complete abandonment of the project on which his heart was set, and remaining as King, or doing as he intimated to me that he was prepared to do, in the talk which I have reported, going, and later on contracting that marriage, if it were possible. During the last days, from that day until now, that has been the struggle in which His Majesty has been engaged. We had many talks, and always on the various aspects of this limited problem.

The House must remember—it is difficult to realise—that His Majesty is not a boy, although he looks so young. We have all thought of him as our Prince, but he is a mature man, with wide and great experience of life and the world, and he always had before him three, nay, four, things, which in these conversations at all hours, he repeated again and again—That if he went he would go with dignity. He would not allow a situation to arise in which he could not do that. He wanted to go with as little disturbance of his Ministers and his people as possible. He wished to go in circumstances that would make the succession of his brother as little difficult for his brother as possible; and I may say that any idea to him of what might be called a King's party, was abhorrent. He stayed down at Fort Belvedere because he said that he was not coming to London while these things were in dispute, because of the cheering crowds. I honour and respect him for the way in which he behaved at that time.

I have something here which, I think, will touch the House. It is a pencilled note, sent to me by His Majesty this morning, and I have his authority for reading it. It is just scribbled in pencil:

> Duke of York. He and the King have always been on the best of terms as brothers, and the King is confident that the Duke deserves and will receive the support of the whole Empire.

I would say a word or two on the King's position. The King cannot speak for himself. The King has told us that he cannot carry, and does not see his way to carry, these almost intolerable burdens of Kingship without a woman at his side, and we know that. This crisis, if I may use the word, has arisen now rather than later from that very frankness of His Majesty's character which is one of his many attractions. It would have been perfectly possible for His Majesty not to have told me of this at the date when he did, and not to have told me for some months to come. But he realised the damage that might be done in the interval by gossip, rumours and talk, and he made that declaration to me when he did, on purpose to avoid what he felt might be dangerous, not only here but throughout the Empire, to the moral force of the Crown which we are all determined to sustain.

He told me his intentions, and he has never wavered from them. I want the House to understand that. He felt it his duty to take into his anxious consideration all the representations that his advisers might give him and not until he had fully considered them did he make public his decision. There has been no kind of conflict in this matter. My efforts during these last days have been directed, as have the efforts of those most closely round him, in trying to help him to make the choice which he has not made; and we have failed. The King has made his decision to take this moment to send this Gracious Message because of his confident hope that by that he will preserve the unity of this country and of the whole Empire, and avoid those factious differences which might so easily have arisen.[5]

It is impossible, unfortunately, to avoid talking to some extent to-day about one's-self. These last days have been days of great strain, but it was a great comfort to me, and I hope it will be to the House, when I was assured before I left him on Tuesday night, by that intimate circle that was with him at the Fort that evening,[6] that I had left nothing undone that I could have done to move him from the decision at which he had arrived, and which he has communicated to us. While there is not a soul among us who will not regret this from the bottom of his heart, there is not a soul here to-day that wants to judge. We are not judges. He has announced his decision. He has told us what he wants us to do, and I think we must close our ranks, and do it.

[Mr. Baldwin, after indicating necessary legislative procedure, then read to the House: (1) his December 9th message to the King in which he had relayed the Cabinet's regretful reaction and their hope that His Majesty might reconsider his intention before issuing a formal decision, and (2) the King's reply further confirming his determination to abdicate. He went on:]

My last words on that subject are that I am convinced that where I have failed

[5] For the King's account of these events and negotiations, see *A King's Story*.

[6] There were nine at dinner that night: the King; Mr. Baldwin; the King's brothers, the Duke of York and the Duke of Kent; Major Thomas Dugdale, Baldwin's Parliamentary Private Secretary; Sir Edward Peacock; and the three men who, at the King's request, had come to stay with him and advise him during the last few days of the crisis —Walter Monckton, personal adviser and liaison with the Prime Minister and Cabinet; Major Ulick Alexander, Keeper of the Privy Purse and a member of the King's Household; and George Allen, his solicitor and personal adviser. (*A King's Story*, pp. 399–400.)

no one could have succeeded. His mind was made up, and those who know His Majesty best will know what that means.

This House to-day is a theatre which is being watched by the whole world. Let us conduct ourselves with that dignity which His Majesty is showing in this hour of his trial. Whatever our regret at the contents of the Message, let us fulfil his wish, do what he asks, and do it with speed. Let no word be spoken to-day that the utterer of that word may regret in days to come, let no word be spoken that causes pain to any soul, and let us not forget to-day the revered and beloved figure of Queen Mary, what all this time has meant to her, and think of her when we have to speak, if speak we must, during this Debate. We have, after all, as the guardians of democracy in this little island to see that we do our work to maintain the integrity of that democracy and of the monarchy, which, as I said at the beginning of my speech is now the sole link of our whole Empire and the guardian of our freedom. Let us look forward and remember our country and the trust reposed by our country in this, the House of Commons, and let us rally behind the new King—[Hon. Members: "Hear, hear"]—stand behind him, and help him; and let us hope that, whatever the country may have suffered by what we are passing through, it may soon be repaired and that we may take what steps we can in trying to make this country a better country for all the people in it.

[At this point, 4:32 p.m., Mr. Attlee moved for a short recess. When the House reconvened at 6 p.m., he was the first speaker.]

Mr. Attlee: [7] This occasion does not, in my view, call for long and eloquent speeches. My words will be few and simple. We have all heard with profound concern the message from His Majesty the King. The Prime Minister has related to us the course of events that have led up to this momentous act. The King has decided that he can no longer continue on the Throne. The whole country will receive the news with deep sorrow, and his subjects in these Islands and throughout the British Dominions beyond the seas will feel a sense of personal loss. I am certain that, throughout these anxious days, he has had the sympathy of all, in the tragic dilemma with which he has been faced. That sympathy is due not only to the nature of the issue, involving as it does the strongest human emotions, but to the personal affection which he has inspired in his people. No British Monarch has been so well known by his subjects. The people not only in this country but throughout the Commonwealth and the Empire, have seen in him, not a remote Ruler, but a man who was personally acquainted with many of them and had visited the places where they live.

[The rest of Mr. Attlee's short speech commented in a complimentary way on Edward as Prince of Wales—on his sympathy with the miners, on his present difficult choice which, once made, had to be accepted by all; and ended with words of sympathy for the Prime Minister, the Royal Family, and for the next King in assuming his new burden.]

[7] Clement Attlee (1883–   ), Member for Limehouse Div. of Stepney; leader of the Labor Opposition in Commons; later Deputy Prime Minister under Churchill during World War II, and Prime Minister, 1946–1951. Now retired as Lord Attlee.

SIR ARCHIBALD SINCLAIR: [8] The whole country and the Empire have been passing through days of stress and tension, and the climax to which events have now marched has aroused in all of us the deepest feelings of grief and frustration. We are bound to our King not only by formal and solemn ties, by our oaths of allegiance and by our recognition of the Crown as the link which unites all the peoples of the Empire, but also by those closer and more personal links which the Leader of the Opposition has so simply and so eloquently described, and which the King has forged between himself and his people—people of all classes, of all creeds and of all races in every part of his Dominions—during nearly a quarter of a century of Royal service. The rupture of those ties is profoundly painful to us all. It must be most painful to those right hon. Gentlemen who, during these brief months of his Reign have been his Ministers and confidential advisers; above all, to the Prime Minister, his closest and most intimate adviser, who deserves our sympathy, and to-day also our gratitude for the grave but clear and moving statement which it was his melancholy duty to make to us this afternoon.

Let us also gratefully and respectfully acclaim the political wisdom which His Majesty has shown in discountenancing any attempt to divide the country on the issues to which his proposed marriage gave rise. It is in large measure due to His Majesty's wise and strong restraint, and to his recognition of the supremacy of Parliament and the constitutional responsibility of Ministers, that the Crown has not become involved in our political controversies, but remains above and aloof from them.

The Leader of the Opposition spoke of the earnestness and the anxiety with which all of us have been exploring the possibility of finding some means by which this conflict could be resolved. The Prime Minister referred to the possibility of a Morganatic Marriage Bill; I think it is only right to tell the House that I could not have supported it. It is not only the law of our country but it is also, I believe, a sound, healthy and essential element in the monarchial principle itself, that the lady whom the King marries must become Queen and share with him, before the whole people, the glorious burden of sovereignty. Such a Bill would, moreover, under the Statute of Westminster, have had to pass through all the Parliaments of the United Kingdom and the Dominions, before it could have become valid in this country or in any of the Dominions, and the attempt to do so would have involved the Throne in prolonged controversy which would have gravely impaired its prestige and dignity. In my judgment the Government had no option but to reject the proposal.

[Sir Archibald then commended the fine qualities of the Duke of York and those of his wife, paid a tribute to the system of constitutional monarchy, and urged prompt action as best serving the interests of all.]

MR. CHURCHILL: [9] Nothing is more certain or more obvious than that recrimination or controversy at this time would be not only useless but harmful and

---

[8] (1890–1956), Member for Caithness and Sutherland; Liberal Parliamentary Party, chairman and leader of the party.

[9] Winston Spencer Churchill, Member for Epping Div. of Essex; Conservative Party; at this time, in the King's words, "a virtual outcast" from the party. See below, pp. 521–23.

wrong. What is done is done. What has been done or left undone belongs to history, and to history, so far as I am concerned, it shall be left. I will, therefore, make two observations only. The first is this: It is clear from what we have been told this afternoon that there was at no time any constitutional issue between the King and his Ministers or between the King and Parliament. The supremacy of Parliament over the Crown: the duty of the Sovereign to act in accordance with the advice of his Ministers: neither of those was ever at any moment in question. Supporting my right hon. Friend the Leader of the Liberal party, I venture to say that no Sovereign has ever conformed more strictly or more faithfully to the letter and spirit of the Constitution than His present Majesty. In fact, he has voluntarily made a sacrifice for the peace and strength of his Realm which goes far beyond the bounds required by the law and the Constitution. That is my first observation.

My second is this: I have, throughout, pleaded for time; anyone can see how grave would have been the evils of protracted controversy. On the other hand, it was, in my view, our duty to endure these evils even at serious inconvenience, if there was any hope that time would bring a solution. Whether there was any hope or not is a mystery which, at the present time, it is impossible to resolve. Time was also important from another point of view. It was essential that there should be no room for aspersions, after the event, that the King had been hurried in his decision. I believe that, if this decision had been taken last week, it could not have been declared that it was an unhurried decision, so far as the King himself was concerned, but now I accept wholeheartedly what the Prime Minister has proved, namely, that the decision taken this week has been taken by His Majesty freely, voluntarily and spontaneously, in his own time and in his own way. As I have been looking at this matter, as is well known, from an angle different from that of most hon. Members, I thought it my duty to place this fact also upon record.

That is all I have to say upon the disputable part of this matter, but I hope the House will bear with me for a minute or two, because it was my duty as Home Secretary, more than a quarter of a century ago, to stand beside His present Majesty and proclaim his style and titles at his investiture as Prince of Wales amid the sunlit battlements of Carnarvon Castle, and ever since then he has honoured me here, and also in war-time, with his personal kindness and, I may even say, friendship. I should have been ashamed if, in my independent and unofficial position, I had not cast about for every lawful means, even the most forlorn, to keep him on the Throne of his fathers, to which he only recently succeeded amid the hopes and prayers of all. In this Prince there were discerned qualities of courage, of simplicity, of sympathy, and, above all, of sincerity, qualities rare and precious which might have made his reign glorious in the annals of this ancient monarchy. It is the acme of tragedy that these very virtues should, in the private sphere, have led only to this melancholy and bitter conclusion. But, although our hopes to-day are withered, still I will assert that his personality will not go down uncherished to future ages, that it will be particularly remembered in the homes of his poorer subjects, and that they will ever wish from the bottom of their hearts for his private peace and happiness and for the happiness of those who are dear to him.

I must say one word more, and I say it specially to those here and out of doors —and do not underrate their numbers—who are most poignantly afflicted by what has occurred. Danger gathers upon our path. We cannot afford—we have no right—to look back. We must look forward; we must obey the exhortation of the Prime Minister to look forward. The stronger the advocate of monarchical principle a man may be, the more zealously must he now endeavour to fortify the Throne and to give to His Majesty's successor that strength which can only come from the love of a united nation and Empire.

MR. MAXTON: [10] I rise to say a few words on this unprecedented situation in which the House of Commons finds itself to-day, and I realise that I am speaking in a House in which an overwhelming proportion of the membership is under feelings of very strong emotion. I respect these emotions, although I do not entirely share them. The monarchical institutions of this land date back to very early times, and by many are regarded as sacrosanct and everlasting. I share with others in this House the human sympathies that go out to His Majesty as a man confronted with the difficulties with which he as a man has been confronted in these recent weeks. I share the same human sympathies with the Prime Minister, who has had to shoulder a task which few if any of the occupants of his office have ever had to shoulder before, and, in the nature of the case, has had to shoulder it alone. The decisions that he has made are, I believe, in strict accordance with his Conservative principles, on which he has been chosen as the leader of this country in the House of Commons, and, therefore, I make no criticism of them whatever. But I do say that, in the very nature of the monarchical institutions on an hereditary basis, circumstances of this kind were bound to arise, and they have arisen now in conditions which have created very grave difficulties for this country and for the Empire over the seas.

It is a question whether now this House will not be prepared to look at this particular political problem that has been forced upon our attention to-day as a practical political problem, one among many that intelligent men in the twentieth century must confront, recognising that the problems of our age cannot be met and solved with the ideas and the institutions which have come down to us from earlier times. We are living in a new kind of world, with new kinds of problems, and the institutions that date back centuries, however much reverence they may inspire because of their ancient origin and the traditions and associations that have become attached to them over the centuries, are not necessarily the institutions which can cope with the problems of modern times. We therefore intend, however it may be against the general run of opinion in this House, to take strongly the view that the lesson of the past few days, and of this day in particular, is that the monarchical institution has now outlived its usefulness. [HON. MEMBERS: "No."] The happenings of the past few days have only indicated the grave perils that confront a country that has as its centralising, unifying figure an hereditary personality who at any time may break under the force of the circumstances that gather round about him. We hope to take the opportunity given us, when steps are being taken to make good the evil and injury that have already been done to try to persuade this House now to face the situation with the idea in their minds that for the future Great Britain and its allied countries across the seas shall become, among other advanced countries in the world, one of the republican nations.

[10] James Maxton (1885–1946), Member for Bridgeton Div. of Glasgow; Independent Labor Party, chairman and leader of the party.

[Colonel Josiah Clement Wedgwood, the Labor Member for Newcastle-under-Lyme, here took the floor to say that he had "put a Motion on the Paper" [11] but that after the Prime Minister's speech, it was dead; that, although he had wished His Majesty could have been allowed to stay as a happily married King, he now accepted the two alternatives as the only possible ones, and he commended the King's choice.]

Mr. GALLACHER: [12] I would like just to remark that the concluding sentence of the right hon. Gentleman the Member for Epping (Mr. Churchill) happened to be the first note that I have in my hand. Danger lies before us, and it is going to be very bad if we close our eyes to that fact. It is very nice to hear right hon. Members talking about the necessity for all standing together, but how was it possible that such a crisis as has arisen should come upon us? The King and Mrs. Simpson do not live in a vacuum. Sinister processes are continually at work.

I would direct your attention to the fact that the Prime Minister told us that he was approached about a morganatic marriage, but he did not tell us who approached him. He told us that, when he went to the King later, the King asked him if he had been approached on this matter. It is obvious that forces were operating, advising and encouraging what was going on. It is a year since I heard about Mrs. Simpson. Perhaps it is the same with other Members. No one paid very much attention to Mrs. Simpson or to what she was doing until more and more difficulties arose in Europe, and then there was a move for a decree nisi. This is not something decided on by the King and Mrs. Simpson on her own. I want to make it understood, if I possibly can, that we have here not an issue between the King and Parliament, for Parliament has never been consulted from beginning to end—interviews, secret and otherwise, but Parliament not consulted and the forces operating, two forces fighting with one another on this issue, as they have been fighting continually on every important issue that has come on foreign policy. I am concerned with the working class. I see terrible dangers arising. There is not an hon. Member here who, if he asks himself the question, believes that this finishes the crisis and that the forces which have been operating behind this will now stop. There is victory for one group at the moment, but they will not stop. The forces will go on.

I want to draw attention to the fact that Mrs. Simpson has a social set, and every Member of the Cabinet knows that the social set of Mrs. Simpson is closely identified with a certain foreign Government and the Ambassador of that foreign Government. [13] [HON. MEMBERS: "No, no."] It is common knowledge, and round about this issue is the issue that is continually arising when other Debates come on. I say it is not an issue between the King and Parliament. It is an issue be-

---

[11] The motion, as cited in Sencourt, p. 156, was: "In the opinion of the House, the oath of allegiance which they have already taken to King Edward VIII is unaffected by the form of Coronation ceremony, or by the presence thereat or by the absence therefrom of any personage whatsoever. Nor will they substitute any other for the King of England."

[12] William Gallacher (1881–   ), Member for Western Div. of West Fife; Communist Party, leading member of the party in Great Britain and the only Communist in the House.

[13] Probably a reference to Germany and to Ribbentrop, who had sometimes been a guest of the Simpsons.

tween two groups which are fighting continually for domination, and it is a thousand pities that the Labour movement should show any signs of falling into the trap. The only hope for the working class is that the Labour movement should adopt an independent policy and pursue it against these groups, accept the proposal of the hon. Member for Bridgeton (Mr. Maxton) and finish with it all. No one can go out before the people of the country and give any justification for clinging to the Monarchy. You all know it. You will not be able, no matter what you do, to repair the damage that has been done to the Monarchical institution. If you allow things to go on as they are going, you will encourage factions to grow, and factions will grow, of a dangerous and desperate character, so far as the mass of the people are concerned. I appeal to the Labour movement to take strong, determined action to arouse the people of the country to the urgent need of uniting all their forces for peace and progress in face of the dangers that lie in their path—the very terrible dangers that are bound to confront us in the very near future.

MR. BUCHANAN: [14] I feel that I ought to express my own view and go a step farther than my hon. Friend the Member for Bridgeton (Mr. Maxton). I should not be honest if I did not do so. I have listened to more cant and humbug than I have ever listened to in my life. I have heard praise of the King which was not felt sincerely in any quarter of the House. I go further. Who has not heard the tittle-tattle and gossip that is going about? If he had not voluntarily stepped from the Throne, everyone knows that the same people in the House who pay lip service to him would have poured out scorn, abuse and filth. Some months ago we opposed the Civil List.[15] To-morrow we shall take the same line. I have no doubt that you will go on praising the next King as you have praised this one. You will go on telling about his wonderful qualities. If he is a tenth as good as you say, why are you not keeping him? Why is everyone wanting to unload him? Because you know he is a weak creature. You want to get rid of him and you are taking the step to-day.

The great tragedy of it is this: If an ordinary workman had been in this mess, everyone in the House of Commons would have been ashamed of him. You would have refused him benefit. You would have ill-treated him. Look at the Minister of Labour sneering at collusive action. [HON. MEMBERS: "No, no!"] Everyone knows it. The whole Law Courts were set at defiance for this man. A divorce case was taken when everyone of you knows it was a breaking of the law. What are you talking nonsense about? The law is desecrated. The law courts are thrust aside. There is an association which everyone of you knows is collusive action. If a little boy in Wales leaves his mother to get 7s. extra, he has to stand the jeers and taunts of a miserable Minister of Labour. Talk to me about fairness, about decency, about equality! You are setting aside your laws for a rich, pampered Royalty. The next set will be pampered too. You will lie and praise them and try to laud them above ordinary men. Instead of having the ordinary frailties that all of us have,

[14] George Buchanan (1890–   ), Member for Gorbals Div. of Glasgow; Independent Labor Party.

[15] All expenses for the sovereign and the royal household are voted by Parliament under the Civil List Act, which derives its name from the fact that in early times the King paid for the civil part of the government (as opposed to the military part); a fixed annual sum for the sovereign is voted by Parliament at the beginning of each reign. The list of expenses, personal and official, is the Civil List.

they will have this additional one, of being surrounded with a set of flunkeys who refuse to let them know the truth as others do. To-morrow I will willingly take the step of going out and saying it is time the people ceased to trust those folk, but only trusted their own power and their own elected authority.

[Captain Sir Ian Fraser, Conservative Member for North St. Pancras, spoke of the respect the King commanded among ex-servicemen and gave assurance of their loyalty and help to his successor. The King's message was then considered, put, and agreed to; the Abdication Bill was brought in and read for the first time; and the House adjourned at 6:41 P.M. until the next day.]

December 11.

THE PRIME MINISTER (MR. BALDWIN): I beg to move, "That the Bill be now read a Second time."

The provisions of this Bill require very few words of explanation from me at this stage. It is a matter which, of course, concerns the Dominions and their Constitutions just as it concerns us. As the House will see, four Dominions—Canada, Australia, New Zealand and South Africa—have desired to be associated with this Bill. As regards the Irish Free State, I received a message from Mr. De Valera [16] yesterday telling me that he proposed to call his Parliament together to-day to pass legislation dealing with the situation in the Irish Free State.

The legal and constitutional position is somewhat complex, and any points with regard to it which anyone desires to raise would more properly be dealt with at a later stage.

[Mr. Baldwin went on to clarify certain clauses in the Bill which effected the King's abdication and provided for the succession of the Duke of York.]

MR. ATTLEE: We on this side desire to support this Bill in order that we may carry out the wishes of His Majesty that this chapter in our history which is closing should be closed with the least possible delay. But a new chapter is being opened, and I want to say a word or two as to why we support this Bill. We are concerned with fundamental economic changes. We are not to be diverted into abstract discussions about monarchy and republicanism. The one essential is that the will of the people should prevail in a democratic country. Further, we want the mind of the nation to return as soon as possible to the urgent problems of the conditions of the people, the state of the world and the great issue of peace.

I want to say one or two words on the lessons which, I think, we should draw for the future. It is not my intention for a moment to glance at the past. I believe that a great dis-service has been done to constitutional monarchy by over-emphasis and by vulgar adulation, particularly in the Press. The interests which stand for wealth and class privilege have done all they can to invest the monarchy with an unreal halo, and to create a false reverence for royalty, and this has tended to obscure the realities of the position. I think, too, the continuance of old-fashioned Court ceremonial, and the surrounding of the Monarch by persons drawn from a narrow and privileged class, have hampered him in his work, and have at times frustrated good intentions. I hope that we shall see a new start

---

[16] Eamon De Valera, president of the Irish Free State.

made. I believe this is necessary if constitutional monarchy is to survive in the present age. Some pomp and ceremony may be useful on occasions, but we believe that the note of monarchy should be simplicity. We as a party stand for the disappearance of class barriers and a moving towards equality, and we believe that in the interests of the Throne, in the interests of the Commonwealth, and in the interests of this country, we should see the utmost simplicity in the monarchy, which will, I believe, bind together people and Monarch more closely than before.

[Mr. Buchanan spoke on a procedural point, and Sir Archibald Sinclair spoke briefly in support of the Bill.]

MR. MAXTON: I beg to move, to leave out from the word "That", to the end of the Question, and to add instead thereof:

this House declines to give a Second Reading to a Bill which has been necessitated by circumstances which show clearly the danger to this country and to the British Commonwealth of Nations inherent in an hereditary monarchy, at a time when the peace and prosperity of the people require a more stable and efficient form of government of a republican kind, in close contact with and more responsive to the will of the mass of the people, and which fails to give effect to the principle of popular election.

[After apologizing for his inability to put the Amendment on the Order Paper because of lack of time and after expressing his opinion that the House should face the political problem involved, Mr. Maxton continued:]

My hon. Friends and I have been sent here, election after election, standing as Socialists, and telling our people frankly that we were Socialists, for the Socialist system of society as a society of equality—economic equality, social equality—with neither Kings, nor courts, nor nobles, nor peers, for a no-class society. Here to-day we are asked to give our consent to the continuation of the outstanding symbol, the very head and front, of a class society. We would be prepared to say—although on every occasion, during Jubilee celebrations, Civil Lists, Oaths of Allegiance, we have always taken what opportunities there were of putting forward our anti-monarchist views—that we have realised in the past that they were not practical politics at the given moment. I say to this House and to the country that after the experiences of these last few weeks republicanism has become more an issue of practical politics than it has been for many years. I know that a large proportion of the Members of this House will do their utmost to place monarchy back in the position it was in some months ago. I want you to remember your childhood's nursery rhyme:

> Humpty Dumpty sat on a wall,
> Humpty Dumpty had a great fall,
> All the King's horses and all the King's men,
> Could not put Humpty Dumpty back again.
> [Hon. Members: "Together again."]

Through three reigns the constitutional monarchy has worked as a reasonable device. Hon. Members of this House are charged with a greater responsibility in these days than any monarch, are asked to face greater problems than ever a monarch was asked to face, and I want them to look at the thing as sane men, as they would look at the ordinary political problems that confront us, and realise that constitutional monarchy is only a device, a device which, I say, worked reasonably well during three reigns, which has not worked well in these last weeks, and which is unlikely ever to have so long a run as it has had of smooth, easy working. As my hon. Friend the Member for West Fife (Mr. Gallacher) said yesterday, this crack-up of a monarch is not merely just the matter of a failure of a man, or the passions or affections of a man, but is something deeper and something more fundamental than that—the whole break-up of social conceptions, the whole break-up of past ideas of a Royal Family clear of the ordinary taints and weaknesses of ordinary men. The King is victim of something that has swept over Europe and the world, and cracked Crowns in every corner of the globe. We here, with the supreme egotism which is perhaps one of our most valuable possessions, say that Great Britain can remain immune, clear of all the movements that sweep over the world.

> Nations not so blessed as we,
> Must in their turn to tyrants fall,[17]

But we are above all that sort of thing.

Let hon. and right hon. Members, if they care, go on living in their fool's paradise. The economic and social forces that are at work in the world will affect this country as they have affected other countries. I have hoped, and I do hope still, that the necessary social and economic changes may take place in this country by more humane, smoother, kindlier methods than have arisen in other countries. That has been my hope; that still remains my hope, but it will be fulfilled only if the representatives of the Commons of this land are prepared to meet their difficulties in advance and create a political structure which can respond speedily and accurately to the will of the mass of the people, so that, through ordinary governmental representative democratic institutions, we can give effect to the changes that have now become necessary in human affairs.

To-day, I say that the step we are taking is a reactionary step, in attempting to set up again a governmental form which pertains to a class society, which pertains to a past age, which has a connection with problems that are not the problems of to-day. We are doing a wrong and a foolish thing if, as a House, we do not seize the opportunity with which circumstances have presented us of establishing in our land a completely democratic form of government which does away with all monarchical institutions and the hereditary principle.

MR. STEPHEN: [18] I beg to second the Amendment.

The issue has appeared to me as one of very great significance for the working people in this country. As I sat and listened yesterday to the Debate I thought of how a few weeks ago the impression was abroad throughout the land that the Monarch was almost a unique personality—[Interruption]

MR. THORNE: [19] On a point of Order. Although I am opposed to the Amendment, is not the hon. Member who is now addressing the House entitled to a fair hearing, and not to be exposed to the buzzing that is going on at present?

---

[17] A slight modification of the first two lines of the second stanza of a British national anthem, "Rule Britannia," by James Thomson (1700–1748).

[18] Cambell Stephen (1884–1947), Member for Camlachie, Glasgow; Labor Party.

[19] Will Thorne (1857–1946), Member for West Ham; Labor Party.

Mr. Stephen: I thank the hon. Member. Possibly the House is just exercising part of its ordinary discretion in this matter. I am not asking for any special favours. I represent a point of view which, I believe, has a very large backing in the country. I was saying, however, that, in my opinion, there was something very humiliating yesterday in the attitude of so many hon. Members of this House who, a short time ago, were prepared for every form of adulation of the Monarch; yet yesterday there was not one of his friends in this House who was prepared to stand up and make an appeal to the Government that those who had gloried in the qualities of the Monarch and had tried to persuade the country that he was a unique personality, should make another appeal to him to change his decision. Not one of his friends was prepared to challenge the assumptions of the Prime Minister that this man, a man of mature age, was not the person best entitled to say who should be his wife and share his Court. I believe that was very significant indeed.

The passage in the Prime Minister's speech was of very great significance, in which he told us how he had put it to His Majesty that a great position had been built up for Monarchy in this country and how, in a short time, all that might be lost. I believe profoundly that this effort being made by the Government in connection with a constitutional issue cannot meet with success and the glamour be restored to this ancient institution. The one argument for its retention is that it remains the only link binding the Dominions and keeping the Empire together. Again and again in recent years an attempt has been made to put that across as being the great function of the Monarch to-day. If your Empire is being held together only by the link of Monarchy, it is held by a very weak link but I do not think it is true. I think it is a complete illusion.

As I see it, the British Commonwealth of Nations is not held together by sentimental attachment to a particular Royal Family, but because of the associations that grew up with the development that took place. What basically keeps them together now is their economic interests. The idea that you can connect these Dominions within a Commonwealth by a particular family appears to me to lead inevitably, in the future, to your Empire fading away. I believe that the determinant is economic—that there is a real economic interest between them, that they will stay together in the Commonwealth, and that this form of government is of no vital importance. The dilemma of the King arose because the King was, like any of the rest of us, a human being. He was only a man like anyone else, and, in spite of all that Governments can do, his successor or successors will also only be human beings, and the problem that has arisen in the present instance may very well arise in the next few years. I know that the new Monarch is a married man, but so was Mr. Simpson, and just as it happened with others, so also it may happen here; and, as the Prime Minister said, another happening such as that of the present time would put an end to the Monarchy. If that be so, is a great mistake now being made by hon. Members here in not facing up to the opportunity that was provided by the present circumstances? Is the opportunity not provided here to-day for intelligent people to devise a form of government that will be a rational form of government, that will be in accordance with the needs and difficulties of to-day?

[Here Mr. Stephen mentioned what some considered royal intervention in the political events of 1931 (referring, no doubt, to the part played by King George V in setting up the "National Government" and its Coalition Cabinet); he pointed out that such intervention was one of the dangers of hereditary monarchy. He continued:]

I realise, with the Leader of the Opposition, that our function here is to deal with great fundamental economic problems, but those great fundamental economic problems are also closely associated with this monarchial system, and the monarchial system has a very great significance with regard to the maintenance of the present economic order. It is for that reason that my friends and myself have always taken the opportunity of pressing upon the House the importance of making your democracy a real democracy from top to bottom—a real democracy in which the will of the people can prevail without question. One question that is debated often enough with regard to the social struggle is whether, within the confines of the present State in a country like this, it is possible to make the transition from the present economic order to a Socialist economic order, and, looking at it quite bluntly, I believe that the forces which render it practically impossible are the forces which gather round the hereditary Monarch, and the association of the Forces—the armed Forces—so particularly with the Crown. It is the King's Army, the King's Navy, the King's Air Force. I know it is our debt, as one of my friends beside me reminds me, but it is of the utmost significance that the forces upon which the State rests, the armed Forces, are so associated with the King. There is one thing also that I would like to say in conclusion, and it has to do with a statement made by the right hon. and gallant Member for Newcastle-under-Lyme (Colonel Wedgwood) yesterday. He said that there will be no nonjurors, and I think it is only right that I should indicate what my view is with regard to the Oath of Allegiance. The Members of this House took the Oath of Allegiance to the present Monarch. Now, by this legislation, the supremacy of Parliament is again being asserted, or, at least, the supremacy of the Cabinet is being asserted, and Members will be released from that Oath of Allegiance. I look upon the Oath of Allegiance very much in the same way as Members here are acting with regard to the Oath of Allegiance. It is an oath to the King, his heirs and successors by law established, and it will be the Government that comes into being according to the circumstances of the time to which allegiance is given. Naturally, we do not think that we have a majority in this House, and, not having a majority in this House, we shall not be able to stop this legislation. We will act as we have always acted, but we believe that behind us in the country there will be a much greater volume of opinion than many people imagine at present. This crisis has revealed the weakness of the hereditary Monarchy. It has destroyed so much of the glamour that has been built up about it, more especially during recent years and there will be many who will join us in saying it is time to put an end to all this flummery and to bring into being a modern form of government, a real democratic government, based on the principle of popular election.

THE SECRETARY OF STATE FOR THE HOME DEPARTMENT (SIR JOHN SIMON): [20] I shall best interpret the general feeling of the House if I do not attempt to deal at any length with this manuscript Amendment. It expresses a sentiment which rouses very deep feelings of resentment in the hearts of most of us, but the condi-

---

[20] (1873–1954), Member for Spen Valley Div. of Yorkshire; Liberal National Party, leader of the party and deputy leader of House of Commons.

tions are such that it can be discussed calmly and, I hope, with dignity, and certainly briefly.

It is a measure of the misfortune of all this business that it should give occasion for such an Amendment. It is true that what has happened has deeply, even inexpressibly, shocked the British people—I do not mean merely the events of yesterday, but the incidents and rumours which led up to the events of yesterday. It is right that this should be so, but the fact that it is so only demonstrates how deeply this conception of constitutional Kingship is embedded in our hearts. If it did not represent an idea deeply cherished and profoundly respected, we should care much less about what has happened than we do.

The institution of the Throne is greater, far greater, than the life or experiences of any individual. If institutions were not greater than our frailty or the inscrutable promptings of an individual human heart, orderly development would be impossible. The hon. Member for Bridgeton (Mr. Maxton) described constitutional Monarchy as a device. Is not the Presidency of a Republic a device? History does not show that Republicanism is a guarantee of stability—certainly not of stability combined with civil liberty.

This conception, created by the genius of the British people and valued as the symbol of Commonwealth unity, can withstand this shock, grievous though it be, and will, I believe, be once again vindicated and strengthened in the new reign. The hon. Member for Bridgeton mistakes a most grievous incident in the history of an institution for the breakdown of the institution itself. The hon. Member for Camlachie (Mr. Stephen) said just now that he supported this Amendment because he desired the will of the people to prevail. The will of the people will prevail, and when this Bill passes to-night, the individual who ascends the Throne is one who has already won our esteem and who, with his wife at his side, will hold in trust for us this precious possession.

SIR AUSTEN CHAMBERLAIN: [21] I ask the indulgence of the House while I say a few sentences. I am the oldest Member in the service of this House present to-day, I have served as one of the confidential advisers to His Majesty's father and grandfather. I was junior Member of the Government in the last decade of Queen Victoria's reign. The House will understand what emotions have pressed upon me in these last days and what are my feelings. But it is not in that capacity that I ask the House to listen to me to-day. I sit for a poor constituency in the second greatest city of this country. West Birmingham is no home of the rich. It is a constituency of poor streets and mean houses, the people living in back courts to a very large extent, all of them very near the hardships and sufferings of life in their cruellest form. That constituency, those people who sent me here, men and women, poor as they may be, suffering as many of them are, see in the King of this country a friend and in the Monarchy their safeguard.

I think it was right that some Member standing for such a poor constituency should repudiate in their name the suggestion of the hon. Member for Bridgeton (Mr. Maxton), that the Monarchy is a castle of class and privilege. In the minds of those whom I represent, it stands higher than all class. They think of it not as an institution or as an individual buttressed with privilege; they think of the Monarchy as the first servant of the nation. When the Monarchy is clouded in sorrow, they are the first to sympathise, and their sympathy is among the

[21] (1863–1937), Member for Birmingham, West; Conservative (Unionist) Party.

most sincere. When there is occasion to rejoice in these back streets, there are no civic processions, no civil declarations. The fête is the people's own fête in honour and affection for the wearer of the Crown. Let it go forth not only here in this country and in the Empire, but let it go forth to all other nations, that our King is the people's King, their guardian and supporter.

Mr. Gallacher: I wish to identify myself with this Amendment. In doing so, I would like to remind the House that 40 years ago Republicanism was quite the thing in this country, and I do not think that I am wrong in saying that a very prominent politician from Birmingham [22] was in the forefront of the Republican movement. What I am concerned most about is that we have the Leader of the Opposition and the Leader of the Liberal party saying that next week we will go on with our ordinary business. There seems to be a tendency to accept this event as something that has happened, and then life will go on as though nothing had actually taken place. But this is the most unparalleled event in the history of this country, and it expresses and represents something. The crisis itself is superficial, but beneath the superficial crisis there is something that demands, and must get, attention.

I have listened to the attempts being made to put a case for the Monarchy. The Home Secretary says that it is an idea deeply cherished. He ought to have said "an idea deeply cultivated." I will confound the Home Secretary, and I will confound every supporter in this House out of the mouth of the principal spokesman. The right hon. Member for West Birmingham (Sir A. Chamberlain) states here that he represents a poor constituency, with poor streets, awful houses, terrible poverty, suffering and hardships, these people living in wretched unhygienic houses, no clothes, no sufficiency of food, part of them broken—he has the audacity to tell us that they look upon the Monarch as their guardian. Guardian of what? Guardian of their poverty; guardian of their suffering.

Mr. Buchanan: What about the means test? [23]

Mr. Gallacher: What cant. What humbug. When we were discussing the Civil List I drew attention to a remark made by the hon. and learned Member for Bristol, East (Sir S. Cripps) wherein he said that if the aristocracy were not removed, then the people, rising against the aristocracy, might overthrow the monarchy. I said that he was wrong and that not anywhere in history was there a case of the workers overthrowing the Monarchy. But the ruling class know no loyalty. As long as the King served their interests, they would keep the King. When the King failed to serve their interests, out the King would go. That was while we were discussing the Civil List. Where is your loyalty to-day? At the time when there is the greatest need for loyalty, it is not there. It is not there because he ceased to serve the interests of a particular group that surrounds the Monarch, the Cabinet at the present time. Their loyalty goes and the King matters nothing, and you cover it all up by talking about the Constitution, but underneath this crisis, this superficial crisis, is the crisis of unemployment, the means test and the derelict areas, and, instead of dealing with the superficial crisis, we ought to be dealing with the real, fundamental crisis. Last night the hon. Member for Gorbals (Mr. Buchanan) made a reference to the effect that a working man

[22] Joseph Chamberlain, father of Sir Austen Chamberlain.

[23] A test of the resources or means of the unemployed to determine their eligibility for payments from other funds once their unemployment insurance payments have been exhausted.

getting into such a mess would be deprived of his benefit, and Members shouted "No, no!" The Minister of Labour has gone away, but I would like to ask him whether, if a working man in any particular town got into a mess, left his job and went to live in another town, he would get Unemployment Benefit? No. In every part of the country workers are suffering from unemployment and the means test—suffering terrible poverty. That is the problem we ought to be discussing, and if we could solve that problem, the superficial problem or the superficial issue would fall into its proper and insignificant place.

Therefore, I want the House to understand that this crisis is not finished. I have a letter in my hand sent to me this morning from Lincoln's Inn,[24] and it represents what will now become customary discussion. This individual wants me to raise what he claims to be the average view among all intelligent people under the age of 45—I do not agree with him about that—but he is for the King—for the past King, if there is a past King—and for Mrs. Simpson. And the peculiar thing is, that up to a couple of weeks ago, the main body of the Members of this House were for the King and Mrs. Simpson. There was not a word against Mrs. Simpson. But this writer of the letter is for the King and Mrs. Simpson, and he has some very queer things to say about the relations of the Cabinet and the new King. This is going to be more and more discussed. All the evil forces will begin to form round about this question.

I cannot describe this event, it is such a unique thing. Never since the time of Cromwell have you had such a situation confronting the House of Commons. It cannot simply pass into history and die. The only way in which we can overcome the forces that represent both sides of this trouble is to unite all the people we can for the purpose of solving the economic problem, the problem of unemployment, the abolition of the means test, the abolition of the unemployment assistance Regulations, construct huge schemes for the derelict areas and get a peace policy based on collective security. Let us get this without the worry and trouble of a Monarchy, and we can win the masses of the people of this country and weld them together as the greatest possible factor for the pacification and progress of Europe. It is on these lines that I appeal to Members of the Labour party to support the Amendment and to go forward with a policy of peace and progress, appealing to the masses of the people, confident of getting their support.

[There followed a question by Mr. Mathers, Labor Member for Linlithgowshire, concerning a technicality; brief remarks by Mr. Cluse, Labor Member for South Islington, on the necessity of abolishing poverty in general and the means test in particular; and comments from Mr. G. Hardie, Labor Member for Springburn Div. of Glasgow, on the folly of allowing heredity to dictate who should fill "the highest posts" in the nation. The question was then put and the Amendment defeated 403 to 5. The second reading of the Bill was followed by discussion and final agreement on specific clauses, on the Schedule to the Bill, and on the Preamble to the Bill. The Prime Minister moved the third and last reading of the Bill.]

THE PRIME MINISTER: I beg to move, "That the Bill be now read the Third time."

[24] One of the London legal societies from which the profession of law operates in England. Presumably, therefore, the letter came from someone connected with the law.

I rise once more to-day, and only for a very few moments, because I do not want this Bill to leave this House without making the few observations which I propose to make. This is the last Bill that will be presented for the Royal Assent during the present reign. The Royal Assent given to this Bill will be the last act of His present Majesty, and I should not like the Bill to go to another place without putting on record what, I feel sure, will be the feeling of this House and of the country, that, though we have this duty to perform to-day, and though we are performing it with unanimity, we can never be unconscious of, and we shall always remember with regard and affection, the whole-hearted and loyal service that His Majesty has given to this country as Prince of Wales and during the short time he has been on the Throne. Like many of his generation, he was flung into the War as a very young man, and he has served us well in trying to qualify himself for that office which he knew must be his if he lived. For all that work I should like to put on record here to-day that we are grateful and that we shall not forget. There is no need on this Bill to say anything of the future. It deals with the fate of him who is still King and who will cease to be King in a few short hours. I felt that I could hardly reconcile it with my conscience or my feelings if I let this Bill go to another place without saying just these few words.

[At this point Mr. Buchanan tried to explain why the Amendment made the day before was late; he was ruled out of order by the Speaker. However, he continued:]

Mr. Buchanan: I only rose for the purpose of explanation and to say that we took the course of giving it to you, Sir, and to the Prime Minister at the earliest possible moment. We will not divide on the Third Reading because we divided on Second Reading. We have registered our opinion, and, as Parliamentarians, we accept the decision of the House. We will, however, take action again when subsequent legislation is produced. We shall take action on the Civil List. I only want now to register our opinion that we do not agree with what the Prime Minister said about unanimity. We still hold the view we held, and we shall preserve our right to oppose subsequent legislation as we have opposed this legislation to-day.

[Question put, and agreed to. Bill read the Third time, and passed. The Prime Minister then outlined the order of business of the House for the next week; this included a meeting the next day at which Members might take the Oath of Allegiance to the new King. The House adjourned at 1:58 p.m.]

～

Edward VIII (1894–   ) and the Farewell Message

December 11, 1936

The abdication had been formally completed by Parliament on Friday, December 11, and at two o'clock the next morning, Edward, whose reign had not been even long enough to include his own coronation,[1] left England.[2] Before he went, he said goodby to the people of the British Empire.

His farewell message was simplicity itself. Read with evident but for the most part controlled emotion, in the slow and deliberate manner[3] once advised by Churchill some seventeen years before, when Edward was first struggling with public speaking,[4] it had the moving dignity of sincerity.

The emotional impact of the speech on its audience was tremendous. It was unique because the speech was unique. Never before had a head of state, or anybody else for that matter, spoken personally to millions of people about a personal problem, and moreover a problem caused by something as easily understood and universally experienced as falling in love. Edward's appealingly simple apologia impressed and touched most of those who heard it. Whether they agreed with his decision, they responded to his own implicit plea for understanding of it with intensely personal sympathy. And this was as true of the knowing American or Frenchman who had been following developments for months in a not always accurate press, as it was of the bewildered Briton who was still trying to sort out his conflicting reactions to the incredible story suddenly thrust upon him only days before.

It was a response reflected in the great majority of the world's newspapers, for the audience itself was virtually world-wide. "In Norway, Sweden, Czechoslovakia, Latin America, the Dutch East Indies, the Empire, and the world at large an estimated 500 million men, women, and children formed the largest audience for a single speech in the history of man."[5]

Edward says that he wrote the speech himself, though he asked Churchill to read it and Churchill "made several admirable suggestions"[6] which he used. He then sent the draft to Baldwin and the Cabinet so that they would know in advance what he was about to say. The farewell message was broadcast from Windsor Castle at 10 P.M. Friday night under the supervision of Sir John Reith,[7] director of the BBC, who made the introductory announcement: "This is Windsor Castle. His Royal Highness, Prince Edward."[8] According to Edward's account,

[1] Edward had been King from January 20 to December 11 of 1936. The Coronation had been set for May 12, 1937, and, in fact, was held then just as planned—with only a change of principals.

[2] He went to Austria and after the divorce decree became final, was married to Mrs. Simpson on June 3, 1937, by a venturesome clergyman who defied his Church of England bishop in order to officiate. The ceremony took place in France at the Chateau de Candé (owned by Charles Bedaux, a French-American, who not many years later was charged with treasonable collaboration with the Nazis and committed suicide).

[3] In his study of the speech, Smith reports that it was read at a rate of about eighty words per minute, and lasted six minutes and forty seconds. (Robert W. Smith, "Rhetoric in Crisis: The Abdication Address of Edward VIII," *Speech Monographs*, XXX (1963), 336.)

[4] *A King's Story*, p. 137.

[5] Smith, p. 337. In the United States alone, according to Smith, more than 300 stations carried the broadcast.

[6] The two specifically mentioned by Edward (*A King's Story*, p. 407) are footnoted in the text of the speech used here.

[7] Edward had requested that he be the one to take charge (*A King's Story*, p. 410).

[8] With his abdication, Edward became a royal prince again, though without any of the royal titles he had previously held as prince. Consequently on this occasion he

Sir John then "slipped out of the room," leaving him alone with Walter Monckton [9] and the radio technicians as, seated at a table, he began to read from his manuscript.

∾

Farewell Message [*]

[1] At long last I am able to say a few words of my own.

I have never wanted to withhold anything, / but until now it has not been constitutionally possible / for me to speak.

[2] A few hours ago I discharged my last duty as King and Emperor, / and now that I have been succeeded by my brother, / the Duke of York, / my first words must be to declare my allegiance to him. // This I do with all my heart. //

[3] You all know the reasons which have impelled me to renounce the Throne, / but I want you to understand that in making up my mind / I did not forget the Country or the Empire, / which, as Prince of Wales and lately as King, / I have for 25 years tried to serve.

[4] But you must believe me when I tell you / that I have found it impossible to carry the heavy burden of responsibility / and to discharge my duties as King, as I would wish to do, / without the help and support / of the woman I love, / and I want you to know that the decision I have made / has been mine, and mine alone. // This was a thing I had to judge entirely [1] for myself. // The other person most nearly concerned has tried, / up to the last, / to persuade me

---

was simply "Prince Edward." Shortly thereafter, George VI made him His Royal Highness, Duke of Windsor. This was a title only, carrying with it no ducal lands or residence, and "Windsor" is merely the family name, having nothing to do with Windsor Castle, which belongs to the Crown.

[9] The barrister friend who had given untiring service as personal adviser and as liaison between Edward and the Prime Minister throughout the crisis.

[*] The text of the Farewell Message is derived from two sources. The first is the transcription of an electronic recording made from the broadcast, which is used by Robert W. Smith for his text in his study of the speech (see Bibliographical Note). The second is the manuscript which Edward used as his reading copy, and from which the paragraphing, capitalization, and punctuation for the present text are taken. Reproduced by photostat in A King's Story (opposite p. 389), the reading manuscript is a typewritten copy with pencilled additions in Edward's hand. In the present text, the pencilled additions are bracketed and footnoted. On the reading copy Edward underlined some words and phrases and inserted slashes after others, apparently as a guide to the use of emphasis and pause in delivery. The reading copy also contains typed arabic numerals, from 1 through 7, along the left-hand margin, each one presumably to indicate the introduction of a new idea. All of these marks and numerals have been retained in the present text; the only marks not retained are four brackets pencilled on the edge of the left-hand margin the length of the two paragraphs comprising 1, the length of the paragraph marked 4, the length of the paragraph marked 5, and the length of the first of the paragraphs comprising 7.

[1] The reading copy omits "entirely"; probably ad-libbed during the reading.

to take a different course.[2] // I have made this, / the most serious decision of my life, / only upon the single thought / of what would in the end be best for all.

[5] This decision has been made less difficult to me / by the sure knowledge that my brother, / with his long training in the public affairs of this Country / and with his fine qualities, / will be able to take my place forthwith / without interruption or injury to the life and progress of the Empire, / and he has one matchless blessing, / enjoyed by so many of you, / and not bestowed on me, / a happy home with his wife and children.[3]

[6] During these hard days I have been comforted by [Her Majesty][4] my Mother and by her [5] by my Family.

The Ministers of the Crown [and in particular Mr. Baldwin],[6] the Prime Minister,[7] have always treated me with full consideration. There has never been

[2] *A King's Story* (p. 406) sheds an interesting sidelight on this sentence. Baldwin had told Walter Monckton to ask the King whether there was anything concerning their negotiations that he would particularly like Baldwin to mention in his Commons report. Edward, appreciating this courtesy, sent Baldwin two notes. One was the note about the Duke of York, which Baldwin read verbatim. (See 318 *H. C. Deb.* 5s., 2183.) The other asked that Baldwin say substantially what the King himself says here about Mrs. Simpson's trying to dissuade him. Baldwin never referred to this. Sencourt defends the omission on the grounds that "it would have turned the whole effort [Baldwin's case for the King, one aspect of which was that the King had been anxious for the 'moral force of the Crown'] into a farce if at that moment Baldwin had sought to enlist the tributes of the House to a woman whose part in the business had already outraged honest opinion in the House of Commons and in the constituencies its Members represented"; and that Baldwin could scarcely have stated that although Mrs. Simpson had offered to give him up, the King still persisted in putting her ahead of all the claims of the Crown which Baldwin had been at pains to show were of great concern to the King. (*The Reign of Edward VIII*, p. 194.) Whether Edward would have used this idea in his own speech if Baldwin had already included it in his, is, of course, a moot question. In any case, Edward's account of an ironic sequel to this incident shows that neither then nor later when he wrote his book had an explanation such as Sencourt's or anybody else's ever occurred to him; it also reveals the bitterness with which he regarded Baldwin's whole speech, as well as the incident itself. Edward writes that a few hours before he was to broadcast, Monckton brought the draft of his speech back from the Government, with the hint that Baldwin "would be gratified if I should stress that he had at all times shown me every possible form of consideration. 'That's a good one,' I said, remembering how he had ignored my simple request the day before that he should do justice in his speech to Wallis. His omission was all the harder to understand because of the apparent benevolence that pervaded his own speech—an autobiographical triumph disguised as a homily on the errors of a King. However, determined not to be petty at the last moment, I incorporated into my broadcast that little item that Mr. Baldwin had valued. Perhaps the rendering of these simple courtesies falls more easily upon kings than upon politicians; after all we do not have to run for office." (*A King's Story*, pp. 408–9.) See note 6, below.

[3] ". . . one matchless blessing . . . children" is one of the phrases contributed by Churchill.

[4] Inserted in pencil in the reading copy.

[5] "by her" is a misreading. Edward saved the sense of the phrase by repeating the preposition and finishing correctly: "by my Family."

[6] Inserted in pencil in the reading copy. Thus did Edward incorporate "that little item that Mr. Baldwin had valued." (See note 2, above.)

[7] The reading copy omits "the Prime Minister"; probably ad-libbed.

any constitutional difference between me and them / and between me and Parliament. / Bred in the constitutional tradition by my Father,[8] / I should never have allowed any such issue to arise. //

Ever since I was Prince of Wales, / and later on when I occupied the Throne, / I have been treated with the greatest kindness by all classes of the people [9] wherever I have lived or journeyed throughout the Empire. // [For that I am very grateful.] [10]

[7] I now quit altogether public affairs / and I lay down my burden. // It may be some time before I return to my native land, / but I shall always follow the fortunes of the British race and Empire with profound interest, / and if, at any time in the future, / I can be found of service to His Majesty in a private station, / I shall not fail. /

And now we all have a new King. //

I wish Him and you, His people, / happiness and prosperity with all my heart.

God bless you all.

God save the King.

☙

BIBLIOGRAPHICAL NOTE

The story of the abdication—from which some details are still lacking—is to be found mainly in the various biographies and personal memoirs of the people involved, and in a few comprehensive accounts.

Foremost among these is Edward's own book, *A King's Story: The Memoirs of the Duke of Windsor* (1951), which is supplemented by that of "the other person most nearly concerned," *The Heart Has Its Reasons: The Memoirs of the Duchess of Windsor* (1956).

Hector Bolitho, a noted biographer, draws upon his acquaintance with Edward in writing *King Edward VIII* (1937), an "intimate biography" which pinpoints the moments of constitutional crisis, supports Baldwin, and sympathizes with "a man of promise who came to disaster through the slow disintegration of his character" (p. 306); his 33-page sketch of Edward in *A Century of British Monarchy* (1951) offers a concise description of Edward's personality and of his great popularity as Prince of Wales. Philip Guedalla records the abdication as the climactic finale in his chronological account of the events of 1936 entitled *The Hundredth Year* (1939). In his *Ordeal in England* (1937) Philip Gibbs devotes a chapter apiece to Edward and the abdication, stressing the reaction of the man-in-the-street and raising a mild question or two about Baldwin's handling of the crisis. Two works on George V, Harold Nicolson's *King George the Fifth: His Life and Reign* (1952) and John Gore's *King George V: A Personal Memoir* (1941), contain brief but illuminating observations on George's relations with his children, including Edward; and pp. 559–83 of James Pope-Hennessy's *Queen Mary 1867–1953* (1959) give some idea of his mother's attitude toward Edward, his abdication, and his marriage. In its narration of events before, during, and after the abdication, a popular book, *Gone with the Windsors* (1953), by Iles Brody, "an-

---

[8] Churchill's phrase.

[9] The reading copy omits "of the people"; probably ad-libbed.

[10] Inserted in pencil in the reading copy.

swers" and challenges *A King's Story*. Robert W. Smith's informative study, "Rhetoric in Crisis: The Abdication Address of Edward VIII" [in *Speech Monographs*, XXX (1963), 335–39], analyzes the speech, discusses its presentation and favorable reception, and supplies the as-delivered text which is one of the two sources for the text given here and for use of which we are indebted to Professor Smith.

Churchill's part in the crisis, including his rebuff in the House, is objectively recounted by Lewis Broad in *The Years of Preparation* (1958), Volume I of his biography, *Winston Churchill;* and it is referred to briefly by Churchill himself in his first volume of *The Second World War*, entitled *The Gathering Storm* (1948), pp. 217–19.

Although various aspects of the authorized biography of Baldwin by George M. Young, *Stanley Baldwin* (1952), have been questioned, even D. C. Somervell, one of its best known critics [see his *Stanley Baldwin: An Examination of Some Features of Mr. G. M. Young's Biography* (1953)], seems to approve the chapter on the abdication. *My Father: The True Story* (1955) by A. W. Baldwin, while allotting only a few pages to the abdication as such, presents an interpretative depiction of the man who dealt with the crisis for the Government. An interesting, though occasionally somewhat obscure, study of Baldwin's December 10th speech in Commons is provided by James C. Ching's "Stanley Baldwin's Speech on the Abdication of Edward VIII," in *The Quarterly Journal of Speech*, XLII (1956), 163–69.

A fascinating report of Beaverbrook's role in the drama, his motives, and his influence is given in "King as Pawn," Chapter 10 of Tom Driberg's book, *Beaverbrook: A Study in Power and Frustration* (1956); this includes a discussion of Beaverbrook's controversial 1952 radio review of *The History of the* [London] *Times*, in which he reopened the subject of the abdication and made what Driberg terms his "principal direct contribution" to the history of the abdication crisis. Beaverbrook later added to the contribution by writing a full and highly readable account of his own part in the crisis; although completed in 1958, the manuscript remained unpublished until after his death when A. J. P. Taylor edited and issued it in 1966 under the title *The Abdication of King Edward VIII.*

Of a more general nature, *The Magic of Monarchy* (1937) by Kingsley Martin is "an examination of the evolution of British opinion about the Monarchy during the last century and, in particular, during the abdication crisis." Chapter 4 investigates newspaper comment on the abdication and analyzes the makeup of the so-called "King's party"; Chapter 5 discusses factors contributing to the abdication and delineates the overall significance of the abdication itself.

The historian Robert Sencourt (pseudonym for Robert Esmonde Gordon George) has written what is probably the most complete narrative of the abdication story to date in *The Reign of Edward VIII* (1962). The book is a painstaking collation of the Windsors' autobiographical accounts with other memoirs (including most of those mentioned here), of material from journalistic and official records, and of information obtained directly from many of the people involved—cemented by personal knowledge and impressions of most of these people. In the course of his narrative Sencourt seeks to right what he believes to be injustices done Baldwin and others in *A King's Story*, but in doing so he tries to be as "unbiased and objective" as he can, often going to some lengths to understand and explain Edward.

If only two books could be read for background to the House of Commons debate on the abdication and to Edward's farewell message, Sencourt's book and *A King's Story* would be the two to read.

Winston Spencer Churchill
(1874–1965)

No brief note can define the distinctive qualities of so complex a figure as Winston Churchill, but three facts had unique significance in inducing the British and the democratic West to turn to him in moments of historic danger. From 1932 to 1939, Churchill had presciently—monotonously, it seemed to many—insisted that European totalitarianism was a military threat to free European societies and an ample justification for their swift rearmament. During the First World War and later, he had demonstrated administrative resourcefulness. In writing and speaking he had proved himself without a peer in articulating what he liked to call "this good cause" of "this Britain and its far-flung association of states and dependencies."

Except for one short interval, Churchill's membership in the House of Commons extended from 1900 to 1963.[1] He attained cabinet rank in 1908, under Lord Asquith. Subsequently he served in the cabinets of David Lloyd George, Stanley Baldwin, and Neville Chamberlain, and he headed two Governments himself (1940–1945, 1951–1955).

Churchill was never a party "regular." He entered Parliament as a Conservative but, finding at low ebb the "Tory democracy" of Disraeli and Lord Randolph Churchill, he soon transferred his allegiance to the Liberals. After some twenty years as a Liberal, he turned back to the Conservatives in 1924. This time, distaste for the Liberals' position on Protection and disdain for their alliance with the Labor Party caused the break. It was the further mark of his independent spirit that he mounted his most important campaign of criticism from within the Conservative Party—against the military and foreign policies of a Conservative Government. Throughout his career Churchill seemed to orthodox politicians a troublesome irregular in periods of political quietism, but a valuable ally in times of crisis.

By common consent Churchill holds place as the greatest master of spoken English in modern times. At his best he combined the precision of Pericles, as we know that orator through Thucydides, with Roman *gravitas* and English wit. In parliamentary debate, he was sometimes prosaic, sometimes discursive, but usually brilliant in moments of high feeling. He had no equal when the need was to find the public meaning of major events, to place that meaning in historical perspective, and to give such conceptions concise and ennobling or attainting expression. Then, as Charles W. Lomas says, he was an "orator-historian"[2] and, in the words of Lord Birkett, "a survivor from the golden age of oratory."[3]

Speaking affected and was affected by Churchill's lifelong activity as a writer, chiefly of history and biography. Amplifications of his major themes in politics

---

[1] Churchill took leave of politics in 1963. Technically, he was still a member of the House in 1964.

[2] "Winston Churchill: Orator Historian," *Quarterly Journal of Speech*, XLIV (1958), 153–60.

[3] "Churchill the Orator," in *Churchill, by His Contemporaries*, Charles Eade, ed. (New York, 1954), p. 289. This essay is a perceptive discussion of Churchill's style.

and oratory are to be found in his six-volume history of the First World War (1923–1931), in *Marlborough, His Life and Times* (six volumes, 1933–1938), *A History of the English-Speaking Peoples* (four volumes, 1956–1958), and especially in *The Second World War* (six volumes, 1948–1953). It is equally true that concepts and language originating in his public speeches became the materials of history for Churchill as writer.

From 1931 until the beginning of the Second World War, Churchill increasingly spoke in the role of Cassandra, the foreteller of misfortunes who was given no credence. He thus described the indecisiveness against which he set himself:

> The British Government which resulted from the general election of 1931 was in appearance one of the strongest, and in fact one of the weakest, in British records. . . . This was one of those awful periods which recur in our history, when the noble British nation seems to fall from its high estate, loses all trace of sense or purpose, and appears to cower from the menace of foreign peril, frothing pious platitudes while foemen forge their arms.[4]

To challenge this indifference to national self-interest Churchill records:

> I . . . went to Parliament from time to time to deliver warning speeches, which commanded attention, but did not, unhappily, wake to action the crowded, puzzled Houses which heard them.[5]

His speech on the Munich agreement, which we print here, is one of the last and probably the greatest of these "warning speeches."

Though Chamberlain and Daladier acceded to Hitler's demands for *lebensraum* by sacrificing Czechoslovakia, Germany declared war on Poland, September 1, 1939. France and Britain responded by declaring war on Germany, September 3, 1939. The peace Chamberlain and Daladier had won in 1938 had lasted but eleven months. Churchill's status changed too:

> It was only in September, with the German attack on Poland and the imminence of war, that Chamberlain asked Churchill to return to his old post as First Lord of the Admiralty. The news was signaled to the Fleet: "Winston is back."[6]

Poland fell quickly. The winter of "twilight war" was succeeded in April 1940 by German invasion of Denmark and Norway. The British-French forces sent to Norway's aid failed, and on May 9, Chamberlain decided to resign from leadership. Churchill promptly formed a new Coalition Government and entered the greatest and most demanding years of his career.

Not least among his wartime achievements were Prime Minister Churchill's speeches to the British people and to the world.[7] "A Solemn Hour" was his first such broadcast. Like similar addresses to follow, this speech was ostensibly a war report; in fact, it was an instrument of war. Of Churchill as broadcaster it has

---

[4] Winston Churchill, *The Gathering Storm* (New York, 1961), pp. 60, 77.

[5] *Ibid.*, p. 74.

[6] Stephen R. Graubard, *Burke, Disraeli, and Churchill* (Cambridge, Mass., 1961), p. 219. Graubard's essays have special value in that the author seeks to relate the writings of his statesmen-orators to the political events in which they participated.

[7] For excerpts from four wartime reports to the House of Commons see *British Orations* (Everyman's Library, No. 714). See *Parliamentary Debates* for complete texts.

been said: "This was surely the art of the microphone, at a level higher than had ever been reached before or has ever been attained since."[8]

&

ON THE MUNICH AGREEMENT [*]

House of Commons
October 5, 1938

If I do not begin this afternoon by paying the usual, and indeed almost invariable, tributes to the Prime Minister for his handling of this crisis, it is certainly not from any lack of personal regard.[1] We have always, over a great many years, had very pleasant relations, and I have deeply understood from personal experiences of my own in a similar crisis the stress and strain he has had to bear,[2] but I am sure it is much better to say exactly what we think about public affairs, and this is certainly not the time when it is worth anyone's while to court political popularity. We had a shining example of firmness of character from the late First Lord of the Admiralty[3] two days ago. He showed that firmness of character which is utterly unmoved by currents of opinion, however swift and violent they may be. My hon. Friend the Member for South-West Hull (Mr. Law),[4] to whose compulsive speech the House listened on Monday—which I had not the good fortune to hear, but which I read, and which I am assured by all who heard it revived the memory of his famous father, so cherished in this House,[5] and made us feel that his gifts did not die with him—was quite right in reminding us that the Prime Minister has himself throughout his conduct of these matters shown a robust indifference to cheers or boos and to the alternations of criticism and applause. If that be so, such qualities and elevation of mind should make it possible for the most severe expressions of honest opinion to be interchanged in

[8] Richard Dimbleby, "Churchill the Broadcaster," in *Churchill, by His Contemporaries*, p. 354.

[*] The text of this speech is from *Parliamentary Debates*, 5th Series, Vol. 339, columns 359–73. The speech occupied about fifty minutes in delivery.

[1] On October 3, 1938, Sir John Simon, Chancellor of the Exchequer, moved that the House approve Chamberlain's negotiations "by which war was averted in the recent crisis." At issue were the agreements reached at Munich, September 29–30, by Édouard Daladier, Neville Chamberlain, Benito Mussolini, and Adolf Hitler: Germany would occupy the Sudetenland section of Czechoslovakia, plebiscites would be held in certain other parts of Czechoslovakia to determine disposition of those areas, Britain and France would guarantee Czechoslovakia's new boundaries.

[2] Churchill presumably refers to his tenure as First Lord of the Admiralty, 1911–1915.

[3] Sir Samuel Hoare, First Lord of the Admiralty and then Foreign Secretary in the Baldwin Ministry, now Secretary for the Home Department under Chamberlain. On October 3, Hoare declared Czechoslovakia indefensible and insisted that any action except negotiations with Hitler would have plunged the world into war. (*Parliamentary Debates*, Vol. 339, columns 150–62.)

[4] Mr. Richard K. Law had opened a speech against the Munich agreement with a tribute to Chamberlain's commitment to principles and his disregard for popular clamor.

[5] Andrew Bonar Law (1858–1923), Prime Minister 1922–1923.

this House without rupturing personal relations, and for all points of view to receive the fullest possible expression.

Having thus fortified myself by the example of others, I will proceed to emulate them. I will, therefore, begin by saying the most unpopular and most unwelcome thing. I will begin by saying what everybody would like to ignore or forget but which must nevertheless be stated, namely, that we have sustained a total and unmitigated defeat, and that France has suffered even more than we have.

[VISCOUNTESS ASTOR: [6] Nonsense.]

When the Noble Lady cries "Nonsense," she could not have heard the Chancellor of the Exchequer admit in his illuminating and comprehensive speech just now that Herr Hitler had gained in this particular leap forward in substance all he set out to gain.[7] The utmost my right hon. Friend the Prime Minister has been able to secure by all his immense exertions, by all the great efforts and mobilisation [8] which took place in this country, and by all the anguish and strain through which we have passed in this country, the utmost he has been able to gain—[HON. MEMBERS: "Is peace."] I thought I might be allowed to make that point in its due place, and I propose to deal with it. The utmost he has been able to gain for Czechoslovakia and in the matters which were in dispute has been that the German dictator, instead of snatching his victuals from the table, has been content to have them served to him course by course.

The Chancellor of the Exchequer said it was the first time Herr Hitler had been made to retract—I think that was the word—in any degree. We really must not waste time, after all this long Debate, upon the difference between the positions reached at Berchtesgaden, at Godesberg and at Munich.[9] They can be very simply epitomised, if the House will permit me to vary the metaphor. £1 was demanded at the pistol's point. When it was given, £2 were demanded at the pistol's point. Finally, the dictator consented to take £1 17s. 6d. and the rest in promises of good will for the future.

Now I come to the point, which was mentioned to me just now from some quarters of the House, about the saving of peace. No one has been a more resolute and uncompromising struggler for peace than the Prime Minister. Everyone knows that. Never has there been such intense and undaunted determination to maintain and to secure peace. That is quite true. Nevertheless, I am not quite clear why there was so much danger of Great Britain or France being involved in a war with Germany at this juncture if, in fact, they were ready all along to sacrifice Czechoslovakia. The terms which the Prime Minister brought back with him—I quite agree at the last moment; everything had got off the rails

[6] Viscountess Nancy Astor, first woman M.P. to sit in the Imperial Parliament. Member for Plymouth, Sutton Division, 1919–1945.

[7] Sir John Simon alleged that whereas Hitler had been prepared to precipitate war, "the Reich is now acquiring the territory he demanded, not indeed by invasion or war, but by cession."

[8] The French Army was partially mobilized in mid-September. The Admiralty ordered mobilization of the British Fleet, September 28.

[9] Chamberlain met Hitler at Berchtesgaden in mid-September and came away believing Hitler wanted only self-determination for the Germans living in Czechoslovakia. Chamberlain was shocked when, a few days later at Godesberg, Hitler rejected a proposal that Czechoslovakia cede any areas in which more than fifty per cent of the population was German.

and nothing but his intervention could have saved the peace, but I am talking of the events of the summer—could easily have been agreed, I believe, through the ordinary diplomatic channels at any time during the summer. And I will say this, that I believe the Czechs, left to themselves and told they were going to get no help from the Western Powers, would have been able to make better terms than they have got—they could hardly have worse—after all this tremendous perturbation.

There never can be any absolute certainty that there will be a fight if one side is determined that it will give way completely. When one reads the Munich terms, when one sees what is happening in Czechoslovakia from hour to hour, when one is sure, I will not say of Parliamentary approval but of Parliamentary acquiescence, when the Chancellor of the Exchequer makes a speech which at any rate tries to put in a very powerful and persuasive manner the fact that, after all, it was inevitable and indeed righteous—right—when we saw all this, and everyone on this side of the House, including many Members of the Conservative Party who are supposed to be vigilant and careful guardians of the national interest, it is quite clear that nothing vitally affecting us was at stake; it seems to me that one must ask, What was all the trouble and fuss about?

The resolve was taken by the British and the French Governments. Let me say that it is very important to realise that it is by no means a question which the British Government only have had to decide. I very much admire the manner in which, in the House, all references of a recriminatory nature have been repressed, but it must be realised that this resolve did not emanate particularly from one or other of the Governments but was a resolve for which both must share in common the responsibility. When this resolve was taken and the course was followed—you may say it was wise or unwise, prudent or short-sighted—once it had been decided not to make the defence of Czechoslovakia a matter of war, then there was really no reason, if the matter had been handled during the summer in the ordinary way, to call into being all this formidable apparatus of crisis. I think that point should be considered.

We are asked to vote for this Motion which has been put upon the Paper, and it is certainly a Motion couched in very uncontroversial terms, as, indeed, is the Amendment moved from the Opposition side. I cannot myself express my agreement with the steps which have been taken, and as the Chancellor of the Exchequer has put his side of the case with so much ability I will attempt, if I may be permitted, to put the case from a different angle. I have always held the view that the maintenance of peace depends upon the accumulation of deterrents against the aggressor, coupled with a sincere effort to redress grievances. Herr Hitler's victory, like so many of the famous struggles that have governed the fate of the world, was won upon the narrowest of margins. After the seizure of Austria in March [10] we faced this problem in our Debates. I ventured to appeal to the Government to go a little further than the Prime Minister went, and to give a pledge that in conjunction with France and other Powers they would guarantee the security of Czechoslovakia while the Sudeten-Deutsch question was being examined either by a League of Nations Commission or some other impartial body, and I still believe that if that course had been followed events would

---

[10] German troops, accompanied by Hitler, entered Austria on March 12, 1938. Shortly thereafter Austria was incorporated into the Reich.

not have fallen into this disastrous state. I agree very much with my right hon. Friend the Member for Sparkbrook (Mr. Amery) [11] when he said on that occasion—I cannot remember his actual words—"Do one thing or the other; either say you will disinterest yourself in the matter altogether or take the step of giving a guarantee which will have the greatest chance of securing protection for that country."

France and Great Britain together, especially if they had maintained a close contact with Russia, which certainly was not done, would have been able in those days in the summer, when they had the prestige, to influence many of the smaller States of Europe, and I believe they could have determined the attitude of Poland. Such a combination, prepared at a time when the German dictator was not deeply and irrevocably committed to his new adventure, would, I believe, have given strength to all those forces in Germany which resisted this departure, this new design. They were varying forces, those of a military character which declared that Germany was not ready to undertake a world war,[12] and all that mass of moderate opinion and popular opinion which dreaded war, and some elements of which still have some influence upon the German Government. Such action would have given strength to all that intense desire for peace which the helpless German masses share with their British and French fellow men, and which, as we have been reminded, found a passionate and rarely permitted vent in the joyous manifestations with which the Prime Minister was acclaimed in Munich.

All these forces, added to the other deterrents which combinations of Powers, great and small, ready to stand firm upon the front of law and for the ordered remedy of grievances, would have formed, might well have been effective. Of course you cannot say for certain that they would. [Interruption.] I try to argue fairly with the House. At the same time I do not think it is fair to charge those who wished to see this course followed, and followed consistently and resolutely, with having wished for an immediate war. Between submission and immediate war there was this third alternative, which gave a hope not only of peace but of justice. It is quite true that such a policy in order to succeed demanded that Britain should declare straight out and a long time beforehand that she would, with others, join to defend Czechoslovakia against an unprovoked aggression. His Majesty's Government refused to give that guarantee when it would have saved the situation, yet in the end they gave it when it was too late, and now, for the future, they renew it when they have not the slightest power to make it good.

All is over. Silent, mournful, abandoned, broken, Czechoslovakia recedes into the darkness. She has suffered in every respect by her association with the Western democracies and with the League of Nations, of which she has always been an obedient servant. She has suffered in particular from her association with France, under whose guidance and policy she has been actuated for so long. The very measures taken by His Majesty's Government in the Anglo-French Agreement to give her the best chance possible, namely, the 50 per cent. clean cut

[11] Mr. Leopold C. M. S. Amery, Secretary of State for India and Burma in Churchill's Government, 1940–1945.

[12] In *The Gathering Storm* Churchill discusses the revolt planned by German generals during the Czechoslovakian crisis, but he does not indicate whether he and others knew of that disaffection during this debate.

in certain districts instead of a plebiscite, have turned to her detriment, because there is to be a plebiscite too in wide areas, and those other Powers who had claims have also come down upon the helpless victim. Those municipal elections upon whose voting the basis is taken for the 50 per cent. cut were held on issues which had nothing to do with joining Germany. When I saw Herr Henlein [13] over here he assured me that was not the desire of his people. Positive statements were made that it was only a question of home rule, of having a position of their own in the Czechoslovakian State. No one has a right to say that the plebiscite which is to be taken in areas under Saar conditions, and the clean-cut of the 50 per cent. areas—that those two operations together amount in the slightest degree to a verdict of self-determination. It is a fraud and a farce to invoke that name.

We in this country, as in other Liberal and democratic countries, have a perfect right to exalt the principle of self-determination, but it comes ill out of the mouths of those in totalitarian States who deny even the smallest element of toleration to every section and creed within their bounds. But, however you put it, this particular block of land, this mass of human beings to be handed over, has never expressed the desire to go into the Nazi rule. I do not believe that even now—if their opinion could be asked, they would exercise such an option.

What is the remaining position of Czechoslovakia? Not only are they politically mutilated, but, economically and financially, they are in complete confusion. Their banking, their railway arrangements, are severed and broken, their industries are curtailed, and the movement of their population is most cruel. The Sudeten miners, who are all Czechs and whose families have lived in that area for centuries, must now flee into an area where there are hardly any mines left for them to work. It is a tragedy which has occurred. I did not like to hear the Minister of Transport yesterday talking about Humpty Dumpty.[14] It was the Minister of Transport who was saying that it was a case of Humpty Dumpty that could never be put together again. There must always be the most profound regret and a sense of vexation in British hearts at the treatment and the misfortunes which have overcome the Czechoslovakian Republic. They have not ended here. At any moment there may be a hitch in the programme. At any moment there may be an order for Herr Goebbels to start again his propaganda of calumny and lies; at any moment an incident may be provoked, and now that the fortress line is given away what is there to stop the will of the conqueror? [*Interruption.*] It is too serious a subject to treat lightly. Obviously, we are not in a position to give them the slightest help at the present time, except what everyone is glad to know has been done, the financial aid which the Government have promptly produced.

I venture to think that in future the Czechoslovak State cannot be maintained as an independent entity. You will find that in a period of time which may be measured by years, but may be measured only by months, Czechoslovakia will be

[13] Konrad Henlein, head of the *Sudetendeutsche Partie* in Czechoslovakia and *Reichskommisar* for the Sudeten areas after German occupation. He visited London on May 12, 1938, and Churchill interviewed him on May 13.

[14] Edward Leslie Burgin, Minister of Transport, said on October 4 that even if the democracies won a war over Czechoslovakia, "they could never put Humpty Dumpty up again" because of political disintegration within the nation. (*Debates*, Vol. 339, columns 183–97.)

engulfed in the Nazi régime.[15] Perhaps they may join it in despair or in revenge. At any rate, that story is over and told. But we cannot consider the abandonment and ruin of Czechoslovakia in the light only of what happened only last month. It is the most grievous consequence which we have yet experienced of what we have done and of what we have left undone in the last five years—five years of futile good intention, five years of eager search for the line of least resistance, five years of uninterrupted retreat of British power, five years of neglect of our air defences.[16] Those are the features which I stand here to declare and which marked an improvident stewardship for which Great Britain and France have dearly to pay. We have been reduced in those five years from a position of security so overwhelming and so unchallengeable that we never cared to think about it. We have been reduced from a position where the very word "war" was considered one which would be used only by persons qualifying for a lunatic asylum. We have been reduced from a position of safety and power—power to do good, power to be generous to a beaten foe, power to make terms with Germany, power to give her proper redress for her grievances, power to stop her arming if we chose, power to take any step in strength or mercy or justice which we thought right—reduced in five years from a position safe and unchallenged to where we stand now.

When I think of the fair hopes of a long peace which still lay before Europe at the beginning of 1933 when Herr Hitler first obtained power, and of all the opportunities of arresting the growth of the Nazi power which have been thrown away, when I think of the immense combinations and resources which have been neglected or squandered, I cannot believe that a parallel exists in the whole course of history. So far as this country is concerned the responsibility must rest with those who have the undisputed control of our political affairs. They neither prevented Germany from rearming, nor did they rearm ourselves in time. They quarrelled with Italy without saving Ethiopia. They exploited and discredited the vast institution of the League of Nations and they neglected to make alliances and combinations which might have repaired previous errors, and thus they left us in the hour of trial without adequate national defence or effective international security.

In my holiday I thought it was a chance to study the reign of King Ethelred the Unready.[17] The House will remember that that was a period of great misfortune,

---

[15] Germany occupied Sudetenland October 1–2, 1938. The Czech President, Eduard Beneš, resigned October 5. Poland seized the Teschen area October 4–5. On November 2, Germany and Italy agreed to give portions of Slovakia and Ruthenia to Hungary. Hitler dissolved Czechoslovakia as a national entity on March 14, 1939.

[16] James Ramsay MacDonald formed a "National Coalition Government" (Labor-Conservative) in 1931. In 1935, MacDonald retired and his chief aide, Stanley Baldwin, became Prime Minister. The "eager search for the line of least resistance" received continued support from Laborites and Conservatives. Baldwin retired in 1937, and Neville Chamberlain succeeded him. Chamberlain seems to have had greater interest in rearmament, though chiefly as a means of strengthening his bargaining position vis à vis the totalitarian powers.

[17] The Old English Chronicle accounts "Aethelred the Unready" (965?–1016) a weak king. During his reign a navy was lost, London captured by the Danes, and Aethelred forced first to flee to Normandy and then to seek restoration of his throne through negotiations with the enemy.

in which, from the strong position which we had gained under the descendants of King Alfred, we fell very swiftly into chaos. It was the period of Danegeld and of foreign pressure. I must say that the rugged words of the Anglo-Saxon Chronicle, written 1,000 years ago, seem to me apposite, at least as apposite as those quotations from Shakespeare with which we have been regaled by the last speaker from the Opposition Bench.[18] Here is what the Anglo-Saxon Chronicle said, and I think the words apply very much to our treatment of Germany and our relations with her.

> All these calamities fell upon us because of evil counsel, because tribute was not offered to them at the right time nor yet were they resisted; but when they had done the most evil, then was peace made with them.

That is the wisdom of the past, for all wisdom is not new wisdom.

I have ventured to express those views in justifying myself for not being able to support the Motion which is moved to-night, but I recognise that this great matter of Czechoslovakia, and of British and French duty there, has passed into history. New developments may come along, but we are not here to decide whether any of those steps should be taken or not. They have been taken. They have been taken by those who had a right to take them because they bore the highest executive responsibility under the Crown. Whatever we may think of it, we must regard those steps as belonging to the category of affairs which are settled beyond recall. The past is no more, and one can only draw comfort if one feels that one has done one's best to advise rightly and wisely and in good time. I, therefore, turn to the future, and to our situation as it is to-day. Here, again, I am sure I shall have to say something which will not be at all welcome.

We are in the presence of a disaster of the first magnitude which has befallen Great Britain and France. Do not let us blind ourselves to that. It must now be accepted that all the countries of Central and Eastern Europe will make the best terms they can with the triumphant Nazi Power. The system of alliances in Central Europe upon which France has relied for her safety has been swept away, and I can see no means by which it can be reconstituted.[19] The road down the Danube Valley to the Black Sea, the resources of corn and oil, the road which leads as far as Turkey, has been opened. In fact, if not in form, it seems to me that all those countries of Middle Europe, all those Danubian countries, will, one after another, be drawn into this vast system of power politics—not only power military politics but power economic politics—radiating from Berlin, and I believe this can be achieved quite smoothly and swiftly and will not necessarily entail the firing of a single shot. If you wish to survey the havoc of the foreign policy of Britain and France, look at what is happening and is recorded each day in the

[18] Mr. Arthur Greenwood (Labour) spoke just before Churchill. Apropos of Sir John Simon's allusions to Shakespeare, Greenwood suggested a better source might be *Henry the Fourth, Part I*, Act II: Gadshill's cry in scene 2, "What, ho! chamberlain!" and Hotspur's lines in scene 3, "The purpose you undertake is dangerous, the friends you have named uncertain; the time itself unsorted." Churchill's retort is a reminder that the Labor party had been more reluctant to rearm than Chamberlain.

[19] From 1919, French foreign policy aimed at maintaining German weakness through central European alliances. Hitler's power constituted defeat of this policy.

columns of the "Times." Why, I read this morning about Yugoslavia—and I know something about the details of that country—

> The effects of the crisis for Yugoslavia can immediately be traced. Since the elections of 1935, which followed soon after the murder of King Alexander, the Serb and Croat Opposition to the Government of Dr. Stoyadinovitch have been conducting their entire campaign for the next elections under the slogan: "Back to France, England, and the Little Entente; back to democracy." The events of the past fortnight have so triumphantly vindicated Dr. Stoyadinovitch's policy. . . .

—his is a policy of close association with Germany—

> that the Opposition has collapsed practically overnight; the new elections, the date of which was in doubt, are now likely to be held very soon and can result only in an overwhelming victory for Dr. Stoyadinovitch's Government.[20]

Here was a country which, three months ago, would have stood in the line with other countries to arrest what has occurred.

Again, what happened in Warsaw? The British and French Ambassadors visited Colonel Beck,[21] or sought to visit him, the Foreign Minister, in order to ask for some mitigation in the harsh measures being pursued against Czechoslovakia about Teschen. The door was shut in their faces. The French Ambassador was not even granted an audience and the British Ambassador was given a most curt reply by a political director. The whole matter is described in the Polish Press as a political indiscretion committed by those two Powers, and we are to-day reading of the success of Colonel Beck's blow. I am not forgetting, I must say, that it is less than 20 years ago since British and French bayonets rescued Poland from the bondage of a century and a half. I think it is indeed a sorry episode in the history of that country, for whose freedom and rights so many of us have had warm and long sympathy.

Those illustrations are typical. You will see, day after day, week after week, entire alienation of those regions. Many of those countries, in fear of the rise of the Nazi Power, have already got politicians, Ministers, Governments, who were pro-German, but there was always an enormous popular movement in Poland, Rumania, Bulgaria and Yugoslavia which looked to the Western democracies and loathed the idea of having this arbitrary rule of the totalitarian system thrust upon them, and hoped that a stand would be made. All that has gone by the board. We are talking about countries which are a long way off and of which, as the Prime Minister might say, we know nothing. [*Interruption.*] The noble Lady says that that very harmless allusion is—

[Viscountess Astor: Rude.]

She must very recently have been receiving her finishing course in manners. What will be the position, I want to know, of France and England this year and the year afterwards? What will be the position of that Western front of which we are in full authority the guarantors? The German army at the present time is more numerous than that of France, though not nearly so matured or perfected.

---

[20] *The Times*, October 5, 1938, p. 13. Churchill quotes the final paragraph of a dispatch from Belgrade, dated October 4.

[21] Jósef Beck, Polish Foreign Minister (1932–1939). Reports of the Polish seizure of the Teschen district were carried in London newspapers on October 5.

Next year it will grow much larger, and its maturity will be more complete. Relieved from all anxiety in the East, and having secured resources which will greatly diminish, if not entirely remove, the deterrent of a naval blockade, the rulers of Nazi Germany will have a free choice open to them in what direction they will turn their eyes. If the Nazi dictator should choose to look westward, as he may, bitterly will France and England regret the loss of that fine army of ancient Bohemia which was estimated last week to require not fewer than 30 German divisions for its destruction.

Can we blind ourselves to the great change which has taken place in the military situation, and to the dangers we have to meet? We are in process, I believe, of adding, in four years, four battalions to the British Army. No fewer than two have already been completed. Here at least 30 divisions which must now be taken into consideration upon the French front, besides the 12 that were captured when Austria was engulfed. Many people, no doubt, honestly believe that they are only giving away the interests of Czechoslovakia, whereas I fear we shall find that we have deeply compromised, and perhaps fatally endangered, the safety and even the independence of Great Britain and France. This is not merely a question of giving up the German colonies, as I am sure we shall be asked to do.[22] Nor is it a question only of losing influence in Europe. It goes far deeper than that. You have to consider the character of the Nazi movement and the rule which it implies. The Prime Minister desires to see cordial relations between this country and Germany. There is no difficulty at all in having cordial relations with the German people. Our hearts go out to them. But they have no power. You must have diplomatic and correct relations, but there can never be friendship between the British democracy and the Nazi Power, that Power which spurns Christian ethics, which cheers its onward course by a barbarous paganism, which vaunts the spirit of aggression and conquest, which derives strength and perverted pleasure from persecution, and uses, as we have seen, with pitiless brutality the threat of murderous force. That Power cannot ever be the trusted friend of the British democracy.

What I find unendurable is the sense of our country falling into the power, into the orbit and influence of Nazi Germany, and of our existence becoming dependent upon their good will or pleasure. It is to prevent that that I have tried my best to urge the maintenance of every bulwark of defence—first the timely creation of an Air Force superior to anything within striking distance of our shores; secondly, the gathering together of the collective strength of many nations; and thirdly, the making of alliances and military conventions, all within the Covenant, in order to gather together forces at any rate to restrain the onward movement of this Power.[23] It has all been in vain. Every position has been successively undermined and abandoned on specious and plausible excuses. We do not want to be led upon the high road to becoming a satellite of the German Nazi

---

[22] Under agreements made following World War I, Great Britain acquired as "mandated" territories such formerly German colonies as Togoland, German East Africa, etc.

[23] Churchill later wrote: "The emphasis which I put upon the two years' lag which afflicted us may well be judged inconsistent with my desire to come to grips with Hitler in October, 1938. I remain convinced, however, that it was right to spur the Government by every means, and that it would have been better in all the circumstances . . . to fight Hitler in 1938 than it was when we finally had to do so in September, 1939." (*The Gathering Storm* [New York, 1961], p. 207.)

system of European domination. In a very few years, perhaps in a very few months, we shall be confronted with demands with which we shall no doubt be invited to comply. Those demands may affect the surrender of territory or the surrender of liberty. I foresee and foretell that the policy of submission will carry with it restrictions upon the freedom of speech and debate in Parliament, on public platforms, and discussions in the Press, for it will be said—indeed, I hear it said sometimes now—that we cannot allow the Nazi system of dictatorship to be criticised by ordinary, common English politicians. Then, with a Press under control, in part direct but more potently indirect, with every organ of public opinion doped and chloroformed into acquiescence, we shall be conducted along further stages of our journey.

It is a small matter to introduce into such a Debate as this, but during the week I heard something of the talk of Tadpole and Taper.[24] They were very keen upon having a general election, a sort of, if I may say so, inverted khaki election. I wish the Prime Minister had heard the speech of my hon. and gallant Friend the Member for the Abbey Division of Westminster (Sir S. Herbert) last night. I know that no one is more patient and regular in his attendance than the Prime Minister, and it is marvellous how he is able to sit through so much of our Debates, but it happened that by bad luck he was not here at that moment. I am sure, however, that if he had heard my hon. and gallant Friend's speech he would have felt very much annoyed that such a rumour could even have been circulated. I cannot believe that the Prime Minister, or any Prime Minister possessed of a large working majority, would be capable of such an act of historic, constitutional indecency. I think too highly of him. Of course, if I have misjudged him on the right side, and there is a dissolution on the Munich Agreement, on Anglo-Nazi friendship, on the state of our defences and so forth, everyone will have to fight according to his convictions, and only a prophet could forecast the ultimate result; but, whatever the result, few things could be more fatal to our remaining chances of survival as a great Power than that this country should be torn in twain upon this deadly issue of foreign policy at a moment when, whoever the Ministers may be, united effort can alone make us safe.

I have been casting about to see how measures can be taken to protect us from this advance of the Nazi Power, and to secure those forms of life which are so dear to us. What is the sole method that is open? The sole method that is open is for us to regain our old island independence by acquiring that supremacy in the air which we were promised, that security in our air defences which we were assured we had, and thus to make ourselves an island once again. That, in all this grim outlook, shines out as the overwhelming fact. An effort at rearmament the like of which has not been seen ought to be made forthwith, and all the resources of this country and all its united strength should be bent to that task. I was very glad to see that Lord Baldwin yesterday in the House of Lords said that he would mobilise industry to-morrow. But I think it would have been much better if Lord Baldwin had said that 2½ years ago, when everyone demanded a Ministry of Supply. I will venture to say to hon. Gentlemen sitting here behind the Government Bench, hon. Friends of mine, whom I thank for the patience with which they have listened to what I have to say, that they have some responsibility for all this

---

[24] Tadpole and Taper are fictional members of Parliament and political gossips created by Disraeli in his novel, *Coningsby*. There had been rumors that Chamberlain might call a general election to capitalize on his success in avoiding war.

too, because, if they had given one tithe of the cheers they have lavished upon this transaction of Czechoslovakia to the small band of Members who were endeavouring to get timely rearmament set in motion, we should not now be in the position in which we are.[25] Hon. Gentlemen opposite, and hon. Members on the Liberal benches, are not entitled to throw these stones. I remember for two years having to face, not only the Government's deprecation, but their stern disapproval. Lord Baldwin has now given the signal, tardy though it may be; let us at least obey it.

After all, there are no secrets now about what happened in the air and in the mobilisation of our anti-aircraft defences. These matters have been, as my hon. and gallant Friend the Member for the Abbey Division [26] said, seen by thousands of people. They can form their own opinions of the character of the statements which have been persistently made to us by Ministers on this subject. Who pretends now that there is air parity with Germany? Who pretends now that our anti-aircraft defences were adequately manned or armed? We know that the German General Staff are well informed upon these subjects, but the House of Commons has hitherto not taken seriously its duty of requiring to assure itself on these matters. The Home Secretary [27] said the other night that he would welcome investigation. Many things have been done which reflect the greatest credit upon the administration. But the vital matters are what we want to know about. I have asked again and again during these three years for a secret Session where these matters could be thrashed out, or for an investigation by a Select Committee of the House, or for some other method. I ask now that, when we meet again in the autumn, that should be a matter on which the Government should take the House into its confidence, because we have a right to know where we stand and what measures are being taken to secure our position.

I do not grudge our loyal, brave people, who were ready to do their duty no matter what the cost, who never flinched under the strain of last week—I do not grudge them the natural, spontaneous outburst of joy and relief when they learned that the hard ordeal would no longer be required of them at the moment; but they should know the truth. They should know that there has been gross neglect and deficiency in our defences; they should know that we have sustained a defeat without a war, the consequences of which will travel far with us along our road; they should know that we have passed an awful milestone in our history, when the whole equilibrium of Europe has been deranged, and that the terrible words have for the time being been pronounced against the Western democracies:

Thou art weighed in the balance and found wanting.[28]

And do not suppose that this is the end. This is only the beginning of the reckoning. This is only the first sip, the first foretaste of a bitter cup which will be

---

[25] The "small band" included Churchill, Sir Austen Chamberlain, Sir Robert Horne, Sir Edward Grigg, Lord Winterton, Mr. Brenden Bracken, Sir Henry Croft, and others. They formed a Conservative subgroup that acted as a unit in many debates and divisions. (*The Gathering Storm*, p. 74.)

[26] Sir Sidney Herbert, Member for Westminster (Abbey Division), had spoken on October 4.

[27] Sir Samuel Hoare.

[28] The allusion is to the Biblical story of the handwriting on the palace wall at Belshazzar's feast. (*Daniel* 5:27.) The prophet translated a portion of the writing: "Thou art weighed in the balances, and art found wanting." (King James translation.)

proffered to us year by year unless by a supreme recovery of moral health and martial vigour, we arise again and take our stand for freedom as in the olden time.[29]

～

A SOLEMN HOUR *

Radio Broadcast
May 19, 1940

I speak to you for the first time as Prime Minister in a solemn hour for the life of our country, of our empire, of our allies and above all of the cause of freedom.[1]

A tremendous battle is raging in France and Flanders.[2] The Germans by a remarkable combination of air bombing and heavily armoured tanks have broken through the French defenses north of the Maginot line[3] and strong columns of their armoured vehicles are ravaging the open country which for the first day or two was without defenders. They have penetrated deeply and spread alarm and confusion in their tracks. Behind them there are now appearing infantry in lorries, and behind them again, the large masses are moving forward. The regroupment of the French armies to make head against and also to strike at this intruding wedge has been proceeding for several days largely assisted by the magnificent effort of the Royal Air Force.[4]

We must not allow ourselves to be intimidated by the presence of these armoured vehicles in unexpected places behind our lines. If they are behind our front, the French are also at many points fighting actively behind theirs. Both sides are therefore in an extremely dangerous position. And if the French army and our own army are well handled, as I believe they will be, if the French retain their genius for recovery and counterattack for which they have so long been famous;

[29] The motion was later carried 366–144, Churchill abstaining.

* This text has been transcribed from a sound recording of the address as broadcast to North America by the British Broadcasting Corporation.

[1] Prime Minister Chamberlain's majority in the Commons fell to 81 on May 8, 1940. On May 10, Churchill was asked to head a Coalition Government and by evening Labor and Liberal leaders had agreed to serve under him. On May 13, Churchill addressed the House of Commons, incorporating in his speech the words: "I would say to the House as I have said to those who have joined this Government: I have nothing to offer but blood, toil, tears, and sweat." On May 16, he flew to Paris to consult French leaders, returning on the 17th with only a faint hope that a total debacle at the battlefront could be averted. In this mood he made his first report to the British people.

[2] The situation was graver than Churchill revealed. General Gamelin thought the situation "lost." The Germans were advancing from Brussels. On the day of his speech, Churchill received word that Lord Gort, Commander in Chief of the British Expeditionary Force, was "examining a possible withdrawal towards Dunkirk if that were forced on him," and that "only four days' supplies and ammunition for one battle were available." [Churchill, *Their Finest Hour* (New York, 1962), pp. 47–51.]

[3] Toward Cambrai and the river Somme.

[4] On the 16th, Churchill secured Cabinet approval for transfer of additional air squadrons from England to the Continent. (*Their Finest Hour*, pp. 44–45.)

and if the British show the dogged endurance and solid Viking power for which there have been so many examples in the past; then, a sudden transformation of the scene might spring into being.[5]

It would be foolish, however, to disguise the gravity of the hour. It would be still more foolish to lose heart and courage or to suppose that well-trained, well-equipped armies numbering three or four millions of men can be overcome in the space of a few weeks, or even months, by a swoop or raid of mechanized vehicles, however formidable. We may look with confidence to the stabilization of the front in France and to general engagement of the masses, which will enable the qualities of the French and British soldiers to be matched squarely against those of their adversaries.

For myself, I have invincible confidence in the French army and its leaders.[6] Only a small part of that splendid army has yet been engaged and only a very small part of France has yet been invaded. There is good evidence to show that practically the whole of the specialized and mechanized forces of the enemy have been already thrown into the battle; and we know that very heavy losses have been inflicted upon them. No officer or man, no brigade or division, which grapples at close quarters with the enemy, wherever encountered, can fail to make a worthy contribution to the general results. The armies must cast away the idea of resisting attacks behind concrete lines or natural obstacles, and must realize that mastery can only be regained by furious and unrelenting assault.[7] And this spirit must not only animate the high command but must inspire every fighting man.

In the air, often at serious odds—often at odds hitherto thought overwhelming— we have been clawing down three or four to one of our enemies; and the relative balance of the British and German air forces is now considerably more favourable to us than at the beginning of the battle.[8] In cutting down the German bombers we are fighting our own battle as well as that of France. My confidence in our ability to fight it out to the finish with the German air force has been strengthened by the fierce encounters which have taken place and are taking place. At the same time our heavy bombers are striking nightly at the tap-root of German mechanized power and have already inflicted serious damage upon the oil refineries on which the Nazi effort to dominate the world directly depends.

We must expect that as soon as stability is reached on the western front, the bulk of that hideous apparatus of aggression which dashed Holland into ruin and slavery in a few days will be turned upon us. I am sure I speak for all when I say we are ready to face it, to endure it, and to retaliate against it to any extent that the unwritten laws of war permit. There will be many men and many women in this island who, when the ordeal comes upon them, as come it will, will feel comfort and even a pride that they are sharing the perils of our lads at the front—

[5] In his history of the war, Churchill indicates that while these hopes existed, they were scarcely confident anticipations.

[6] Churchill had little confidence in General Maurice Gamelin. He hoped French strategy would improve when General Maxime Weygand arrived from the Near East to replace Gamelin. (*Their Finest Hour*, pp. 50–51.)

[7] Churchill was irritated by the defeatist and defensive thinking he encountered among French military leaders.

[8] In a message to President Franklin D. Roosevelt, sent the day after this speech, Churchill used essentially these same words but added, "they have still a formidable numerical superiority." (*Their Finest Hour*, p. 50.)

soldiers, sailors, and airmen, God bless them—and are drawing away from them a part at least of the onslaught they have to bear. Is not this the appointed time for all to make the utmost exertions in their power?

If the battle is to be won, we must provide our men with ever-increasing quantities of the weapons and ammunition they need. We must have and have quickly more airplanes, more tanks, more shells, more guns. There is imperious need for these vital ammunitions. They increase our strength against the powerfully armed enemy. They replace the wastage of the obstinate struggle; and the knowledge the wastage will speedily be replaced enables us to draw more readily upon our reserves and throw them in now that everything counts so much.

Our task is not only to win the battle—but to win the war. After this battle in France abates its force, there will come the battle for our island—for all that Britain is and all that Britain means. That will be the struggle. In that supreme emergency we shall not hesitate to take every step, even the most drastic, to call forth from our people the last ounce and last inch of effort of which we are capable.[9] The interest of property, the hours of labor—now nothing compares to the struggle for life and honour, for right and freedom, to which we have vowed ourselves.

I have received from the Chiefs of the French Republic, and in particular from its indomitable Prime Minister, M. Reynaud, the most sacred pledges that whatever happens they will fight to the end, be it bitter or be it glorious. Nay, if we fight to the end, it can only be glorious.

Having received His Majesty's commission, I have formed an administration of men and women of every party and of almost every point of view.[10] We have differed and quarreled in the past, but now one bond unites us all: to wage war until victory is won and never to surrender ourselves to servitude and shame, whatever the cost and the agony may be.

If this is one of the most awe-striking periods in the long history of France and Britain, it is also beyond doubt the most sublime. Side by side, unaided except by their kith and kin in the great Dominions, and by the wide Empires which rest beneath their shield—side by side, the British and French people have advanced the rescue, not only of Europe, but mankind from the foulest and most soul-destroying tyranny which has ever darkened and stained the pages of history. Behind them, behind the armies and fleets of Britain and France—gather a group of shattered states and bludgeoned races: the Czechs, the Poles, the Norwegians, the Danes, the Dutch, the Belgians—upon all of whom the long night of barbarism will descend unbroken even by a star of hope, unless we conquer, as conquer we must—as conquer we shall.

Today is Trinity Sunday. Centuries ago words were written to be a call and a spur to the faithful servants of truth and justice. "Arm yourselves, and be ye men of valour, and be in readiness for the conflict; for it is better for us to perish in battle than to look upon the outrage of our nation and our altars. As the Will of God is in Heaven, even so, let it be."

∽

[9] On May 22, Parliament passed a bill giving the Government "practically unlimited power over the life, liberty, and property of all His Majesty's subjects in Great Britain." (*Their Finest Hour*, p. 55.)

[10] In Churchill's new Government the Labor Party held eight, the Liberals three, Independents four, and Conservatives nineteen of the highest places.

Bibliographical Note

The literature concerning Sir Winston Churchill is already massive, but major studies of his career have only begun to appear. The first volume of Peter de Mendelssohn's projected ten-volume biography *The Age of Churchill* was published in 1961. C. L. Broad's two-volume *Winston Churchill* (1958–1963) is a more popular study. Of the many other works, *Churchill, by His Contemporaries,* Charles Eade, ed. (1954); H. L. Steward's *Winged Words: Sir Winston Churchill as Writer and Speaker* (1954); and Robert Lewis Taylor's *Winston Churchill* (1954) contain the most valuable comments on Churchill's speaking. Churchill's own six-volume history, *The Second World War,* is an indispensable source. Of the more than twenty volumes of his speeches, the series edited by his son, Randolph S. Churchill, constitutes the most systematic collection. Three essays analyzing Churchill's speaking have special value: Halbert E. Gulley, "Churchill's Speech on the Munich Agreement," *Quarterly Journal of Speech,* XXXIII (1947), 284–91; Halbert E. Gulley, "Winston Churchill: In Crisis, Eloquence," *ibid.,* XLI (1955), 64–67; and Charles W. Lomas, "Winston Churchill: Orator-Historian," *ibid.,* XLIV (1958), 153–60.

Index of Speakers

Entries include all speakers represented by texts or mentioned significantly in the introductions and notes. Page numbers for texts of speeches appear in italics.

Aelfric (955-1025), 2, *14-20*, 21
Alderman, Edwin of Deira's (c. 627), 2, 7; *see also* Edwin of Deira
Andrewes, Launcelot (preacher), 66, 69, 156
Arnold, Dr. Thomas (teacher, lecturer), 321
Ascham, Roger, 70
Asquith, Herbert Henry (Earl of Oxford and Asquith), 440, 445n, 461, 462
Astor, Viscountess Nancy (M.P.), *524, 530*
Attlee, Clement Richard (Earl Attlee and Viscount Prestwood), 440, 492, 493, *501, 507-08*
Augustine, Saint (Apostle of the English, d. 604), 1, *3-4*

Bacon, Francis (Baron Verulam and Viscount St. Albans), 68, *90-103*
Baldwin, Stanley (Earl Baldwin of Bewdley), 441, *491-501*, 507, *514-15*, 516-20 *passim*
Balfour, Arthur James (Earl of Balfour), 445n, 467
Ball, John (the "mad priest of Kent," d. 1381), 2, *42-45*
Barnard, Sir John (M.P.), *182*, 183n
Barnes, Dr. E. W. (preacher, Bishop of Birmingham), 478n
Barré, Colonel Isaac (M.P.), 244, 249n
Barrow, Isaac (preacher), 66, 157
Bates, William (preacher), 66
Bathurst, Henry (M.P.), *179-81*
Baxter, Richard (preacher), 66
Beaconsfield, Earl of; *see* Disraeli, Benjamin
Beard, Thomas (Puritan zealot), 144
Bede, The Venerable (d. 735), 2, 3-7 *passim*, *7-14*
Belhaven (John Hamilton), Baron (Scottish nationalist), 174
Belloc, Hilaire, 474-90 *passim*
Best, William Draper (trial lawyer), 296n
Bevan, Aneurin (M.P., Labour leader), 440-41
Bevin, Ernest (M.P., Labour leader), 440
Blair, Hugh (writer on rhetoric, preacher), 173, 175

Bolingbroke (Henry St. John), Viscount, 176, 211n
Brickdale, Matthew (M.P. for Bristol), 214n
Bright, John, 318, 320, 387n, *398-413*
Bromley, Sir Thomas (Lord Chancellor), 78
Brougham, Henry Lord, 256, 317, 320, 321, *322-58*
Buchanan, George (M.P.), *506-07*, 508, *513*, *515*
Buckingham, Duke of; *see* Villiers, George
Buller, Sir Francis (legal pleader), 295
Bullock-Webster, Canon G. R. (theological controversialist), 478n
Bunyan, John, 69
Burgin, Edward Leslie (M.P.), 527n
Burke, Edmund, 173, 174, 175, 201, 202, 205n, *211-44*, 245, 246, 249n, 254, 255, 258n, 276n, 277n, 278n, 281, 292, 319
Burnet, Bishop Gilbert, 156-57, 227n
Burns, John (M.P., anti-suffragist), 450n, 451
Butler, Bishop Joseph, 175

Camden (Charles Pratt), Earl (lawyer), 278n
Campbell, George (writer on rhetoric, preacher), 173
Campbell-Bannerman, Sir Henry (Prime Minister), 445n, 462
Canning, George, 317
Cartwright, Thomas (the *Admonition* to Parliament), 77, 80, 85n
Castlereagh (Robert Stewart), Viscount, 362-63
Cecil, Sir Robert (parliamentary speaker), 91
Cecil, William (Lord Burghley), 71
Chalmers, Thomas (Scottish preacher), 321
Chamberlain, Sir Austen, *512-13*, 533n
Chamberlain, Joseph (M.P., father of Sir Austen and Neville), 319, 513n
Chamberlain, (Arthur) Neville, 522, 523n
Chatham, Earl of; *see* Pitt, William, the Elder
Chesterfield (Philip Dormer Stanhope), Earl of, 174, 177-78, 195n
Chesterton, Gilbert Keith, 440, *474-90*

Chillingworth, William (Calvinist theologian), 156

Churchill, Lord Randolph (M.P., father of Sir Winston), 319, 521

Churchill, Sir Winston Spencer, 201, 319, 441, 442, 462, 491n, 492, 493, 502–04, 516, 519n, 520, 521–37

Cobden, Richard, 318, 320, 374n, 380n, 387n, 399–400, 413

Coifi, pagan high priest (c. 627), 6

Cole, Dr. Henry (1500–1580, preacher, Provost of Eton), 60–61

Combe, Richard (Burke's opponent at Bristol), 214n, 242

Cranmer, Thomas (d. 1556), 1, 46, 60–64

Cromwell, Oliver, 65, 144–55, 173

Cruger, Henry (Burke's colleague for Bristol), 213, 214n, 242

Curzon, (George) Nathaniel (Baron and Marquis of Curzon and Kedleston), 319

Defoe, Daniel, 174

Denman, Thomas (Baron Denman) (M.P.), 401n, 406n, 412n

Devereux, Robert (Earl of Essex), 91, 104

Dickens, Charles, 321

Digby, George Lord (Commons' prosecutor of the Earl of Strafford), 131

Disraeli, Benjamin (Earl of Beaconsfield), 318, 319, 320, 371–92, 413, 414, 415–21 passim, 521

Donne, John, 66, 109–23, 156

Drummond, Mrs. Flora Gibson ("The General," suffragist), 444, 455

Dunning, John (lawyer, M.P.), 222n, 249n

Edward VIII, King, 440, 491–515 passim, 515–20

Edwin of Deira (fl. 627), 2, 5–7

Eliot, Edward Granville (Earl of St. Germans) (politician), 367

Eliot, Sir John, 123–31, 173

Eliot, T. S., 442

Elizabeth I, Queen, 65, 68, 69–79, 80–81, 85n, 90, 104, 124

Erskine, Lord Thomas, 213n, 260n, 294–315, 442

Essex, Earl of; see Devereux, Robert

Ethelbert (c. 600), 1, 3–5

Ewart, William (M.P.), 402–03, 410n

Fazakerly, Nicholas (M.P.), 184–85

Fisher, Bishop John (1459–1535), 1, 61

Fitzgibbon, John (Earl of Clare) (M.P.), 364n

Flood, Henry (Irish leader), 220n, 244–46, 254, 274n

Foster, John (Baron Oriel) (M.P.), 364n

Fox, Charles James, 175, 202, 213, 245, 246, 249n, 254–81, 282, 283

Fraser, Sir Ian (M.P.), 507

Gaitskell, Hugh (M.P., Labour leader), 440

Gallacher, William (M.P.), 505–06, 513–14

Gladstone, Herbert (M.P., son of William E.), 444, 458n

Gladstone, William E., 318, 319, 320, 359, 371, 375–76, 413–21, 462

Glanville, Sir John (lawyer, M.P.), 275n

Glyn, John (Commons' prosecutor of the Earl of Strafford), 131

Goodwin, Thomas (preacher), 147n

Graham, Sir James (M.P., minister), 373, 383n

Grattan, Henry, 210n, 220n, 244–54, 358

Greenwood, Arthur (M.P., Labour), 529n

Grenville, George, 230n, 272n

Grey, Charles, Earl, 255, 256, 318

Grindal, William (teacher of Queen Elizabeth), 70, 74n

Harcourt, Lewis (M.P., anti-suffragist), 451n

Hardie, G. (M.P., Labour leader), 494, 514

Hardie, Keir (Labour leader), 440

Hawkesbury (Robert Jenkinson), Lord, 256n, 263, 280n

Hay, William (M.P.), 181

Herbert, Sidney (Baron Herbert of Lea), 377

Herbert, Sir Sidney (M.P.), 532, 533n

Hoare, Sir Samuel, 523–34 passim

Hoby, Sir Edward (parliamentary speaker), 91, 92n

Hooker, Richard (preacher and theologian), 66

Hunt, Henry "Orator" (lecturer, agitator), 321

Huskisson, William (parliamentary leader), 385

Huxley, Thomas Henry, 321

James I, King, 67, 90, 91, 104, 123–24

Jenkinson, Robert; see Hawkesbury, Lord

Johnson, Dr. Samuel, 173, 174, 177–78, 212

Kames (Henry Home), Lord (writer on rhetoric and criticism), 173

Kingsley, Canon Charles, 321, 392–98

Lansdowne, Marquis of; see Shelburne, Earl of

Latimer, Hugh (d. 1555), 1, 2, 3, 45–59, 60

Laud, Charles (Archbishop of Canterbury), 131–32, 138, 150n

Law, (Andrew) Bonar, 463, 523n

Law, Richard K. (M.P.), 523n

Lennox, Lord Henry Charles George Gordon (M.P.), 401n, 410n

Liddon, Henry P. (preacher), 321

Lilburne, John (spokesman of the Levellers), 148n

Lloyd George, David (Earl of Dufor), 440, 444, 461–73

Lyttleton, George (M.P.), 189

Macaulay, Thomas B., 318, 324
MacDonald, James Ramsey, 528n
Mackintosh, Sir James (author of *Vindiciae Gallicae*), 277n, 406n
Macklin, Charles (actor and teacher of oratory), 174
MacLaren, Alexander (preacher), 321
Mansfield (William Murray), Earl of (lawyer), 303n, 331, 334, 442
Maxton, James (M.P.), 504, 508–09
Maynard, John (Commons' prosecutor of the Earl of Strafford), 131
Milton, John (as controversialist), 68
Mitford, Sir John (lawyer), 296n, 297n, 298n, 302n, 304n, 315n
More, Sir Thomas (1478–1535), 1, 2, 61
Morley, John (Viscount Morley of Blackburn), 319, 413, 421
Morris, William (lecturer), 45, 321, 422–37
Morrison, Herbert S. (politician), 440

Newman, John Henry, Cardinal, 321, 393
North, Frederick Lord, 176, 203n, 254

Oastler, Richard (social agitator), 321
O'Connell, Daniel, 317, 318n, 320, 358–71
O'Connell, John (Irish agitator), 366

Paine, Thomas, 174
Palmer, Geoffrey (Commons' prosecutor of the Earl of Strafford), 131
Palmerston (Henry John Temple), Viscount, 318, 319
Pankhurst, Dame Christabel (daughter of Emmeline), 442, 443, 444, 455
Pankhurst, Mrs. Emmeline G., 440, 442–61, 463
Paulinus, Bishop (d. 644), 6
Peel, Sir Robert, 318, 371, 372, 373–91 *passim*, 407n, 413, 414
Pelham, Henry (parliamentary leader), 188–89
Perry, Micajah (M.P.), 183
Pitt, William, the Elder, Earl of Chatham, 176, 177, 178–79, 186–87, 188, 201–10, 230n
Pitt, William, the Younger, 213, 246, 255, 256, 269n, 281–94, 319, 364n
Plunket, William C. (Chancellor of Ireland), 362
Pym, John, 131, 132, 173

Raleigh, Sir Walter, 104–09
Rider, Sir Dudley (M.P.), 185
Ridley, Nicholas (1500–1555, preacher, martyr), 46, 60
Robertson, Frederick William (preacher), 321
Roe, Grace (suffragist), 455n
Rose, William Anderson (M.P., Lord Mayor), 410n

Rosebery (Archibald Primrose), Earl of, 319, 414
Ruskin, John, 321, 422
Russell, Lord John, 331, 371

St. John, Oliver (Commons' prosecutor of the Earl of Strafford), 131
Salisbury (Robert Cecil), Marquis of, 319
Saurin, William (politician), 363
Savile, Sir George (parliamentary leader), 229, 279
"Sermon for the Third Sunday After Trinity" (preacher unknown) (c. 1400), 31–38
Shaftesbury (Anthony Ashley Cooper), Earl of (19th-century reformer), 318, 321
Shaw, George Bernard, 321, 436, 440, 474–90
Sheil, Richard Lalor, 317, 318n, 359n, 370
Shelburne (Sir William Petty), Earl of (later Marquis of Lansdowne), 222n, 249n, 282
Sheridan, Richard Brinsley, 173, 175, 244, 255, 256n, 279n, 281
Sheridan, Thomas (teacher of speaking), 175
Simon, Sir John, 511–12, 523–34 *passim*
Sinclair, Sir Archibald, 493, 502, 508
Smith, Adam (writer on oratory), 173
Smith, Dr. Richard (1500–1563, preacher), 2
Smith, Thomas Berry Cusack (politician), 367
Smith, Dr. Thomas Southwood (physician), 393
South, Robert (preacher), 66, 157, 158n, 175
Spurgeon, Charles Haddon (preacher), 321, 442
Stephen, Cambell (M.P.), 509, 510–11
Strafford, Earl of; see Wentworth, Thomas
Swift, Jonathan (preacher, controversial writer), 174, 245, 247n

Taylor, Jeremy (preacher), 66, 157
Thompson, Colonel Perronet (radical editor), 377–78
Thorne, Will (M.P.), 457n, 509
Thurlow, Edward (Lord Chancellor), 235n
Tierney, George (colleague of Fox), 282–83, 284–85, 290–91
Tillotson, John, 66, 68, 69, 156–72
Tone, Wolfe (Irish agitator), 260n
Townshend, Charles, 230n
Tyler, Wat (agitator, d. 1381), 43

Villiers, George (Duke of Buckingham), 123, 126n, 128n, 129n, 131

Walker, John (teacher of speaking), 175
Walpole, Horace (Sir Robert's son), 176
Walpole, Horatio (Sir Robert's brother), 177, 185n, 186
Walpole, Sir Robert, 176–77, 181, 281
Webb, Sidney James (Baron Passfield), 440, 487n

Wedgwood, Colonel Josiah Clement (M.P.), 505

Wellington (Arthur Wellesley), Duke of, 366, 368

Wells, H. G., 440

Wentworth, Peter, 79–89, 173

Wentworth, Thomas (Earl of Strafford), 131–44

Wesley, Charles (brother of Samuel), 175, 190

Wesley, John, 175, 190–200

Whitefield, George, 175, 190–91, 200

Whitelocke, Bulstrode (Commons' prosecutor of the Earl of Strafford), 131, 133

Whitgift, John (Archbishop of Canterbury), 77

Wilberforce, William (M.P., humanitarian reformer), 282, 283

Wilkes, John (M.P., agitator), 174

Wilkins, John (homiletician), 156, 157, 158n

William the Conqueror, 2, 27–30

Winnington, Thomas (M.P.), 187–88

Wood, Sir George (legal pleader), 295

Wulfstan (d. 1023), 3, 21–27

Wyclif, John (d. 1384), 3, 38–42, 46

Yonge, Sir William (M.P.), 183–84